CONTENTS

PREFACE

The Walker Art Gallery's collection of foreign paintings needs little introduction. It is the outcome of over 150 years discriminating local collecting and a record of the concern of local benefactors to enhance their city's cultural life. Our collection has been built up primarily in the form of gifts and in more recent years through the aid of monetary donations. Its far-famed nucleus is that embodying William Roscoe's collection from the Liverpool Royal Institution, long on loan here and finally presented in 1948. Merseyside owes a great debt to collectors such as Emma Holt, the Rathbone family, James Smith, Arnold Baruchson, Lord Wavertree and the like. In more recent years local firms and trusts such as the Amelia Chadwick Trust, Beausire Trust, Eleanor Rathbone Trust, Granada T.V., Imperial Chemical Industries, Liverpool Daily Post & Echo, the former Martins Bank, Ocean Transport & Trading (P. H. Holt Trust), Royal Insurance, Tate and Lyle, Tetley Walker, and Messrs. Tophams, to name but a few, have been a highly important element in the financing of our purchases. In conjunction with these local sources we owe a great deal to the National Art-Collections Fund and the Pilgrim Trust.

This catalogue, unlike its predecessor of 1963, contains all foreign works of art in the collection from oil paintings to silver and incorporates many revisions and new attributions. The most exciting of these is the proposition that *Christ and the Woman of Samaria*, now in the process of restoration, is by Michelangelo.

The compilers of the catalogue, Edward Morris, Keeper of Foreign Art, and Martin Hopkinson, Assistant Keeper of Foreign Art, have asked me to thank their predecessors and the countless people who have been good enough to help and make suggestions. Most of these are referred to in the entries. I would also like to thank Sally Berry who typed the bulk of the entries.

This collection owes much to the sympathetic work of J. Coburn Witherop who will shortly be retiring after over 25 years as restorer here. Some of the subsequent evaluation of the collection has arisen from his work.

This year of publication marks our centenary and it is to be hoped that the next 100 years will see a continuation and expansion of the tradition of regional collecting recorded in this catalogue.

TIMOTHY STEVENS
Director

HISTORY OF THE COLLECTION

The most remarkable group of pictures in the Walker Art Gallery's Collection are the early Italian and Netherlandish works collected by William Roscoe[1] between about 1804 and 1816. Of them Roscoe wrote in 1816:[2] "The following works have been collected during a series of years chiefly for the purpose of illustrating by reference to original and authentic sources the rise and progress of the arts in modern times as well in Germany and Flanders as in Italy. They are therefore not wholly to be judged of by their positive merits but by a reference to the age in which they were produced. Their value chiefly depends on their authenticity and the light they throw on the history of the arts yet as they extend beyond the splendid aera of 1500 there will be found several productions of a higher class which may be ranked amongst the chef d'oeuvres of modern skill . . . Hopes had been indulged by the present possessor (Roscoe) that the works of . . . Art included in this catalogue might have formed the basis of a more extensive collection and have been rendered subservient to some objects of public utility but the circumstances of the times are not favourable to his views . . ." Indeed Roscoe was compelled by the threat of bankruptcy to sell his collection in 1816.[3] At the sale lots 1-62 were particularly described as "pictures illustrating the rise and progress of Painting in Italy" and lots 78-122 as "pictures illustrating the rise and progress of Painting in Germany, Flanders etc"; lots 1-62 were offered together at £1,000 and 78-122 together at £500 before the sale began but there were no takers[4] and the following note was published immediately after the sale:[5]

"When we view in the large and opulent town of Liverpool, so many public Institutions and such large sums instantly raised, and lavishly expended, to carry them into effect, is it not to be wondered at and much to be regretted, that the truly patriotic wishes of the late intelligent possessor of this highly valuable Collection, so feelingly and so forcibly expressed (at the end of the Advertisement), *when the sum required was so small*, should not have met with a correspondent feeling, in a few of the more enlightened and public spirited Individuals of the place, *to have carried them into effect?* more especially, when the incalculable advantages, resulting from the constant view of such a combination, both of the curious and excellent in Art, are taken into consideration; and the gratifying prospects, which such a Collection, (continually encreasing) would have held forth, both to the present and rising generation, for the cultivation and improvement of an elegant and correct taste, in one of the highest and most rational enjoyments of refined life.

Fertilis assiduo si non renovetur aratro,
Nil nisi cum spinis gramen habebit ager—Ovid."

However a group of subscribers led by William Rathbone[6] acquired thirty-five of these paintings including 12 which had failed to sell at the 1816 sale,[7] and by 1819 had presented them to the Liverpool Royal Institution which was formed between 1814 and 1817. In 1819 a *Catalogue of a Series of Pictures Illustrating the Rise and early Progress of the Art of Painting in Italy, Germany etc. Collected by William Roscoe Esq. and now deposited in the Liverpool Royal Institution* was published

1

with this introduction: " A few individuals conceiving that as the following Pictures form a series from the commencement of the Art to the close of the fifteenth century their value would be enhanced by their being preserved together have united in purchasing and presenting them to the Liverpool Royal Institution; in the hope that by preventing the dispersion of a collection interesting to the history and exemplifying the progress of Design they may contribute to the advancement of the Fine Arts in the Town of Liverpool." The Liverpool Royal Institution contained, then, the first permanent notable public collection of Old Master paintings in Great Britain bought in order to improve public taste. Under the guidance of Thomas Winstanley more pictures including some formerly owned by Roscoe but not acquired in 1819 were added to the Royal Institution's Collection by gift and purchase particularly during the years 1840-1842 while a new Art Gallery was being built for the Institution; however interest in the collection waned and in 1850-1851 abortive negotiations took place between the Royal Institution and the Liverpool Town Council to enable the Council to take over both Gallery and collection.[8] Eventually in 1893, 1915 and 1942 most of the collection was deposited on loan at the Walker Art Gallery which had been built for the Town Council 1874-1877 and these paintings were finally presented to the Gallery in 1948. Included in this gift were the Royal Institution's drawings most of which were presented by David Pennant between 1836 and 1841.[9]

Meanwhile from 1852 the Liverpool Town Council and (later) its Walker Art Gallery had also been acquiring foreign paintings and sculpture by gift and purchase. A considerable number of foreign Pictures were exhibited at the annual *Liverpool Autumn Exhibitions of Modern Paintings* held by the Council from 1871 until 1938 (from 1877 onwards at the Walker Art Gallery) and from the profits from these exhibitions and from other gifts some of these foreign paintings were acquired for the Walker Art Gallery.[10] From 1952 until 1970 the Gallery devoted most of its funds, derived by then partly from individual gifts and partly from rates levied by the Council, towards the purchase of foreign paintings and sculpture.

FOOTNOTES

[1]For Roscoe see Henry Roscoe, *The Life of William Roscoe*, 1833. For his activity as a collector see Michael Compton, *William Roscoe and early Collectors of Italian Primitives*, Liverpool Bulletin Vol. 9, 1960-1961, pp. 27ff, and T. Fawcett, *The Rise of English Provincial Art*, 1974, pp. 94-9.

[2]*Catalogue of the Genuine and Entire Collection of Drawings and Pictures the Property of William Roscoe which will be sold by Auction by Mr Winstanley at his rooms in Marble Street Liverpool 23 September and five following days*, 1816, Advertisement.

[3]The sale catalogue is cited above in footnote 2.

[4]Memoranda stuck into Manchester City Libraries copy of sale catalogue cited in footnote 2.

[5]Memoranda *op. cit.*

[6]*Donations to the Liverpool Royal Institution* in *Resolutions Reports and Bye Laws of the Liverpool Royal Institution*, 1814-1822, p. 17 list the following as the principal subscribers: W. Ewart, G. P. Barclay, R. Benson, C. Tayleur, Jos. Sandars, Jos. Reynolds and B. A. Heywood. William Rathbone is not included but Henry Roscoe, *The Life of William Roscoe*, Vol. 2, 1833, pp. 123-4, 140 implies that he was the leader of the group.

[7]S. H. Spiker who was in Liverpool during the sale remarked in his *Travels through England, Wales and Scotland in the Year 1816*, 1820 p. 309 that "contrary to expectation the pictures and drawings sold for a mere trifle." Fawcett, *op. cit.*, p. 98 states that Roscoe bought them in at the sale through local dealers and that then the subscribers acquired them. Certainly on 16 June 1818 Roscoe wrote to T. S. Traill offering for sale to the subscribers "my collection of Pictures at the Institution" for 1200 guineas (Roscoe Papers 4861 A)—presumably these were the 35 acquired in 1819 by the Liverpool Royal Institution. But the 1816 Sale was stated to be "without reserve" and William Ford, a dealer who bought some of the 35 pictures was not acting on Roscoe's behalf (Roscoe Papers 1560); a printed price list is in the Manchester City Libraries.

[8]Henry A. Ormerod, *The Liverpool Royal Institution*, 1953, pp. 32ff.

[9]See Walker Art Gallery, *Old Master Drawings and Prints*, 1967, pp. 4-5. The gift is first mentioned in the 1843 Catalogue p. 34.

[10]See Edward Morris, *Philip Henry Rathbone and the purchase of contemporary foreign paintings for the Walker Art Gallery, Liverpool, 1871-1914*, Annual Report and Bulletin of the Walker Art Gallery, Vol. 6 1975-6, pp. 59ff.

ABBREVIATIONS AND NOTES ON THE CATALOGUE

B.F.A.C.	Burlington Fine Arts Club.
C.I.	Courtauld Institute.
L.A.E.	Walker Art Gallery, Liverpool Autumn Exhibition.
L.R.I.	Liverpool Royal Institution.
L.R.I. Archives	Archives of the Liverpool Royal Institution now in the University of Liverpool.
Lugt	Frits Lugt, *Les Marques de Collections de dessins*, Amsterdam, 1921, *Supplement*, La Haye, 1956.
R.A.	Royal Academy.
Roscoe Sale	*Catalogue of the Genuine and Entire Collection of Drawings and Pictures the Property of William Roscoe Esq. which will be sold by auction by Mr Winstanley at his rooms in Marble Street, Liverpool Monday 23rd September and five following days*, Liverpool 1816.
Roscoe Papers	Roscoe Papers MSS Liverpool City Libraries.
Vasari ed. G. Milanesi	*Le vite de' piu' eccellenti pittori, scultori ed architettori* (1568), G. Milanesi, ed., 9 vols. Florence 1878-1885.
W.A.G.	Walker Art Gallery.
1816 Catalogue	*Catalogue of the Genuine and Entire Collection of Prints, Books of Prints etc., the Property of William Roscoe Esq., which will be sold by auction by Mr. Winstanley at his rooms in Marble Street, Liverpool, Monday 9th September and ten following days*, Liverpool 1816 and Roscoe Sale 1816 cited above.

1819 Catalogue	*Catalogue of a Series of Pictures Illustrating the Rise and Early Progress of the Art of Painting in Italy, Germany etc. Collected by William Roscoe Esq. and now deposited in the Liverpool Royal Institution,* Liverpool 1819.
1836 Catalogue	*Catalogue of the Pictures, Casts from the Antique etc. in the Liverpool Royal Institution,* Liverpool 1836.
1843 Catalogue	*A Catalogue of the Paintings, Drawings and Casts in the Permanent Gallery of Art, Royal Institution, Liverpool opened in January 1843,* Liverpool.
1851 Catalogue	*Catalogue of the Paintings, Drawings and Casts in the Permanent Gallery of Art Royal Institution,* Liverpool 1851.
1859 Catalogue	*Descriptive and Historical Catalogue of Pictures, Drawings and Casts in the Gallery of Art of the Royal Institution,* Liverpool 1859.
1882 Catalogue	Corporation of Liverpool, Walker Art Gallery, *Descriptive Catalogue of the Pictures* compiled by Charles Dyall, Curator, 1882.
1885 Catalogue	Corporation of Liverpool, Walker Art Gallery, *Descriptive Catalogue of the Permanent Collection of Pictures,* compiled by Charles Dyall, Curator, 1885.
1893 Catalogue	Corporation of Liverpool, Walker Art Gallery, *Catalogue of the Roscoe Collection deposited by the Trustees of the Royal Institution,* 1893.
1915 Catalogue	Corporation of Liverpool, Walker Art Gallery, *Catalogue of the Roscoe Collection and other pictures, deposited by the Trustees of the Liverpool Royal Institution,* 1915.
1927 Catalogue	Corporation of Liverpool, Walker Art Gallery, *Catalogue of the Permanent Collection,* 1927.
1928 Catalogue	Corporation of Liverpool, Walker Art Gallery, *Catalogue of the Roscoe Collection and other Paintings, Drawings and Engravings Deposited by the Trustees of the Liverpool Royal Institution,* 1928.
1963 Catalogue	Walker Art Gallery, *Foreign Schools Catalogue,* Liverpool, *Text,* 1963, *Plates,* 1967.
1967 Catalogue	Walker Art Gallery, *Old Master Drawings and Prints,* 1967.

The Roscoe Sale Catalogues of 1816 and the 1819 Catalogue were by Roscoe himself probably with help from Thomas Winstanley. The 1836 and 1843 Catalogues were by Thomas Winstanley. The 1851 and 1859 Catalogues were by Theodore W. Rathbone and include attributed comments from George Scharf, Director of the National Portrait Gallery, Solomon Alexander Hart, Librarian and Professor of Painting at the Royal Academy, G. F. Waagen, Mrs Anna Jameson, Henry Clark Barlow, G. B. Cavalcaselle and others. Cavalcaselle's comments of 1851 appear to be his first published contributions to art history. The 1882,

1885 and 1893 Catalogues were by Charles Dyall, the 1915 Catalogue was by E. Rimbault Dibdin, the 1927 Catalogue was by Arthur Quigley, all Curators of the Walker Art Gallery and the 1928 Catalogue was by Maurice Brockwell. The 1963 Catalogue was by Michael Compton, then Senior Assistant Keeper at the Walker Art Gallery, with assistance from other members of the staff. The 1967 Catalogue was by Timothy Stevens and Edward Morris, then Keeper and Assistant Keeper of Foreign Art.

The destruction of most of the Liverpool Royal Institution archives during the second World War has resulted in considerable uncertainty about the provenances of those paintings acquired by the Liverpool Royal Institution. Exhibitions before 1900 at which the Gallery's paintings appeared are listed; only the more important 20th Century exhibitions are noted.

All works of art by foreign artists in the Gallery are included in this catalogue. An artist is regarded as foreign if he was born, educated and trained outside the present Commonwealth and South Africa; Benjamin West is however excluded as his America was a British Colony, and so is John Henry Fuseli since virtually no paintings by him pre-date his arrival in this country; copies by British artists after works by foreign artists are excluded unless the foreign artist concerned already appears in the catalogue.

Notes on the condition of works of arts are minimal as detailed records have only recently been kept. Drawings and watercolours are on white paper unless otherwise stated.

All works of art in this catalogue except the prints and photographs are reproduced in Walker Art Gallery, Liverpool, *Foreign Catalogue*, *Plates*, 1977.

CATALOGUE OF PAINTINGS

ABBEY, Edwin Austin, 1852-1911

109 O Mistress Mine, where are you roaming?

Canvas, 156.1 × 246.4 cm

Signed: *E. A. Abbey 1899*

Completed in the spring of 1899[1] but the linings of the sleeves of the female figure were repainted by the artist after the closure of the 1899 Royal Academy Exhibition.[2]

The title is taken from the Clown's Song in Act 2, Scene 3 of Shakespeare's *Twelfth Night* but No. 109 does not appear to represent any event in that scene nor in any other scene from that play.[3] It is simply an imaginary illustration of the song itself.[4] In 1896 the artist had illustrated this play more literally in *The Comedies of William Shakespeare with drawings by E. A. Abbey*, Vol. 2.

Mr T. Mayoh owned a watercolour version of No. 109 in 1953,[5] and a sketch for the female figure was reproduced in the *Art Journal*, 1902, p. 361. 10 studies for No. 109 are at Yale University; they are 1937.2248 (oil on panel), 1937.2249 (oil on canvas), 1937.2254 (two pen and ink studies), 1937.2255 (pencil—the lovers only), 1937.2256 (pen, ink and watercolour—the earliest study), 1937.2257 (background arch only), 1937.2250 (oil on canvas—background and female figure), 1937.2251 (oil on canvas—background, female figure and clown), 1937.2252 (oil on canvas—early study for background only), 1937.2253 (oil on canvas).[6] The pergola in No. 109 was taken from one onto which the rooms of the artist and his wife opened while they were staying in Ravello, Italy, in 1891.[7]

The *Art Journal* critic[8] reviewing No. 109 at the 1899 R.A. remarked that it "will however cause many visitors to pass straight from the second to the fourth gallery in which it is to be seen." The *Magazine of Art* critic observed: "Romantic grace covers a very wide field of imaginative work and of "costume subject." Mr Abbey's "O Mistress Mine, where are you roaming" is perhaps finer than anything that he has done in respect to expression—the wistful yearning on the girl's face is masterly in its pathetic realisation but the composition is not so graceful as a good deal he has done."[9]

Prov: Purchased from the 1899 L.A.E. (£1,000).
Exh: R.A. 1899 (289); L.A.E. 1899 (1022); R.A. 1912 (338).

Ref: **1.** E. V. Lucas, *Life and Work of Edwin Austin Abbey R.A.* 1921, II, p. 344.   **2.** Lucas, *op. cit.*, p. 345.   **3.** As the *Art Journal* 1902, p. 366 pointed out in a considerable review.   **4.** For the song see Peter J. Seng, *The Vocal Songs in the Plays of Shakespeare; a critical history*, 1967, pp. 96-100.   **5.** Letter 26 July 1953. It is now in the Baker-Pisano Collection, New York and shows the sleeve linings green and gold — before repainting.   **6.** Kathleen A. Foster, letter, 24 June 1976.   **7.** Lucas, *op. cit.*, p. 245.   **8.** *Art Journal*, 1899, p. 182.   **9.** *The Magazine of Art*, 1899, pp. 388-390.

ALMA-TADEMA, Sir Lawrence, 1836-1912

178   A Bacchante

Panel, 25.8 × 19.7 cm

Signed: *L. Alma Tadema OP CLII*

Dircks[1] lists this picture as *There he is* (following Standing)[2] under the year 1875 in his chronological list. It's "opus" number would suggest that it was painted around the middle of that year.

No. 178 is reviewed in general terms in the *Magazine of Art*, Vol. 1, 1878, p. 110.

Engr: A Blanchard published 1 October 1875 by Pilgeram and Lefevre.
Prov: J. F. Hutton in 1878; Kaye Knowles sold Christie's 14 May 1887 lot 76 bt. Agnew £577 10s and thence to George Holt (bill, 7 December for 22 October 1887, MS, W.A.G.) £787 10s; bequeathed by Emma Holt 1944.
Exh: Grosvenor Gallery Summer Exhibition 1878 (25) as *A Bacchante*;[3] Grosvenor Gallery, *Exhibition of the Works of Sir Lawrence Alma-Tadema*, 1882 (65).
Ref: **1.** Rudolf Dircks, *List of Works by Alma-Tadema*, The Art Journal, Christmas Number 1910, p. 27.   **2.** P. C. Standing, *Sir Lawrence Alma-Tadema*, 1905, p. 58 (repr.) who also seems to describe No. 178 as *He is coming* (p. 57).   **3.** Reproduced in Henry Blackburn, *Grosvenor Notes*, 1878 p. 14, with some explanatory verses.

9098   Confidences

Panel, 55.3 × 37.6 cm

Signed: *L Alma Tadema MDCCCLXIX*

Reproduced by Standing as *In Confidence*[1] and listed by Dircks as Opus 72.[2]

Prov: (?) Gambart,[3] F. W. Cosens sold Christie's 17 May 1890 lot 119 bt. Tooth £451 10s Lord Joicey; N. Mitchell; Frederick Barnes Waldron who bequeathed it 1976.
Exh: Grosvenor Gallery, *Exhibition of the Works of Sir Lawrence Alma-Tadema* 1882 (51); Arthur Tooth and Sons, *Spring Exhibition of Selected Pictures*, 1891 (88); R.A., *Exhibition of Works by the Late Sir Lawrence Alma-Tadema*, 1913 (9).
Ref: **1.** P. C. Standing, *Sir Lawrence Alma-Tadema*, 1905, p. 36.   **2.** R. Dircks, *List of Works by Alma-Tadema*, Art Journal, Christmas Number, 1910, p. 27.   **3.** Most of Alma Tadema's works at this period were painted for Gambart; see J. Maas, *Gambart*, 1975, pp. 215ff.

ANDERSON, Mrs Sophie (Walter), (nee Gengembre) born 1823[1]

110 Elaine

Canvas, 158.4 × 240.7 cm

Signed: *Sophie Anderson 1870*[2]

Illustrates lines 1146-54 from Tennyson's *Lancelot and Elaine* from the *Idylls of the King* first published in 1859.

Then rose the dumb old servitor and the dead
Oar'd by the dumb went upward with the flood
In her right hand the lily, in her left
The letter—all her bright hair streaming down—
And all the coverlid was cloth of gold
Drawn to her waist and she herself in white
All but her face, and that clear featured face
Was lovely, for she did not seem as dead
But fast asleep, and lay as tho' she smiled

The second half of line 1146 and line 1147 were quoted in the R.A. and L.A.E. Catalogues (see under *Exhibitions*) but with "steered" for "oar'd" as in all editions of *Lancelot and Elaine* before the 1870 edition. In No. 110 the dumb old servitor is certainly steering not rowing although Elaine had said: "he can steer and row" (line 1121). Tennyson's account is based closely on Malory's *Le Morte Arthur* XVIII, 19.

The Art Journal critic wrote of No. 110: "large and effective; the subject has become trite; and this picture might have been better managed".[3] The Illustrated London News commented: "a very able work on a scale seldom attempted by a female artist, yet revealing no trace of weakness or technical immaturity."[4]

Prov: Bought from the 1871 L.A.E. £315.
Exh: R.A. 1870 (482); Glasgow, *Institute of Fine Arts* 1871 (480) L.A.E. 1871 (323).
Ref: 1. Walter Anderson (her husband) letter 19 December 1877. Her date of death does not seem to have been recorded.   2. The last two digits of the date are not now visible.   3. *Art Journal*, 1870, p. 168.   4. *Illustrated London News*, 28 May 1870, p. 562.

ARAEEN, Rasheed, born 1935

7188 BOO/69

Painted wood, 183 × 122 cm

The artist issued the following statement[1] about his work *8bS* and has stated[2] that it is also generally applicable to No. 7188:

Description and Method of Working: The components are glued (wood-working resin "W") together to form unit structures, and further secured firm by screwing. After all the unit structures are constructed, they are given two coats of Polyurethane paint (mat finish).

Since no production/marketing facility has been available to manufacture the structures industrially, I construct the structures myself in the workshop directly without any drawings. Ideally these structures are more suitable/intended to be manufactured from the drawings. All my work so far has been done in hardwood, which is available in market as standard moulding sections (manufactured product), but standard aluminium/steel sections can be used if the suitable method of their construction in these metals is available.

Visual Properties: The SPACE is defined by the structural COMPONENTS, in which they are visually INTER-RELATED by TIME. The COMPONENTS of the whole STRUCTURE shift in INTER-RELATIONSHIP in response to the MOVEMENT of the SPECTATOR in a continuous changing equilibrium, establishing a non-static/changing RELATIONSHIP with the SPECTATOR, while the whole STRUCTURE is physically STATIC.

Random Thoughts: Art must be manufactured. Technology/Engineering is the reality of today. Hand-made art (painting/sculpture) is obsolete and ought to be considered/categorised as a handicraft. In my work I do not seek the beauty of hand-made objects, neither of painting nor sculpture. This beauty has nothing to do with art. I am only interested in the TRANSFORMATION of the functional structures of technology/engineering into the non-functional visual situation/confrontation, so that they could achieve new AWARENESS when reversed to their original/additional functional capacities. Art should not only be manufactured but mass produced to make it accessible to everybody, so that in the end art is no longer a sacred/precious object, but it becomes an IDEA.

Prov: Purchased from the 1969 John Moores Liverpool Exhibition where it won a £300 prize.
Exh: W.A.G., Liverpool, *John Moores Liverpool Exhibition* 1969 (13).
Ref: **1.** Apparently in 1970; the parts of the statement relating specifically to *8bS* alone are omitted.   **2.** Letter 5 June 1970.

ARTHOIS, Jacobus d', 1613—after 1686

1183 Landscape

Canvas, 57.7 × 75.7 cm

Formerly attributed to Lucas van Uden.[1] The site represented may have been in the Foret de Soignes.[2]

Prov: Bequeathed by George Audley 1932.
Exh: W.A.G., *Cleaned Pictures*, 1955 (30)
Ref: **1.** *Cleaned Pictures op. cit.* on the suggestions of Dr. Roland verbally 30 March 1954. For the present attribution see particularly Musées royaux des Beaux-Arts de Belgique, Bruxelles, *Le paysage brabancon au XVIIe siècle*, 1976, Nos. 5-12, pp. 21-2.   **2.** Dr. W. Laureyssens, *letter*, 6 March 1977.

ASSELIJN, Jan, 1610-1660, follower of

869   Travellers Resting

Canvas, 54.8 × 66.5 cm

Dating from the 1660's and close to but not by Willem Schellinks and the anonymous artist of nos. 268, 298, 309 and 331 in Anne Charlotte Steland-Stief, *Jan Asselijn*, 1971.[1]

Prov: Presented to the L.R.I. 13 October 1842 by William Lassell as by Berchem;[2] deposited at the W.A.G. 1893; presented to the W.A.G. 1948.
Ref: **1.** Anne Charlotte Steland-Stief, *letter*, 21 April 1972, see also A. C. Steland-Stief, *Jan Asselyn und Willem Schellinks,* Oud Holland, Vol. 79, 1964, p. 99. **2.** L.R.I. Archives 41.

ASSERETO, Giovacchino, 1600-1649, after

2754   Christ among the Doctors

Canvas, 137 × 174 cm

A copy after the original by Assereto in Santa Croce, Genoa.[1]

Prov: William Earle sold Winstanley 17-18 April 1839 (60) as by Caravaggio[2] £100 5s 0d bt. Mrs Jones; Mrs Benjamin Heywood Jones who presented it to the L.R.I. by 1843;[3] deposited at the W.A.G., 1893; presented to the W.A.G., 1948.
Ref: **1.** G. N. Castelnuovi, *letter*, 9 December 1953.   **2.** The copy of the sale catalogue in the Manchester City Libraries has Caravaggio replaced by Assereto in MS against lot 60 and in the same hand: "Mrs Jones intends to be presented to a permanent gallery".   **3.** Listed in the 1843 Catalogue (No. 88) as by Assereto.

BALDUCCI, Giovanni, active 1590, died 1603

6177   The Preaching of St. John the Baptist

Panel, 27.9 × 21.5 cm

The attribution is due to Philip Pouncey.[1] Berenson had previously attributed it to Beccafumi.[2]

Balducci is recorded by Baglione as having painted a *Preaching of St. John the Baptist* in the cloister of San Giovanni Decollato, Rome,[3] but neither that painting nor the preparatory study for it in the Bowdoin College Museum of Art[4] is very much related in style or composition. 6177 belongs rather to the period of the Hampton Court *Charles Martel doing penance,*[5] the modello for the fresco in San Giovanni de'Fiorentini, Rome. The group of the mother and child in the right foreground is a favourite one of the artist.[6]

The prime inspiration for 6177 is Andrea del Sarto's Scalzo fresco.[7] But there is also a debt to Vasari's *Preaching of the Baptist* in the Chapel of the Quartiere of Leo X in the prominent figure in the left foreground.[8]

6177 is probably a decorative panel in its own right. The preciosity of colour reminds one of Balducci's decorations in Volterra Cathedral.

Prov: Charles Loeser; sold Sotheby's 9 December 1959 (2) bt. Agnews £480; Senator McGuire of Dublin;[9] purchased from Agnews 1963.

Ref: **1.** Philip Pouncey, orally.   **2.** Bernard Berenson, *Italian Pictures of the Renaissance*, 1932, p. 65.   **3.** Giovanni Baglione, *Le Vite de'pittori, scultori et architetti*, Roma, 1642, p. 78.   **4.** James Phinney Baxter Fund 1932-42. Nor is his later *Preaching of St. John the Baptist*, in S. Giovanni de' Fiorentini, Naples.   **5.** Philip Pouncey, *A 'Modello' at Hampton Court for a fresco in Rome*, Burlington Magazine, 1951, p. 323.   **6.** Compare for instance *Way to Calvary* (photograph in Witt Library. C.I.Neg. 191/54/28), Uffizi 1090F and Santa Maria Novella, Chiostro Grande, *Entrance of Saint Antoninus into Florence.*   **7.** *Between Renaissance and Baroque*, City Art Gallery, Manchester, 1965 p. 14 (18).   **8.** Paola Barocchi, *Vasari Pittore*, 1964, pl. 62.   **9.** Letter from Thos. Agnew and Son, 31 January 1975.

BALDUNG GRIEN, Hans, 1485-1545

1221   Mercenary Love

Panel painted up to the edge at the left but not elsewhere, 28.6 × 23 cm

Signed: *HBG* (in monogram) *1527*[1]

The attribution was first suggested by Waagen,[2] regarded as doubtful by Eisenmann[3] but confirmed by the discovery of the monogram in 1955.[4]

The satirical theme was common in Germany[5] and the Netherlands in the late 15th and 16th Centuries.[6]

Prov: William Roscoe;[7] acquired by the L.R.I. between 1836 and 1843;[8] deposited at the W.A.G. 1893; presented to the W.A.G. 1948.

Exh: Staatliche Kunsthalle Karlsruhe, *Hans Baldung Grien* 1959 No. 50.

Ref: **1.** The last two digits are not now legible but can be read on an infra-red photograph of 1955.   **2.** G. Waagen, *Treasures of Art in Great Britain*, 1854, III, p. 237.   **3.** J. Meyer, *Kunstlerlexikon* 1878, II, p. 629, No. 12.   **4.** Walker Art Gallery Catalogue, *Cleaned Pictures*, 1955, No. 15.   **5.** For example Baldung's engraving of 1507 (K. T. Parker, *The Engravings of Hans Baldung Grien*, Print Collector's Quarterly, 1925, Vol. 12, p. 432, No. 1) and his painting *Ungleiches Liebespaar* of 1528 (Staatliche Kunsthalle, Karlsruhe, *Katalog Alte Meister*, 1966, p. 37). **6.** For the theme see Eugen Diederichs, *Deutsches Leben der Vergangenheit* etc, 1908, I plates 83, 84, 219, 464, 465 etc. and Georges Marlier, *Érasme et la peinture flamande de son temps*, 1954, pp. 228-50. **7.** Not at his sale Winstanley's Liverpool 1816 but in his MS draft for his 1816 Sale Catalogue, p. 11 (Roscoe Papers No. 3897) as *An old man addressing a young woman* by Antonello da Messina, panel 11 × 9 ins. **8.** Not in 1836 Catalogue, but No. 27 in 1843 Catalogue as *Age and Youth* by Antonello da Messina.

BALESTRA, Antonio, 1666-1740

619 Raising of Lazarus

Canvas, 172.5 × 162.5 cm

One of a group of paintings including No. 2798 by Pittoni (q.v.).

Prov: See No. 2798 by Pittoni, N.A.A.F.I. Aldershot sold Sotheby 30 April 1947 (83) bt. Berendt £5; H. O. Molesworth from whom purchased 1956.

BAROCCI, Federico, 1526-1612, after

6945 St. Francis receiving the Stigmata

Canvas, 158.4 × 119.5 cm

Traditionally attributed to Agostino Carracci[1] presumably on the strength of his engraving of 1586,[2] No. 6945 is in fact a copy, but with a completely different background, after Barocci's altarpiece of 1594-5 now in the Galleria Nazionale delle Marche, Urbino.[3]

Prov: Richard Vaughan Yates. William Rathbone who presented it to the L.R.I. 1863; presented to the W.A.G. 1969 by the University of Liverpool.
Exh: Liverpool Mechanics Institution, *1st Exhibition of Objects Illustrative of the Fine Arts etc.*, 1840 (103) (as Ludovico Carracci).
Ref: **1.** Old Label. **2.** Adam Bartsch, *Le Peintre Graveur*, 1818, Vol. 18 p. 72, No. 69. **3.** For full details see Bologna, Museo Civico, *Federico Barocci*, 1975, pp. 182-4, No. 220.

BARTOLOMMEO di Giovanni, active 1485-1510

2756 A legend of St. Andrew

Panel, 25 × 52 cm

According to the Golden Legend St. Andrew posthumously appeared as a pilgrim and saved a bishop particularly devoted to him, who was entertaining a devil disguised as a woman traveller. A maid at the door is asking the saint one of the three questions posed by the devil before he was allowed admission.[1]

Exh: Manchester, *Art Treasures,* 1857 (70).

Ref: 1. Jacopo da Voragine, *The Golden Legend . . .* , I, ed Frederick S. Ellis, Hammersmith, 1892, pp. 252-4; George Kaftal, *Iconography of the Saints in Tuscan Painting,* Florence, 1952, col. 40.

2755   Martyrdom of St. Sebastian

Panel, 25.4 × 52 cm

Sebastian in fact survived his ordeal with the arrows, but was then beaten to death by maces. His martyrdom took place in the Campus Martius in Rome during the reign of Diocletian. Somewhat unusually the artist has attempted to give an authentic flavour by setting the figures against a background of familiar Roman buildings. The Colosseum, the Arch of Titus, the Torre della Milizia and the Pantheon are clearly recognisable.[1]

Berenson was the first to suggest Alunno di Domenico as the artist of 2755 and 2756,[2] subsequently revealed by documents as Bartolommeo di Giovanni. Another panel owned by the Mount Trust representing the *Resurrection* (24.8 × 52 cm) may have been the centre-piece of the predella to which 2755 and 2756 once belonged.[3] But although the measurements match, the style is not entirely consonant with our panels.

An altarpiece in San Andrea, Camoggiano represents *The Crucifixion with Saints Sebastian, Peter, Mary Magdalen, Andrew and a Bishop Saint.*[4] It could have had a predella consisting of 5 panels of the size of 2755 and 2756. The presence of 5 Saints would rule out the possibility of a *Resurrection* as centrepiece.

The drawing in the Louvre,[5] which has been suggested as possibly a study for one of the archers, is not particularly close to any of them.

Prov: With 2756, Littlehales Sale, a collection of Italian pictures "recently consigned from Rome", Christie, 2 March 1804 (13) and (14) bt. Bryan 6 gns.; Fagan and Grignon Sale, Squibb's, 29 May 1806 (1) bt. Jackson 1 gn.; Jackson of Ebury House, Chelsea, Sale, Christie, 7 April 1807 (25) and (26) bt. Winstanley £2 and £2 12s 6d respectively (for 2755 and 2756); Roscoe sale, 1816 (14) and (15) passed; presented to the L.R.I. by 1819;[6] deposited at the W.A.G., 1893;[7] presented to the W.A.G., 1948.

Exh: Manchester, *Art Treasures,* 1857 (69).

Ref: 1. 1963 Catalogue p. 14. Other painters like Pollaiuolo use classical buildings to identify Rome, but do not represent specific Roman buildings.   2. Bernard Berenson, *Florentine Painters,* 1909, p. 98.   3. First suggested by Horace Buttery, letter 5 December 1938 and by Hans Gronau, letter of Horace Buttery, 23 November 1951; see also Denys Sutton, *The Mount Trust Collection,* The Connoisseur, CXLVI, October 1960, p. 466.   4. 180 cm. 1963 Catalogue p. 14. Reproduced as fig. 2 in Everett Fahy, *Bartolommeo di Giovanni reconsidered,*

Apollo, XCVII, 1973, pp. 462-469, who agrees with Sutton over the Mount Trust picture and with Compton over the *Crucifixion*, and Everett Fahy, *Some followers of Domenico Ghirlandajo* (Doctoral Thesis, Harvard University, 1968), 1976, pp. 37-38, 133, 142-143 (43, 44).   **5.** 1963 Catalogue, *op. cit.* Illustrated in Raimond Van Marle, *The Development of the Italian School of Painting*, XI, 1929, p. 444, fig. 278.   **6.** 1819 Catalogue (8) and (9).   **7.** 1893 Catalogue p. 9 (17) and (18).

BASSANO, Francesco da Ponte, the Younger, 1549-1592

1217   The Betrayal of Christ

Canvas, 97.5 × 142.9 cm

Of the same height as a picture attributed to Jacopo and Francesco Bassano in the Sambon Gallery, Paris in 1929 of *Saint Veronica presenting her kerchief to Christ on his way to Calvary*.[1] Possibly they formed part of a set.

As in the case with 1218, there are a number of versions repeating parts of the composition, of which the prime source appears to be a painting of upright format now in Cremona Museum (inv. 189), signed by Francesco.[2] This painting once formed part of a cycle devoted to The Passion in the Gesu, Brescia.[3]

Although both the 1859[4] and 1893[5] Catalogues attribute 1217 to Jacopo and note that it was "inscribed", no inscription is now visible, and the execution appears to be very close to Francesco.[2]

Prov: William Earle; his sale, Winstanley's, 17 April 1839 (20) £43; presented by John Miller to the L.R.I. by 1843;[6] deposited at the W.A.G., 1893;[5] presented to the W.A.G., 1948.

Ref: **1.** A. Sambon, *Les Bassano, Catalogue des oeuvres des ces artistes exposées à la Galerie Sambon*, 1929, (Witt Library photograph) 97 × 127 cm.   **2.** Edoardo Arslan, *I Bassano*, Milan, 1960, I, p. 349. The attribution is accepted by Pallucchini and Ballarin orally 19 October 1967.   **3.** Arslan, *op. cit.*, p. 207 and Carlo Ridolfi, *Le Maraviglie dell'arte*, I, 1648 p. 379 as Jacopo.   **4.** 1859 Catalogue p. 51 (96).   **5.** 1893 Catalogue p. 31 (88).   **6.** 1843 Catalogue p. 21 (75).

BASSANO, Francesco da Ponte, the Younger, after

1218   The Element of Fire

Canvas, 107.3 × 143.4 cm

Inscribed: on the base of a column left. *FRANC/BASSANO/PINX*.

Probably one of a set of four elements. It is on a slightly smaller scale than the two sets, parts of which were both once in the Liechtenstein Collection.[1] Ridolfi mentions part of a set in the collection of Carlo Scagliari, great nephew of Jacopo Bassano.[2] There was another complete set[3] and an individual picture of *The Element of Fire,* 'sbozzato' in the inventory of the studio made after Jacopo's death.[4] There was also a Vulcan listed in that inventory.[5]

Despite the signature 1218 is probably a copy,[6] although Wart Arslan holds it to be a studio work[7] and Edoardo Arslan regards it as by Francesco himself.[8]

As in the case with 1217 motifs in the composition can be found in a number of works from the Bassano family studio.

Prov: Entered the L.R.I. Collection between 1836 and 1843;[9] deposited at the W.A.G., 1893;[10] presented to the W.A.G., 1948.

Exh: Manchester, *Art Treasures,* 1857 (284).

Ref: **1.** W. E. Suida, *A Catalogue of Paintings in the John and Mable Ringling Museum of Art, Sarasota,* 1949, p. 85 (a) Sarasota Ringling Museum 86 and 87 *Fire,* 55 × 71⅝ in and *Water* 55½ × 71¾ in; Berlin Kaiser Friedrich Museum n. 1956 *Air* (destroyed in the war) 123 × 182 cm (b) Vaduz 232 *Fire,* 234 *Earth* 145 × 187 cm.   **2.** Carlo Ridolfi, *Le Maraviglie dell'Arte,* I, 1648, p. 398.   **3.** Giambatista Verci, *Intorno alla vita e alle opere de'pittori . . . di Bassano,* 1775, p. 95 (80).   **4.** Verci, *op. cit.,* p. 93, (48).   **5.** Verci, *op. cit.,* p. 99 (165).   **6.** Pallucchini and Ballarin, orally, 19 October 1967.   **7.** Wart Arslan, letter, 9 November 1958.   **8.** E. Arslan, *I Bassano,* I, 1960, p. 218.   **9.** 1843 Catalogue p. 24 (84).   **10.** 1893 Catalogue p. 32 (89).

BASSANO, Jacopo da Ponte, active 1535, died 1592

1219   The Sacrifice of Noah

Canvas, 119.7 × 86.3 cm

The subject is taken from Genesis VIII 20. Noah is offering burnt sacrifice in the left distance in thanks for his deliverance from the Flood. The figures in the foreground are presumably Noah's sons building a house.

1219 may be a fragment from one of a set of pictures devoted to the Story of Noah. The composition is very similar to the versions at Kromeriza[1] and in the Escorial;[2] both of which form parts of complete sets. One set is mentioned in the inventory of the studio drawn up on Jacopo's death,[3] as is a single picture of the *Sacrifice of Noah.*[4] Possibly the same *Sacrifice of Noah* was owned by Carlo Scagliari, great nephew of Jacopo.[5]

1219 is probably a late autograph work.[6] But Edoardo Arslan postulates some studio assistance.[7]

Prov: Mrs Vere Wright, Shelton Hall, Newark;[8] her sale Turner, Fletcher and Essex, Shelton Hall, 5 July 1951 (297) with "the Temple of Minerva Media (sic) at Rome", purchased from Messrs Colnaghi, 1952.

Versions: Kromeriz 049;[1] Escorial; [2] Palazzo Pitti No. 386,[9] Museo Stibbert 369.[10]

Ref: **1.** Vaclav Tomasek, *Umeleckohistoricke Muzeum Obrazarna Kromerizs-kehozamku*, 1964, p. 49, 049. 134 × 179 cm. signed: IAC BASSAN.   **2.** Juan José Luna Fernandez, *Acotaciones a la serie de "El Diluvio" de los Bassano*, Archivo Espanol de Arte, XLIV, 1971, p. 328.   **3.** Giambatista Verci, *Notizie intorno alla vita e alle opere de'pittori . . . di Bassano*, 1775, p. 95 (84).   **4.** Verci, *op. cit.*, p. 98 (152).   **5.** Carlo Ridolfi, *Le Maraviglie dell'Arte*, 1648, p. 389.   **6.** Bernard Berenson, *Venetian School*, 1957, p. 18; Wart Aslan, letter, 6 January 1958 and Ballarin orally 19 October 1967.   **7.** Edoardo Arslan, *I Bassano*, I, 1960, p. 169. Pallucchini suggests orally 19 October 1967 that the figures were by Jacopo and the landscape by Francesco.   **8.** Colnaghi, *Old Master Paintings*, 1952 (11).   **9.** 93 × 124 cm. Art. Iahn-Rusconi, *La R. Galleria Pitti in Firenze*, 1937, p. 60 as Francesco Bassano.   **10.** Giuseppe Cantelli, *Il Museo Stibbert a Firenze* II, 1974, pl. 128.

BATIST, Karel, active 17th century

822   Flower Piece

Canvas, 99 × 73.6 cm

823   Flower Piece

Canvas, 99 × 73.6 cm

No. 822 includes a lily, chrysanthemum and roses and No. 823 has daffodils, a rose, chrysanthemum, pink, tulip, etc. The attribution of both is traditional.

Prov: Mrs Theodore Rathbone, presented by Miss May Rathbone, 1913.

BEERS, Jan van, born 1852

313   Girl's Head

Panel, 28.5 × 22.8 cm

Signed and dated: *Jan van BEERS/PARIS/1878*

Prov: Bought from Everard by Agnew's November 1878;[1] thence to George Holt, 15 January 1879 (receipt dated 26 June, MS, W.A.G.) £45; bequeathed by Emma Holt 1944.

Ref: **1.** Agnew's Stock Book.

BELLINI, Giovanni, active c. 1459, died 1516

2757 Portrait of a Young Man

Panel, 35.1 × 27 cm

Condition: Right side of face much worn; left eye and areas of the sky and parapet damaged.[1] Pentimenti reveal that the sitter's right shoulder was once without the flap, that the left shoulder was once higher and that the cap was once larger.

Inscribed: *IOANNES BELLINVS*. on parapet

A characteristic Bellini type, bust length turned left behind a parapet with a view of the sky behind.[2]

Suggestions as to attribution made before the radical attention to 2757 in 1950 should be disregarded because of extensive repainting. Its present condition especially in the important area of the face induces caution; several scholars including Berenson[3] and Heinemann[4] accept it as autograph. The delicacy of the painting of the sky supports their conclusion. The technique suggests a date before the Loredan[5] and Hampton Court[6] portraits, that is in the last two decades of the fifteenth century.[7]

The costume is unusual; the type of hat is found in a group of Germans in Gentile Bellini's *Corpus Christi Procession* of 1496.[8]

A self portrait attributed to Giovanni Bellini was in the Muselli collection in 1662.[9] When first recorded 2757 was thought to be a self portrait.[10]

Prov: Entered L.R.I. Collection between 1836 and 1843;[10] deposited at the W.A.G., 1893;[11] presented to the W.A.G., 1948.

Ref: **1.** W.A.G., *Cleaned Pictures*, 1955, pp. 29-30.   **2.** The formal structure is conceived in the same way as in the Uffizi portrait. In ultra-violet photographs a pentimento is visible on the right shoulder which originally would have been rounded without the interruption of the cape.   **3.** Bernard Berenson, *Italian Pictures of the Renaissance: Venetian School*, I, 1957, p. 31 as late.   **4.** Fritz Heinemann, *Giovanni Bellini e I Belliniani*, I, 1959, p. 79 no. 293 as towards 1510.   **5.** Martin Davies, *National Gallery, Earlier Italian Schools*, 1961, pp. 55-6.   **6.** Georg Gronau, *Giovanni Bellini*, 1930, p. 163.   **7.** For a discussion of the chronology of the portraits, Giles Robertson, *Giovanni Bellini*, 1968, pp. 106-8, who considers 2757 to be a studio work.   **8.** Mrs Newton, orally, June 1972.   **9.** Giuseppe Campori, *Raccolta di Cataloghi ed Inventari inediti . . .*, 1876, p. 187.   **10.** 1843 Catalogue p. 12 (40).   **11.** 1893 Catalogue p. 13 (33).

BERTIERI, Pilade, 1874-1965

2739 Lady in Black Furs (La Dame aux Fourrures Noires)[1]

Canvas,[2] 222.2 × 131.5 cm

Signed: *Bertieri*

The sitter was the artist's wife Genevieve (1887-1969) daughter of John and Mary Sutherland Wilson of New York whom he married in 1906;[3] Bertieri painted a considerable number of other portraits of his wife[4] including one in which she wears the same clothes as in No. 2739 but is standing up[5] and another full length seated portrait.[6] No. 2739 probably dates from 1910.[7]

Prov: Purchased from the L.A.E., 1914, £100.

Exh: Paris, *Société Nationale des Beaux Arts*, 1912 (130) plate 77 as *Portrait de Mme Pilade Bertieri*; Brighton, *Autumn Exhibitions*, 1913 (58); London, Dowdeswell Galleries, *Portraits, Landscapes and Drawings by Pilade Bertieri*, 1914 (8); L.A.E. 1914 (60).

Ref: 1. This French title first appears in the 1913 Brighton Catalogue (see Exhibitions).   2. Stretcher stamped 568.   3. Information from press cuttings particularly the New York Herald 14 January 1906 from the artist's studio communicated by Mrs G. B. M. Anderson the artist's daughter.   4. Press Cuttings, *op. cit.*, Dowdeswell Galleries, *Portraits, Landscapes and Drawings by Pilade Bertieri*, 1914 (41 and 42).   5. *La Femme qui Passe* (Paris, Société Nationale des Beaux Arts, 1913 (112) plate 162).   6. Dowdeswell Galleries, *op. cit.* (15) See *The Standard* 30 May 1914.   7. Mrs G. B. M. Anderson letter 22 July 1970.

BERTOIA, Jacopo, 1544-1574

2795   Female Figure

Lime plaster with gilded background, 35.7 × 17.2 cm

The 1804 Sale Catalogue described it as "Corregio. A Nymph, in Fresco, cut from a Cornice in the Palazzo Vecchio at Parma."[1] The figure probably formed part of a frieze and appears to be the sole surviving piece of an otherwise unknown room decoration. A plumb line was incised in the plaster by the artist to construct the figure.

The Palazzo Vecchio has been identified with the Palazzo del Giardino on the grounds that the palace was built on the site of the old Visconti fortress.[2] It may, however, only have come from "an old palace."

The connection with the artists who painted in the Palazzo del Giardino was first made by Andrews.[3] Vasari said that Girolamo Mirola worked there,[4] and fragments surviving in the Gallery at Parma are generally attributed to Bertoia.[5] It is not yet clear what Mirola's style was like. Shearman was the first to specifically attribute 2795 to Bertoia.[6] In fact the closest points of contact are with the frieze in the grand salone of the Palazzo Lalatta,[7] a work which must be close to 1566 in view of resemblances with the fragment of the *Coronation of the Virgin* painted on the outside of the Palazzo del Comune for the visit of Princess Maria Daviz of Portugal, who arrived on 24 June 1566.[8]

Prov: Parma, Palazzo Vecchio?;[1] Col. Matthew Smith Sale, Christie's 12 May 1804 (6), bt. Roscoe £2 2s 0d; Roscoe sale (38) bt. Robinson £8 18s 6d; Thomas H. Robinson, his sale, Winstanley, Manchester, 17 May 1820 (4); Thomas Winstanley, who presented it to the L.R.I., 1829;[9] deposited at the W.A.G., 1893;[10] presented to the W.A.G., 1948.

Ref: **1.** Col. Matthew Smith Sale, Christie's, 12 May 1804 (6).   **2.** 1963 Catalogue, p. 21.   **3.** Keith Andrews orally, and reiterated by letter 7 December 1963.   **4.** Vasari, ed. Milanesi, VII, 1881, p. 422.   **5.** Augusta Ghidiglia Quintavalle, *Il Bertoia*, 1963, p. 52 as c. 1572-4.   **6.** Professor J. Shearman, orally, 1958.   **7.** Quintavalle, *op. cit.*, pl. IV and V. A comparison suggested by Quintavalle, *letter*, 27 February 1967, who also suggests that 2795 may have formed part of the decoration of that palace, *letter*, 5 May 1967.   **8.** Quintavalle, *op. cit.*, pl. III and p. 10 citing A. M. Edoari Da Herba, *Compendio Copiosissimo dell'origine, antichità, successo e nobiltà della città di Parma, suo popolo e territorio*, Parma, 1572.   **9.** L.R.I. Annual Report, 1829, p. 24.   **10.** 1893 Catalogue p. 32 (90).

BICCI DI LORENZO, 1373-1452, studio of

2759 St. Peter

Panel (poplar), 25.7 cm diameter

Prov: See 2760.

2760 St. Paul

Panel (poplar), 25.7 cm diameter

Two roundels probably from the gables of a polyptych, first attributed to Bicci di Lorenzo in the 1963 Catalogue.[1] A Saint Paul and Saint Peter very similar in type and style, though superior in quality, occur in roundels at the top of the Crawford Polyptych in Westminster Abbey.[2] The tooling of the haloes of two panels in the Galleria Nazionale, Rome representing Saints John the Baptist and Nicholas of Bari, and Saints Anthony Abbot and (?)Julian[3] is so close to that of 2759 as to suggest that they are from the same punches. The Crawford polyptych is closely linked in style with a polyptych, the main part of which is now divided between the Badia, Grottaferrata, the Robert Lehmann Collection and the Gallery at Parma.[4] This altarpiece dated 1433 is documented as being painted by Bicci di Lorenzo, with the collaboration of Stefano d' Antonio (1405-1483), for the monastery of San Niccolo in Cafaggio in Florence. It was valued on January 14, 1435.[5] In 1433 Stefano d'Antonio is also documented as in course of painting in association with Bicci di Lorenzo a chapel and a panel for San Marco, and an altarpiece and chapel for the Cante Compagni in Santa Trinità.[6]

It is possible that 2759 and 2760 belonged to the same polyptych as the two panels in Rome or to the San Niccolo in Cafaggio polyptych occupying analogous positions to those occupied by the Crawford roundels. Certainly their style is of the mid 1430's.

The *St. Mark* in Indianapolis, however, cannot belong to the same polyptych as 2759 and 2760 on account of the difference in size[7] and haloes as well as of style.

Prov: Thomas Winstanley, who presented them to the L.R.I. between 1836 and 1843;[8] deposited at the W.A.G., 1893.[9]

Ref: **1.** 1963 Catalogue pp. 21-22 followed by Bernard Berenson, *Italian Pictures of the Renaissance, Florentine School*, I, 1963, p. 30.   **2.** St. John Gore, *The Art of Painting in Florence & Siena from 1250 to 1500*, Wildenstein, London, 1965, pp. 20-21 (34) fig. 32.   **3.** Raimond Van Marle, *The Development of the Italian Schools of Painting*, IX, 1927, p. 41.   **4.** Berenson, *op. cit.*, I, pl. 506.   **5.** W. Cohn, *Maestri sconosciuti del quattrocento fiorentino, II — Stefano d'Antonio*, Bolletino d'arte, XLIV, 1959, pp. 61, 67, doc V.   **6.** Cohn, *op. cit.*, pp. 65-66 doc IV, 68 n. 14.   **7.** 5¹/₄ ins (diameter). Dwight Miller, *Catalogue of European Paintings, Indianapolis Museum of Art*, 1970.   **8.** 1843 Catalogue pp. 4-5 (10-11); the L.R.I. Presents Book (L.R.I. Archives 37) notes 6 Old Masters presented by Winstanley, 11 February 1838 and a specimen of Early Italian painting deposited by him 2 April 1838, but does not specify their painters or subjects.   **9.** 1893 Catalogue pp. 5-6 (9 and 10).

BIONDO, Giovanni del, *c.* 1356-1392, studio of

2782   Coronation of the Virgin

Panel, 42.9 × 51.1 cm

Prov: Roscoe Sale, Winstanley, (2) bt. Crompton, £10 10s 0d; presented to the L.R.I., 1819;[1] deposited at the W.A.G., 1893;[2] presented to the W.A.G., 1948.

Exh: Manchester, *Art Treasures*, 1857, (18)

6119
6120   Angels playing musical instruments

Panel, 33.1 × 38 cm and 32.8 × 29.5 cm (respectively)

Prov: Roscoe Sale (9), bt. Ford[3] £6 6s 0d; E. Grindley, 73 and 75 Church Street, Liverpool;[4] (?)Wedells Collection, Hamburg;[5] bt. in London by Carlo Sestieri and taken to Rome;[6] purchased from Carlo Sestieri, 1962.

2782, 6110 and 6120 probably formed the central part of a large altarpiece,[7] cut up before 1816. The top of 2782 and the legs of Christ and the Virgin have been lost. Despite the identical embroidery patterns Roscoe failed to relate 6119 and 6120 to 2782.[8]

Berenson was the first to suggest Giovanni del Biondo,[9] and Offner regards it as a workshop product.[10] The composition is similar to that of the 1372 *Coronation of the Virgin,* once in the Cook Collection.[11] 2782 is probably somewhat later. Offner suggests about 1375 or a little later,[12] whilst Boskovits puts it as late as 1380-1385.[13]

Variations of the pattern of the throne hanging were very popular with Giovanni del Biondo,[14] whilst that on the drapery of both Christ and the Virgin is a variation of an arabesque pattern ultimately of Persian origin, which first appears in Italian painting in the circle of Bernardo Daddi in the 1340's.[15]

The musical instruments played by the angels are a portable organ, a viol and a lute.

Ref: 1. 1819 Catalogue (1).   2. 1893 Catalogue p. 4 (5).   3. Identified in the British Museum copy of the Roscoe Sale Catalogue as William Ford, bookseller of Manchester, for whom see C. W. Sutton in *Dictionary of National Biography*.   4. Label on reverse of 6120. Grindley, a dealer in works of art and in artists' materials is registered in Gore's Directory as having a shop with the address 73 and 75 Church Street from 1872 to 1891.   5. Bernard Berenson, *Florentine School*, 1963, p. 85. For the collection see Alfred Rohde *Die Galerie Wedells in Hamburg,* Cicerone, Vol 1, 1922, pp. 506-8. It is possible that 6119 and 6120 are the "zwei kleine Bildchen der Giottoschule" mentioned on p. 506. They are not mentioned by Gustav Paoli *Sammlung Wedells in Hamburg*, Pantheon, 1937, pp. 133-8.   6. Carlo Sestieri, *letter*, 18 January, 1962.   7. Federico Zeri, *letter* 11 July 1961 and *Una predella ed altre cose di Giovanni del Biondo*, Paragone, XIII, no. 149, 1962, pp. 19-20.   8. Roscoe Sale (9) The width inadvertently was printed first in the sale catalogue.   9. Bernard Berenson, *Due Illustratori Italiani della Speculum Humanae Salvationis*, Bolletino d'Arte, V, 1925/6, pp. 314, 320 as c. 1390.   10. Richard Offner, *A Ray of Light on Giovanni del Biondo and Niccolo di Tommaso*, Mitteilungen des Kunsthistorisches Institutes in Florenz, VII, 1956, p. 189, and Richard Offner and Klara Steinweg, *A Corpus of Florentine Paintings*, Section IV, Vol. V, Part II, 1969, pp. 163 and 166.   11. Theo Melville, *Some recent acquisitions*, Liverpool Bulletin, 10, 1962 p. 13.   12. Offner and Steinweg, op. cit., p. 163.   13. Miklos Boskovits, *Pittura Fiorentina alla vigilia del Rinascimento 1370-1400*, 1975, p. 311.   14. Brigitte Klesse, *Seidenstoffe in der italienischen Malerei des vierzehnten Jahrhunderts*, 1967, p. 365 Kat 318 lists 5 other examples of paintings by Giovanni del Biondo with similar patterns.   15. Klesse, op. cit., pp. 234-6 Kat 121.

BISSOLO, Francesco, active 1492-died 1554, studio of

2784   Virgin and Child with Saints Michael and Veronica and a donor

Panel, 69.4 × 94.6 cm

Until 1893, 2784 was held to be a *Marriage of Saint Catherine*, when the compiler of the L.R.I. Annual Report identified the Saints. The attribution to Bissolo was first made by Fairfax Murray.[1] A superior version convincingly attributed to Bissolo is at York.[2]

The suggestion that 2784 is by Pietro degli Ingannati put forward first by Waagen[3] and supported by Berenson[4] and Heinemann[5] seems unwarranted. The influence of Palma evident in 2784 confirms the attribution to the circle of Bissolo, rather than Ingannati.

Prov: Possibly the picture, which Winstanley exchanged with Roscoe for a Titian;[6] Roscoe Sale (64) bt. Mason £99 15s 0d; presented to the L.R.I. by 1819;[7] deposited at the W.A.G., 1893;[8] presented to the W.A.G., 1948.

Ref: **1.** L.R.I. Annual Report 1893, p. 49 (85).   **2.** *Catalogue of Paintings*, City of York Art Gallery, I, 1961, p. 10, pl. 12. The attribution is disputed, however, by Fritz Heinemann, *Giovanni Bellini e I Belliniani*, I, 1962, p. 109, S147a. The Madonna and Child are repeated in a painting at Vercelli, Vittorio Viale, *Catalogo: I Dipinti Museo Civico Francesco Borgogna*, Vercelli, 1969, p. 77, no. 117, pl. 122.   **3.** On a visit to Liverpool in 1835 G. F. Waagen, *Works of Art and Artists in England* III, 1838, p. 184 and *Art Treasures in Great Britain*, III, 1854, p. 237 no. 75.   **4.** Bernard Berenson, *Italian Pictures of the Renaissance: Venetian School,* 1957, p. 92.   **5.** Fritz Heinemann, *Giovanni Bellini e I Belliniani,* I, 1963, p. 109, s. 147 as youthful work; and *letter* 9 July 1968.   **6.** Roscoe Papers, no. 5315.   **7.** 1819 Catalogue (20).   **8.** 1893 Catalogue p. 28 (79).

BLANCHARD, Pascal, active 19th century

3086   Samson and Delilah

Canvas, 180 × 272 cm

Signed: *Pascal Blanchard 1886.*

Prov: Unknown.
Exh: Paris, *Societé des Artistes francais,* 1886 (242).

BOLOGNESE School, 17th century

2860   Death of St. Joseph

Copper, 21.5 × 16.7 cm

2861   A Saint with a Chain around his Neck

Copper, 16.5 × 12.3 cm

2862   St. Francis receiving the Stigmata

Copper 21.7 × 16.5 cm

Of low quality. The attribution is traditional.

Prov: Acquired together from J. Sanderson of 10 Mount Pleasant, Liverpool by the L.R.I.; deposited at the W.A.G. 1893; presented to the W.A.G. 1948.

2863   Meleager and Atalanta

Panel, 15.2 × 20.2 cm

Attributed in 1843 to Guido Reni in his "Guercino or middle manner",[1] No. 2863 has been more recently attributed to Tiarini.[2]

Prov: Acquired by the L.R.I. between 1836 and 1843; deposited at the W.A.G. 1893; presented to the W.A.G. 1948.
Ref: **1.** 1843 Catalogue No. 112.   **2.** 1963 Catalogue p. 190.

2900   Holy Family with St. Anne

Canvas, 143 × 135.5 cm

Dr. Erich Schleier suggests that No. 2900 is by Pierfrancesco Mola.[1]

Prov: Presented by T. Arthur Hope 1882.
Ref: **1.** Letter 25 January 1969.

BOMPIANI, Roberto, 1821-1908

3033   An Italian Girl

Canvas, 73.6 × 61.5 cm

Signed: *Rto. Bompiani ft.*

Bonfigli recorded in Bompiani's studio in the Via di S.Claudio "A Seated Girl, holding a tambourine, representing a young Baccante".[1]

Prov: Transferred from the Toxteth Branch Library 1918.
Ref: **1.** F. S. Bonfigli, *Guide to the Studios of Rome,* 1860, p. 46.

BONHEUR, Auguste, 1824-1884

181   Ploughing, Early Morning

Canvas, 69.8 × 120 cm

Signed: *A Bonheur* (initials in monogram)

Prov: Bought by George Holt from W. G. Herbert, either 1871[1] (bill dated 28 November for *Pictures* by Auguste Bonheur, £270), or possibly 1872/3 (bill dated 4 February for *Ploughing,* £320, both bills MSS, W.A.G.); bequeathed by Emma Holt 1944.
Exh: Liverpool Art Club, *Modern Oil Paintings by Foreign Artists* 1884 No. 28.
Ref: **1.** This earlier date and lower price are given in Holt's MS *Catalogue,* W.A.G.

182 Paysage d'Auvergne

Canvas, 79.7 × 116.2 cm

Signed and dated: *A Bonheur/1852*. (initials in monogram)

Described under this title in the Morny Sale Catalogue (see provenance) and as *Landscape, Auvergne* while in the Holt Collection, but No. 182 can be identified as the *Ruines du Chateau d'Apchon* of the 1853 Paris Salon (see exhibitions) and the castle on the hill in No. 182 certainly is Apchon.[1]

In 1842 Auguste Bonheur's father married his second wife who came from Mauriac, the arrondissement in which Apchon stands, and the Bonheur family appear to have visited that area frequently thereafter. Auguste Bonheur was patronized by the Duc de Morny, Minister of the Interior in France, 1851-2, President of the Corps Legislatif, 1854-1865, at the request of Rosa Bonheur, his sister.[2]

Prov: Duc de Morny sold Paris, 31 May 1865 (1), bt. Gambart 4350 francs. Bought by George Holt from Agnew's 1868 (bill 6 October, MS, W.A.G.) £235; bequeathed by Emma Holt 1944.

Exh: Paris, *Salon*, 1853 (133) *Ruines du Chateau d'Apchon* (appartenant a M. le comte de Morny).

Ref: 1. Archives Photographiques, Caisse Nationale des Monuments Historiques, No. 70776.   **2.** Anna Klumpke, *Rosa Bonheur, sa vie, son oeuvre* 1908, p. 226, note 1.

BONHEUR, Rosa, 1822-1899

183 Sheep and Lambs

Panel, 33 × 43.5 cm

Signed and dated: *Rosa Bonheur/1886*

Another version of No. 183, almost identical to it but slightly more finished, was published as a photograph in the *Musee Goupil et Cie*, No. 738, n.d. This version was signed and dated 1866 and entitled *Brebis et Agneaux*.

Prov: (?)Marquis de Santurce, sold Christie's 25 April 1891 (99), bt. West £672. (?)Messrs Murrieta sold Christie's 14 May 1892 (31) bt. Agnews £514 10s 0d. Bought from Agnew's, London by George Holt, £600;[1] bequeathed by Emma Holt 1944.

Exh: Cork, 1902; Bristol, 1908 (79).

Ref: 1. No bill extant; price noted in Holt's Price List, MS, W.A.G.

184   Arab and Dead Horse

Canvas, 20 × 34 cm

Signed and dated: *R. Bonheur 1852*

Prov: Anon, sold Christie's 16 June 1877 (46) bt. Morley. W. G. Herbert from whom it was bought by George Holt 1877 (bill 4 October, MS, W.A.G.), £45; bequeathed by Emma Holt 1944.

185   Le Retour du Moulin

Canvas, 27.3 × 35.5 cm

Signed: *Rosa Bonheur*

Prov: F. T. Turner sold Christie's 4 May 1878 (56) bt. Agnew £598 10s 0d; bought by George Holt from Agnew's 1889 (bill 30 September, MS, W.A.G.), £600; bequeathed by Emma Holt 1944.
Exh: Birmingham, *Exhibition of French Pictures*, 1898 (27); Guildhall London, 1898 (125); Whitechapel Art Gallery, London, *Animals in Art*, 1907 (108).

BOR, Paulus, 1600-1669

958   The Magdalen

Panel, 65.7 × 60.8 cm

The attribution is generally accepted[1] but the names of P. de Grebber, Lievens[2] and the young Salomon de Bray[3] have also been suggested.

Prov: At Penayre, Brecon by 1879 as the property of Sir Anthony Cleasby and his son Richard Cleasby;[4] by descent to J. O. M. Hill; sold to W. J. Price October 1946; anon sold Christie's 31 January 1947 (135) as Rembrandt bt. Leggatt from whom purchased 1952.
Exh: Antwerp, *Caravaggio and the Netherlands,* 1952 (22).
Ref: **1.** Benedict Nicolson, *Caravaggio and the Netherlands,* Burlington Magazine 1952, p. 252; Dr. A. Blankert, letter 10 May 1972. B. Nicolson, *Provisional List of Caravaggesque Pictures in Public and Private Collections in Great Britain and Northern Ireland*, Burlington Magazine, Vol. 116, 1974, p. 56.   **2.** Vitale Bloch, *I Caravaggeschi a Utrecht e Anversa*, Paragone, No. 33, 1952, p. 19, plate 8.   **3.** Nicolson, 1952, *op. cit.*   **4.** MS inventory compiled by Mrs Cleasby in 1879 listed as *A Magdalene* (J. O. M. Hill, letters, 19 August 1954 and 14 September 1954).

BOUCHET, Auguste, born 1831

1028   Le Mahboul

Canvas, 100 × 150.8 cm

Signed: *Ate Bouchet 1877*

A Mahboul was a North African visionary and the word "maboul" came to mean mad in French.

Prov: Montague West who paid £140 for No. 1028;[1] presented by Mabel West, 1922.
Exh: Paris, *Société des Artistes francais*, 1877 (261) with the alternative title *Fou arabe*; W.A.G., *Grand Loan Exhibition*, 1886 (1284).
Ref: 1. Rev. A. Elwell, letter, 13 May 1922.

BOUGHTON, George Henry, 1833-1905

190   The Miners

Canvas, 66.4 × 56.1 cm

Signed: *G. H. Boughton 1878*

Another version of No. 190 with the woman in the foreground, no baby and other differences was exhibited at the Grosvenor Gallery Summer Exhibition 1878 No. 115 as *The Rivals*.[1]

Did Boughton see Henry Wallis's *The Stonebreaker* (now Birmingham City Art Gallery) at the Philadelphia Centennial Exhibition 1876 (No. 177 lent by Temple Soames)?

Prov: Bought by George Holt from Agnew's 1878;[2] bequeathed by Miss Emma Holt in 1944.
Ref: 1. Reproduced in Henry Blackburn, *Grosvenor Notes* 1878 p. 39 and reviewed by Henry James in *The Grosvenor Gallery* 1878 (*Nation,* 23 May 1878 reprinted *The Painter's Eye*, 1956, p. 165). According to George Holt's *Catalogue* (MS, W.A.G.) this version belonged to G. Dobell. It was exhibited at the Walker Art Gallery, Liverpool, *Grand Loan Exhibition*, 1886, No. 765, lent by George C. Dobell and was sold by R. B. Dobell, Christie's, 16 May 1929 lot 14, 51 × 38 ins. bt. Sampson £5 5s 0d. It was described in the *Magazine of Art*, 1878, Vol. 1., p. 81.   2. MS *Account* Christmas 1878 for 30 August by exchange (W.A.G.).

769   Nut Brown Maids

Canvas, 41 × 51 cm

Signed: *G. H. Boughton*

The title of No. 769 was supplied by George Audley (see Provenance) who identified it with *A Nut Brown Maid* exhibited at the New Gallery 1903[1] (see Exhibitions). It is however more likely to have been the *Nut Brown Maids* exhibited at the Dudley Gallery in 1878[2] (see Exhibitions). Another version of No. 769 entitled *Dort Holland, Girls Nutting*[3] is identical to No. 769 except that a male and female figure recline on the grass beneath the large clump of trees and the girl on the right in the foreground has a hat on. The artist was at Dort in 1880.[4] Dutch scenes by Boughton are however rare before his visit to Holland in 1880.

Prov: William Foulds 1914. George Audley who presented it 1925.

Exh: ?Dudley Gallery, *Winter Exhibition of Cabinet Pictures in Oil*, 1878 (289) as *Nut Brown Maids*; ?New Gallery 1903, *Summer Exhibition* No. 99 as *A Nut Brown Maid*.

Ref: 1. George Audley, *Collection of Pictures*, 1923 No. 11.   2. Described in the *Athenaeum*, 1878, p. 694 as "girls walking in a meadow during summer".   3. Indistinctly annotated photograph in the Witt Library.   4. G. H. Boughton, *Sketching Rambles in Holland*, 1885, pp. 6ff. The date 1880 is provided by E. V. Lucas, *Life and Work of Edwin Austin Abbey* 1921, p. 107.

2740   The Lady of the Snows

Canvas, 107.3 × 87 cm

Signed: *G. H. Boughton R.A.*

The *R.A.* of the signature suggests a date after 1896, when the artist was made an academician. The title presumably contains a humorous reference to the miracle whereby the Virgin indicated the future site of S. Maria Maggiore by causing snow to fall on a site on the Esquiline Hill in the reign of Constantine. This miracle was revived as a subject for artists around 1900—compare, for example, E. R. Frampton's *Our Lady of the Snows* of 1916 in the Walker Art Gallery.

Prov: Mrs Greenwood;[1] George Audley[2] who presented it 1924.

Exh: *Franco British Exhibition*, London, 1908 (419); L.A.E., 1923 (932).

Ref: 1. The lender to the 1908 Franco British Exhibition (see Exhibitions); George Greenwood M.P. and Hamar Greenwood M.P. were both on the general committee of that exhibition.   2. George Audley, *Collection of Pictures* 1923, No. 9 p. 4.

3073   The Road to Camelot

Canvas, 137 × 246 cm

Signed: *G. H. BOUGHTON 1898*

Illustrates these lines[1] from Part II, of Tennyson's *The Lady of Shalott*:

> And there the surly village churls
> And the red cloaks of market girls
>   Pass onward from Shalott
> Sometimes a troop of damsels glad
> An abbot on an ambling pad
> Sometimes a curly shepherd lad
> Or long-hair'd page in crimson clad
>   Goes by to tower'd Camelot
> And sometimes thro' the mirror blue
> The knights come riding two and two
> She hath no loyal knight and true
>   The Lady of Shalott

On the left are the "market girls", on the right the "damsels glad" in the distance the knights "riding two and two" and in the centre foreground the "long-hair'd page"

A. C. R. Carter reviewing the 1898 Royal Academy for the Art-Journal[2] wrote of No. 3073: "The spirit of medievalism which animates much of Mr Boughton's compositions has not been lacking in the singularly decorative conception of 'The Road to Camelot', which is reproduced here as an extra plate. He has chosen his theme from Tennyson's 'Lady of Shalott', and it is interesting to mark the difference between the inspiration which the poet has afforded Mr Boughton on this occasion and Mr Waterhouse previously. In 'Mariana in the South', and the 'Lady of Shalott', we have the intensely tragic side of Tennyson's verse fully illustrated. The passage to Camelot for Mr Waterhouse is that broad stream flowing thither on which the corpse of the lady, "lying robed in snowy white," floated down. For Mr Boughton, the wondrous vision of picturesque life and movement passing down to Camelot, on which the lady was forbidden to look, save as reflected in the clear mirror before her, has been the attraction, and has called forth his powers of conjuring up its realization on canvas. Thus we have a picture faithfully depicting the gayer side of Tennyson's poem when the 'shadows of the world' which appear on the highway are those of a happy and careless throng, the entire scheme being a tender harmony of colour decoration. The fair-haired page, decked in crimson, and holding a hound in leash, makes a fine centerpiece for the composition, and to the right and left are symmetrically balanced groupings of glad court damsels, with minstrels, and red-cloaked market girls. Across the stream the knights riding two and two fulfil the composition with gay touches of colour on the streamers of their lances, and the simple background of landscape, with the grey-towered Camelot in the distance, sends into relief the figures in the foreground, the colours of whose costumes are subtly blended and form an effective scheme in which pale salmons, blue greys, and warm pinks are predominant, with here and there a stray purple. So truly is the picture attuned and composed that it seems a ready answer to the charge—alas! too often true—that the national idea of composition is to see a picture "par morceaux detachés," for the simple reason that too frequently there is no unity." The Athenaeum critic[3] however attacked "the want of animation and virility, colour and natural life. For the last a prevailing chalkiness is a poor substitute and the colours are too scattered to be effective;" he also denounced the poor anatomy of the figures.

The dress of the two girls nearest the dog is closely related to "Aesthetic" dress — so is the shoulder-cape of the foremost peasant girl in the group on the left."[4]

Prov: Purchased from the L.A.E., 1898 (£700).
Exh: R.A., 1898 (216); L.A.E., 1898 (1006).[5]
Ref: **1.** An even longer quotation appears in the R.A. *Catalogue* cited above. **2.** *Art Journal* 1898 p. 166. No. 3073 was the subject of the extra illustrated plate in that Art Journal. A less interesting review appeared in The Studio, *A Record of Art in 1898*, 1898, p. 112. **3.** *The Athenaeum*, I, 1898, p. 701. **4.** Mrs S. M. Newton, letter, 5 December 1974. **5.** Where it hung "on the end wall of the Grosvenor Room", letter from the Curator of the W.A.G. to the artist 26 August 1888.

BOURDON, Sebastien, 1616-1671, after

9125 Bacchus and Ceres with nymphs and satyrs

Canvas, 83.8 × 111.7 cm

Another version displaying small variations is in Budapest 798 (691).[1] Several elements in the composition also occur in a picture with Frank Sabin in 1952 also attributed to Bourdon.

Prov: Entered the collection of the L.R.I. between 1836 and 1843;[2] from whom transferred by the University of Liverpool, July 1976.
Exh: Manchester, *Art Treasures*, 1857 (617). ?Leeds, 1868.[3]
Ref: **1.** Klara Garas, *Katalog der Galerie Alter Meister*, I, 1967, p. 90. Charles Ponsonailhe, *Sebastien Bourdon, sa vie et son oeuvre*, 1883, p. 298 and Henri Stein, in Ulrich Thieme and Felix Becker, *Allgemeines Lexikon der bildenden Künstler,* IV, 1910, p. 459 mention No. 9125 as by Bourdon. Fairfax Murray was the first to note that it is a copy, L.R.I. *Annual Report*, 1893, p. 53.   **2.** 1843 Catalogue p. 26 (93).   **3.** 9125 does not appear in the catalogue, but a Leeds 1868 Exhibition label is on the stretcher.

BRESCIAN School, *c.* 1530-1535

2869 Visit to a prison

Panel, 23.8 × 49.7 cm

The style is close to that of Floriano Ferramola, for instance, the painting attributed to him of *The Meeting of the Betrothed* in Brescia.[1] The costume indicates a date in the early 1530's.[2] Ferramola died in 1528 and the resemblance is to be explained by his influence.

Prov: Roscoe sale, (44) bt. Mason £9 19s 6d; presented to the L.R.I. by 1819;[3] deposited at the W.A.G., 1893;[4] presented to the W.A.G., 1948.
Ref: **1.** Letter from Dott. Gaetano Panazza, 17 January 1963.   **2.** Letter from Mrs Stella Newton, 22 April 1958.   **3.** 1819 Catalogue (26).   **4.** 1893 Catalogue p. 31 (87).

BRIDGMAN, Frederick Arthur, 1847-1928

1777 The Diligence

Canvas, 98 × 130.5 cm

Signed: *F. A. Bridgman 1873*

Inscribed: *Pyrenees*

The artist was living in the Pyrenees between 1870 and 1873[1] but spent the winter of 1872-3 in Algeria. A study entitled *Diligence Horse* presumably for No. 1777 was exhibited as No. 156 at the Art Institute of Chicago 1890 *Catalogue of Pictures and Studies of Frederick Arthur Bridgman.* He exhibited *In the Pyrenees* at the National Academy of Design, New York (No. 424) in 1875.[2] The Art Journal critic wrote of No. 1777 when exhibited at the Liverpool Autumn Exhibition: "F. A. Bridgman, a young American painter studying in Paris, sends a sketchy picture, *The Diligence,* after the French School, clever and lively . . ."

Prov: Purchased from the L.A.E. 1874 (£105).

Exh: Paris, Salon, 1874, No. 261 as *Un Voyage aux Pyrenees*; L.A.E. 1874 (373).

Ref: **1.** Clara Clement and L. Hutton, *Artists of the 19th Century* 1879, Vol. I, p. 94 say 1870-1872. *The Dictionary of American Biography*, Vol. III, 1929, p. 37 says 1871-3. He exhibited a number of other paintings with Pyrenean themes at the Paris, *Salons* and at the New York, *Society of American Artists* in the 1870's.   **2.** No. 1777 was listed as *Diligence in the Pyrenees* in the Art Institute of Chicago, *Catalogue of Pictures and Studies of Frederick Arthur Bridgman* 1890, p. 8.   **3.** *Art Journal* 1874 p. 335.

BROWN, Mather, 1761-1831

7041   John Bridge Aspinall

Canvas, 76 × 64.5 cm

Signed: *Mather Brown/pinxt*

The sitter (died 1830) was Mayor of Liverpool in 1803, he was a plumber and glazier with works in Park Lane and a house in Duke Street; politically he was a Tory and a supporter of General Gascoigne at various Liverpool Parliamentary elections. He died at Bath and is buried in the Abbey Church there.[1]

The artist was living in Liverpool 1810-1813.[2]

Prov: By descent in the family of the sitter to one of his great grandsons.[3] Presented to Liverpool Corporation by Captain O. Addison William Williamson probably after 1922; transferred to the W.A.G. from City Estates Committee 1967.

Exh: ?Liverpool Academy 1810 (52).

Ref: **1.** See J. A. Picton, *Memorials of Liverpool* 1873, Vol. 2, p. 312 and 1903 Vol. I, p. 283, (Aspinall) *Liverpool a few years since*, 1885, p. 33, A. Lewin, *Clarke Aspinall: a biography*, 1893, pp. 42, 50, *Liverpool's Legion of Honour*, 1893, p. 139.   **2.** Typescript copies of the artist's correspondence with his aunts (1777-1831) are in Massachusetts Historical Society, Boston.   **3.** Old Label, partially obscured on verso.

BROWNE, Henriette or Mme Jules de Saux, 1829-1901

191 A Nun

Oil on canvas,[1] 92.4 × 73.6 cm

Signed and dated: *Henriette Browne*

Prov: John Heugh, sold Christie's 24 April 1874 (157), bt. Agnew £336;[2] thence to George Holt, 1874 (bill Xmas for 30 October MS, W.A.G.), £400 with an exchange; bequeathed by Emma Holt, 1944.

Exh: ?Paris Salon, 1859 (434) as *Une Soeur.* ?French Gallery, 1866, *Artists of the French and Flemish Schools* (30).[3] Liverpool Art Club, *Modern Oil Paintings by Foreign Artists*, 1884 (27).

Ref: **1.** Stamped on back: 30 Ancienne Maison Valle Bellayoine Success, 3 Rue de l'Arbre-Sec Paris. **2.** Agnew's Stock Book. **3.** Where the picture was reviewed at length in the *Saturday Review,* 16 June 1866, p. 720.

BRUEGHEL, Pieter the elder, active 1551-1569, after

1177 The Resurrection

Panel, 147 × 109.8 cm

A simplified copy, probably contemporary, after the engraving of 1562, published by Hieronymus Cock and probably made by Philipp Galle.[1]

The distant landscape in No. 1177 differs from that in the engraving; a specifically alchemical motif in the print, the sun rising over this landscape on the right,[2] is much less conspicuous in No. 1177.

Prov: ?Joseph Brooks Yates sold Winstanley, Liverpool 14 May 1857 (37) bought by Richard Rathbone[3] and certainly presented by him to the L.R.I. 1857-8;[4] deposited at the W.A.G. 1893; presented to the W.A.G. 1948.

Ref: **1.** R. van Bastelaer, *Les estampes de Peter Bruegel L'ancien*, 1908, (No. 114). No. 1177 is described as a copy in F. Grossmann, *The Drawings of Pieter Brueghel the elder in the Boymans Museum*, Bulletin Museum Boymans, Rotterdam, Vol. 5, No. 2, 1954, p. 62. **2.** Jacques van Lennep *L'alchimie et Pierre Brueghel l'ancien*, Bulletin, Musées royaux des Beaux Arts de Belgique, 1965, pp. 115-6. **3.** Annotated Sale Catalogue, Liverpool City Libraries. **4.** *Annual Report of the Liverpool Royal Institution* 1857-8.

BUKOVAC, Vlaho, 1855-1923

1779 Mrs Richard Le Doux

Canvas, 200 × 111.5 cm

Signed: *V. BUKOVAC L'pool 1892*

The artist visited Marfield, West Derby, Liverpool, the home of the Le Doux family both in 1891 and 1892; on the second occasion he stayed for a month and painted both No. 1779 and a portrait of Richard Le Doux, the sitter's husband,[1] who owned a considerable collection of his work, including another seated portrait of Mrs Le Doux, all now lost except No. 1779.[2]

In a letter dated 11 February 1893 Mrs Le Doux wrote to the artist to tell him that many of her friends were going to Paris to see No. 1779 exhibited at the Salon[3] where it was extensively reviewed.[4]

Prov: Acquired between 1927 and 1958 from an unknown source.
Exh: L.A.E. 1892 (1255) Paris, *Société des Artistes Francais,* 1893 (290).
Ref: **1.** Vlaho Bukovac, *Moj Zivot,* Zagreb 1918 pp. 132-3.   **2.** Bukovac family papers, Cavtat, near Zagreb.   **3.** Bukovac family papers, *op. cit.*   **4.** *Revue des Beaux Arts,* Paris, 4 April 1893, *Daily Chronicle,* London 29 April 1893, *Le Public,* Paris, 30 April 1893, *Evénement,* Paris, 6 May 1893, *Souverenité,* Paris, 9 May 1893, *Revue Internationale,* Rome, 14 July 1893, Louis Cardou, *Salon de 1893,* 1893, P. de Kelou, *Salon,* 1893, I am indebted to G. A. Newby and more particularly Dr. Vera Kruzic Uchytil for all these references.

BYZANTINE, GRECO-VENETIAN School, late 15th or 16th century

3051   Madonna and Child

Panel, 33.2 × 27.9 cm

The attribution is due to Talbot Rice.[1] Like 3045 the image is that of the Glykophilousa or Eleousa Virgin.

Prov: Lord Wavertree, who bequeathed it to the W.A.G., 1933.
Ref: **1.** Professor D. Talbot Rice, confirmed by Professor O. Demus 21 March 1955.

BYZANTINE, GRECO-VENETIAN School, late 16th century

2870   Madonna and Child with 6 Saints

Panel, 53 × 40 cm

Saints John the Evangelist and John the Baptist sit on the same raised parapet as the Madonna, whilst below in front of it stand Saints Peter, Francis, Dominic and Paul.

As Compton notes,[1] this is by far the most Venetian of the icons in the Collection. A number of paintings in a similar style are in the Museo Correr, Venice.[2] Since the earliest attribution of 2870 in the Liverpool Royal Institution was to Domenico Ghirlandaio,[3] it may have been the picture, which was sent to Roscoe as a Domenico Ghirlandaio along with 1180.[4]

Prov: Possibly William Carey;[4] possibly William Roscoe;[4] in the L.R.I. Collection by 1819;[3] presented to the W.A.G., 1955.

Ref: **1.** 1963 Catalogue, p. 36.   **2.** Giovanni Mariacher, *Il Museo Correr di Venezia*, 1957, p. 140-3. Inv. n. 255, 1288, 2192.   **3.** 1819 Catalogue (14).   **4.** Roscoe Papers 735-737 letters from William Carey. First mentioned 11 July 1814. Note dated 31 August 1814 on letter dated 30 August 1814 mentions price of £17 17s.

3043   St. Joseph and the Child Christ

Inscribed: *St. ISEPPO*

Panel, 51.3 × 39.3 cm

Scharf thought that 3043 was Wallachian.[1] Talbot Rice suggested that it was painted on the eastern side of the Adriatic and that possibly the red curtains behind the Saint were repainted.[2] The name of the saint is written in Venetian dialect.[3] The Church in the distance at the left also has a distinctly Venetian character.

Prov: Joseph Mayer, who presented it to the L.R.I., 1844;[4] deposited at the W.A.G., 1893;[5] presented to the W.A.G., 1948.

Ref: **1.** Scharf, notes to proof Catalogue published 1859. L.R.I. Archives 63.   **2.** Prof. D. Talbot Rice, letter, 28 June 1959.   **3.** 1963 Catalogue, p. 37.   **4.** L.R.I. Presents Book, 24 April 1844 (L.R.I. Archives 37).   **5.** 1893 Catalogue p. 3(1).

BYZANTINE, GRECO-VENETIAN School, late 16th or early 17th century

3044   The Virgin holding a Crucifix

Inscribed: At the top $\overline{M} - \dot{P}$ and   V (Greek for Mother of God). On the label on the Cross *I.N.B.I.* (INRI). On the arms of the Cross *IC̄ XC̄* (Jesus Christ).

Panel, 40 × 32 cm

The attribution is due to Talbot Rice, who compares it with icons in San Giorgio dei Greci, Venice.[1] The icon is of the type sometimes known as a Pieta. A similar one also bearing a Greek inscription is in the Russisches Museum, Leningrad,[2] whilst there are examples at Altenberg[3] and Ravenna[4] bearing Latin inscriptions.

The three gold stars on the Virgin's forehead, and shoulders allude to her Virginity, before, during and after the Birth of Christ.[5]

Prov: Thomas Winstanley, who presented it to the L.R.I. between 1819 and 1836;[6] deposited at the W.A.G., 1893;[7] presented to the W.A.G., 1948.

Ref: **1.** Professor D. Talbot Rice, letter, 28 June 1959. **2.** Philipp Schweinfurth, *Geschichte der russischen Malerei*, 1930, p. 447, pl. 160. **3.** Robert Oertel, *Frühe Italienische Malerei in Altenberg*, 1961, p. 214 pl. 108. **4.** Sergio Bettini, *Pitture Cretesi-Veneziane Slave e italiane del Museo Nazionale di Ravenna*, 1940, p. 59 pl. 21. **5.** Ann Plogsterth, *A Reconsideration of the Religious Iconography in Hartt's History of Italian Renaissance Art,* Art Bulletin, 1975, p. 436 citing L. H. Appleton and S. Bridges, *Symbolism in Liturgical Art*, 1959, p. 96 and A. Dean Mackenzie, *Greek and Russian Icons and Other Liturgical Objects in the Collection of Mr Charles Bolles Rogers*, 1965, p. 26. **6.** 1836 Catalogue (13). **7.** 1893 Catalogue p. 4 (4).

3052 Madonna and Child with Saint Roche

Panel, 32 × 26.3 cm

The Virgin suckles her Son. The type is known as Galaktotrophusa.

Talbot Rice suggests that the artist was a Greek working in Venice.[1] Heinemann points out the faint influence of Bellini.[2] There are a number of examples in Ravenna of the suckling Virgin accompanied by a saint at the right.[3]

Prov: Lord Wavertree, who bequeathed it to the W.A.G., 1933.

Ref: **1.** Professor D. Talbot Rice, notes 21 March 1955. **2.** Fritz Heinemann, *Giovanni Bellini e i Belliniani*, 1959, p. 278, V 415. **3.** Sergio Bettini, *Pitture Cretesi-Veneziane, Slave e italiane del Museo Nazionale di Ravenna*, 1940, pp. 81-2, fig, 34.

BYZANTINE GREEK School, 17th century

3045 Madonna and Child enthroned with two angels holding the instruments of the Passion

Inscribed: In Greek *Mother of God* above the Madonna and above the angels in Greek *The Hope of the World*.[1]

Panel, 49.8 × 33.9 cm; painted area, 44 × 28 cm

The Madonna pressing her cheek against her Son's is the traditional image of the Glykophilousa or Eleousa (affectionate or pitying) Virgin. The gesture reminds the worshipper that later she was to press her cheek to the face of the dead Christ, as he is lowered into the tomb.[2] This image is combined here with that of the Child blessing.

Talbot Rice pointed out the Italian influence in the tooled haloes, and dated it in the fifteenth century,[3] but Mrs McGeorge thinks that it is Ionian of the seventeenth century.

Prov: Joseph Mayer, who presented it to the L.R.I., 1844;[4] deposited at the W.A.G., 1893;[5] presented to the W.A.G., 1948.

Ref: **1.** The compiler is indebted to Mrs E. McGeorge for help in deciphering and translating the inscription letter 29 January 1976.   **2.** Dorothy C. Shorr, *The Christ Child in Devotional Images in Italy during the XIV Century*, 1954, p. 34.   **3.** Professor D. Talbot Rice, letter, 28 June 1959.   **4.** L.R.I. Archives 37 Presents Book 24 April 1844.   **5.** 1893 Catalogue p. 3 (2).

3053   St. Jerome

Panel, 29.2 × 22.8 cm

Inscribed: On the cross *INRI*

Talbot Rice pointed to the Cardinal's hat as evidence that the iconography is Italian, but suggested that the artist is perhaps Dalmatian or East Italian.[1]

Prov: Lord Wavertree by 7 April 1921,[2] who bequeathed it to the W.A.G., 1933.
Ref: **1.** Professor D. Talbot Rice, notes, 21 March 1955.   **2.** Label on reverse.

BYZANTINE GREEK School, 18th century

3055   St. George slaying the dragon and fourteen episodes from his life

Inscribed: in Greek upper left *Saint George*; the two angels crowning him bear scrolls inscribed, *Hail great martyr and soldier* (left), *hail Champion of Christ the trophy bearer* (right); above each scene from the saint's life an identifying inscription: (1) *The saint casts down the idols* (2) *The Saint by prayer is freed from the chains* (3) *he is cast into the pit of lime* (4) *the Saint receives poison and remains unharmed* (5) *thongs lash his flesh* (6) *Christ appears to Saint George* (7) *the sword rebounds from his head* (8) *the Saint opens the coffin of a dead man* (9) *the Saint is brought to the King for the second time* (10) *the Saint is being presented to the King* (11) *the Saint is put in prison* (12) *a slab is placed on the Saint's chest* (13) *the Saint is put on the wheel* (14) *the Saint is freed from the wheel by an angel.*[1]

Panel with lobed top made in one piece with a rectangular frame with columns at the sides and carved spandrels; 106.8 × 76.1 cm; painted area 90.2 × 62.1 cm.

The attribution is due to Talbot Rice, who assigned it to the Greek mainland or the Ionian islands.[2] Mrs McGeorge, however, points out that it is painted in Laiki (folk) style and that it does not belong to any of the main schools of Byzantine iconography.[3]

St. George, a Roman soldier of Cappadocian origin was martyred in 287 A.D. during the rule of the Emperor Diocletian, either at the orders of Diocletian himself, or at the orders of Datian or Dacian in some accounts described as a Roman prefect and in others as the Emperor of the Persians.

The central scene of St. George slaying the dragon does not form part of the original St. George legend, but was probably appropriated from the life of Saint Theodore, another military saint.[4] To pacify a dragon which threatened the country, the people of Silene, Libya were compelled to give up to it a man or child everyday. Eventually the victim chosen was the King's daughter, who was rescued from her fate by St. George.

Only three of the scenes occur in the *Golden Legend* by Jacopo da Voragine, the casting down of the idols, the poisoning, and the wheel.[5] Most of the other scenes can be paralleled in a manuscript in the Vatican dated 916 (MS Vatican 1660 fol 272-288),[6] but the order of the narrative is different and the literary source is surely to be sought in the Greek rather than the Western world.

Prov: Lord Wavertree, who bequeathed it to the W.A.G., 1933.
Ref: **1.** Aid in translation provided by Mrs E. McGeorge.   **2.** Professor D. Talbot Rice, undated notes and notes dated 21 March 1953.   **3.** Mrs E. McGeorge, letter 29 January 1976.   **4.** J. B. Aufhauser, *Das Drachenwunder des hl. Georg in der griechischen und lateinischen Ueberlieferung*, Byzantinisches Archiv, V, 1911, pp. 237ff.   **5.** *The Golden Legend of Jacobus de Voragine*, translated by Granger Ryan and Helmut Rippenger, 1941, pp. 235-7.   **6.** Hippolyte Delehaye, *Les légendes grecques des saints militaires*, 1909, pp. 56-8.

BYZANTINE GREEK School, late 18th century

3054   Virgin and Child with Orb

Panel, 17 × 13.2 cm

The attribution is due to Talbot Rice.[1]

Prov: Lord Wavertree, who bequeathed it to the Gallery, 1933.
Ref: **1.** Professor D. Talbot Rice, notes, 21 March 1955.

CAMPIN, Robert, 1378/9-1444, after

1178   The Descent from the Cross

Three panels, centre panel 59 × 60.2 cm, left panel 59.9 × 26.5 cm, right panel 59.6 × 26.3 cm

Inscribed: *S. IVLIANVS and S. JOHES. BAPTA*

The centre panel has the *Descent from the Cross,* the left panel a crucified thief[1] with St. John the Baptist on the reverse, the right panel another crucified thief with St. Julian on the reverse.

Generally regarded as a crude but fairly accurate 15th century copy after a large triptych probably by Campin[2] of which only a fragment now survives.[3] The reverses of the two side panels with the figures of St. John the Baptist and St. Julian are, however, probably original works of the copyist;[4] in the original the sky was gold not blue and the figure of the donor in late fifteenth century dress in the left panel together with the coat of arms in the right panel were both additions by the copyist. Numerous other copies and derivatives exist,[5] but No. 1178 is the only accurate record of the entire composition.[6]

Prov: Perhaps from the hospice of St. Julian, Bruges.[7] Roscoe Sale, 1816, lot 81 as by Memlinc bt. Crompton £15 14s 6d; presented to the L.R.I. 1819; deposited at the W.A.G., 1893; presented to the W.A.G., 1948.

Exh: Manchester, *Art Treasures,* 1857 (412); New Gallery 1899-1900 *Winter Exhibition* (94); Bruges, *Exposition de Primitifs flamands,* 1902 (22).

Ref: **1.** The good thief, for the controversy over the identification of the thieves see E. Panofsky, *Early Netherlandish Paintings,* 1953, p. 168. M. S. Frinta, *The Genius of Robert Campin* 1966 pp. 52-3 (whose idea that the Descent in No. 1178 is seen from behind is contradicted by the nails visible in the Cross). Martin Davies, *Rogier van der Weyden* 1972, p. 249 and S. N. Blum, *Early Netherlandish Triptychs* 1971, p. 140, note 32 all with further references.   **2.** Max J. Friedlander, *Early Netherlandish Painting,* Vol. II *Rogier van der Weyden and the Master of Flemalle,* 1967, No. 59, Panofsky, *op. cit.,* p. 167, Davies, *op. cit.,* p. 249.   **3.** At the Stadelsches Kunstinstitut, Frankfurt.   **4.** The grisaille on the reverse of the original Frankfurt panel (repr. Davies, *op. cit.,* plate 139) does not resemble the St. Julian of No. 1178; see Blum, *op. cit.,* p. 119.   **5.** Listed in Panofsky, *op. cit.,* p. 423, Davies, *op. cit.,* p. 250 and 1963 Catalogue, p. 41.   **6.** Although H. Beenken, *Rogier van der Weyden,* 1951, pp. 24, 48 and others have suggested that the central panel of the original represented a *Crucifixion* not a *Deposition.*   **7.** James Weale in his introduction to the catalogue *Exposition de Primitifs flamands,* Bruges 1902, p. xix apparently first suggested this provenance. Certainly the coat of arms on the right panel resembles that of Bruges, although the Lion in that coat of arms is neither crowned nor collared and the colours are now very indistinct, and the hospice of St. Julian was owned by the City of Bruges; St. Julian moreover appears on the reverse of the right panel. In a charter of 1465 (now in the archives of St. Julian) a benefactor called Jan de Koninck stipulated that the fraternity of this hospice must burn candles in the chapel of St. Julian "before the panel of St. John"; St. John was the patron saint of Jan de Koninck who may have been the donor in the left panel (Dr. J. Geldhof, letter, 22 September 1974). Did Roscoe attribute No. 1178 to Memlinc knowing that it came from Bruges? Other copies after Campin's triptych are associated with Bruges (see Davies *op. cit.* p. 250) and the original may have been commissioned for Bruges. In 1798 the hospice of St. Julian was taken over by the *Commission des Hospices Civils de Bruges* and at that date a lot of paintings, including possibly No. 1178 left the Hospice (Dr. J. Geldhof, letter, 17 January 1975). K. Garas, *The Ludovisi Collection of Pictures in 1633,* II, Burlington Magazine, Vol. 109, 1967, p. 343, No. 60 suggests that No. 1178 may have been in the Ludovisi Collection in 1633 and then sold from it in 1684 by Giambattista Ludovisi; the evidence does not seem convincing.

CARRACCI, Annibale, 1560-1609, after

2767   Crucifixion

Panel, 32.3 × 23.1 cm

A copy of the painting of 1594 now at Dahlem, Berlin[1] (No. 364).

Prov: Acquired by the L.R.I. 1836-1843;² deposited at the W.A.G., 1893; presented to the W.A.G., 1948.

Ref: **1.** Donald Posner, *Annibale Carracci*, Vol. II, 1971, No. 81, p. 34.   **2.** 1843 Catalogue No. 110.

2893   St. Roche distributing alms

Copper, 50.7 × 66 cm

The immediate original of No. 2893 was probably Guido Reni's etching of 1610¹ after Annibale's painting, now at Dresden, No. 305², because both No. 2893 and the etching have two extra figures at the extreme right. In other respects they are both identical to No. 305 at Dresden but in reverse. Reni painted a version of this composition on copper³ but probably neither No. 2893 nor the version at the Prado⁴ can be identified with it.

Prov: Edward Rogers sold Vernon's Liverpool 24-25 July 1797 (54) bought Hilary for W. Clarke;⁵ probably given to William Roscoe by 1816,⁶ presented by Mrs A. M. Roscoe 1950.

Ref: **1.** A. Bartsch, *Le Peintre Graveur*, 1818 Vol. 18 No. 53; C. C. Malvasia, *La Felsina Pittrice*, 1841, I. pp. 87 and 93; H. Bodmer *Die Graphische Kunste*, 1938, III pp. 109-11 plate 9; M. Calvesi and V. Casale, *Le Incisione dei Carracci* 1965, No. 209.   **2.** Donald Posner, *Annibale Carracci* 1971 II No. 86, p. 35.   **3.** Malvasia *op. cit.* II, p. 8, then owned by Count Livio Zambeccari.   **4.** For which see Alfonso E. Perez Sanchez, *Pintura Italiana del Siglo XVII en Espana*, 1965, p. 108 who attributes it tentatively to Domenichino.   **5.** Roscoe Papers No. 1127.   **6.** Roscoe Sale, 1816, engraving lot 752; Roscoe papers No. 3897 where No. 2893 is listed in Roscoe's MS draft for his 1816 Sale Catalogue of pictures. No. 2893 has a metal plate on the back engraved *Amico Conservatori/1801*. The meaning is obscure, unless it refers to the gift of No. 2893 to Roscoe from W. Clarke, his banking partner. Was, however, No. 2893 the "Guido" mentioned by Roscoe in a letter of 1819 to Mr Smith as purchased from Mr Hill in Greek Street, London valued at £50 and not included in the 1816 Sales (Roscoe papers No. 574)? Roscoe certainly owned No. 2893 by 1820 for it is listed in his inventory of that date as a present (Roscoe Papers No. 3906) — suggesting that it was not the picture purchased from Mr Hill.

CASANOVA, Francesco Giuseppe, 1727-1802

2768   Landscape

Canvas, 94.5 × 158 cm

The subject is presumably a view in the Campagna.¹

Prov: A. W. Aldridge; sold 15th August 1878² to T. A. Hope who presented it to the W.A.G., 1882.

Ref: **1.** Noted, surely wrongly, as an English Landscape in Heinrich Leporini, *Francesco Casanova*, Pantheon, XXII, 1904, p. 175 plate 4.   **2.** Label on reverse.

CATENA, Vincenzo di Biagio, active c. 1500-1531

2769 Madonna and Child with Saints Catherine (?), Nicholas and Francis

Panel, 72.4 × 110.5 cm

Inscribed: *VINCENCIVS CHATENA P* on lower edge at left

In view of the provenance of 2769 and since there were churches in Parenzo dedicated to Saints Nicholas (on the island of San Niccolo), Francis and Catherine, as well as to the Madonna and Child (Cathedral), it may have been painted for a church in Parenzo.[1]

An early work,[2] like 2770 packed with borrowings from Bellini and Cima.[3] The Madonna was probably adapted from the figure in the Budapest *Holy Family*.[4] She also reappears in a *Madonna and Child* sold in New York in 1933.[5]

The orphrey worn by Saint Nicholas is like, though not the same as, that worn by Saint Louis of Toulouse in the Berlin Staatliche Museen *Madonna and Saints*.[6] Similar standing saints beneath large ribbed domes also occur on the embroidered orphrey belonging to a cope in the Cathedral at Gandino.[7]

A note on a photograph mount in the Witt Library identifies the donor as a notary. Indications of dress in 2769 are insufficient to be so precise. The most that can be said is that he is in official dress.[8]

Copies: Pen drawings of the complete work and of each of the heads, Saint Catherine and the Madonna, the Child and Saint Francis by G. B. Cavalcaselle, Victoria and Albert Museum MS.

Prov: Monsignor Negri, Bishop of Parenzo (died 1778);[9] Consul John Strange, private sale at 125 Pall Mall, 10 December 1789 (95); and 27 May 1799 (116); Roscoe sale (63), passed at 42 gns; presented to the L.R.I., 1819;[10] deposited at the W.A.G., 1893;[11] presented to the W.A.G., 1948.

Exh: Manchester, 1857, *Art Treasures* (67); New Gallery, 1894, *Venetian Art* (99).

Ref: 1. Letter of Dr. A. Sonje, 16 January 1976. 2. Giles Robertson, *Vincenzo Catena*, 1954, no. 10, pp. 19ff. 3. 1963 Catalogue pp. 44-5. 4. Robertson, *op. cit.*, p. 45. 5. Leger Sale, American Art Association, New York, 2 March 1933 19½ × 16 ins. 6. Ruth Gronwoldt, *Studies in Italian Textiles — II: Some Groups of Renaissance Orphreys of Venetian Origin*, Burlington Magazine, 1965, p. 236. 7. Gronwoldt, *op. cit.*, pp. 236, 240. 8. Mrs Newton, letter 7 August 1975. 9. Consul Strange sale catalogue which states "collected by him chiefly at Rome and purchased of his executors by the present Proprietor". 10. 1819 Catalogue (23). 11. 1893 Catalogue p. 29 (81).

2770 Madonna and Child

Panel, 43.2 × 34.3 cm

Condition: Two vertical cracks down the centre of the panel, probably of linden wood. Areas of damage extending to the priming in the face of the Madonna and on the parapet. The flesh areas, formed of transparent glazes laid directly over the tinted priming have become thin, revealing the under drawing. Damage to the blue overgarment. Painted up to the edges on all sides.[1]

First attributed to Catena by Fairfax Murray.[2] An early work of the artist[3] of characteristic asymmetrical design replete with derivations from the paintings of Giovanni Bellini[4] and Cima.[5] The style is close to that of two signed works, *The Madonna and Child with two donors,* in the Pospisil Collection, Venice, and the Budapest *Holy Family.*[6]

The same pose was used for the Madonna in Catena's painting at Glasgow,[7] in a painting at Indianapolis, attributed to Rondinelli,[8] in a picture at Krakow,[9] and in a picture at Berlin (n. 126),[10] the latter being the closest to 2770, but with alterations to the Madonna's gaze and without the landscape background.

Versions: Copy by G. B. Cavalcaselle, Biblioteca Marciana, Venice, Cod. It. IV 2033 (=12274) fasc. 22.[11]

Prov: Bought by Roscoe from Thomas Winstanley, July 1811, £21;[12] Roscoe sale (21) passed at 8 gns; in L.R.I. Collection by 1819;[13] deposited at W.A.G., 1893;[14] presented to the W.A.G., 1948.

Exh: Leeds, 1868 (64).

Ref: 1. Technical report, J. C. Witherop.   2. L.R.I. Annual Report, 1893, p. 48.   3. Giles Robertson, *Vincenza Catena*, 1954, pp. 16, 42.   4. cf Georg Gronau, *Giovanni Bellini*, 1930, pl. 86, 119 or its putative prototype p. 211.   5. National Gallery no. 2506; Martin Davies, *The Earlier Italian Schools*, 1961, pp. 146-7; borrowing noted by Robertson *op. cit.*, p. 16n.1.   6. Robertson, *op. cit.*, p. 42.   7. Robertson, *op. cit.*, no. 9 pl. 8, 89 × 114 cm.   8. Fritz Heinemann, *Giovanni Bellini e I Belliniani*, 1963, I p. 30, 118n, II pl. 296. 76.2 × 58.7 cm.   9. Letter of Dr. J. Banach, 1 August 1975, no. XII 202/old inv. V 299. 66 × 54 cm.   10. Peter Murray undated note in Gallery files; reproduced Heinemann, *op. cit.* II, fig. 610. Formerly on loan Cologne, Wallraf-Richartz Museum. 75 × 70 cm.   11. Letter of E. Covi 17 November 1975. The album in which it is kept bears the date 1865.   12. Roscoe Papers 5316.   13. 1819 Catalogue (16).   14. 1893 Catalogue p. 30 (13).

CAVAILLES, Jules, 1901-1977

3032   Poppies (Les Pavots)

Canvas, 81 × 50 cm

Signed: *J. Cavailles*

Painted in the spring of 1952, one of a series of three pictures on the same theme.[1]

Prov: Arthur Tooth and Sons Ltd, from whom purchased 1954.

Exh: Arthur Tooth and Sons, *Le Tour des Ateliers,* 1953 (8).

Ref: 1. Jules Cavailles, letter, 11 August 1959.

CAVALLINO, Bernardo, 1622-1654

2771   Rape of Europa

Canvas, 101 × 133.7 cm

Acquired by the Walker Art Gallery as by Romanelli[1] and first attributed to Cavallino by Denis Mahon.[2]

De Dominici[3] noted a picture of this subject, four palmi high by three palmi wide, together with its pendant an *Erminia and the Shepherds* in the Caputi Collection. An *Erminia and the Shepherds,* canvas 101 × 125 cm is now at Capodimonte, Naples (No. 1717).[4] For the condition of No. 2771 see the *Cleaned Pictures* Catalogue cited under *Exhibitions*.

Prov: Alexander Nowell of Underley Park,[5] Westmorland, sold Winstanley, Liverpool 12 July, 1842,[6] T. A. Hope who presented it to the W.A.G., 1882.
Exh: W.A.G., *Cleaned Pictures*, 1955, No. 28, plate VII.
Ref: **1.** Walker Art Gallery, *Descriptive Catalogue of the Permanent Collection of Pictures*, 1885, No. 288, p. 63.   **2.** Letter 22 November, 1954.   **3.** Bernardo de Dominici, *Vite de Pittori, Scultori etc.*, 1742, Vol. 2, p. 40.   **4.** It was presented to the Italian State about 1900 by the heir of the Santangelo di Pollena Trocchia family of Naples (Raffaello Causa, letter, 8 February 1973).   **5.** Old Label. For Nowell see Alexander Pearson, *Annals of Kirkby Lonsdale in Bygone Days*, 1930.   **6.** No catalogue survives but the sale was reported in the *Liverpool Mercury* of 8 July, 1842, as including a work by Romanelli. A handbill for the sale exists in the files of the Walker Art Gallery.

CENTRAL ITALIAN School, late 15th century

2751   Madonna and Child

Panel, 63.7 × 49.5 cm

The child clasps a gourd, a symbol of the Resurrection,[1] and not a globe as thought by Van Marle.[2]

Roger Fry first attributed 2751 to the Umbrian School, noting relationships with the art of "Antoniazzo Romano, Balducci and Fungai."[3] Van Marle made a more definite association with Antoniazzo.[2] A number of Madonnas are related to 2751 in composition, the picture in the Hoving and Winberg sale, Stockholm, 27-29 September 1917, where the Child holds a ball, is the closest and may be by the same hand. In the case of the Madonnas owned by the Norton Simon Foundation[4] and the derivation from it once in the Spiridon Collection,[5] the style is different, although the pose of the Child is related to 2751. A third picture with a different composition which may be by the painter of 2751[6] is a *Madonna and Child* in Altenburg.[7] Zeri has associated a group of works around this work and 2751 and baptized the artist, the Master of the Liverpool Madonna.[8] Links with the certain works of Antoniazzo are explicable in terms of distant influence.

Prov: Entered the collection of the L.R.I. between 1836 and 1843;[9] deposited at the W.A.G., 1893;[10] presented to the W.A.G., 1948.

Ref: **1.** George Ferguson, *Signs and Symbols in Christian Art*, 1974, p. 31 refers to *Jonah* IV 10-11. **2.** Raimond Van Marle, *The Development of the Italian Schools in Painting*, XV, 1934, p. 298. **3.** Catalogue of B.F.A.C. Exhibition, 1909, *Umbrian School* (49). **4.** Bernard Berenson, *Italian Pictures of the Renaissance, Central Italian and North Italian Schools*, III, 1968, pl. 1064. **5.** Sotheby's 27 November 1963 (110); reproduced A. Venturi, *Storia dell'Arte Italiana*, VII, ii, 1913, fig. 212. **6.** This link was noted independently by Federico Zeri, *Appunti sul Lindenau-Museum di Altenburg*, Bollettino d'Arte, 1964, pp. 52-3 and *Italian Paintings in the Walters Art Gallery*, I, 1976, pp. 166-167. **7.** Robert Oertel, *Frühe Italienische Malerei in Altenburg*, 1961, p. 168, pl. 71. **8.** Zeri, 1976, *op. cit*. But not all the works he lists seem to be by the same hand. **9.** 1843 Catalogue, p. 13 (43). **10.** 1893 Catalogue, p. 14 (34*).

CENTRAL ITALIAN School, early 16th century

2866   Adoration of the Magi

Panel, 12.8 × 61.3 cm

A predella panel by an artist influenced at some distance by Perugino. Compton tentatively suggested Sinibaldo Ibi as its author,[1] whilst Longhi maintained that it was by the same hand as 2751.[2] Berenson thought of Eusebio di San Giorgio.[3]

The *Adoration of the Magi* attributed to Pinturricchio in Roscoe's collection might be the same picture as 2866.[4]

Prov: Seal with a coronet and the number 388 on reverse; entered the collection between 1836 and 1843;[5] deposited at the W.A.G., 1893;[6] presented to the W.A.G., 1948.

Ref: **1.** 1963 Catalogue, p. 194. **2.** R. Longhi, letter, 29 October 1959. **3.** Bernard Berenson, *Italian Painters of the Renaissance* I, 1932, p. 178 (also p. 258 as Girolamo dai Libri) and Bernard Berenson, *Central Italian and North Italian Schools*, 1968, p. 123. **4.** MS draft for Roscoe's 1816 Sale Catalogue p. 12 (Roscoe Papers 3897). **5.** 1843 Catalogue, p. 7 (20). **6.** 1893 Catalogue, p. 16 (8).

CEREZO, Mateo the younger, 1635-1685 after

6173   The Penitent Magdalen

Canvas, 104 × 82.5 cm

A copy after the painting of 1661 in the Rijksmuseum Amsterdam (No. 688-B-1)[1] or after the version signed and dated 1668 in the Salzburger Residenzgalerie (No. 314).[2]

Prov: Messrs Saxon's Ltd. Liverpool, from whom purchased 1963.

Ref: **1.** See P. Van Vliet, *Spaanse Schilderijen in het Rijksmuseum etc.* Bulletin van het Rijksmuseum, 1966, No. 4, p. 136. plate 4.   **2.** *Katalog der Salzburger Residenzgalerie*, 1962, No. 30, plate 39.

CEZANNE, Paul, 1839-1906

6242 The Murder

Canvas, 65.4 × 81.2 cm; painted area 63.8 × 78.8 cm

One of a group of early dark paintings with violent subjects; it is usually dated to 1870,[1] a date first suggested by Meier-Graefe, but Venturi and Barnes and De Mazia suggest 1867-70.[2] *La Femme Etranglée*[3] (Musee du Jeu de Paume, Paris) and a watercolour *Le Meutre*[4] (Mme Ernest Rouart Collection) are related. No. 6242 was well known in Germany 1913-1933[5] and may have influenced German Expressionism. For the sources of No. 6242 see particularly J. Rewald, *Zola et Cezanne*, 1936, p. 46.

A sheet of drawings including some for No. 6242 is in the Basel Kunstmuseum, Inv. No. 1934.192 recto, dateable to 1864-7.[6]

Prov: Bought by Cassirer from A. Vollard October 16, 1916;[7] Sally Falk, Mannheim;[8] bought back by Paul Cassirer April 1918;[9] sold to Julius Elias, Berlin May 3, 1918;[10] Frau Elias; Wildenstein, from whom purchased 1964 with the aid of the National Art-Collections Fund.

Exh: Berlin, *Katalog der XXVI Ausstellung der Berliner Secession*, 1913 p. 16, and repr. No. 24A. Dresden, Galerie Ernest Arnold, *Französische Ausstellung*, 1914, No. 8. Berlin, Paul Cassirer, *XVI Jahrgang Sommeraustellung*, 1914, No. 8 (repr.). Berlin, Paul Cassirer, *Cezanne-Ausstellung*, Nov.-Dec., 1921, p. 31. No. 1 and repr. Chicago, Art Institute, *Cezanne*, Feb 7-Mar. 16, 1952, No. 2 and repr. New York, Metropolitan Museum of Art, *Cezanne*, Apr. 1-May 16, 1952. No. 2 and repr. Aix-en-Provence and Nice, *Cezanne: peintures, aquarelles, dessins.* 1953, No. 2, p. 27, and repr. opp. p. 22. Baltimore, Museum of Art, *Man and his years*, Oct. 19-Nov. 21, 1954, p. 34, No. 95 and repr. and cited p. 19. Washington D.C., The Corcoran Gallery of Art, *Visionaries and Dreamers*, Apr. 7-May 27, 1956, p. 8. No. 37. Zurich, Kunsthaus, *Paul Cezanne*, Aug. 22-Oct. 7, 1956, p.23, No. 5. Munich, Haus der Kunst, *Paul Cezanne*, Oct.-Nov. 1956, No. 2 and repr. Vienna, Osterreichische Galerie, *Paul Cezanne*, Apr.14-June 18 1961 (4). London, Institute of Contemporary Art, *Study for an Exhibition of Violence in Contemporary Art*, 1964, No. 01.

Ref: **1.** J. Meier-Graefe, *Cezanne und sein Kreis*, 1920, p. 92.G. Riviere, *Le Maitre Paul Cezanne*, 1923, p. 199. J. Rewald letter, 1 November 1971.   **2.** L. Venturi, *Cezanne*, 1936, Volume I, p. 94, No. 121. A. Barnes and V. De Mazia, *The Art of Cezanne*, 1939, p. 404, No. 20.   **3.** Venturi, *op. cit.*, No. 123.   **4.** Venturi, *op. cit.*, p. 349, repr. J. Rewald, *Correspondence de Paul Cezanne*, 1937, plate 14.   **5.** See provenance and exhibitions, also *Kunst und Kunstler*, XI, 1912-13, p. 512 (review by Emil Waldmann); *Kunst und Kunstler*, XII, 1914, p. 279 (repr.); *Die Kunst fur Alle*, 1914, Volume 29, p. 480, Paul Schumann, *Franzosische Austellung in Dresden*; J. Meier-Graefe, *op. cit.*, p. 14 describing No. 6242 as a "kirmesbildartigen Mord"; K. Pfister, *Cezanne, Gestalt, Werk, Mythos*, Potsdam, 1927, plate 20; Karl Scheffer, *Geschichen der Europaischen Malerei*, Berlin, 1927, Volume II, p. 90; *Sammeren*, 1929, Volume VII, plate 20.   **6.** Adrien Chappuis, *Les Dessins de Paui Cezanne au Cabinet des Estampes du Musee des Beaux Arts de Bale*, 1962, I, p. 32, No. 4, repr. II, p. 3 and *The Drawings of Paul Cezanne*, 1973, No. 162, p. 83.   **7.** J. Rewald, *letter*, 1 November 1971.   **8.** H. Lutjens, *letter*, 3 March 1969.   **9.** H. Lutjens, *op. cit.*   **10.** H. Lutjens, *op. cit.*

CLAUDE Gellée, 1600-1682, after

142 Landscape

Canvas, 90.3 × 125.2 cm

A copy after the composition recorded in the *Liber Veritatis*, No. 8,[1] probably based on the etching by Vivares of 1741 to which No. 142 is closer than to the painting now in the Metropolitan Museum of Art, New York.

Prov: An old version at Allerton Priory, Liverpool in 1858.[2] Mrs E. E. Cubbin who bequeathed it 1955.

Ref: 1. M. Rothlisberger, *Claude Lorrain, The Paintings,* Vol. I, No. 8, pp. 109-110.   2. Rothlisberger, *op. cit.*, Mrs Cubbin's family came from Liverpool.

COLEMAN, Enrico, 1846-1911

1788 Oxen drawing a block of marble to the Studio of John Warrington Wood in Rome

Canvas, 45.8 × 69.8 cm

Signed: *H. Coleman/Roma 1872*

Inscribed: *WARRINGTON WOOD/SCULPTOR* (on door)

The view is taken from the Via Sistina where it enters the Piazza S. Trinita dei Monti looking into the Piazza; on the right is Warrington Wood's studio at 7 Trinita dei Monti[1] and then the church of S. Trinita dei Monti, in the centre is the Roman Obelisk erected in 1788 by Pope Pius VI.

Perhaps the marble in No. 1788 was for Wood's *Proserpine gathering flowers in the Elysian fields startled by Pluto* and/or *St. Michael and Satan*,[2] Nos. 1309 and 1314 at the 1875 Royal Academy, both there in marble.

Prov: Presented by Mrs John Warrington Wood 1900.
Ref: 1. The address given for Wood in Royal Academy Catalogues 1868-74.   2. Now in Warrington Museum and Art Gallery.

COROT, Jean Baptiste Camille, 1796-1875

202 La Vache a l'Abreuvoir

Panel 27 × 37.3 cm

Signed: *COROT*

Apparently to be identified with Robaut No. 2302,[1] which is dated to

1870-1873 and given the above title. No. 202 was sold to Holt as *The Lake near Ville d'Avray*.

Prov: Jules Warnier-David (1883).[2] M. Duche (1887).[3] M. Gerard fils (1892).[4] Bought
         from Cremetti by George Holt 1892 (bill 28 October, MS, W.A.G.), £650;
         bequeathed by Emma Holt 1944.
Ref: **1.** Albert Robaut, *L'Oeuvre de Corot*, 1905, Vol. III, p. 355, (repr.).   **2.** *J.
         Warnier 1 April 1883* is inscribed on the reverse of the panel.   **3.** Robaut, *op.
         cit.*   **4.** Robaut, *op. cit.*

COSSAAR, Jacobus Cornelis Wynardus, born 1874

566   Commercial Shipping, Rotterdam

Canvas, 25.3 × 38.3 cm

Signed: *J. COSSAAR*

567   On the River Schie

Canvas, 25.3 × 38.3 cm

Signed: *J. COSSAAR*

Prov: Purchased from the Goupil Gallery about 1910-1911[1] by Denys Hague[2] who
         presented them 1918.
Ref: **1.** This Gallery had contracted to take all Cossaar's work from 1903 until about
         1910 (the Goupil Gallery, *letter*, 11th March 1918).   **2.** Denys Hague *letter*
         19th March 1918.

COURBET, Gustave, 1819-1877

6111   Marée Basse à Trouville

Canvas, 59.6 × 72.6 cm

Signed: *G. Courbet*

Generally dated to the mid 1860's.[1] The identification of the beach as Trouville is traditional.

Prov: E. L. T. Mesens. Reid and Lefevre in 1936; Mrs Chester Beatty; Sir Alfred Ches-
         ter Beatty; on loan to the National Gallery, London 1955-1961; purchased from
         Sir Alfred Chester Beatty 1961 with the aid of a grant from the National Art-
         Collections Fund.
Exh: Glasgow, Reid and Lefevre, at the McLellan Galleries, *French Art of the 19th
         and 20th Centuries*, 1937;[2]

Ref: **1.** Courbet exhibited 10 *Marines Diverses, Trouville,* 1865 at the Champs Elysees, *Exposition des Oeuvres de M. G. Courbet,* 1867 (57-66) and 25 Trouville seascapes are mentioned in a letter from the artist to Castagnary of 5th July 1869 (G. Mack, *Courbet,* 1951, p. 230). There were however both earlier and later seascapes by Courbet see *Courbet and the Naturalistic Movement* ed George Boas, 1938, p. 124   **2.** No catalogue appears to survive.

COURTOIS, Jacques, 1621-1676

2763   Battle Scene

Canvas, 95.9 × 183.5 cm

Attributed on entry into the collection to Salvator Rosa,[1] No. 2763 could equally well be by Jacques Courtois.[2]

The battle appears to involve the Turks.

Prov: Purchased by William Earle in Naples;[3] presented by Charles Langton, his nephew, 1869.
Ref: **1.** 1882 Catalogue, No. 107, but in the 1963 Catalogue as after Salvator Rosa.   **2.** Luigi Salerno *letter* 3 May 1972.   **3.** Liverpool Corporation; Libraries, Museums and Arts Committee 5 August 1869, letter from the donor.

CRANACH, Lukas, 1472-1553 or Hans died 1537

1223   The Nymph of the Fountain

Panel, 51.3 × 78 cm (51.3 × 76.8 cm painted area)

Signed: with a snake with upright wings

Inscribed: *FONTIS NYMPHA SACRI SOMNVM NE RVMPE QVIESCO* and dated *1534*

The sources and iconography of this subject first painted by Cranach in about 1515[1] have been extensively discussed.[2] Briefly a latin text was fabricated in the 15th Century and passed off as antique; it was stated to be an inscription on a fountain with a statue of a sleeping guardian nymph beside it on the Danube;[3] an abbreviation of this text appears on No. 1223. Visual sources included perhaps a lost *Venus resting from the hunt* by Giorgione,[4] various actual fountains with carved nymphs[5] and more certainly one of the woodcuts from the *Hypnerotomachia Poliphili* published in Venice in 1499.[6] Later versions including No. 1223 often have deer or a bow and arrows or both suggesting a subject similar to Giorgione's lost *Venus resting from the Hunt* where Venus personifies life and energy; in the same way the patridges symbolise Venus or Luxuria but

47

Luxuria in the sense of luxuriant growth not voluptuousness.[7] No. 1223 is however exceptional among later versions in that the fountain of the earliest versions is not replaced by a natural spring and the striped cushion is another very artificial element unusual in the whole group. The apple tree may be a reference to the Fall of Man;[8] the bow and arrows could refer to Venus and Cupid or to a follower of Diana;[9] the sleeping nymph at least in the early versions may be interpreted as a sleeping Helen.[10] A connection, particularly in the case of No. 1223 rather than the other versions, can also be made with the alchemist Bernardus Trevisanus.[11]

In 1534 No. 1223 could have been painted by Hans Cranach unlike most of the other versions which were either painted after his death or when he was probably too young. Friedlander and Rosenberg would not commit themselves over this[12] and Koepplin and Falk say "vielleicht von Hans Cranach stammend."[13]

The relationship between Cranach's treatment of the Nymph of the Fountain theme and mannerism is discussed briefly by Liebmann[14] and extensively by Koepplin and Falk.[15]

Prov: ?Thomas Wilkinson junior sold Winstanley and Son, 34 Russell Square, London, 29 June 1811 lot 53, *The Fountain Nymph exquisitely finished by Lucca Cranach* £13 2s 6d. *A Venus by Lucas Cranach*, "lately brought from the continent" was sold by Winstanley's Liverpool on 16-17 November 1815.[16] Thomas Winstanley.[17] Acquired by the L.R.I. between 1843 and 1851[18] presumably from Winstanley; deposited at the W.A.G., 1893; presented to the W.A.G., 1948.

Exh: Manchester, *Art Treasures*, 1857, No. 457. Leeds, *National Exhibition*, 1868, No. 539.

Ref: **1.** The version in the Jagdschloss Grunewald, Berlin Staatlicher Schlosser und Garten, Dieter Koepplin and Tilman Falk, *Lukas Cranach*, 1974-6, No. 543, p. 636 is now dated to that year. The version at Leipzig (Max J. Friedlander and Jakob Rosenberg, *Die Gemalde von Lucas Cranach*, 1932, No. 100, p. 49) is dated 1518. Other later versions are Friedlander and Rosenberg No. 101, which is Koepplin and Falk No. 544 now in the Batthyany-Thyssen Collection at Lugano-Castagnola, Friedlander and Rosenberg Nos. 323 and 324, Friedlander and Rosenberg No. 324c which is Koepplin and Falk No. 547 now in Besancon Musée des Beaux Arts et d'Archeologie; other later versions are Koepplin and Falk Nos. 545, 546 and 548; there was also the drawing formerly at Dresden but destroyed during the second World War, see Jakob Rosenberg, *Die Zeichnungen Lucas Cranachs D.A.* 1960, No. 40, p. 22. **2.** There are critical references to all the literature in Koepplin and Falk *op. cit.* pp. 421ff and pp. 631ff. **3.** There are other antique and pseudo antique sources and the story about the nymph can vary. See particularly Elizabeth B. Macdougall, *The Sleeping Nymph, Origins of a Humanist Fountain Type*, Art Bulletin, 1975, Volume 57, pp. 357ff., Koepplin and Falk, *op. cit.*, p. 428, Otto Kurz, *Huius Nympha Locis,* Journal of the Warburg and Courtauld Institutes 1953, Volume 16, No. 3, pp. 171ff and Harry Murutes, *Personifications of Laughter and Drunken Sleep in Titian's Andrians*, Burlington Magazine, 1973, Vol. 115, pp. 518ff. **4.** Kurz, *op. cit.*, and *Holbein in a 17th Century Collection*, Burlington Magazine Vols. 82-3, 1943, pp. 281-2 but see Michael Liebmann, *On the Iconography of the Nymph of the Fountain*, Journal of the Warburg and Courtauld Institutes 1968, Vol. 31, p. 434 for the relationship between Giorgione's *Venus* at Dresden and Cranach's *Nymph of the Fountain.* **5.** Macdougall, *op. cit.* **6.** Liebmann, *op. cit.*, p. 435 with a reproduction of the woodcut in question; it is inscribed (in Greek): "To the all-bearing." Werner Schade, *Die Malerfamilie Cranach* 1974 p. 70 argues that the pose of the nymph in No. 1223 as also in the Berlin version suggests a Venetian source. **7.** For all this see Liebmann, *op. cit.*, Koepplin and Falk, *op. cit.*, pp. 421ff are more sceptical about the relevance of humanist Symbolism to Cranach but suggest other sources as well as later derivatives; the nymph could have been simply a follower of Diana. **8.** Koepplin and Falk, *op. cit.*, p. 633. **9.** Koepplin and Falk, *op. cit.*, p. 633 noting that hunting was traditionally associated with the pursuit of love. **10.** Koepplin and Falk, *op. cit.* p.

632. **11.** Schade, *op. cit.* p. 69 with further references to the works of Jung. **12.** *Op. cit.* No. 211 and No. 100 p. 49. **13.** *Op. cit.*, p. 635. **14.** *Op. cit.*, p. 436. **15.** *Op. cit.*, pp. 421ff. **16.** No catalogue survives but the sale was reported in the *Liverpool Mercury* 10 November 1815. **17.** A letter of 9 March 1858 from M. Bewley and Son to the President of the L.R.I. (L.R.I. Archives 17) refers to a portrait of Lucca Cranach (sic) "belonging to the late Mr Winstanley." No. 1223 was believed to be a portrait of Cranach's wife in the 1851 and 1859 Catalogues (Nos. 52 and 50). **18.** 1851 Catalogue No. 52.

CREDI, Lorenzo di, 1456/9-1537, follower of

2772 Madonna suckling the Child

Panel, 86.5 × 62 cm

Attributed to Lorenzo di Credi by Cavalcaselle before 1851.[1] Crowe and Cavalcaselle later considered it a workshop production.[2] A superior version is at Elton Hall,[3] and a copy at Cincinnati (1927.388).[4]

A drawing in the British Museum (pp.1-30), probably by Picro di Cosimo for a Madonna and Child surrounded by angels has a Child, which is very close to that in 2772,[5] and to that in Princeton University's tondo *Madonna and Child with two angels*,[6] a work by an unknown artist influenced by Credi. A very similar child occurs in reverse in Credi's Dresden *Madonna and Saints*.[7]

Prov: Thomas Winstanley from whom bought by the L.R.I., 1835;[8] deposited at the W.A.G., 1893;[9] presented to the W.A.G., 1948.

Ref: **1.** MS comments on the L.R.I. Collection (L.R.I. Archives 63.4). **2.** J. A. Crowe and G. B. Cavalcaselle, *A History of Painting in Italy*, III, 1866, p. 414. **3.** Tancred Borenius and Rev. J. V. Hodgson, *Catalogue of the Paintings at Elton Hall*, 1924, p. 7 (2) 28 × 22½ in. **4.** Gigetta Dalli Regoli, *Lorenzo di Credi*, 1966, p. 184 (186) fig. 237. **5.** A. E. Popham and Philip Pouncey, *Italian Drawings in the Department of Prints and Drawings of the British Museum*, *Fourteenth and Fifteenth Century*, 1950, pp. 127-8. **6.** Dalli Regoli, *op. cit.* fig. 233. **7.** Dresden n. 15. Dalli Regoli, *op. cit.* fig. 200. **8.** Bill from Winstanley dated 3 August 1836 (L.R.I. Archives 63). **9.** 1893 Catalogue, p. 11 (24).

CUNEO, Cyrus Cincinatto, 1878-1916

699 The Diners

Board, 60.9 × 48 cm

Signed: *CYRUS CUNEO*

Prov: Purchased from the 1913 L.A.E. (£20)
Exh: R.A. 1913 (425); L.A.E. 1913 (327).

DAGUERRE, Louis Jacques Mande, 1787-1851

3034 Ruins of Holyrood Chapel

Canvas, 211 × 256.5 cms.

Daguerre exhibited dioramas of this subject at Paris from 20 October, 1823 until 21 February 1824,[1] in London from March 1825,[2] in Liverpool in 1825-7,[3] in Bristol in September 1825[4] and no doubt elsewhere as well. Three other paintings by Daguerre as well as No. 3034 represent Diorama subjects and in each case the oil painting succeeds the diorama and is not a study for it.[5]

No. 3034 appears not to be the *Ruines de la Chapelle de Holyrood*, No. 400 at the 1824 Paris Salon[6] for it lacks the figure of the Comtess de L . . . recorded in the Salon picture as visiting the tomb of her former friend Louise Francoise Gabrielle Aglaede Polignac, Duchesse de Grammont,[7] who died in exile at Holyrood in 1803 and was buried in the royal vault in the south east corner of Holyrood Chapel.[8] This figure also appeared in the London and Paris Dioramas.[9] Gernsheim argues that the precise detail in No. 3034 is to be explained by Daguerre's use of a camera oscura while working on No. 3034 at Holyrood itself.[10] However Daguerre is not recorded as ever visiting Scotland and by 1816 the tracery in the east window had in fact been repaired.[11] As early as 1818 the view by moonlight of Holyrood Chapel was already famous.[12]

Prov:　Bought "recently" on the continent by Arnold Baruchson[13] who presented it, 1864.

Ref:　1. H. and A. Gernsheim, *L. J. M. Daguerre*, 1956, p. 176.　2. Gernsheim *op. cit.*, p. 178. Francis Danby apparently saw the London showing which probably influenced his *Sunset through a Ruined Abbey* (Tate Gallery, London) according to Eric Adams, *Francis Danby, Varieties of Poetic Landscape* 1973, p. 75.　3. *A Stranger at Liverpool*, 1825, p. 189 *Liverpool Courier* August 2 1826. Liverpool Mercury 23 February 1827.　4. *Bristol Mirror*, September 17, 1825 — I owe this reference to Francis Greenacre.　5. Gernsheim *op. cit.*, p. 25.　6. As stated in Gernsheim *op. cit.*, p. 25 and the 1963 Catalogue.　7. *Explication des ouvrages etc. exposés au Musée Royal des Arts*, 1824, p. 47, No. 400.　8. *Historical Description of the Monastery or Chapel Royal at Holyroodhouse, with a short account of the Palace and Environs*, 1818, p. 58. Her remains were taken away from Holyrood in 1825 and returned in state to France at the expense of the French Government and the Duke of Hamilton (*Historical and Descriptive Account of the Palace and Chapel Royal of Holyroodhouse* 1826, p. 14).　9. A woodcut of them is reproduced by Gernsheim *op. cit.* plate 12. In London the figure was not understood. A guide entitled *Diorama, Regents Park, Two Views, Ruins of Holyrood Chapel, A Moonlight Scene painted by M. Daguerre etc*, 1825, p. 4 observed: "the figure of the woman in contemplation with the lamp burning on a monument on the right hand side of the picture (is) only to give more interest and show the effect of light." (p. 4).　10. H. Gernsheim, *History of Photography* 1955, p. 49.　11. Historical and Descriptive Account *op. cit.* plate 8, and Historical Description, *op. cit.*, p. 35. The 1825 guide cited in footnote 9 remarked that Daguerre deliberately showed the tracery unrepaired "to give a more picturesque effect" (p. 4).　12. Historical Description *op. cit.*, p. 35. An undated moonlight view close to No. 3034 is reproduced in Ministry of Works, *The Palace of Holyroodhouse, An Illustrated Guide*, 1960, p. 15.　13. Liverpool Corporation Libraries Museums and Arts Committee 23 June 1864.

DAHL, Michael, 1656-1743

2359 Portrait of Henrietta Maria, Lady Ashburnham (1686/7-1718)

Canvas, 231.8 × 136 cm

Signed: *M. Dahl : 1717*

The sitter was Henrietta Maria first daughter and co-heiress (from 1714 sole heiress) of William 9th Earl of Derby. She married first John 4th Earl of Anglesey in 1706 and then John 3rd Baron Ashburnham in 1714. In 1714 on the death of her sister Elizabeth she became Baroness Strange in her own right.[1]

The meaning of the orange tree—if it has one—is not clear. The sitter was the great granddaughter of James 7th Earl of Derby and the mother of his wife, Charlotte de la Tremouille, was a daughter of William of Orange but the relationship is very distant. The Barony of Ashburnham was one of the first creations of William III (1689) and the 3rd Baron, the sitter's husband, strongly supported the Protestant Succession in 1714 although a Tory.[2]

The companion portrait of the sitter's husband, also by Dahl but not apparently signed or dated, was lot 104 at Sotheby's Sale 15 July 1953 (Bt. Gooden and Fox). It probably dates from 1714.[3] No. 2359 would presumably therefore have been painted to match it.

Prov: By descent to the Trustees of the Ashburnham Settled Estates etc. sold Sotheby's 15 July 1953, lot 108[4] bt. Agnew; presented by Major Philip R. England 1954.

Ref: 1. *The Complete Peerage* ed. GEC, Vol. 1, 1910, pp. 135, 272, Vol. 4, 1916, pp. 215-6.   2. Henry Horwitz, *Revolutionary Politicks*, 1968, p. 242.   3. He is dressed in Baron's Coronation Robes—suggesting that it was painted on the occasion of George I's Coronation in 1714 and there is an entry for 25 February 1714 in a cash book formerly at Ashburnham: "Paid Mr Dahl painter for my lord's whole length picture £44 10s 0d" (Note in Sotheby's Sale Catalogue cited under *provenance*). George I was crowned on 20 October 1714 but 25 February 1714 (old style) would mean 25 February 1715 (new style).   4. Lot 109 at that sale was another full length portrait of the sitter in No. 2359 by Dahl but smaller (43 × 30 ins). It also had an orange tree.

DEGAS, Edgar, 1834-1917

6645 Woman Ironing

Canvas, 80 × 63.5 cm

Inscribed: *Degas*[1]

Dated by Lemoisne to 1885 and described by him as *Repasseuse à Contre Jour;*[2] there are two other *Repasseuses à Contre Jour* close to No.

6645, one in the Metropolitan Museum of Art (H. O. Havemeyer Collection No. 29.100.46) dating from about 1874,[3] the other in the collection of Mme Georges Durand Ruel dating from about 1882.[4]

Degas was painting laundry women throughout most of his working life.[5]

Prov: 1 er Vente Degas, Galerie Georges Petit, 6-8 May 1918. p.21 (32). Georges Viau. Paris. César M. de Hauke, New York.[6] Jacques Seligmann, New York; Wildenstein and Co. 1930; Hon. Mrs A. E. Pleydell-Bouverie, 1942; sold Sotheby's 3 July 1968 (13); purchased by the W.A.G., with the aid of the National Art-Collections Fund.

Exh: New York, Jacques Seligmann Gallery, *Courbet to Seurat*, 1937 (7). National Gallery, *Nineteenth Century French Paintings*, 1942, (37). Edinburgh Festival and Tate Gallery, *Degas* 1953 (22). Tate Gallery, *The Pleydell Bouverie Collection* 1954 (15). Tate Gallery, *Private Views*, 1963 (152).

Ref: 1. Mark of 1 er Vente Degas (see provenance) Lugt No. 658.   **2.** P.A. Lemoisne, *Degas et son Oeuvre*, 1946, No. 846.   **3.** Lemoisne, *op. cit.* No. 356.   **4.** Lemoisne *op. cit.* No. 685.   **5.** E. Degas, *Letters,* ed Guerin, 1947, p. 18 and p. 218. For the subject itself see particularly Erich Steingraber, *La Repasseues zur fruhesten Version des Themas von Edgar Degas,* Pantheon, Vol. 32, 1974, pp. 47-53, and Theodore Reff, *Degas: the Artist's Mind*, 1976 pp. 82ff. and pp. 166ff. for the influence of Daumier and Zola.   **6.** Apparently de Hauke never actually owned No. 6645, Germain Seligmann *letter* 28 December 1968.

DELAROCHE, Hippolyte (Paul), 1797-1856

2990 Napoleon Crossing the Alps

Canvas, 279.4 × 214.5 cm

Signed: *Paul Delaroche / Nice 1850*

Commissioned by Arthur George, 3rd Earl of Onslow in 1848 as a historically accurate corrective to Jacques Louis David's version[1] of the same subject.[2] Delaroche's source was A. Thiers, *Histoire du Consulat,* I, 1845, pp. 375-6,[3] although the artist also apparently studied the site in the Alps itself.[4] On its arrival in England in 1850 No. 2990 was unfavourably reviewed in the Athenaeum.[5]

For a more extensive discussion of No. 2990 see Edward Morris, *Napoleon Crossing the Alps by Paul Delaroche,* Walker Art Gallery Annual Report and Bulletin, Vols. 2-4 1974 pp. 65ff, which however does not mention A. F. Girard's engraving, *Bonaparte passant le Saint Bernard,* after Steuben of 1847, which is very close in conception to No. 2990.

A *Tete d'Etude* for No. 2990 was lithographed by Emile Lassalle.

Eng: A Francois (1851); Gautier (mezzotint)
Prov: Arthur George, 3rd Earl of Onslow sold Christie's 22nd July 1893 (15) bought Henry Yates Thompson who presented it 1893.

52

Exh: Messrs. Leggatt and Co., Cornhill, London, 1850;[6] Alexander Hill's Rooms, Edinburgh, 1850-51.[7]

Ref: **1.** The best version is in the Musée National de Malmaison.   **2.** C. E. Vulliamy, *The Onslow Family* 1953, p. 244. Jules Goddé and Henri Delaborde, *Oeuvre de Paul Delaroche*, 1858, plate 53. The delay in completing No. 2990 was caused by the artist's departure from Paris on the outbreak of the 1848 revolution. N. D. Ziff, *Paul Delaroche*, 1977, pp. 226ff, 296ff Nos. 164-169, 179-80, however states that there were earlier (?) versions begun and completed in 1848.   **3.** Goddé *op. cit.* An illustrated edition of Thier's *Histoire de Consulat* published in 1845 contains an engraving by Outhwaite after Karl Girardet of the same subject as No. 2990 and very close to it.   **4.** Vulliamy *op. cit.* No. 2990 is signed *Nice*.   **5.** *The Athenaeum* 1850, October 19, p. 1098, but possibly referring to John Naylor's version of 1851 (?) exhibited at Palais des Beaux Arts, *Exposition des Oeuvres de Paul Delaroche*, 1857 (40), last seen at Christie's 7 May 1971 lot 86; other versions are certainly not autograph; however the version at the John Dillon Sale, Christie's, 17 April 1869, lot 90, also lent by John Dillon to the Art Treasures Exhibition, Manchester, 1857 (659), was sold "with an autograph letter of the painter's in reference to it".   **6.** The Times 23 December 1850.   **7.** I am indebted to Basil Skinner for this reference.

DELOBBE, Francois Alfred, 1835-1920

3035   Haymakers Resting

Canvas, 119.4 × 207.6 cm

Signed: *A. Delobbe*

Damaged in 1904 but repaired by the artist in 1904-5, No. 3305 was finally destroyed in the Second World War.

Prov: Purchased from the 1901 L.A.E. (£80).

Exh: Paris, *Société des artistes francais* 1901 (613) as *Le Repos des Faneuses;* L.A.E. 1901 (401).

DENIS, Maurice, 1870-1943

6234   Rocher du Skevel

Cardboard, 25.5 × 30.8 cm

Signed in monogram: *MAUD*

The subject, the Rocher du Skevel, Ploumanach near Perros-Guirec was identified by Dominique Maurice-Denis in 1966.[1] Hitherto the picture had been entitled *Les Rochers Roses*. Denis stayed at Perros-Guirec in June and July 1893[2] and this seems a likely date for No. 6234.[3] The closest dated picture to No. 6234 is probably *Le Roi Arthur et Saint Efflam* (Collection Louis Hautecoeur, Paris) of 1891.[4]

Prov: Mme Jean Follain (the artist's daughter); Wildenstein, from whom purchased 1964.

Exh: Paris, Galerie Beaux Arts, 1963 (108); Wildenstein, London, *Maurice Denis,* 1964 (9).

Ref: **1.** Letter 9 June 1966.   **2.** Maurice Denis, *Journal,* I, 1957, p. 100.   **3.** Dominique Maurice-Denis, letter *op. cit.*   **4.** *Maurice Denis,* Orangerie des Tuileries, 1970 (28).

DERAIN, André, 1880-1954

2874   L'Italienne[1]

Canvas laid on plywood, 91 × 72 cm

Signed: *a derain*

Painted from an Italian model in the artist's studio, rue Bonaparte, Paris about 1920-24; Derain was in Italy in 1921 but did not work from the posed model there.[2] The same model seems to have been used in the *Frauen-Brustbild,* Prague,[3] the *Head of a Girl,* (R. Hauert Collection)[4] and *La Bohemienne* (ex Elie Faure Collection).[5] No. 2874 is discussed in detail by John Jacob, *L'Italienne by Andre Derain,* Liverpool Bulletin, Vol. VII, No. 3, 1958-9 pp. 314ff. and by Denys Sutton.[6]

Prov: Valentine Gallery, New York; Hirschorn Barbee Collection, U.S.A. sold Parke Bernet, New York 10 November 1948 (54) bt. J. J. Mage 500 dollars. Mayor Gallery, London, from whom purchased 1959.

Exh: Edinburgh Festival, *Derain,* 1967 (70)

Ref: **1.** Title suggested by Denys Sutton, *Derain,* 1959, No. 47, p. 152.   **2.** Alice Derain, *letter,* 10 May 1959. Italian models, often women in national costume, were common in Paris at least around 1900 see Jacques Letheve, *Daily Life of French Artists in the Ninteenth Century* 1972, p. 76 with further references.   **3.** National Gallery, Prague No. 0-3211.   **4.** Denys Sutton, *op. cit.* plate 45.   **5.** Sold Sotheby's 6 December 1961 (62a) bt. Mauradian.   **6.** *Op. cit.,* pp. 37 and 152 dating No. 2874 more precisely to the period after the artist's return from Italy in 1921 and discussing the "softening" of the artist's "monumentality" through the influence of Corot and Renoir.

DIEST, William van, 1610-1673

2897   Sea Battle

Canvas, 97.8 × 146.6 cm

Signed: *W. V. Diest 165(3?)*

Another version, varying slightly from it, of No. 2897 was sold at Parke-Bernet, New York, 7-8 March 1952, lot 80, 33 × 63 ins, signed and dated 1657. The subject appears to be the Battle of Scheveningen on 31 July 1653.[1]

Prov: Presented by Everton Public Library 1923.

Ref: 1. E. H. H. Archibald, *letter,* 16 March 1971 confirmed by an annotated photograph in the Rijksbureau voor Kunsthistorische Documentatie, The Hague noted by Dr. R. M. Vorstman 4 August 1971.

DOLCI, Carlo, 1616-1686, after

2903 St. Mary Magdalen

Canvas, 73.7 × 58.5 cm

Inscribed: on reverse *I.P.P./Egisto Manzuoli/Firenze*

A copy of the picture in the Uffizi. Manzuoli may only have been the picture-dealer and not the copyist.[1]

Prov: Transferred from the Toxteth Branch Library, January 1918.[2]

Ref: 1. See under 2841 After Raphael for full discussion. 2903 like 2841 has a printed label on the stretcher giving Manzuoli's address as Casa Machiavelli and calling him 'pittore'. 2. W.A.G. Stock Book I p. 129. This contradicts the statement that it was presented in *Walker Art Gallery Illustrated Catalogue of the Permanent Collection,* 1927, p. 126. Probably it was presented to the Toxteth Library before 1918.

DORÉ, Louis Christophe Paul Gustave, 1833-1883

2282 Flower Sellers

Canvas, 221 × 134.6 cm

Signed: *Gve Dore*

Identical to Doré's etching *Marchande de Fleurs a Londres* of 1876[1] apart from the right hand figure.

Jerrold relates that during the artist's stay in London, 1869-1873 "he made some studies of the flower girls by the Royal Exchange but when he painted or drew them afterwards he put French baskets on their arms and was impatient when I pointed this out."[2]

A number of other *Marchandes de Fleurs, Londres* by Doré are recorded.[3]

Prov: Purchased from the artist by Henry Thompson 1875[4] who presented it 1880.

Ref: 1. H. Béraldi, *Les Graveurs du 19 me siècle,* 1885, vol. 15, No. 15, reproduced in Konrad Farner, *Gustave Doré,* Dresden, n.d. plate 223. 2. Blanchard Jerrold, *Life of Gustave Doré,* 1891, p. 191. 3. See Henri Leblanc, *Catalogue de l'oeuvre complet de Gustave Doré,* 1931, p. 535, and Gustave Doré and Blanchard Jerrold, *London,* 1872. 4. Jerrold, 1891, *op. cit.,* Appendix II, p. 409 who notes that Thompson bought No. 2282 for presentation to the "Walters Gallery" (sic).

D'ORSAY, Count Alfred, 1801-1852

662   Portrait of the Duke of Wellington (?)

Canvas, 76.2 × 62.8 cm

Exhibited as the *Duke of Wellington at Walmer Castle*[1] and tradition-ally described as the *Duke of Wellington wearing the Insignia of the Lord Warden of the Cinque Ports*.[2] The church in No. 662 however does not resemble Walmer Church—nor that at Stratfield Saye, Hampshire, the Duke's country house—and his dress and insignia do not resemble those of the Lord Warden of the Cinque Ports.[3]

Many portraits of this sitter by this artist are recorded and known; none is identical to No. 662.[4]

Prov: Presented by Lord Wavertree 1928
Exh: L.A.E. 1928 (222) as *Duke of Wellington at Walmer Castle*.
Ref: **1.** See exhibitions.   **2.** Gallery files.   **3.** J. M. Melhuish *letter*, 7 March 1972 relying on the relics of the Duke of Wellington at Walmer Castle.   **4.** See Lord G. Wellesley and J. Steegman, *The Iconography of the first Duke of Wellington*, 1935, p. 8.

DOUVEN, Frans Bartolomaeus, 1688-1726

1190   Christ on the Cross

Panel, 27.6 × 20.8 cm

Signed: *F. B. Douve(n)* (F B D in monogram)

Prov: Purchased from Mrs E. Clare Evans 1952.

DRURY (or DURY), Tony, born 1819

2590   Portrait of Andrew Commins

Canvas, 61.5 × 51 cm

The sitter (1829/32-1916) was a barrister practising in Liverpool. He became a Liverpool Town Councillor in 1876 and Alderman in 1892; he was M.P. for Roscommon in 1880-92 and for Mid Cork 1893-1900.

Prov: Presented by Mrs Commins, 1917.
Exh: L.A.E. 1879 (591).

DUGHET, Gaspard, 1615-1675

1310 Landscape with Pyramus and Thisbe

Canvas, 100 × 145 cm

The subject is taken from Ovid's *Metamorphoses,* IV, 55-165. No. 1310 is clearly influenced by Nicolas Poussin's landscapes of the 1650's, but may show Dughet moving away from Poussin's classicism—at its peak in Dughet's works around 1653-4—towards a more baroque approach and can thus be dated to about 1656.[1]

Prov: ?Walsh Porter sold Christie's 22 March 1803, lot 40 as Gaspar Poussin, *A noble landscape embellished with the story of Pyramus and Thisbe, one of the most elegant* bought for the Earl of Suffolk[2] £126. W. H. Grenfell by descent to Lord Desborough sold Christie's 9 April 1954 lot 68 bought Agnew, purchased by the W.A.G., 1954.

Exh: ? British Institution 1858 (153) as *Landscape*; lent by the Earl of Suffolk, Royal Academy 1878 (127).

Ref: 1. Marie–Nicole Boisclair, *Gaspard Dughet: une chronologie revisée*, Revue de l'Art, Vol. 34, 1976, pp. 35 and 41.   2. Waagen noted in about 1850 in the collection of the Earl of Suffolk: "Francois Millet. A Fine Hilly Landscape in the taste of his great model Gaspard Poussin (G. F. Waagen, *Art Treasures in Great Britain*, 1854, III, p. 170). The 17th Earl dies in 1876 and W. H. Grenfell exhibits No. 1310 at the Royal Academy in 1878 (see Exhibitions). It therefore seems likely that No. 1310 was in the Earl of Suffolk's Collection. It did not appear at the Earl's sale at Christie's of 9 June 1877.

DURER, Albrecht, 1471-1528, after

1224 The Birth of the Virgin

Panel, 36.7 × 27.6 cm

A copy without the angel after Durer's woodcut of about 1504.[1] It probably dates from the late 16th or 17th Century and suggests Durer as a source of 17th Century genre painting.

Prov: ? A Gentleman deceased from Buckinghamshire sold Christie's 2 February 1805 (73) bt. Thompson £5 0s 0d. Mr Jackson sold Christie's 7 April 1807 (106) bt. Winstanley £3 0s 0d. Acquired by the L.R.I. between 1836 and 1843;[2] deposited at the W.A.G., 1893; presented to the W.A.G., 1948.

Exh: Manchester, *Art Treasures*, 1857 (484). Leeds, *National Exhibition*, 1868 (513).

Ref: 1. A. Bartsch, *Le Peintre Graveur*, Vol. VII, 1866, No. 80.   2. 1843 Catalogue No. 67 where it is already listed as a copy after Durer "in a free and able style".

DUTCH School, 17th century

817 Marine View

Panel, 22.8 × 30.5 cm

The principal ship is flying the Dutch flag. Attributed on entry to the Gallery to Willem van der Velde the younger.[1]

Prov: Bequeathed by Mrs Margaret Harvey, 1878.
Ref: **1.** 1882 Catalogue p. 64.

820   The Butcher's Shop

Canvas, 75.5 × 57.5 cm

Attributed in the 1927 Catalogue (p. 178) to Jan Steen.

Prov: Presented by Alderman E. Samuelson 1886.

831   Landscape with a Foot Bridge

Canvas, 77.5 × 110.5 cm

The 1963 Catalogue suggested an attribution to Adrian, Jansz Ockers. The costume of the figures suggests a date in the 1650's.[1]

Prov: Bequeathed by Mrs E. E. Cubbin 1955.
Ref: **1.** Aileen Ribeiro *letter* 22 February 1973.

956   Landscape with Tower

Panel, 54.5 × 68.5 cm

An Italianate landscape attributed to a follower of Jan Both in the 1963 Catalogue. Dr. Anne Charlotte Steland-Stief suggests a date around 1640 and believes No. 956 to have been painted at Rome.[1]

Prov: Presented by Hugo Rathbone, Lady Warr and Reynolds Rathbone in memory of Mrs E. E. Rathbone, 1954.
Ref: **1.** *Letter* 22 September 1975.

962   Portrait of a Boy

Canvas, 57 × 50.1 cm

An old label on the back describes it as a Portrait of the Prince of Orange by De Bray.

Prov: Bequeathed by Mrs A. M. Kingsley 1953.

DUTCH School, early 18th century

1024   Landscape with Horseman

Canvas, 75.2 × 101.6 cm

Attributed on entry into the Liverpool Royal Institution to Lingelbach and Wynants[1] but the 1963 Catalogue suggested Dionys Verburgh;[2] neither attribution seems convincing and No. 1024 can only be dated to around 1720-1730 on the basis of the costume.[3]

Prov: Presented to the L.R.I. 1874 by Mrs Macaulay; deposited at the W.A.G. 1942; presented to the W.A.G. 1948.

Ref: 1. *Annual Reports of the Liverpool Royal Institution* 1874 and 1893. 2. For this artist see H. C. Hazewinkel, *De Rotterdamsche Schildersfamilie Verburgh,* Oud Holland, Vol. 55, 1938, pp. 217ff. 3. Anne Buck, letter, 12 June 1972.

DYCK, Sir Anthony van, 1599-1641, studio of

1191 Portrait of the Infanta Isabella-Clara-Eugenia

Canvas, 143.5 × 114.3 cm

The sitter (1566-1633), dressed as a member of the Third Order Regular of St. Francis,[1] was Archduchess of Austria and Regent of the Netherlands.

In December 1628 the artist received a gold chain worth 750 guilders for a portrait of the sitter.[2] This portrait was probably the full length portrait now at the Galleria Sabauda, Turin[3] of which No. 1191 is a variant.[4] Versions and variants of this portrait were being painted as late as 1634.[5] Apparently Van Dyck was unable to secure a sitting from the Infanta and had to depend for his likeness on Rubens's portrait of 1625 (autograph versions in the collection of Lord Aldenham, the Thyssen-Bornemisza Collection, Lugano, and the Pitti Palace No. 4263),[6] to which indeed No. 1191 is very close. This dependence was first observed by R. Oldenbourg, *Die Flamische Malerei des 17 Jahrhunderts,* 1918, p. 63.

Prov: Bought for £300 by Mr Philipe, a London print dealer, in Holland from the descendants of the family to whom the sitter had given the portrait;[7] Mrs Philipe; Andrew Geddes;[8] Earl of Hopetoun in 1821 (350 guineas); by descent to the Marquis of Linlithgow; sold Christie's 18 June 1954 lot 39; presented by the Royal Insurance Company.

Exh: R.A. 1872 (64); R.A. 1900 (43); R.A. *Flemish Pictures,* 1953-4 (446).

Ref: 1. She entered the order in 1621 see Luke Wadding, *Annales Minorum,* ed. Quaracchi, Florence, 1934, XXV, p. 430, p. LXXIV. 2. M. de Maeyer, *Albrecht en Isabella en de Schilderkunst,* 1955, pp. 387-388, No. 224. 3. *Antoon Van Dyck, Tekeningen en Olieverfschetsen* (ed. Roger-A d'Hulst and Horst Vey), Rubenshuis, Antwerp, 1960, p. 17. 4. Ludwig Burchard MSS documentation on Van Dyck, Rubenianum, Antwerp, notes No. 1191 as "eine selbstandige Variante nicht eine Teilreplik der Ganzfigur" (R.-A. d'Hulst, letter, 7 September 1972); there are numerous other variants and versions of which the fullest list is in Schaeffer, *Van Dyck, Klassiker der Kunst* 1909, Nos. 291-293. Presumably a very good version three-quarters length like No. 1191, but without the pilaster, appears in the 2 paintings of about 1647 by David Teniers *The Picture Gallery of Archduke Leopold Wilhelm of Austria* (Prado, Madrid, Inv. No. 1813) and *The Picture Gallery of the Archduke Leopold Wilhelm of Austria with the royal portraits* now at Munich. The Archduke was also a Regent of the Netherlands (1646-1655). 5. The City of Antwerp was seeking a version from Van Dyck in 1634 (F. J. van den Branden, *L'Histoire de la Peinture Anveroise,* 1883,

c

and Charles I of England paid for a full length version in 1632 (W. H. Carpenter, *Pictorial Notices etc*, 1844, p. 71). **6.** Max Rooses, *L'Oeuvre de P. P. Rubens*, 1890, Vol. IV, p. 196, No. 970. (L. Burchard) *A Loan Exhibition of Peter Paul Rubens*, Wildenstein, London, 1950, No. 32, p. 39-40. **7.** *Memorandum of the portrait of Isabella by Sir Anthony Vandyke etc.* written by Andrew Wilson MSS Marquess of Linlithgow and the Hopetoun Manuscripts Trust (kindly communicated by Basil Skinner 1968.) **8.** *Memorandum of pictures bought 1820 to 1821*, MSS *op. cit.* See also Basil Skinner, *Andrew Wilson and the Hopetoun Collection*, Country Life, Vol. 144, 1968, p. 372.

DYCK, Sir Anthony van, after

1182   Venus beseeching Vulcan to forge arms for Aeneas

Canvas, 188 × 142.3 cm

A copy after the painting in the Louvre No. 1965.

Prov: Don Miguel of Spain.[1] T. Arthur Hope who presented it 1882.
Ref: **1.** Old Label.

ERCOLE de 'Roberti, active 1479, died 1496

2773   Pietà

Panel; 34.3 × 31.3 cm

A pentimento is visible running from the Virgin's head to her left elbow.[1] There is also an apparent pentimento at the left where the artist seems to have originally drawn the tomb projecting diagonally from a cave.

2773 is first mentioned with an implied attribution to Ercole by Pietro Lamo in 1560 who saw it 'above the high altar' of San Giovanni in Monte, Bologna accompanied by two panels, the *Betrayal* and the *Road to Calvary*,[2] now in Dresden (Gemaldegalerie 45 and 46). [3] Also on the altar was an altarpiece by Costa,[4] a *Coronation of the Virgin with Saints John the Baptist, Jerome, George, Sebastian, John the Evangelist and Luke*, signed and dated 1501, which is still there, and above the *peduccio*—the predella formed by 2773 and the Dresden panels, twelve terracotta busts of apostles gilded to give the appearance of bronze by Zaccheria da Volterra.[1]

Zaccheria (1473-1544) is first recorded in Bologna in 1516[5] and Costa's panel postdates Ercole's death.[6] So Lamo's description is not much of a guide to the intended appearance of the whole altarpiece when Ercole executed his panels. Bargellesi has in fact disputed the association of his three panels and the Costa on the grounds that Lamo meant that the Costa was elsewhere in the chapel.[7] This runs contrary to the literal reading of the passage.[8] Costa's altarpiece is 283cms wide and the predella panels together 267cms.[9] A series of terracotta busts of apostles, now at least ungilded, sit on top of the choir stalls in the Cappella Maggiore and have been there from the nineteenth century[10] usually attributed to Alfonso Lombardi.[11]

The busts may have rested on a screen behind and above the predella as they are clearly too large and too many to have ever sat directly on top of the predella. Behind them on the back wall of the chapel may have been the *Coronation of the Virgin,* which would have been also an *Assumption* witnessed by the Apostles. The whole artistic ensemble would have had iconographic unity in showing the Virgin at the lowest depths and highest peak in her life.

The delay in the completion of the altarpiece makes it possible that the Costa formed part of a new campaign in the Cappella Maggiore following the erection of the cupola in 1496.

The panels were repeatedly moved and reconstructed until 1695 when the predella was placed in the small sacristy. In 1750 the other two predella panels were removed for the Duke of Saxony through the agency of Luigi Crespi, Canon of Santa Maria Maggiore.[12]

Cavalcaselle was the first to realize the association of 2773 and the Dresden panels and to return to the attribution of Ercole,[13] which had been first made explicitly by Vasari.[14] The latter said that Ercole painted it at the same time as the frescoes in the Garganelli Chapel in San Petronio (an error for San Pietro). These lost frescoes are assigned to the years 1482 to 1486. Nevertheless various dates have been given to the predella ranging from c.1482[15] to c.1495-6.[16] But the strong influence of Mantegna and Tura, and the resemblances with the style of the surviving fragment from the Garganelli chapel indicate that Vasari's dating is to be preferred.[17]

The drawing in the British Museum attributed to Ercole appears to be a development from 2773 rather than a study for it.[18] It was used for a painting attributed to Mazzolino.[19] The weak drawings in the Uffizi and the British Museum published by Longhi[20] and suggested by Compton[21] as of a type related to ones used in 2773 are not connected to 2773 and are probably Florentine.[22]

The Pietà, the Virgin holding the body of her Son in her lap is included in Jacopo da Voragine's *Sermo de Passione* and there are numerous references to this unbiblical event in the writings and teachings of fourteenth and fifteenth century writers. In the text of the Breviary the Virgin holding her Son on her knees is compared to the Shunamite, who in the fourth book of II Kings held her sick son on her knees. The Pieta is an act of sacrifice on the part of the Virgin who offers Him for the Redemption of mankind.[23]

The Pietà can also refer back to the Incarnation, since according to San Bernardino, when the body of her dead Son rested in the Virgin's lap, she was reminded of the Nativity and the shroud in which she enveloped him, held in her right hand in 2773 she imagined to be the swaddling clothes.[24]

A Pietà, now lost, by Roger Van der Weyden, was seen by Cyriac of Ancona in 1449 in the Este Collection at Ferrara[25] and may have been seen by Ercole.[26] The composition of 2773 appears to have been inspired by Tura's *Pietà* in the Museo Correr. A Giovanni Bellini *Pietà* (Bergamo private collection) has also been claimed as a source.[27] All three artists probably knew a number of pieces of sculpture of Northern origin on the theme of the Vesperbilder. One such group is in San Giovanni in Monte.[28] The type, however, of the Virgin holding Christ on her lap in front of the tomb already existed in Italian painting in the fourteenth century as shown by an example once in the Martin Le Roy Collection, attributed to Giovanni da Milano.[29] Meiss interprets the atmospheric sketchiness of the setting compared with the two central figures and the tomb as an attempt by Ercole to convey the memory that haunts the mind of the Virgin of the past event of the Crucifixion.[30] Tura also combined the two events in one painting. The Virgin is dressed in a black mantle as she was in the annual productions of religious dramas held by the *Confraternita del Gonfalone* in the Colosseum in the late fifteenth century.[31]

Versions: Enlarged copy, Pinacoteca Nazionale, Bologna;[32] lead pencil and pen drawing by G. B. Cavalcaselle, Venice, Bibliotheca Marciana.[13] Two pen drawings by G. B. Cavalcaselle, Victoria and Albert Museum.[13]

Prov: San Giovanni in Monte, Bologna;[2] said to have come from the Riccardi Palace;[33] Roscoe Sale, (18), bt. Crompton £4 14s 6d; presented to the L.R.I., 1819;[34] deposited at the W.A.G., 1893;[35] presented to the W.A.G., 1948.

Exh: Manchester, *Art Treasures*, 1857 (91); Burlington Fine Arts Club, *Works of the School of Ferrara-Bologna*, 1894 (8); New Gallery, 1898 (138).

Ref: **1.** This is visible with the naked eye, but even more apparent from the X-rays taken by Ruhemann in 1935. **2.** Pietro Lamo, printed in *Graticola di Bologna*, Bologna, 1844, p. 13 n. 7. **3.** Picture Gallery, *Dresden Old Masters*, 1962, p. 87. Both 35 × 118 cm. **4.** Ranier Varese, *Lorenzo Costa*, 1967, p. 66 (23) pl. IX. **5.** N. Rasmo, s.v. Zacchi, Zaccaria, *Thieme-Becker*, XXXVI, 1947, p. 373. **6.** F. Filippini, *Ercole Grandi da Ferrara*, 1914, p. 31 argues that the difference in date means that the Dresden panels and 2773 were not part of the same altarpiece. **7.** Giacomo Bargellesi, *Ercole da Ferrara*, XII, 1934, p. 7. **8.** Filippini, *op. cit.* p. 30. **9.** Guido Zucchini, L'altare maggiore e la predella di Ercole da Ferrara in *La Chiesa di S. Giovanni in Monte di Bologna*, 1914, pp. 31 ff who gives the history of the altarpiece in detail. The measurements given by Varese, *op. cit.*, p. 66 are wrong. **10.** Girolamo Baruffaldi, ed. Domenico Taddei, *Vite de pittori e scultori Ferraresi*, 1844, I, p. 218 note. **11.** For instance Carlo Malvasia, *Le Pitture di Bologna*, 1686, p. 290. **12.** Zucchini, *op. cit.*, p. 35. **13.** Cavalcaselle in his copy of the 1857 Manchester, *Art Treasures* exhibition catalogue crossed out the name of Mantegna and replaced it 'sia Cossa o Grandi', finally plumping for Cossa, but on a drawing in Venice Cod. Marciana It. IV 2033 (=12274) fasc 22 which is a rough copy of 2773 he wrote 'Mantegna-no.. Ercole Grandi vedi Dresda.' Lina Moretti, *G. B. Cavalcaselle, Disegni da antichi maestri*, Florence, Galleria degli Uffizi, Gabinetto dei disegni, 1973, p. 88 (59). The album in which it is, bears the inscription "Liverpool 1865". Above one of the two copies in the Victoria and Albert Museum Collection of Ms notes a similar inscription appears attributing 2773 to Ercole. **14.** Vasari, ed. Milanesi, III, p. 145. **15.** Rosemaria Molajoli, *L'Opera Completa di Cosmè Tura e i grandi pittori ferraresi del suo tempo*, 1974, n. 112; Zucchini, *op. cit.*, pp. 87ff and implicitly Sergio Ortòlani, *Cosmè Tura, Francesco del Cossa, Ercole de'Roberti*, 1941, pp. 183, 188. **16.** Roberto Salvini and Leone Traverso, *Predelle dal '200 al '500*, 1959, p. 223 following C. Gamba, *Ercole da Ferrara*, L'Esposizione della Pittura Ferrarese del rinascimento, March, 1933, pp. 13-14. **17.** As for instance Benedict Nicolson, *The Painters of Ferrara*, 1950, pp. 14-15 and Mario Salmi, *Ercole de' Roberti*, 1960, p. 28. **18.** A. E. Popham and Philip Pouncey, *Italian drawings in the British Museum, The fourteenth and fifteenth centuries*, 1950, pp. 140-1, B.M. 1892-4-11-5. **19.** Conte Vittorio Cini Collection, Silla Zamboni *Ludovico Mazzolino*, 1968, pl. V, 12a, pp. 56-7.   **20.** Roberto Longhi, Ampliamenti nell' Officina Ferrarese, 1940, *Officina Ferrarese,* 1956, pp. 133-4, figs. 315-319.   **21.** 1963 Catalogue, p. 63.   **22.** Popham and Pouncey, *op. cit.,* p. 177.   **23.** Tadeusz Dobrzeniecki, *Medieval sources of the Pietà,* Bulletin du Musée National de Varsovie, VIII, 1967, pp. 5 ff, espec. 6-15.   **24.** Emile Male, *L'Art Religieux de la fin du Moyen-âge en France,* 1925, pp. 124-5 see also Erwin Panofsky, *Reintegration of a Book of Hours executed in the workshop of the Maitre des Grandes heures de Rohan,* Mediaeval Studies in Memory of A. Kingsley Porter, 1939, II, p. 491.   **25.** Cyriac d' Ancona 8 July 1449 reprinted in Michael Baxandall, *Giotto and the Orators,* 1971, p. 108, n. 49, who also prints the description in Bartolomeo Fazio's *De Pictoribus.*   **26.** Michael Levey, lecture at the Walker Art Gallery, 15 October 1964.   **27.** Ridolfo Pallucchini, *Giovanni Bellini,* 1959, p. 26, fig. 19.   **28.** Werner Korte, *Deutsche Vesperbilder in Italien,* Kunstgeschichtliches Jahrbuch der Bibliotheca Hertziana, I, 1937, p. 118. nr. 13 pl. 52.   **29.** Roberto Longhi, *Una 'riconsiderazione' dei primitivi italiani a Londra,* Paragone, XVI, 183, May, 1965, p. 13 pl. 1. There is also a *Pietà* of this type with the Madonna in black, signed and dated July 26, 1368 by Simone da Bologna in the Palazzo Davia, Bologna (173). The Madonna is also in black in Botticelli's Munich Alte Pinakothek *Pietà.*   **30.** Millard Meiss, *Giovanni Bellini's St. Francis in the Frick Collection,* 1964, p. 30   **31.** Stella Mary Newton, *Renaissance Theatre costume and the sense of the historic past,* 1975, p. 146 cites Marco Vatasso, *Per la Storia del dramma sacro in Italia,* 1903, pp. 95-6, 98-9.   **32.** E. Mauceri, *Il Comune di Bologna,* 1934, I, pp. 74-5.   **33.** Roscoe sale (18), but not mentioned in subsequent nineteenth century catalogues.   **34.** 1819 Catalogue (12).   **35.** 1893 Catalogue p. 12 (28).

EVERSDIJK, Willem, 1617-1671, after

826   Allegory of the Herring Fisheries

Canvas, 13.4 × 169.5 cm

Noted by Luttervelt[1] as a contemporary copy of Eversdijk's picture now in the Rijksmuseum, Amsterdam, No. 118 A15, and as evidence of the picture's popularity in the seventeenth century. The original can be dated to the period of prosperity for the Dutch herring fishery between the end of the war with England in 1667 and the Treaty of Dover in 1670.[2] No. 826 differs from the original in that the view of Flushing in the original is omitted in No. 826.

Prov: Presented by William Thompson Mann 1872 (as by an unknown artist).[3]

Ref: 1. R. van Luttervelt, *Herinneringer aan Michiel Adriaenszoon de Ruyter in het Rijksmuseum,* Bulletin van het Rijksmuseum, Amsterdam, 1957, Vol. II, p. 63.   2. Luttervelt *op. cit.,* with full details of the subject including an identification of the figures in No. 826.   3. 1882 Catalogue No. 148, p. 38 and Liverpool Corporation Libraries Museums and Arts Committee 24 December 1872 (the date is wrongly given as 1874 in early inventories and catalogues of the W.A.G.).

FABRITIUS, Carel, 1622-1654

959   Portrait of a Bearded man

Panel, 22.8 × 19.3 cm

Apparently by the same hand as the *Head of an Old Man* at the Mauritshuis (No. 828) also attributed to Carel Fabritius.[1] Neither however can be regarded as certainly by the same artist as the signed self portrait in the Boymans Museum, Rotterdam, No. 1205.[2]

Prov: Said to have been in the Collection of William Roscoe but apparently not at his sale 1816 (unless lot 114 *His own Portrait; in chiaroscuro* by Van Dyck, 9 × 7 ins.); Mrs. A. M. Roscoe who bequeathed it 1950.

Ref: 1. Sheila Somers first suggested this attribution 1956; Captain Eric C. Palmer supported it, letter 19 July 1957 and Professor K. Bauch saw No. 954 as a weak work by Carel Fabritius, letter 7 May 1963.   2. The *Head of an Old Man* at the Mauritshuis was exhibited as by Fabritius at the exhibition *Rembrandt after three hundred years,* Art Institute of Chicago, 1969, No. 58, p. 66. It bears an illegible signature, not clearly identifiable as that of Carel Fabritius.

FARASYN, Edgard, 1858-1938

508   The Cheat

Canvas, 85.4 × 114.3 cm

Signed: *FARASYN 1878*

A copy after *The Cardplayers* by Theodor Rombouts now at the Musée des Beaux Arts, Antwerp No. 358.

Farasyn was a pupil at the Antwerp Academy in 1878 and *The Cardplayers* had been at the Musée des Beaux Arts since 1847.[1]

Prov: Presented by George Wharton 1929.
Ref: 1. Van der Borch—van Cam Bequest.

FERRARESE School, early 16th century

2778   Madonna suckling the Child

Panel, 29.5 × 23.8 cm

Condition: Extensive damage in the area of the child's right hand and undergarment over her right breast. Vertical cracking of panel caused by penetration of woodworm.[1]

One of a number of Ferrarese small devotional pictures with asymmetrical compostions, apparently inspired by the work of Boccaccio Boccaccino.[2] 2778 is close to the early work of Garofalo,[3] when he was under the influence of Francia,[4] and Costa. The position of the Child on the parapet is akin to that of the Child in the fresco of *The Presentation in the Temple* in the Oratory of the Conception.[5] But the clumsiness of the child in 2778 raises a little doubt, and in the absence of documented or signed works of this type, it would be unwise to rule out alternative candidates such as Domenico Panetti, to whom a series of Madonnas with children standing on parapets is attributed.[6] 2778 does, however, seem to be closer to works associated with Garofalo than to these.

Prov: Entered the L.R.I. between 1836 and 1843;[7] deposited at the W.A.G., 1893;[8] presented to the W.A.G., 1948.

Ref: 1. Revealed on cleaning by J. C. Witherop, 1971.   2. Compare the Madonnas in the Ca d'Oro, Venice and in Padua, Museo Civico. Alberto Puerari, *Boccaccino*, 1957, pl. 33, 34.   3. Bernard Berenson, *North Italian Pictures of the Renaissance*, 1907, p. 226 as Garofalo?; Bernard Berenson, *Central and North Italian Schools*, I, 1968, p. 156 as early—attribution accepted by G. Bargellesi, letter, 6 January, 1970.   4. Influence noted by W. M. Conway, *The Gallery of the Royal Institution*, 1884, pp. 13-14.   5. Maurizio Calvesi, *Nuovi affreschi Ferraresi dell'Oratorio della Concezione*, II Bollettino d'Arte, 1958, p. 318, fig. 11.   6. Calvesi, *op. cit.*, pp. 322 figs 15, 16; 323, fig. 17 note 1.   7. 1843 Catalogue, p. 11 (34).   8. 1893 Catalogue p. 11(26).

FERRI, Ciro, 1634-1689

2774   Holy Family, Rest on the Flight into Egypt

Canvas, 116.2 × 86 cm

First attributed to Ferri in 1952[1] and dated by Roderick Thesiger to the period 1659-1665.[2]

The figures of the Virgin and Child are identical to those in a painting formerly in the Dusseldorf Gallery, another *Rest on the Flight into Egypt* by Ferri.[3] Pascoli[4] records the existence of two paintings of this subject by Ferri, one large one and a smaller one at S. Andrea del Noviziato a Montecavallo.

Prov: Sir George Oliver Colthurst[5] of Blarney Castle; by descent to Sir Richard Colthurst sold Sotheby's 27 February 1952 lot 145 (as by Maratta) bought Thesiger £35 from whom it was purchased 1953.

Ref: 1. *Notable Works of Art Now on the Market*, Burlington Magazine, 1952, plate IX.   2. *Letter*, 10 November, 1953.   3. Nicolas de Pigage and Chrétien de Mechel, *La galerie electorale de Dusseldorf etc*, 1778, No. 194, plate 15, 6ft. 4 in × 6ft 3 in. This picture did not accompany the rest of the Dusseldorf Gallery to Munich in 1806, Rolf Kultzen, letter, 19 January 1973; it may have been the *Rest on the Flight into Egypt* by Ferri at the Musée Fesch, Ajaccio until the Second World War.   4. Lione Pascoli, *Vite de Pittori etc*, 1730, Vol. 1, p. 172.   5. *Oliver* is painted on the back of No. 2774.

FISHER, William Mark, 1841-1923

2283 Harlow Mill

Canvas, 89 × 130 cm

Signed: *Mark Fisher*

Nearly identical to the *Harlow Mill* exhibited by Fisher at the 1912 Royal Academy (no. 179)[1] and presumably a near contemporary repetition of it. The artist had moved to Hatfield Heath, near Harlow in 1902. Harlow Mill, the building just to the right of centre, was burnt down in the 1940's and only the foundations remain; just to the left of it is the old grain store now the Harlow Mill Restaurant; to the right of the Mill is the lock keeper's house; the barn at the extreme left had been demolished by 1921.[2]

Prov: Purchased from the Beaux Arts Gallery, London 1939.

Exh: ?Leicester Galleries, *Memorial Exhibition of Works by the late Mark Fisher* 1924 No. 57 as *Harlow Mill.* An old label on the back of No. 2283 refers to the 1928 R.A. *Exhibition of Works by Late Members* etc. but 2283 does not appear in the catalogue although a large section of this exhibition was devoted to the work of Mark Fisher. No. 74 at this exhibition was described in the catalogue as *Harlow Mill,* owned by Mrs. Mark Fisher measuring 18 × 25½ in and exhibited at the 1912 R.A. The 1912 R.A. *Harlow Mill* however measured 36 × 44 in[3] and No. 74 at the 1928 exhibition may have been the sketch both for the 1912 R.A. *Harlow Mill* and for No. 2283. Another old label refers to the 1907 Dublin Irish International Exhibition at which No. 2283 was not exhibited.

Ref: **1.** *Royal Academy Pictures and Sculpture* 1912, p. 6.   **2.** Correspondence in the *Harlow Gazette and Citizen* 29 November 1974-13 December 1974; one correspondent dated No. 2283 to 1910.   **3.** *Royal Academy Pictures and Sculpture, op. cit.*

FLEMISH School, 17th century

2873 Crucifixion

Canvas, 167 × 110.3 cm

Prov: Sir William Stanley Massey Stanley sold in Hooton Hall sale of 1849.[1] Henry Steele who presented it 1851.[2]

Ref: **1.** A former label on the back and the Gallery records refer to Hooton Hall, Cheshire, and a sale took place there in 1849 when Sir William Stanley Massey Stanley sold the estate to R. C. Naylor see White's *Cheshire Directory* 1860, p. 609. The Liverpool Albion December 17, 1849 describing the sale referred to a *Crucifixion* by Murillo or Rubens sold for £27:16:0.   **2.** Liverpool Corporation Libraries, Museums and Art Committee 28 November 1851 and 29 April 1852 with an attribution to Rubens. The early catalogues and inventories of the Walker Art Gallery give the date wrongly as 1853.

6944 Crucifixion

Panel, 121 × 90 cm

Inscribed: *R. P. IOES VAN GHINDERTAL/S. BP IN RUBEA VALLE DD* and with the van Ghindertaelen arms.[1]/*JESUS NAZARENUS REX JUDAEORUM* and in Greek and Hebrew.

X-rays reveal the presence of a female (?) figure on a column and of a Bishop's Mitre under the Crucifixion.

Johannes van Gindertal was sub prior at the Priory of the Augustine Canons at Rouge Cloitre, near Brussels from 1649 until 1654.[2] For the iconography of No. 6944 see Emile Male, *L'art religieux de la fin du XVI siecle, du XVII siecle et du XVIII siecle,* 1951, pp. 270, 276.

Prov: Rouge Cloitre was suppressed in 1784 and its contents sold or confiscated.[3] No. 6944 is not identifiable in the inventories then drawn up.[4] Acquired by the L.R.I. 1836-1843;[5] presented to the W.A.G. by the University of Liverpool 1969.

Ref: 1. As recorded in Rietstap, *Armorial General* under *Ghindertaelen.* 2. Gaspare Ofhuys MSS *Primordiale Rubeae Vallis* (Catalogus Fratrum Choralium Rubeae Vallis) Bibliotheque Royale Albert I, Brussels, (II-480) published in Societe des Bollandistes *Anecdota ex codicibus Johannes Gielemans,* Brussels, 1895, pp. 197-303. I owe this reference to A. Maes. 3. A. Maes, *Rouge Cloitre,* 1964, p.61. 4. A. Maes letter 2nd October, 1972; the inventories are in the Archives Generales du Royaume de Belgique; there was a public auction of the best pictures from Rouge Cloitre in Brussels in June 1785 but No. 6944 was apparently not included. 5. No. 6944 first appears in the 1843 Catalogue (No. 74) as by Rubens and with a note that it was painted for the Church of the Bernardines at Antwerp.

FLINCK, Govaert, 1615-1660

960 Portrait of an Oriental

Canvas, 82.5 × 66.5 cm

Purchased by the L.R.I. as Aert de Gelder,[1] No. 960 was attributed by Waagen[2] to Salomon de Koninck. Flinck was preferred at Leyden in 1956[3] and von Moltke[4] confirmed this attribution and dated No. 960 to about 1642. This attribution cannot, however, be regarded as established.[5]

Prov: ?John W. Gibson. William Brett of Liverpool (?) from whom it was purchased for £20 by the L.R.I. 7th April, 1842;[6] deposited at the W.A.G. 1893; presented to the W.A.G. 1948

Exh: ?L.R.I., *Exhibtion of Old Master Paintings,* 1823 (79) as *Head of an Old Man* by Flinck lent by J. W. Gibson. Leeds 1868 (592) (as Aert de Gelder). Leyden *Rembrandt als Leermaster* 1956 (52).

Ref: 1. Minute Book of the Gallery of Art Committee 1841-5, L.R.I. Archives 41.   2. G. F. Waagen, *Art Treasures*, 1854, Vol. III, p. 240 but K. Lilienfeld, *Aert de Gelder,* 1914, p. 238, No. XXIV denied that No. 960 was either by Aert de Gelder or Salomon de Koninck.   3. See Exhibitions.   4. J. W. von Moltke, *G. Flinck*, 1965, p. 25, No. 183.   5. No. 960 could be an 18th Century Rembrandt pastiche; von Moltke. *op. cit.* notes the low quality of the painting apart from the head itself.   6. Minute Book *op. cit.* For William Brett see Neil Maclaren. *The Dutch School, National Gallery Catalogues,* 1960, p.347 and Nos. 2748-50 (Vincenzo) p. 222.

FLORENTINE School, second half of the 14th century

2857   Two wings of a triptych. Crucifixion right; Adoration of the Magi and of the Shepherds left. Above the Annunciation, Mary right, Gabriel left.

Panel, 55.2 × 25.7 cm each

Both panels have been cut very slightly at the top at the point at which the wings fold in to meet the missing central panel. Both panels are painted on their backs, the *Crucifixion* blue or green around a circle, the *Adoration* red around a light blue circle.

In the Crucifixion scene the Virgin is supported by St. John and one of the Holy Women, in the background is St. Longinus on horseback, his hands clasped in prayer. Offner notes the left wing as an early instance of the merging of the Nativity and the Adoration in one scene.[1]

The outer wings of a portable triptych. Offner attributes it to the School of Maso di Banco and identifies the centrepiece with a panel, once in the Lazzaroni Collection, Paris.[1] Berenson assigns 2857 to Jacopo di Cione and his workshop.[2] The patterning of the tooling around the edges of the scenes, and of the haloes is similar to that in a portable triptych in Edinburgh (1958) attributed by Berenson to the same workshop.[3]

A Madonna with eight saints, the centre of a portable triptych by the same hand was in Christie's sale at the Villa d'Este, Como, 1 June, 1971 (396).[4] Its measurements, however, preclude any suggestion that it belonged to 2857.

Prov: Thomas Winstanley, who presented it to the L.R.I. probably 2 April 1838;[5] in the L.R.I. Collection by 1843;[6] deposited at the W.A.G. 1893;[7] presented to the W.A.G., 1948.

Exh: Manchester, *Art Treasures,* 1857 (19).

Ref: 1. Richard Offner, *A Corpus of Florentine Painting,* Section III, Vol. V, 1947, p. 212 note 1.   2. Bernard Berenson, *Italian Pictures of the Renaissance, Florentine School,* I, 1963, p. 105.   3. Berenson, *op. cit.,* p. 103.   4. Painted surface, 45 × 22.5 cm; total size 68 × 30.5 cm.   5. L.R.I. Archives 37. Presents Book.   6. 1843 Catalogue p. 5 (14).   7. 1893 Catalogue p. 6 (11).

FLORENTINE School, *c.* 1420-1430

2761   Pentecost

Panel, 34.8 × 59 cm

Berenson was the first to suggest Bicci di Lorenzo as the author of this predella panel.[1] The style, however, is not very close to certain works by Bicci.

The composition goes back to the 14th Century.[2]

Prov: Purchased by the L.R.I. from Thomas Winstanley in 1835;[3] deposited with the W.A.G., 1893;[4] presented to the W.A.G., 1948.
Exh: Manchester, *Art Treasures*, 1857 (33).
Ref: **1.** Bernard Berenson, *Italian Pictures of the Renaissance*, 1932, p. 85.   **2.** 1963 *Catalogue*, p. 22.   **3.** Liverpool Royal Institution Presents Book. Bill dated 3 August 1836 for paintings supplied in 1835 (L.R.I. Archives 63).   **4.** 1893 Catalogue p. 6 (11a).

FLORENTINE School, *c.* 1480-1490

2809   Adventures of Odysseus

Top 1. Odysseus and his crew escape from the Laestrigonians, below they land on Circe's island, in the 1. centre she restores them to human form. Above Odysseus and three girls (?Odysseus in the land of the Cimmerians or Odysseus receiving instructions about his voyage from Circe), to the r. he consults Teiresias in Hades. Far r. the episode of the Sirens, and above, that of Scylla and Charybdis.

Panel, 42.8 × 153 cm

Conditions: Poor. Much rubbed and abraded.[1]

The story is taken from Homer's *Odyssey* Book 10. 144 ff, 11.155 ff and 12.166 ff. It is not clear what scene is represented in the right background. Odysseus when in the land of the Cimmerians speaks with the spirit of his mother Anticleia alone, and then throngs of women appear, thirteen of whom are addressed by Odysseus. The three women may be Anticleia and two representatives of the women met by Odysseus. But Circe in both the preceding scenes is accompanied by two women, and it is possible that it is these three again, particularly since Odysseus appears to reach the entrance to Hades only in the next scene. Circe would then be instructing Odysseus how to reach Hades and warning him of the dangers of the Sirens and of Scylla and Charybdis.

2809 is a panel from a Cassone,[2] still bearing at the top marks where the keys struck the surface as the lock was opened.

69

The previous attribution has been to the Dido Master,[3] a name covering a heterogeneous group of works. Weisbach was the first to note a link with two panels devoted to the Argonauts in the Metropolitan Museum.[4] Fahy thinks that the artist who painted 2809 and the first Metropolitan panel is identical with Offner's Master of the Porta Romana Lunette.[5] But while there are undoubtedly similarities between 2809 and the first Metropolitan panel, the condition of 2809 precludes any positive identification of the artist. Callmann reasonably suggests a date in the 1480's,[6] but her contention that 2809 is a reflection of the Lanckorowski *Odyssey* seems unwarranted.

Prov: A Customs stamp of Florence on the reverse. Said to have been in the collection of William Roscoe;[2] entered the collection of the L.R.I. between 1836 and 1843;[7] deposited at the W.A.G., 1893;[8] presented to the W.A.G., 1948.

Exh: Manchester, *Art Treasures*, 1857 (74),

Ref: **1.** Concern was expressed about its state by Philip Westcott in a letter to Theodore Rathbone 24 January 1854 (Liverpool University L.R.I. Archives 17). **2.** Already noted in 1859 Catalogue p. 15 (21) but not identifiable in the Roscoe Sale or among the pictures mentioned in the Roscoe Papers. **3.** 1963 Catalogue, p. 106 **4.** Werner Weisbach, *Francesco Pesellino und die Romantik der Renaissance*, 1901, p. 125. **5.** Everett Fahy, *letter*, 28 July 1967. **6.** Ellen Callmann, *Apollonio di Giovanni*, 1974, p. 17 n. 61 and p. 41 n. 12. **7.** 1843 Catalogue, p. 7 (22). **8.** 1893 Catalogue, p. 10 (21).

FLORENTINE School, *c*. 1515-1525

2868   Virgin, Child and infant St. John the Baptist

Panel, 62.2 × 59.5 cm

Condition:— An addition to the upper half has turned 2868 from a circular into a slightly oval shape.

This picture, if correctly identified, was described as 'unfinished' in one of the Sanford Catalogues.[1] When it was copied for Sanford the landscape at the left came up to the level of the bridge of St. John's nose and more detail was visible in the landscape at the right.[2]

There is a superior rectangular version at Grenoble (no. 516),[3] attributed by Berenson to Puligo.[4] 2868 has also been attributed to Puligo.[5] The design appears to have been evolved for a rectangular rather than a circular shape. Neither version, however, is close to Puligo's known work.[6] The composition derives from Albertinelli's *Madonna, Child and Infant St. John,* the best version of which is the Earl of Harewood's signed and dated 1509.[7] The physical types are Sartesque—compare for instance the head of the Brussels *Leda*[8]—and there are resemblances with the lost *Madonna and Child with Saint John under a baldacchino.*[9] But the curls of the children's hair approach those of the mature Rosso, suggesting possibly a slightly later date.

Prov: Geri Bocchineri;[10] Tom. Bandini, 22 May 1621;[10] the Rev. John Sanford (possibly purchased by him in November 1832 'Tondo di Andrea' for p. 10 10[11] or £23;[1] his sale Christie's 9 March 1839 (82) bt. Norton; in the L.R.I. Collection by 1843;[12] deposited at the W.A.G., 1893;[13] presented to the W.A.G., 1948.

Ref: **1.** *A list of paintings the property of the Revd John Sanford in the Casino Torrigiani Novr–1834* No. 43 (MSS Corsham Court). **2.** Watercolour copy by Giuseppe Gozzini, Corsham W158. **3.** 57 × 46 cm, letter of Mme. Gabrielle Kueny 15 March 1967. **4.** Bernard Berenson, *Florentine School,* I, 1963, p. 184 doubtfully. **5.** Note by V. Pace on a photograph in the Witt Library. **6.** An opinion shared by S. Bruce-Lockhart, orally, 11 May 1974. **7.** Bernard Berenson, *op. cit.,*II, pl. 1317. **8.** John Shearman, *Andrea del Sarto,* 1965, I, pl. 35b. **9.** Shearman, *op. cit.,* I, pl. 30c. **10.** Inscription on reverse: *Questo tond. è di Geri Bocchineri et l'ha consegnan al S. Tom . . . .? Bandi . . questo di 22 di Maggio 1621 in fiorenza et il d° Geri/ . . . . qui di suo proprio magno S.* A Geri Bocchineri is recorded as active between 1632 and 1641 and as the secretary to the Grand Duke of Tuscany (*16 Poligrafo Gargani* Florence, Biblioteca Nazionale, 320, 321, citing *Carteggio galileano inedito . . .* G. Campori 1881 p. 341). **11.** Rev. John Sanford Account Book (Barber Institute) p. 21 between the 5th and 23rd November (letter from Prof. H. Miles, March 1975) but a pencil addition in *Catalogue of Paintings purchased by the Revd John Sanford during his residence in Italy—1830/and following years* No. 43 (MSS Corsham Court) gives dimensions 30 × 18½. **12.** 1843 Catalogue p. 29 (104). **13.** 1893 Catalogue p. 25 (69).

FLORENTINE School, mid 16th century

2859 Madonna and Child with the infant St. John the Baptist

Panel, 68 × 48.5 cm

A compilation after a product of Andrea del Sarto's workshop in the National Gallery of Canada, Ottawa[1] and a Sartesque picture at Chatsworth.[2]

Prov: Entered the Collection of the L.R.I. between 1836 and 1843;[3] deposited at the W.A.G., 1893;[4] presented to the W.A.G., 1948.

Ref: **1.** John Shearman, *Andrea del Sarto,* II, 1965, p. 290. **2.** John Shearman, undated note in Gallery files. **3.** 1843 Catalogue p. 23 (80). **4.** 1893 Catalogue p. 25 (67).

FLORENTINE School, third quarter of the 16th century

2852 Saints Peter, Paul and Jerome

Panel (poplar), 136 × 153.5 cm

Condition: Poor. Considerable damage due to the warping of the three planks on which it is painted. Probably cut at the top—part of Peter's head is missing—and at the sides.[1]

Inscribed: *886* (bottom right)

The saints were first identified by Scharf.[2] The subject is enigmatic. It has been suggested that 2852 might be the bottom of a large altarpiece, possibly showing the *Virgin and Child in Glory*[3] or a *Disputa*. But the blue green veined marble background demands an explanation. Possibly there was once a companion panel with another three saints.

The artist appears to have used the same model for each of the three figures, turning him round and making slight alterations. There is a pentimento in the torso of Saint Jerome, who was originally clothed.[1]

The traditional attribution is to Vasari,[4] most recently supported by Pouncey and Gere.[5] Naldini's name has also been suggested,[6] but 2852 lacks the flickering brushwork to be found even in his earliest paintings and resemblances with works like the San Simone *Deposition*[7] are most plausibly explicable in terms of common sources rather than common authorship. 2852 has clearly been influenced by Pontormo, particularly that master's *Saint Jerome* in Hanover.[8] Links with Vasari's secure works are likewise not strong enough to justify so definite an attribution. David McTavish has suggested that 2852 might be a very late work by Francesco Salviati.[9]

Prov: Inventory number of an unknown collection; Massimi-Colonna family;[10] probably the late James Johnston Esq. of Straiton and Champfleurie, N.B., Rainy, 14 Regent Street, 29 June 1842, lot 77 Vasari, St. Peter, St. Mark and St. Jerome;[11] purchased by the L.R.I., October 1842;[12] deposited at the W.A.G., 1893;[13] presented to the W.A.G., 1948.

Ref: **1.** Technical report, J. C. Witherop. **2.** MS notes on 1858 proof catalogue (72) (L.R.I. Archives 63.14). **3.** Peter Cannon-Brookes, note in Gallery files. **4.** Minute Book of Art Gallery Committee, 17 October 1842 (L.R.I. Archives 41). **5.** Letter of P. M. R. Pouncey, 15 November 1974. **6.** Peter Cannon-Brookes, letter, 19 February 1968. **7.** Francoise Viatte, *Two studies by Naldini for the 'Depositon' in S. Simone, Florence*, Master Drawings, V, 1967, pp. 383-5, figs 1 and 2. **8.** Janet Cox Rearick, *The drawings of Pontormo*, II, Cambridge, Massachusetts, 1964, pl. 273. **9.** Orally, 12 June 1976. **10.** Seal on the reverse of a noble of the Massimi family of the branch descended from the marriage of Luca Massimi with Virginia di Giulio Colonna. Pompeo Litta, *Celebri Famiglie Italiane*, II, 1819, s.v. Colonna di Roma tavola VI. **11.** But it does not appear in the *Catalogue of the Johnston Gallery of Pictures . . . Straiton House, Wemyss Place, Edinburgh*, opened 23 December 1833, 2nd edition 1835. **12.** Possibly from Winstanley since deposited by him. Minute Book of Art Gallery Committee, 17 October 1842 (L.R.I. Archives 41). **13.** 1893 Catalogue p. 24 (66).

FLORENTINE School, 17th century

2840 Mythological Figure

Canvas, 104 × 82 cm

Later overpainting including drapery, a wooden cross and a pot was removed in 1962 and No. 2840 formerly described as *The Magdalen* can now probably be identified as a fragment of *Diana slaying Chione, Cephalus slaying Procris* or *Apollo slaying Coronis*,[1] all from Ovid's *Metamorphoses*.

P. Pouncey has suggested that No. 2840 is "terribly near the style of or by Baldassare Franceschini."[2]

Prov: ?William Roscoe.[3] Acquired by the L.R.I. between 1836 and 1843;[4] deposited at the W.A.G. 1893; presented to the W.A.G. 1948.

Ref: 1. See particularly Jane Costello, *Poussin's Drawings for Marino and the new Classicism,* Journal of the Warburg and Courtauld Institutes, Vol. 18, 1955, pp. 311ff for all these subjects.   2. Letter 25 July 1968. Independently Mina Gregori, *letter,* 31 July 1957 made the same suggestion adding that it might be a late work while Evelina Borea published it as by this artist in *Dipinti alla Petraia per don Lorenzo de Medici: Stefano della Bella . . . e altri,* Prospettiva, Vol. 2, 1975, pp.24ff.   3. Roscoe's draft for his 1816 Sale Catalogue included a Magdalen by Pasinelli (deleted), Roscoe Papers No. 3897.   4. 1843 Catalogue No. 87. Possibly No. 2840 was the Magdalen "after Guido" lent to the 1840 *First Exhibition of Objects Illustrative of the Fine Arts etc,* Liverpool Mechanics Institution 1840, No. 320 by R. V. Yates.

FLORIS Frans, 1516-1570, School of

6942 Crucifixion

Panel, 117.5 × 99 cm

The attribution was suggested by L. de Vries[1] and Professor Julius Held.[2]

Prov: Joseph Brooks Yates sold Winstanley's Liverpool 14th May 1857 (38) as by Van Eyck. Presented to the L.R.I. by William Rathbone between 1857 and 1859[3]; presented to the W.A.G. 1969.

Ref: 1. Letter 3rd February 1970.   2. Verbally 1973   3. Listed in the 1859 Catalogue No. 58.

FONTANA, Lavinia,1552-1614 after Buonarotti, MICHELANGELO, 1475-1564

2853 Silentium

Copper, 28 × 21.1 cm

The attribution first made by Longhi[1] is supported by comparison with the signed and dated Borghese *Silentium* of 1591 (inv. 437),[2] and the signed and dated 1589 Escorial *Silentium.*[3] The composition derives from a design by Michelangelo, much copied by Marcello Venusti and other followers.[4] Pouncey, in fact, attributes 2853 to Venusti.[5] Langedijk identifies the figure on the left in the Welbeck drawing by Michelangelo as Harpocrates.[6] He is in fact the infant St. John with the attributes of Harpocates,[7] the wolf's skin and the finger pressed to his lips.

The Virgin is in the act of unveiling the body of her Son, an action that recalls the lifting of the cloth that covers the chalice in the Mass,[8] the cloth that represents the winding sheet in which Christ was removed from the Cross.[9] There may also be a reference to the Neo-Platonic view that the body is a cloak which is shed when the soul is liberated by death.[10] Christ is slumped across his mother's knees in a pose that prefigures the Pieta. The hourglass symbolizes that Christ's life span will run out just like that of an ordinary man.

A *Holy Family, attended by angels* attributed to Lavinia Fontana was lent to the Liverpool Royal Institution Old Masters Exhibition of 1823 (10) by J. W. Gibsone, who presented no. 2854 to the L.R.I.

Prov: Entered the L.R.I. Collection between 1836 and 1843;[11] deposited at the W.A.G., 1893;[12] presented to the W.A.G., 1948.

Exh: Manchester, 1857, *Art Treasures* (224); Leeds, 1868 (168).

Ref: **1.** R. Longhi, letter, 29. 10. 1959.   **2.** Paola della Pergola, *Galleria Borghese, I Dipinti*, I, 1955, p. 36, pl. 44.   **3.** Rómeo Galli, *Lavinia Fontana Pittrice, 1552-1614*, 1940, p. 63, fig. 4.   **4.** W. Burger, *Trésors d'art en Angleterre*, 1860, p. 43 confuses 2853 with another copy, when he states that 2853 was engraved by Charles Pye.   **5.** Philip Pouncey, orally, 8.7.1968.   **6.** Karla Langedijk, *Silentium*, Nederlands Kunsthistorisch Jaarboek, 15, 1964, pp. 15-16.   **7.** Cecil Gould, *The National Gallery Catalogues, The Sixteenth Century Italian School*, 1975, p. 155.   **8.** Gizella Firestone, *The Sleeping Child in Italian Renaissance Representations of the Madonna*, Marsyas, II, 1942, p. 43-62.   **9.** Yrjo Hirn, *The Sacred Shrine*, 1958, p. 69.   **10.** Firestone, *op. cit.*, p. 62, n. 57 refers to William Lameere, *Un Symbole pythagorien dans l'art funeraire de Rome*, Bulletin de Correspondence Hellenique, LXIII, 1939, pp. 81ff. For *Silentia* bearing inscriptions fron the Psalms and the Song of Solomon see Christopher Lloyd, *A Catalogue of the Earlier Italian Paintings in the Ashmolean Museum*, 1977, pp. 13-14 and Millard Meiss, *The Painter's Choice*, 1976, pp. 119, 129, note 70.

FORMILLI, T. G. Cesare

6003   Woman in classical draperies seated in a wood

Plaster, 182.3 × 75 cm

Signed: *CF*

Also at the 1903 L.A.E. Formilli exhibited a *Sgraffito Panel in Polychrome, on real wall* (No. 1434). A. Lys Baldry, *Modern Mural Decoration*, 1902, pp. 105-8 discusses the artist's combination of fresco painting and incised line decoration.

Prov: Presented by the artist, 1903.

Exh: L.A.E. 1903 (1418) as *Sgraffito Panel in Monochrome–on real wall.*

FOURNIER, Louis Edouard, born 1857

749   The Funeral of Shelley

Canvas, 129.5 × 213.4 cm

Signed: *Louis Edouard Fournier 1889*

The event is described in E. J. Trelawny, *Recollections of the Last Days of Shelley and Byron*, 1858, Chapter XII, and in his Appendix to the *Records of Shelley, Byron and the Author*, 1878. No. 749 differs from Trelawny's description: there is no furnace in No. 749, the body of Shelley has not decayed in No. 749; the event took place on a hot August day not on a cold day as Fournier suggests. The three figures round the pyre are Trelawny, Leigh Hunt and Byron as recorded by Trelawny himself; Leigh Hunt, however, who is depicted as an old man, was only 38.

This subject was also painted by Jean Leon Gerome in 1881, but the picture was never finished. It was still in his studio in 1892.[1] Trelawny sent details of the Funeral to Gerome[2] but Fournier did not profit from them if indeed he had access to them.

Prov: Bought from the artist by William Gordon, a banker in 1889.[3] Presented by William Moore first to the National Liberal Club, Whitehall Place, London and then to the Walker Art Gallery 1905.[4]

Exh: Paris, *Société des artistes francais*, 1889 (1068)[5] with this note: "Le poète anglais Shelley périt dans un naufrage entre la Spezia et Lerici. Son corps rejeté sur la grève ayant été retrouvé par ses amis Lord Byron, Hunt et Trelawny ils le brûlèrent sur un bûcher voulant lui rendre ainsi les honneurs d'une crémation antique (1822)".

Ref: **1.** Mrs. F. F. Hering, *Gerome, The Life and Work of J. L. Gerome*, 1892, p. 226.   **2.** *Letters of Edward John Trelawny*, 1910, pp. 268 ff.   **3.** Undated letter from the artist.   **4.** Letter from the Secretary of the National Liberal Club 30 April, 1924.   **5.** The artist received a second class medal at this salon.

FRENCH School, about 1500

1315   Lamentation over the Dead Christ

Panel, 93.7 × 76 cm

Inscr: *Chy gist agnes du bois qui* (?) *fust veuve* (?) *en son tamps* (?) *De feu* (?) *jehan datinghin et vesqui quarat ants* (?) *Elle* (?) *a* (?) *veduite depuis quil trespassa Puis lan mil et dc IIII maiis. dellaissa Le victime* (?) *dapuri* (?) *che siecle miserable Pries dieu quil lui dnt la* (?) *vie prdurable*

In bad condition; there are large fillings down the two joins in the panel.

St. John and the Virgin support Christ; one of the holy women is in the centre. At the right is a kneeling female "donor", probably the Agnes Dubois of the inscription, behind her are St. Francis(?) and St. Barbara.

With ligatures and abbreviations resolved the inscription should read:—[1]

> Chy gist Agnes Dubois, qui fust veuve en son tamps
> De feu Jehan d'Atinghin et vesqui quarat ants.
> Elle a véduite depuis qu'il trespassa.
> Puis, l'an mil et DC. IIII maiis., dellaissa
> Le victime dapuri(?) che siecle miserable.
> Pres Dieu qu'il lui doint la vie perdurable.

This could be translated: "Here lies Agnes Dubois who was widowed in her time by the late Jehan d'Atinghin and lived forty years. She remained a widow from the time he died. Then in the year 1500 on 4 May she died the victim of this unhappy century. Pray God that He give her eternal life." Presumably the picture originally hung over the grave of Agnes Dubois and its purpose was intercessionary.

The Atinghin of the inscription may be the modern Attigny in the Ardennes—close to Picardy in the dialect of which the inscription is written.[2]

Prov: ?William Roscoe;[3] acquired by the Liverpool Royal Institution by 1819; presented to the Walker Art Gallery 1948.

Exh: Manchester *Art Treasures* 1857 No. 470

Ref: **1.** Dr. M. J. Freeman, *letter* December 1974 agreeing very closely with the reading suggested by Charles Sterling letter 15 May 1958. **2.** Charles Sterling letter *op. cit.*, again confirmed by Dr. M. J. Freeman *op. cit.*, who believes that modern Attigny is a plausible identification. **3.** Not apparently at his 1816 sale but all the pictures in the 1819 Catalogue, where No. 1315 was No. 37 attributed to the French School, are there stated to have come from Roscoe's Collection. **4.** 1819 Catalogue No. 37.

FRENCH School, about 1530

1308 Portrait of a Lady with a Parrot

Panel, 62.1 × 52.6 cm

Thomas Winstanley first suggested an attribution to Jean Clouet[1] and Passavant proposed identifying the sitter with Marguerite de Valois (or d'Angouleme or de Navarre) (1492-1549) sister of Francis I.[2] Gustav Gluck reconstructed an "Ambroise Clouet"[3] as the artist but L. Dimier believed that it must be by an Italian.[4] Paul Wescher believes No. 1308 to be a portrait of Marguerite de Valois by Jean Clouet dating from about 1527.[5]

The parrot may be a symbol of eloquence or prophecy[6] or could simply by a fashionable pet.[7] *Les Epitres de l'Amant Vert* by Jean Lemaire de Belges, written in 1505 and first published in 1511 are the imaginary love songs of the green parrot of Marguerite d'Autriche (1480-1530) addressed to her; she could therefore be the sitter but the green parrot of Jean Lemaire de Belges had a "colier vermeil et purpurin" (line 67 of first epistle); on the other hand taken together with the cupid in the hat of the sitter this reference might suggest that love is implied in this portrait,[8] and that it represents someone's wife or mistress.

The costume suggests a date between 1515 and 1520.[9]

Prov: Roscoe sale 1816 lot 75 bt. Crompton £26 5s 0d; presented to the L.R.I. 1819; deposited at the W.A.G. 1893; presented to the W.A.G. 1948.

Exh: Manchester *Art Treasures* 1857 (510); Leeds *National Exhibition* 1868 (543).

Ref: **1.** 1836 Catalogue No. 1.   **2.** *Tour of a German Artist in England,* Vol. 2, 1836, pp. 18-19. See also G. Waagen in *Art and Artists in England* 1838, Vol. III, pp. 183-4.   **3.** In Zeitschrift fur Bildende Kunst, Vol. XXVIII, 1917, p. 177 (republished in *Aus Drei Jahrhunderte Europaischer Malerei,* 1929, Vol. 2 pp. 254 ff, plate III).   **4.** L. Dimier, *Histoire de la peinture de Portrait en France au XVIe siecle,* II, 1925, p. 359, No. 1476. He dated the portrait to about 1520 and listed the sitter as "perhaps Marguerite de Valois."   **5.** Paul Wescher, *New Light on Jean Clouet as a Portrait Painter,* Apollo, Vol. 103, 1976, pp. 20 ff. A drawing by Clouet (?) of this sitter in old age is at Chantilly see most recently Raoul de Broglie, *Les Clouet de Chantilly* Gazette des Beaux Arts, Vol. 77, 1971, No. 204, p. 305 and Peter Mellen, *Jean Clouet,* 1971, p. 230, No. 124.   **6.** As argued in the *1963 Catalogue,* p. 71. But the parrot could also symbolize virginity, see E. K. J. Reznicek, *De Reconstructie van "t'Altaer van S. Lucas" van Maerten van Heemskerck,* Oud Holland, Vol. 70, 1955, pp. 233ff.   **7.** The so-called *Portrait of Mary of Guise* attributed to Sir Antonio Moro, No. 232 at the Royal Academy, *Flemish and Belgian Art* 1927 is another portrait of woman with a parrot.   **8.** The parrot is entirely (and implausibly) green and green was the colour for passionate love—see Jean Lemaire de Belges, *Les Épitres de l'Amant Vert,* 1948, ed Frappier, p. xxi.   **9.** Mrs. Stella Newton, letter 9 January 1975.

FRENCH School, late 18th century

1309 Head of an Old Man

Canvas, 66.3 × 54.8 cm

Attributed first to Rubens[1], in 1836 to de Crayer as a study for an *Adoration of the Magi*[2] and in 1963 to Fragonard,[3] No. 1309 would seem to be by an unknown French artist working towards the end of the 18th Century.[4]

Prov: ?Mr. Hill of Greek Street. ?William Roscoe[5]. Presented to the L.R.I. by Thomas Hargreaves[6] between 1819 and 1835; deposited at the Walker Art Gallery 1893; presented to the Walker Art Gallery 1948.

Exh: Walker Art Gallery, *Cleaned Pictures* 1955 (36).

Ref: **1.** 1819 annotated Catalogue (MSS, National Gallery, London) note *Head by Rubens.*   **2.** 1836 Catalogue No.3. The annotation in the 1819 Catalogue, probably inspired by Samuel Woodburn (see No. 1016 under Netherlandish School) has *Rubens: de Crayer.*   **3.** 1963 Catalogue p. 70.   **4.** Jacques Wilhelm, *letter,* 28 February, 1972.   **5.** Letter from William Roscoe to Mr. Smith of 1819 mentioning a "Rubens Head" not included in Roscoe's Sale of 1816 and now for sale; it was valued at £100 during Roscoe's Sale and was purchased from Mr. Hill of Greek Street (Roscoe Papers No. 574).   **6.** Henry Smithers *Liverpool its Commerce, Statistics and Institutions* 1825, p. 342 and 1819 annotated Catalogue *op. cit.*

FRERE, Pierre Edouard, 1819-1886

226   Cottage Scene

Oil on panel,[1] 45 × 36.8 cm

Signed and dated: *Edouard Frere. 1867*

Prov: Bought by George Holt from Agnew's, 1869 (bill Xmas for 29 September, MS
W.A.G.), £262 10s 0d; bequeathed by Emma Holt 1945.
Exh: Southport, 1892, *National Art Treasures,* No. 298
Ref: 1. Winsor and Newton prepared panel.

FRIESEKE, Frederick Carl, 1874-1939

941   Lady in Pink

Board, 46.3 × 38 cm

Signed: *F. C. Frieseke Paris 1902*

Prov: Bequeathed by Mrs. Barbara Jean Paterson 1935.
Exh: Société Nationale des Beaux Arts, Paris, 1903 (539) as *Femme en Rose.*

GAMBARDELLA, Spiridione, ?1815-1886

2165   Portrait of James Pownall

Canvas,[1] 92 × 71 cm

Inscribed: (verso): *JAMES POWNALL ESQre. / ETAT 52 / GAM-BERDELLA* (sic) / *PINXt*

The sitter (?1792-1855) was a merchant and last Bailiff of Liverpool
before the Municipal Reform Act.

Prov: Presented by James Tabley Pownall, son of the sitter, 1882.
Ref: 1. Canvas stamp of Charles Roberson, Long Acre.

7140   Portrait of Edward Rushton

Canvas, 127 × 101.5 cm

The sitter (1795-1851) began his career as a politician but was called to the bar in 1831, becoming Stipendiary Magistrate of Liverpool in 1839.[1]

Eng: T. H. Maguire (litho)
Prov: Painted at the request of the Bench of Magistrates of the Borough of Liverpool for presentation to St. George's Hall, hung in the Magistrates Court; transferred to the Gallery by City Estates Committee 1969.
Exh: Liverpool Academy 1844 (104[2].) Old Post Office Place, Liverpool 1848.[3]
Ref: 1. *Letters of a Templar* ed. W. Lowes Rushton 1903 passim with many further details.   2. Where it was reviewed in the Liverpool Albion 4 November 1844.   3. Liverpool Albion 14 February 1848.

GAROFALO, Benvenuto Tisi, called, ?1481-1559, after

2777   The Circumcision

Panel, 31.7 × 27.5 cm

Painted up to the edges left and right; unpainted margin top and bottom.

A copy with slight alterations to clothing and positions of the heads, of the central part of the predella for the altarpiece of the *Massacre of the Innocents* painted for S. Francesco, Ferrara.[1] The original predella panel is now in the Louvre,[2] and was much copied.[3]

Prov: Entered the L.R.I. Collection between 1836 and 1843;[4] deposited at the W.A.G., 1893;[5] presented to the W.A.G., 1948.
Exh: Manchester, *Art Treasures*, 1857 (203).
Ref: 1. G. Bargellesi, *Notizie di opere d'arte ferraresi*, 1955, pp. 91-4.   2. Paris, Louvre, no. 1550; 35 × 49 cm.   3. A number of the copies are listed by Federico Zeri, *Italian Paintings in the Walters Art Gallery*, II, 1976, pp. 369-370.   4. 1843 Catalogue p. 22 (79).   5. 1893 Catalogue p. 27 (77).

GARRIDO, Leandro Ramon, 1868-1909

1327   His First Offence (En Conseil de Famille)

Canvas, 105.5 × 52 cm

Signed: *L. R. Garrido*

Painted at Etaples from local models in 1904.[1] On 28 June, 1905 the artist wrote to Mrs. Bate from Etaples. "My pictures in the Paris Salon have caused my election to full membership this year with the privilege, which is an undue one, of six pictures, three on the line. I am taking the liberty to send you a photo of one of them (No. 1327), the best. It has by the way been invited to Liverpool. I refused £120 for it, but hope they will find a purchaser there. In fact I believe it is worthy of going to the Permanent Collection of that town though that is probably a matter of opinion."[2] A sketch for No. 1327 is in the Art Gallery and Museums, Brighton, No. 328.

Prov: Purchased from the L.A.E. 1905 (£80).

Exh: ?Royal Institute of Oil Painters 1904.[3] Société Nationale des Beaux Arts, Paris, 1905 (537).[4] L.A.E. 1905 (315).

Ref: **1.** J. Quigley, *Leandro Ramon Garrido,* 1913, p. XV and 98-9   **2.** Quigley, *op. cit.,* p. 120.   **3.** Quigley *op. cit.,* p. XV states that No. 1327 was at this exhibition but it does not appear in the catalogue.   **4.** The reproduction on page 175 of the catalogue is entitled *En Conseil de Famille;* it does not represent No. 1327 and presumably refers to *Les Geoliers,* No. 538 in the catalogue.

GARZI, Luigi, 1638-1721 and another hand

151   Flight into Egypt

Canvas, 127.5 × 182.5 cm

Both the William Earle Sale Catalogue (see provenance) and the 1843 Catalogue[1] attribute No. 151 to Luigi Garzi and Salvator Rosa jointly, the 1843 Catalogue specifying the figures as by Garzi and the landscape by Rosa. Certainly the figures seem to be by a different hand from the landscape and are possibly by Garzi.[2] George Scharf[3] and Waagen[4] however attributed the whole picture to Garzi.

Prov: William Earle sold Winstanley's Liverpool 17-18 April 1839 lot 119 £162 15s 0d, bt. Jones. Presented to the L.R.I. by John Pemberton Heywood between 1839 and 1843; deposited at the W.A.G., 1942; presented to the W.A.G., 1948.

Ref: **1.** No. 91.   **2.** Luigi Salerno *letter* 3 May 1972. But the illustrations in Giancarlo Sestieri, *Per la Conoscenza di Luigi Garzi,* Commentari, Vol. 23, 1972, pp. 89 ff do not seem close to No. 151—particularly the *Sacrifice of Marcus Curtius* at the Glasgow City Art Gallery. Garzi provided figures for Pietro Francesco Garoli who specialized in painting architecture; the latter might be responsible for the rest of No. 151.   **3.** 1859 Catalogue No. 119.   **4.** G. F. Waagen, *Art Treasures,* 1854, III, p. 240, No. 109.

GEETS, Willem, 1838-1919

1030   Awaiting an Audience

Panel, 70 × 110 cm

The costume probably represents the artist's idea of Switzerland around 1530-1540.[1] No. 1030 was noted in the *Magazine of Art,* 1886, p. xlvi.

Prov: Seen by the Chairman of the Libraries, Museums and Arts Committee of the Liverpool Town Council in the artist's studio and specially invited to the 1886 L.A.E.;[2] purchased from the L.A.E. 1886 (£315).
Exh: L.A.E. 1886 (No. 833).
Ref: 1. Anne Buck letter 20 March 1972.   2. Letter from the Curator of the W.A.G. to the artist 30 June, 1886.

GERARD, Baron Francis, 1770-1837, Studio of

8626   King Charles X of France

Canvas, 86.7 × 73.8 cm

A copy of the oval portrait of the King in his coronation robes now in the Louvre (inv. 4768).[1] The original was commissioned in 1825, the year of the King's coronation at Rheims. In 8626 the base of the column behind the King is higher than in the original. The King is wearing the Order of the Holy Spirit.

King Charles X (1757-1836) lived in exile in Britain for over twenty years after the French Revolution. In this period of exile, when still Comte d'Artois, he was entertained by members of the English aristocracy.[2] He paid an annual visit to the second Earl of Sefton at Croxteth Hall and during his stay would regularly attend the Roman Catholic church of St. Swithin's, Gillmoss which was patronized by the Molyneux family. His seat on the gospel side of the church later became known as "the King of France's seat."[3]

Prov: King Charles X of France, who presented it to the 2nd Earl and Countess of Sefton, 1826;[4] purchased from the executors of the estate of the 7th Earl of Sefton, 1974.
Ref: 1. *Catalogue des Peintures*, I, *Ecole Francaise*, 1972 p. 177, 84.5 × 77.2 cm.   2. Full length portraits deriving from the 1824 portrait are at Hatfield and Apsley House.   3. Dom F. O. Blundell O.S.B., *Old Catholic Lancashire*, I, 1925, p. 73 quotes a manuscript note on the back of the baptismal registers of St. Swithin's in the handwriting of the Rev. Joseph Emmott S. J. (now in Liverpool Public Record Office) referring to a visit in September 1812.   4. Inscribed on the frame DONN E. PAR. S. M. CHARLES X. A. LORD & LADY SEFTON. 1826. It was thus presented in the same year as the portrait by Gerard given by Charles X to the Duke of Wellington (Evelyn Wellington, *A Descriptive Catalogue of Pictures and Sculpture at Apsley House*, Vol. 2, 1901, pp. 389-91).

GEROME, Jean Leon, 1824-1904

230   Circus Maximus

Canvas, 16.1 × 32.3 cm

Signed: *J. L. Gerome*

Hitherto entitled *Chariot Race*,[1] No. 230 is apparently a sketch for Gerome's *Circus Maximus,* Harding Museum, Chicago, reproduced in Earl Shinn, *Gerome, A Collection of the Works of J. L. Gerome in 100 photogravures* edited by Edward Strahan 1881, n.p. when owned by Mrs. A. T. Stewart of New York and listed among Gerome's unexhibited paintings by Gustave Haller.[2]

For his circus scenes Gerome collaborated with a former winner of the Prix de Rome in architecture, who was a good archaeological draughtsman.[3] Gerome's collaborator may have been Viollet-le-Duc.[4]

Mrs. Hering noted that the Palace of the Caesars was to be seen on the left and that the Septizonium towered loftily in the background against the hills; the artist undertook apparently "profound research" in reconstructing the Circus Maximus.[5]

Prov: ?T. F. Walker sold Christie's 21 April 1883 (95) bt. Martin £105. Bought from James Polak by George Holt, 1885 (bill 24 June, MS Walker Art Gallery) £80; bequeathed by Emma Holt 1944.

Ref: 1. George Holt, MS Catalogue. (W.A.G.).   2. Gustave Haller, *Nos grands peintres,* 1899, pp. 100 ff. See also *Jean Leon Gerome*, Exhibition at the Dayton Art Institute and elsewhere, 1972, no. 27 pp. 73-4.   3. Charles Moreau-Vauthier, *Gerome,* 1906, p. 150.   4. Henry James, *Parisian Sketches,* 1958, p. 98.   5. F. F. Hering, *Gerome,* 1892, p. 236. Dr. Ackerman's help is acknowledged.

GIANFRESCO da Rimini, active 1441-1464, dead by Dec. 1470

2781   Madonna and Child with Angels

Panel, 62.1 × 47 cm

Inscribed: at throat of Madonna's dress *AVE MARIA*

The attribution was first made by M. L. Berenson,[1] followed by B. Berenson[2] and Rezio Buscaroli.[3] It is closely related to the signed National Gallery *Madonna* of 1461 and the signed *Madonna* in San Domenico, Bologna of 1458 or 9.[4] The compressed composition suggests the influence of relief sculpture. Compare for instance, the reliefs of Agostino di Duccio.

Prov: Purchased for the L.R.I. by Thomas Winstanley 1835;[5] deposited W.A.G., 1893; presented to W.A.G., 1948.

Ref: 1. M. L. Berenson, *Ancora di Giovanni Francesco da Rimini,* Rassegna d'Arte, VII, 1907, p. 53.   2. B. Berenson, *Central Italian Painters,* 1909, p. 175.   3. Rezio Buscaroli, *La Pittura Romagnola del Quattrocento,* 1931, p. 57, with slight reservations.   4. Serena Padovani, *Un Contributo alla cultura Padovana del primo rinascimento: Giovan Francesco da Rimini,* Paragone, Vol. 259, 1971, p.30 note 46 implicitly dates No. 2781 to this period of his career.   5. L.R.I. Archives 63 Bill dated 3 August 1836 from Winstanley for pictures supplied in 1835.

GIMIGNANI, Giacinto, 1611-1681

150   Flight of Cloelia

Canvas, 169.1 × 256.5 cm

For No. 150 the artist has consulted Plutarch, *Lives*, XIX, 2 and Livy, *History of Rome*, XIII, 6[1]. Valerius Publius greets Cloelia who is accompanied by the guard whom she has tricked. In the background on the other side of the Tiber is the Etruscan camp and pursuing Etruscans.

No. 150 was attributed to Romanelli on its entry to the L.R.I.[2] but the present attribution first suggested by Zeri and Emiliani[3] can be regarded as established.

The strong influence of Poussin apparent in No. 150 suggests that it is an early work of about 1640.[4]

Prov: Acquired by the L.R.I. between 1836 and 1843; deposited at the W.A.G., 1942; presented to the W.A.G., 1948.

Ref: 1. For full details of the iconography see R. M. Ogilvie, *A Commentary on Livy*, Books 1-5, 1965, p. 267 and A. Pigler, *Barockthemen*, 1956, Vol. II, pp. 363-5.   2. 1843 Catalogue No. 90.   3. Verbally July 1959; confirmed by Ursula Fischer, *letter*, 30 July, 1969,   4. Fischer *op. cit.*, see L. Pascoli, *Vite de Pittori*, 1730, Vol. II p. 299.

GIORDANO, Luca, 1632-1705, Studio of

144   Dionysus, Tyrant of Syracuse

Canvas, 177.8 × 252.7 cm

Always attributed to Giordano[1] but of too low a quality to be autograph.[2] Dionysus the younger returned to Syracuse in B.C. 350 but was again expelled by Timoleo; he is then supposed to have become a schoolmaster at Corinth.

Prov: ?William Noel Hill, 3rd Lord Berwick sold Winstanley, Liverpool 29 October, 1839.[3] Presented to the L.R.I. by J. B. Yates between 1841 and 1843 deposited at the W.A.G., 1893; presented to the W.A.G., 1948.

Exh: Liverpool Mechanics Institution, *First Exhibition of Objects Illustrative of the Fine Arts* 1840 (252) (as by Giordano).

Ref: 1. See exhibitons, 1843 Catalogue No. 73, G. F. Waagen, *Art Treasures*, Vol. III, p. 240 etc.   2. Oreste Ferrari and Giuseppe Scavizzi, *Luca Giordano*, Vol. II, 1966, p. 293.   3. No catalogue of this sale survives but see *Liverpool Mercury* 25 October, 1839 for an account of the sale. Lord Berwick was ambassador at Naples 1824-1833 and the Liverpool Mercury *op. cit.*, stated that he bought his pictures there.

GIORDANO, Luca, 1632-1705, after

145   The Entombment

Canvas, 259 × 206.6 cm

A copy after the painting of 1677 now in the Pio Monte della Misericordia, Naples.[1]

Prov: Purchased by the L.R.I. from Thomas Winstanley 17 October, 1842 (as Ribera);[2] deposited at the W.A.G., 1893; presented to the W.A.G., 1948.

Ref: **1.** Oreste Ferrari and Giuseppe Scavizzi, *Luca Giordano*, Vol. II, 1966, p. 293.   **2.** *Minute Book of Gallery of Art Committee*, L.R.I. Archives 41.

GIULIO ROMANO, 1494-1546, after

1314   The Triumph of Scipio Africanus

Canvas, 52 × 61.5 cm

Condition: Concern was expressed about its state in 1854.[1]

Already identified as after Giulio Romano in 1857.[2] It is a copy of the modello in the Louvre (3524) for one of the set of tapestries representing the triumph of Scipio Africanus.[3] The scene represents animals being led to sacrifice[4] and follows the description of Appian *Punic Wars* VIII. 9.66.[5]

It is probably French of the 17th Century.[6]

Prov: Count Altamira, his sale, "consigned direct from Madrid" Stanley 1 June 1827 (14) Julio Romano, one of "Three paintings in *chiaroscuro*, touched with gold and silver painted by order of the Duke of Mantua to be copied in Tapestry" £4 8s 0d;[7] by 1827, Joseph Strutt of Derby;[8] his sale T. Winstanley & Son, Exchange, Manchester, 15 May 1828 (87), *"Giulio Romano Chiaroscuro/ Painted for the Duke of Mantua, and copied in tapistry, from Count Altamira's Collection. Painted with gold"*; John Douglas of Gyrn, near Holywell, Flintshire;[9] his sale T. Winstanley, Gyrn, 26 August 1840 (4) 4 gns; in the L.R.I. Collection by 1843;[10] deposited at the W.A.G., 1893;[11] presented to the W.A.G., 1948.

Exh: Manchester, *Art Treasures*, 1857 (185).

Ref: **1.** Letter of Philip Westcott to Theodore Rathbone 24 Janurary 1854 (L.R.I. Archives 17).   **2.** Manchester, *Art Treasures*, 1857 (185).   **3.** J. Shearman, verbally, 1959. Reproduced in Frederick Hartt, *Giulio Romano*, 1958, II, fig. 475. A number of changes were introduced in the cartoon at Leningrad, which is in reverse direction (inv. 46406).   **4.** John Douglas of Gyrn sale (4).   **5.** Hartt, *op. cit.*, I, pp. 227-9.   **6.** Letter of John Gere, 19 November 1952 giving the opinion of P. M. R. Pouncey.   **7.** There was a sale of landed property after the death of the Marquis of Astorga, Count of Altamira, held in Madrid on 21 Janurary 1820. Possibly the picture left Spain at about this date.   **8.** *Catalogue of Paintings, Drawings, Marbles, Bronzes, Alabaster and Plaster Busts and figures, China ornaments &c &c in the collection of Joseph Strutt*, Derby, 1827 (572) or (574). Strutt owned three of these 'chiaroscuros', only one of which (573) was in his 1835 Catalogue.   **9.** There is a faint possibility that 1314 was in the John Bartie of Newman Street sale, Foster, 20 June 1838 (243) "Giulio Romano. An allegorical subject with many figures".   **10.** 1843 Catalogue, p. 33 (122).   **11.** 1893 Catalogue, p. 27 (75).

GLEYRE, Marc Gabriel Charles, 1806-1874, after

2876 The Evening Hymn

Canvas, 98.5 × 155 cm

Inscribed: *C. Gleyre 1851*

A copy after *Le Soir* or *Les Illusions Perdues* acquired for the Luxembourg Museum in 1843, but now lent by the Louver to the Musee d' Arras (Inv. 10039). It was exhibited in England at the 1862 International Exhibiton.[1]

No. 2867 is not listed by Clement and the signature is probably spurious; according to Clement the only version by Gleyre of this composition apart from the original at the Louvre, is the one now in the Walters Art Gallery, Baltimore, No. 184.[2]

Prov: Presented by George Audley[3] 1924.

Ref: 1. For its enthusiastic reception see Francis Haskell *Un monument et ses mysteres*, Revue de l' Art, 1976, p. 69. 2. Charles Clement, *Gleyre, Etude biographique et critique*, 1878, p. 399, No. 38. 3. George Audley, *Collection of Pictures*, 1923, No. 58, p. 22.

GOYEN, Jan van, 1596-1656, Follower of

613 River Scene

Panel, 39 × 61.2 cm

Signed: *V. G. 1638* (?)

The scene has been identified as Overschie in the province of South Holland.[1] This signature and date are now difficult to decipher and may not be original; Dr. Hans Ulrich Beck believes No. 613 to be by an unidentifiable follower of Van Goyen.[2]

Prov: Countess Andre Mniszech.[3] Edward R. Bacon, New York;[4] Mrs. Virginia Purdy Bacon sold Christie's 12th December 1919 lot 76 bought Agnew's £840; Mrs. A. B. Williamson who presented it through the National Art Collections Fund 1957.

Ref: 1. See N. Maclaren, *National Gallery Catalogues, The Dutch School*, 1960, No. 151, p. 135 for a full discussion of this problem and for a list of other versions to which may be added a version attributed to an imitator of Van Goyen in the Metropolitan Museum of Art, No. 65.181.11 (A. Lehman gift). But Hans Ulrich Beck, *Jan Van Goyen*, I, 1972, p. 268, Nos. 845/55, 845/57 (Kronig drawings) notes that the inscriptions *Oudeschie* on which the identification relies are by a later hand and so not accurate necessarily. 2. Letter 5 December 1973. 3. Dr. Hans Ulrich Beck letter 1 December 1960. 4. *Memorial Catalogue of Paintings by old and modern masters etc. owned by Edward Rathbone Bacon*, New York, 1919, p. 164 No. 210.

GOYEN, Jan van, Imitator of

1486 River Scene

Oak, 57 × 89 cm

Of very low quality.

Prov: Unknown, first recorded in the collection 1957.

GRANACCI, Francesco, 1477-1543, Associates of

2783   Scenes from the Life of St. John the Baptist:—Naming; taking leave of his parents; venturing into the wilderness; blessing by Christ; collecting water from a spring

Panel; 77.4 × 228.6 cm

No. 2783 was together with two other panels, with scenes from the life of St. John,[1] in the collection of Samuel Woodburn until after 1850.[2] The height of all three is similar, as is that of a fourth panel in Cleveland, once in the Gerini Collection in Florence.[3] A fifth panel, now lost, also once in the Gerini Collection, has been associated with the four already mentioned.[4] It is probable that some, if not all, of these panels formed part of a scheme for the decoration of an interior, and that further panels with important episodes in the life of the Baptist are lost.[5] The size of the panels approaches those attributed to Granacci known to have been in the Borgherini room,[6] which may indicate that they had a similar location. Their size, certainly, make it improbable that they came from Cassoni. The three panels in the Woodburn sale are said to have been owned by the Tornabuoni family. That provenance may only have been suggested by the clear relationship with the Santa Maria Novella frescoes of Domenico Ghirlandaio, since they were then attributed to him and No. 2783 was thought to be a sketch for the frescoes.[7] But the fact that Woodburn was active as a dealer in Florence and that a number of Tornabuoni pictures appeared on the market at about the same time enhances credit in the alleged provenance of 2783.[8]

The attribution of No. 2783 to Granacci's own hand[9] has rightly been questioned.[10] Comparison with the Metropolitan Museum panel with the *Birth,* securely related to Granacci, shows considerable divergencies in the figure style. However, the distant landscapes in each, both of high quality, are probably by the same hand. More than one hand is visible in

2783 as is also the case with the Metropolitan *Birth*. Certain of the figures in 2783, particularly the infant Christ and Baptist are close to the style of Bugiardini (1475-1554), like Granacci a pupil of Domenico Ghirlandaio and a friend of the young Michelangelo. The other panels in the Metropolitan[11] and at Cleveland[12] are markedly different from each other and from the others in the style both of figure and landscape. But this need not militate against the theory that they all came from the same ensemble. All the panels appear to date from c. 1505-1510.[13] The architecture in No. 2783 is close to that in a pair of panels showing *Scenes from the Life of Tobias* in Berlin (142 and 149) where however the figure style is different.

Prov: Tornabuoni family?; Samuel Woodburn;[14] his sale, Christie's 9 June 1860, lot 77 bt. Pearce £420; Wynn Ellis by 1868;[15] Wynn Ellis Sale, Christie's 17 June 1876, (91) bt. Cox £72 9s 0d. William Graham sale, Christie's 8 April 1886 (217), bt. P. H. Rathbone £142 16s 0d, who bequeathed it to the W.A.G., 1895, passed to the collection 1905.

Exh: Leeds 1868 (4).

Ref: 1. Now Metropolitan Museum of Art, New York (1) *The Birth of the Baptist with the Annunciation to Zacharias and the Visitation* 80 × 152 cm; (2) *Preaching of the Baptist* 75.5 × 210 cm.   2. Federico Zeri, *Italian Paintings, A Catalogue of the Metropolitan Museum of Art, Florentine School,* London, 1971, pp. 183, 186.   3. No. 44.91 *Maidservant with the infant Baptist*. Painted surface 76 × 33 cm, see Christian Von Holst, *Three Panels of a Renaissance Room Decoration at Liverpool and a new work by Granacci,* Walker Art Gallery, Liverpool, Annual Report and Bulletin, Vol. I, 1970-1, p. 34; and Christian Von Holst, *Francesco Granacci,* 1974, p. 134.   4. F. Zeri, *op. cit.,* p. 182.   5. C. Von Holst, 1970-1, *op. cit.,* pp. 32 ff, and F. Zeri, *op cit.,* pp. 181 ff.   6. John Shearman, *Andrea del Sarto,* 1965, Vol II, pp. 231-2.   7. Christie's 7 June 1860, lot 77, and a label on the reverse.   8. Among these Woodburn himself owned Bartolommeo di Giovanni's *The Story of Jason and the Golden Fleece* and its companion panel *The Story of Jason* dated 1487. *Natale Labia Collection on Loan to the South African National Gallery,* n.d. (but 1976). Other Tornabuoni pictures, which may have been dispersed at about the same time include Domenico Ghirlandaio's *Lucrezia Tornabuoni* in the National Gallery of Art, Washington (Kress Collection) Fern Rush Shapley, *Paintings from the Samuel H. Kress Collection Italian School XIII-XV Century* 1966, p. 125 and *Giovanna Tornabuoni* in the Thyssen collection, Rudolf J. Heinemann, *Sammlung Schloss Rohoncz Castagnola,* 1958, pp. 39-40 (150).   9. G. Fiocco, *La data di Nascita di Francesco Granacci e un'ipotesi Michelangiolesca,* Rivista d'Arte, XIII, 1931, p. 130.   10. C. Von Holst, 1970-1, *op. cit.,* p. 37 and 1974, *op. cit.,* p. 133; F. Zeri, *op. cit.,* p. 183.   11. MS note in *Ashburnham House Catalogue,* 1878, states that A. Venturi had ascribed *the Preaching* to Raffaellino del Garbo. F. Zeri, *op. cit.,* p. 185 more reasonably suggested early Raffaello Botticini, under the influence of Granacci. Von Holst, 1974, *op. cit.,* p. 133 as between Granacci and Raffaello Botticini.   12. Everett Fahy, and F. Zeri, *op. cit.,* pp. 182-3 attribute it to the Master of the Spiridon Story of Joseph which is more convincing than the attribution to Granacci of Von Holst, 1970-1, *op. cit.,* p. 34, and 1974, *op. cit.,* pp. 134-5. But Edmund P. Pillsbury, *Florence and the Arts Five Centuries of Patronage,* Cleveland Museum of Art, 1971 (12) accepts the association.   13. Von Holst, 1970-1, *op. cit.,* p. 37 and 1974, *op. cit.,* p. 133 dates the whole cycle in the first decade of the 16th Century whilst Zeri, *op. cit.,* p. 183 dates it 'around 1510, if not sometimes earlier.'   14. MS *List of Mr Woodburn's Collection of Early Italian Pictures* (National Gallery) No. 24 "Domenico Ghirlandaio The history of St. John, one of the series so fully described by Vasari."   15. Leeds, 1868 Catalogue (4). Pearce often bought pictures for Wynn Ellis, Neil Maclaren, *National Gallery Catalogues, The Dutch School,* 1960 p. 22 s.v. Berchem 1004 note 2. No. 2783 also appears in R. U. Wornum, *The Schedule of the Wynn Ellis Pictures at No. 30 Cadogan Place* (MS 1876 National Gallery Library) p. 14 at 76 Newman Street (75) Ghirlandaio, *Life of St. John.*

GRONLAND, Theude, 1817-1876

2901   Fruit and Flowers

Canvas, 90 × 118 cm

Signed: *Th. Gronland 1851*

Included in No. 2901 are melons, plums, black and green grapes, pineapple, cherries, peach, pear, pomegranate, roses, camelia, frittillaria, azalea, diletrium, sunflower, sweet pea, ipomoea, a grass hopper, goldfinch and swallow tail butterfly.

For the artist's symbolism in this type of picture see Lilli Martius, *Schleswig—Holsteinische Malerei im 19 Jahrhundert,* 1956 pp. 326-8, with many further references.

Prov: Presented by Alderman J. G. Livingston, 1883.
Exh: ?R.A. 1852 (410) as *Fruit and Flowers.*[1].
Ref: 1. No. 2901 was not No. 109 at the 1853 Liverpool Academy: see the long review in *The Albion* 12 September 1853 p. 6.

GUARDI, Francesco, 1712-1793

6273   Merit

Panel, 127.6 × 73 cm

6274   Abundance

Panel, 127.6 × 73.6 cm

Formerly cupboard doors.[1] F. Watson,[2] D. Mahon,[3] J. Byam Shaw[4] and T. Pignatti[5] support the present attribution but P. Zampetti,[6] and A. Morassi[7] favour Gian Antonio Guardi.

Zampetti[8] dates 6273 and 6274 to 1740-1750, Mahon[9] to about 1750 and Morassi to 1730-1735.[10] A drawing in the British Museum (1910-10-13-6)[11] corresponds closely to the upper half of 6274. The identification of 6273 as merit rests on a drawing by G. B. Tiepolo at Trieste inscribed *Merito.*[12]

Prov: ?A. Collection in Northern France;[13] Baroni Collection, Paris; P. and D. Colnaghi; purchased 1965 by the Gallery with the aid of a contribution from the National Art-Collections Fund.
Exh: Venice, *Mostra dei Guardi*, 1965 (17-18).
Ref: 1. The hinges and locks were removed in 1965.   2. Francis Watson, *The Guardi Family of Painters*, Journal of the Royal Society of Arts, 1966, p. 283.   3. Denis Mahon, *The Brothers at the Mostra dei Guardi: Some Impres-*

sions of a Neophyte, Problemi Guardeschi, 1967 p. 113.   **4.** Verbally 1965.   **5.** Venice, Mostra dei Guardi, 1965, Nos. 17-18, p. 31 but in a letter of 3 August 1966 he prefers Francesco.   **6.** Mostra dei Guardi, op. cit.   **7.** A. Morassi, Guardi, (1973), I, pp. 111-2 and 329, Nos. 114-5, repr. II. figs 134-5.   **8.** Mostra dei Guardi, op. cit.   **9.** Mahon op. cit.   **10.** Morassi, op. cit.   **11.** J. Byam Shaw, The Drawings of Francesco Guardi, 1951, plate III.   **12.** G. Vigni, Disegni del Tiepolo, 1942, No. 8.   **13.** According to information given to Morassi, op. cit.

GUERCINO IL, Barbieri, Giovanni Francesco, 1591-1666, after

2779   St. Jerome and a Rabbi

Canvas, 102.2 × 133 cm

On the right hand page can be read in Hebrew the heading "Psalms" and the opening lines of Psalm I[1] St. Jerome's second revision of the Psalms was made at Bethlehem from A.D. 385; there he was assisted by a Jew, Bar Ananias, who worked with him at night for fear of his fellow Jews.[2]

No. 2779 has been attributed to Benedetto Gennari since it entered the L.R.I.[3] but is more likely to be a copy after a lost painting by Guercino.[4] There is another version of No. 2779 identical in size and composition in the Museo Arqueologico, Burgos, which is attributed to Guercino.[5]

Prov: Presented to the L.R.I. by M. D. Lowndes between 1836 and 1843; deposited at the W.A.G. 1893, presented to the W.A.G. 1948.

Ref: **1.** A. R. Millard, letter, 12 April 1972.   **2.** Letters of St. Jerome ed Wace and Schaff, 1893, letter 84, p. 176.   **3.** 1843 Catalogue No. 114 and subsequent catalogues; G. F. Waagen, Art Treasures, 1854, III, p. 239, No. 97.   **4.** Denis Mahon, verbally 1969, saw it closer to Guercino than to Gennari.   **5.** Exhibited in Prado, Madrid, Pintura Italiana del Siglo XVII, 1970 (97) repr.

GUSSOW, Carl, 1843-1907

2877   Old Man's Treasure (Das Katzchen)

Panel, 107.3 × 90.8 cm

Signed: C. GUSSOW/Bl'n 1876

The artist was appointed to the staff of the Berlin Academy in 1876 as part of the reforms of the new Director, Anton von Werner, and sent No. 2877 together with two other similar genre pictures with life size figures, Der Blumenfreund and Verlorenes Gluck to the Royal Berlin Academy in that year: there they were seen there as "ein geharnischter fehdehandschuh des Realismus ... ein starker Protest der naturlichen Empfindung gegen der unnaturliche falsche Pathos des Nachtreter eines Piloty und Kaulbach".[1]

Prov: Purchased from the L.A.E. 1879 (£500).
Exh: Royal Berlin Academy 1876 (290); L.A.E. 1879 (65).
Ref: 1. See K. Pietschker, *Karl Gussow und der Naturalismus*, 1898, pp. 12 ff. For further reviews see *Art Journal* 1902, p. 16 and *The Academy* 4 October 1879, p. 254; No. 2877 was reproduced in the *Supplement* p. 1.

HAMDI, Osman Bey, 1842-1910

2953 A Young Emir Studying

Canvas, 120.7 × 222.2 cm

Signed: *O Hamdy Bey/1905*

Apparently exhibited at Paris as *Jeune Croyant lisant la Bible*[1] but listed by Thalasso more plausibly as *Jeune Croyant lisant le Coran.*[2] Inscribed in the wall on either side of the niche are the first verse of the Koran and fragments of other well known Islamic prayers; the young Emir is reading the Koran and in his niche are other sacred Islamic books including the *Diwan Hafez* and the *Moshtawa Sherif;* wrapped around the candle is a prayer in Kufic script and at the bottom of the candlestick appears again the first verse of the Koran.[3] Hamdi's *La Liseuse*[4] is almost identical to No. 2953 except that the figure reading is female.

There is a review in the *Art Journal*, 1906, p. 168.

Prov: Purchased from the L.A.E. by Sir John Brunner who presented it 1906.
Exh: ?Paris, Société des artistes francais, 1905 (908). R.A. 1906 (237). L.A.E. 1906 (23).
Ref: 1. See Exhibitions.   2. A. Thalasso *L'art ottoman*, *Les peintres de Turquie*, 1911, p. 25; the script in the book read by the Emir is certainly arabic.   3. I am indebted to Mr. Said Gohary for all this information.   4. Thalasso *op. cit.*, p. 9.; in 1911 *La Liseuse* was owned by the *Union francaise de Constantinople*.

HARPIGNIES, Henri Joseph, 1819-1916

7274 Bord de Loing

Canvas, 116 × 165 cm

Signed: *h harpignies 91*

The title is traditional. The river Loing was a favourite subject of this artist.

Prov: *L'Aube* was sold by the artist to Arnold and Tripp in January 1891 for 3,000 francs and sold by them to M. Guyotin in February 1891 for 10,800 francs.[1] Henry Vasnier owned *L'Aurore* at the 1891 Salon (see exhibitions) (?) J. B. Tattegrain; (?) Monsieur de Celles[2]. Purchased from Wildenstein and Co. 1970.

Exh: ?Paris, Société des artistes francais 1891 (806) as *L'Aurore*

Ref: 1. Jean Dieterle, *letter*, 2 July, 1970 quoting Arnold and Tripp stock number 2995, No. 7274 did not appear at the Guyotin Sale, Hotel Drouot, Paris 6 February, 1918.   2. Names written in chalk on stretcher.

HAYDEN, Henri, born 1883

3024   Green Island

Canvas, 46 × 55.5 cm

Signed: *Hayden/58.*

No. 3024 was painted in the summer of 1958 at Changis—St. Jean on the Marne; it represents an island in the Marne there, called by the artist the "Green Island".[1] A number of similar views were painted by artist at the same time.[2]

Prov: Purchased from the Waddington Gallery 1959.

Exh: Waddington Gallery, *Henri Hayden*, 1959 (7).

Ref: 1. Letter from the artist 27 July, 1959.   2. Letter *op. cit.*, *Le Marne à Changis* exhibited at the Musée de Lyon, *Hayden*, 1960 (93) from the artist's collection and *Les Meules à Changis* reproduced as plate 74 in Jean Selz, *Hayden*, 1964 also from the artist's collection are examples.

HEEREMANS, Thomas, about 1640-after 1697

961   Winter Scene

Panel, 47.3 × 63.4 cm

Signed: *T H MANS 1669* (first three letters in monogram)

Prov: Christie's Sales 11 June 1831(3), 9 March 1835(25), 4 April 1835(52), 13 February 1836(6), 27 May 1836(64), 22 June 1838(4) could all be identified with No. 961. Acquired by the L.R.I. between 1836 and 1843;[1] deposited at the W.A.G. 1893; presented to the W.A.G. 1948.

Exh: Manchester *Art Treasures* 1857 (1612).

Ref: 1. 1843 Catalogue No. 96.

D.

HEMESSEN, Jan Sanders van, about 1504-before 1566, after

1179   The Mocking of Christ

Panel, 127.6 × 103.8 cm

A copy after the signed painting of 1544 in the Bayerischen Staats-gemaldesammlungen (No. 1408).[1]

Prov: Prince William of the Netherlands (later King William II) in 1815.[2] King William of the Netherlands sold the Hague 12 August 1850 lot 56 (as by an unknown artist) bt. De Haan 66 guilders. Presented to the W.A.G. by Malcolm Guthrie 1884.

Ref: **1.** Alte Pinakothek, Munich, *Deutsche und Niederlandische Malerei zwischen Renaissance und Barock*, 1961 p. 39 listing No. 1179 as a repetition as well as other copies and further references.   **2.** A seal on the back of No. 1179 is of a type only used by Prince William in that year (A. van Schendel, *letter* 30 January 1958). A rather similar but slightly smaller *Christ carrying the Cross* by Hemessen (M. J. Friedlander, *Die Altniederlandische Malerei*, XII, 1925 p. 185, No. 193) is still owned by the Dutch Royal Family and was already in that collection by 1847 (L. van Dorp, *letter*, 8 April 1975), while a *Descent from the Cross* nearly identical in size to No. 1179 (123 × 94.5 cm) by Hemessen is now in the Musees Royaux des Beaux Arts de Belgique (Inv. No. 6909); it was noted by Friedlander *op. cit.*, XIV, p. 128.

HONDECOETER, Melchior d', 1636-1695, after

870   The Poultry Yard

Canvas, 102.6 × 129.7 cm

A copy after the signed picture in the National Gallery of Ireland, No. 509.

Prov: D. Macaulay;[1] presented to the L.R.I. by Mrs. Mary L. Macaulay 1861;[2] deposited at the W.A.G., 1893; presented to the W.A.G., 1948.

Exh: Liverpool Mechanics Institution, *Third Exhibition of Objects Illustrative of the Fine Arts*, 1844 (85).

Ref: **1.** See Exhibitions.   **2.** Letter from the donor to the L.R.I. of 11 May, 1861, L.R.I. Archives 17.

ISENBRANDT, Adriaen, active 1510, died 1551

1017   Virgin and Child

Panel, 36.6 × 30.7 cm

Apparently unfinished in the dress of the Virgin and elsewhere. Probably by the artist identified by Friedlander[1] and others as Adriaen Isenbrandt; another version of No. 1017 but with an entirely different background is also attributed to this artist.[2]

In the background is the *Massacre of the Innocents* and the tree behind the Virgin and Child may pre-figure the Cross.[3]

Prov: Roscoe Sale 1816 lot 29[4] bt. Mason £5 5s 0d; presented to the L.R.I. 1819; presented to the W.A.G. 1955.

Exh: Manchester, *Art Treasures*, 1857 No. 485.

Ref: 1. Max. J. Friedlander, *Die Altniederlandische Malerei*, 1933, Vol. XI pp. 79ff. This attribution is supported by Robert Koch, letter, 5 February 1975.   **2.** Now at the William Hayes Ackland Memorial Art Center, Chapel Hill, University of North Carolina, No. 65.9.1.   **3.** As suggested in the 1963 Catalogue p. 91.   **4.** as *Madonna and Child* by Ridolfo Ghirlandaio panel, 14 × 12 ins; in his MS draft for the 1816 sale catalogue (Roscoe Papers No. 3897 p. 20). Roscoe described lot 29 as *Virgin and Child in the background a landscape with the Slaughter of the Innocents.*

ITALIAN School, 17th century

2991 Portrait of a Man

Panel, 54.5 × 40 cm

Inscribed on spine of book *Horace* (?)

The gown, cravat and hair date this portrait to about 1665 to 1670.[1]

Prov: Perhaps William Roscoe; Mrs. A. M. Roscoe who bequeathed it 1950.

Ref: 1. Aileen Ribeiro, *letter*, 22 February 1973.

5608 Nymph

Canvas, 77.5 × 66.5 cm

Prov: Unknown; found in the Gallery 1960.

ITALIAN School, 18th century

136 Reconciliation of Jacob and Esau

Canvas, 229.9 × 328.9 cm

Acquired as by an unknown artist[1] No. 136 was attributed to the Venetian School but Anthony Clark suggests an artist close to the style of Mariano Rossi.[2] For the subject see Genesis XXXIII verses 1-15. The male figure third to the left of the main group might be a self portrait of the artist.

Prov: Presented by Henry Steele 1853; in 1854 it was hanging in the Free Public Library Reading Room.[3]

Ref   1. 1882 Catalogue No. 185.   **2.** Letter 27 March 1972.   **3.** *Liverpool as it is or a Guide for the Stranger and Resident* 1854, p. 92.

2802 Virgin and Child with Angels

Canvas, 162 × 118.3 cm

Attributed on entry into the L.R.I. and thereafter to Solimena,[1] No. 2802 could perhaps more probably be allocated to the Genoese School.[2]

Prov: William Noel Hill, 3rd Lord Berwick sold Winstanley's Liverpool 29 October 1839;[3] purchased by the L.R.I. between 1836 and 1843; deposited at the W.A.G., 1893; presented to the W.A.G., 1948.

Ref: **1.** 1843 Catalogue No. 78; G. F. Waagen, *Art Treasures*, 1854, III, p. 240, No. 108 but the 1963 Catalogue suggests Michele Rocca (p. 166).   **2.** Stephen Pepper, *verbally*, 22 February, 1971. F. Bologna, *Francesco Solimena*, 1959, p. 295 denies that No. 2802 is by Solimena or is even Neapolitan; he suggests tentatively Giuseppe Passeri.   **3.** No catalogue survives; see the *Liverpool Mercury* 25 October 1839 p. 4 for an account of the sale. Lord Berwick was ambassador at Naples 1824-33 and the Liverpool Mercury, *op. cit.*, stated that he bought his pictures there.

3419 Venus and Cupid

Canvas, 130.5 × 190.5 cm

Attributed on entry to the Walker Art Gallery to Luca Giordano[1]; No. 3419 was attributed in the 1963 Catalogue to Corrado Giaquinto.[2] This suggestion has not proved acceptable[3] and No. 3419 is in any event not of high quality.

Prov: Presented by James L. Bowes 1878.

Ref: **1.** 1882 Catalogue No. 20. p. 10.   **2.** Oreste Ferrari and Giuseppe Scavizzi, *Luca Giordano*, 1966, Vol. II, p. 293 support this attribution with qualification.   **3.** Dwight C. Miller, verbally 1962, denied it and Stephen Pepper, verbally 1971, thought that No. 3419 was probably Venetian.

9128 Portrait of a man

Canvas, 79.8 × 59.5 cm

The costume would suggest that the date assigned to No. 9128 in 1893 is too early.[1]

Prov: Entered the collection of the L.R.I. in 1893;[1] from whom transferred by the University of Liverpool, 1976.

Ref: **1.** L.R.I. Annual Report 1893, p. 53 (121A) as 16th Century *Portrait of an ecclesiastic.*

JENKINS, Paul, born 1923

6174 Phenomena Votive

Canvas, 195 × 150 cm

The artist's "Phenomena" paintings began in 1958 and he wrote of them: "The sensation of the experience happened within me, not outside of me, as though it were done by a medium. The discovery came within the act, not arbitrarily before the act . . . it comes in the workings, in the discovery with paint—images move unceasingly caught with purpose[1]"

No. 6174 is dated by Elsen to 1962-3.[2]

Prov: Purchased from Arthur Tooth and Sons Ltd. 1963.

Exh: Arthur Tooth and Sons, *Paul Jenkins,* 1963 (3) repr.

Ref: 1. Paul Jenkins, *A Cahier Leaf.* It is, No. 2. Autumn 1958 p. 13 and *An Abstract Phenomenist,* Painter and Sculptor, Winter-Spring 1958-9, p. 5. See also Albert Elsen, *Paul Jenkins,* New York (1973) p. 21 for further explanations of the term *Phenomena* and Jean Cassou, *Jenkins,* 1963, passim where No. 6174 (repr. as No. 51) is dated to 1962/3. **2.** Elsen *op. cit.,* plate 68.

JONES, Hugh Bolton, 1848-1927

915 Silver Birches

Canvas, 138.4 × 91.7 cm

Signed: *H. BOLTON JONES 1878*

Painted during the artist's European tour of 1876-1880 presumably at Pont Aven.[1]

The Athenaeum critic wrote: "we turn with zest to a manifestation of the influence of Corot, hardly less conventional and yet most exquisite art and poetry. This is to be found in Mr. H. B. Jones's autumnal landscape No. 449 where nearly leafless beeches grow in a rocky meadow by a brook and a rude bridge. The drawing of the trees is admirable; indeed so good as to be worthy of Mr. Macwhirter's attention".

Prov: (?)Thomas B. Clarke, but not in his sale, New York, 14-18 February 1899; presented by Walter C. Clarke 1904.

Exh: R.A. 1880 (449) as *"When drop the leaves from branches sere/As fade the hopes of a vanished year."*

Ref: 1. The R.A. Catalogues of 1878-80 give the artist's address as Pont Aven, Finisterre. There is a brief account of his movements in the *Dictionary of American Biography* Vol. X p. 175. **2.** The Athenaeum, I, 1880 p. 702 in its review of the R.A. Summer Exhibition.

KABEL, van der, Adrian, 1630/31-1705

868 Wooded Landscape

Canvas, 85 × 108.3 cm

No. 868, formerly attributed to Cornelis Huysmans is virtually identical to an etching by Kabel inscribed *Adr. Vander Cabel jn. et fecit.* etc/*N. Rob(ert). ex.* etc.

Prov: Presented to the Liverpool Royal Institution by Henry Lawrence between 1851 and 1857,[2] deposited at the Walker Art Gallery 1893; presented to the Walker Art Gallery 1948.

Ref: **1.** A. Bartsch, *Le Peintre Graveur*, Vol. 4, 1854, No. 38, p. 252 as *Le pecheur a la ligne* in the artist's *Septieme Livre des Paisages*. I am indebted to Dr. An Zwollo for drawing my attention to this etching which, together with No. 868 will be fully discussed in her forthcoming article in *Oud Holland.*   **2.** It is No. 139 in a proof copy of the 1859 Catalogue dateable to about 1857 (Liverpool University Library L.R.I. Archives 63)—attributed there to Huysmans.

KAUFMANN, Wilhelm, born 1895

1110   Portrait of William Armstrong

Canvas, 76.2 × 63.5 cm

Signed: *WK* (in monogram) *1929*

The sitter (1882-1952) was producer and director at the Liverpool Playhouse from 1914 to 1944; from 1945 to 1947 he was assistant director at the Birmingham Repertory Theatre. The artist described by the sitter simply as Wilhelm Kaufmann,[2] can be more precisely identified from the monogram.[3]

Prov: Presented by William Armstrong 1949.

Ref: **1.** Obituaries in the *Liverpool Echo* 6 October 1952 and in the *News Chronicle* 7 October 1952.   **2.** Letter to John Tilney 19 April 1949 (typescript copy in Walker Art Gallery).   **3.** Franz Goldstein, *Monogram Lexikon*, 1964, p. 782.

KITAJ, Ronald B., born 1932

6115   The Red Banquet

Canvas, 152.5 × 152.5 cm

Inscribed on a sheet of paper stuck to the canvas:

In February, 1854 Mr. Saunders, the /American Consul, gave a banquet to a dozen/of the principal foreign refugees in London.

Among the guests were Alexander Herzen,/Garibaldi, Mazzini, Orsini, Kossuth,/Ledru-Rollin, Worcell, and other refugee/leaders. The party was completed by the/American Ambassador James Buchanan, a/future President of the United States.

Herzen is apostrophised on the left in/this picture with the image of Michael/Bakunin planted in his midsection . . ./(Bakunin was not present but arrived in London/late in 1861.)

This "Red Banquet" is described by/E. H. Carr in his book "The Romantic Exiles"/(Penguin, 1949).

The scene has been set in a house based/on a photo of Le Corbusier's House at Garches,/near St. Cloud, 1927/28.

R. B. Kitaj

and under snake: *Don't tread on me* and around snake: *c/sc /nc/v/p/m/nj/ny*

On the left is the figure of Alexander Herzen[1] above that of Michael Bakunin; Bakunin has half obliterated sticks of dynamite on his chest. On the right of these two figures is the American Ambassador James Buchanan; on his chest appears a rattlesnake inscribed with the initial letters of the first union of American States and with the motto: *Don't tread on me*—a device used on early naval flags of the revolting American colonies in 1776 and thus symbolizing, like the dynamite, revolutionary change. The cloudburst above the head of the American Ambassador is connected with this rattlesnake as the snake has often been seen as a symbol of lightning.[2] The identification, interpretation and symbolism of the figures and objects on the right must remain conjectural as the artist had apparently forgotten their sources and intentions by 1972.[3]

No. 6115 was painted in 1960.[4]

Prov: Presented by John Moores 1961.
Exh: W.A.G., *John Moores Liverpool Exhibition*, 1961 (61).
Ref: 1. This elucidation of No. 6115 is wholly based on Richard Francis, *The Red Banquet by R. B. Kitaj*, Annual Reports and Bulletin of the Walker Art Gallery, Liverpool, Vols. 2-4, 1971-4, pp. 84ff. Francis also considers Kitaj's debt to Ezra Pound and T. S. Eliot in his aggregation of images, facts and ideas and his relationship to realism, abstract expressionism and to American Indian pictography. The photograph of Le Corbusier's House at Garches to which Francis refers (note 1) was published in Fritz Saxl, *Lectures*, 1957, plate 62a.   2. Aby Warburg, *A Lecture on Serpent Ritual*, Journal of the Warburg and Courtauld Institutes, Vol. 2, No. 4, 1939, pp. 282ff—a source certainly used by the artist.   3. Francis *op. cit.*, p. 87—who does however offer some possible interpretations.   4. Museum Boymans-van Beuningen Rotterdam, *R. B. Kitaj*, 1970, No. 104.

KNELLER, Godfrey, 1646-1723

3023   Charles II

Canvas, 224.7 × 142.8 cm

Signed: *GODFREY KNELLER/ad VIVUM fecit/Ad 1685*

Probably a version of the *Portrait of Charles II* by Kneller in the collection of James II, later hung in St. James's House where it was last recorded by Horace Walpole in 1758[1] and possibly that original (?) portrait itself.[2]

Kneller's last portrait of Charles II completed after the death of the sitter (despite the very unusual form of signature).[3] Details of other portraits of Charles II by Kneller appear most conveniently in Stewart.[4]

The bust on the left is stated to be that of Charles II's Queen, Catherine of Braganza.[5] The King wears Garter Robes. The pose in No. 3023 is very similar to that in Lely's portrait of the same sitter of about 1675 (now Euston Hall, Suffolk).

Another version of this portrait is owned by the Earl of Powis.[6]

Engr: I. Beckett, T. Chambers, B. Picart, John Smith, R. Williams etc.[7]

Prov: See above. Sir Cuthbert Quilter Bt. Bawdsey Manor, Suffolk. Lord Brocket sold Sotheby 16 July 1952 lot 57 bt. for Walker Art Gallery.

Exh: New Gallery, *Monarchs of Great Britain and Ireland*, 1901-2, No. 115. Walker Art Gallery, *Kings and Queens*, 1953 No. 21.

Ref: **1.** Oliver Millar, *Pictures in the Royal Collection, Tudor, Stuart and Early Georgian Pictures*, 1963, p. 141 gives a detailed history of this portrait with extensive references. **2.** J. D. Stewart, *Sir Godfrey Kneller*, National Portrait Gallery, 1971, p. 50 identifies No. 3023 as the original portrait (presumably that described by Millar *op. cit.,*) but Millar *op. cit.*, himself does not give priority either to No. 3023 or to the portrait formerly in the Royal Collection (if not No. 3023). **3.** 1685 (old style) means after March 25, 1685 (new style) and Charles II died on 6 February 1685 (new style)—see the correspondence in *The Times* 1955, 11 May and 14 May between E. H. Ramsden and David Piper over this. **4.** Stewart *op. cit.* **5.** Sotheby's Sale Catalogue (see provenance). **6.** Royal Academy *The Age of Charles II*, 1960-1961, No. 294, p. 91. **7.** F. O'Donoghue *Catalogue of Engraved British Portraits*, 1908, I, p. 398, Nos. 48-53.

6272   William Clayton, later Lord Sundon

Canvas, 127 × 101.5 cm

Signed: *G. Kneller f./1719* (initials in monogram)

The sitter (1671-1752) was appointed Clerk to the Auditor of the Receipt in 1688 and after various other official appointments became a member of parliament in 1716 for New Woodstock and remained in parliament for various constituencies until his death; he was created Baron Sundon of Ardagh (an Irish peerage) in 1735.[1] He can be identified first from the coat of arms on No. 6272[2] (the Clayton Arms[3] with the Dyve Arms,[4] the Clayton Motto, *Probitatem quam Divitias*[5] and a Baron's Coronet[6]) and secondly from the inscription *Wm. Clayton Baron Sundon of Ardagh* on another version of No. 6272.[7]

Prov: Bequeathed by Arthur George Isaacson through his son Brian H. Isaacson, 1965.

Ref: **1.** See *The Complete Peerage* ed. G.E.C., Vol. 12, part 1, 1953, pp. 490-1, B. Burke, *The Genealogical History of the dormant Peerages of the British Empire*, 1883, p. 122 and particularly Romney Sedgwick *The House of Commons, 1715-54*, Vol. 1, 1970, p. 558 where his political activities are described in detail. **2.** It seems to be painted over an earlier coat of arms. **3.** Burke *op. cit.*, p. 122 and B. Burke, *General Armory*, 1884, p. 201. **4.** General Armory, *op. cit.*, p. 311. Before 1714 the sitter married Charlotte Dyve for whom see *Dictionary of National Biography* under Clayton. **5.** General Armory, *op. cit.* **6.** The coat of arms must therefore have been painted in after 1735 when the sitter was elevated to the peerage. **7.** Sold Sotheby's 2 November 1955 lot 95 bt. Tallent £6; sold Sotheby's 1 February 1956 lot 142 bt. Rich £10. On both occasions a portrait of Charlotte, Lady Sundon was sold with the portrait of Lord Sundon. Perhaps they were the pair given to Dr. Freind in 1728 (Dictionary of National Biography *op. cit.*). For Lady Sundon see particulary *Memoirs of Viscountess Sundon etc.* ed Mrs Thomson, 1847 where however no portraits by Kneller are mentioned.

KNELLER, Godfrey, Studio of

8564 Portrait of Alexander Pope

Canvas, 74 × 60.7 cm

The only signed and dated version (now owned by Lord Home) of this portrait is dated 1721 and is presumed to be the first.[1] A drawing on oiled paper in the British Museum[2] is probably a studio copy after this version for making repetitions, among them No. 8564. The allusions to antiquity, the snake biting its tail, the Roman toga, the profile pattern all' antica, the short hair and the crown of ivy are discussed by Wimsatt.[3]

Prov: At Croxteth Hall, the Liverpool seat of the Earls of Sefton at least by 1863,[4] Croxteth Hall Sale, Christie's 19 September 1973, lot 1020 bt. Walker Art Gallery.

Ref: **1.** W. K. Wimsatt, *The Portraits of Alexander Pope*, 1965, pp. 52-55, Nos. 6.2 and 6.4.   **2.** E. Croft Murray and P. Hulton, *Catalogue of British Drawings*, I, *XVI, and XVII Centuries*, 1960 No. 11.   **3.** *Op. cit.* See also J. D. Stewart, *Sir Godfrey Kneller* National Portrait Gallery, 1971, p. 65, No. 82.   **4.** There is a photograph of No. 8564 dated 27 November 1863 at the National Portrait Gallery; it is possible that No. 8564 was commissioned by one of the Molyneux family (later Earls of Sefton) from Kneller since both that family and the sitter were then Catholics and Pope's close friend John Caryll was related to the Molyneux. No. 8564 is not however listed in the Croxteth Inventory of 1745 (MSS Lancashire Record Office, Preston).

KNELLER, Godfrey, after

2537 Matthew Prior

Copper, 18.6 × 16 cm

Copy after the head and shoulders only of the portrait by Kneller,[1] now in Trinity College Cambridge.

Prov: ?William Roscoe presented by Mrs. A. M. Roscoe, 1950.

Ref: **1.** For which see Lord Killanin, *Sir Godfrey Kneller and his times, 1646-1723*, 1948, plate 51; D. Piper, *Catalogue of the 17th Century Portraits in the National Portrait Gallery 1625-1714*, 1963, p. 288 and particularly J. D. Stewart, *Sir Godfrey Kneller,* National Portrait Gallery, 1971, No. 80, p. 63.

KOLLER, Guillaume, 1829-1884/5

248   A Marriage Scene

Panel, 55.5 × 79 cm

Signed and dated: *G. Koller 186(–)*

No. 248, the subject of which has not hitherto been identified, can probably be described as the *Marriage of Count Sickingen* which appeared in the two sales listed below. Franz von Sickingen, 1481-1523, was best known as one of the protectors of Martin Luther.

Prov: ?J. Latty Bickley sold Christie's 14 February 1863 lot 60 bt. Dowling £115 10s 0d. Anon sold Christie's 29 May 1875 lot 175 bt. Polak £120 15s 0d. Bought by George Holt from Polak 1875 (receipt 26 June MS W.A.G.) £450. Bequeathed by Emma Holt 1944.

Exh: Liverpool Art Club, *Modern Oil Paintings by Foreign Artists*, 1884 No. 54 as a *Hungarian Marriage Scene*.

KRELL, Hans, active about 1522-1586

1222   Portrait of Princess Emilia of Saxony (1516-1591)

Panel, 31.5 × 25.9 cm

Identified by H. Zimmermann[1] as an engagement portrait of Princess Emilia of Saxony, who married the Margrave George of Ansbach in 1532, and attributed by him to Krell; the clasped hands on the central necklace and bodice indicate an engagement portrait and the Saxon coat of arms on the upper necklace a Saxon princess; the central figure of the triple portrait at Vienna by Lucas Cranach the elder,[2] dateable from costume to about 1535, is derived from No. 1222 and represents the same sitter.

The necklaces in No. 1222 are discussed in general terms by Joan Evans in *A History of Jewellery 1100-1870*, 1953, pp. 98-9. No. 1222 is painted up to the edges all round.

Prov: ?William Young Ottley sold Christie's 25 May 1811 lot 9 *A Princess of Saxony* by Cranach bt. Walker £4 16s 0d. Probably the Mrs. Cranach[3] for which William Roscoe paid J. Ashton Yates £7 7s 0d, on 22 August 1812;[4] Roscoe Sale 1816 lot 97 (as Portrait of Lucas Cranach's Wife by Lucas Cranach). Joseph Brooks Yates who presented it to the L.R.I. 4 July 1842;[5] deposited at the W.A.G., 1893; presented to the W.A.G., 1948.

Exh: Leeds, *National Exhibition*, 1868, (539).

Ref: **1.** Heinrich Zimmermann, *Zur Ikonographie von Damenbildnissen des alteren und des jungeren Lucas Cranach*, Pantheon, Vol. XXVII, No. 4, 1969, pp. 284ff. This hypothesis seems plausible but by no means conclusive.   **2.** V. Oberhammer, *Katalog der Gemaldeglerie*, Kunsthistorisches Museum, Vienna, II, 1958, p. 37, No. 111; the other two figures in this portrait are, according to

Zimmermann, *op. cit.*, p. 284 Princess Sidonia (1518-1575) and Princess Sibylla (1515-1592) the sisters of Princess Emilia. **3.** No. 1222 has on its back an old inscription stating that it was a portrait of Margaret Rauschen the wife of Lucas Cranach by Lucas Cranach. **4.** Roscoe Papers, No. 5405, it was contained in a parcel of prints sent to Yates by Mr. Dodd on 18 August 1812. **5.** L.R.I. Archives 41.

LAMORINIERE, Jean Pierre Francois, 1828-1911

2878 Landscape

Panel, 124.5 × 188 cm

Signed: *Fcois Lamoriniere/XX 1869*

If No. 2878 has been correctly identified (see exhibitons) the river in it would be the Meuse.

Prov: Mrs. Alfred Morrison sold Christie's 28 January 1899 lot 76 (as *A Belgian Village, Autumn*) bought Jevons £52 10s 0d bequeathed by Arthur Jevons 1906.
Exh: ?Expositon Générale des Beaux Arts, Brussels,1869 (691) as *L'Automne, vue prise aux environs d'Hastière*. Liverpool Art Club *Modern Oil Paintings by Foreign Artists* 1884 No. 59 or No. 150.

3036 Sunset

Canvas, 135 × 296 cm

Signed: *F. Lamoriniere 1849 Anvers*

Prov: Purchased "recently" on the continent and presented by Arnold Baruchson 1864.[1]
Exh: ?Salon d'Anvers, 1849 (332) as *Les Derniers Rayons de soleil.* ?Exposition Générale des Beaux Arts, Brussels, 1851 (734) as *Les bruyères de Putte en Hollande, effet de soleil couchant.*
Ref: 1. Liverpool Corporation, Libraries Museums and Arts Committee 23 June 1864.

LANGENMANTEL, Ludwig, 1854-1922

1337 The Outposts

Canvas, 81.5 × 110 cm

Signed: *Langenmantel Munchen 84*

Prov: Presented by Mrs. Fanny Park, 1929

LE BRUN, Charles, 1619-1690

2898 Atalanta and Meleager

Canvas,[1] 212.5 × 280.5 cm

One of a series of cartoons for the tapestries commissioned by Jean Valdor in 1658.[2] Two other cartoons from the same series illustrating the story of Meleager are now in the Louvre, *The hunt of the Calydonian Boar* (Inv. No. 2899) and *The Death of Meleager* (Inv. No. 2900). Engravings after the tapestries were published by Picart in 1714 from the set then owned by the Duke of Orleans[3] and six of another set survive in the Swedish Royal Collections.[4]

Two drawings of dogs by Le Brun for No. 2898 are in the Louvre.[5] However it must be assumed that Le Brun collaborated with other artists in painting No. 2898.[6]

Jennifer Montagu[7] argues that No. 2898 represents not the original presentation of the head and hide of the Calydonian Boar by Meleager to Atalanta but its second presentation to her after the murder by Meleager of his jealous uncles as recounted in Isaac de Benserade's *Méléagre* of 1641; neither this second presentation nor *The Crowning of Atalanta*, which appears in the series of 1658 but not in the engravings of 1714, is to be found in Ovid's *Metamorphoses* VIII, 267-546 but both are recounted by Benserade. Certainly the prominence accorded to the bloody sword and the presence in the background of at least one dead body, perhaps an uncle, supports this hypothesis; the boar was killed with a spear, the uncles with a sword.

A small copy after no. 2898 is pen, ink and watercolour by Biagio Rebecca (1738-1808) is in the British Museum (Inv. No. 1911-2-23-3)

Prov: Jean Valdor.[8] ?Everhard Jabach.[9] Princes Louis Napoleon[10] sold Christie's. 10 March 1852, lot 71 (as Venetian School) bt Benjamin £5 10s 0d B. Benjamin of London[10] who presented it 1852.

Ref: **1.** For a technical discussion see J. Coburn Witherop, *Atalanta and Meleager by Charles Le Brun*, Liverpool Bulletin, Vo. 12, 1967, pp.28ff.   **2.** C. Nivelon, *Vie de Charles Le Brun et description détaillée de ses ouvrages*, Paris, Bibliotheque Nationale MSS fr. No. 12987, p. 106-7. For the material in this entry the compiler is indebted to Dr. Jennifer Montagu who discusses No. 2898 at length in *Atalanta and Meleager: A newly identified painting by Le Brun*, Liverpool Bulletin, 1967, Vol. 12, pp. 17ff.   **3.** The engravers were J. Folkema, L Surugue, Q. Fonbonne, S. Thomassin and E. Jeaurat.   **4.** John Bottiger, *Svenska Statens Samling af vafda Tapeter/La Collection des tapisseries de l'etat suédois,* Stockholm, 1898, Vol. III, p. 38, plates XXIV—XXVI, XLVIII, Vol. IV, pp. 81 and 86.   **5.** F. Lugt, *Musée du Louvre, Invéntaire general des dessins des ecoles du nord, école flamande*, 1949, nos. 41 and 42 there attributed to Pieter Boel.   **6.** The list of the tapestries woven at the Gobelins drawn up in 1692 states: "Les tableaux ont esté fourni par feu M. Valdor; je ne sçay pas par qui il les avoit fait peindre. Les *Pensées* sont de M. Lebrun" (J. J. Guiffrey, *Les Manufactures parisiennes de tapisseries au XVII siècle*, Memoires de la société de l'histoire de Paris et de l'ile—de—France, XIX, 1892, p. 238), but Nivelon wrote: "M. Le Brun fit pour luy (Valdor) six grands tableaux pour etre executé en tapisserie" and adds that Le Brun's pen drawings of the same subject were made "de la meme maniere sans

changements et les paysages sont de l'habile M. Bellin qui vivoit dans ce tems"
(Nivelon *op. cit.*). Possibly Bellin (presumably Francois Bellin, died 1661)
worked on the paintings not the drawings (Montagu, *op. cit.*, p. 26 who also suggests the collaboration of an artist trained in the tradition of Snyders).　**7.**
Montagu *op. cit.*, pp. 23ff.　**8.** J. J. Guiffrey *op. cit.*, p. 238.　**9.** The inventory drawn up on Jabach's death included "Meleagre portant la teste du sanglier a
Atalante" (no. 518) valued at 20 livres; at his death his collection passed to his
son Henry Jabach (Vicomte de Groucy, *Everhard Jabach, collectionneur
parisien,* Memoires de la société de l'histoire de Paris et de l'ile de France, XXI,
1894, pp. 275-6 and Edmund Bonaffe, *Dictionnaire des Amateurs francais au
XVIIe Siecle,* 1884, p. 144). Jabach may also have owned a set of finished pen
drawings by Lebrun made after the cartoons (for which see Montagu *op. cit.*, pp.
25-26 and Bonaffe *op. cit.*, p. 317).　**10.** Minutes of the Libraries, Museums
and Art Gallery Committee, Liverpool Corporation, 10 June 1852.

LEGRAS, Auguste, 1818-1887

255　Girl with Birds

Canvas, 40.5 × 28.8 cm

Signed: *A. Legras* (initials in monogram)

Prov:　　Sewell M. Barker, Manchester, sold Christie's 31 May 1875 (90), bt. Agnew,
£21; thence to George Holt (no bill extant), for £32 according to his Price List,
MS W.A.G. bequeathed by Emma Holt 1944.

Exh:　　Paris Salon, 1861 (1895) as *La Fille aux Oiseaux* with this quotation from George
Sand's *Teverino:* "Une jeune montagnarde grimpait la pente escarpée qui con-
duisait à la roche verte et cette enfant marchait littéralement dans une nuée
d'oiseaux qui voltigeaient autour d'elle."

LEGROS, Alphonse, 1837-1911

2593　Study of a Head

Canvas, 57.5 × 43 cm

No. 962 at the Liverpool Autumn Exhibition of 1878 was Legros's
Study of a Head, painted before the students at the Slade School of fine arts
and presumably in connection with this work Legros offered to come to
Liverpool on 25 November 1878 "to paint a picture for the benefit of the
Art Students of the town and to present the said study to the (Walker) Art
Gallery";[1] 120 tickets were issued and No. 2593 was painted in 1 hour 40
minutes before Liverpool Art Students in the "lower room" of the
Walker Art Gallery on 27 November 1878.[2] The sitter was Joseph Davies
a joiner at the Gallery (1818-1893).[3]

Studies from the heads of living models done by the master in front of his pupils were part of the French Academic tradition.[4]

Prov: Presented by the Artist 1878.

Ref: **1.** Arts and Exhibitions Sub Committee of the Liverpool Town Council MSS Minutes W.A.G. 19 November 1878.   **2.** Sub Committee Minutes, *op. cit.*, 26 November 1878 and MS notes in W.A.G. Accessions Book, and Charles Dyall, *First Decade of the Walker Art Gallery*, 1888, p. 18; to attend the students had to have certificates of advanced studies in painting and drawing. For further references on the artist's teaching methods see p. 256, 392-3   **3.** Information from John Hibbert former attendant at the Walker Art Gallery.   **4.** A. Boime, *The Academy and French Painting in the Nineteenth Century*, 1971, p. 37, figs 14-17 for examples by Charles Gleyre and Thomas Couture.

3090   The Pilgrimage

Canvas, 137.2 × 226 cm

Signed: *A. Legros/1871*

The subject was a favourite one of the artist going back to his *Ex-Voto* of 1860.[1] Also characteristic of Legros is the fact that the figure of the crucified Christ, the cause of the religious emotion on the faces of the peasants, is omitted from the picture.[2] The head-dress of the two peasants on the left is that of Boulogne-sur-Mer, perhaps reflecting the influence of the *Boulonaises* of his friend the sculptor Dalou.[3] The general influence of Courbet is clear.

At the R.A. No. 3090 was extensively and favourably reviewed. The Art Journal critic[4] wrote: "Legros touches upon certain convictions of the French School which are the very antipodes of some leading principles entertained by ourselves . . . . . . The women . . . . . . are placed in one attitude and all looking towards the shrine. This is instanced as the only composition in the exhibition based on the simple principles that governed the studies of the earliest painters. Those uncompromising whites and blacks ignore entirely those rules of practice which have been in force for centuries but which are now not infrequently repudiated in the universal stirring after what is considered originality." The Athenaeum[5] referred to the "simple earnest and quaint faces" as "intensely pathetic", to the picture's "solemnity and breadth of colouring not less than the fine feeling for expression it exhibits and its largeness of style." "The figures of the women" it went on "are rather uncouth not to say dumpy and to this result the bulky costume contributes not a little; yet on the other hand we are bound to remember that this very ungracefulness adds to the homely and naive pathos of the design . . ." Much later Ford Madox Brown[6] described No. 3090 as "a very fine picture great in style."

A drawing entitled *Le Pélerinage* is recorded by Soulier.[7] No. 3090 was repaired or restored by the artist in 1875.[8] It was later severely damaged in 1957.

Prov: Presented by P. H. Rathbone 1873.

Exh: R. A., 1872 (184); L.A.E., 1872 (54); The Society of French Artists 1875 (80).

Ref: **1.** R. A. 1864 (230); favourably reviewed by F. T. Palgrave *Essays on Art* 1866, p. 52. Now in the Musée des Beaux Arts, Dijon; for full details see Dijon, Musée des Beaux Arts, *Alphonse Legros* 1957 (2) p. 15. **2.** Monique Geiger, *La peinture d'Alphonse Legros en Angleterre*, Mem. de l'Académie de Dijon, Vol. 112, 1954-6, p. 78. **3.** Geiger *op. cit.*, and letter 2 December 1975. **4.** The *Art Journal* 1872, p. 153. **5.** *The Athenaeum* 1872, p. 596. **6.** *The Progress of English Art as Not Shown at the Manchester Exhibiton*, Magazine of Art, 1888, p. 123. **7.** Gustave Soulier, *L'Oeuvre gravé et lithographié de Alphonse Legros*, 1904, No. 5 under *Dessins*. **8.** Extracts of the Libraries, Museums and Art Committee of the Liverpool Town Council 27 April, 1875.

LELY, Peter, 1618-1680

2945 Josceline Percy, 11th Earl of Northumberland

Canvas, 127 × 101.6 cm

Inscribed: *IOSCELINE PIERCY 11th EARL OF/NORTHUMBER-LAND/DIED AT TURIN 21st May 1670/AETAT*

Probably painted in about 1660 when the sitter was 16 and still Lord Percy.[1] The sitter, 1644-1670, was made Lord Lieutenant of Northumberland (jointly with his father) in 1660 and Lord Lieutenant of Sussex in 1668; he became Earl of Northumberland on the death of his father in 1668. Other portraits of him by Lely exist[2].

Prov: Possibly passed out of the Northumberland family into the Carlisle family in 1688 when the 3rd Earl of Carlisle married Lady Anne Capel, niece of the sitter; Hon. Geoffrey W. A. Howard (from Castle Howard) sold Christie's 18 February 1944 lot 51 bt. Arcade £27 6d 0d, purchased from the Arcade Gallery 1945.

Ref: **1.** For the sitter see particularly *The Complete Peerage* ed G.E.C. Vol. 9, 1936, p. 739. An inventory of his personal estate on his death with notes of the pictures then at Northumberland House, Petworth and Syon survives among the papers of the Duke of Northumberland see The Historical Manuscripts Commission, *Third Report*, 1872, *Appendix*, pp. 109-10. "A Picture of Sr. Jocelin Percy to the Knees" is there listed as at Syon. I am indebted to Mr. R. M. Gard for looking at this inventory for me. **2.** R. B. Beckett *Lely*, 1951, Nos. 390-393. No. 2945 is No. 392, there dated to 1659.

LE SIDANER, Henri Eugene Augustin, 1862-1939

2373 St. Paul's from the River: Morning Sun

Canvas, 90 × 116 cm

Signed: *Le Sidaner*

Painted in London in the winter of 1906-7.[1] Pencil "squaring" of the canvas can be seen showing through the paint.

Prov: Purchased at the L.A.E. 1911 (£200) from William Marchant and Co.

Exh: Goupil Gallery, London, *Hampton Court and London by Henri Le Sidaner,* 1908 (10) as *St. Paul's from the River, Morning Sun in Winter;* Paris, Société Nationale des Beaux Arts, 1908 (729); Carnegie Institute, Pittsburgh, *13th Annual Exhibition,* 1909 (170); L.A.E. 1911 (212).

Ref: 1. Louis Le Sidaner, *Letter,* 26 November 1957, C. Mauclair, *Le Sidaner,* 1928, pp. 130, 256, repr. p. 59.

6588   L'lle Madre, Clair de Lune

Canvas, 89.5 × 117 cm

Signed: *Le Sidaner*

Painted in the winter of 1908-9 from Stresa; the subject is the Isola Madre in Lake Maggiore.[1]

Prov: Purchased from the L.A.E. by J. D. Johnston (£350)[2]; sold Sotheby's 14 November, 1956 lot 68 bought in £50; purchased from Mrs. Florence Johnston 1967 (£100).

Exh: Paris, Société Nationale des Beaux Arts, 1909 (763) as *Isola Madre (Clair de lune);* L.A.E. 1909 (305). On loan to the Royal Photographic Society c. 1930-1955.

Ref: 1. Louis Le Sidaner, letter, 26 November 1957, C. Mauclair, *Le Sidaner,* 1928, pp. 40 and 54 (repr.)   2. Account Sales Books, MSS W.A.G. An Old label gives the Galeries Georges Petit Stock No. 4374.

LEVENSTEDE, Hinrik the Younger, active 1497-1520

1231   The Holy Family with Angels

Panel, 92.9 × 61.5 cm

Inscribed: *JHESUS MARIA JHESU*

1230   The Family of St. Elizabeth

Panel, 91.5 × 60.5 cm

Inscribed: *MARIA ELISABES*

Two panels from a dismembered polyptych;[1] a third *The Family of Mary Cleophas* is in a private Dutch Collection and a fourth *The Family of Mary Salome* presumably existed;[2] Mary Salome and Mary Cleophas were the sisters of the Virgin and St. Elizabeth was her cousin; the overall subject was therefore the Holy Kinship. The figures in 1230 are presumably St. Elizabeth with the infant St. John the Baptist on her lap greeting the Infant Christ and Zacharias[3] behind the wall.

The painted dividing stips visible at the top of No. 1230 and at the bottom of No. 1231 suggest that No. 1231 originally was placed above No. 1230; their gold backgrounds suggests that they were visible only when the polyptych was opened out;[4] both are gilded on their backs and No. 1230 has some grisaille painting there as well.

Gmelin believes that Nos. 1230-1231 date at least from before 1516.[5]

Prov: Acquired by the L.R.I. between 1843 and 1851;[6] deposited at the W.A.G., 1893; presented to the W.A.G., 1948.
Exh: Manchester, *Art Treasures*, 1857 (417)
Ref: 1. H. G. Gmelin, *Hinrik Levenstede der jungere und Werke der Luneberger Malergilde um 1500*, Niederdeutsche Beitrage zur Kunstgeschichte, Vol. X, 1971, pp. 121ff; according to Gmelin the polyptych was an altarpiece with a double pair of shutters.   2. Gmelin, *op. cit.*, pp. 122-3.   3. Gmelin, *op. cit.*, p. 122 says Joachim.   4. Gmelin, *op. cit.*, p. 122.   5. Gmelin, *op. cit.*, p. 124.   6. 1851 Catalogue Nos. 35-36. The contents of the Nikolaikirche in Luneburg were sold between 1831 and 1840 (Gmelin, *letter*, 22 March, 1968).

LEYS, Jean August Henri, 1815-1869, Imitator of

723   Interior of an Artist's Studio

Canvas, 52 × 63 cm

Inscribed: *H. Leys ft. 1849*

A pastiche of pictures by Leys such as *The Burgomaster Six visiting the Studio of Rembrandt* of 1850 (now lost).[1]

Prov: Purchased from the Samuel Huggins Sale, Branch and Leete, 7 July, 1891 Liverpool (£38 17s 0d).
Exh: ?Agnew's, Exchange Galleries, Liverpool, 1872 (128) *An Interior.*
Ref: 1. Alma-Tadema doubted that No. 723 was by Leys (note in Gallery records).

LIEBERMANN, Max, 1847-1935

5599   Cottage Interior with seated Woman

Panel, 29.7 × 15.8 cm

Signed: *M. Liebermann*

Dated by Carl-Wolfgang Schumann to around 1875[1]

Prov: Found in the Gallery in 1958
Exh: Louis Bock und Sohn, Hamburg[2];? Venice, Biennale.[3]
Ref: 1. Letter 18th February 1972.   2. Old Stamp on stretcher.   3. Old label: *Giuseppe Biassutti, Venice, depository of pictures.*

LINDHOLM, Berndt, 1841-1914

3041 Forest in Finland

Canvas, 148.5 × 223 cm

Signed: *B. Lindholm*

Probably painted early in the 1870s and representing the district of Porvoo (South Finland)[1]

Prov: Arnold Baruchson who presented it 1875.
Ref: 1. Herlmiriitta Sariola, letter, 13 February, 1973.

LIPPI, Filippino, 1457/8-1504, Follower of

2775 Virgin and Child

Panel, 90.1 cm diameter

Condition: badly stained.

Cleaning in 1966 revealed that the panel had originally included an infant St. John the Baptist to the left and below the Virgin.[1] The pointing finger of the Virgin's right hand and the gaze of the Christ Child were directed at him. The Baptist is not recorded in the watercolour copy made for the Rev. John Sanford,[2] but appears to have become visible before the Graham sale in 1886. St. John was removed at some time between 1886[3] and 1893.[4]

As in 2751 the Christ Child holds in his hands a gourd, symbolic of the Resurrection.[5]

Schmarsow suggested that 2775 was close to Raffaellino del Garbo,[6] while Fahy attributed it to the Master of the Naumburg Madonna.[7] That artist seems closer to Lorenzo di Credi, and not all the paintings listed by Fahy appear to be by the same hand. The Madonna and Child in 2775 derive from Filippino Lippi's 1496 *Adoration of the Magi* in the Uffizi. Fairfax Murray[8] was the first to attribute it to a follower of Filippino.

Versions: Watercolour copy by Giovanni Fanciullacci Corsham Court W79;[2] Palazzo Pitti, tondo, *Madonna and Child holding a pomegranate with St. John* and a different background; Davis Collection, Newport, 19½ × 15½ ins set in an interior with a landscape seen to the left; H. Young sale, New York, 1928, *Madonna and Child with a pomegranate* 29½ × 19 ins.
Prov: A seal on the reverse of the Hapsburg-Lorraine Grand Dukes of Tuscany;[9] Rev. John Sanford;[10] his sale, Christie's 9 March 1839 (109) bt. Sherrard; William Graham sale, Christie's 8 April 1886 (244) bt. Philip Rathbone £105; in the Collection of the L.R.I. by 1893;[11] deposited at the W.A.G., 1893;[11] presented to the W.A.G., 1948.

Ref: **1.** Technical report by J. C. Witherop, 1966. **2.** Benedict Nicolson, *The Sanford Collection,* Burlington Magazine, XCVII, 1955, p. 213 (24). **3.** William Graham Sale, Christie's 8 April 1886 (244). Florentine School The Virgin and Child—Circular. The Virgin is seated, holds the Infant, who grasps a pomegranate. St. John lifts both hands in adoration. **4.** 1893 Catalogue p. 14 (35). **5.** George Ferguson, *Signs and Symbols in Christian art,* 1974, p. 31 cites *Jonah* IV 10-11. **6.** August Schmarsow, notes on 1893 Catalogue. **7.** Everett Fahy, *The Master of the Naumburg Madonna,* Fogg Art Museum, Acquisitions, 1966-7, pp. 15, 17. and *Some followers of Domenico Ghirlandajo* (Doctoral Thesis, Harvard University, 1968) 1976, p. 186. **8.** Fairfax Murray, *L.R.I. Annual Report,* 1893, p. 48; an opinion shared, independently by Nicolson, *op. cit.,* p. 213 (24). **9.** Much defaced; probably a customs seal. **10.** Probably *Catalogue of Paintings purchased by the Revd John Sanford during his residence in Italy—1830/and following years* MSS Corsham Court no. 87. Filippo Lippi Virgin and Child/unnumbered £27. 0s. 0d. **11.** L.R.I. 1893 Catalogue p. 14 (35).*

LOUTHERBOURG, Philippe Jacques, 1740-1812

2899 Landscape with Figures

Canvas, 114 × 194 cm

Signed: *P. J. LOUTHERBOURG/1763*

Loutherbourg's paintings at the 1763 Salon (see Exhibitions) were very well received[1] and No. 2899 in particular received extravagant praise from Diderot, establishing the artist's reputation.[2]

"Voyez à gauche ce bout de forêt: il est un peu trop vert, à ce qu'on dit, mais il est touffu et d'une fraicheur delicieuse. En sortant de ce bois et vous avançant vers la droite, voyez ces masses de rochers, comme elles sont grandes et nobles, comme elles sont douces et dorées dans les endroits ou la verdure ne les couvre point, et comme elles sont tendres et agréables où la verdure les tapisse encore! Dites-moi si l'espace que vous decouvrez au dela de ces roches n'est pas la chose qui a fixé cent fois votre attention dans la nature. Comme tout s'éloigne, s'enfuit, se dégrade insensiblement, et lumières et couleurs et objets! Et ces boeufs qui se reposent au pied de ces montagnes, ne vivent-ils pas? ne ruminent-ils pas? N'est-ce pas la vraie couleur, le vrai caractère, la vraie peau de ces animaux? Quelle intelligence et quelle vigueur! Cet enfant naquit donc le pouce passé dans la palette? Où peut-il avoir appris ce qu'il sait? Dans l'âge mûr, avec les plus heureuses dispositions, après une longue experience, on s'élève rarement a ce point de perfection. L'oeil est partout arrêté, recréé, satisfait. Voyez ces arbres; regardez comme ce long sillon de lumière éclaire cette verdure, se joue entre les brins de l'herbe et semble leur donner de la transparence. Et l'accord et l'effet de ces petites masses de roches détachées et repandues sur le devant ne vous frappent-ils pas? Ah! mon ami, que la nature est belle dans ce petit canton! arrêtons-nous-y; la chaleur du jour commence à se faire sentir, couchons-nous le long de ces animaux. Tandis que nous admirerons l'ouvrage du Créateur, la conversation de ce pâtre et de cette paysanne nous amusera; nos oreilles ne dédaigneront pas les sons rustiques de ce bouvier, qui charmé le silence de cette solitude et trompe les ennuis de sa condition en jouant de la flûte. Reposons-nous; vous serez à côté de moi, je serai à vos pieds tranquille et en sûreté, comme ce chien, compagnon assidu de la vie de son maître et garde fidèle de son troupeau; et lorsque le poids du jour sera tombé nous continuerons notre route, et dans un temps plus éloigné, nous nous rappellerons encore cet endroit enchanté et l'heure délicieuse que nous y avons passée."[3]

There is a study for No. 2899 dated 1762 at the Kestner Museum, Hannover (Inv. No. Slg N. 60).

Prov: Sir Richard Glyn, Bart; C. Marshall Spink, presented by C. F. J. Beausire, 1952.

Exh: Paris, Salon 1763 (154) as *Un Paysage avec Figures et Animaux. L'heure du jour est le matin.*[4] Tableau de 6 pieds[5] de largeur sur 3 pieds 6 pouces de hauteur. Greater London Council, Kenwood, The Iveagh Bequest 1973 *Philippe Jacques de Loutherbourg* (2).

Ref: **1.** Diderot, *Salons,* ed. Seznec and Adhemar, 1957, pp. 152 and 186. **2.** Kenwood Catalogue cited under *Exhibitions* which also notes the debt to Berchem in No. 2899. **3.** Diderot, *op. cit.*, pp. 225-6. Neither in the 1957 edition, *op. cit.*, nor in the 1975 edition (pp. 186-7) do Seznec and Adhemar identify No. 2899 as No. 154 at the 1763 Paris Salon and as the picture described by Diderot but this identification seems entirely convincing, it is accepted in the Kenwood Catalogue (cited under *Exhibitions*). For other reviews see Diderot *op. cit.*, pp. 186-7. Philip Conisbee in Greater London Council, Kenwood, The Iveagh Bequest, *Claude Joseph Vernet,* 1976, No. 40, argues that Diderot's attitude to No. 2899 conditioned his much less favourable response to Vernet's *Shepherdess of the Alps*, No. 92 at the same 1763 *Salon.* **4.** The *Mercure de France*, 1763, November, p. 203 wrote of No. 2899: "il parait que M. Loutherbourg s'est attaché a l'imitation des differens effects de la lumière dans les differentes heures du jour. On a lieu d'applaudir aux progrès qu'il a déjà faits dans cette utile étude." **5.** In Diderot *op. cit.*, p. 186 there is a misprint *pouces* for *pieds*.

LUCAS van Leyden, active 1508, died 1533, after

1184 Man of Sorrows

Panel, 32 × 25.3 cm

1185 The Virgin

Panel, 26.6 × 21.2 cm

Copied with a few alterations from Lucas van Leyden's woodcut[1] or, more probably Simon Wynout Frisius's etching of 1522.[2]

Prov: No. 1184 has a collector's mark HB. Acquired by the L.R.I. between 1859 and 1893;[3] deposited at the W.A.G. 1893; presented to the W.A.G. 1948.

Ref: **1.** F. W. H. Hollstein, *Dutch and Flemish Etchings, Engravings and Woodcuts,* Vol X, n.d. p. 219, No. 35 **2.** Hollstein *op. cit.,* VII n.d. p. 35, No. 194 **3.** Possibly Nos. 1184-5 were "the two very interesting paintings of the early German School" presented in 1865 by Theodore Rathbone (*Annual Report of the Liverpool Royal Institution,* 1865).

LUCCHESE School, late 15th century

2780 Madonna and Child with Saints Nicholas, Sebastian, Roch and Martin

Panel transferred to canvas and now laid down on composite board; 169 × 149.5 cm

Inscribed: along the lower edge *S. NICHOLAVS S.SEBAS-TIANVS.AVE. GRATIA. PLENA. DNS. TECV. S. ROCHVS. S. MARTINVS.*

Condition: Vertical cracks down centre, each side of the throne and through the two episcopal saints. Extensive damage in other areas, especially the head of St. Sebastian and the lower left edge, the latter obliterating the inscription identifying the left hand Saint. Badly rubbed generally.

The composition is close to the altarpiece in the Sacristy of the Duomo, Lucca, convincingly attributed to Domenico Ghirlandaio, *the Madonna enthroned with Saints Peter, Clement, Sebastian and Paul.*[1] Certain of the figure types are also close to Ghirlandaio. The influence of Filippino Lippi, who worked in Lucca,[2] is to be seen in the types of the Madonna and Child and in the treatment of the drapery. The angling of the bishops' croziers and of St. Sebastian's arrow recalls the angling of St. Roch's staff, Saint Helena's cross and St. Sebastian's arrow in his altarpiece in San Michele, Lucca.[3]

No. 2780 has been associated with a group of works assembled under the name of the Lucchese Master of the Immaculate Conception.[4] It certainly appears to be by the same hand as the Barcelona *Madonna and Child enthroned with Saints Peter and Paul,*[5] *the Madonna and Child enthroned with Saint James and an angel*[6] and the destroyed Berlin *Madonna and Child enthroned with two angels, Saints Vincent, Nicholas, Dominic and Peter Martyr.*[7] But 2780 has much less in common with the altarpiece of the Immaculate Conception.[8] The lack of control in the handling of the forms would suggest that if 2780 was by the same hand it must be an early work; yet in such early work one would expect to see Filippino's influence to be particularly prominent.

2780 does, however, seem to be by a Lucchese artist, as first suggested by Zeri.[9]

Fahy has tentatively associated with 2780 a lunette with Christ blessing accompanied by two angels.[10] By analogy with the Ghirlandaio altarpiece in the Sacristy of the Duomo at Lucca,[11] a lunette probably crowned 2780; but though the measurements are close, there seems to be insufficient grounds for accepting the proposal. The lunette does appear to be by the same hand as the *Immaculate Conception.*

The Operaio of the Cathedral, San Martino, was authorized to sell a number of pictures in 1595 after they had been replaced by more up to date altarpieces.[12]

Since Saints Sebastian and Roch are both plague saints, it is possible that 2780 was commissioned at a time of plague.

The carpet on the steps of the Madonna's throne is of the so-called Holbein type probably coming from the Ushak region of W. Anatolia.[13]

Prov: William Graham sale, Christie's 8 April 1886 (255) bt. P. H. Rathbone £215 5s 0d; bequeathed by P. H. Rathbone to the W.A.G., 1895; passed to the collection, 1905.

Ref: **1.** J. A. Crowe and G. B. Cavalcaselle, ed. R. Langton Douglas *A History of Painting in Italy*, IV, 1911, p. 331.   **2.** Filippino according to Vasari "In Lucca lavoro . . .alcune cose . . ." Vasari, ed. G. Milanesi, III, p. 466.   **3.** Katharine B. Neilson, *Filippino Lippi*, 1938, fig. 11.   **4.** The Master was originally identified by Offner and following his ideas, the altarpiece of the Immaculate Conception from San Francesco, Lucca, now in the Villa Guinigi with a small group of other works was published by S. Simeonides, *"An Altarpiece by the Master of the Immaculate Conception,"* Marsyas, VIII, 1957-9, p. 55-66. Everett P. Fahy identified the Master with Michele Ciampanti, a late fifteenth century Lucchese artist, in *Paragone*, XVI no. 185/5, July 1965, p. 14, and Everett Fahy, *Some followers of Domenico Ghirlandajo* (Doctoral Thesis, Harvard University, 1968), 1976, p. 177.   **5.** Barcelona Museo de Arte, No. 64978 ex Spiridon Collection. Raimond Van Marle, *The Development of the Italian Schools of Painting*, XIII, 1931, fig. 85 and F. J. Sanchez Canton, *La Colleccion Cambo*, 1955 pp. 28, 60, plate 23.   **6.** Lepke Sale, Berlin 24 February, 1914.   **7.** Berlin, no. 87; *Beschreibendes Verzeichnis der Gemalde im Kaiser-Friedrich Museum und Deutschen Museum*, 1931, pp. 180-1. Van Marle, *op. cit.*, XII, fig. 279.   **8.** Licia Bertolini Campetti in *Catalogo del Museo di Villa Guinigi*, 1968, pp. 164-6, pl. VI.   **9.** Federico Zeri, letter 7 August 1959.   **10.** Present whereabouts unknown, with Paolini, 1924; 145 × 64 cm. Fahy, *Some followers of Domenico Ghirlandajo, op. cit.*, p. 179.   **11.** Isa Belli Barsali, *Guida di Lucca*, 1970, p. 63.   **12.** Janet Ross and Nelly Erichsen, *The Story of Lucca*, 1912, pp. 170 and 172 note 2. Bibliotheca Statale, Lucca, Miscellanea Lucchese, secolo XV-XIX. MS, 1552 p. 12 dated 11 September, 1595.   **13.** For carpets with similar pseudo-kufic arabesque decoration of the borders and rows of octagons with interlaced outlines alternating with other interlaced patterning compare Kurt Erdmann, *Seven Hundred Years of Oriental Carpets*, 1970, pp. 52-56, 141, 145, figs 42, 47, 177, 184 and Kurt Erdmann, *Oriental Carpets, An account of their history*, 1960, fig. 29. On the use of oriental rugs on the steps of thrones in Italian pictures see M. S. Dimand, *Oriental Rugs in the Metropolitan Museum of Art*, 1973 pp. 173-183, citing further literature.

MARCHAND, Jean Hippolyte, 1883-1940

2136 Nocturne

Canvas, 93 × 73.7 cm

Signed: *J. H. Marchand* (initials in monogram)

Painted in 1915. No. 2136 was one of a group of paintings with still life subjects seen against a window of 1913-1915.[1] The flowers have been accurately described as "genets blancs";[2] friesias also appear in No. 2136. The vase has been repainted at an unknown date to make it flatter and more cubist.[3]

Prov: French Private Collection.⁴ Leon Marseille; Galerie Marseille Paris; Crane Kalman Gallery; Arthur Crosland sold Christie's 3 February 1956 (165) bt. Kalman £33 12s 0d, purchased from the Crane Kalman Gallery 1958.

Exh: Venice, Cavallino Gallery, 1957 (lent by the Crane Kalman Gallery).

Ref: 1. René Jean, *Jean Marchand*, 1920, p. 45.   **2.** Jean, *op. cit.*   **3.** Compare the illustration of No. 2136 in Jean, *op. cit.*, p. 9 where No. 2136 already bears the title *Nocturne.*   **4.** Jean *op. cit.*, p. 45 presumably referring to Leon Marseille, a friend of the artist.

MARTINI, Simone, *c.* 1284-1344

2787   Christ discovered in the Temple

Inscribed: on the book *filii/qui/feci/stin/bis/../../*

Signed: on the frame, *SYMON. DE. SENIS. ME. PINXIT, SVB. A.D.M.C. (CC.) XL. II.*

Panel, 49.6 × 35.1 cm

The inscription in the book comes from the Vulgate, Saint Luke II, 48 "Fili, quid fecisti nobis sic? ecce pater tuus, et ego dolentes quaerebamus te" (Son, why have you dealt with us like this, behold, your father and I have sought you, sorrowing). These were Mary's words when his parents found Jesus in the Temple.

Denny points out the unusualness of the emphasis on the humility of Mary, rather than on that of Christ, which contrasts strongly with most medieval commentaries on the passage.¹ He argues that 2787 follows the interpretation of Ubertino of Casale (c. 1259-c. 1329/1341) of the scene in his *Arbor vitae crucifixae Jesus Christi* of 1304/5 in the concentration on "Christ's revelation of divine paternity at the expense of his devotion to Joseph and Mary." He suggests that Provence had been a stronghold of the Spiritual Franciscans, of whom Ubertino was a leading figure and that support for his thought may have lingered on in Avignon despite papal attempts at repression in the 1330's.² Van Os, however, objects that Ubertino's text says very little about the scene represented in 2787 and nothing about the sorrow of Mary, so evident in the picture. He also notes that Ubertino preached in Florence and not in Siena.³ He puts forward the more plausible suggestion that 2787 is in key with the Prayer of Mary in the *Meditationes Vitae Christi,* a text that first appeared at the beginning of the fourteenth century in the Siena area and was much read in Siena. The position of the Virgin seated on a low cushion, akin to that of a Madonna of Humility is in keeping with the spirit of the prayer. According to Van Os the book that Christ holds in his arms is a reference to his knowledge of Holy Writ with which he has just astonished the learned Doctors. The gestures of Joseph and Mary are the ceremonial ones of offering and acceptance, whilst Christ already has his mind on the business of his Father in heaven.⁴ It is difficult, however, to be certain in the present state of knowledge about the language of gestures about their meaning in this picture. It could equally well be argued that Joseph and Mary were gently reproving their errant son.

Denny notes that an angel in Simone's fresco of *The Dream of St. Martin* in the Lower Church of St. Francis at Assisi also has his arms folded across his chest and is in a similar formal relationship to Christ, as Christ is to his parents in 2787. Denny also suggests that the resolute pose of Christ asserting his independence was in part inspired by the example of Pietro Lorenzetti's lost *Presentation of the Virgin,* one of a cycle of frescoes on the facade of the Ospedale di S. Maria della Scala, Siena.[5]

Brink has attempted to reconstruct an altarpiece with 2787 at the centre flanked by the Antwerp *Crucifixion* and Berlin *Entombment* on its right and the Louvre *Way to Calvary* and Antwerp *Deposition* on its left.[6] Van Os and Rinkleff-Reinders correctly reject his attempt.[7] 2787 still has its original frame. There is no evidence from the sides of the frame that 2787 was ever linked physically to other panels either side. Furthermore Brink's reconstruction means that the altarpiece bore two signatures.[8] The panel is painted on the reverse with a fictive marbling[9] which suggests that it was portable. The top of the frame does have a number of nail holes in it of uncertain date. It should be noted that at the sale of 1804 there was a companion picture of a *Virgin and Child* painted on a gold ground.[10]

2787 is the last dated work of Simone and the only dated work extant from his Avignon period. It was painted in the year in which Pierre Roger de Beaufort (1291-1351) became Pope Clement VI, and in the year in which one of his nephews, also called Pierre Roger de Beaufort (1329-1378) was aged twelve, the age traditionally ascribed to Christ at the time of his discovery in the Temple. Clement VI created his nephew Cardinal at the very early age of 18, a creation which he justified at some length in the Sacred College.[11] This Cardinal later became Pope Gregory XI. In view of the subject matter of 2787, the first assertion of Christ's manhood, it is possible that it was commissioned by the Pope as a gift for his nephew.

Brink has pointed to the similarity in proportions between 2787 and other late works by Simone such as the Petrarch Virgil frontispiece and the Orsini polyptych and claims that they measure a root-two rectangle.[12]

Eng: George Scharf.[13]

Prov: Colonel Matthew Smith; his sale, Christie's 12 May 1804 (40) bt. Roscoe £5 5s 0d(?);[10] his sale (8) passed; presented to the L.R.I. by 1819;[14] deposited at the W.A.G., 1893; presented to the W.A.G., 1948.

Exh: Manchester, *Art Treasures*, 1857 (31); R.A., 1881 (225); New Gallery, 1894 (79).

Ref: **1.** Don Denny, *Simone Martini's The Holy Family*, Journal of the Warburg and Courtauld Institutes, XXX, 1967, pp. 140-3.   **2.** Denny, *op. cit.,* pp 143-5.   **3.** H. W. Van Os, *Marias Demut und Verherrlichung in der sienesischen Malerei*, 1300-1450, 1969, pp. 117-118 n. 130. It should be noted, however that Ubertino of Casale was chaplain to Napoleone Orsini and Brink argues that he was the source for the iconography of the Orsini polyptych *Simone Martini's Orsini Polyptych,* Jaarboek van het Koninklijk Museum voor Schonen Kunsten

Antwerpen, 1976, pp. 18-23.   **4.** Van Os, *op. cit.*, p. 118.   **5.** Denny, *op. cit.*, p. 138-9.   **6.** J. E. Brink, unpublished doctoral thesis, Art Department, John Hopkins University, Baltimore, Maryland. Photograph of proposed reconstruction in gallery files. Brink has subsequently dropped this hypothesis. Brink, *op. cit.*, p. 14 n. 7.   **7.** Henk Van Os—Marjan Rinkleff-Reinders, *De Reconstructie van Simone Martini's Zgn. Polyptiek van de Passie*, Nederlands Kunsthistorisch Jaarboek, 1972, p. 24-25.   **8.** Giovanni Paccagnini, *Simone Martini*, 1955, p. 110 The Antwerp *Crucifixion* is signed PINXIT, the *Descent from the Cross* SYMON.   **9.** Also noted by Julian Gardner, *Saint Louis of Toulouse, Robert of Anjou and Simone Martini,* Zeitschrift fur Kunstgeschichte, 1976. Heft I p. 12 n. 7. See also Julian Gardner, *The back of the panel of Christ Discovered in the Temple by Simone Martini*, to be published in Vol. 7 of the Annual Report and Bulletin of the Walker Art Gallery.   **10.** Seal of Col. Matthew Smith, his sale, Christie's 12 May 1804 lot 39 bt. Vernon. Lot 39 is described as "The Virgin and Child, painted on a gold ground," whereas lot 40 is described as "The Virgin, St. Joseph and Christ, the Companion." The latter would appear to be 2797, although the Christie marked sale catalogue notes that Roscoe bought the former for £5 5s 0d. and that the latter was bought by Vernon for £5 7s 6d. There appears to be an error, therefore, in either the catalogue numbering or more probably in the MS annotation. An alternative explanation is that Roscoe acquired 2787 from Vernon (who may have been the Liverpool dealer) after the sale, perhaps exchanging it for its companion. The latter may be the S. Memmi The Virgin and Child *a curious early specimen* in the sale of Woodburn, Christie 27 January 1809 (91) bt. W. £1 18s 0d possibly bt in.   **11.** Bernard Guillemain, *Le Cour Pontificale d'Avignon,* 1962, pp. 175, 188, 208 who states that no other Cardinal of this period was created at such an early age .   **12.** Brink, *op. cit.*, p. 7 note 1.   **13.** George Scharf, *On the Manchester Art-Treasures Exhibition, 1857,* 1858 (read 15 April 1858 to The Members of the Historic Society of Lancashire and Cheshire) between pp. 280 and 281, and E. Kugler, *Handbook of Paintings. The Italian Schools*, I. 1885, between pp. 156 and 157 woodcut signed GS.   **14.** 1819 Catalogue (4).

MARTINO, Eduardo de, 1838-1912

220   The Quay at Naples

Canvas, 40.5 × 26.6 cm

Signed and dated: *E. De Martino/86*

The view is taken from near Mergellina; in the distance is Pizzofalcone with the Theatine Church of S. Maria degli Angeli.

Prov: Bought by George Holt from the artist, 1886 (receipt, 8 November, with another picture, *The Maskelyne* at Lisbon, £62, MS W.A.G.); bequeathed by Emma Holt 1944.

MASTER OF THE AACHEN ALTARPIECE, active about 1480-1520

1225   Pilate washing his hands
(reverse) Mass of St. Gregory

1226 Lamentation over the dead Christ
(reverse) Two kneeling donors

Panels, 109.1 × 54.2 cm; 106.8 × 54 cm

Inscribed: (on the scabbard of the soldier right foreground of No. 1225): *EO HRM TX* (and on the pot held by the Magdalen in No. 1226): *AVE*

Two wings of an altarpiece the central panel of which is No. 1049 at the National Gallery, London.

In No. 1225 can be seen Pilate washing his hands with perhaps a self portrait of the artist looking over the shoulder of the soldier with the inscribed scabbard,[2] top left Christ mocked and the Flagellation, top centre the release of Barabbas (?), top right Christ presented to the people; in No. 1226 centre the Lamentation with left to right Mary Magdalen, one of the Holy Women, the Virgin, another Holy Woman, Nicodemus, Joseph of Arimathea and Christ supported by St. John, top left the Ascension and top right the Resurrection; on the reverse of No. 1225: the Mass of St. Gregory[3] with Christ as the Man of Sorrows surrounded with the Instruments of the Passion and on His right the Denial of St. Peter (?), on His left Judas Iscariot, Pilate, Caiaphas and between Pilate and Caiaphas an unidentified figure, perhaps Malchus, the servant of Caiaphas; on the reverse of No. 1226 the two donors Hermann Rinck and his wife Druitgin van Dalen.[4] Behind them are three younger male figures—perhaps their three sons.[5] This is the earliest portrait of any Burgermeister of Cologne.[6] Friedlander, Stange and most authorities date Nos. 1225-6 to just before the Aachen Altarpiece itself.[7] For Stange in particular Nos. 1225-6 are largely compilations of other artist's ideas.[8]

An area deeply burnt by a candle in the upper part of the reverse of No. 1225 has not been restored.

Prov: In the Parish Church of St. Kolumba, Cologne in 1806 with the central panel.[9] Acquired by the L.R.I. between 1836 and 1843;[10] deposited at the W.A.G. 1893; presented to the W.A.G. 1948.

Exh: Manchester, *Art Treasures*, 1857 Nos. 405-6. Leeds *National Exhibition*, 1868 No. 512a (No. 1225 only). R.A., *Winter Exhibition of Works by the Old Masters*, 1881 Nos. 228 and 231; New Gallery, London, *Winter Exhibition*, 1899 Nos. 19 and 248; Wallraf Richartz Museum Cologne, 1961 *Kolner Malerei der Spatgotik* Nos. 40B and 40C.

Ref: **1.** The connection and attribution were first made by Max Friedlander, *Die Leihausstellung der New Gallery in London*, Repertorium fur Kunstwissenschaft 1900, p. 258. The artist is named after a triptych with scenes from the Passion now in the Munsterschatz, Aachen (Kunsthalle, Cologne, *Herbst der Mittelalters*, *Spatgotik in Koln und am Niederrhein*, 1970, No. 36 p. 49). Theodor Rensing, *Der Meister des Aachener Altars*, Wallraf Richartz Jahrbuch, Vol. XXVI, 1964, pp. 229ff identified him with a certain Hermann Sotmann, a Cologne goldsmith but this hypothesis has not met with support—see John Jacob, *The Master of the Aachen Altarpiece, A Discovery*, Liverpool Bulletin Vol 11 1963-6, pp. 7ff and Fedja Anzelewsky, *Zum Problem des Meisters des Aachener Altars*, Wallraf Richartz Jahrbuch, Vol. XXX, 1968, pp. 185ff. who suggests an identification with an engraver, the Master PW, and Kunsthalle, Cologne 1970 *op. cit.*, p. 49. **2.** Friedlander, *op. cit.*, p. 118 and A. Stange, *Deutsche Malerei der Gotik,*

V, 1952, p. 118.   **3.** The Mass of St. Gregory, at which Christ is supposed to
have appeared to Pope Gregory the Great as he was celebrating Mass, was very
popular as a subject in the 15th and early 16th Centuries—see Louis Reau,
Iconographie de l'Art Chretien, 1958, III, II, pp. 614ff with many further references.   **4.** Franz Irsigler, *Hansekaufleute—Die Lubecker Veckinchusen und
die Kolner Rinck* in Kunsthalle Koln, *Hanse in Europa*, 1973, p. 327. They married in 1454 and he died in 1495. He was a leading merchant of Cologne—Burgermeister in 1480, 1483, 1488, Rentmeister in 1481 and 1482; for
full details see Irsigler, *op. cit.,* p. 324.   **5.** They had four sons, the youngest
was born in 1472; the eldest in 1458; the first to die did so in 1516; for full details
see Irsigler, *op. cit.,* p. 328.   **6.** Dr. Werner Schafke, *letter,* 7 April 1975.   **7.**
M. J. Friedlander, *Der Kolner Meister des Aachener Altars,* Wallraf Richartz
Jahrbuch, Vol. I, 1924, p. 102. Stange *op. cit.,* p. 118, Cologne 1961 Catalogue
cited under exhibitions; Kunsthalle Cologne 1970 *op. cit.,* p. 49, No. 36 the two
latter with many further references. The date of the Aachen Altarpiece itself is
more controversial; it dates perhaps from about 1505 suggesting that Nos.
1225-6 were painted well after the death of the donor Hermann Rinck. Their
purpose was presumably intercessionary; see particularly Emile Male, *L'art
religieux de la fin du moyen age en France,* 1908, pp. 96-7.   **8.** Stange, *op. cit.,*
pp. 118-9 with the fullest description of the style of Nos. 1225-6 and their relationship to the works of other artists particularly to the triptych by Dirck Baegert
also containing scenes from the Passion painted for the Church of St. Lawrence at
Cologne in 1489 and now at the Staatsgemaldesammlungen Munich Nos. WAF
223-4 and at Musees Royaux, Brussells, No. 1004.   **9.** Ludwig von Bullingen,
Urkunden, Inschriften und Notizen uber die Kirchen und Kapellen der Stadt Koln,
c. 1800, 2 Vols mentioned in *Kunstdenkmaler der Stadt Koln,* Vol. I, 1916 part 4,
p. 213 and preserved in the Stadt-Archiv Koln *Chroniken und Darstellungen* 181
and 182, especially 182a p. 330. I am indebted for this reference to Dr. Hans M.
Schmidt, letter, 19 July 1975. The Rinck Family were generous patrons of this
church in the late 15th Century see Irsigler, *op. cit.,* p. 325. The central panel was
brought from Flanders to England "at the time of the French Revolution," and
was later with an art dealer in Manchester from whom it was bought by a Mr.
Dixon, a merchant of Newcastle; it was bought from his executors by Edward
Shipperdson who presented it to the National Gallery 1847 (Michael Levey, *The
German School National Gallery Catalogues* 1959, p. 64); at what point the wings
were separated from the central panel is not known. The archiepiscopal see of
Cologne was left vacant in 1801 and not filled until 1821; presumably the triptych
left Cologne between these dates.   **10.** 1843 Catalogue, Nos 62 and 64.

MASTER OF APOLLO AND DAPHNE, late 15th century

2808   Susannah and the Elders

Panel, 58.5 × 163.2 cm

The panel illustrates the Apocryphal book of Susannah verses 15 to 22.
Susannah goes into the garden to bath, accompanied by her two maids
(centre); her maids go out by the side doors, having shut the garden doors
(right); the two elders appear from their hiding place, surprise Susannah
bathing and blackmail her (left).

No. 2808 almost certainly formed part of a large decorative ensemble
devoted to the story of Susannah, which included three panels in the
Walters Art Gallery, Baltimore, and a panel in the Yale University Art
Gallery with the young Daniel.[1] Schubring considered No. 2808 as a
'Sopraporta'.[2]

The artist is close to Bartolommeo di Giovanni, and like him is a follower of Domenico Ghirlandaio, influenced also by Botticelli.[1]

Zeri dates the series of paintings to the mid 1490's.[3] Another version of the story of Susannah from the workshop is in Chicago.[4]

Prov: William Graham, Christie's 8 April 1886, lot 238, bt. P. H. Rathbone, £36 15s 0d; who bequeathed it to the W.A.G., 1895, passing to the collection 1905.

Ref: 1. Everett Fahy, *The Master of Apollo and Daphne*, Museum Studies 3, 1968, pp. 21ff. and independently F. Zeri, see Fern Rusk Shapley, *Paintings from the Samuel H. Kress Collection Italian Schools XIII—XV Century*, 1966, pp. 129-130. A pair of panels in the Ryerson Collection, Chicago Art Institute representing the same story, are very closely connected in style, see also Everett Fahy, *Some followers of Domenico Ghirlandajo*, (Doctoral Thesis, Harvard University, 1968), 1976, pp. 11-17, 108-109 (16) who emphasizes the judicial character of the scheme and suggests that the series might have been a civic commission.   2. P. Schubring, *Cassoni*, 1915, p. 301, No. 350 as workshop of Ghirlandaio (?Cosimo Rosselli).   3. Federico Zeri, *Italian Pictures in the Walters Art Gallery*, I, 1976, p. 104.   4. Fahy, *op. cit.*, p. 36.

MASTER OF FORLI, early 14th century

3042   The Crucifixion

Panel, 53.6 × 34.4 cm; painted area 51.4 × 31.7 cm

Probably the right wing of a diptych[1] since there are traces of hinge marks on the left side of the panel. Garrison suggests as its companion a panel in the Hermitage (N6314) with the Agony in the Garden above and the Madonna with Saints Lucy and Catherine of Alexandria below.[2] Although that panel has traces of hinge marks on its right side, its measurements are not identical, and its back, unlike that of 3042 is painted with octagonal stars on a black field divided by squares.[3] Kermer suggests that the left wing was a Madonna enthroned.[4] Offner was the first to make the attribution, when the artist was known as the Master of the Griggs Spoliation.[5] Garrison dates it c. 1325,[6] a dating also accepted by Cuppini.[7]

˙ The composition with both the Virgin and Saint John on the left, whilst Saint Longinus is on the right, is rare.

Prov: Benson Rathbone, who presented it to the L.R.I., 21 December 1876;[8] deposited at the W.A.G., 1893;[9] presented to the W.A.G., 1948.

Ref: 1. Edward B. Garrison, *Italian Romanesque Panel Painting*, 1949, p. 102 (260).   2. Edward B. Garrison, *Il Maestro di Forli*, Rivista d'Arte, XXVI, 1950, p. 70. n. 7.   3. Letter of Tatiana Kustodieva, 20 November 1975.   4. W. Kermer, *Studien zum Diptychon in Sakralen Malerei*, 1967, part II, p. 66 (63) as c. 1325.   5. Evelyn Sandberg Vavala, *Italo-Byzantine Panels at Bologna*, Art in America, XVIII, 1929, pp. 83-84 cites Offner's opinion.   6. Garrison, *Italian Romanesque Panel Painting*, p. 102; Rivista d'Arte, 1950, p. 81; though pp. 60, 64 he gives a date c. 1300-1325.   7. Luciano Cuppini, *Aggiunte al Maestro di Forli e al Maestro di Faenza*, Rivista d'Arte, XXVII, 1951-2, p. 18. n. 2.   8. L.R.I. Archives 37.   9. 1893 Catalogue p. 3 (4).

MASTER OF FRANKFURT, 1460-about 1520

1020   Holy Family with Music Making Angels

Panel, 156.2 × 155.9 cm

The centre of an altarpiece[1] of which the wings *St. Catherine* and *St. Barbara* are now in the Mauritshuis.[2] Many versions exist of both wings and centrepiece;[3] the best but not necessarily the earliest is the triptych in the Museu Nacional de Arte Antiga, Lisbon No. CX116 generally attributed to Mabuse and dated about 1505.[4]

The monkey in the foreground presumably represents sin enchained by the incarnation.[5] The dress, particularly in the two wings, is closely related to contemporary theatrical costume.[6]

Prov: William Graham sold Christie's 8 April 1886 lot 12 bt. Rathbone; P. H. Rathbone who bequeathed it to the W.A.G. 1895, passed to the Gallery 1905.

Ref: 1. Max J. Friedlander, *Early Netherlandish Painting*, Vol. VII, 1971, p. 83, Supplement No. 118.   2. Netherlandish State Collection on loan to the Mauritshuis; Friedlander *op. cit.*, p. 77, No. 137. Dated by Friedlander *op. cit.*, p. 56 to about 1510.   3. See Michael Compton, *A Triptych by the Master of Frankfurt*, Liverpool Bulletin Vol. 7 No. 3, 1958-9 pp. 5ff.   4. Max J. Friedlander, *Die Altniederlandische Malerei*, 1930, Vol. VIII, pp. 29ff and 150 No. 1. A further pair of wings are in the Museo Cerralbo, Madrid, see Guias de los Museos de Espana, *Museo Cerralbo*, 1969, pp. 21-2, repr.   5. See E. Kirschbaum, *Lexikon der Christlichen Ikonographie* 1968, pp. 76ff.   6. Stella Mary Newton, *Renaissance Theatre Costume*, 1975, p. 228.

MASTER LD

821   Portrait of a Burgomaster

Panel, 75.6 × 59.7 cm

Signed: *LDFE/06*[1]

The dress suggests a date between 1610 and 1620.[2]

Prov: Purchased from J. R. Bell 1890.
Ref: 1. Noted about 1954, no longer visible.   2. Aileen Ribeiro, *letter*, 22 February 1973.

MASTER P.L.

1031   Harbour Scene

Panel, 23.1 × 32.8 cm

Signed *P.L.*

Probably by an unidentified follower of Matthys Schoevaerts or of

Boudewyns. The harbour appears to be Italian. Formally attributed to Lingelbach.

Prov: Arthur Earle; presented by Miss Lilian Earle 1942.

MASTER OF THE VIRGO INTER VIRGINES, active 1480-1495

1014   The Entombment[1]

Panel, 55.2 × 56.3 cm

On the left are the Virgin supported by St. John together with the two Holy Women, Mary Salome and Mary Cleophas; on the right supporting the dead Christ are Nicodemus and Joseph of Arimathea with Mary Magdalen holding her long hair. No. 1014 is regarded by Friedlander[2] as the most characteristic work by this artist and it is dated by him early in the artist's middle period[3]—presumably therefore about 1486.

No. 1014 is not painted up to the edges (painted area 53.8 × 52.9 cm).

Prov: Count Truchsess (the Truchsessian Gallery) sold Skinner, Dyke and Co. 24-26 April 1806 (43) £3 13s 6d.[4] Roscoe Sale lot 78 (as by Jan Van Eyck) bt. Mason £4; presented to the L.R.I. 1819; deposited at the W.A.G. 1893; presented to the W.A.G. 1948.
Exh: Manchester, *Art Treasures*, 1857, No. 443.
Ref: 1. As Max J. Friedlander, *Early Netherlandish Painting*, V, 1969, p. 39 says, the subject of No. 1014 is in fact "a moment between the Deposition and the Lamentation." The artist was very fond of this subject see Friedlander *op. cit.*, pp. 80-81, p. 90 and p. 98.   2. Friedlander, *op. cit.*, with long and detailed analysis of the painting.   3. Friedlander *op. cit.*, p. 43. K. G. Boon, *De Meester van de Virgo inter Virgines*, Oud Delft, n.d. pp. 17 and 31 seems to agree with this dating.   4. *Catalogue of the Truchsessian Picture Gallery*, 1803, p. 75 as by Israel van Mecheln with dimensions 1ft 8ins × 1ft 8ins. *Summary Catalogue of the Pictures etc, at the Truchsessian Gallery*, 1804, No. 802, p. 32 with the same attribution.

MATISSE, Henri, 1869-1954

6216   Le Pont

Canvas, 35.5 × 28 cm

Signed: *Henri Matisse*

Identified by Marguerite G. Duthuit, the artist's daughter, as *Viaduc d'Arcueil, near Paris* and dated by her to 1904.[1] In style No. 6216 appears a little earlier.

Prov: R. W. B. Maurice who sold it through Alex Reid and Lefevre to Paul Cross on 9 April 1943 (£295);[2] bought from the estate of G. G. O. Cross 1964.
Ref: **1.** *Letter* 6 May 1972. The viaduct spans the Valleé de la Bièvre (Seine).   **2.** G. S. Corcoran, *letter*, 28 October 1968.

MAYAN, Theophile Henri, born 1860

1532   Ajoncs en Fleur

Canvas, 66.6 × 101 cm

Signed: *Theo H. Mayan*

The view is taken from the banks of the Etang de Berre, Provence.[1] The artist regarded it as one of his best works.[2]

Prov: Purchased from the L.A.E., 1904 (£50).
Exh: Paris, *Société des Artistes Francais*, 1904 (1250), L.A.E., 1904 (350).
Ref: **1.** L.A.E. Catalogue (see exhibitions).   **2.** *Letter* 9 October 1912.

MAYER-MARTON, George, 1897-1960

3157   The Weir, Summerbridge

Canvas, 61.3 × 81.5 cm

Painted in 1952.[1] Summerbridge is three and a half miles south of Pately Bridge, West Yorkshire. A photograph of this subject, taken by the artist, is in the W.A.G.

Prov: Purchased from the artist, 1953.
Exh: W.A.G., 1953, *Liverpool Academy* (62); Agnew, 1955, *Walker Art Gallery Acquisitions*, 1945-55 (42); W.A.G. and Derby, 1961, *Memorial Exhibition* (19).
Ref: **1.** W.A.G. and Derby, 1961, *Memorial Exhibition* (19). The title and date appear in Mayer-Marton's MS workbook. Collection of Mrs. H. J. Braithwaite.

MAZONE, Giovanni, active 1453-1510, dead by 1512

2788   St. Mark enthroned between Saints Catherine and John the Baptist (left), Saints Paul and Giustina (right)

Panel, 123.2 × 175.3 cm (painted surface 121.5 × 174 cm)

The saints were first identified by Scharf.[1] Details such as the open coffered loggia and the tooling of the haloes link 2788 with Mazone's documented polyptych of the *Annunciation* in S. Maria di Castello, Genoa and the signed polyptych of the *Nativity* in Savona Pinacoteca Civica. Berenson was the first to suggest his name.[2] It would certainly seem to be an early work[3] and Castelnovi claims that it is his earliest known.[4]

St. Mark was the first bishop of Alexandria, the city that gave its name to Mazone's home town, Alessandria.

Prov: Joseph Brooks Yates,[5] who bought it for 80 guineas;[6] his sale, Winstanley's, 14 May 1857 (36); Samuel H. Thompson, who presented it to the L.R.I., 1857-8;[7] deposited at the W.A.G., 1893;[8] presented to the W.A.G., 1948.

Exh: Leeds, 1868 (10).

Ref: 1. MS notes on 1858 proof Catalogue (8) L.R.I.Archives 63.14).   2. Bernard Berenson, *Italian Pictures of the Renaissance*, 1932 p. 338.   3. R. Longhi, *Carlo Bracceso*, 1942 p. 25 note 25; Letter of Angelo Dalerba, 11 March 1969.   4. Gian Vittorio Castlenovi in *La Pittura a Genova e in Liguria*, 1970, p. 91.   5. Joseph Brooks Yates was travelling in Northern Italy for the first time in the spring of 1826 during which time he acquired some works of art. Roscoe Papers 343, 344, 2939.   6. J. B. Yates Sale Catalogue, 14 May 1857.   7. Annual Report 1857-8.   8. 1893 Catalogue p. 7 (13).

MAZZOTTA, Federico,[1] 19th century

729   A Mean Advantage

Canvas, 62 × 91.2 cm

Signed: *F. Mazzotta 1879*

Prov: Presented by William Preston, 1883.

Ref: 1. Listed in the 1963 Catalogue as Francesco.

MEIFREN, Eliseo, born 1859

2828 Pasajes, Guipuzcoa

Canvas, 80.7 × 101 cm

Signed: *E. Meifren*

Exhibited as *Night Pontevedra* at the Liverpool Autumn Exhibition[1] and acquired as such; No. 2828 in fact represents *Pasajes, Guipuzcoa*.[2]

Prov: Purchased from the L.A.E. 1908 (£100).

Exh: L.A.E. 1908 (341).

Ref: **1.** See exhibitions   **2.** No. 2828 is reproduced by Leonard Williams, *Eliseo Meifren, A Spanish Painter of Today*, The Studio, Vol. 40, 1907, p. 192 as *Pasages Guipuzcoa* and on p. 197 in the same article there is reproduced the same scene from a slightly different viewpoint with the same title. Jose Filgueira Valverde, *letter* 30 June 1971 confirms that No. 2828 does not represent a scene either in the city or province of Pontevedra and Isobel Cucurella Esteve, *letter* 15 October 1972 confirms that No. 2828 does represent *Pasajes*. A considerable number of Pontevedra scenes by Meifren do exist (see Williams *op. cit.*, or the *Pontevedra de noche, vista desde la Caeira* at the Seville Museum) and these were evidently confused with No. 2828.

MENGS, Anton Raphael, 1728-1779

1227   Self Portrait

Panel, 73.5 × 56.3 cm

Inscribed: (on the back) RITRATTO D'ANTONIO RAFFAELLO MENGS/FATTO DA LUI MEDESIMO PER LORD NASSAU[1] CONTE DI COWPER/IN FIRENZE L'ANNO 1774

Mengs was in Florence from the autumn of 1773 until the summer of 1774;[2] a portrait of the 3rd Earl Cowper also dates from this stay.[3] See also No. 1513 (by Zoffany).

The monochrome sketch partly visible in No. 1227 is related to Mengs' *Perseus and Andromeda*, now in the Hermitage, Leningrad No. 1328; No. 1227 provides evidence that this painting, finished in 1777,[4] was started as early as 1774 and indicates that it may also have been painted for Earl Cowper.[5] The head in No. 1227 is identical to the head in another *Self Portrait* of 1773 now in the Bayerische Staatsgemaldesammlungen, Munich, Inv. No. 1058. Many other similar self-portraits exist.

Prov: Listed in the Inventory of Pictures at Florence belonging to William 3rd Lord Cowper of about 1779 as No. 28 *Ritratto del Cavre MENGS FATTO DAL MEDMO;*[6] probably brought back to England in 1826 on the death of Earl Cowper's widow; seen at Panshanger by Miss M. L. Boyle in 1885;[7] by descent to Lady Desborough sold Christie's 16 October 1953 lot 92 bt. Agnew; purchased from Agnew by W.A.G., 1953.

Versions: Professor J. Singer, London, 1941, panel 69 × 58.5 cm, probably the picture in the Erzherzog Friedrich Sale, A. Kende, Vienna 8-10 Janurary 1933 lot 155, oil, 71 × 58 cm.

Ref   **1.** Earl Cowper claimed this title in 1777, see particularly *Horace Walpole's Correspondence*, ed Lewis, 1967, Vol. 24, pp. 298ff.   **2.** Dieter Honisch, *Anton Raphael Mengs*, 1965 p. 63.   **3.** Hermann Voss, *Die Malerei des Barock in Rom*, 1924, p. 659 as in the collection of Prince Corsini, Florence. See Honisch, *op. cit.*, p. 150 for references to sources. A version "from the Collection of Lord Cowper, Panshanger" was sold at Sotheby's 26 February 1958 lot 59 bt. Betts £65.   **4.** Honisch, *op. cit.*, p. 94, No. 104 and Giuseppe Niccola d'Azara, *Opere di Antonio Raffaelle Mengs*, 1780 p. XXXV.   **5.** *Perseus and Andromeda* was commissioned for England but was captured by the French on the journey home; see Honisch, *op. cit.*, and Giuseppe Niccola d'Azara, *Oeuvres Completes d'Antoine Raphael Mengs*, 1786 pp. 30-1, note by the translator H. Jansen for further details. Herbert von Einem, *Ein unveroffentliches Selbstbildnis von Anton Raphael Mengs etc.*, Wallraf-Richartz-Jahrbuch, Vol. 35, 1973, p. 350 states that it was painted for Cowper.   **6.** Denys Sutton, *Paintings at Firle Place*, The Connoisseur, 1956, p. 83 reproduces the inventory.   **7.** M. L. Boyle, *Biographical Catalogue of the Pictures at Panshanger*, 1885, p. 442.

E

MERLE, Hugues, 1823-1881

270   Girl with Fruit

Canvas, 81.3 × 65 cm

Prov: Bought from Agnew's by George Holt 1872 (bill Xmas, MS. W.A.G.), £472 10s
0d; bequeathed by Emma Holt 1944.
Exh: Liverpool Art Club, *Modern Oil Paintings by Foreign Artists*, 1884, No. 35.

MEULENER, Pieter, 1602-1654, follower of

2992   Battle Scene

Canvas transferred to panel, 33.7 × 77.7 cm

The attribution was suggested by Dr. F. Hutteman;[1] the signed *Cavalry Skirmish* at the National Gallery, Prague, No. 0-9823 has very similar figures and horses.

Prov: Transferred from the Liverpool Public Library 1932.
Ref: 1. *Letter*, 26 November, 1973.

MICHELANGELO Buonarotti, 1475-1564

2789   Christ and the Woman of Samaria

Panel (poplar), 77.7 × 69.2 cm

Condition: Poor, concern was expressed about its state in 1854.[1] The panel is split vertically roughly into thirds. A heavy brown varnish was applied to it at some date probably between 1859[2] and 1893,[3] since by the latter date its quality was no longer apparent and it no longer received much attention from scholars.

2789 is a bistre drawing of a highly finished character on gesso and a greenish brown ground giving it a similarity to a grisalle. Another panel associated with Michelangelo bearing a bistre drawing on a green prepared gesso ground is Ashmolean 278, *The Return of the Holy Family from Egypt*, which has a similar provenance.[4] This, however, unlike 2789 could be interpreted as an under-drawing for a painting. An engraving of 2789 (?) by Normand fils published in 1811[5] and an anonymous engraving published in 1857[6] both reveal a landscape background not visible in this century until cleaning was begun.

Michelangelo painted a *Woman of Samaria* for Vittoria Colonna between c. 1536/8 and 1542[7] after which there is a well known engraving by Nicolas Beatrizet[8] as well as several copies.[9] There are no known drawings by Michelangelo for the composition still extant.[10] The Biblical source for the subject is John IV 5-26.

Vittoria Colonna wrote a sonnet on *Christ and the Woman of Samaria at the well*,[11] of which de Tolnay interprets the significance as that "prayer should be made direct and not through the Church as intermediary."[12]

Roscoe assumed that his picture was the original painted for Vittoria Colonna and recorded by Vasari and stated that it had been in the collection of the King of Naples at Capo di Monte.[13] This latter statement was based on the second Ottley sale catalogue's description of 2789 as "the finished preparation for a picture, on board, from the collection of the King of Naples at Capo di Monte,"[14] a provenance that is also given in the 1801 sale catalogue.[15]

Waagen was the first to assert that 2789 is not by Michelangelo, although he remarked on its high quality.[16] Waagen's opinion was followed by Kugler,[17] Mrs. Jameson[18] and Scharf. The latter associated it with the famous copy of the *Battle of Cascina* by Aristotile da Sangallo at Holkham.[19] But others such as Thore-Burger[20] accepted it as a Michelangelo when it was shown in Manchester in 1857. Later opinion[21] was less favourable although de Tolnay regarded it in its uncleaned state as the closest of the copies to the Beatrizet engraving.[22] The style of 2789 is close to that of the *Crucifixion* in the British Museum, also once owned by Ottley and supposed to be the work Michelangelo did for Vittoria Colonna.[23]

Eng: Nicolas Beatrizet: Adam Ghisi; Mario Cartaro; Ferando Bertelli;[24] Antoine Lafrery;[25] C. P. Normand[26] and an anonymous engraver in 1857.[27]

Prov: King of Naples, Capo di Monte; William Young Ottley;[28] his sale, Christie, 16 May 1801 (7) bt. W. Young[29] 26 gns; Col. Crewe, Christie, 2 February 1811 (93) bt. Soloman £7 12s 0d or £8 12s 0d;[30] William Young Ottley, Christie 25 May 1811 (34) £8 15s 0d (purchaser illegible); William Roscoe sale (52) bt. Dr. T. S. Traill[31] £52 10 0d; presented to the L.R.I. by 1819;[32] presented to the W.A.G., 1955.

Exh: 118 Pall Mall, late the Milton Gallery, c. 1801 (52);[33] Manchester, *Art Treasures*, 1857 (184); Leeds, 1868 (95).

Ref: **1.** Letter from Philip Westcott to Theodore Rathbone, 24 January 1854 (L.R.I. Archives 17).   **2.** 1859 Catalogue p. 40 (69) as Michael Angelo.   **3.** L.R.I. Annual Report 1893 p. 53 (69) as after Michael Angelo.   **4.** Christopher Lloyd, *A Catalogue of the earlier Italian Paintings in the Ashmolean Museum*, 1977, pp. 116-119. A copy of the Last Judgement in chiaroscuro attributed to Marcello Venusti described as 'un dissegno in quadretto' or 'un quadro in carta disegno' is recorded as having been in the Aldobrandini Collection in the inventories of 1603, 1626 and 1682. Cesare d'Onofrio, *Inventario dei dipinti del Cardinal Pietro Aldobrandini compilato da G. B. Agucchi nel 1603*, II, Palatino, 1964, p. 162; Paolo della Pergola, *Gli inventari Aldobrandini*, Arte antica e moderna, 1960, p. 430 and Paolo della Pergola, *Gli inventari Aldobrandini: l'inventario del 1682*, Arteantica e moderna. 1962, p. 318. The famous Holkham Hall copy of the *Battle of Cascina* by Artistotile da Sangallo of 1542 is also 'in chiaroscuro'. But the handling is very different from 2789. Vasari ed. G. Milanesi, VI, pp. 433ff.   **5.** C. P. Landon, *Vies et oeuvres des peintres les plus celebres des toutes les écoles, Oeuvre de Michelange*, I, 1811, pl. XXXVIII.   **6.** *Art-Treasures Examiner*, 1857, p. 155.   **7.** Letter of 20 July 1542 from Vittoria Colonna to Michelangelo. Vittoria Colonna, *Carteggio*, raccolto e pubblicato da Ermanno Ferrero e Giuseppe Muller, 1892, pp. 268-269 see also Vasari, ed. G. Milanesi, VII, p. 275.   **8.** Maria Catelli Isola in *Fortuna di Michelangelo nell' incisione*, Benevento Museo del Sannio, 1964, pp. 68-69 (42) pl. 26 and Charles de Tolnay, *Michelangelo*, V, 1960, p. 133 note 27, fig. 334.   **9.** Henry Thode, *Michelangelo Kritische Untersuchungen uber seine Werke*, II, 1908, p. 464 gives the most complete list, which is supplemented by de Tolnay, *op. cit.*, p. 133 note 27 fig. 335-6. The painting listed in a Devonshire collection is in fact in the Devonshire Collection, Chatsworth and is probably by a Northern artist. Other copies include a painting once in the Watney Collection at Cornbury (Christie 23 June 1967 (36) 17 × 13¼" as Marcello Venusti), a painting once in the collection of Sir Arundell Neave Bt. (Sotheby 19 November 1975 (157)), a painting attributed to Sebastiano del Piombo, once at Alton Towers, now in the Houben Collection (letter of Dr. W. Houben 16 March 1969). and Christie. 14 January 1977 (77) Copper 36 × 26.5 cm, a copy after Beatrizet's engraving possibly by a Flemish artist.   **10.** Bernard Berenson, *The drawings of the Florentine Painters*, II, 1938, p. 162 note 2 wrongly connects a drawing of a hand on a sheet now in the Fitzwilliam Museum Cambridge with the composition. The drawing is discussed and reproduced in Luitpold Dussler, *Die Zeichnungen des Michelangelo*, 1959, pp. 49-50 (3) pl. 116.   **11.** Johann J. Wyss, *Vittoria Colonna Leben Wirken Werke*, Frauenfeld, 1916, p. 87 prints the sonnet, also printed by Domenico Tordi, *Sonetti inediti di Vittoria Colonna*, Rome, 1891, LXXXIX.   **12.** Charles de Tolnay, *Michelangelo Sculptor Painter Architect*, 1975, p. 111.   **13.** William Roscoe, *Life of Leo X*, III, 1827 p. 229 note *c*.   **14.** Christie, 25 May 1811 (34). Ottley interpreted the Ashmolean panel as forming part of a series of designs by Michelangelo of New Testament subjects including *Christ and the Samaritan Woman at the Well,* intended for the wide walls of the Sistine Chapel, *The Italian Schools of Design*, London, 1823, p. 31. Roscoe also owned a drawing attributed to Raphael of *the Madonna, Child, Saint Elizabeth and John*, which was previously in the Naples Royal Collection and Ottley's Collection, Roscoe sale, Winstanley, 24 September 1816 (168) bt. Esdaile £3 13s 6d.   **15.** Christie, 16 May 1801 (7). 1963 Catalogue p. 118 mistakenly interpreted the Ottley sale catalogue as meaning that a picture painted from 2789 had been in the Naples Royal Collection. 2789 probably did not pass directly from the Naples Royal Collection to Ottley in view of the statement in the catalogue of the exhibition at 118 Pall Mall referred to in note 33 below.   **16.** Gustav Waagen, *Works of Art and Artists in England*, III, 1838, p. 184 and *Treasures of Art in Great Britain*, III, 1854, p. 237 as "imbued in an unusual manner with the spirit of Michael Angelo and therefore certainly by one of his best scholars."   **17.** Franz Kugler, *Handbuch der Geschichte der Malerei seit Constantin dem Grossen*, (ed. Jacob Burckhardt), I, 1847, p. 538 and F. Kugler, (ed. Sir Charles L. Eastlake), *Handbook of Painting. The Italian Schools*, II, 1855, p. 309 as "by one of his best scholars."   **18.** 1859 Catalogue p. 40 (69).   **19.** 1859 Catalogue p. 41 (69) "remarkably bold in conception, but with the same peculiarities and faults as the famous *chiaroscuro* design from MICHAEL ANGELO'S Cartoon at Pisa—now at Holkham."   **20.** W. Burger, *Tresors d'art en Angleterre*, 1860, pp. 39-40.   **21.** L.R.I. Annual Report, 1893, p. 53 (69); Ernest Steinmann, *Die Sixtinische Kapelle*, II, 1905, p. 502, note 1; Thode, *op. cit.*, II, p. 464; de Tolnay, *op. cit.*, V, p. 133 note 27.   **22.** Charles de Tolnay, *letter*, 20 September, 1971.   **23.** Johannes Wilde, *Italian Drawings in the Department of Prints and Drawings in the British Museum Michelangelo and his studio*, London, 1953, pp. 106-7 (67) pl. CIII.   **24.** Thode, *op. cit.*, II, p. 464. Georges Duplessis, *Les Gravures de Michel-ange*, Revue universelle des arts, 22, 1865-1866, pp. 154-155 mentions two copies in reverse, one of which may be that mentioned by R. Duppa, *The Life of Michel Angelo Buonarotti with his poetry and letters*, 1807, pp. 326-327.   **25.** Landon, *op. cit.*, II, p. 3.   **26.** Landon, *op. cit.*, I, pl. XXXVIII. It is possible that Normand only had access to Beatrizet's engraving and not Michelangelo's picture.   **27.** *Art-Treasures Examiner*, 1857, p. 155.   **28.** W. Buchanan, *Memoirs of Painting*, II, 1824, p. 20 states that Ottley's collection was formed in Italy in 1798 and 1799 and that it was brought to England in 1800. Ottley in a letter to Miss Flaxman of December 18, 1826 (B.M.Add MS 39782 f. 223) states that his work on Italian art had begun at Rome as early as 1792.   **29.** Ottley was a grandson of Sir William Young (see Christie, 16 May 1801 (49) p. 10). Sir Richard Ottley, Chief Justice of Ceylon, married the daughter of Sir William Young, second baronet of Dominica (1749-1815) (see *Burkes Peerage, Baronetage and Knightage*, 1970, s.v. Young of North Dean). He may have been buying the pictures in at the sale. The Victoria and Albert Museum copy of the Catalogue appears to note an expected price in the range 30 guineas or pounds to 140 guineas or pounds. 2789 does not appear in the sale on Sir William Young's death, Coxe, 20 May 1802.   **20.** The prices given in marked sale catalogue differ.   **31.** A MS note at the front of E. K. Waterhouse's copy of Roscoe's sale catalogue states that Traill bought on behalf of Mr. Coke of Norfolk—that is Thomas Coke of Holkham Hall. If this is true,

Coke may have been persuaded to present 2789 to the L.R.I. **32.** 1819 Catalogue (19). **33.** *A Catalogue of Paintings from the Colonna, Borghese and Corsini Palaces &c &c., purchased in Rome in the years 1799 and 1800 now in exhibition and sale by private contract at No. 118 Pall Mall, late the Milton Gallery* (52) among pictures grouped under the heading "Under circumstances of the rapid changes of Property in Italy, it has not been possible to ascertain with accuracy the precise collections of which the following Pictures formed a part."

MIEREVELDT, Michiel, 1567-1641

2997   Portrait of Sir Edward Cecil, Viscount Wimbledon 1572-1638

Panel, 113.4 × 85 cm

Inscribed on the baton: *Chi non puol quel che vuol che puol*[1]

The head of No. 2997 is almost identical with that of Miereveldt's portrait inscribed and dated 1610 formerly in the royal collections and now owned by Mrs D. Yeats Brown,[2] and probably derives from the same sitting.

The sitter in No. 2997 was first identified by Cust;[3] hitherto No. 2997 had been described as a portrait of Sir Walter Raleigh.

The General's baton in No. 2997 suggests that No. 2997 certainly dates from after 1610 when Cecil was made a General and the costume suggests a date around 1610-1612.[4]

No. 2997 was formerly attributed to Paul van Somer, an attribution first suggested by Waagen.[5]

The sitter was the 3rd son of the 1st Earl of Exeter, served in the Netherlands 1596-1610, was treasurer to Queen Elizabeth of Bohemia 1613, commanded the Spanish expedition 1625, was made Viscount Wimbledon in 1626, commanded in Holland 1627-31 and was Governor of Portsmouth 1630-38.

Prov: (?)Edward Hyde, 1st Earl of Clarendon, by descent to the 3rd Earl and his son Lord Cornbury; Catherine Duchess of Queensbury and transferred to Amesbury 1786; Archibald Douglas, later 1st Baron Douglas and transferred 1818 to Bothwell Castle, Lanarkshire;[6] Lord Douglas sale Christie's 20 June 1919 lot 147 bt. Agnew £567; Lord Brassey at Apethorpe Hall by 1921; Apethorpe Hall sale October 1947 lot 1373 bt. Wheeler £130; Arthur Tooth from whom purchased 1947.

Ref: **1.** A misquotation from Giambattista Guarini's *Pastor Fido*, 1590, where Amarilli says "chi non può quel che vuol, quel che può, voglia" (Act 3, Scene 3). It is not listed among the mottoes in C. N. Elvin, *Handbook of Mottoes* 1860 or in Fairbairn's *Crests*. It means roughly: let that man that cannot do what he wants to do want to do what he can do. Its significance is unclear. **2.** So Dr. Malcolm Rogers (letter, 22 November 1976) of the National Portrait Gallery believes. The iconography of Sir Edward Cecil will be fully discussed in his forthcoming National Portrait Gallery Catalogue; he believes the elucidation in Charles Dalton, *Life and Times of General Edward Cecil*, 1885, Vol. 2 pp. 359-361 to be misleading.

Mrs. D. Yeats Brown's picture is noted in W. Bathoe, *A Catalogue of the Collection of Pictures etc. belonging to King James the Second*, 1758, No. 1011, p. 86, in the *Vertue Notebooks*, Vol. 1, Walpole Society, 1929-30 p. 54 as by Cornelius Johnson and in Horace Walpole, *Letters*, ed Toynbee, 1903-5 Vol. 4, p. 180.   **3.** Lionel Cust, *The Portraits of Sir Walter Raleigh*, Walpole Society, Vol. 8, 1920, p. 14.   **4.** Mrs. Stella Mary Newton, letter, 21 November 1961.   **5.** G. F. Waagen, *Treasures of Art*, 1857, Supplement, p. 464.   **6.** The provenance this far is derived from Cust *op. cit.*, Waagen *op. cit.*, Lady Theresa Lewis, *Lives of the Friends and Contemporaries of Lord Chancellor Clarendon*, 1852, Vol. 3 p. 250 and passim and *Diary of John Evelyn*, ed Bray, 1906, Vol. 3, pp. 435-6; it should be regarded as doubtful.

MIEREVELDT, Michiel, after

819   Christian, Duke of Brunswick

Panel, 66.6 × 56.7 cm

Identified by comparision with the engraving by Delff after Miereveldt of 1623.[1] The 1963 Catalogue suggested Wybrandt van der Geest as the artist of No. 819. Another version is now at Hardwick Hall, Derbyshire.[2] O. Millar believes that No. 819 may also be a version of the portrait of the Duke of Brunswick by Michael Johnson in the collection of Charles I.[3]

Prov: Stated to have been in the Aston Hall Sale[4] (Sir Arthur Ingram Aston sold Churton 6 August 1862) but not identifiable in the catalogue of that sale. H. Graves; Studley Martin sold Branch and Leete, Liverpool, 28 January 1889 lot 431. Angus Watson,[5] by descent to Miss Dalziell MacKay from whose estate it was purchased, 1947.

Ref: 1. F. W. H. Hollstein, *Dutch and Flemish Etchings, Engravings and Woodcuts*, Vol. V., p. 150. The original painting for the engraving is not at Hampton Court as stated by Hollstein (Oliver Millar, *letter*, 14 July 1975).   **2.** The National Trust, *Hardwick Hall, Biographical notes on the Portraits at Hardwick*, 1975, No. 45 there attributed to an unknown artist.   **3.** O. Millar, *Abraham van der Doort's Catalogue of the Collection of Charles I*, Walpole Society, Volume 37, 1958-1960, pp. 174, 234.   **4.** Branch and Leete Sale Catalogue.   **5.** According to the family of Miss Dalziell MacKay.

MOLENAER, Klaes, 1620-1676

874   The Village Festival

Panel, 72.7 × 107.7 cm

Signed: *K. Molenaer 1671*

The first old master painting purchased by the W.A.G.

Prov: William Duff.[1] John King of Renshaw Street from whom it was purchased 1880.

Ref: 1. William Duff lent *A Dutch Fair with a Mountebank* by Molenaer, identified in the catalogue as John Molinaer, to the *Exhibition of Old Master Paintings* at the Liverpool Royal Institution 1823, No. 24.

MOMPER, Jan de, early 18th century

835 Ruined Keep

Canvas, 40.6 × 72.7 cm

Attributed in the 1843 Catalogue to "John Momper—usually called Momperts of Italy", No. 835 is probably by the artist of at least some of the paintings assembled by Longhi and identified by him variously as Christian Reder,[1] Monsu X,[2] and finally as Jan de Momper.[3]

Prov: Acquired by the L.R.I. between 1836 and 1843, deposited at the W.A.G., 1893; presented to the W.A.G. 1948.

Exh: Central Museum, Utrecht, *Italianate Landscape Painters*, 1965 (151).

Ref: 1. *Monsu Bernardo*, Critica d'Arte, 1938, p. 130. 2. *Monsu X, Un Olandese in Barocco*, Paragone, 1954, No. 53, pp. 39ff. 3. *Chi era Monsu X*, Paragone, 1959, No. 109, pp. 65-6. As well as No. 835 the *Paesaggio*, No. 544 at the Galleria Doria Pamphili, Rome bears an old attribution to "Mompair" and is clearly by the artist assembled by Longhi (see Ettore Sestieri, *Catalogo della Galleria ex–fide–commissaria Doria Pamphili*, 1942, No. 544, p. 356 and Utrecht exhibition catalogue cited above). No. 53 in the Istituto Finanziario per l'Arte Milan, *Catalogo 61*, May 1969, there attributed to Momper is close to No. 835. W. G. Constable, *Richard Wilson*, 1953, pp. 83-4 also discusses the identity of the Momper who influenced Wilson, presumably also the artist assembled by Longhi; No. 835 has also been attributed to William Hodges, a pupil of Wilson (old label on frame).

MONET, Claude, 1840-1926

6133 Break-up of the ice on the Seine, near Bennecourt (Débâcle de la Seine, près Bennecourt)

Canvas, 65 × 100 cm

Signed: *Claude Monet*

The title is traditional[1] and the view in No. 6133 corresponds with the Seine just above Bennecourt.[2] Bennecourt is only 3 miles from Giverny where Monet lived from 1883.[3]

A date of 1893 for No. 6133 was first suggested by Douglas Cooper[4] relying largely on the *Debacle de la Seine a Giverny* (John A. Brown Collection, Baden) dated 1893 and *Neige et Glacons* (Private Collection, Paris) dated 1893 (or possibly 1895).[5] Monet was certainly painting thaw scenes in the winter of 1892-3 and on 24 January 1893 he wrote to Durand Ruel:[6] " . . . j'ai peiné tous ces temps derniers à peindres dehors malgre le grand froid, mais le dégel est arrivé trop tôt pour moi. N'ayant pas travaillé depuis si longtemps je n'ai fait que des mauvaises choses que j'ai dû detruire, et ce n'est qu' à la fin que je parvenais à m'y retrouver. Resultat; quatre ou cinq toiles seulement, et encore elles sont loin d'etre complètes, mais je ne désespère pas de pouvoir les reprendre" and he exhibited *Les Glacons (Bennecourt)* and *Effet d'hiver sur la Seine (Bennecourt)* in 1895.[7]

A *Paysage d'hiver a Bennecourt (Le Debacle)* nearly identical to No. 6133 was lot 142 in the Wormser Sale, American Art Association, New York, 16-19 January 1917, was later sold at Parke Bernet, 19-20 May, 1948, lot 86 (ex James F. Sutton Collection), and was later exhibited at the Marlborough Fine Art, London, *Selected European Masters* 1973 No. 48. A *Bennecourt,* signed and dated 1893 with the same view as in No. 6133 but with more included to the left was in the collection of Mrs. C. H. Tweed, New York.

Prov: With Durand Ruel early this century.[8] ?Georges Bernheim. Albert Pra sold Charpentier Paris 17 June 1938 lot 43,80,000 Fr; Georges Seligmann; Jacques Seligmann & Co; Mrs. M. Thompson-Biddle sold Charpentier Paris 14 June 1957 lot 26; Wildenstein from whom purchased 1962.

Exh: New York, Wildenstein, 1945, *Claude Monet* (35).

Ref: 1. It appears in the Pra Sale Catalogue (see provenance). 2. Visit to Bennecourt by Hugh Scrutton, 1964. 3. Monet had however been to Bennecourt in 1866; see Rudolph Walter, *Critique d'Art et Vérité; Emile Zola en 1868,* Gazette des Beaux Arts, Volume 73, 1969, pp. 225ff; Bennecourt had first been popularised by Daubigny; see also Rudolph Walter, *Cezanne à Bennecourt en 1866,* Gazette des Beaux Arts, Volume 59, 1962 pp. 103ff. and Claire Joyes, *Monet at Giverny,* 1975. 4. Letter, November 22 1962. 5. Reproduced in M. Matingue, *Claude Monet,* Monaco, 1943, p. 136 also a Bennecourt view according to Cooper, *op. cit.* 6. L. Venturi, *Les Archives de l'Impressionisme,* 1939, I, p. 348. 7. Galeries Durand Ruel, *Exposition de Tableaux de Claude Monet,* Paris 1895, Nos. 40 and 46. The catalogue states that No. 40, *Les Glacons Bennecourt* was then owned by Henri Vever, but it was in the care of M. Gillot of 79 rue Madame according to Monet's correspondence with Durand Ruel over this exhibition (published in Venturi, *op. cit.,* pp. 357-9); this correspondence also makes it plain that No. 46 *Effet d'hiver sur la Seine (Bennecourt)* was returned to the artist after the exhibition unsold. 8. No. 6133 is the subject of Durand Ruel photograph No. 11582. Comparison between this photograph and No. 6133 suggests that the latter has somewhat faded or been over-cleaned or that the paint has become more transparent.

MONNOYER, Jean-Baptiste, 1636-1699

180   Flower Piece

Canvas, 73 × 59.6 cm

The flowers represented include parrot tulips, peonies, stock, hyacinths, lilac, gentians, ipomoea, cornflower, and boraginaceae. Another version identical to No. 180 was in the Firmin Collection[1] and was last recorded in the possession of Messrs. W. Turner Lord & Co. of 19 Mount Street, London W1 (1928).[2]

No. 180 may be by a follower or imitator of Monnoyer.[3]

Prov: Given to George Holt by Miss Annie Archer[4] of 21 Mulgrave St., Liverpool, 1895, bequeathed by Emma Holt 1944.

Ref: 1. Photograph in the Witt Library, London. 2. A. E. Francis, Leggatt Brothers, *letter* 9 October 1970. 3. But it is accepted by S. H. Paviere, *Jean Baptiste Monnoyer,* 1966 No. 126, p. 25 (ill.). 4. George Holt, MS Catalogue, W.A.G.

MONTAGNA, Bartolomeo, before 1459-1523, Studio of

6369 St. Augustine

Canvas, 284.6 × 137.3 cm

6370 St. Bartholomew

Canvas, 284.6 × 137.3 cm

Both panels suffered deterioration as a result of bomb damage to the glass of Westminster Cathedral in the Second World War. Their state before and after their cleaning by Alfred Bartlett is recorded in the *Illustrated London News*, June 5, 1954, p. 573.

The internal faces of a pair of organ shutters from San Bartolomeo, Vicenza.[1] The external faces, with *The Annunciation* which became separated from 6369 and 6370 in the 19th Century, are now in New College, Oxford. The church of San Bartolomeo belonged to the Canonici Lateranensi, Augustinian Canons.[3] Hence the presence of St. Augustine.

Montagna executed several important paintings for San Bartolomeo, including the high altar piece.[4] The organ shutters may have formed part of a general campaign of decoration assigned to the Montagna workshop. 6369 and 6370 are first mentioned in 1779 without an attribution,[5] but throughout the 19th Century were assigned to Montagna. Berenson was the first to question this, giving the execution to Francesco da Ponte under the supervision of Montagna.[6] This connection, more recently supported by Puppi,[7] cannot be sustained[8] and was withdrawn by Berenson who gave the Saints to Montagna and *The Annunciation* to his pupil, Giovanni Speranza.[9] The style is close to Montagna's works of the first decade of the 16th Century. Notice for instance the simplification of forms and the gentle curvilinear insistence in the drapery of St. Augustine comparable to that of *San Biagio blessing* in the Cappella di San Biagio in S.S. Nazzaro e Celso, Verona, documented to 1504-1506.[10] The forms of the windows are reminiscent of those in the Panshanger *Madonna*.[11]

There is, however, a hesitancy in the drawing suggestive of studio responsibility for the execution. The hand is certainly distinct from that responsible for *The Annunciation*.

Prov: San Bartolomeo, Vicenza:[1] still in Vicenza, 1834;[12] no longer there in 1871;[13] Ricchetti, Venice;[14] ?Passaro, Venice;[15] G.A.F. Cavendish-Bentinck sale, Christie, 11 July 1891 (580 and 581) bt. Davis £78 15s 0d; Duke of Norfolk by 1894;[16] presented by him to Westminster Cathedral c. 1910; Sotheby's 6 July 1966 (33) bought in; purchased 1966 through Sotheby's from Westminster Cathedral with the aid of a contribution from the National Art-Collections Fund.

Exh: New Gallery, *Venetian Art*, 1894/5 (36) and (45).

Ref: 1. Count E. Arnaldi, *Descrizione delle Architetture, Pitture e Scolture di Vicenza . . .*, Mosca, I, Vicenza, 1779, p. 5 2. Bernard Berenson, *Italian Pictures of the Renaissance, Venetian School*, I, 1957, pl. 505. Both faces were copied in watercolours by Bartolomeo Bongiovanni dated 18 May 1834. Museo Civico Vicenza, D. 403-406. G. G. R. Radcliffe, *Dismembered Italian Masterpiece*, Country Life, CXI, 1952, p. 101. First noted by Antonio Magrini, *Elogio di Bartolomeo Montagna*, Atti dell 'Accademia di Belle Arti in Venezia dell' anno 1862, 1863, p. 39. The external panels were acquired in Venice or Verona during

131

the early 19th Century by E. C. Cheney and taken to Badger Hall, Bridgnorth. They were sold to New College, Oxford when the house was sold. *Illustrated London News*, June 5, 1954, p. 573.   **3.** Ottavio Bertotti Scamozzi, *Il Forestiere Istruito nelle cose . . . di Vicenza*, Vicenza, 1761, p. 108.   **4.** Lionello Puppi, *Bartolomeo Montagna*, 1962, pp. 136-8.   **5.** *Descrizione, op. cit.*, p. 5. noted by Tancred Borenius, *I Pittori di Vicenza 1480-1550*, 1912, p. 84, n. 1.   **6.** Bernard Berenson, *Venetian Paintings chiefly before Titian (at the exhibition of Venetian Art, New Gallery, 1895)*, republished in *The Study and Criticism of Italian Art*, 1901, p. 116.   **7.** Puppi, *op. cit.*, p. 167 and Lionello Puppi, *Giovanni Speranza*, Rivista dell' Istituto Nazionale d'Archeologia e Storia dell' Arte, 1963, pp. 408-9.   **8.** Michael Levey, *Two organ doors from S. Bartolomeo at Vicenza*, Burlington Magazine, XCVI, 1954, p. 181.   **9.** Berenson, *Italian Pictures*, *op. cit.*, I, pp. 117, 166.   **10.** G. Biadego, *La Cappella di S. Biagio nella Chiesa dei S.S. Nazzaro e Celso di Verona*, Nuovo Archivio Veneto, II, pl. 2, 1906, pp. 116-119.   **11.** Puppi, *op. cit.*, p. 167 fig. 119.   **12.** Since they are recorded in the watercolours by Bongiovanni dated May 18, 1834. A group of pictures from San Bartolomeo were deposited with the Comune of Vicenza in 1820 (Franco Barbieri, *Il Museo Civico di Vicenza Dipinti e Sculture dal XIV al XV secolo*, 1962, pp. 165, 169. According to E. Arslan, *Catalogo delle cose d'Arte e di Antichita d'Italia: Vicenza, I, Le Chiese*, 1956, pp. 5-6 the church was largely demolished in 1838, but an 1842 guide lists it as still standing and containing various works of art. *Il Forestiere Instruito nelle visita della R. Citta di Vicenza*, 1842, p. 27. A watercolour by Bongiovanni shows its interior appearance in the early 19th Century—Arslan, *op. cit.*, pl. II.   **13.** J. A. Crowe and G. B. Cavalcaselle, *A History of Painting in North Italy*, II, 1871, p. 435 note citing Magrini p. 39 and describing all four figures as missing.   **14.** Levey, *op. cit.*, p. 178 identifies the Ricchetti mentioned in the Cavendish Bentinck sale catalogue with a dealer active in Venice in the 1850's. Sir Charles Eastlake MS *Note-books* (National Gallery Library) 1854. (1) p. 8 and MS. *Diary of Otto Mundler* (National Gallery Library) I, p. 70 recto October, 23 and 31, 1854, p. 70 verso November 2, 1856. He is probably the seller of Venetian curiosities and objects of art and vertu, listed in Murray's *Handbook for Travellers in Northern Italy . . .*, 1860, p. 332; 1869, p. 377; 1873, p. 377 at the Palazzo Marcello, Canal Grande. He may be the dealer Consiglio Ricchetti who owned a number of Venetian pictures now in Boston, which he sold to Isabella Stewart Gardner in the 1890's. Philip Hendy, *European and American Paintings in the Isabella Stewart Gardner Museum*, *Boston*, 1974, pp. 32, 174, 277.   **14.** Levey, *op. cit.*, p. 178 identifies the Pajaro mentioned in the Cavendish Bentinck sale catalogue, with another Venetian dealer, Passaro.   **15.** New Gallery, *Venetian Art*, 1894 (36 and 45).

MONTAGNA, Bartolomeo, after

2776   St. Jerome in the desert

Panel, 55.2 × 68.8 cm

In the background is the Nativity.

A copy after the Montagna[1] in the Brera, Milan;[2] it is slightly larger than the original.[3] Some authorities have considered it as an autograph Montagna;[4] Berenson suggested that it is the work of Marcello Fogolino.[5]

Prov: Entered the L.R.I. between 1836 and 1843;[6] deposited at the W.A.G., 1893;[7] presented to the W.A.G., 1948.

Exh: New Gallery, London, 1894 (62).

Ref: 1. Fairfax Murray in L.R.I. Annual Report, 1893, p. 48 (36). 2. B. Berenson, *Venetian Painting chiefly before Titian,* Exhibition of Venetian Art, New Gallery, 1895; republished in *The Study and Criticism of Italian Art,* London, 1901, p. 110. Another copy was once in the Lanz Collection, Amsterdam. Hermann Nasse, *Gemalde aus der Sammlung des Univ-Professors Dr. Freih. Fr W. Von Bissing II,* Munchener Jahrbuch der Bildende Kunst, 6, 1911, pp. 110-112. 3. 51 × 58 cm. 4. A. Venturi, *Studi dal Vero,* Milan, 1927, pp. 252-3. 5. B. Berenson, *Italian Pictures of the Renaissance: Venetian School,* I, London 1957, p. 77 followed by Lionello Puppi, *Bartolommeo Montagna,* Venice 1962, p. 109, and in this author's *Marcello Fogolino,* Venice, 1966, p. 59. 6. 1843 Catalogue p. 13 (44). 7. 1893 Catalogue p. 14 (35).

MONTICELLI, Adolphe Joseph Thomas, 1824-1886

1126 Scene from Boccaccio

Panel, 40.5 × 59.3 cm

Signed: *A. Monticelli*

The 'A' of the signature suggests a date before 1859 but the style of No. 1126 would support a considerably later date.[1] The first of Monticelli's mature *Decameron* scenes seem to date from 1869.[2] Represented in No. 1126 are the seven women and three men who retired into the country from the plague in Florence to tell the stories of Boccaccio's *Decameron.*

Prov: Bequeathed by James Smith 1927.
Exh: W.A.G., *Jubilee Autumn Exhibition* 1922 (829).
Ref: 1. A. M. Alauzen, *letter,* 26 August 1971. 2. A. M. Alauzen and P. Ribert, *Monticelli, sa vie et son oeuvre,* 1969, fig. 162, p. 120 but see also fig. 48. p. 53.

1127 After the Cock Fight

Panel, 39 × 18 cm

Signed: *Monticelli*

Close in style to works of 1869—1870 but perhaps even later than the *Grand Combat de Coqs*[1]. at the Musee de Gap of 1880.

Prov: Bequeathed by James Smith 1927.
Ref: 1. A. M. Alauzen, *letter,* 26 August 1971. See A. M. Alauzen and P. Ribert, *Monticelli, sa vie et son oeuvre,* 1969, fig 309, p. 225.

1128 Ladies playing with Oranges

Panel, 33.2 × 61 cm

Signed: *Monticelli*

The eccentric signature and the vigour of style suggest a date around 1880.[1]

Prov: Probably bought from the artist by Alex Reid;[2] bought from Alex Reid in 1892 by James Smith who bequeathed it 1923.

Exh: W.A.G. *Jubilee Autumn Exhibition* 1922 (825).

Ref: 1. A. M. Alauzen, *letter,* 26 August 1971.   2. See footnote 2 of No. 1130 *The Door of a Mosque* by Monticelli.

1129   Ladies in a Garden

Panel, 38.7 × 61.7 cm

Close in style to works of 1869-70.[1]

Prov: Perhaps bought from W. B. Paterson 1896 by James Smith;[2] bequeathed by James Smith 1923.

Ref: 1. A. M. Alauzen *letter,* 26 August 1971.   2. MS note by Elizabeth Smith, his widow (W.A.G.).

1130   The Door of a Mosque

Canvas, 46.5 × 38 cm

Signed: *A. Monticelli*

The 'A' of the signature suggests a date before 1859.[1]

Prov: Probably bought by Alex Reid from the artist;[2] bought from Alex Reid in 1902 by James Smith who bequeathed it 1923.

Exh: W.A.G., *Jubilee Autumn Exhibition*, 1922 (795). Scottish Arts Council, *A Man of Influence*, *Alex Reid*, 1967 (34).

Ref: 1. A. M. Alauzen, *letter,* 26 August 1971.   2. Reid was buying pictures by Monticelli certainly in 1888, see *La Correspondance de Vincent Van Gogh*, 1960, letter 464, A. M. Alauzen and P. Ribert, *Monticelli, sa vie et son oeuvre*, 1969, pp 441—2 and Scottish Arts Council, cited under exhibitions.

MORO, Antonio, 1519-1575, after

827   Portrait of Anne van Buren

Panel, 48.5 × 35.5 cm

The sitter was the first wife of William of Orange. The original of 1555 is now lost but many other copies survive.

Prov: Bequeathed by Lord Wavertree 1933.

Ref: 1. R. van Luttervelt, *Een schilderij van Anna van Buren en andere portretten uit haar omgeving*, Oud Holland, Vol. 74, 1959, pp. 183ff.

MOSCOW, School of, 18th century

3046 Presentation of the Virgin in the Temple

Panel, 30.1 × 26.9 cm; painted area 22.2 × 20 cm.

Inscribed: on raised margin at the top, indecipherable inscription and above the head of St. Anne and St. Joachim *Saint Anne* and *Saint Joachim* (in Russian).

In the background an angel carries heavenly food to the Virgin Mary represented at a window against a gold background.[1]

The attribution is due to Talbot Rice.[2]

Prov: Mrs. E. L. Broadbent, from whom it was purchased, 1953.
Ref: 1. Icons showing this scene are in the Leningrad Russisches Museum, W. N. Lasarew in *Geschichte der Russischen Kunst*, II, 1958, p. 154 pl. 134 and a signed one by Theodore Pouliakis (?1622-1692) in San Giorgio dei Greci, Venice; Manolis Chatzidakis, *Icônes de Saint-Georges des Grecs et de la collection de l'Institut*, 1962, p. 144, n. 124 (88).   2. Professor D. Talbot Rice, notes, dated 21 March 1955.

MOSCOW, School of, 18th or 19th century

3050 Divine Wisdom

Inscribed: in Slavonic top left, *angels;* top right, *angels* ; top centre, *Jesus Christ*; centre above the figure of Divine Wisdom, *Virgin Soul*; above the Madonna, *Mother of God;* above St. John, *John*; on St. John's scroll undeciphered inscription.

Panel with a silver border attached; 36 × 31 cm, painted area 29.5 × 23.8 cm.

Meyendorff[1] has explained how the subject of the Divine Wisdom, originally derived from *Proverbs IX*, 1ff "Wisdom hath builded a house . . .", developed into a symbolic representation of the Logos or Word under the form of Wisdom incarnate enthroned in imperial dress. On her left stands the Madonna holding the image of her infant Son of the type Christ Emmanuel and on her right stands St. John the Baptist. The three principal figures thus form a Deesis. Above are the three persons of the Trinity, Christ blessing, the dove of the Holy Spirit, and the Father holding an orb, accompanied by groups of three angels either side of an altar or table.

Talbot Rice described 3050 as an Allegory of the Resurrection and attributes it to the School of Moscow in the 18th Century.[2] Demus prefers a later date[3] as did Mary Chamot.[4]

Prov: ?Purchased by William Archibald Propert in Petrograd;[5] Fine Art Society;[6] from whom purchased May 1917 for £26 5s by Lord Wavertree;[7] who bequeathed it to the W.A.G., 1933.

Exh: Fine Art Society, *Russian Icons*, 1917 (6).

Ref: **1.** Jean Meyendorff, *L'Iconographie de la Sagesse Divine dans la tradition Byzantine*, Cahiers Archéologiques, X, 1959, pp. 259-277.   **2.** Professor D. Talbot Rice, notes dated 21 March 1955.   **3.** Professor O. Demus, notes dated 21 March 1955.   **4.** Hove Museum of Fine Art, 1961 *Russian Life and Art* (34).   **5.** Letter of Peyton Skipworth 22 April 1976, who quotes the minute book of the Board of Directors of the Fine Art Society for 8 December "Russian Ikons: it was reported that a sum of £100 had been telegraphed to Mr. W. E. Propert at Petrograd upon receipt of a letter from him that he could usefully employ the same in the purchase of old Russian Ikons" W. A. Propert was a Director of the Fine Art Society from 1909 to 1919.   **6.** MS Label on back Fine Art Society/No. 6.   **7.** Letter of S. F. Growse, 27 August 1959.

MOSTAERT, Jan, about 1475-1555/6

1018   Portrait of a Young Man

Panel, 96.6 × 73.7 cm

The attribution was first suggested by Gluck[1] and established by Friedlander[2] who implies that No. 1018 is a mature work.

In the background is the *Conversion of St. Hubert.*[3] A *Portrait of a Woman* by Mostaert now in the Rijksmuseum (Inv. No. 1674A1) also has this subject in the background and both sitters may have belonged to a confraternity dedicated to St. Hubert. This seems more likely than that St. Hubert was the "name Saint" of the sitter as suggested by Friedlander.[4] The *Portrait of a Man* No. 538 at the Musees Royaux des Beaux Arts, Brussells by Mostaert has the same costume as No. 1018—perhaps it was a uniform of some sort.[5]

Prov: Griffier Fagel (of The Hague);[6] Henry Fagel sold Phillips 15 March 1813 lot 41 as by Lucas van Leyden bt. Emerson £29 8s 0d. Roscoe Sale 1816 lot 149 bt. Crompton £48 6s 0d; presented to the L.R.I. 1819; deposited at the W.A.G. 1893; presented to the W.A.G. 1948.

Exh: Manchester, *Art Treasures*, 1857 No. 452. Leeds, *National Exhibition*, 1868, No. 519. New Gallery, London, *Winter Exhibition* 1899 No. 91. Royal Academy, *Flemish Art*, 1927 No. 119.

Ref: **1.** G. Gluck, *Zeitschrift fur bildende Kunst,* 1896, Vol. VII, pp. 265 ff.   **2.** Max J. Friedlander, *Die Altniederlandische Malerei*, 1934, Vol. X, p. 123 No. 38.   **3.** By the 15th Century the story of the conversion as in No. 1018 had become attached to both St. Eustace and St. Hubert; Durer called his engraving of about 1501, on which No. 1018 to some extent depends, *The Conversion of St. Eustace* but No. 1018 does probably represent St. Hubert who was especially venerated in the Netherlands, see E. van Heurck, *Saint Hubert et son culte en Belgique*, 1925 and Dom Rejalot *Le culte et les reliques de S. Hubert*, 1928. For further details of the iconography see Erwin Panofsky, *Durer's St. Eustace*, Record of the Art Museum, Princeton University, Vol. IX, No. 1, 1950, pp. 2-10.   **4.** Friedlander, *op. cit.*   **5.** Mrs. S. M. Newton, letter 15 May 1975, suggests that both sitters may have been "city councillors or regents of charitable organizations or perhaps both." G. J. Hoogewerff *De Noord Nederlandsche Schilderkunst*, 1937, Vol 2, p. 468 however describes the sitter as a young nobleman.   **6.** For this collection see W. Buchanan *Memoirs of Painting*, 1824, Vol. 1, pp. 297ff.

MOUCHERON, Frederick de, 1633-1686, Studio of

867   The Two Bridges

Canvas, 87.3 × 110.8 cm

Presented to the L.R.I. as by Moucheron[1] and accepted as such by Waagen,[2] No. 867 seems on grounds of quality to be from the artist's studio.[3]

Prov: Presented by Richard Rathbone to the L.R.I. between 1836 and 1843; deposited at the W.A.G., 1893; presented to the W.A.G., 1948.
Ref: 1. 1843 Catalogue No. 95.   2. G. F. Waagen, *Art Treasures*,1854, III, p. 240.   3. 1963 Catalogue p. 125.

MULLER, Charles Louis Lucien, 1815-1892, after

754   Roll Call of the Last Victims of the Terror

Canvas, 105.5 × 195.5 cm

A copy after the painting of 1851 at the Musée National de Versailles (No. MV 6327). The colours in No. 754 do not correspond with those of the original.[1] It may therefore have been copied from one of the numerous engravings after the original.[2]

Prov: Bequeathed by Mrs. E. E. Cubbin, 1955.
Ref: 1. J. Vilain, *letter*, 4 October 1972.   2. There is an etching by Edmond Hedouin, and an engraving by M. A. Riffaut appeared in *L'Artiste*, serie 5, tome 5, 1851, p. 241. The original painting was lavishly praised in the *Athenaeum*, 1851, p. 359, while at the Salon, and a version(?) was exhibited at the French Gallery, London 1860 (164).

MURILLO, Bartolome Esteban, 1618-1682

1351   Virgin and Child in Glory

Canvas, arched top, 236 × 169 cm

Dated by Mayer to between 1665 and 1675[1] and identified in the 1963 Catalogue[2] with an altarpiece painted in 1673.

The central upper part of No. 1351, including the upper part of the Virgin and all of the Child, was cut out in 1810-1812 and then re-united with the original canvas in 1862-3 by Pinti, a restorer at the National Gallery, London.[3]

There is a sketch or copy in the Loyd Collection.[4]

Prov: Possibly the altarpiece in the lower oratory of the Seville Archiepiscopal Palace commissioned by Archbishop Don Ambrosio Spinola in 1673 at a price of 1000 ducats.[5] No. 1351 was removed from this or another building in Seville by Marshal Soult during his occupation of Seville 1810-1812;[6] the original central upper part of No. 1351, including the upper part of the Virgin and all of the Child, was cut out in Seville either by thieves or at the orders of Soult,[7] —or had it already been cut out? see footnote 5—then sent to Paris but lost on the way there to the English perhaps after the Battle of Vitoria in 1813;[8] by 1824 it was in the collection of Edward Gray of Harringhay[9] and in 1838 it was bought by Lord Overstone;[10] the rest of the picture was successfully sent to Paris by Soult presumably in about 1813 and there a new central upper part, copying the then lost original, was painted by Louis Francois Lejeune and inserted into the original canvas at the orders of Soult;[11] W. Buchanan tried to sell the painting, now with Lejeune's copy inserted, on behalf of Soult to the British Government in 1823-4 without success;[12] it was bought in at 5,000 francs at Soult's Sale in 1852;[13] Lord Overstone, by now the owner of the original fragment cut out in 1810-1812, tried to buy Soult's painting in 1855 through Otto Mundler and eventually succeeded in buying it through Sir Charles Eastlake in 1862 from Soult's heirs the Duc de Dalmatie and the Marquis de Morny;[14] the two original parts of the canvas, now both owned by Lord Overstone were reunited in 1862 by Pinti, a restorer at the National Gallery;[15] by descent to Lord Wantage, Lady Wantage, A. T. Loyd, C. Loyd; presented by the National Art-Collections Fund 1953.

Engr: Hardouin Coussin before 1760.[16] J. M. Leroux 1845. Maggi.

Exh: British Institution 1863 (1); Royal Academy 1885 (164); Birmingham City Art Gallery, *Paintings and Tapestries from Lockinge House, Wantage* 1945 (24).

Ref: **1.** A. L. Mayer, *Murillo*, 1913, pp. 171 and 288.   **2.** p. 126, for further details see *Provenance*.   **3.** For further details see *Provenance*.   **4.** *The Loyd Collection of Paintings and Drawings*, 1967, No. 47, p. 31. It was also formerly owned by Edward Gray of Harringhay see *Provenance*.   **5.** Cean Bermudez, *Diccionario Historico* 1800, II. p. 62 described this altarpiece as a "Virgen con el nino de cuerpo entero" with a "gracioso trono de angeles" but Soult in 1810-12, who certainly used Bermudez's *Diccionario* (see below) would also have read there (*op. cit.*) that the upper central portion of that altarpiece—including the upper part of the Virgin and all of the Child—had already been cut out and a new spurious copy substituted.   **6.** W. Buchanan, *Memoirs of Painting*, 1824 I, pp. 346 and 349.L. B. Curtis, *Velazquez and Murillo*, 1883, p. 149, No. 79. Mayer *op. cit.*, I. H. Lipschutz, *Spanish Painting and the French Romantics* 1972, p. 37 with many further references. For further details of Soult's confiscations see Richard Ford, *Handbook for Travellers in Spain,* 1855 Vol. 1, pp. 180 and 190 and Conde de Toreno, *Historia del Levantamiento, Guerra y Revolucion de Espana* 1872, pp. 239ff. No. 1351 is not however listed in M. Gomez Imaz, *Inventario de los Cuadros sustraidos por el Gobierno intruso en Sevilla,* 1917.   **7.** Buchanan, *op. cit.*, The *Catalogue Raisonne des Tableaux de la Galerie de feu M. le Marechal General Soult dont la vente aura lieu à Paris dans l'ancienne galerie Lebrun . . .19, 21, 22 Mai 1852*, p. 20, No. 59 states that robbers broke into the place where the picture was being stored and cut out the upper central portion and Curtis, *op. cit.*, charitably, also adopts this explanation but implies that the cutting out took place after Soult had first removed the picture. G. Redford, *Descriptive Catalogue of the Pictures at Lockinge House,* 1875, No. 1 exonerates Soult completely but G. F. Waagen, *Galleries and Cabinets of Art in Great Britain*, 1857 Supplement p. 140 blames "a French Officer" but Mayer, *op. cit.*, and Lipschutz, *op. cit.*, blame Soult who cut out this portion, apparently, because the whole picture would have taken too long to transport to Paris.   **8.** Lipschutz, *op. cit.*   **9.** Buchanan, *op. cit.*, p. 349 or at least he knew where it was in 1824. Soult had apparently tried to recover it, see Mayer, *op. cit.*   **10.** A. G. Temple, *Catalogue of Pictures forming the Collection of Lord and Lady Wantage*, 1905, No. 152, pp. 104-5.   **11.** Curtis, *op. cit.* For Lejeune and his copy see No. 1352, p. 139 in this catalogue and Lipschutz, *op. cit.*   **12.** Buchanan, *op. cit.*, pp. 43-4.   **13.** Soult Sale Catalogue 22 May lot 59. Unsuccessful attempts were made to try to persuade Lord Overstone to buy the picture at this sale see *The Athenaeum*, 1852, pp. 609-10. For Soult's earlier attempts to sell his collection see Ary Scheffer's letter of 16 April 1835 quoted in Marthe Kolb, *Ary Scheffer et son temps,* 1937, pp. 167-8. For the influence on French painting of Soult's paintings see Lipschutz, *op. cit.,* passim.   **14.** Temple, *op. cit.,*   **15.** Temple, *op. cit.*   **16.** According to Temple *op. cit.,* but the compiler has not found an impression.

MURILLO, Bartolome Esteban, after

1352 Virgin and Child

Canvas, 89 × 66 cm set into a rectangle 104 × 82 cm

Commissioned by Marshall Soult to replace the cut out upper centre part of No. 1351. The copyist responsible for No. 1352 who used an engraving, probably the one by Hardouin Coussin, if it existed, was a Monsieur Le Jeune.[2] He is probably to be identified with Louis Francois Lejeune, general and artist, who knew Soult in Seville 1810-1812[3] when the picture was removed by Soult. No. 1352 was removed from No. 1351 when the original upper centre part was restored to it in 1862-3.[4]

Prov: Marshall Soult; Lord Overstone; by descent to C. Loyd; presented by the National Art Collections Fund 1953.

Exh: Birmingham City Art Gallery, *Paintings and Tapestries from Lockinge House, Wantage*, 1945 (25).

Ref: 1. See no. 1351 p. 138 in this catalogue.   2: (G. Redford) *Descriptive Catalogue of the Pictures at Lockinge House*, 1875 No. 1. L. B. Curtis, *Velazquez and Murillo*, 1883, p. 149 No. 79 gives no further details.   3. Louis Francois Lejeune, *Memoires*, II, 1895, p. 84. This identification is confirmed by I. H. Lipschutz, *Spanish Paintings and the French Romantics*, 1972, p. 37.   4. For further details see No. 1351 p. 138 in this catalogue.

NEAPOLITAN School, 17th century

119 Joseph Embracing his Father and Benjamin

Canvas, 133.4 × 181 cm

120 Joseph Taken into Egypt

Canvas, 132.4 × 180.5 cm

Both were originally attributed to Luca Giordano.[1] For No. 119 this attribution is rejected by Ferrari and Scavizzi.[2] No. 119 is taken from Genesis XLVI, 29,[3] No. 120 from Genesis XXXVII, 28.

Prov: Presented by John George Woodhouse, 1876.

Ref: 1. 1882 Catalogue Nos. 98 and 100.   2. Oreste Ferrari and Giuseppe Scavizzi, *Luca Giordano*, II, 1966, p. 293.   3. See also A. Pigler, *Barockthemen*, 1956, I, p. 88.

2865 Portrait of a General

Canvas, 128 × 90.3 cm

Purchased by William Noel Hill, 3rd Lord Berwick in Naples,[1] No. 2865 has been attributed to Velazquez[2] and to Carlo Maratti.[3] The costume suggests a date around 1670.[4] Thomas Winstanley described the sitter as a Spanish General.[5]

Prov: Purchased by Lord Berwick in Naples probably in 1824-1833;[6] probably sold Christie's 1 December 1827 lot 109 *Portrait of a Spanish General* by Velazquez probably bought in £17 6s 6d; presented by Thomas Winstanley to the L.R.I. 25 June 1842; deposited at the W.A.G., 1893; presented to the W.A.G., 1948.

Exh: Liverpool Mechanics Institution, *1st Exhibition of Objects Illustrative of the Fine Arts etc.*, 1840 (51) as *Portrait of a Spanish General* by Velazquez.

Ref: **1.** 1843 Catalogue No. 101.   **2.** The 1843 Catalogue, *op. cit.*, says: "From the collection of Lord Berwick who purchased it at Naples where it was said to be by Velazquez."   **3.** 1963 Catalogue p. 102.   **4.** Aileen Ribeiro, *letter*, 22 February 1973.   **5.** Minute Book, Gallery of Art Committee, L.R.I. Archives 41.   **6.** See footnote 1; Lord Berwick was British Ambassador in Naples 1824-1833.

NEAPOLITAN School, 18th century

3420   Adoration of the Magi

Canvas, 180.5 × 261.7 cm

Attributed since its entry into the Collection to Luca Giordano[1] but Ferrari and Scavizzi[2] state that No. 3420 is by a Neapolitan artist, between Giordano and Solimena, working at the beginning of the 18th Century.

Another *Adoration of the Magi* attributed to Giordano is at Hampton Court.[3]

No. 3420 contains many pentimenti; the central King's pose has been altered and a large column painted out in the right centre.

Prov: Presented by Horace Collins 1908.
Exh: W.A.G., *Cleaned Pictures*, 1955 (32).
Ref: **1.** 1928 Catalogue, p. 60.   **2.** Oreste Ferrari and Giuseppe Scavizzi, *Luca Giordano*, Vol. II, 1966, p. 293,   **3.** See M. Levey, *Pictures in the Royal Collection, The Later Italian Pictures*, 1964, No. 514, p. 83 with further references.

NERI di Bicci, 1419-1491

2790   Virgin and Child enthroned with Saints Mary Magdalen, John the Evangelist, Paul and Barbara

Panel, 88.8 × 92.7 cm

Berenson first pointed out that the elderly bearded saint writing in a book is St. John the Evangelist.[1]

A characteristic work, already attributed to Neri di Bicci in 1879.[2] Santi dates it considerably later than 1475, the year which concludes the painters's diary.[3]

Prov: Seal on the back inscribed DA ... OBA COLLI (perhaps a customs stamp); Kenneth Muir Mackenzie;[2] his father-in-law, William Graham; his sale, Christie, 8 April 1886 (204) bt. P. H. Rathbone £24 13s 6d; P. H. Rathbone, who bequeathed it to the Gallery, 1895; passed to the collection, 1905.

Exh: Nottingham Castle, 1879-1886.[2]

Ref: **1.** Bernard Berenson, *Italian Pictures of the Renaissance, Florentine School*, I, 1963, p. 155.   **2.** Midland Counties Art Museum, City of Nottingham Museum, Loan Ledger, (79).   **3.** Bruno Santi, *letter*, 9 October 1967.

NETHERLANDISH School, late 15th century

1186 Christ Nailed to the Cross

Panel, 68 × 59.7 cm

Apparently cut at the sides and certainly painted right up to the edges. The shape suggests that it was part of a large composite altarpiece. The prominent standing figure at the left holding a staff is probably Pilate.[1]

Attributed by K. G. Boon to the Master of the Jesse Tree in the Buurkerk, Utrecht, an artist working in Utrecht between 1455 and 1470 who may have been Hillebrandt van Rewijk.[2]

Prov: Acquired by the L.R.I. by 1819 as an early German picture;[3] deposited at the W.A.G., 1942; presented to the W.A.G., 1948.

Ref: **1.** John XIX, 19 states that Pilate was present at the Crucifixion; he is certainly there in the *Diptych with Scenes from the Passion*, Dutch School 15th Century, No. 16 at the Royal Academy *Dutch Pictures 1450-1750*.   **2.** K. G. Boon, *Een Utrechtse schilde uit de 15 de eeuw de Meester van de Boom van Jesse in de Buurkerk*, Oud Holland, 1962, p. 51ff.   **3.** 1819 Catalogue No. 17. No. 1186 cannot be identified in the Roscoe 1816 Sale Catalogue but all the paintings in the 1819 Catalogue are there stated to have come from William Roscoe's Collection.

NETHERLANDISH School, about 1500

833 Virgin and Child with St. Anne

Panel, 34.8 × 21 cm

Attributed in 1958 to the Master of Alkmaar[1] and in the 1963

Catalogue to the School of Haarlem, No. 833 is of a type common in the Netherlands in the 15th and early 16th Centuries.[2]

The top 3.5 cm of the panel is a modern addition. The panel is painted right up to the edge all round except at the top.

Prov: Presented to the L.R.I. by Thomas Winstanley 8 December 1823;[3] deposited at the W.A.G., 1942; presented to the W.A.G., 1948.

Ref: **1.** Rijksmuseum, Amsterdam, *Middeleeuwse Kunst der Noordelijke Nederlanden*, 1958, No. 93, p. 91.   **2.** The earliest example appears to have been Fol. 333b in the Breviary of Philip the Good (Bibliotheque royale, Brussels, No. 9026) reproduced in Abbe Victor Leroquais, *Le Brevaire de Philippe le Bon*, 1929, II, plate XIII and attributed by Leroquais to the studio of Guillaume Vrelant in about 1450 (Otto Pacht, *verbally*, 1959). Another later example very close to No. 833 was No. 6 at Colnaghi, *Paintings by Old Masters*, 1959, attributed to the Master of Alkmaar and later owned by Mrs. R. Popham.   **3.** *Correspondence and Papers relating to Gifts and Deposits at the Liverpool Royal Institution*, L.R.I. Archives 61.21.

1021   Rest on the Flight into Egypt

Panel, 81.4 × 59 cm

One of a number of Netherlandish variants, the best though perhaps not the first of which is probably the *Virgin and Child with St. Barbara and St. Catherine* (No. 58.196) at the Museum of the Rhode Island School of Design, Providence, after a lost Italian, probably Lombard original of about 1500. The background in No. 1021 with the figure of St. Joseph is not found in any of the other variants.[1]

The story of the palm tree bending down for St. Joseph is taken either from Chapters 20-21 of the Gospel of the Pseudo St. Matthew or from the Golden Legend.[2] The foreground flowers are the iris for royalty and the columbine for the Holy Ghost.[3]

Prov: ?The Property of three distinguished families in Sicily recently consigned from the Mediterranean sold Christie's 12 May 1810 lot 5 *Virgin holding the Infant Christ and seated in a luxuriant landscape; St. Joseph in the background gathering fruit* by A. Durer Roscoe Sale lot 20 bt. Ballantyne £37 16s 0d; presented to the L.R.I. 1819; deposited at the W.A.G. 1893; presented to the W.A.G. 1948.

Exh: Manchester, *Art Treasures*, 1857, No. 505. Leeds *National Exhibition*, 1868, No. 518. New Gallery, London, *Winter Exhibition*, 1899, No. 76.

Ref: **1.** The most extensive discussion of this composition and list of variants is H. Pauwels, *Een nieuwe toeschrijving aan Ambrosius Benson*, Federation des Cercles d'Archeologie et d'Histoire de Belgique, Annales 43rd Congress, Sint Niklaas, 1974, pp. 291ff who attributes the *Virgin and Child with St. Barbara and St. Catherine* at Providence to Ambrosius Benson and who suggests that No. 1021 is by the same artist as the *Virgin and Child with St. Barbara,* yet another variant and now at the Mittelrhein Museum, Koblenz (Inv. No. M16 see E. Schaar, *Niederlandische Meister, Kataloghefte des Mittelrhein-Museums Koblenz,* I, 1968, p. 26). The variant at the Accademia Carrara, Bergamo, No. 330, is signed by Bernardino de Conti and is dated 1501. Wilhelm Suida, *Leonardo und sein Kreis*, 1929, p. 272 identifies the Italian original as a work of Leonardo of before 1499. Other versions are also listed by J. A. Crowe and G. B. Cavalcaselle, *History of Painting in North Italy*, 1912, II, p. 394 in H. Bodmer, *Leonardo, Klassiker der Kunst*, 1931, p. 373 and in the 1963 Catalogue pp. 92-3.   **2.** Ed. Ryan and Ripperger, 1941, p. 66.   **3.** Elizabeth Haig, *Floral Symbolism of the Great Masters*, 1913, pp. 31, 168 and 198.

NETHERLANDISH School, early 16th century

873   Martyrdom of St. Lawrence

Panel, ogee arched top, 90.2 × 64.9 cm

Severely damaged; a new strip ¼ in wide was inserted down the centre of the panel from top to bottom running through the judge's staff, the back of the dog and the groin of the saint; lacunae in the landscape and in the judge's hat have been filled in; the faces of the evil looking figures had been defaced.

Probably by an Antwerp Mannerist working in the first quarter of the 16th Century.[1]

Prov: Sold by Winstanley and Taylor, 17 November 1812, to William Roscoe;[2] his sale, 1816, lot 96 bt. Ford £5 15s 6d; presented to the L.R.I. 1819; deposited at the W.A.G., 1893; presented to the W.A.G., 1948.

Ref: 1. The 1963 Catalogue p. 110 suggested an attribution to the Master of the Groot Adoration for whom see Max J. Friedlander, *Die Altniederlandische Malerei*, XI, 1933, pp. 35ff, and noted the similarity between the figure of the executioner in No. 873 and one of the figures in Lucas van Leyden's *Mohammed and Sergius* of 1508 (A. Bartsch, *Le Peintre Graveur*, 1803/21, Vol. VII, No. 126).   2. Roscoe Papers No. 5318.

NETHERLANDISH School, 16th century

818   Prodigal Son

Panel, 38.8 × 57.2 cm

Attributed in the 1963 Catalogue to a follower of the Brunswick Monogrammist[1] and perhaps by the same artist as *The Prodigal Son* at the Museo di Palazzo Venezia, Rome.[2]

Prov: Roscoe Sale, 1816 lot 100 as Holbein bt. Ford £25 4s 0d; presented to the L.R.I. 1819; deposited at the W.A.G., 1893; presented to the W.A.G., 1948.

Exh: Manchester, *Art Treasures*, 1857, No. 469.

Ref: 1. For this artist see Simone Bergmans, *Le Probleme du Monogrammiste de Brunswick*, Bulletin, Musees royaux des Beaux Arts de Belgique, 1965, pp. 143 ff. and Musees royaux des Beaux Arts de Belgique, *Le Siecle de Bruegel*, 1963, pp. 174-6, Nos. 251-2.   2. Museo di Palazzo Venezia, Rome, *Dipinti* (1948), p. 40 fig. 42 also attributed to the Brunswick Monogrammist.

829   The Massacre of the Innocents

Panel, 56.4 × 36.7 cm

Strips about 3 cm wide at either side are later additions.

Prov: Bequeathed by Lord Wavertree, 1933.

1012   St. Mary Magdalen

Panel, 52.7 × 20.3 cm

1013   St. Catherine

Panel, 52.5 × 20.3 cm

Extensively restored especially in the top left corner of 1012 and the top right corner of 1013. Both are painted up to the edges on the two long sides.

Other versions of these triptych wings are in the Pallavicini Gallery, Rome[1] and were on the art market in 1958;[2] the centrepiece of the former pair is a copy after Raphael's *Madonna del divino Amore* while the centrepiece of the latter pair is a copy after Marcantonio's *Virgin and Child with St. Anne*[3]. Further versions were at Panshanger (thence by descent to Rosemary, Lady Ravensdale), now on the art market.

Prov: Roscoe Sale 1816 lot 82 bt. Crompton £4; presented to the L.R.I. 1819; deposited at the W.A.G. 1893; presented to a the W.A.G. 1948.

Exh: Leeds *National Exhibition*, 1868, No. 56 (No. 1013 only). New Gallery, *Winter Exhibition* 1899-1900 No. 41 (No. 1012 only).

Ref: **1.** Federico Zeri, *La Galleria Pallavicini in Rome*, 1959 No. 186, p. 111.   **2.** Now untraced, photograph in the Rijksbureau voor Kunsthistorische Documentatie, The Hague.   **3.** A. Bartsch, *Le Peintre Graveur*, Vol. 14, 1813 No. 63. Another copy after this engraving is in the Staatliche Gemaldegalerie, Kassel (*Katalog der Staatlichen Gemaldegalerie zu Kassel*, 1958, No. 25, p. 107). Did it too have wings similar to Nos, 1012-1013? Or were indeed Nos. 1012-1013 its original wings; they are about 15 cm shorter than the height of the sides of the Kassel picture but may have been cut down.

1016   The Nativity

Panel, 31.6 × 25.5 cm; painted up to the edge all round.

Attributed in the 1963 Catalogue to a follower of Cornelius Engelbrechtsz.[1]

Prov: (?)C. F. Greville;[2] Roscoe Sale, 1816 bt. Mason 3 gns; presented to the L.R.I., 1819; deposited at the W.A.G., 1893; presented to the W.A.G., 1948.

Exh: Manchester, *Art Treasures*, 1857 (460) as by Krug.

Ref: **1.** An attribution first suggested by Samuel Woodburn in 1835 see his MSS notes (National Gallery, London, in an 1819 Catalogue). Walter S. Gibson, *letter*, 18 April 1977, sees No. 1016 as a work of about 1510 painted under the influence of Englebrechtsz.   **2.** "It was in Col. Greville's Collection where it was called *Jan Van Eyck*", Samuel Woodburn, notes, *op. cit.,* No. 1016 did not however appear at any of the Greville sales listed by F. Lugt, *Repertoire des Catalogues de Vente*, 1600-1825, 1938.

1188   Portrait of a Merchant

Panel, 101 × 76.8 cm

Inscribed on shield: *GPS*

The costume suggests a date between 1555 and 1565.[1]

Prov: Bought by William Roscoe from Thomas Winstanley 12 April 1810.[2] Roscoe Sale 1816 lot 148 bought Lord Stanley[3] £13 13s 0d; by descent[4] to the 18th Earl of Derby sold Christie's 22 April 1955 lot 40 bt. Agnew; from whom purchased 1955.

Ref: 1. Aileen Ribeiro, *letter,* 22 February 1973.   2. Roscoe Paper No. 5314, Liverpool City Libraries.   3. Later the 13th Earl of Derby.   4. G. Scharf, *A Catalogue of the pictures at Knowsley Hall,* 1875, No. 275.

1189   Virgin and Child with Angels

Panel, 33.8 × 25.2 cm

In the background at the left is the Visitation and at the right the Annunciation. An apple[1] passes between the Virgin and Child or is it repelled by Christ? Christ holds a Rosary.

The panel is painted up to the edges at the right and top.

Prov: ?Lewis J. Hart sold Winstanley, Liverpool, 24 September 1839.[2] Acquired by the L.R.I. between 1836 and 1843;[3] deposited at the W.A.G. 1893; presented to the W.A.G. 1948.

Exh: New Gallery, *Winter Exhibition,* 1899-1900, (77).

Ref: 1. The iconography seems unusual; see Ernst Guldan, *Eva und Maria,* 1966, pp. 108-116 for a full discussion of the problem.   2. The Liverpool Mercury, 20 September 1839, contains Winstanley's advertisement for this sale for which no catalogue survives; according to the advertisement the sale included "The Virgin and Child seated in a Landscape, a very rare and beautiful quality of picture by Hans Hemmelinkc" to whom, *sic,* No. 1189 was attributed in the 1843 Catalogue No. 65.   3. 1843 Catalogue, No. 65.

1192   St. John the Baptist presenting a donor and St. Mary Magdalen

Panel, 108.6 × 83.7 cm

Possibly two wings of an altarpiece made up in the 19th Century (?) into a single picture by adding new (?) decorated dividing strip and borders[1] but more probably conceived and executed in its present state in the 16th Century.[2]

In the background of the scene with St. John the Baptist is that saint preaching and in the background of the scene with Mary Magdalen is a wayside shrine with worshippers and (?) St. Jerome.

Prov: Joseph Brooks Yates sold Winstanley Liverpool 14 May 1857 lot 39. Presented to the L.R.I. by Richard Rathbone by 1859; deposited at the W.A.G. 1893; presented to the W.A.G. 1948.

Exh: Leeds, *National Exhibition,* 1868 (549).

Ref: 1. As suggested in the 1963 Catalogue, p. 48   2. No. 1192 is composed of several separate panels but the joins do not invariably coincide with the lines joining the pictorial areas with the decorative areas. No. 1192 seems to have reached its present state at least by 1859 and probably by 1857 (see provenance and 1859 Catalogue No. 62).

145

1193   The Nativity

Panel, 37.6 × 29.2 cm

Inscribed on banner held by angels: *GLORIA IN ALTISSIMIS DEO*

Attributed to Marcellus Coffermans in the 1963 Catalogue on the basis of the signed (?) *Adoration of the Shepherds*, No. 17.190.3 at the Metropolitan Museum of Art.[1]

The panel is painted up to the edges all round.

Prov: A worn seal on the back, possibly a falcon. William Roscoe;[2] presented by Thomas Winstanley to the L.R.I. between 1816 and 1819;[3] deposited at the W.A.G. 1942; presented to the W.A.G. 1948.

Ref: 1. Metropolitan Museum of Art, New York, *A Catalogue of Early Flemish, Dutch and German Paintings*, 1947, p. 154.   2. Perhaps the *Nativity* by Correggio or Parmigianino listed in Roscoe's draft MS for the 1816 Sale Catalogue (Roscoe Papers no. 3897). See 1819 Catalogue No. 21; all the pictures in that catalogue are there, stated to have come from Roscoe's collection.   3. Correspondence and Papers relating to Gifts and Deposits at the Liverpool Royal Institution L.R.I. Archives 61.21.

NETHERLANDISH School, about 1600

825   The Judgment of Paris

Panel, 83.8 × 126.4 cm

Dated from dress and hair style to between 1600 and 1605

Prov: Presented by C. E. Taylor, 1883
Ref: 1. Mrs. Harris, report, 1 August 1958.

NETHERLANDISH School, early 17th century

834   The Murder of Abel

Copper, 26.3 × 20.4 cm

Attributed to Rottenhammer in 1851[1] but G. Scharf disputed this attribution in 1859.[2]

Prov: William Roscoe;[3] presented by W. S. Roscoe to the L.R.I. 1843-4;[4] deposited at the W.A.G., 1893; presented to the W.A.G., 1948.

Ref: 1. 1851 Catalogue No. 60.   2. 1859 Catalogue No. 66.   3. No. 834 was presumably the *Picture of Cain slaying Abel* listed as a gift in Roscoe's 1820 Inventory (Roscoe Papers no. 3906).   4. *Annual Report of the L.R.I.*, 1843-4.

NEWTON, Gilbert Stuart, 1794-1835

2571 Portrait of James Maury

Canvas, 91.4 × 71 cm

The sitter (1746-1840) was born in Virginia, settled in Liverpool as a merchant about 1786 and was appointed American Consul there in 1796.[1]

Eng: R. Lane (litho)
Prov: Presented by subscribers to the American Chamber of Commerce in Liverpool 1825; presented to the Gallery by Sir John Gray Hill on behalf of the Chamber 1908.
Exh: W.A.G., *700th Anniversary of Liverpool*, 1907.
Ref: 1. For further details see particulary W. O. Henderson, *The American Chamber of Commerce in Liverpool*, Transactions of the Historical Society of Lancashire and Cheshire, Vol. 85, 1933, pp. 2, 6, 56 and *Papers of Thomas Jefferson*, ed. J. P. Boyd, 1950-55, Vol. 10, pp. 387-8, p. 619.

NICCOLO Liberatore or Alunno da Foligno, active *c.* 1456, died 1502, studio of

2791 Coronation of the Virgin

Panel with elaborate cresting; painted surface; main field 84.5 × 51 cm tympanum 46 × 41 cm

First attributed to Niccolo da Foligno by Byam Shaw,[1] 2791 is a workshop product, close in composition to the *Coronation of the Virgin* in the upper tier of the polyptych in the Cathedral at Nocera Umbria signed and dated 1483. Omelia dates it circa 1495-1500.[2] Zeri has noted similar elaborate cresting on six small panels in the Walters Art Gallery, Baltimore, which, however, are of superior quality.[3]

Prov: Probably first Viscount Pery of Limerick;[4] Kenneth Muir Mackenzie (later Lord Muir-Mackenzie);[5] his father-in-law, William Graham; his sale, Christie's 8 April 1886 (180) bt. P. H. Rathbone £18 7s 6d; P. H. Rathbone, who bequeathed it to the Walker Art Gallery, 1895; passed to the collection, 1905.
Exh: Nottingham Castle, 1879-1881;[3] W.A.G., 1886.[6]
Ref: 1. J. Byam Shaw, orally, 1952.   2. John F. Omelia, letter 22 March 1967.   3. Federico Zeri, *Italian Paintings in the Walters Art Gallery*, I, 1976, pp. 160-1, pl. 178.   4. Seal before his ennoblement in 1785 on the reverse.   5. Midland Counties Art Museum, City of Nottingham Museum, Loan Ledger, (95).   6. Label on reverse; a number of Rathbone pictures appear to have been lent, but no catalogue can be found.

NIKICH—KRILICHEVSKII, Anatolii Yurevich, born 1918

6254   Still Life with Drawings by the Artist's Son.[1]

Canvas, 110 × 100 cm

Signed in Russian script and dated *63*.

Part of a cycle of works under the general title "In the Studio"; this cycle was begun in the late 1950's and is still continuing; so far it consists of about 12 pictures.[2]

Prov: Purchased from the Grosvenor Gallery 1964.
Exh: W.A.G., *Aspects of Contemporary Soviet Art*, 1964 (not numbered)
Ref: **1.** Reproduced in *A. Nikich*, Moscow, 1968, cover as *Still Life with Peaches and Son's Pictures* 1963.   **2.** Letter from the artist, 28 September 1976.

NORMANN, Adelsteen, 1848-1918

755   A Norwegian Fjord

Canvas, 120.5 × 193 cm

Signed: *A Normann 76* (date no longer visible)

The subject may be the Sogne Fjord, the subject of the artist's painting at the 1885 Royal Academy (No. 93).[1]

Prov: Presented by R. R. Rathbone, 1891.
Exh: ?Exchange Buildings Liverpool *Exhibition of High Class Paintings* 1890 No. 78A.
Ref: **1.** Reviewed in the *Art Journal*, 1885, p. 226. This might be No. 755 or the *Sognefjord*, No. 77 in the Leeds City Art Gallery which has a composition similar to No. 755.

NORTH ITALIAN School, *c.* 1520

2765   Three Saints

Copper, 22.1 × 17.1 cm

It has been suggested that the saints are from left to right St. Robert of Chaise Dieu, St. Vitale and St. Gervase.[1] St. Gervase however, generally appears with his brother and fellow martyr, St. Protasius, both young and beardless.

The third Saint, Vitale, was their father.[2] All three are patron saints of Milan, to which the tower on the standard may refer. San Vitale would be the Saint on the left, distinctly older than the other two. An alternative would be San Satirus, another Milanese Saint, who appears alongside Gervase and Protasius holding the host in Ambrogio Borgognone's altarpiece in the Certosa at Pavia. He, however, wears a hermit's costume rather than a deacon's habit. The buildings in the background may allude to the town or church for which 2765 was painted.

Mullaly[3] attributes 2765 to Antonio Brenzoni comparing it with a signed triptych of 1533 with the Madonna and Saints Jerome and George in the third chapel on the left of the nave in the Duomo at Verona. Berenson has suggested Caroto.[4] Pouncey,[5] however, thinks that it is close to Gerolamo da Santa Croce. A group of three Saints at Princeton attributed to Giolfino may be by the same hand.[6]

Prov: Entered the collection of the L.R.I. between 1836 and 1843;[7] deposited at the W.A.G., 1893;[8] presented to the W.A.G., 1948.

Ref: 1. 1963 Catalogue, p. 200. G. Scharf identified the saint on horseback as St. Victor of Milan (Notes on proof catalogue of the L.R.I. 1857, National Portrait Gallery annotated copy); compare Engelbert Kirschbaum, *Lexikon der Christlichen Ikonographie*, VIII, 1976, pp. 556-7.   2. George Kaftal, *Iconography of the Saints in Tuscan Paintings*, 1952, 133 col. 449. San Vitale appears bearded and on horseback, together with his sons, Gervase and Protasius in Carpaccio's signed and dated 1514 altarpiece in San Vitale, Venice. Jan Lauts, *Carpaccio*, 1962, p. 249 (76) pl. 177.   3. Orally.   4. Bernard Berenson, *Italian Pictures of the Renaissance, Central Italian and North Italian Schools*, I, 1968, p. 79 as partly autograph.   5. Orally, 8 July 1968.   6. J. Paul Richter, *The Cannon Collection of Italian Paintings of the Renaissance*, 1936 p. 23 (16), *St. George between St. Zeno and a Martyr Saint*.   7. 1843 Catalogue, p. 10 (31).   8. 1893 Catalogue, p. 27 (76).

NORTH ITALIAN School, 16th century

2871   Annunciation

Panel, 33.5 × 25.6 cm

The composition derives in reverse from the engraving attributed to Marco Dente da Ravenna[1] omitting God the Father and the accompanying cherubim and with alterations to the architectural setting. Landon published it as after Raphael.[2] The original design may have been made by Baldassare Peruzzi.[3]

Other derivations from the engraving are Gerolamo da Santacroce's *Annunciation* at Breslau (191),[4] an intarsia in the Cathedral at Genoa and reverse-painted glass panels in Sarasota,[5] and Naples, Museo Nazionale di Capodimonte, de Ciccio Collection 1284.

Prov: Entered the L.R.I. (as by Pulzone) between 1836 and 1843;[6] deposited at the W.A.G., 1893;[7] presented to the W.A.G. 1948.

Exh: Manchester, *Art Treasures*, 1857 (142).

Ref: **1.** Adam Bartsch, *Le Peintre Graveur*, XIV, 1867, p. 16 (15) as Raimondi and
Dean A. Porter in *The Age of Vasari*, Notre Dame, Indiana and Binghamton,
1970, p. 150 (G2) rep. p. 154.   **2.** C. P. Landon, *Vie et oeuvre complète de
Raphael Sanzio*, III, 1813, pl. CLI.   **3.** F. Zeri, letter, 19 April 1956.   **4.**
*Katalog der Gemalde u. Skulpturen, Schlessisches Museum der bildende Kunste
Breslau*, 1926, p. 70.   **5.** Kent Sobotik, *after Marco Dente da Ravenna*, Ring-
ling Museums News letter, September, 1972, pl. 1.   **6.** 1843 Catalogue p. 24
(83).   **7.** 1893 Catalogue p. 28 (78).

NORTH ITALIAN School, *c.* 1550

1187   A warrior saint in a red cuirass holding a spear

Panel (soft wood), 81.3 × 37.7 cm

1187 has probably been cut on all four sides. It appears once to have
formed part of an altarpiece. The lining of the blue drapery in the upper
left has been misinterpreted as a cross and the saint, therefore, identified
as the centurion, Longinus. The fact that the drapery appears at a higher
level than the Saint and that he is looking up suggests that 1187 may be a
fragment of an Assumption or Virgin in Glory.

1187 was attributed to van Heemskerk in 1893,[1] but the style bears a
strong influence from Giulio Romano[2] and the panel is of soft wood.

Prov: William Roscoe owned a painting described as a "Roman warrior looking
upwards his hands joined in adoration and holding a standard, his head encircled
with a glory, panel by Giulio Romano."[3] Mrs. James Yates by whom presented to
the L.R.I. in 1872;[4] deposited at the W.A.G., 1893;[1] presented to the W.A.G.,
1948.

Ref: **1.** 1893 Catalogue, p. 25 (68).   **2.** Compare for instance the work of Giulio
and Giovanni Taraschi in Modena, A. Venturi, *Storia dell 'Arte Italiana*, IX, part
VI, 1933, fig. 370-371.   **3.** MSS draft for Roscoe's 1816 Sale Catalogue, Roscoe Papers 3897.   **4.** L.R.I. Annual Report, 1872 where 1187 is also stated to
have been owned by Roscoe.

NORTH ITALIAN School, *c.* 1600

This group of thirty-nine portraits of famous men and women are
mostly copies of a set of portraits, collected at Como by Paolo Giovio,
bishop of Nocera (1483-1552).[1] His collection is not completely recorded
and has been dispersed, but a large proportion of the copies made by Cris-
tophano degli Altissimi between 1552 and 1568 for Duke Cosimo de
Medici are now in the Uffizi. Another set of copies in watercolour painted
for the Archduke Ferdinand[2] is now in the Munzkabinett at Vienna,
whereas Tobias Stimmer (1539-1582) made drawings for the wood

engravings published in the illustrated Basle edition of Giovio's *Elogia* in two volumes in 1575 and 1577 and in Theobald Muller's book on Giovio's Museum in 1578. Bernardino Campi made a set, now lost, for Donna Ippolita Gonzaga at the same time as the Altissimi set. Cardinal Federico Borromeo commissioned another set about 1619, which survives in the Ambrosiana, and some copies of Jurists were executed for the Marquis of Mantua. An inventory of 1598 records another lost set.[3]

Although some of the Liverpool set clearly once belonged to the Community of the Rosary in Venice and later to Gustavus Brander,[4] it is by no means certain that all the portraits have the same original provenance. The *Erasmus* (3285) is said to have been purchased at the sale of the Prince de Conti,[5] whilst William Roscoe acquired the *Fiammetta* (3288)[6] and the *Can Grande della Scala* (3306)[7] from different sources than the rest. The oval shape of *Jacopo Sannazzaro* also suggests a different origin. All the rest are approximately the same size the largest difference being c. 0.3 cm. The only exception is *Cosimo dei Medici* (3296), on which no inscription survives. It may therefore have been cut at the bottom.

William Roscoe owned 40 of these portraits in 1820. So one at least of his set has disappeared.[8] A portrait probably from the same set was once in the Crespi Collection, Milan.[9]

At some stage the inscriptions were standardized and traces of earlier and larger inscriptions or tablets for inscriptions can be seen in 3306, 3311, 3283, 3289, 3293, 3299, 3300, 3301, 3303, 3304, 3314.

The portraits fall into a number of groups according to the form of their inscriptions.

(a) Large lettering with wide M's, S's and compressed R's with a flourish, 3278, 3279, 3281, 3285, 3286, 3287, 3288, 3297, 3298, 3309, 3306 and 3311.

(b) Large lettering with straight R's and L's 3284, 3291, 3294, 3295, 3307.

(c) Large lettering with compressed M and no flourish 3276.

(d) Small lettering with no flourishes save for an extended lower stroke of the R. 3277, 3280, 3282, 3290, 3292, 3302, 3308, 3310, 3312, 3313.

(e) Small lettering with flourishes to R's, L's and S's. All in this group once had larger inscriptions. 3283, 3289, 3293, 3299, 3300, 3301, 3303, 3304, 3314.

Some of the differences can be accounted for by repainting of the inscriptions, and it does not seem that the variations are very much guide in indicating hands. Clearly there are a number of different painters, but the quality of the pictures renders a precise division hazardous.

Prov: For the whole group; additions and exceptions are given in the individual entries.
Community of the Rosary attached to the Church of S.S. Filippo and Giacomo,

Venice;[4] Gustavus Brander sale, Christie, 11-12 December 1789 part of lot 22 (43 heads) bt. Sat or Saj £5 0s 0d; William Roscoe by 9 July 1820;[5] by descent to Mrs. A. M. Roscoe by whom bequeathed, 1950.

Exh: Liverpool Royal Institution, 1844, accompanying (32) *Portrait of Roscoe* lent by Mrs. W. S. Roscoe.

Ref: **1.** Ralph Fastnedge and A. F. Donaldson, *A Note on an early portrait of Politian*, Liverpool Bulletin, III, nos. 1 & 2, 1953, pp. 4-11.   **2.** Friedrich Kenner, *Die Portratsammlung des Erzherzogs Ferdinand von Tirol*, Jahrbuch des Kunsthistorischen Kunstsammlungen des allerhöchsten Kaiserhauses, XV, 1894; XVII 1896, XVIII, 1897, XIX 1898.   **3.** Franz von Reber, *Die Bildnisse der herzoglich bayerischen Kunstkammer nach dem Fickler' schen Inventar von 1598*, Sitzungsberichte der mathematisch-physikalischen Classe der k.b. Akademie der Wissenschaften zu Munchen, 1893, espec. pp. 8, 36, 41-43.   **4.** Seals on the backs of some of the portraits indicated under individual entries.   **5.** Inscription on reverse. Untraceable in the sales of the Prince de Conti.   **6.** Colonel Matthew Smith sale, Christie, 12 May 1804 (17) bt. Roscoe 2 gns.   **7.** Roscoe Papers 5317 bill from Winstanley. Bought 29 September 1812 for 25s.   **8.** Roscoe Papers 3906. Inventory of Household Furniture of William Roscoe 8 July 1820, p. 14. The portrait of Ino. de Caza listed separately may or may not have been another picture in the set. The set hung in his study Henry Roscoe, *Life of William Roscoe*, Vol. 2, 1833, p. 379.   **9.** Bernard Berenson, *Lorenzo Lotto*, 1956, p. 37, pl. 85. 22 × 17 cm, sold Galerie Petit, 4 June 1914 (32), and with Tooths 1932.

3276   Alfonso d'Avalos

Panel, 22.6 × 16.8 cm

Inscribed: *ALFONSVS VASTVS MARC.*

(1502-1546) Marquis of Vasto, successor to Antonio di Laeva (q.v.) as imperial general.

Not based on any of the surviving portraits by Titian, unlike the copy painted for the Archduke Ferdinand, which is based on the Titian,[1] now in the Collection of the Marquis de Ganay, Paris.[2]

Version: Uffizi 125.
Ref: **1.** Karl Wilczek, *Ein Bildnis des Alfonso Davalos von Tizian*, Zeitschrift für bildende Kunst, LXIII, 1929, pp. 240-7.   **2.** Harold E. Wethey, *The Paintings of Titian*, II, 1971, p. 79 pl. 56.

3277   Daniele Barbaro or Lorenzo Beccadelli

Panel, 22.8 × 16.8 cm

Inscribed: *DANIEL BARBARO EELEC. A QVIL*

(1514-1570) Venetian ambassador to England, Patriarch of Aquileia, Commentator on Vitruvius and writer of *La Pratica della Prospettiva*.

The portrait of Daniele Barbaro painted for Giovio was in the Molinary Collection. Pietro Aretino sent it to Giovio in 1545.[1]

But 3277 is not based on any of the surviving portraits by Titian (Ottawa;[2] Prado, Madrid)[3] and Veronese (Florence, Pitti Palace).[4] The features of the sitter are much closer to those of Lorenzo Beccadelli (1501-1572), Archbishop of Ragusa, poet and biographer of Petrarch and member of the reforming party in the Catholic Church. The resemblance to the Titian portrait dated 1552 (Uffizi) even extends to the pose.[5]

Ref: **1.** Luigi Rovelli, *L'Opera storica ed artistica di Paolo Giovio*, 1928, p. 186.   **2.** Harold E. Wethey, *The Paintings of Titian*, II, 1971, pp. 80-1, pl. 95.   **3.** Wethey, *op. cit.*, p. 81 pl. 94.   **4.** Giuseppe Fiocco, *Paolo Veronese*, 1928, p. 191, fig. 80.   **5.** Wethey, *op. cit.*, p. 81, pl. 164.

3278   Angelo Beolco, called Ruzzante

Panel, 22.8 × 16.7 cm

Inscribed: *RVGIANS POET. COM. PAT.*

(c. 1500-1542) Paduan poet and writer of comedies as the Latin inscription explains.

No versions are known of this portrait, though two other types are recorded.[1]

Ref: **1.** Iacobus Philippus Tomasinus, *Elogia Iconibus Exornata*, Padua, 1630, p. 30, and *Enciclopedia Italiana*, XXX, p. 3582 reproduces the engraving published in E. Lovarini, *Una Poesia musicata del Ruzzante*, Miscellanea in onore di V. Crescini, Cividale, 1913.

3279   Cardinal Bessarion

Panel, 22.8 × 16.7 cm

Inscribed: *BESSARION CAR. NICENVS*

(1403-1472) Born at Trebizond. Theologian and humanist, collector of codices and advocate for the unity of the Church.

Vasari says that Giulio Romano painted a portrait of him for Giovio after the fresco, attributed to Piero della Francesca in the Stanza d'Eliodoro in the Vatican.[1] The fresco was destroyed when Raphael and his studio redecorated the room.

The Basle edition engraving though not exactly the same is clearly based on the same prototype.[2]

Versions: Vienna 22 (756),[3] Uffizi 356; Ambrosiana, Milan.
Ref: **1.** Vasari ed. Milanesi, II, 1878, p. 492.   **2.** Paolo Giovio, *Elogia Virorum literis illustrium*, 1577, p. 43.—also in Isaac Bullart, *Academie des Sciences et des Arts*, 1682, I p. 9.   **3.** Kenner, *op. cit.*, XVII, 1896, pp. 156-7.

3280 St. Carlo Borromeo

Panel, 22.8 × 16.7 cm

Inscribed: *S. CAROLVS BORROMEVS*

(1538-1584) Archbishop of Milan and leading figure in the Counter Reformation.

3280 derives from the Figino bust portrait[1] in the Biblioteca Ambrosiana, Milan with small alterations that make the sitter look older.

The portrait in the Ambrosiana series of famous men, however, differs slightly from 3280.

Ref: **1.** *Enciclopedia Italiana*, IX, 1931, p. 35 (reproduced), and Roberto Paola Ciardi, *Giovan Ambrogio Figino*, 1968, pp. 96, 223 (13).

3281 Leonardo Bruni of Arezzo

Panel, 22.8 × 16.7 cm

Inscribed: *(LE)ONARDVS (A)RETINV(S)*

(1370-1444) Chancellor of Florence 1427-1444, humanist and historian.

Probably ultimately based on his tomb by Antonio Rossellino in S. Croce, Florence. Giovio's portrait was in the Signora Palumba Cerboni collection.[1] The engraving in the Basle edition of the *Elogia* is based on the same prototype as 3281, although Bruni's hat is different and he is wearing a laurel wreath.[2]

Vasari painted a portrait of Bruni in the ceiling of the Sala di Lorenzo il Magnifico in the Palazzo Vecchio, Florence.[3]

The portrait in the Ambrosiana differs from 3281.

Versions: Uffizi
Ref: **1.** Luigi Rovelli, *L'opera storica ed artistica di Paolo Giovio*, 1928, p. 180.   **2.** Paolo Giovio, *Elogia* . . ., Basle, 1577, p. 19.   **3.** Vasari, ed. G. Milanesi, VIII, 1882, p. 117.

3282 Bartolommeo Cocles della Rocca

Panel, 22.8 × 16.8 cm

Inscribed: *BARTHOLOMEVS COCLES*

(1467-1504) Of Bologna. Hermetic philosopher, chiromancer, physiognomist.

3283 Cardinal Contarini

Panel, 22.8 × 16.7 cm

Inscribed: *GASPAR CONTARENVS CARD*

(1483-1542) Venetian Cardinal, with Sadoleto (q.v.), one of the leading reformers of the Church.

The engraving in the Basle edition of the *Elogia* displays minor differences from 3283, but is clearly based on the same source,[1] which may be Titian's portrait in the *Submission of Frederick Barbarossa to Pope Alexander III* in the Doge's Palace, destroyed in the fire of 1577.[2]

Vasari painted portraits of Contarini in his *Meeting of Charles V and Pope Clement VII* in the Sala di Clemente VII in the Palazzo Vecchio[3] and in his *Pope Paul III rewarding merit* in the Cancelleria of the Palazzo di San Giorgio, Rome.[4]

Versions: Uffizi 567; Ambrosiana.
Ref:　1. Paolo Giovio, *Elogia* . . ., 1577, p. 184.　2. Carlo Ridolfi, *Le Maraviglie dell 'arte*, I, 1648, p. 140.　3. Vasari ed. G. Milanesi, VIII, 1883, p. 169.　4. Vasari ed. G. Milanesi, VII, 1883, p. 679.

3284 King David II of Abyssinia

Panel, 22.8 × 16.8 cm

Inscribed: *DAVID MAX. ABISSINVS. A ETIOPV̂ REX*

(1497-1540). Succeeded in 1507.

David II gave Pope Clement VII his portrait in 1524 together with the golden cross which he holds in the engraved version in the Basle edition of the *Elogia*.[1]

Versions: Vienna 31;[2] Uffizi 1; Rovelli Collection.[3]
Ref:　1. Paolo Giovio, *Elogia Virorum bellica virtute illustrium* . . ., 1575, p. 355.　2. Kenner, *op. cit.*, XIX, 1898, pp. 141-2.　3. Rovelli, *op. cit.*, p. 177.

3285 Erasmus of Rotterdam

Panel, 22.6 × 17.2 cm

Inscribed: *ERASMVS ROTERODAMVS TVRPIS ME*

(1466-1536). Humanist and reforming theologian.

The inscription is ungrammatical and probably refers to Erasmus's illegitimate birth.

The type appears to be derived from the woodcut of Hans Wenditz of

155

Strassbourg of 1523[1] or that of Hans Holbein of 1532.[2] Other profile portraits are an alabaster relief in the Basle Historisches Museum,[3] the Quentin Matsys medal,[4] the Louvre Holbein[5] and an Upper German woodcut dated 1522.[6]

Both the Ambrosiana and the Uffizi portraits on the other hand are based on the three quarter view of the Longford Castle Holbein type.

Prov: Said to have been purchased at the sale of the Prince de Conti.[7]
Ref: 1. Dr. Emil von Major, *Erasmus von Rotterdam*, n.d, pl. 4. First published in *Ulrichi ab Hutten cum Erasmo Roterodamo expostulatio*, Strassburg, 1523. 2. Von Major, *op. cit.*, pl. 5. 3. Von Major, *op. cit.*, fig. 16. 4. Von Major, *op. cit.*, fig. 2. 5. Von Major, *op. cit.*, fig. 5. 6. Paul Ganz, *The Paintings of Hans Holbein*, 1950, pl. 66. 7. Inscription on reverse.

3286   Cardinal Ippolito d'Este

Panel, 22.8 × 16.8 cm

Inscribed: *HIPPOLITVS ESTENSIS. CAR.*

(1509-1572) Son of Alfonso I, Duke of Ferrara and Lucrezia Borgia. Patron of the arts and sciences.

A head of Ippolito was listed in the 1624 inventory of Cardinal Alessandro d'Este,[1] and a portrait of him attributed to Bronzino was in the sale of "a personage of very high rank", Christie, 10 June 1872 (107).

Ref: 1. Giuseppe Campori, *Raccolta di cataloghi ed inventari inediti . . .*, 1870, p. 69.

3287   Isabella d'Este

Panel, 22.8 × 16.8 cm

Inscribed: *ISABELLA ESTENSIS. MANT.*

(1474-1539) Wife of Francesco Gonzaga, Marquess of Mantua. Patron of the arts and letters.

The portrait is based on the lost Titian once in King Charles I's collection. It is best known through the copy in Vienna, made by Rubens when it was at Mantua.[1]

Roscoe owned another portrait of Isabella d'Este attributed to Titian.[2]

Ref: 1. Harold E. Wethey, *The Paintings of Titian*, II, 1971, p. 197 pl. 231. 2. Roscoe Sale 65, 1ft × 9 in, bt. Crompton £26 5s 0d.

3288   Fiammetta

Panel, 22.8× 16.6 cm

Inscribed: *FLAMMVLA. JOAN. BOCACII.*

(c. 1310-1350) The heroine of Giovanni Boccaccio's early poem, *L'Amorosa Visione* and of his prose elegy *La Fiammetta*, Boccaccio's mistress. Said to have been the daughter of Tommaso Count of Aquino or of Robert of Anjou, King of Naples.

Portraits of Fiammetta and Boccaccio attributed to Giorgione from the Borghese Palace were in the sale of John Heugh Esq. of Upper Brook Street, Christie, 11 May 1878 (276).

Prov: Col. Matthew Smith;[1] his sale, Christie, 12 May 1804 (17) bt. Roscoe 2 gns.
Ref: **1.** Seal on the reverse.

3289   Marcilio Ficino

Panel, 22.8 × 16.8 cm

Inscribed: *MARSILIVS FICINVS*

(1433-1499) Florentine humanist and Neoplatonic philosopher.

The portrait owned by Giovio was in the Molinary Collection.[1] The ultimate source for 3289 was Domenico Ghirlandaio's fresco in Santa Maria Novella, *The Annunciation to Zachariah*,[2] to which 3289 is closer than the engraving in the *Elogia*.[3] Vasari drew on the same prototype for his portrait on the ceiling of the Sala di Lorenzo il Magnifico[4] and in his picture of *Ficino presenting his works to Cosimo il Vecchio*, in the Sala di Cosimo il Vecchio, both in the Palazzo Vecchio, Florence.[5]

Versions: Vienna 88 (497);[6] Uffizi 172; Ambrosiana.
Ref: **1.** Rovelli, *op. cit.*, p. 182.   **2.** Jan Lauts, *Domenico Ghirlandaio*, 1943, pl. 79.   **3.** Paolo Giovio, *Elogia* . . ., 1577 p. 84.   **4.** Vasari, ed. Milanesi, VIII, p. 116.   **5.** Vasari, ed. Milanesi, VIII, p. 100.   **6.** Kenner, *op. cit.*, XVIII, 1897, p. 227.

3290   Marcantonio Flaminio

Panel, 22.8 × 16.5 cm

Inscribed: *MARCANT (ONIVS F) LAMIN (IVS)*

(1498-1550) Humanist, poet and theologian.

Version: Brooklyn Museum 32.781, probably identical with picture in E. Kraemer Sale, Georges Petit, Paris 2-5 June 1913 (11).[1]
Ref: **1.** Letter of Dora Bentley-Cranch 17 January 1967.

3291   Doge Antonio Grimani

Panel, 22.8 × 16.8 cm

Inscribed: *ANTONIVS GRIMANO VENETIAR. D*

(1436-1523). Blamed for the defeat by the Turks at Sonchio and stripped of his offices, but elected Doge 1521.

The prototype is a lost three quarter length portrait by Titian[1] which is recorded in a number of versions.[2] The engraving in the Basle edition of the *Elogia* is the reverse of 3291.[3] The Uffizi portrait is of Cardinal Domenico Grimani, not the Doge.

Versions: Rovelli Collection.[4]
Ref: **1.** Vasari, ed. Milanesi, 1881, VII, p. 437. **2.** (a) Walter Toscanelli, New York, 1939, ex. Palazzo Grimani. Harold E. Wethey, *The Paintings of Titian*, II, 1971, pp. 169-170 (b) Vercelli, Museo Borgogna. Vittorio Viale, *Civico Museo Francesco Borgogna, I Dipinti*, 1969, p. 73, pl. 113. (c) Lord Rothermere (d) Lord Rosebery, Mentmore (e) Reverend John Sanford Sale, Christie 9 March 1839 (124) recorded by a watercolour copy at Corsham Court. **3.** Paolo Giovio, *Elogia . . .*, 1575, p. 257. **4.** Rovelli, *op. cit.*, p. 173.

3292 Cardinal Wolsey

Panel, 22.8 × 16.7 cm

Inscribed: *HENRICVS ANGLIE REX VIII*

Another version inscribed *ARIGO VII/RE DI IN/GILTE/RA* was in the collection of the Earl of Ellenborough.[1] But 3292 does not represent the features of either Henry VIII or Henry VII, but rather resembles portraits of Cardinal Wolsey,[2] such as that in the National Portrait Gallery (32).[3] The sitter wears a badge in his cap of a rider on a horse.

The prototype of 3292 in Giovio's collection[4] was engraved as a portrait of Henry VIII as early as 1575, which implies that the error over identity occured very early.

The Uffizi portrait of Cardinal Wolsey is not based on the same source as 3292.

Versions: Ex. Earl of Ellenborough Collection.[1]
Ref: **1.** Sotheby's 11 June 1947 (48) bt. R. Ward. **2.** Letter of Roy Strong 8 September 1971. **3.** Roy Strong, *Tudor and Jacobean Portraits*, 1969, I, p. 335, II, pl. 622. **4.** Paolo Giovio, *Elogia . . .*, 1575, p. 338 and Theobald Muller, *Musaei Ioviani Imagines*, 1577, n.p.

3293 Pope Julius II

Panel, 22.8 × 16.7 cm

Inscribed: *IVLIVS II. PONT. MAX*

(1443-1513) Pope 1502-1513.

Based on the same prototype as the drawing in the Recueil d'Arras.[1] A similar, but larger painting, was formerly in the collection of Conte Bruschi, Corneto Tarquinia.[2] The Pope is wearing a short beard and the woollen hat or cuffiotto which he wore on campaign at the siege of Mirandola in January 1511 as Klaczko pointed out.[2] The portraits in the Uffizi and other series are derived from the Raphael in the National Gallery.

Ref: **1.** 11898 (Bibliotheque Municipale d'Arras) Photograph A. Girardon. **2.** J. Klaczko, *Rome et la Renaissance: Jules II,* 1898, p. 281. A reference pointed out to the Gallery by John Shearman in a letter, 7 October 1971.

3294   Antonio da Laeva

Panel, 22.8 × 16.8 cm

Inscribed: *ANTONIVS DA LEVA*

(c. 1480-1536) Condottiere, born in Spain. Predecessor of Alfonso d'Avalos as general of the imperial forces.

Titian painted a portrait of Laeva in Bologna in 1530, probably identical with a picture in the collection of Pietro Mattei in Venice in the 17th Century,[1] which was engraved in Spain in the 18th Century as by Leonardo.[2] Vasari used the same portrait as the basis for his portrait in the *Meeting of the Emperor Charles V and Pope Clement VII at Bologna* in the Palazzo Vecchio, Florence.[3]

The portrait owned by Giovio engraved in his *Elogia* is based on the same prototype as 3294.[4]

A half length portrait attributed to Dosso Dossi of Antonio di Laeva in armour was in Lord Methuen's sale, Christie, 16 May 1840 (21) bt. Foster.

Versions: Uffizi; and probably John Rushout, Baron Northwick Sale, Phillips, 9 August 1859 (857).[5]

Ref: **1.** Vasari, ed. Milanesi, VII, p. 450 and Carlo Ridolfi, *Le Maraviglie dell' Arte*, I, 1648, pp. 154, 178.   **2.** *Retratos de Espanoles con un epitomo de sus vidas*, 1711.   **3.** Vasari, ed. Milanesi, VIII, p. 173.   **4.** Paolo Giovio, *Elogia . . .*, 1575, p. 316; Theobald Muller, *Musaei Ioviani Imagines*, 1577, n.p. and Aliprando Capriolo, *Ritratti di cento capitani illustri*, 1596, opp. p. 99.   **5.** "ALTISSIMO. Portrait in profile of Antonio di Leva, the celebrated Spanish general." bt. Bennett £15 15s 0d. This picture is probably identical with that in the collection of the Duke of Lucca, *Society of Painters in Water Colours*. July 1840 (42) inherited by his Royal Highness from his Grandfather, Charles IV of Spain. Signed. H(eight) 1. 1 W15.

3295   Galeotto Malatesta

Panel, 22.8 × 16.8 cm

Inscribed: *GALEOTTV (S) MA . . .*

The inscription has been read to refer to Galeotto Malatesta (?-1385) of Rimini, but the reading is uncertain and the features resemble those of Galeazzo Maria Sforza (1444-1476), ruler of Milan, as they appear in the engraving of the Basle edition of the *Elogia* in reverse[1] and in several medals.[2] The prototype, however, is not the same as for the Uffizi portrait of Sforza.

According to Vasari Benedetto da Maiano produced a portrait of Galeotto Malatesta, when he was working in the Romagna,[3] and a standing terracotta statue of Malatesta wearing friar's robes is recorded at San Agostino, Cesena.[4]

Ref: **1.** Paolo Giovio, *Elogia . . .*, 1575, p. 151.   **2.** George Francis Hill, *A Corpus of Italian medals of the Renaissance before Cellini*, 1930, I, 284, 635, 669, 675, II, pl. 45, 112, 116, 117.   **3.** Vasari, ed. G. Milanesi, III, p. 339.   **4.** Vasari, ed. G. Milanesi, III, p. 339 n. 1

3296   Cosimo dei Medici

Panel, 20.9 × 16.5 cm

(1389-1464) Il Vecchio. Ruler of Florence.

The prototype was the Pontormo portrait,[1] which is in turn based on the relief and medal.[2] The portrait owned by Giovio was engraved where the sitter is more upright.[3]

Versions: Vienna 2 (372);[4] Rovelli Collection;[5] Bronzino in Museo Mediceo, Florence.
Ref: **1.** Janet Cox Rearick, *The Drawings of Pontormo*, 1964, pl. 83.   **2.** George Francis Hill, *A Corpus of Italian medals of the Renaissance before Cellini*, 1930, I 910; II pl. 147.   **3.** Paolo Giovio, *Elogia . . .*, 1575, p. 131.   **4.** Kenner, *op. cit.*, XVIII, 1897, pp. 145-6.   **5.** Rovelli, *op. cit.*, p. 168.

3297   Giuliano dei Medici

Panel, 22.6 × 16.8 cm

Inscribed: *IVLIANVS MEDICES*

(1453-1478) Brother of Lorenzo il Magnifico and grandson of Cosimo il Vecchio (q.v.).

The prototype is the portrait by Botticelli.[1] The portrait in the Giovio collection showed a dagger in Giuliano's breast referring to his assassination in the Pazzi conspiracy.[2]

Versions: Vienna 8 (378);[3]
Ref: **1.** Vasari, ed. G. Milanesi, III, 315. Berlin version reproduced Wilhelm Bode, *Sandro Botticelli*, 1925, pl. XXV.   **2.** Paolo Giovio, *Elogia . . .*, 1575, p. 159 and Theobald Muller, *Musaei Ioviani Imagines*, 1577, n.p.   **3.** Kenner, *op. cit.*, XVIII, 1897, p. 149.

3298   Lorenzo dei Medici, Duke of Urbino

Panel, 22.6 × 16.8 cm

Inscribed: *LAV(R) EN (TI) VS VRBINI. D.P.F.*

(1492-1519) Great grandson of Cosimo il Vecchio (q.v.). Ruler of Florence from 1513.

The prototype is the portrait by Raphael of which very many copies are known.[1] Vasari used it in his *Leo X creating cardinals in Consistory* and in his *Triumphal entry of Leo X into Florence,* both in the Sala di Leone X in the Palazzo Vecchio, Florence.[2]

Version: Vienna 14 (384);[3] Bronzino in the Museo Mediceo, Florence.
Ref: 1. Vasari, ed. Milanesi, IV, p. 352-3 completed by 5 February 1518. Giovanni Gaye, *Carteggio inedito d'artisti dei secoli XIV, XV, XVI*, II, 1839, p. 146. 2. Vasari, ed. G. Milanesi, VIII, p. 143. 3. Kenner, XVIII, p. 153.

3299 Francesco Panigarola

Panel, 22.8 × 16.7 cm

Inscribed: *FRANCISCVS. PANIGAROLA*

(1548-1594) Bishop of Asti, theologian and preacher.

The portrait in the Ambrosiana is not based on the same prototype.

3300 Pietro Pitato

Panel, 22.8 × 16.8 cm

Inscribed: *PETRVS PITATVS ASTRO. SCIEN.*

(active 1544-1568) Veronese astrologer.

3301 Angelo Poliziano

Panel, 22.8 × 16.8 cm

Inscribed: *ANGELVS POLITIANVS*

(1454-1494) Humanist scholar and poet.

The original Giovio portrait was in the collection of Signora Palumbo Cerboni.[1] The prototype is Domenico Ghirlandaio's portrait in his Santa Maria Novella fresco, *The Annunciation to Zachariah,*[2] a source also used by Vasari for his portrait in the ceiling of the Sala di Lorenzo il Magnifico in the Palazzo Vecchio.[3]

Versions: Uffizi 191; Ambrosiana.
Ref: 1. Rovelli, *op. cit.*, p. 182. Engraved, Paolo Giovio, *Elogia . . .*, 1577 p. 73. 2. Vasari ed. G. Milanesi, III, 1878, p. 266. Jan Lauts, *Domenico Ghirlandaio*, 1943, pl. 79. 3. Vasari ed. G. Milanesi, VIII, 1883, p. 116.

3302 Luigi Pulci

Panel, 22.5 × 17 cm

Inscribed: *ALOVSIVS PVLCIVS*

(1432-1484) Poet and humanist.

Derived in reverse from the head of the man on the extreme right in the group of the *Raising of the Emperor's Nephew by St. Peter* by Filippino Lippi in the Brancacci Chapel, Santa Maria del Carmine, Florence.[1] Vasari drew on the same prototype for his portrait for his ceiling in the Sala di Lorenzo il Magnifico in the Palazzo Vecchio.[2]

Version: Uffizi
Ref: **1.** Vasari, ed. G. Milanesi, III, p. 463. Repr. Katherine B. Neilson, *Filippino Lippi*, 1938, fig. 15. **2.** Vasari, ed. G. Milanesi, *I Ragionamenti e le lettere*, Florence, 1883, VIII, p. 116.

3303 Vincenzo Ruffo

Panel, 22.8 × 16.6 cm

Inscribed: *VINCENCIVS RVFVS MVS.*

(1510-1587) Veronese singer and composer.

There is an unidentified seal on the back.

3304 Jacopo Sadoleto

Panel, 22.6 × 16.7 cm

Inscribed: *IACOBVS SADOL(ET)VS*

(1477-1547) Humanist, Professor of Civil Law at Ferrara. Cardinal in the reforming party.

The ultimate prototype is the same as that used by Vasari for his portrait in *Leo X's entrance into Florence* in the Palazzo Vecchio.[1] According to Kenner, Vasari also used the same source in his *Paul III rewarding merit* in the Cancelleria of the Palazzo di San Giorgio.[2]

Versions: Ambrosiana; Uffizi; Vienna 32 (761).[2]
Ref: **1.** Vasari, ed. Milanesi, VIII, p. 142. Count Baldesar Castiglione, *The Book of the Courtier*, 1901, pl. 48. **2.** Kenner, *op. cit.*, XVI, 1896, p. 163. Vasari, ed. G. Milanesi, VII, p. 679.

3305 Jacopo Sannazzaro

Panel, 21.8 × 16.8 cm

(1456-1530) Neapolitan poet and scholar.

The Giovio portrait was in the collection of Signora Palumbo Cerboni.[1] 3305 differs from the portrait engraved in the Basle edition of the *Elogia . . .*[2] The sitter is not the same man as in the so-called *Sannazzaro* by Titian at Hampton Court.[3] There is some resemblance in the features in the portrait attributed to Giovanni Paolo di Agostini at New Orleans.[4] The sitter appears rather older, but with a very similar hairstyle and in a very similar pose in Vasari's *Entry of Leo X into Florence* in the Palazzo Vecchio.[5] He is also older in the bust on his tomb in Santa Maria del Parto, Naples.

Marcantonio Michiel records a portrait in the collection of Pietro Bembo attributed to Sebastiano del Piombo after another portrait[6] which may be that which appeared in the Ventura Collection sale, Milan 6 April 1932 lot 47.[7] In this portrait too the sitter is older than in 3305. 3305 is closest to a picture engraved by Luigi Morghen when in the Lancelotti Collection.[8]

Both the Ambrosiana and the Uffizi portraits differ from 3305 as does the portrait in the Recueil d'Arras (11917). The Vienna portrait is reported to be like the engraving.[9]

The portrait in Titian's lost *Submission of Frederick Barbarossa to Pope Alexander III* is probably the source of one of these types.[10]

Ref: **1.** Rovelli, *op. cit.*, p. 184.   **2.** Paolo Giovio, *Elogia . . .*, 1577, p. 149.   **3.** Harold E. Wethey, *The Paintings of Titian*, II, 1971, p. 138, pl. 19.   **4.** Fern Rusk Shapley, *Paintings from the Samuel H. Kress Collection, Italian Schools, XV-XVI Century*, 1968, p. 51, fig. 114.   **5.** Vasari, ed. G. Milanesi, VIII, p. 142; Count Baldesar Castiglione, *The Book of the Courtier*, 1901, pl. 17.   **6.** The Anonimo, *Notes on pictures and works of art in Italy made by an anonymous writer in the 16th Century*, translated by Paolo Mussi, edited by George C. Williamson, 1903, p. 22.   **7.** Luitpold Dussler, *Sebastiano del Piombo*, Basel, 1942, pp. 146-147.   **8.** Lionello Venturi, *Gian Paolo de Agostini a Napoli*, L'Arte XXI 1918, pp. 49-52, fig 1; the picture is dated 1516 and was then attributed to Raphael, see J. D. Passavant, *Raphael d'Urbin*, 1860 Vol. 2, p. 364. The engraving appears on the title page of Colangelo, *Vita di G. Sannazaro*, Naples 1819.   **9.** Kenner, *op. cit.*, XVIII, 1897, pp. 250-1.   **10.** Carlo Ridolfi, *Le Maraviglie dell'arte*, I, 1648, p. 140.

3306 Cangrande della Scala

Panel, 22.8 × 16.8 cm

Inscribed: *CANIS MAGNVS*
CANIS SCALIGER/C(O)GNOMENTO MAGNI

(1291-1329) Ruler of Verona, and later of Vicenza and Padua.

A portrait by Giotto is recorded by Vasari[1] and Kenner thinks that Altichiero used this for his fresco in Verona.[2] This seems a more probable prototype than the equestrian statue in Verona.[3]

3306 is not based on the portrait engraved in the Basle edition of the *Elogia*, where Scaliger is bearded and not in armour.[4]

Versions: Vienna 145 (694); Uffizi 80; Rovelli Collection.[5]
Prov: Bought from Winstanley by Roscoe 29 September 1812 £1 5s 0d.[6]
Ref: **1.** Vasari, ed. G. Milanesi, 1878, I, p. 388.   **2.** Kenner, *op. cit.*, XVII, 1896, pp. 244-6.   **3.** Julius von Schlosser, *Ein veronesischer Bildenbuch und die höfische Kunst des XIV Jahr.*, Jahrbuch des Allerhochsten Kaiserhauses, XVI, 1895, p. 181 suggests that the Vienna and Uffizi versions are based on a lost fresco in the Palazzo della Signoria, Verona.   **4.** Paolo Giovio, *Elogia . . .*, 1575, p. 64.   **5.** Rovelli, *op. cit.*, p. 165.   **6.** Roscoe Papers 5317 bill from Winstanley.

3307   Giacomuzzo Attendolo, Count of Cotignola, called lo Sforza.

Panel, 22.8 × 16.8 cm

Inscribed: *SFORTIA COTTIGNOIA*

(1369-1424) Soldier. Founder of the Sforza family.

3307 is based on the same prototype as the Giovio portrait.[1] The Vienna portrait, however, is based on a different source.[2]

Versions: Uffizi 101; Ambrosiana; Rovelli Collection.[3]
Ref: **1.** Kenner, *op. cit.*, XVIII, 1897, p. 253.   **2.** Paolo Giovio, *Elogia . . .*, 1575, p. 120; Theobald Muller, *Musaei Ioviani Imagines*, 1577, n.p.; and Paolo Giovio, *Vitae Illustrium Virorum*, 1578, p. 105.   **3.** Rovelli, *op. cit.*, p. 167.

3308   King Sigismund I of Poland

Panel, 22.8 × 16.8 cm

Inscribed: *GISMVNDVS REX POL*

(1467-1548) King of Poland from 1506. Soldier.

The ultimate prototype is the portrait in Hans von Kulmbach's *Adoration of the Kings* in Berlin.[1] Giovio's portrait was engraved.[2]

Version: Uffizi.
Ref: **1.** Friedrich Winkler, *Hans von Kulmbach*, 1959, pl. 35.   **2.** Paolo Giovio, *Elogia . . .*, 1575, p. 353 and Theobald Muller, *Musaei Ioviani Imagines*, 1577, n.p.

3309 Alessandro Tartagni da Imola

Panel, 22.8 × 16.6 cm

Inscribed: *ALEXANDER IMOLA. I.V.C.*

(1424-1477) Jurist and professor of civil law. The abbreviations stand for *Iuris consultus.*

According to Kenner, the Mantua copy was dated 1467 and differed from that in Vienna, which is a version of 3309. The ultimate prototype for 3309 was probably the portrait on his tomb by Francesco di Simone Ferrucci in San Domenico, Bologna or his death mask.[1] Another portrait of Tartagni based on the same prototype is in the album of drawings made by Bartolomeo Passarotti of Bolognese jurists.[2]

Versions: Vienna 135 (483).[1]
Ref: **1.** Kenner, XVIII, 1897, pp. 256-7. **2.** Stanza del Borgo, Milan and Florence, 1970, *Vise e figure in disegni italiani e stranieri dal Cinquecento al Ottocento* (18). Christie, 6 December, 1972 (42). *Burlington Magazine* Supplement to December 1976 pl. XII.

3310 Benedetto Varchi

Panel, 22.8 × 16.8 cm

Inscribed: *BENEDICTVS VARCHIVS*

(1503-1565) Florentine historian, poet and humanist.

Although the sitter is not the same man as the so-called Varchi by Titian in Vienna,[1] and the portrait is not based on the Domenico Poggini medal,[2] the features agree with those in the Uffizi portrait where Varchi is looking upwards.

Ref: **1.** Harold E. Wethey, *The Paintings of Titian*, II, 1971, pl. 83. **2.** Wethey, *op. cit.*, pl. 84.

3311 Fra Giovanni da Verona

Panel, 22.5 × 16.7 cm

Inscribed: *F. IOHANNES VER. VERMIGVLATO/OPERE CELEBRIS./FRATER IOAANNES VERMICULATOR VER.*

(1457-1525) Decorative artist, who worked in intarsia, wood, stone and bronze. The inscription refers to his prowess in *opus vermiculatum.*

The top inscription is the earlier.

3312 Francesco Accursio

Panel, 22.8 × 16.7 cm

Inscribed: *ACCVRSI. GIO. FIOR*

(1182/1185-1259/1263) Jurist. Compiler of the *Glossa Magna* of the *Corpus Iuris Civilis*. Florentine by birth, but worked in Bologna.

GIO is probably an error for GLO made by a restorer strengthening the inscription.[1]

The portrait in the Ambrosiana is of Marcangelo Accursio not Francesco. The Uffizi portrait (271) is based on a different source from the source of 3312. The portrait once at Mantua bore the date 1236; another portrait is recorded at Vienna 40 (476).[2] and yet others are listed by Friedrich Carl von Savigny.[3]

Ref: 1. Ralph Fastnedge, *Cleaned Pictures*, W.A.G., 1955, p. 52 (26).   2. Kenner, *op. cit.*, XVIII, 1897, pp. 187-8.   3. Friedrich Carl von Savigny, *Geschichte des Römische Rechts in Mittelalter*, V, Heidelberg, 1829, p. 238.

3313 Andrea Alciati

Panel, 22.8 × 16.8 cm

Inscribed: *ANDREAS ALCIATVS*

(1492-1550) of Milan. Jurist and historian of the law.

Giovio asked Ercole II of Ferrara for a copy of the portrait in his collection in 1544.[1] That portrait was probably not painted before 1542 when Alciati arrived in Ferrara.[2]

3313 is not based on the same prototype as the Vienna[3] or the Ambrosiana version. Abbondanza lists a number of other portraits of Alciati.[4]

Versions: Uffizi 207.

Ref: 1. P. Iovii. *Epistularum pars prior* ed. G. G. Ferrero, 1956, n. 177. Noted by Eugene Muntz, *Le Musée des portraits de Paul Jove*, 1900, p. 13.   2. R. Abbondanza, s.v. Alciato, Andrea in *Dizionario Biografico degli Italiani*, II, 1960, p. 75.   3. Kenner, *op. cit.*, XVIII, 1897, p. 188.   4. Abbondanza, *op. cit.*,

3314 Giovanni Andrea dell' Anquillara

Panel, 22.8 × 16.2 cm

Inscribed: *IOANNES AND ANQVILARA*

(c. 1517-c. 1572) Poet and translator, best known for his translation of Ovid's *Metamorphoses*.

NORTH RUSSIAN School, late 17th or early 18th century

3049   The Archangel Michael with Saints Laurus and Florus

Panel, 72 × 52.5 cm; painted area, 59.5 × 44 cm

Inscribed: in Slavonic on the margin at the top *Holy Martyr Flor, Archangel Michael, Holy Martyr Lavr.* Above the leading horseman, undeciphered inscription.

Saint Florus and Laurus were patrons of horses and horsebreeders.[1] Russians dedicated chapels in the neighbourhood of stables and markets to them.[2] The saints stand in front of the walls of the city of Kvestendil, Bulgaria where St. Michael halted a pestilence that affected the horses. The three riders on the left are Speusippos, Jeleusippos and Meleusippos, who are frequently associated with Saints Florus and Laurus in icons. Their Phrygian caps betray their Cappadocian origin. The three horsemen took their horses to pagan festivals, but were persuaded to alter their ways when God appeared to them in their dreams and asked them to take care of their "immortal animals." The cult of Florus and Laurus came to Russia from the Balkans.[3]

Icons in an Oslo private collection[4] and in the Russisches Museum[5] also combine these three saints and horsemen with the city walls of Kvestendil.

Talbot Rice at differing dates suggested attributions to the Novgorod[6] and Pskov Schools.[7] Chamot dated 3049 to the late 16th Century.[8] G. D. Petrova, however, dated 3049 to the late 17th or early 18th Century on the grounds of the shape of the faces. She suggested that it was painted in one of the North Russian provinces.[9]

Prov: ?Purchased by William Archibald Propert in Petrograd;[10] Fine Art Society;[11] from the whom purchased for £22 by Lord Wavertree, May 1917;[12] who bequeathed it to the W.A.G., 1933.

Exh: Fine Art Society, *Russian Icons*, 1917, (14).[10]

Ref: **1.** W. N. Lasarew, *Die Malerei und die Skulptur Nowgorods*, in *Geschichte der Russischen Kunst*, II, 1958, pp. 170-2.   **2.** Louis Réau, *L'Art Russe des origines à Pierre le Grand*, 1921, p. 159.   **3.** P. Gussew, *Die Ikonographie der Heiligen Flor und Laurus in der Nowgoroder Kunst*, Arbeiten des XV Archäologen—Kongresses in Nowgorod, 1914, p. 97 and N. Malizki, *Altrussische Kulte der Heiligen der Landwirtschaft nach Kunstdenkmälern*, Nachrichten der Staatliche Akademie für die Geschichte der materiellen Kultur, XI, 1932, pp. 12-14.   **4.** Helge Kjellin, *Ryska Ikoner*, 1956, p. 132, pl. XLVIII.   **5.** Helskini Ateneum, 1974, *Venäjän Taidetta 900-1600-Luvuilta* (138).   **6.** Professor D. Talbot Rice, undated notes in the Walker Art Gallery file.   **7.** Talbot Rice, notes dated 21 March 1955.   **8.** Hove Museum of Art, 1961, *Russian Life and Art* (6).   **9.** G. D. Petrova, letter, 24 October 1975.   **10.** Letter of Peyton Skipwith 22 April 1976. For further details see 3050 (p. 136).   **11.** Label on reverse Fine Art Society/No. 14.   **12.** Letter from S. F. Growse, 27 September 1959.

NOVGOROD, School of, 16th or 17th century

3048   Saint George killing the dragon and other saints Around him in smaller rectangular fields. Above: St. Michael, the Virgin, Christ

and St. John and Gabriel; to the left; Saints Nicholas, an unidentified saint, ?Saint Nicophoros; to the right; Saint Athanasios, Demetrios of Thessalonica, Stephen or Spiridon. Below: Saints Cosmas, Damian, Pyaatnitsa, Catherine and Barbara.

Panel, 86.3 × 52.3 cm

Inscribed: with the names of the saints in Slavonic: *Saint George, Michael, Mother of God, Jesus Christ, John, Gabriel, Saint Nicholas, . . ., N. k . . ., Athanasios, Demetrios, Stefan, . . .smas, Damian, Pyaatnitsa, Ecaterina, Barbara.*

Condition: much worn throughout

The grouping of Christ between the Virgin and St. John who intercede for the sins of the world is that of the Deesis.[1] Saint Pyaatnitsa (Friday) is also known as Saint Paraskeva.

Talbot Rice at different times, attributed it to the Serbian School of the 15th Century or 16th Century,[1] and the Novgorod School of the 17th Century in a primitive style fairly close to a Greek prototype.[2] Demus thought that it was possibly of the 16th Century.[3]

Prov: ?Purchased by William Archibald Propert in Petrograd;[4] Fine Art Society;[5] from whom purchased in May 1917 for £26 5s 0d. by Lord Wavertree;[6] who bequeathed it to the W.A.G., 1933.

Exh: Fine Art Society, *Russian icons*, 1917, (5).[4]

Ref: **1.** Professor D. Talbot Rice, undated notes in the gallery files. **2.** Talbot Rice, notes dated 21 March 1955. **3.** Professor O. Demus, notes dated 21 March 1955. **4.** Letter of Peyton Skipwith 22 April 1976. For further details see 3050 (p. 136). **5.** Label on the back Fine Art Society/No. 5. **6.** Letter of S. F. Growse, 27 August 1959.

OTTOMAN School, 18th century

3047   The Pantocrator with two small angels

Panel, 63.1 × 48.5 cm

Inscribed: on the halo *O CO   P (O SOTHR*—The Saviour (Greek)). Beside the two angels two circular medallions inscribed in Arabic.

Condition: Very poor; blessing hand of Christ is completely lost.

According to Talbot Rice, the appellation "The Saviour" is very rare.

He also suggested that 3047 is a 14th Century picture perhaps from one of the Greek communities of Southern Asia Minor, the medallions and the lower part of Christ's Costume repainted in the 17th Century in North Syria or Anatolia.[1] He later suggested that it was Syrian of the 18th Century,[2] whereas Demus considered it Turkish "and by a local painter not earlier than the 17th Century."[3]

Prov: Purchased in Baalbec by J. W. Thompson, who presented it to the W.A.G., 1939.
Ref: **1.** Professor D. Talbot Rice, letter of 18 August 1939. **2.** Letter of 28 June 1959. **3.** Notes by Professor O. Demus, 21 March 1955.

PALMA, Jacopo, il Giovane, 1544-1628, Follower of

2848 The Dead Christ supported by an angel

Copper, 24 × 20.1 cm, with an addition of 3 cm to top and bottom

Fairfax Murray thought it possibly a copy after Palma Giovane.[1] It certainly derives from his style.

Prov: Entered the collection of the L.R.I. between 1836 and 1843;[2] deposited at the W.A.G., 1893;[3] presented to the W.A.G., 1948.
Ref: **1.** L.R.I. Annual Report 1893 p. 50 (102). **2.** 1843 Catalogue p. 30 (108). **3.** 1893 Catalogue p. 33 (92).

PALMEZZANO, Marco, 1458/1463-1539, Studio of

2793 Virgin and Child enthroned with Saints Francis, Matthew, Louis of Toulouse (left), John the Evangelist, Anthony Abbot and Peter Martyr[1] (right)

Panel, 82.5 × 156 cm

The ground is strewn with heads of pink flowers of the poppy family, a symbol of death, whilst meadow rue, a symbol of grace, and a fig tree,[2] a symbol of life, grow out of the wall either side of the Virgin and Child. Hence there is an allusion to Christ's death and resurrection bringing grace to mankind.

The coats of arms at the lower corners are those of the Michiel and Donà families.[3] 2793 may have been painted to celebrate the marriage in 1526 between Giovanni Michiel and Donata Donà.[4]

The attribution to Palmezzano's workshop was first suggested by Cavalcaselle.[5] The style is close to that of his late work. For instance compare St. Matthew with St. John the Baptist in the signed and dated 1536 *Baptism* once in the Mensing Collection.[6]

Heinemann's attribution to Giovanni Mansueti is unconvincing.[7]

Prov: Anonymous sale, Robins, 20 April 1812 (29) £31 15s 0d. Entered the collection of the L.R.I. between 1836 and 1843;[8] deposited at the W.A.G., 1893;[9] presented to the W.A.G., 1948.

Ref: 1. First identified by Mrs Jameson, Notes on 1851 L.R.I. Catalogue (L.R.I. Archives 63.2).   2. Mrs Greenwood helped to identify the flower and herb, orally 23 July 1976, and August 11, 1976.   3. 1812 sale catalogue identified St. Francis as Giovanni Michiel and St. Thomas a Becket (i.e. St. Peter Martyr) as Tomaso Donato, which suggests that the coat of arms may already have been identified.   4. Letter from the Direttore of the Archivio di Stato, Venice, 23 November 1951.   5. J. A. Crowe and G. B. Cavalcaselle, *A History of Painting in North Italy*, I, 1871, p. 116. Cavalcaselle had earlier considered it a fake. MS comments (L.R.I. Archives 63.4).   6. W. M. Mensing Collection Sale, Amsterdam, 1938; previously Smallenburg Sale, Fred Muller, 6 May 1913.   7. Fritz Heinemann, *Bellini e I Belliniani*, I, 1963, p. 247 v. 193; confirmed by letter, 9 July 1968.   8. 1843 Catalogue p. 12 (37).   9. 1893 Catalogue p. 12 (29).

PANINI, Giovanni Paolo, 1691/2-1765

2794   Ruins of Rome

Canvas, 173 × 221 cm

Signed: *I. PAV PANINI/ROMAE/174(?)*

A *capriccio* or *veduta ideata* with, from left to right, the Temple of Hadrian, the Pantheon, the Obelisk now in the Piazza del Popolo, the Arch of Janus Quadrifrons in the Forum Boarium, the so-called Temple of Fortuna Virilis also in the Forum Boarium, and the Column of Trajan. In the left foreground is the statue of a Goddess now in the Museo Nazionale, Naples but to be found in the 18th century in the courtyard of the Palazzo Farnese.[1] Panini has "reconstructed" some of these antique buildings; the Temple of Hadrian has been disengaged from the Dogana di Terra into which Francesco Fontana had built it in 1695 and the cornice and entablature extended;[2] the Pantheon has been deprived of Bernini's two bell towers and of the railings between the columns erected under Alexander VII (1655-67), some entablatures have been restored to the Arch of Janus Quadrifrons;[3] Trajan's Column however retains the statue of St. Peter erected in 1588. In other respects the buildings and inscriptions are accurately recorded; the scale of the figures supporting the inscription on Trajan's Column has however been increased.

Arisi suggests 1740 or 1741 as the date for No. 2794.[4]

Variants are in the collection of Mrs P. de Koenigsberg of Buenos Aires (dated 1735), in the John Herron Art Museum, Indianapolis (dated 1735), formerly with Knoedlers, New York (dated 1741) and in the Appleby Collection, London (undated). A copy[5] was formerly in the collection of Raymond Richards, Esq., (ex. Lord Crawford of Balcarres) sold Christie's, 4 December, 1964, lot 125.

Prov: William Earle, sold Winstanley, Liverpool, 17-18 April 1839 (44) £107 12s 6d.;
       James Aikin who presented it 1876.

Exh: *1st Exhibition of Objects Illustrative of the Fine Arts*, Mechanics Institution,
       Liverpool 1840 (241); British Institution 1864 (116); W.A.G., *Cleaned Pictures*,
       1955 (37).

Ref: 1. Identified by Ferdinando Arisi, *Gian Paolo Panini*, 1961, pp. 165 and
       181.   2. See for example G. Piranesi, *Vedute di Roma, Veduta della Dogana di
       Terra a Piazza di Pietra*, No. 26, 1753.   3. See for example G. Cassini, *Nuova
       Raccolta delle migliori Vedute antiche e moderne di Roma*, 1755, fol. 62 repro-
       duced in Ernest Nash, *Pictorial Dictionary of Ancient Rome*, 1968, I, p. 504, plate
       620.   4. Arisi, *op. cit.*, p. 165.   5. A considerable number of pentimenti can
       be detected in No. 2794.

PARTON, Ernest, 1845-1904

412 A Woodland Home

Canvas, 95.2 × 128 cm

Signed: *Ernest Parton 1879*

Prov: Purchased from the 1879 L.A.E. (£126 6s 0d.).
Exh: L.A.E. 1879 (16).

PASINELLI, Lorenzo, 1629-1700, after

2872 Coriolanus taking Leave of his Wife and Children

Canvas, 100.4 × 138.5 cm

Probably a copy after the painting commissioned by Annibale Ranuzzi
for the Casa Ranuzzi in Bologna and described thus by Zanotti, "Marzio
Coriolano quando alla presenza del suo Esercito accampato sotto le mura
di Roma corre ad incontrare la Madre che con la Moglie e con Figlio viene
ad implorare da Lui compassione e pietà por la Patra angustiata ed
oppressa dalle sue Armi".[1] The original is lost. It was completed by May
1, 1672 when Annibale Ranuzzi became Gonfaloniere of Bologna.[2]

Prov: Presented by John George Woodhouse, 1876.
Ref: 1. G. P. Zanotti, *Nuovo fregio di gloria a Felsina . . . nella vita di Lorenzo Pasinelli*
       etc. 1703, pp. 30-1. The original is also noted in the *Catalogo dei quadri della Casa
       Ranuzzi di Bologna*, 1698, published by G. Campori, *Raccolta di Cataloghi
       Inediti*, 1870, p. 410. See also A. Pigler, *Barockthemen*, II, p. 366.   2. L. Cres-
       pi, *Vite de pittori bolognesi*, 1769, p. 132.

PERUGINO, Pietro, 1445-1523

2856 The Birth of the Virgin

Panel, 18.7 × 41 cm

This predella panel had a companion picture in both the Cawdor and
Matthew Smith Sales, which Anne Cooke identified as a panel now at
Polesden Lacey.[1] Sinibaldi,[2] Camesasca[3] and Passavant,[4] however, all still

accept the association of 2856 with the predella of the Verrocchio work-shop altarpiece at Pistoia, first proposed by Valentiner.[5] Measurements,[6] provenance, style and the identical red and white painted marble frames however confirm the association with the Polesden Lacey *Miracle of the foundation of Santa Maria Maggiore* and invalidate the association with the proposed Pistoia altarpiece predella. The subject matter of the Poles-den Lacey panel, the miraculous fall of snow forming the shape of the church of Santa Maria Maggiore in Rome suggests that the altarpiece of which it once formed a part was probably painted for a church or altar dedicated to the Madonna of the Snow.

Generally 2856 has been identified as *The Birth of the Baptist.* Roscoe, however, was perhaps correct in calling it *"the Nativity of the Virgin"*.[7] It is not possible to sex the child. It would be iconographically unusual for the *Birth of the Baptist* to appear alongside a *Foundation of Santa Maria Maggiore* in a predella. The latter subject fits much more comfortably into a predella illustrating the life and miracles of the Virgin. For instance, one finds the *Birth of the Virgin*, the *Foundation of Santa Maria Maggiore* and other scenes from the life and miracles of the Virgin in the predella to Jacopo Bellini's altarpiece of the *Annunciation* in San Alessandro, Bres-cia.[8]

There are a number of representations of the *Miracle of the Foundation* in Florence dating from the fifteenth century. The series of stained glass windows in Orsanmichele devoted to the Miracles of the Virgin include *The Foundation*,[9] and there is a fresco of it by Lorenzo Monaco in another cycle devoted to the Virgin's life and miracles in Santa Trinita.[10]

The attribution to Perugino was first made by Berenson,[11] was followed by Zeri[12] and has been generally accepted since. It has been doubted occasionally whether the Polesden Lacey panel is by the same hand, and the names of Filippino Lippi and Raffaellino del Garbo have been associated with it.[13] But most recently Zeri[14] and Longhi[15] have accepted the authorship of Perugino for both panels. They are clearly related in style to the Perugia *Miracles of San Bernardino*, 2856 especially to the *Freeing of a Prisoner* and *The healing of the Paralytic*, the Polesden Lacey panel to *The healing of the daughter of G. A. da Rieti* and *The miracle of the blind man*. Both are Verrocchiesque, particularly 2856, where the child is very reminiscent of the Child in the Gambier-Parry *Madonna and Child*.[16]

Prov: Cappella in Casa Pucci, Florence;[17] bought by Tresham;[17] Lord Cawdor sale, Skinner and Dyke, 6 August 1800 (26); Colonel Matthew Smith sale Christie, 12 May 1804 (42) bt. Roscoe £9 9s 0d.; Roscoe sale (11) passed; presented to the L.R.I. by 1819;[18] deposited at the W.A.G., 1893;[19] presented to the W.A.G., 1948.

Exh: Manchester, *Art Treasures*, 1857 (105).

Ref: 1. Anne Cooke, *A Companion to Liverpool's "Birth of the Baptist,"* Liverpool Bulletin 10, 1962, pp. 14-22. Her conclusions have been accepted most recently by Martin Davies in *European Paintings in the Collection of the Worcester Art Museum, Text*, 1974, pp. 384-385 n. 11.   2. Giulia Sinibaldi, *Drawings by Perugino*, Master Drawings, II, 1964, p. 31.   3. Ettore Camesasca, *L'opera completa di Perugino*, 1969 (13).   4. G. Passavant, *Verrocchio*, 1969, p. 213. App. 54.   5. R. Langton Douglas, *Leonardo da Vinci*, 1944, pp. 61ff and p. 109.   6. Cooke, *op. cit.*, p. 16, 20. The Polesden Lacey panel, 18.7 × 40 cm; Louvre *Annunciation* 14 × 59 cm; Worcester *Miracle of San Donato* 16.2 × 34.8 cm.   7. Roscoe sale, (11); followed by the 1819 Catalogue (6) the 1843

172

Catalogue p. 8 (24), and by the 1851 Catalogue p. 6 (20).   **8.** Bernard Berenson, *Italian Pictures of the Renaissance, Venetian School*, I, 1957, pl. 60-64.   **9.** Werner Cohn, *Zur Ikonographie der Glasfenster von Orsanmichele*, Mitteilungen des Kunsthistorischen Institutes in Florenz, Neunter Band,—Heft I, 1959, p. 8 fig. 8.   **10.** Bernard Berenson, *Italian Pictures of the Renaissance, Florentine School*, I, 1963, p. 119.   **11.** Bernard Berenson, *Italian Pictures of the Renaissance*, 1932, p. 432; though R. Longhi's attribution in a letter of 29 October 1959 was based on notes made in 1930.   **12.** Federico Zeri, *Il maestro della Annunciazione Gardner*, Bollettino d'Arte, 1953, pp. 134-5.   **13.** St. John Gore, *The Art of Painting in Florence & Siena from 1250 to 1500*, Wildenstein, London, 1965, pp. 33 (57) and 38-9 (66), and his *Polesden Lacey*, 1964, p. 18-19 quoting also the opinion of Luisa Vertova. He now, however, accepts that they are by the same hand in *Polesden Lacey*, 1974, pp. 23-4. Carlo L. Ragghianti, *Firenze 1470-1480 Disegni dal modello*, 1975, p. 42 n. 34 thinks that it is close to Monte di Giovanni.   **14.** Federico Zeri, *Italian Primitives at Messrs. Wildenstein*, Burlington Magazine, 1965, p. 255.   **15.** Roberto Longhi, *Una 'Riconsiderazione' dei Primitivi Italiani a Londra*, Paragone, XVI, No. 183, May, 1965, p. 16.   **16.** Sir Anthony Blunt, *The Gambier-Parry Collection, Provisional Catalogue*, 1967, p. 19 (62) pl. I. Noted also by Passavant, *op. cit.*, p. 210.   **17.** MS note on reverse as from Casa Pucci. Colonel Smith Sale 12 May 1804 (42) as from Capelle Pucci, in Florence. Henry Tresham went to Italy with John Campbell of Cawdor (later 1st Lord Cawdor). He returned to London in 1789. Ulrich Thieme and Felix Becker, *Allgemeines Lexikon der Bildenden Kunstler*, XXXIII, 1939, p. 381 s.v. Tresham.   **18.** 1819 Catalogue (6).   **19.** 1893 Catalogue p.10 (22).

PERUGINO, Pietro, follower of

1600   Madonna and Child with Saint John and two angels

Canvas laid down on panel, 79.5 × 63.5 cm

A much damaged work by an unidentified follower of Perugino,[1] possibly once a banner. The Madonna and Child are derived from Perugino's *Madonna of the Brotherhood of Saint Peter Martyr* in Perugia.[2]

Prov: Unidentified seal bearing the initials BC; purchased in Italy by Henry Clark of Bromborough House, Cheshire c. 1860; by descent to Bishop Herbert Gresford Jones; presented by the latter, with his son, Bishop Michael Jones, 1947.[3]

Ref: **1.** 1963 Catalogue p. 152 as a nineteenth century copy or pastiche or fake, but Prof. S. Rees-Jones, orally, November 1976 considers that it is a sixteenth century work, and no Perugino prototype of this composition appears to be extant.   **2.** Walter Bombe, *Perugino*, 1914, p. 177.   **3.** MS label on reverse.

PESELLINO, Francesco di Stefano, called, *c.* 1422-1457, follower of

2796   Madonna and Child enthroned

Panel, 70 × 48.1 cm

The attribution is due to Berenson who suggested that 2796 came from the same cartoon as the Madonna in the Johnson Collection.[1] There the Madonna and Child are in reverse and the Child kicks out with his left foot. There are also differences in the position of the Madonna's hands. A similar group is in the Fogg Museum, where the Child holds a pomegranate and the hands are in different poses.[2]

Prov: Entered the L.R.I. Collection between 1836 and 1843;[3] deposited at the W.A.G., 1893;[4] presented to the W.A.G., 1948.

Ref: 1. Bernard Berenson, *Catalogue of the Johnson Collection I, Italian Paintings*, 1913, p. 23 (36). **2.** Bernard Berenson, *Quadri senza casa*, II, Dedalo, XII, 3, 1932, p. 678. Attributed to the Master of the Pomegranate by Fahy, letter of Mrs Phoebe Peebles, 7 August 1975. **3.** 1843 Catalogue, p. 6 (18). **4.** 1893 Catalogue, p. 8 (14).

2797 Head of a Woman

Panel, 36.8 × 30.2 cm

Concern about the condition of No. 2797 was expressed in 1854.[1] The blueish green background is entirely repainted and a strip about 2 cm wide around the edges appears to have been painted over more recent gesso. The unusual thickness of the panel may have led Roscoe to believe that it had once been set into wainscotting.[2]

2797 derives from the Virgin in Filippo Lippi's Munich *Madonna and Child* (647). The same head was used again as a Saint Catherine in Budapest's *Madonna and Child with the infant Saint John, Saint Catherine and five angels* (50.752)[3] and in Yale's *Madonna, Child, four angels and Saint Catherine* (1871.43).

The absence of a halo might indicate that this was intended to be a portrait rather than a Madonna or Saint. Berenson in fact suggested that the original might have been a lost portrait of Filippo Lippi's mistress, Lucrezia Buti.[4] But it is more probable that 2797 is a fragment from a larger composition.

Prov: Probably Mr Pinney from whom purchased by William Roscoe after July 1811, possibly after May 1812;[5] Roscoe sale 1816 (16) passed, in the L.R.I. by 1819;[6] deposited at the W.A.G., 1893;[7] presented to the W.A.G., 1948.

Ref: 1. Letter from Philip Westcott to Theodore Rathbone 24 January 1854 (L.R.I. Archives 17). **2.** William Roscoe sale catalogue (16), as "a panel cut from the wainscott of the Palazzo Riccardi, formerly the palace of the Medici at Florence". **3.** Klara Garas, *Katalog der Galerie Alter Meister*, I, 1967, p. 539, 99 × 60.5 cm. **4.** Bernard Berenson, *Florentine Painters*, 1909, p. 169. **5.** Roscoe Papers, No. 5315, 5316. Pinney may be the man who bought a Berchem in the National Gallery (820). **6.** 1819 Catalogue (11). **7.** 1893 Catalogue p. 9 (19).

2890 Madonna and Child with St. John and three angels

Panel, 64.1 × 49.5 cm

Traces of squaring are still visible.

The goldfinches held by the Christ Child and on the parapet are symbols of the Passion,[1] whilst the open pomegranate is a symbol of immortality.[2] The lily is particularly associated with the angel Gabriel in the Annunciation, and may identify him in 2890, but may simply be a symbol of purity.

The composition of 2890 was extremely popular in the late fifteenth century. There are a large number of paintings from the same studio which are related, some probably taken from the same cartoon. All the participants in 2890, occur, for instance in the *Madonna, Child, St. John and another Saint with God the Father and the Dove*, once in the Fitzgerald collection, where one of the angels is no longer half obscured.[3] The closest picture to 2890, however, is that in Budapest, (Inv. 2539(55)) in which foliage has replaced the two angels at top right.

The St. John the Baptist derives from Filippo Lippi's Berlin *Adoration of the Child* (No. 69), whilst the central group is inspired by a *Madonna and Child* of the type found in the Isabella Stewart Gardner Museum, Boston,[4] in a recent Christie sale[5] and in the Keresteny Museum, Esztergom,[6] which is developed from Filippo Lippi's Pitti *tondo* in reverse.

Pictures of this type generally are attributed to Pseudo Pier Francesco Fiorentino, a figure to whom a large and disparate group of works deriving from paintings by Pesellino and Lippi emanating from several studios have been assigned. Berenson was the first to associate 2890 with this group.[7]

Prov: Roscoe, sale, (17) passed at £10 17s 6d.; in the L.R.I. by 1819;[8] deposited at the W.A.G., 1893;[9] presented to the W.A.G., 1948.

Exh: Manchester, *Art Treasures*, 1857 (837).

Ref: 1. Herbert Friedman, *The Symbolic Goldfinch*, 1946 p. 9. E. F. Wilson, *Review of Friedman op. cit.*, Speculum, XXIII, 1948, pp. 121-125 also points out that the lating for goldfinch "lucina or lucinia" may mean "bringer of light" (i.e. of grace).   2. Friedman, *op. cit.*, p. 120.   3. Sothebys 3 July 1963 (18) 34½ × 19¼ in.   4. Philip Hendy, *The Isabella Stewart Gardner Museum, Catalogue of the Exhibited Paintings and Drawings*, 1931 p. 257-9, 60 × 39 cm and Philip Hendy, *European and American Paintings in the Isabella Stewart Gardner Museum, Boston*, 1974, pp. 179-180 listing a large number of derivations.   5. Christie 26 June 1970 (61) bt. Stringer, 21 × 16½ in.   6. Bernard Berenson, *Italian Pictures of the Renaissance, Florentine School*, II, 1963, pl. 835 and Czobor Aynes, *Az Esztergomi Kereszteny Museum Kiallitasakanak Vezetoje*, 1955, p. 8.   7. Bernard Berenson, *Florentine Painters*, 1909, p. 169 and *Italian Pictures of the Renaissance*, 1932, p. 451.   8. 1819 Catalogue (10).   9. L.R.I. Annual Report 1893, p. 48 (23).

PICKNELL, William Lamb, 1853-1897

175   Wintry March

Canvas, 125.7 × 202 cm

Signed: *W. L. Picknell 85*

Picknell was painting in the New Forest in 1881-3 and No. 175 could well represent that area; however he apparently returned to the U.S.A. in 1883, returning thereafter for the winters occasionally to Europe but only to the Mediterranean.[1] The R.A. catalogues however give Picknell's address as Winston House, Ealing for 1885-7 and the canvas of No. 175 has a London stamp.[2] Millicent Garrett-Fawcett[3] described at length the appeal of the New Forest to artists of the 1880's.

Prov: Purchased from the L.A.E., 1885 (£250).
Exh: R.A. 1885 (1121). L.A.E. 1885 (1008). London, *American Exhibition*, 1887.
Ref: 1. *Dictionary of American Biography* XIV, p. 572. *The Catalogue of Paintings by William L. Picknell*, Museum of Fine Arts, Boston, 1898 (introduction by Edward W. Emerson), pp. 7-8, states that Picknell painted for the one or two winters of 1881-1883 in and near the New Forest and that No. 175 was painted there in that period. See also the same author's *An American Landscape Painter*, The Century Magazine, Vol. 62, 1901, p. 711. The date on No. 175 suggests that this must be incorrect but No. 175 could have been started there or based on sketches made there. Apparently in the New Forest while painting in the winter he used a shed with one side glazed in order to paint in bad weather directly from the subject. 2. *Newman, Soho Square,* stamped twice. 3. In *The New Forest,* Magazine of Art, Vol. 8, 1885 pp. 1ff and pp. 45ff.

PIGNONE, Simone, 1611-1698

6261   The Vestal Virgin Tuccia

Canvas, 99 × 85.2 cm

The attribution is accepted by Dr Gerhard Ewald.[1] Accused of breaking her vow of chastity the Vestal Virgin Tuccia carried water in a sieve from the Tiber to the Temple of Vesta to prove her innocence.[2]

Prov: Purchased from the Sabin Galleries, London 1964.
Ref: 1. Letter 22 May 1964. 2. See C. Ripa, *Iconologia*, 1610, pp. 74-5 under *Castita*, also A. Pigler, *Barockthemen*, 1956, II, p. 332 and G. de Tervarent, *Attributs et Symboles dans l'art profane*, 1959, II, p. 369.

PISSARRO, Lucien, 1863-1944

3144   Cerisiers en fleur

Canvas, 61 × 73 cm

Signed in monogram and dated 1931

Listed in the artist's MS Catalogue[1] under April 1931 with the number T.20 and as painted while the artist was at the Campagne Orovida, Chemin de l'Hubac, Dardennes, Toulon. Letters from the artist and from his wife Esther of 4, 7, 14, 20 April and 3 May[2] reveal that the artist was able to work during the middle weeks of April because the weather was fine during that period.

No. 3144 was painted from the terrace of the Campagne Orovida looking north west; the mountain in the background is Le Bau des Quatre Heures.[3]

Prov: Purchased from the artist at the 1934 L.A.E. (£136 10s 0d.).
Exh: L.A.E. 1934 (997); Arts Council, *Lucien Pissarro*, 1963 (58) pl. 8.
Ref: 1. Now owned by Mr John Benusan-Butt to whom I am indebted for this information. 2. All in the Ashmolean Museum, Oxford. I am indebted to Christopher Lloyd and Mrs Anne Thorold for these references. 3. Carel Weight, *letter*, 14 December 1976 and John Benusan-Butt, *letter*, 19 December 1976.

PITTONI, Giovanni Battista, 1687-1767

2798   Solomon and the Queen of Sheba

Canvas, 174.6 × 163.2 cm

One of a group of pictures sold together from a single source in 1947[1] including also No. 619 by Balestra (q.v.), Balestra's *Death of Abel*,[2] I. Spolverini's *Destruction of the Army of Sennacherib*, G. A. Boni's *Christ Healing the Blind* and *Christ in the House of Simon* and Pittoni's *Christ and the Woman taken in Adultery*.[3] These seven pictures probably formed part of a larger group whose theme was justice and mercy. Balestra's *Death of Abel* is signed and dated 1733. No. 2798 was attributed at the 1947 sale to S. Ricci but is certainly by Pittoni. A drawing published as a sketch for the head of Christ in Pittoni's *Miracle of the Loaves and Fishes*[4] may be a sketch for the head of Solomon.

Prov: Obtained in Italy by Algernon William Bellingham Greville[5] 1815-1887; at the sale of his widow, Louisa Fanny, died 1904.[6] N.A.A.F.I. Aldershot sold Sotheby's 30 April 1947 (88) bt. Arcade £38; Philip Toynbee; Richard Wollheim from whom purchased 1955.

Exh: R.A., *Italian Art in Britain* 1960 (444).

Ref: 1. Catalogue of Sotheby's Sale 30 April 1947 lots 82-88.   2. Now Graves Art Gallery, Sheffield.   3. Now Graves Art Gallery, Sheffield attributed to G. A. Boni at the 1947 sale.   4. R. Pallucchini, *I Disegni di Giambattista Pittoni*, 1945, plate 45.   5. Old label on the back of Balestra's *Death of Abel* presumably referring also to the whole group. The stretcher of No. 2798 bears a monogram: AG:. For Algernon William Bellingham Greville see Burke's *Peerage* under *Warwick*. See also Sotheby's Sale Catalogue, 30 April, 1947 catalogue note after lot 88.   6. The same old label states that Balestra's *Death of Abel* was bought at "Mr Greville's sale 1904"—this sale has not been identified.

POST, Kerstin von, 1835-1917

824   A Fishing Village in Flanders

Canvas, 97.1 × 138.4 cm

Attributed on accession to the Gallery to Franz Post[1] but not by him. The donor gave the artist's name as "Poste"[2] and No. 824 is by a 19th century artist with this name. It was exhibited at Leeds in 1868 as by "Mdlle C. de Post (Swedish)" presumably Kerstin von Post (1835-1917) but this attribution cannot yet be substantiated.[4]

Prov: Presented by Robert Hutchison 1865.

Exh: Leeds 1868, *National Exhibition* (1771).

Ref: 1. 1882 Catalogue No. 114, p. 30.   2. Proceedings of the Libraries Museum and Art Galleries Committee, 23 March, 1865.   3. See Exhibitions.   4. Gorel Cavalli-Bjorkman, *letter*, 7 September 1976.

POUSSIN, Nicolas, 1593/4-1665, follower of

1313 Landscape with Arcadian Shepherds

Canvas, 102.5 × 133.3 cm

Attributed by Anthony Blunt most recently to the painter of the *Amor Vincit Omnia* in the Cleveland Museum of Art,[1] this painting has itself been attributed to Pierfrancesco Mola[2] and Blunt had earlier attributed a group including No. 1313 and the *Amor Vincit Omnia* to an artist in the circle of Cassiano dal Pozzo who might be Pietro Testa or Mola.[3] Denis Mahon however believes No. 1313 to be an autograph work of Poussin of about 1627.[4] Grautoff[5] and Jamot[6] had earlier made the same attribution Grautoff suggesting 1630-1635 and Jamot to the period just before 1624.

No. 1313 has suffered considerable losses particularly in the foreground.[7]

Prov: Acquired by the L.R.I. 1836-1843 (as Poussin);[8] deposited at the W.A.G., 1893; presented to the W.A.G., 1948.

Exh: Leeds, *National Exhibition of Works of Art*, 1868 (415). Whitechapel Art Gallery, *French Art*, 1907 (50). Paris, Petit Palais, *Paysage Francais*, 1924 (272). W.A.G. *Cleaned Pictures*, 1955 (29).

Ref: **1.** Anthony Blunt, *The Paintings of Nicolas Poussin*, 1966, *Critical Catalogue*, p. 178. R119.   **2.** E. Schaar, *Eine Poussin-Mola-Frage*, Zeitschrift fur Kunstgeschichte XXIV, 1961, pp. 184ff. The attribution to Mola is denied both by Richard Cocke, *A Note on Mola and Poussin,* Burlington Magazine, Vol, 111, 1969, p. 712 and *Pier Francesco Mola*, 1972, p. 65, R. 14 and by Anne Sutherland Harris, *Notes on the Chronology and Death of Pietro Testa,* Paragone, No. 213, November 1967, pp. 39-40 who believes that it may be by Testa.   **3.** Anthony Blunt, *Poussin dans les Musees de Province*, La Revue des Arts, 1958, p. 12 and *Poussin Studies XI, Some Addenda to the Poussin Number*, Burlington Magazine, Vol. CII, 1960, p. 396.   **4.** Denis Mahon, *Poussiniana*, 1962, p. 18, note 49.   **5.** Otto Grautoff, *Nicolas Poussin*, 1914, pp. 107-108, No. 36.   **6.** Paul Jamot, *Nouvelles Etudes sur Nicolas Poussin*, Gazette de Beaux Arts, 1925, Vol. II, p. 73.   **7.** See W.A.G., *Cleaned Pictures*, 1955 No. 29.   **8.** 1843 Catalogue No. 86.

POUSSIN, Nicolas, after

1311 Landscape with Rebecca and Eliezer

Canvas, 89.1 × 127 cm

The central group is copied nearly exactly from the *Rebecca quenching the Thirst of Eliezer* attributed to Nicolas Poussin.[1] The smoking castle and distant landscape are also both derived from Poussin. No. 1311 was presented to the Gallery with an attribution to Gaspard Dughet[2] to whose style the landscape is certainly close.[3]

Prov: Alexander Nowell of Underley Park Westmorland sold Winstanley, Liverpool 12 July, 1842 bt. T. Arthur Hope[4] who bequeathed it 1882.

Exh: Whitechapel Gallery, *French Art*, 1907 (51).

Ref: 1. Denis Mahon, *Nicolas Poussin's Rebecca al Pozzo*, Apollo, Vol. 81, 1965, p. 196, pl. III. **2.** 1885 Catalogue No. 289 p. 63. **3.** Marie-Nicole Boisclair, *letters*, 21 March and 21 April 1975. **4.** Old Label gives the name of Nowell, no catalogue of this sale survives but it was reported in the *Liverpool Mercury* of 8 July, 1842. The same old label also states that Winstanley, the auctioneer, believed No. 1311 to be by Orizonte and that he had sold it before for £30. A handbill for the sale is in the Gallery files and lists a work by Van Blomen (sic).

PRAT, Loys Joseph, born 1879

756 Idylle

Canvas, 161.3 × 200.5 cm

Signed: *Loys PRAT*

Prov: Purchased from the L.A.E. 1907 (£80).
Exh: Paris, *Société des artistes francais*, 1907 (1292); L.A.E. 1907 (326).

PRETI, Mattia, 1613-1699

2799 Christ in the House of Simon

Canvas, 229 × 302.2 cm

A drawing for this composition is owned by Wildenstein (stock No. 19571).

2887 The Marriage at Cana

Canvas, 229 × 302 cm

2888 The Nativity

Canvas, 227.4 × 298 cm

2889 The Adoration of the Magi

Canvas, 226.6 × 301.3 cm

B. Dargaville[1] suggests an attribution to Gregorio Preti for No. 2889. Nos. 2799, 2887-9 may all be versions of earlier compositions, made in Preti's studio late in his career.[2] Paintings with the subjects of Nos. 2799 and 2887 are recorded late in the artist's career by de Dominicis.[3]

Prov: "A Princely collection in Naples."[4] Presented to the L.R.I., 1829 by John Ashton Yates, Joseph Brooks Yates, John Gladstone, Arthur Heywood, John Philips, R.N., John William Gibson, Thomas Winstanley, Samuel Winstanley, Nathaniel George Philips, George Drinkwater and Gilbert Henderson.[5]
Ref: 1. Verbally, 1972. **2.** B. Dargaville verbally 1972. **3.** Bernardo de Dominicis, *Vite de Pittori*, 1742, Vol. 2, pp. 374-5. **4.** 1836 Catalogue, note following No. 46. **5.** *Annual Report of the Liverpool Royal Institution and Address by Thomas Stuart Traill*, 1829.

PROCACCINI, Giulio Cesare, 1570-1625, after

2800　Marriage of Saint Catherine

Canvas, 144.2 × 152 cm

A copy[1] of the picture in the Brera.[2] The Virgin's bodice and skirt are whiteish whereas in the Brera picture they are red and grey respectively. The considerable variation in tonality from the picture and minor modifications in pose suggest that 2800 may be a studio version.

A Procaccini *Marriage of Saint Catherine* was in Anon sale, Christie, 19 April 1811 (88).

Prov:　Probably sold Thomas Winstanley's, Liverpool, 21-22 January 1840;[3] J. W. Gibsone, who presented it to the L.R.I., 30 April 1845;[4] deposited at the W.A.G., 1893;[5] presented to the W.A.G., 1948.

Ref:　1. Ralph Fastnedge, *Cleaned Pictures*, W.A.G., 1955, p. 48 (20). More recently supported by P. Pouncey orally 8 July 1968; P. Cannon-Brookes, *letter*, 7 July 1975 and H. Brigstocke, *letter*, 7 July 1975. 　2. 145 × 149 cm. Peter Cannon-Brookes, *Lombard Paintings c. 1595-c.1630. The Age of Federico Borromeo*, Birmingham City Museum and Art Gallery, 1974, p. 177. 　3. *Liverpool Mercury*, January 10, 1840, 4th page column 4. 　4. L.R.I. Archives 11 Committee Minute Book. John William Gibsone, merchant is recorded in Liverpool from 1818 until 1841, and was Prussian Consul from 1827 until 1841. 　5. 1893 Catalogue, p. 35 (99).

PULINCKX, Louis, 1843-after 1901

3038　The Way in the Wood: View near Antwerp

Canvas, 157 × 211.5 cm

Prov:　Submitted by the artist to the 1881 L.A.E. but apparently not exhibited there;[1] purchased 1882 (£25).

Ref:　1. Letter from the artist to the curator, 23 July 1882, MS W.A.G.

RAPHAEL Sanzio, 1483-1520, ascribed to

2867　Votive Picture

Panel, 22.7 × 32.7 cm; painted area, 22.7 × 31.6 cm

Inscribed: On a white label in the foreground:
B·R·VERONEN · VIRGIN. M. . ./OB·VALETVDINEM· (IN) ·EXTREMIS·/RESTITVTAM·

Condition: Much rubbed and worn

This panel is an ex-voto offered to the Virgin in thanks for the return to health of a woman from Verona. Other pictures of this type close in date are in Columbia, Missouri,[1] and in the Museo Poldi Pezzoli, Milan (649).[2]

The date 1495 or 1496 in Arabic numerals to be seen in old photographs was found on cleaning to be a restoration. It could record an older tradition or inscription.

2867 was traditionally attributed to Raphael.[3] The attribution was revived by A. Venturi[4] and supported by Clark.[5] More recently Shearman has thought it a possibility as a juvenilium.[6]

The condition makes it difficult to make a definite attribution, but the handling of the space and atmosphere appear to indicate a major artist, and the style is not incompatible with Raphael's earliest known works. Furthermore it is hard to imagine that in the nineteenth century Raphael's name could become attached to a panel of so lowly a character without the support of some tradition. The colours appear to indicate an artist trained in the Marches rather than Umbria.[7] Other suggestions for the artist in recent years have been a Sienese, under Umbrian influence[8] and Domenico Morone.[9]

The Gallery owns two canvases by Tom Phillips which are free variations after 2867 painted in 1972-3 (8487 and 8488).[10] A further variation by Phillips is in the Gemeentemuseum, The Hague,[11] and he has also produced a screenprint.[12]

Prov: Entered the collection of the L.R.I. between 1836 and 1843;[3] deposited at the W.A.G., 1893;[13] presented to the W.A.G., 1948.

Ref: **1.** Kress Collection K1182. Fern Rusk Shapley, *Paintings from the Samuel H. Kress Collection, Italian Schools, XV-XVI Century.* 1968, pp. 67-68, fig. 167.   **2.** Franco Russoli, *La Pinacoteca Poldi Pezzoli*, 1955, p. 189, pl. 93. For the history and type of votive pictures see Lenz Kress-Rettenbeck, *Das Votivbild*, 1958, pp. 108-134.   **3.** 1843 Catalogue p. 10 (30).   **4.** A. Venturi, *Storia dell'arte Italiana*, IX, ii, 1926, pp. 72-75 and XI, i, 1938, pp. 180-181.   **5.** K. Clark orally, 1954.   **6.** Letter 25 July 1975.   **7.** 1963 Catalogue, pp. 192-3.   **8.** Angiolo Santoni, *letter*, 16 February 1953.   **9.** Giles Robertson, *letter*, 29 September 1960; opinion reconfirmed orally, 1972.   **10.** Charles Spencer, *Tom Phillips*, Alecto Monographs 2, 1973, pp. 11ff for full details.   **11.** Part of *Forty recapitulatory paintings 1962-1974*, reproduced Spencer, *op. cit.*, p. 9 and 14.   **12.** Reproduced, Spencer, *op. cit.*, p. 14.   **13.** 1893 Catalogue p. 12 (27).

RAPHAEL, after

2807   Venus

Canvas, 64.7 × 50.1 cm

After part of the *Venus, Ceres and Juno* in the Loggia di Psiche in the Villa Farnesina, Rome, as B. R. Haydon first noticed.[1]

Prov: Presented by William Lowndes to the L.R.I. 1842-1843;[2] deposited at the W.A.G. 1893; presented to the W.A.G. 1948.

Exh: Leeds, *National Exhibition*, 1868 No. 150.

Ref: **1.** "I have been much amused to see that some of these profound gentlemen (in Liverpool) have attributed to Guido a copy of Raphael's Venus in his *Cupid and Psyche*. I shall say not a word and somebody by and by will find it out and their profundity will receive a fall. This is unchristian but I really cannot help it." (B. R. Haydon, *Correspondence and Table Talk*, 1876 Vol. 1, p. 446, letter to his wife, Liverpool, 1 April, 1844). The attribution to Sassoferrato (see 1963 Catalogue p. 178) is not supported by Parks Campbell, *verbally*, 11 August 1975.   **2.** No. 2807 is one of the "pictures added since this catalogue was printed" in the 1843 Catalogue No. 127.

2841   Madonna della Sedia

Canvas, 74.2 × 73.5 cm

Inscribed; on reverse: *I.P.P./Egisto Manzuoli/Firenze*

A copy of the famous painting in the Palazzo Pitti.[1] Although a printed label on the stretcher describes Manzuoli as "pittore", the copy may only have been sold by him. His address was Casa Machiavelli, 16 Via Guiccardini, Florence.[2] A picture dealer called Manzuoni is listed at the same address in Murray's handbooks of 1874[3] and 1875.[4] It is likely that he is the same man, assuming that the difference in spelling is due to a misprint.

The inscription I.P.P. might be an abbreviation for I.P.pinxit. A certain Pompignoli is listed as a drawing master and copyist at No. 3 Piazza di Santa Croce from 1858 to 1875.[5]

Copying regulations at the Pitti permitted only one copyist at a time to have access to the *Madonna della Sedia*, and each copyist was allowed two months. Therefore, as Charles Weld noted, many copies were not done directly from the original.[6]

Prov: Egisto Manzuoli.[2] Acquired before 1927.[7]

Ref: **1.** Palazzo Pitti 151; Art. Iahn-Rusconi, *La R. Galleria Pitti in Firenze*, 1937, p. 216.   **2.** Printed label on stretcher.   **3.** *A Handbook for travellers in Central Italy,* Murray, 1874, p. XIX.   **4.** *A Handbook for travellers in Central Italy*, Murray, 1875, p. XIX.   **5.** *A Handbook for travellers in Northern Italy*, Murray, 1858, p. 521; *A Handbook for travellers in Central Italy*, Murray, 1861, pp. 81-3; 1864 edition, pp. 85-86; 1867 edition, p. 87; 1874 and 1875 editions pp. XIX-XX.   **6.** Charles Richard Weld, *Florence The New Capital of Italy*, 1867, p. 217.   **7.** 1927 Catalogue, p. 151 states 2841 was bequeathed by Mrs Grosvenor Stopford in 1902; but it does not appear in any of the catalogues before 1927, nor in the Gallery Stock Book and Register and 1963 Catalogue, p. 101 says that it was transferred from the Free Library (?).

2842   Madonna del Cardellino

Canvas, 56.3 × 40.5 cm

A nineteenth century copy of the original in the Uffizi Gallery, Florence.

Prov: P. H. Rathbone by 1886;[1] who bequeathed it to the W.A.G., 1895; passed to the collection, 1905.

Ref: **1.** *The Athenaeum*, September 18, 1886, p. 376.

2843   Madonna del Divino Amore

Panel, 140.7 × 108.6 cm

A copy of the picture by Raphael, of which the best known version is in the Galleria Nazionale, Naples. It may be the same as the *Holy Family* after Raphael exhibited at the Liverpool Mechanics Institute in 1840 lent by R. V. Yates.[1]

Prov: Joseph Brooks Yates; his sale, Winstanley's 14 May 1857 (8) bt. Theodore W. Rathbone, who presented it to the L.R.I. in 1857/8;[2] deposited at the W.A.G., 1893;[3] presented to the W.A.G., 1948.

Ref: 1. Liverpool Mechanics Institute, 1840, *Catalogue of the Exhibition of objects illustrative of the Fine Arts, Natural History, Philosophy, Machinery, Manufactures, Antiquities etc*, VII, Picture Gallery (20).   2. L.R.I. Annual Report, 1857/8.   3. 1893 Catalogue, p. 27 (74).

2844   The Transfiguration

Panel, 144.5 × 113.4 cm

A copy, perhaps of the eighteenth century or later, of the original in the Vatican.[1]

There are many copies of that famous picture. In the 1840 Liverpool Mechanics Institute exhibition a copy owned by Richard Vaughan Yates was exhibited.[2] And in the 1844 Liverpool Mechanics Institute exhibition three copies were exhibited, all owned by the Misses Yates and R. V. Yates. Only the third, described as a "modern copy of the finished picture in the Vatican" could be 2844.[3] It should be noted that 2843, another Raphael copy owned by T. W. Rathbone has a Yates provenance.

Prov: Theodore W. Rathbone, who presented it to the L.R.I., 1857/8;[4] deposited at the W.A.G., 1893;[5] presented to the W.A.G., 1948.

Ref: 1. Already noted as a copy in the 1859 Catalogue p. 43 (78).   2. *Descriptive Notes of some of the most interesting articles at the exhibition now open at the Mechanics Institute, Liverpool,* Liverpool Journal, June 18, 1840, p. 11, and Liverpool Mechanics Institute, 1840 *Catalogue of the Exhibition of objects illustrative of the Fine Arts, Natural History, Philosophy, Machinery, Manufactures, Antiquities etc.,* VII, Picture Gallery (8).   3. Liverpool Mechanics Institution, 1844, *Third Exhibition of objects illustrative of the Fine Arts,* (196).   4. L.R.I. Annual Report, 1857/8.   5. 1893 Catalogue, p. 26 (73).

2845   Madonna di Loreto

Canvas, 118.5 × 88.5 cm

A copy after Raphael's lost picture,[1] the best known versions of which are in the Louvre and the Getty Collection.[2] There seems to be no evidence to support Compton's suggestion the 2845 was in the collection of Queen Christina of Sweden.[3]

Engr: A. Romanet;[4] E. Lingée;[5] A. N. Foin;[6] G. Bouillard.[7]
Prov: Duc d'Orleans by 1727;[8] sold Bryan's Gallery, Pall Mall, 26 December 1798 (85), bt. Willett 700 guineas; Willett Willett Esq., sold Peter Coxe & Co., 2 June 1813 (122) bt. Lord Bolingbroke;[9] sent to auction to George Stanley, 1835;[10] ?bt. in or bt. by Bolingbroke's son, Rev. G. F. St. John; sent to George Stanley by 20 October 1843;[11] sold by Rev. St. John to James Marshall, 1845; by descent to Mrs Victoria Marshall, who presented it to the W.A.G., 1926.

Exh: Leeds, 1868 (143).

Ref: **1.** G. Waagen, *Treasures of Art in Great Britain*, II, London, 1854, p. 494 was the first to note that it is a copy. C. P. Landon, *Annales du Musée*, XVI, Paris, 1808, pp. 109-110 thought that it was possible that 2845 was the original but more likely that with the Louvre version it reflected a lost original.   **2.** Alfred Scharf, *Raphael and the Getty Madonna*, Apollo 79, 1964 pp. 114-121, pl. 2, 4, 10 and Burton Fredericksen *New Information on Raphael's Madonna di Loreto* J. Paul Getty Museum Journal III, 1976, pp. 1-45.   **3.** 1963 Catalogue p. 161.   **4.** J. Couché, *Galerie du Palais Royal Gravée . . .*, I, Paris, 1786.   **5.** Landon, *op. cit.*, opp p. 109.   **6.** C. P. Landon, *L'Oeuvre de Raphael*, III, Paris, 1809, pl. 148.   **7.** J. D. Passavant, *Raphael d'Urbin et son père Giovanni Santi*, II, 1860, p. 103.   **8.** L. F. Dubois de Saint Gelais , *Description des tableaux du Palais Royal*, Paris, 1727, p. 430.   **9.** George Stanley in a letter to Rev. G. F. St. John 27 October 1843 (MS. W.A.G.) states that he sold the picture to Lord Bolingbroke in 1813. The picture owned by Lenoir Debreuil cannot be the Orleans version because of its dimensions (Fredericksen, *op. cit*, p. 42).   **10.** G. F. Waagen, *Works of Art and Artists in England*, I, 1838, p. 328 and Passavant, *op. cit.*   **11.** George Stanley, letter to Rev. G. F. St. John, 27 October 1843.

REMBRANDT van Rijn, 1606-1669

1011   Portrait of the Artist as a Young Man

Panel, 69.7 × 57 cm

Inscribed: *Rembrandt . f*

Identified by Ursula Hoff[1] as the painting in the collection of Charles I listed by van der Doort as "Item above my Lo: Ankrom's doore the picture done by Rembrandt being his owne picture done by himself in a black capp and furred habit with a little goulden chaine uppon both his shouldrs. In an oval and square black frame. 28 × 23 in. Given to the Kinge by my Lo: Ankrom".[2] Van der Doort's very precise description of Charles I's painting leaves no reasonable doubt that No. 1011 or a version of it was that painting. No. 1011 might have been given to Lord Ancram by Frederick Henry of Orange, the Stadtholder of the Netherlands, possibly through his secretary Constantyn Huyghens, on Ancram's official journey to the King of Bohemia in 1629;[3] by 1633 Ancram probably had given it to Charles I.[4] However No. 1011 has most recently been dated on stylistic grounds to 1630/1631.[5] In 1650/51 No. 1011 was valued at St. James's as No. 128 and sold to Major Edward Bass in the Commonwealth Sale of 19 December, 1651 for £5.[6] No. 1011 and the *Portrait of the Artist's Mother* (now at Windsor) were the first paintings by Rembrandt to reach England and are evidence of his early reputation.[7]

X-rays of No. 1011 reveal under it the standing figure of a man plausibly attributable to Rembrandt helping to confirm the attribution of No. 1011: the signature is however certainly a much later addition.[8]

Prov: See above. The pictures acquired by Philip, Lord Lisle later 3rd Earl of Leicester at the Commonwealth Sale seem to have been returned to Charles II[9] but "A Man's Head by Rimbrant" is included in the MSS inventory at Penshurst of the Earl of Leicester's house in Leicester Field, 14 October 1737[10] and "A Head, by Rembrandt" is included in a MSS undated inventory now in the National Portrait Gallery of the Pictures at Penshurst taken by Mr George Montague of Sawsey Forest and sent to Thomas Barrett-Lennard 17th Lord Dacre (died 1786);[11] "a fine picture of a head by Rembrandt" is noted at Penshurst in Cobran's *New Guide for Tunbridge Wells*, 1840, p. 190 by James Phippen; Lord de L'Isle and Dudley sold Sotheby's 14 April 1948 lot 144; Mrs Borthwick Norton from whom purchased 1953.

Versions: Ten Cate Collection 74 × 59 cm (H. E. van Gelder, *Rembrandt en zijn Portret*, n.d. p. 11);[12] Berlin Art Market 1921 (see W. R. Valentiner, *Rembrandt Wiedergefundene Gemalde*, 1921, p. XV, pl. 6); Private Collection Italy (attributed to Bernard Keil), Rolando Celesti letter April 27, 1970; Private Collection Belgium (R. H. Marijnissen letter 30 September 1960): Fischer Sale, Lucerne, 5 November, 1955, lot 2130, 60 × 46 cm; Christie's Sale 3 May, 1929, 29¾ × 24¼ in oval; Delaroff Collection (photo Rijksbureau); Hamburg? (photo Kunsthalle, Hamburg) sd. Rembrandt F 16 . . . Private Collection, Sweden, auction Stockholm (Bukowski) June 1969.

Ref: **1.** Ursula Hoff, *Rembrandt und England*, Hamburg, 1935, p. 33ff. **2.** *Abraham Van der Doort's Catalogue of the Collections of Charles I* ed Millar, Walpole Society, 1958-1960, Vol. 37, p. 57. Millar says No. 1011 is "probably" Charles I's picture; B. Haak, *Rembrandt*, 1969, p. 47 says "possibly". Christopher Wright, *Rembrandt and his Art*, 1975, p. 25 says "virtually certain." Kurt Bauch, *Rembrandt Gemalde*, 1966, No. 297 p. 16 says "may have been". H. Gerson, *Rembrandt*, 1968, p. 490, No. 41 and in A. Bredius, *Rembrandt*, revised by H. Gerson, 1969, p. 547, No. 12 says "can be identified as" Charles I's picture. *Rembrandt Research Project* draft catalogue entry kindly communicated by Professor J. Bruyn 15 September 1976 says that "it is hardly doubtful that it is." **3.** Hoff, *op. cit.* see also Christopher White, *Did Rembrandt ever Visit England*, Apollo, LXXV, 1962, pp. 177ff and B. Haak *op. cit.* p. 47. **4.** A label on the back of Rembrandt's *Portrait of the Artist's Mother* also given to Charles I by Lord Ancram reads "given by Sir Robert Ker" and he was made Lord Ancram in 1633 (O. Millar letter 9 Febraury 1954). **5.** Rembrandt Research Project, *op. cit.*, earlier dates are given by the following: W. R. Valentiner, *Rembrandt Wiedergefundene Gemalde*, 1921, pl. 6, Kurt Bauch, *Die Kunst des jungen Rembrandt*, 1933, pl. 189, p. 210 who both suggest 1630; A. Bredius, *The Paintings of Rembrandt*, 1937, No. 12 who suggests 1630; A. Bredius, *Rembrandt*, revised by H. Gerson, 1969, No. 12, p. 547, who suggests 1629. **6.** O. Millar, *letter*, 9 February 1954. O. Millar, *The Inventories and Valuations of the King's Goods, 1649-1651*, Walpole Society, Vol. 43, 1972, p. 264. **7.** Seymour Slive, *Rembrandt and his Critics*, 1953, pp. 27ff. **8.** Rembrandt Research Project, *op. cit.* **9.** Historical Manuscripts Commission, Vol. 77, *De L'Isle and Dudley Manuscripts*, Vol. VII, 1626-1698, 1966, pp. 502-3. ed. G. D. Owen. **10.** O. Millar, *letter*, 29 April 1972. **11.** William Perry (died 1757) married Elizabeth, heiress of Penshurst but he collected Italian pictures and antique sculpture (John Britton, *The Beauties of England and Wales, Kent*, 1801-15, p. 1310 and James Dallaway, *Anecdotes of the Arts in England*, 1800, p. 382). **12.** Now untraced; perhaps an error by the author, B. Haak, *letter*, 4 July 1972.

REMBRANDT van Rijn, School of

957 The Angel Appearing to Hagar

Canvas, 109.5 × 100.5 cm

Hitherto attributed to Bol[1] but probably not by him although close to his work of the 1640's and dateable to about 1645.[2]

Drawings possibly related to No. 957 are in the Frits Lugt Collection,[3] the Collection of Professor E. Perman[4] and another was in the Rudolf Goldschmidt Collection.[5]

The subject was very popular in Rembrandt's circle.[6]

185

Prov: Acquired by the L.R.I. 1836-1843; deposited at the W.A.G. 1893; presented to the W.A.G. 1948.

Exh: Manchester, *Art Treasures*, 1857 (674). Leyden, *Rembrandt als Leermeester* 1956 (19) pl. 6. Chicago and Detroit, *Rembrandt after Three Hundred Years* 1969 (32) ill. p. 124.

Ref: **1.** 1843 Catalogue No. 116; G. F. Waagen, *Treasures of Art in Great Britain*, III, 1854, p. 240, and exhibition catalogues cited above. **2.** Dr. A. Blankert, *letter*, 17 April 1972; Dr. C. Hofstede de Groot also doubted the attribution to Bol but preferred B. Fabritius (Dr. A. Blankert *op. cit.*). **3.** J. G. Van Gelder, *Prenten en tekeningen*, 1958, No. 83 as Bol. **4.** Laren, Singer Museum, *Oude Tekeningen uit de Nederlanden verzameling Prof. E. Perman*, 1962, p. 8, No. 11, fig. 33 as Bol. **5.** Sold Frankfurt 4-5 October 1917 No. 185 as Eeckhout (see H. van de Waal, *Hagar in de Woestijn door Rembrandt er zijn School*, Nederlandsch Kunsthistorisch Jaarboek, Vol. I, 1947, p. 151). **6.** See particularly van de Waal *op. cit.*

1019   The Betrothal

Canvas, 90.8 × 121.7 cm

At the Royal Academy in 1910 James Greig[1] and C. H. Collins Baker[2] saw Bol's signature on No. 1019 and Greig saw a date, 1656. Neither signature nor date is now visible. No. 1019 was traditionally attributed to Rembrandt[3] but Sir Walter Armstrong attributed it to Gerrit Willem Horst;[4] W. R. Valentiner dismissed this attribution[5] and Dr. A. van Schendel suggested Bol or Gerbrandt van Eeckhout;[6] subsequently Dr. A. Blankert saw No. 1019 as close both to Bol and to Govaert Flinck but he preferred to describe it as "circle of Rembrandt."[7]

B. Haak dates No. 1019 to about 1650 and notes it as an interesting case of a portrait of a married couple suggesting, unlike Rembrandt's *Jewish Bride* of 1665, no scriptural allusions.[8] Both figures are, however, wearing theatrical or fancy dress, the man's costume having details from early 16th Century fashions; costume and hair style date No. 1019 to about 1640.[9]

Prov: Probably bought by A. Wauchope about 1850;[10] by descent to Mrs Wauchope of Niddrie Marischal, Edinburgh; Trustees of the Wauchope Settlement Trust sold Christie's 12 May 1950 lot 16; bought for the Walker Art Gallery.

Exh: R.A. 1910 (117) as Rembrandt.

Ref: **1.** *Morning Post*, 17 February 1910. **2.** *Outlook*, 26 February 1910 and *The So-called Rembrandt and Saskia at Burlington House*, Burlington Magazine, Vol. 16, 1909/10, p. 351. **3.** The Royal Academy Catalogue 1910 (117) notes a signature by Rembrandt, *R*. **4.** Burlington Magazine, Vol. 20, 1911/12, pp. 258ff; according to Armstrong, Bredius and Hofstede de Groot suggested Jan Victors. **5.** *Zum Werk Gerrit Willemsz Horsts*, Oud Holland, Vol. L, 1933, p. 241. **6.** Letters 18 May 1951 and 6 July 1951. **7.** Letter 10 May 1972. **8.** B. Haak, *Rembrandt*, 1969, p. 322, pl. 542, apparently supporting an attribution to the "School of Rembrandt". **9.** Aileen Ribeiro, *letter*, 22 February 1973. **10.** Colin Thompson, *letter*, 7 October 1958.

RENI, Guido, 1575-1642, after

127   St. Jerome

Canvas, 168.7 × 127.8 cm

A copy after the St. Jerome in the *Virgin and Child enthroned with*

Saints No. 328 at Dresden.[1] The setting and colour of the mantle have been changed.

Prov: Presented by Mr Isaac on behalf of Henry Steele 1853.[2]
Ref: 1. Reproduced in C. Gnudi and G. C. Cavalli, *Guido Reni*, 1955, pl. 100.   2. Liverpool Corporation Libraries, Museums and Art Gallery Committee Minutes 17 February 1853, with an attribution to Lanfranco.

141 Saint Cecilia

Canvas, 97.2 × 74.5 cm

A copy after the original now in the Chrysler Collection, New York.[1]

Prov: Presented by Abel Boadle 1864.
Exh: Liverpool Society of Fine Arts, *Exhibition of Ancient and Modern Paintings*, 1860 (205); R.A., *Italian Art*, 1930 (779).
Ref: 1. O. Kurz, *Jahrbuch der Kunsthistorischen Sammlungen in Wien*, N.F. XI, 1937, p. 214.

2801 The Infant Christ asleep on the Cross

Copper, 22.8 × 30 cm

The best version of this composition is now in the Art Museum, Princeton University.[1]

Prov: ?T. Winstanley sold Christie's 15 March 1805 lot 64 bt. Lewene £6. ?Sale of a Collection formed a few years ago by a man of Taste in Italy, Christie's 17 April 1812 lot 16 *A Sleeping Christ* from the Zambeccari Collection of Bologna bt. Neville £73 10s 0d. Presented to the L.R.I. by W. S. Roscoe in 1843-4;[2] deposited at the W.A.G., 1893; presented to the W.A.G., 1948.
Ref: 1. Richard Spear, *Guido Reni at Princeton*, Record of the Art Museum, Princeton University, XXII, 1963, No. 2, pp. 35ff for the other versions and iconography. See also Émile Male *L'Art religieux de la fin du XVIe siecle, du XVIIe siecle* etc., 1951, p. 331.   2. *Annual Report of the Liverpool Royal Institution*, 1843-4.

2894 Salome with the Head of the Baptist

Canvas, 128.3 × 100 cm

A copy after the original in the Corsini Gallery, Rome.

Prov: ?R. V. Yates; presented to the L.R.I. by S. H. Thompson 1861; deposited at the W.A.G., 1893; presented to the W.A.G., 1948.
Exh: ?Liverpool Mechanics Institution, *2nd Exhibition of Objects Illustrative of the Fine Arts, etc.*, 1842, (564) lent by R. V. Yates.
Ref: 1. *Annual Report of the Liverpool Royal Institution*, 1861, as "a very fine picture of the School of Guido".

2895 Nativity

Canvas, 99.7 × 101 cm

A copy in very bad condition, after the original, probably the version now in the Hermitage, Leningrad.[1]

Prov: Presented by John Mure in 1852.[2]
Ref: **1.** Stephen Pepper, *letter*, 27 July, 1970. **2.** Liverpool Corporation Libraries Museums and Art Committee, 28 October, 1852.

RICHIR, Herman, born 1866

2689 En Blanc

Canvas, 150.5 × 85 cm

Signed: *Herman Richir*

Prov: Purchased from the L.A.E., 1906 (£180).
Exh: Paris *Société Nationale des Beaux Arts*, 1906 (1030); L.A.E., 1906 (258).

ROMAN School, 17th century

1023 Landscape

Canvas, 72.6 × 96.5 cm

Attributed to "Poussin" in the 19th century[1] No. 1023 would certainly appear to have been influenced by the work of Gaspard Dughet.

Prov: Presented by Mrs Macaulay to the L.R.I. 1874;[2] deposited at the W.A.G. 1942; presented to the W.A.G., 1948.
Ref: **1.** *Annual Reports of the Liverpool Royal Institution*, 1874 and 1893. **2.** Annual Report *op. cit.*, 1874.

ROMAN School, about 1700

2858 Death of Lucretia

Canvas, 139 × 105.8 cm

Prov: ?William Roscoe.[1] J. B. Yates, presented by his daughter Mrs Bostock 1895.
Ref: **1.** Letter to the curator from Mrs Bostock 22 June 1895: No. 2858 was "thought to be " formerly owned by William Roscoe.

ROOS, Philipp Peter, 1657-1706, called Rosa da Tivoli

134 Cattle and Sheep

Canvas, 152.4 × 226.8 cm

Prov: ?John Miller sold Branch and Leete, Liverpool 3 May 1881 lot 174, *Cattle and Sheep* 59 × 87½ in. Presented by William Bennett 1881.

1220   The Shepherd and his Horse

Canvas, 66 × 88.6 cm

Formerly attributed to Benedetto Castiglione;[1] the present attribution was suggested by H. Gerson.[2]

Prov: Acquired by the L.R.I. between 1836 and 1843; deposited at the W.A.G., 1942; presented to the W.A.G., 1948.
Exh: W.A.G., *Cleaned Pictures*, 1955 (34).
Ref: **1.** 1843 Catalogue No. 103 and G. F. Waagen, *Art Treasures*, 1854, III, p. 240, No. 111.   **2.** Letter 15 March 1954.

1228   The Stag Hunt

Canvas, 122 × 162.6 cm

The waterfall in the background does not resemble very closely the falls at Tivoli (see prov.).

Prov: ?Anon sold Christie's 7 May 1842, lot 33 *Stag Hunt at Tivoli*. Acquired by the L.R.I. between 1836 and 1843; deposited at the W.A.G., 1893; presented to the W.A.G., 1948.

ROSA, Salvator, 1615-1673

2891   Landscape with Hermit

Canvas, 78.8 × 75.5 cm

Another version, identical to No. 2891, is at the Musee Condé, Chantilly.[1] Both are presumably late works.

Prov: Presented by Miss G. I. Anson 1933.
Ref: **1.** Luigi Salerno, *letter*, 3rd May 1972, believes both to be autograph.

ROSA, Salvator, follower of

2892   St. John Preaching in the Wilderness

Canvas, 66.1 × 90.2 cm

An attribution to Pietro Montanini was suggested in the 1963 Catalogue.

Prov: ?George Peters.[1] George Audley who bequeathed it 1932.
Ref: **1.** On the back of No. 2892 is a seal bearing a coat of arms close to that granted to George Peters of the City of London in 1748 (The College of Arms, *letter*, 23rd February 1972).

ROSSELLI, Cosimo, 1439-1507

2803 A martyr Saint, probably St. Lawrence

Panel, 64.8 × 37.8 cm; painted area, 63.7 × 36.2 cm

The saint was first identified as St. Lawrence by Cavalcaselle.[1] But the object at the bottom left hand corner cannot be identified with certainty. St. Vincent of Saragossa is also represented as a young deacon and appears with a grill with nail points, the instrument of his martyrdom.[2] Saint Lawrence is more likely as the better known Saint.

Fairfax Murray attributed 2803 to Rosselli.[3] It is a characteristic work, probably of the early 1470's judging by the facial type. The position of the hand holding the palm recalls the mannered elegance of Pollaiuolo's *St. Vincent* of the Cardinal of Portugal's Chapel. Busignani, however, associated 2803 with the style of the Salutati frescoes.[4]

A St. Lawrence attributed to Giotto was purchased by Roscoe from Winstanley in July 1811.[5]

Prov: ?Thomas Winstanley;[5] William Roscoe;[6] entered the L.R.I. Collection between 1836 and 1843;[7] deposited at the W.A.G., 1893;[8] presented to the WA.G., 1948.
Exh: Manchester, *Art Treasures* 1857 (53); Leeds, 1868 (6).
Ref: 1. G. B. Cavalcaselle notes on 1843 Catalogue (19). (L.R.I. Archives 63.14).   2. Louis Réau, *Iconographie de l'art chrétien*, III, part III, 1959, pp. 1326-1327.   3. Fairfax Murray, L.R.I. Annual Report, 1893, p. 47.   4. Alberto Busignani, *Educazione di Cosimo Rosselli*, Arte Figurativa, 1958, p. 23 n. 13.   5. Roscoe Papers, 5316.   6. 1859 Catalogue, p. 11 (15).   7. 1843 Catalogue, p. 7 (19).   8. 1893 Catalogue, p. 8 (16).

ROSSO Fiorentino, Giovanni Battista di Jacopo di Gaspare, called 1495-1540

2804 Portrait of a young man with a helmet

Panel, 88.6 × 67.3 cm (painted area 81.3 × 65.1 cm)

Signed: below right forearm of sitter *RUBEUS/FACIEBAT*

The signature came to light when it was cleaned in 1950.[1]
2804 is probably the earliest of the extant portraits by Rosso. The hatching of the flesh is simpler than in the other portraits. The style is closest to that of the portrait of a man dated 1518 in an English private collection.[2] The picture surface of the Kress *Portrait of a man* in Washington is more highly worked and closer to that in the Christ of the Volterra *Deposition*. The hands, too, in 2804 are nearer to those in the 1518 Uffizi altarpiece than to those in the *Pala Dei* of 1521. A date of 1518 would seem likely.[3] Carroll, however, suggests 2804 is of c. 1522.[4]

Mrs Newton suggested, "between 1519 and 1524" on the evidence of costume, but pointed out that "the hairstyle, hat, sleeve, high-necked shirt and high-necked tunic *could* have been worn by a young man in the height of fashion as early as 1517." Hat, sleeve, shirt and tunic all find parallels in the dated portrait of that year in the Liechtenstein Collection, often attributed to Franciabigio. It is only the gathering of the tunic in folds that persuades her to suggest a later date.[5]

Copy: Drawing by G. B. Cavalcaselle, Biblioteca Marciana, Venice, Cod. It. IV 2033 (=12274) fasc. 22.[6]

Prov: Schmidt of Amsterdam, sold Christie's, 12 June 1811 (29), bt. Pinney,[7] £7 7s 0d; probably purchased by Roscoe with another picture now at Holkham, attributed to Giorgione at Winstanley 1811;[8] Roscoe Sale lot 72, *bt. Crompton[9] £48 6s 0d; passed to the L.R.I. by 1819;[10] deposited at the W.A.G., 1893;[11] presented to the W.A.G., 1948.

Exh: Naples, *Fontainebleau e la maniera Italiana*, 1952 (5); Florence, Palazzo Strozzi, *Mostra del Pontormo e del primo manierismo Fiorentino*, 1956, (157), R.A., *Italian Art and Britain*, 1960 (101).

Ref: **1.** Ralph Fastnedge, *Two Cleaned Pictures from the Roscoe Collection*, Liverpool Libraries, Museum and Arts Committee Bulletin, I, 1950, pp. 15-19.   **2.** Colnaghi, *Paintings by Old Masters*, 1965 (7).   **3.** Herbert Keutner, *Zu einigen Bildnissen des frühen Florentiner Manierismus*, Mitteilungen des Kunsthistorischen Institutes in Florenz, VIII, 1959, p. 143 proposed a date soon after the Uffizi altarpiece, 1518/19.   **4.** Eugene A. Carroll, *The Drawings of Rosso Fiorentino*, (Doctoral thesis presented to Harvard University, 1964), I, 1976, Book II, pp. 44, 127, a date already suggested by Donato Sanminiatelli, *The Pontormo Exhibition in Florence*, Burlington Magazine, 1956, p. 240 as against 1517-1521 favoured by Fastnedge, *op. cit.*, pp. 17-19 and Paola Barocchi, *Il Rosso Fiorentino*, 1950, p. 253; as before 1521 by E. K. Waterhouse, in *Italian Art and Britain*, Royal Academy, 1960, p. 50 (101); as shortly before Rosso went to Rome by Ferdinando Bologna and Raffaello Causa in *Fontainebleau e la Maniera Italiana*, Naples, 1952, p. 6 (5) and Luciano Berti, in *Mostra del Pontormo e del Primo Manierismo Fiorentino*, Florence, Palazzo Strozzi, 1956, p. 126 (157).   **5.** Mrs Stella Newton, *letter*, 27 March 1950.   **6.** Letter of E. Covi, 17 November 1975. The album in which it is kept bears the date 1865.   **7.** Roscoe Papers, 5315, account from Winstanley. 2804 occurs together with the double portrait attributed to Giorgione, both in 1811 and in 1816. Pinney was probably a dealer and perhaps the same man who bought a Jan Steen, now at Upton House, in 1818. St. J. G(ore), *Upton House. The Bearsted Collection: Pictures*, 1964, p. 39 (130).   **8.** The Collector's mark on the reverse of 2804, T or J B in a circle suggests that it may have been acquired via John R. Blakey from whom Roscoe bought a number of pictures at his sale Winstanley 10-11 October 1811 (advertisements Liverpool Mercury 27 September and 11 October 1811). Old Masters from J. R. Blakey's collection were also sold at Winstanley's on 21 and 22 July 1814 (Advertisement for the sale in the Liverpool Mercury 15 July 1814 p. 20.) He had a further sale on 22 November 1815 at Mr Stoakes' Room, Church Street, Liverpool under the hammer of Mr Branch of Manchester (Advertisement in Liverpool Mercury, November 17, 1815, p. 157.) J. R. Blakey is probably John Blakey, corn merchant listed in Liverpool street directories from 1813 to 1814 and 1816 to 1817. A Thomas Blakey, corn merchant, who owned a warehouse is listed in Liverpool from 1800 to 1816 and may have been his father. The picture at Holkham is by Pietro Zacchia.   **9.** Perhaps Dr Peter Crompton of Eton House, near Liverpool, who stood unsuccessfully as a Whig for Nottingham in 1796, 1807 and 1812, Preston in 1818 and Liverpool in 1820 and 1823 (William Wardell Bean, *The Parliamentary Representation of the Six Northern Counties of England*, Hull, 1890, p. 416.) A manuscript note in the British Museum copy of the Roscoe Sale Catalogue identifies him as Crompton M.P. or M.D. of Liverpool.   **10.** 1819 Catalogue (22).   **11.** 1893 Catalogue p. 30 (82).

RUBENS, Peter Paul, 1577-1640

4097   The Virgin and Child with St. Elizabeth and the Child Baptist

Canvas, 180 × 139.5 cm

There are numerous pentimenti including the head of St. Joseph which can be seen under the curtain. No. 4097 is apparently unfinished at the left.

Oldenbourg's dating[1] of about 1630-1635 for No. 4097 is generally accepted; he held No. 4097 to be largely a studio work[2] but M. Jaffe[3] among others now holds it to be autograph. See John Jacob, *The Liverpool Rubens and other related Pictures*, The Liverpool Bulletin, Vol. 9, 1960-61, pp. 4-25 for a full discussion of No. 4097. John Shearman[4] believes that No. 4097 and other Holy Families by Rubens depend on Andrea del Sarto's Medici *Holy Family* now in the Palazzo Pitti, Florence, Inv. No. 81.

A copy with putti in the top corners formed part of the original decoration of the Great Room at Marble Hill, Twickenham, of 1724-1725. This copy was removed in the late 19th Century.[5]

Engr: Jan Witdoeck (with the figure of St. Joseph and other alterations) and Jaspar Isac.[6]

Prov: Recorded at Devonshire House in the Collection of the Duke of Devonshire in 1760;[7] Agnew's; purchased by the W.A.G., 1960 with the aid of a special Treasury Grant and contributions from the National Art Collections Fund, various trusts, firms and private individuals, 1960.

Exh: R.A., 1895 (124), 1912 (113), *17th Century Art in Europe*, 1938 (77).

Ref: **1.** R. Oldenbourg, *Rubens*, Klassiker der Kunst, 1921, p. 469, repr. p. 342. Max Rooses, *L'Oeuvre de P. P. Rubens*, 1886, I, No. 230, pp. 304-5 had suggested about 1615 and Edward Dillon, *Rubens*, 1904, p. 232 suggested 1630. John Jacob, *The Liverpool Rubens and other related Pictures*, Liverpool Bulletin, Vol. 9, 1960-61, suggests 1632-4.   **2.** Oldenbourg, *op. cit.* S. A. Strong, *The Masterpieces in the Duke of Devonshire's Collection* also considered No. 4097 largely a studio work but Rooses, *op. cit.*, does not appear to have doubted that it was autograph.   **3.** Verbally, 1960.   **4.** *Andrea del Sarto*, 1965, Vol. 2, p. 280.   **5.** John Jacob, *letter*, 26 August 1976.   **6.** G. Voorhelm Scheevoogt, *Catalogue des Estampes gravees d'apres Rubens*, 1873, p. 86, Nos. 106-7.   **7.** Horace Walpole, *Catalogue of the Collection of Pictures of the Duke of Devonshire* etc. 1760, p. 5. William Kent's frame for No. 4097, part of the decoration of the Devonshire House Gallery (Ballroom) made about 1735-1737, survives at Chatsworth; this suggests that No. 4097 was in Devonshire House by about 1737 but Vertue did not see it on his 1743 visit to Devonshire House (*Vertue Notebooks V*, Walpole Society Vol. 26, 1938, p. 23). No. 4097 is also noted in Dodsley, *London and its Environs Described*, 1761, II, p. 227 and in (Martyn) *The English Connoisseur*, 1766, I, p. 49.

RUBENS, Peter Paul, after

1181 Meleager and Atalanta

Panel,[1] 55.6 × 38.3 cm

A good probably contemporary copy after the *Meleager and Atalanta* at Munich (Inv. No. 355)[2] or after the versions at Dresden (Inv. No. 973)[3] and in the Alphonse de Rothschild Collection.[4]

Prov: ?John Humble[5] sold Christie's 11 April 1812, lot 14, bt. Sir William Curtis £39 18s 0d; Sir William Curtis sold Christie's 19 June 1847 lot 14 as "a beautifully finished sketch by Rubens" bt. Pernandwith £6 6s 0d. ?Sir Charles Scarisbrick sold Christie's 11-25 May, 1861, lot 678, bt. Polak, £21, as *Venus and Adonis*; Sir Charles Scarisbrick sold Hatch and Fielding, Southport, 12-13 March, 1923, lot 775; George Audley[6] who presented it 1932.

Ref: **1.** With a panel makers stamp *WI* or *NV* in monogram.   **2.** Max Rooses, *L'Oeuvre de P. P. Rubens*, 1886, Vol III, No. 640.   **3.** Rooses, *op. cit.*, No. 641.   **4.** Rooses, *op. cit*, No. 642.   **5.** Arms close to the Nugent arms appear on the back of No. 1181; Sir John Nugent Humble, 1785-1834, created a baronet in 1831, was the son of the heiress, Elizabeth, daughter of Edward Nugent Shanaghan of Cloncoskoraine, County Waterford, who married Captain Charles Humble (see *Burke's Peerage*, 1924 under Nugent of Cloncoskoraine).   **6.** George Audley, *Catalogue of my Pictures*, 1923 No. 137 p. 46.

RUISDAEL, Jacob van, 1629-1682, after

177 The Stag Hunt

Canvas, 100.3 × 132.7 cm

A copy after *The Hunt*, No. 1492 at Dresden.

Prov: Presented by Mrs Lewis, Berkeley Street, Liverpool, 1934.

RUYSDAEL, Salomon van, 1602-1670

1022 River Scene with a Ferry Boat

Canvas, 106 × 152 cm

Signed: *S v Ruysdael 1650*

W. Stechow, *Salomon van Ruysdael*, 1938, No. 426.

Prov: Lord Savile of Rufford Abbey sold Christie's 18 November 1938 (18) bt. Gooden and Fox £4,200; E. E. Cook of Bath who bequeathed it with his collection to the National Art Collections Fund, which allocated it to the Gallery 1955.
Exh: R.A. 1885 (152).

SANTACROCE, Girolamo da, active 1516-died *c.* 1556

2806 The Martyrdom of Saint Blaise

Panel, 33 × 30.8 cm

Blaise, Bishop of Sebaste in Cappadocia was tortured by curry combs. He is normally represented as an old man, and with a tonsure; Scharf, however, notes that there are exceptions.[1] He appears unbearded, though tonsured in an early sixteenth century French *Martyrdom* in Chalon sur Saône Museum, whilst a middle aged, tonsured and bearded Saint appears in three scenes from the life of Saint Blaise in Vicenza Museo Civico (A. 162). Saint George, a younger Saint, was also tortured with iron combs as can be seen in the altarpiece of St. George attributed to

193

Marzal de Sas in the Victoria and Albert Museum.² There, however, he is tied to a cross, not a column.

Waagen's attribution to Girolamo da Santacroce is convincing,³ although Heinemann suggested Francesco da Santacroce il Giovane, comparing 2806 with a *Resurrection* in the Kunstmuseum, Basle.⁴ Connections are strongest with signed works by Girolamo in Dalmatia. Compare, for instance, the facial types and gestures in the Ognissanti altarpiece at Blat (Korcula island)⁵ and the peculiarities in the scale of the figures in the reliquary now in the Cathedral of S. Trifone, Kotor.⁶

The prime seat of devotion for St. Blaise was Ragusa, also in Dalmatia, where the Cathedral is dedicated to him.⁷ A St. Blaise attributed to Girolamo da Santacroce bought in Ragusa was once in the collection of Count Teodoro Lechi together with a companion picture of the same size of Saints Peter and Paul.⁸

Prov: Entered the collection of the L.R.I. between 1836 and 1843;⁹ deposited at the W.A.G., 1893; ¹⁰ presented to the W.A.G., 1948.

Ref: **1.** 1859 Catalogue, p. 21 (34).   **2.** C. M. Kauffmann, *Victoria and Albert Museum, Catalogue of Foreign Paintings*, I, 1973, pp. 179-184 and C. M. Kauffmann, *The altarpiece of St. George from Valencia*, Victoria and Albert Museum Yearbook, 2, 1970, p. 83.   **3.** G. F. Waagen, *Art Treasures in Great Britain*, III, 1854, p. 234 No. 31.   **4.** Fritz Heinemann, *Giovanni Bellini e I Belliniani*, I, 1959, p. 186, s. 693; opinion confirmed by letter 9 July 1968.   **5.** Kruno Prijatelj, *Le Opere di Girolamo e Francesco da Santacroce in Dalmatia*, Arte Lombarda, XII, 1967, pp. 55-56.   **6.** Prijatelj, *op. cit.*, pp. 57-58.   **7.** Louis Réau, *Iconographie de l'art chrétien*, III, I, 1958, p. 229.   **8.** Fausto Lechi, *I quadri delle collezioni Lechi in Brescia*, 1968, pp. 119 n. 28, 191 n. 145. 162 × 81 cm.   **9.** 1843 Catalogue p. 12 (14).   **10.** 1893 Catalogue p. 14 (34).

SANTACROCE, Girolamo da, studio of

2805   The Resurrection with St. Catherine of Alexandria, St. Benedict and a female donor

Canvas, 62 × 76.8 cm

The iconography is remarkable. Representations of the Resurrected Christ with Saints and donors do occur in the Veneto.¹ But in No. 2805 Christ clearly holds out a ring in his right hand, presumably a reference to the Mystic Marriage of Saint Catherine.² There is no technical evidence that this is a later addition. The rabbits in the foreground as in 2762 symbolize mankind whose hope for salvation lies in Christ and his Passion.³

Waagen first advanced the attribution to Girolamo da Santacroce.⁴ Heinemann thinks that he only painted Christ and the landscape with the castle to the right. The rest he assigns to Francesco da Santacroce.⁵ The whole landscape, however, seems to be typical of Girolamo. the rabbits are almost literally repeated in the *Noli Me Tangere* which was with F. A. Drey in 1949. The colour is very close to the *Rest on the Flight* in Padua (Museo Civico 44), in which the type of St. Joseph is comparable to St. Benedict in 2805.

194

When first definitely recorded in 1836 2805 is described as "Christ ascending from the Tomb."[6] So it is possible that it is identical with the "Ascension of Christ" attributed to Antonio Bartolotto already in the collection of the Liverpool Royal Institution in 1823. That work had been presented by Thomas Winstanley.[7]

An early Italian *Resurrection of Christ with Saints* was lot 27 in the sale of Thomas Jones Esq., of Shrewsbury lately deceased, and that of an officer in the army, also deceased, held by Winstanley at Manchester, 24 August 1821.

Prov: Said to have come from the Palazzo Riccardi, Florence; Thomas Winstanley who presented it to the L.R.I. Collection between 1819 and 1836;[6] deposited at the W.A.G., 1893;[8] presented to the W.A.G., 1948.

Ref: 1. For instance Cariani's *Resurrection with Ottaviano Visconti and his wife* in the Brera, Milan. Bernard Berenson, *Italian Pictures of the Renaissance, Venetian School*, 1957, I, p. 54, II, pl. 729.   2. First noticed by Professor Archer and G. Scharf notes 1859 Catalogue pp. 46-47 (86).   3. George Ferguson, *Signs and Symbols in Christian Art*, 1974, p. 20.   4. Dr Waagen on his first visit to Liverpool, 1835, *Works of Art and Artists in England*, III, 1838, p. 186, *Art Treasures in Great Britain*, III, 1854, p. 238.   5. Fritz Heinemann, *Giovanni Bellini e I Belliniani*, Venice, 1963 p. 168, s. 530; opinion confirmed by letter 9 July 1968.   6. 1836 Catalogue (8). MS addition to Winstanley's annotated copy of the 1819 Catalogue p. 15, "In addition to these are the ascension of Christ by *Domo Ghirlandaio*".   7. Written into a copy of the 1819 Catalogue in the possession of the W.A.G., before the valuation by Winstanley of 17 January 1824. L.R.I. Archives 61.21 "A work earlier presented to the L.R.I. by Winstanley and then attributed to Bellini now appears to be by Antonio Bartolotto from whom Correggio received instructions and who painted about the year 1510" (8 December 1823).   8. 1893 Catalogue p. 29 (80).

SARGENT, John Singer, 1856-1925

2634 Vespers

Canvas, 71 × 91.5 cm

Signed: *John S. Sargent*

Probably painted during the artist's visit to Corfu in the autumn of 1909.[1] Another version very close to No. 2634 but without the right hand side of it was formerly owned by Sir Frank Swettenham.[2] Two sketches related to No. 2634 survive in the collection of the artist's family.[3]

A. C. R. Carter wrote of the landscape exhibited by Sargent at the 1910 R.A.:[4] "With the temporary secession of Mr Sargent from portraiture to landscape the Academy gains in curiosity what it loses in strength. Manifestly brilliant studies of sunlight, these exercises do not yet take us far on the road which the painter has doubtless planned for himself in the future." E. A. Abbey wrote to Walter James in November 1909: "I hear that J.S.S. did some beautiful things in Corfu."[5]

Prov: Bought from the artist by Sir Thomas Brock 1910;[6] Sir Thomas Brock sold Christie's 4 May 1928 lot 88 bt. Frederick Brock £882; purchased by George Audley who presented it 1928.

Exh: R.A., 1910, No. 529.

Ref: **1.** For the visit see Richard Ormond, *John Singer Sargent*, 1970, p. 76. No. 2634 is listed by C. M. Mount, *John Singer Sargent*, 1957 p. 360 No. K0914.   **2.** Exhibited at the R.A., *Exhibition of Works by the late John S. Sargent, R.A.*, 1926, No. 313 as *Landscape in Corfu*; Mount, *op. cit.*, No. K096, p. 359; sold Christie's 22 November 1946 lot 25 as *Sunshine and Shadow Corfu* bt. Bollen £36 15s 0d; sold Sotheby's 11 December 1957 lot 127 as *The White House Corfu* bt. Strachen £200.   **3.** C. M. Mount, *letter*, 4 December 1974. These sketches are listed in C. M. Mount, *John Singer Sargent*, 1969, p. 468 as done in Constantinople in 1891.   **4.** *Art Journal*, 1910, p. 168.   **5.** E. V. Lucas, *The Life and Work of Edwin Austin Abbey*, Vol. 2, 1921, p. 460.   **6.** Frederick Brock, *letter*, 23 June 1928.

SARGENT, John Singer, after

955   Lord Wavertree

Canvas, 91.5 × 71 cm

For biographical notes on Lord Wavertree see the portrait by G. di Fenilé 9167 (p. 248). The sitter is in his peer's parliamentary robes. The head like 9167 is based on Sargent's drawing of 1919[1] but the drapery etc. is unlikely to relate to Sargent.[2]

Prov: Presented by Lord Wavertree, 1927.
Exh: L.A.E., 1927, (898) rep. p. 29.
Ref: **1.** L.A.E., 1925 (164) rep. p. 29.   **2.** Letter from C. M. Mount, 4 December 1974.

3017   Portrait of Field Marshal Earl Roberts

Canvas, 163.8 × 106 cm

This copy by Frank Markham Skipworth was commissioned by Colonel W. Hall Walker (later Lord Wavertree) in 1917;[1] it is after the presentation portrait by Sargent of 1904 now in the National Portrait Gallery (No. 3927).

Prov: Presented by Colonel W. Hall Walker, 1917.
Ref: **1.** Colonel W. Hall Walker, *letter*, 25 September 1917; he had just sent another copy of this portrait also by Skipworth to the Carlton Club; he left yet another copy in his Will to either the Royal Military Academy Woolwich or to Wellington College (Captain J. G. Ferguson, *letter*, 8 July 1975).

SCARSELLINO, Ippolito Scarsella, called, 1551-1620

2792   The Entombment of Christ

Canvas, 96.5 × 118.7 cm

Joseph of Arimathaea or Nicodemus supports Christ's head, whilst Saint Mary Magdalen holds his right hand.

The attribution to Scarsellino made by Zeri,[1] has received support from Emiliani[2] and Nicolson.[3] Pallucchini thought that it was by the same hand as a *Deposition* in the Brass Collection, Venice temporarily deposited at the Abbazia della Misericordia, Venice.[4] The strong Venetian flavour of 2792 has been noted both by Pallucchini[4] and Pouncey.[5] Pallucchini suggested that it came from the studio of Tintoretto, and was possibly by El Greco or Scarsellino, when they were working there.[4] The attribution to Tintoretto was the traditional one.[6] The influence of Tintoretto is clear, but there are also links with the style of Palma Giovane noted by Pouncey.[5]

Prov: ?The late Allan Gilmore of Portland Place, Phillips, 2 May 1843 (44), Tintoretto *The Entombment*; entered the collection of the L.R.I. between 1836 and 1843;[6] deposited at the W.A.G., 1893;[7] presented to the W.A.G., 1948.

Ref: 1. F. Zeri, orally, July 1959. 2. A. Emiliani, *letter*, 21 August 1959. 3. Benedict Nicolson, *Burlington Magazine*, Vol. 107, 1965, p. 172. 4. Professor R. Pallucchini, verbally, 19 October 1967. Reproduced Erich von der Bercken *Die Gemalde des Jacopo Tintoretto*, 1942, pl. 203. 5. *Letter*, 26 June 1975. 6. 1843 Catalogue p. 22 (76) as Tintoretto. 7. 1893 Catalogue p. 31 (85).

SCHEFFER, Ary, 1795-1858, studio of

298 Ruth and Naomi

Panel, arched top, 55.8 × 40.8 cm

Signed: *Ary Scheffer*

Inscribed: Ruth, Chapter I, verses 15.16, were written on the frame in French by Agnew's, 1873. An undated Paris Customs Seal appears on the reverse.

A reduced version of the painting of 1854-1855, which in 1859 was in the collection of Mme. La Baronne de Rothschild[1] No. 298 is not listed by Kolb[2] nor does it appear in the list of works by Scheffer drawn up by his legatee in 1859;[3] it is probably a studio version. Another small replica is in the Stadelsches Kunstinstitut, Frankfurt-am-Main.

Eng: J. G. Levasseur (for Goupil) 1859 (after the original)
Prov: Bought by Thomas Agnew and Sons from Goupil, 1858, sold by Agnew's to Sam Mendel 1859. Bought by George Holt from Agnew's 1873, £945;[4] bequeathed by Emma Holt 1944.
Exh: Royal Manchester Institution, *Exhibition of Works by Modern Artists* 1865 (703). Liverpool Art Club, *Modern Oil Paintings by Foreign Artists* 1884, No. 92.
Ref: 1. Marthe Kolb, *Ary Scheffer et son Temps*, 1937, p. 478. This original painting was praised extravagantly in the *Athenaeum* 1857, No. 1524, pp. 55-6 where it is reported as just finished. 2. Kolb, *op. cit.* 3. Museum Ary Scheffer, *Catalogus*, 1934, pp. 95ff. For the distinction between replicas, copies and versions of Scheffer's works see particularly Mrs Grote, *Memoir of the Life of Ary Scheffer*, 1860, Appendix D, pp. 155ff. For Scheffer's assistants see Kolb, *op. cit.*, p. 211 and Thomas Armstrong, *A Memoir*, ed Lamont, 1912 pp. 3ff. 4. Agnew's Stock Book for all these transactions.

6584 Temptation of Christ

Canvas,[1] 222.5 × 151.6 cm

Signed: *Ary Scheffer 1854* (?)

An unrecorded[2] version of the 1854-7 original commissioned by the French Ministry of the Interior in 1849 and now in the Louvre (lent to the Musee d'Arras).

Engr: A. Francois (for Goupil) 1860, after the original, engraved in England.[3]

Prov: Bought by John Naylor in Paris in 1855 before its final completion by Scheffer (£630);[4] sold Harrods 18 March 1931 (451) bt. in; presented by J. M. Naylor, 1967.

Ref: **1.** Canvas stamp: Deforge, Boulevard Montmarte, 8e.   **2.** Not in the lists of versions in M. Kolb, *Ary Scheffer et son Temps*, 1937, p. 478 or in the list of works drawn up by the artist's legatee in 1859 and published in the Museum Ary Scheffer, *Catalogus*, 1934, pp. 95ff. The small version in the National Gallery of Victoria, Melbourne is also dated 1854. For the distinctions between replicas, copies and versions of Scheffer's works see particularly Mrs Grote, *Memoir of the Life of Ary Scheffer*, 1860, Appendix D, pp. 155ff. For Scheffer's assistants see Kolb, *op. cit.*, p. 211 and Thomas Armstrong, *A Memoir*, ed Lamont, 1912, pp. 3ff. For the original picture see particularly Kolb, *op. cit.*, p. 390ff.   **3.** The original painting came to England in 1860 (Kolb *op. cit.*, p. 393, Grote, *op. cit.*, p. 105 and *Art Journal*, 1860, p. 126).   **4.** Edward Morris, *John Naylor and other Collectors of Modern Paintings in 19th Century Britain*, Annual Report and Bulletin of the W.A.G., 1974-5, p. 95, No. 164. Naylor must therefore presumably have acquired No. 6584 directly from the artist.

SCHEFFER, Henri, 1798-1862, after

2885 The Arrest of Charlotte Corday

Canvas, 129.5 × 162.5 cm

After the original painting of 1830 first exhibited at the 1831 Salon, and now lent to the Musée de Peinture et de Sculpture, Grenoble (Inv. 938) by the Musee du Louvre.[1] By 1859 the original picture, then in the Luxembourg Museum had already been copied 1200 times.[2]

Prov: ?"A Collection of Pictures just received from Paris" sold Foster 9 December 1858 (79) bt. Mably £39 18s 0d. Presented by the executors of the late James Mander, 1874.

Ref: **1.** Jacques Foucart, *letter*, 2 March and 12 June 1976. Louvre Inv. No. 7868. The destroyed picture formerly at Brest recorded in Thieme Becker, *Kunstler-Lexikon*, Vol. 30, 1936, p. 5 and elsewhere was only ever a replica.   **2.** Antoine Etex, *Ary Scheffer*, 1859, p. 4.

SCHERREWITZ, Johan, born 1868

2641 Homewards Winter

Canvas, 80 × 125.8 cm

Signed: *J. Scherrewitz*

Prov: Presented by the executors of Alfred Booth, 1921.

SCHEX, Joseph, 1819-1894

3039 Cromwell refusing the Crown

Canvas, 179 × 215 cm

Signed: *J. Schex 1861*

Cromwell refused the Crown in a speech to Parliament given at the Banqueting House, Whitehall in the morning of 8 May, 1657.

Prov: Presented by Edward Stanley Arkle, 1878.

SCHLOESSER, Carl, 1836-after 1914

2648 The Village Lawyer

Canvas, 163.2 × 115 cm

Signed: *Carl Schloesser*

A long review and an engraving were published in the Illustrated London News.[1]

Prov: Purchased from the L.A.E., 1880 (£315).
Exh: ?Vienna World Fair 1873 as *Rat in Not*;[2] ?Royal Berlin Academy 1874 (713) with the same title; ?Frankfurt Academy (Stadelschen Institut) 1875 (not numbered)[2] with the same title; R.A., 1876 (1305) as *The Village Lawyer*; ?Paris, International Exhibition 1878 as *Cherchant Conseil*; L.A.E., 1880 (238).
Ref: **1.** 16 September 1876, pp. 265-6.   **2.** See F. von Boetticher, *Malerwerke des Neunzehnten Jahrhunderts*, 1891-1901, II, 2, p. 584.

SCHONGAUER, Martin, about 1430-1491, after

1015 Agony in the Garden

Panel, 30.4 × 41.7 cm

All the figures are taken directly from Schongauer's engraving *The Agony in the Garden*[1] from his *Passion* series. The angel with the cup in Schongauer's engraving seems to have been once present but to have been painted out. The landscape is vaguely reminiscent of the work of Joachim Patenir. No. 1015 was attributed in the 1963 Catalogue to Adriaen Isenbrandt, an attribution still upheld by Robert Koch.[2]

No. 1015 is painted up to the edges.

Prov: Roscoe Sale, 1816, lot 83, bt. Mason £3; presented to the L.R.I. by 1819; deposited at the W.A.G., 1893; presented to the W.A.G., 1948.
Ref: **1.** A. Bartsch, *Le Peintre Graveur*, 1803, Vol. VI, No. 9. Roscoe himself noticed this—see his sale catalogue under provenance.   **2.** *Letter*, 5 February 1975 "warrants no more than the 'attributed to ' qualification that it now (1963) bears".

SCHUPPEN, Jacob van, 1670-1751

1195   The Guitar Player

Canvas, 90.2 × 117.5 cm

Signed: *Jacque van Schuppen pinxit*

The sitters have not been identified. The guitar was probably made by one of the Voboam family, guitar makers in 17th Century Paris.[1]

Prov: Acquired by the L.R.I. between 1836 and 1843;[2] deposited at the W.A.G., 1893; presented to the W.A.G., 1948.
Exh: Manchester, *Art Treasures*, 1857 (964); W.A.G., *Cleaned Pictures*, 1955 (35).
Ref: **1.** Mary Anne Evans, *letter*, 7 February 1976.   **2.** 1843 Catalogue No. 115.

SEGANTINI, Giovanni, 1858-1899

2127   The Punishment of Luxury

Canvas, 99 × 172.8 cm

Signed: *G. Segantini 1891*

The first of a number of compositions on this theme[1] No. 2127 has had various titles, notably *Nirwana, Il Castigo delle Lussuriose, Il Nirvana delle Lussuriose, Le Madri Snaturate*—The present title of No. 2127 is an inexact translation—it should be *The Punishment of Lust.*[2]

With No. 2127, probably begun in late 1899[3] and completed by February 1891[4] Segantini moved decisively away from naturalism towards symbolism;[5] this movement and possibly the composition of No. 2127 in particular[6] provoked a quarrel with Vittore Grubicy, Segantini's friend and dealer, who apparently liked the landscape but not the figures in it.

No. 2127 and its related paintings were inspired by Luigi Illica's translation of the so-called Indian poem Pangiavahli.[7] No. 2127 shows mothers who have forsaken their children for a life of luxury or who have obtained abortions for themselves for the same purpose wandering in pain in an icy dismal valley representing an after life. The related painting at the Kunsthistorisches Museum, Vienna, No. MG 269 shows a subsequent event in the same poem when the face of the neglected child appears in the tree and the forgiven mother and the child are re-united in the tree. The Vienna picture was wrongly entitled *Per le cattive Madri (prima del Nirvana)*[8] at Milan in 1894 and presumably the events in No. 2127 strictly precede Nirvana, while those in the Vienna picture both precede Nirvana and represent Nirvana.

Segantini lost his mother at the age of seven and thereafter received little care from his family, this presumably influenced Segantini's choice of subject in No. 2127.[9] Servaes argues further that Segantini's contention is that modern bourgeois life makes women selfish and flirtatious rather than good mothers and Servaes sees No. 2127 as representing the negative and pernicious side of motherhood while *Il Frutto dell' Amore* of 1889 shows the positive side.[10]

The landscape in the background shows Maloja, Engadina.[11]

Prov: Apparently seen by a member of the Committee of the Free Public Library Museum and W.A.G. of the City of Liverpool at the Grafton Gallery 1893[12] (see *Exhibitions*) brought up to Liverpool at the City's expense for the 1893 L.A.E.; purchased there for £315.[13]

Exh: Berlin, *Internationale Kunstausstellung Veranstaltet vom Verein Berliner Kunstler*, 1891 (2865)[14] as *Nirwana*, Milan, Galleria Grubicy, 1891-2;[15] Grafton Gallery, *First Exhibition consisting of Painting and Sculpture*, 1893 (102).[16] L.A.E., 1893 (935); International Society of Sculptors, Painters and Gravers, *Exhibition of International Art*, 1898 (30) repr. as *The Punishment of Infanticide*; Aberdeen, *Artists Society*, 1898; Glasgow, *Institute of Fine Arts*, 1902; Edinburgh, *Society of Scottish Artists*, 1903; Dublin, *Irish International Exhibition*, 1907; St. Gallen, *Giovanni Segantini*, 1956 (83); Munich, *Secession*, 1964 (504).

Ref: **1.** T. Fiori and F. Bellonzi, *Archivi del Divisionismo*, 1968, II, p. 40, II. 353 pl. 432, (Kunsthaus, Zurich) is a variant of No. 2127; *Archivi del Divisionismo*, II. 312 pl. 359 (Kunsthistorisches Museum, Vienna) is closely related to No. 2127 and *Archivi del Divisionismo*, II. 354 pl. 439 (Kunsthaus, Zurich) is a version of the Vienna picture. A drawing, distinct from these four works, *Le Cattive Madri*, *(Nirvana)* was exhibited as No. 51 in *Esposizione di alcune opere di G. Segantini*, Milan, 1899.   **2.** Most of these titles are given in *Archivi del Divisionismo*, II, 281. No. 2127 was first exhibited at Berlin under the title *Nirwana*. A. P. Quinsac, verbally 1975, first pointed out the mistranslation—*Luxury* instead of *Lust*—in the present title.   **3.** A. P. Quinsac, verbally 1975 F. Servaes, *G. Segantini, Sein Leben und Sein Werk*, 1907, p. 149 says 1890.   **4.** Implied in the artist's letter to Alberto Grubicy of 27 February 1891, *Archivi del Divisionismo*, I, p. 336.   **5.** See particularly Segantini's letter of 2 May 1891 to Vittore Grubicy in *Archivi del Divisionismo*, 1. p. 338 with a description of No. 2127; one line has been accidentally ommitted from this text of the letter; it can be supplied from *Giovanni Segantini, Scritti e Lettere*, 1910, p. 186.   **6.** Servaes *op. cit.*, p. 153 and P. Leir, *Il primo ed il secondo Segantini*, 1900, p. 40 but see the editor's note in *Archivi del Divisionismo*, 1, p, 326 and particularly Segantini's letter of 24 February 1910 to Benvenuto Benvenuti in *Archivi del Divisionismo*, I, p. 108 dating the quarrel to late 1889, the date of Segantini's first symbolist painting *Il Fruto dell Amore*, *Archivi del Divisionismo*, II, II. 243.   **7.** *Archivi del Divisionismo*, I, p. 359 where Illica's text is quoted; Pangiavahli in fact never existed—the poem was by Illica (A. P. Quinsac, verbally, 1975). The artist however wrote to the Curator of the Walker Art Gallery on 26 September 1893 thus: "the subject is not taken from any book, nor is in any of my works, but has been created to symbolize (sic) part of a Buddistic (sic) conception from Nirvana, and the truth of this is that at first I gave to my picture the title of 'Nirvana' (MSS Walker Art Gallery).   **8.** Milan, Castello Sforzesco, *Catalogo delle Esposizioni Riunite*, 1894, No. 66. A. P. Quinsac, verbally, 1975, stated that this title was not Segantini's.   **9.** See particularly Karl Abraham, *Clinical Papers*, 1955, pp. 210ff. and Servaes *op. cit.*, p. 154. A. P. Quinsac, verbally, 1975, gave seven not five as the age at which the artist lost his mother.   **10.** Servaes, *op. cit*, pp. 155-7.   **11.** A. P. Quinsac, *letter*, 6 April 1972.   **12.** Letter from the Curator of the W.A.G. to the artist, 19 May 1893, MSS W.A.G. P. H. Rathbone is likely to have been the main instigator of the purchase of No. 2127; see his obituary in the *Liverpool Courier*, 23 November 1895; he was in London with the curator in March 1893 looking at studios and exhibitions for the Autumn Exhibition (*Liverpool Review*, March 18 1893, p. 11) and in that month the Grafton Gallery Exhibition opened.   **13.** No. 2127 was one of the first of Segantini's pictures to be acquired by a public gallery outside Italy, the Galleria Nazionale d'Arte Moderna, Rome had bought *Alla Stanga* in 1888. The Liverpool Clergy are stated to have supported the purchase of No. 2127 (see St. Gallen Exhibition Catalogue, *Giovanni Segantini*, 1956, No. 83), so are Henrietta Rae and David Murray, two of the artists advising the hanging committee of the 1893 L.A.E. (see Arthur Fish, *Henrietta Rae*, 1905, p. 70).   **14.** No. 2127 was not well received at Berlin (Servaes, *op. cit.*, p. 152 and *Kunstchronik*, 1890-1891, Neue Folge, p. 435, 463, 508 where No. 2127 is not even mentioned in Adolf Rosenberg's reviews) and the artist wrote on 5 August 1891 to the organizers asking that his name be omitted from the list of "Honourable Mentions" (Giovanni Segantini, *Scritte e Lettere*, 1910, p. 188—for the full list of awards see Kunstchronik, *op. cit.*, p. 570).   **15.** Seen there by Gaetano Previati who described No. 2127 in a letter of 24 December 1891 to his brother Giuseppe (*Archivi del Divisionismo*, I, p. 267).   **16.** In London the reviewers were more interested in No. 2127. C. W. Furse wrote in *The Studio*, Vol. 1, 1893, p. 34. "The painting of M. Segantini however is mechanical to the last degree and shows none of that delight in oil paint which characterises most great work but the result is dignified and personal". A. L. Baldry wrote in the Art Journal, 1893, p. 146 specifically of No. 2127 "a curious commingling of quaint fancy and earnest observation. In technicalities it is quite the finest of the painter's contributions and in colour it is especially refined". The correspondent of *The Artist* (1 April, 1893, p. 125) wrote: "In this vision of figures floating with closed eyes as in a trance of levitation there is something unearthly and dreamlike in the beauty and serenity of the lone and level snowfields and snowy mountains under the sun and the blue of the most freezing sky" and he added on the news that No. 2127 had been acquired by the W.A.G. that it was a piece of erratic genius which quite deserves a place in a public gallery (4 November, 1893, p. 350). The *Saturday Review*, (4 March 1893, p. 235, Vol. 75) referred to No. 2127 as "A singular purgatorial scene etc." and referred to the artist as "a realist turned to mysticism".

SEURAT, George Pierre, 1859-1891

6112 Ville d'Avray, Maisons Blanches

Canvas, 33 × 46 cm

A *croqueton* generally dated to 1882.[1] The building at the right also appears in a similar view in *Maison dans un Paysage, Environs de Paris* (Gift of Mme. Albert Marquet to the Musées Nationaux, France).[2]

Impressionist influence in paintings like No. 6112 is generally assumed.[3]

The title of No. 6112 is traditional. Jacques Emile Blanche stated that in 1882 Seurat was sketching near the fortifications outside Paris, near the factories of Suresnes and on the island of La Grande Jatte.[4]

Prov: Henri Lebasque; Eugene Garlot; Alex Reid and Lefevre (1936); Mrs Chester Beatty; purchased from Sir Chester Beatty in 1961 with the aid of a contribution from the National Art Collections Fund.

Exh: Bignou Gallery, New York, *The Post-Impressionists*, 1937 (8); Lefevre Gallery, *Delacroix to Dufy*, 1946 (49).

Ref: **1.** H. Dorra and J. Rewald, *Seurat*, 1959, No. 34, p. 33; C. M. de Hauke, *Seurat et son Oeuvre 1961*, Vol. 1, No. 20, p. 12.   **2.** Hauke *op. cit.*, No. 18.   **3.** W. L. Homer, *Seurat's Formative Period 1880-1884*, The Connoiseur, 1958, p. 58 dates this influence to 1882. See also Dorra, *op. cit.*, pp. LXXIX, LXXX and particularly W. L. Homer, *Seurat and the Science of Paintings*, 1964, pp. 16, 17, 54, 266-8 for further references, Hauke, *op. cit.*, p. XXI for Seurat's letter to Felix Feneon of 20th June 1890 and Paul Signac, *D'Eugène Delacroix au Neo-Impressionisme*, 1911, p. 70 dating the first influence of impressionism on Seurat to 1884.   **4.** *De Gauguin a la revue nègre*, 1928, p. 37.

SIGNORELLI, Luca, 1441-1523

2810 Madonna and Child

Panel (poplar), 59.1 × 50.1 cm

Cleaning in 1955 revealed the quality of 2810. A margin of about 3 cm previously concealed by the rebate retains the original colour of the landscape.[1] 2810 had already been linked to Signorelli by Cavalcaselle[2] and Waagen.[3] Fastnedge claimed that 2810 derives from the same cartoon as the *Madonna and Child* in the Metropolitan Museum.[1] Salmi considered it a work of Signorelli executed considerably later than the latter picture,[4] whilst Scarpellini dated it probably after 1500.[5] 2810 may be as late as the Arcevia altarpiece dated 1507 and documented as completed in 1508.[6] Its style certainly antedates the Cortona *Communion of the Apostles* dated 1512.[7]

The suggestion that 2810 was once in the Casa Tommasi, Cortona appears to arise from a confusion with the Metropolitan picture.[8]

Version: Metropolitan Museum of Art, New York, ex. Bache Collection, 51.4 × 47 cm.

Prov: Thomas Winstanley, from whom purchased in 1835 by the L.R.I.;[9] deposited at the W.A.G., 1893;[10] presented to the W.A.G., 1948.

Exh: Burlington Fine Arts Club, *Exhibition of the Work of Luca Signorelli and his school*, 1893 (9).

Ref: **1.** Ralph Fastnedge, *A restored work by Signorelli*, Burlington Magazine, 1953, p. 273-4. **2.** Cavalcaselle notes on 1843 Catalogue. **3.** G. F. Waagen, *Art Treasures in Great Britain*, III, London, 1854, p. 238 (78). **4.** Mario Salmi, *Signorelli*, 1953, p. 32. **5.** Pietro Scarpellini, *Luca Signorelli*, 1964, pp. 135, 141. **6.** Margherita Moriondo, *Mostra di Luca Signorelli*, Cortona and Florence, 1953, p. 87 (44). **7.** Moriondo, *op. cit.*, p. 99 (50). **8.** Moriondo, *op. cit.*, p. 77 (39). **9.** L.R.I. Archives 63. Bill dated 3 August 1836 from Winstanley to the L.R.I. for pictures supplied in 1835. **10.** 1893 Catalogue p. 11 (25).

SLABBAERT, Karel, about 1618-1654

871 Portrait of a Boy

Panel, 23 × 18.7 cm

The attribution was suggested by H. Gerson.[1] No. 871 was formerly attributed to Gerard Dou.

Prov: Bequeathed by Mrs Margaret Harvey, 1878.
Ref: **1.** *Letter*, 24 May 1957.

SOLIMENA, Francesco, 1657-1747

2846 The Birth of the Baptist

Canvas, 40.3 × 32.4 cm

Another version of No. 2846 is in the Museo Civico, Teramo[1] and there is a drawing varying slightly from both versions in the Louvre, Inventory No. 12583.[2] Bologna[3] prefers No. 2846 to the Teramo version, dates No. 2846 to about 1715 and identifies it with the painting on copper for Cardinal Ottoboni.[4]

Prov: Anon[5] sold Sotheby's 28 January 1953 (141) bt. Barnett £80. Purchased from Colnaghi's, 1953.

Exh.   P. and D. Colnaghi, *Paintings by Old Masters*, 1953 (18). Royal Academy, *Italian Art in Britain*, 1960 (439). Art Institute of Chicago, *Painting in Italy in the 18th Century*, 1970 (102).

Ref: **1.** G. Carandente, *Il Museo Civico di Teramo*, 1960 p. 21 No. 40.   **2.** Musee du Louvre, *Le dessin a Naples du XVI Siecle au XVIII Siecle*, 1967, p. 44 No. 77.   **3.** F. Bologna, *Francesco Solimena*, 1959, pp. 112 and 255, fig. 154.   **4.** See B. de Dominici, *Vite de Pittori etc.*, 1840-1846, IV, p. 427.   **5.** From the Beaumont Collection according to the photograph in the Witt Library.

6366   Diana and Endymion

Canvas, 179 × 232.8 cm

Another version of No. 6366, identical to it but measuring only 146 × 196 cm, now in the Handelhaus, Halle[1] (Staatliche Galerie Moritzburg Inv. No. I 1560) is signed by Jean Baptiste Van Loo and is presumably a copy after No. 6366. No. 6366 would appear to be a late work but it seems unlikely that Van Loo would have copied a picture of this type after about 1720.

Yet another version of No. 6366 again 150 × 205 cm, was sold anonymously at Sotheby's 24 October 1973 lot 45 (bt. Moretti £2,500); in the Sotheby's Catalogue it was described as by an assistant of Solimena and seemed slightly inferior in quality to No. 6366; it came from a local auction in Germany.[2]

Prov: Purchased by P. and D. Colnaghi at a sale in Amsterdam about 1966; purchased from Colnaghi's 1966 with the aid of a contribution from the National Art Collections Fund.

Ref: **1.** Dr. H. W. Keiser, *letter*, 22 January 1968.   **2.** John Somerville, *letter*, 14 October 1973.

SPANISH School, 16th century

1180   Pieta

Panel, 71.4 × 55.3 cm

This type of composition was common in the circle of Quentin Matsys and of Gerard David and was then extensively imitated in Spain,[1] particularly in the circle of Morales.[2]

No. 1180 is not painted up to the edges (painted area 70.2 × 53.1 cm).

Prov: Count Truchsess (the Truchsessian Gallery).[3] William Carey who sold it to William Roscoe August 1814 for 14 guineas;[4] Roscoe Sale, 1816, lot 85 passed at 3 guineas presented to the L.R.I., 1819, deposited at the W.A.G., 1942, presented to the W.A.G., 1948.

Ref: 1. Diego Angulo Iniguez, *Pintura del Renacimiento*, Ars Hispaniae, 1954, p. 240.   2. Ingjald Backsbacka, *Luis de Morales*, 1962, pls. 20, 65, 66, 67, 68, 69, 70, 71, 72, 85, 96, 101, 113, 161, 162, 163, 164, 165, 166. H. Gerson, verbally, 1958 considered No. 1180 Spanish.   3. 1843 Catalogue No. 59, p. 17. Presumably *Catalogue of the Truchesessian Picture Gallery*, 1803, p. 131, *Mater Dolorosa* by Daniele da Volterra, 2 ft 4 in × 1 ft 9 in on wood and *Summary Catalogue of the Pictures etc. at the Truchsessian Gallery*, 1804, No. 579, p. 23 with the same title and attribution but not at the Skinner Dyke & Co. Sale of 24-26 April 1806.   4. Roscoe Papers Nos. 735-737, Liverpool City Libraries.

SPANISH School, 17th century

6126   St. Francis in Ecstasy

Canvas, 169 × 123.5 cm

Attributed to Juan Simon Gutierrez since its entry into the collection,[1] but not apparently by this artist.[2]

Prov: Presented to the L.R.I. by Thomas Barber between 1836 and 1843; purchased from Liverpool University, 1962.

Exh: Manchester, *Art Treasures*, 1857 (646).

Ref: 1. 1843 Catalogue No. 82; G. F. Waagen, *Art Treasures*, 1854, Vol. III, p. 240.   2. Diego Angulo Iniquez, *letter*, 1 February 1972; for the problems of attributions with Gutierrez see Diego Angulo Iniquez, *Pintura del Siglo XVIII*, *Ars Hispaniae*, 1971, p. 366. No. 6126 has an old MS label: *Spanish Picture by the Slave/Thomas Barber/17 Erskine Street* but an attribution to Juan de Pareja seems no more promising.

SPINELLO Aretino, active 1373-1410/1

2752   Salome

Fresco, 39.5 × 31 cm

2752 and 2753 formed part of two frescoes of the Life of the Baptist in the Manetti Chapel in the Church of the Carmine, Florence. The chapel was decorated under the will of Vanni Manetti, drawn up in 1348; he was still alive in 1357.[1] A fire on 28/29 January 1771 largely destroyed the church, but the frescoes were relatively undamaged. They were removed from the walls by Thomas Patch in 1771. He made engravings of the six frescoes and of details of some of the figures, including 2752.[2] Vasari held the frescoes to be by Giotto.[3] Vitzthum was the first to attribute them to Spinello.[4]

There are six other fragments in the Ammanati Chapel in the Camposanto, Pisa,[5] one in the Museum Boymans-van Beuningen, Rotterdam;[6] one in the National Gallery, London;[7] one recently on the American art market;[8] and another possibly from the same chapel in the Museo Malaspina, Pavia.[9]

2752 is part of the *Feast of Herod*. Herod's head was recently on the American art market,[8] whilst the head of the harp player is at Pisa.[5]

The frescoes probably date close to 1390.[10]

Prov: Manetti Chapel, S. Maria del Carmine, Florence sawn from the wall by Thomas Patch after 29 January 1771; possibly Towneley Collection;[11] probably William Young Ottley; his sale, Christie's 25 May 1811 (28), bt. Lambert £9; William Roscoe, his sale (7), bt. in £10 0s 0d; presented to the L.R.I., 1819;[12] deposited at the W.A.G., 1893;[13] presented to the W.A.G., 1948.

Exh: Manchester, 1857, *Art Treasures*, (32); R.A., 1881 (226).

Ref: 1. Ugo Procacci, *L'Incendio della Chiesa del Carmine del 1771*, Rivista d'Arte, 1932, pp. 141ff; espec. 212ff.   2. Thomas Patch, *The Life of Giotto*, 1772, No. XI (*head of Salome*); VI (*Feast of Herod*); III (*Naming of the Baptist*).   3. Vasari, ed. Milanesi, I, 1878, p. 376.   4. Conte Giorgio Vitzthum, *Un ciclo di affreschi di Spinello Aretino perduti*, L'Arte, IX, 1906, p. 199.   5. Procacci, *op. cit.*, pp. 218, 221-4, fig. 12-15; for the two fragments not reproduced by Procacci see Raimond van Marle, *The Development of the Italian Schools of Painting*, III, 1924, fig. 331, 332.   6. H. W. Van Os and Marian Prekken, *The Florentine Paintings in Holland 1300-1500*, 1974, p. 103 (63).   7. Martin Davies, *National Gallery, The Early Italian Schools*, 1961, pp. 498-500.   8. Federico Zeri, *Italian Primitives at Messrs. Wildenstein*, Burlington Magazine, Vol. 107 1965, p. 255, and Adams, Davidson & Company, 1967 *Catalogue*, p. 29 (77).   9. Procacci, *op. cit.*, p. 223 fig. 18.   10. Procacci, *op. cit.*, pp. 228-9 dates the frescoes close to the cycles of San Miniato al Monte and Santa Caterina all'Antella; Van Os and Prekken, *op. cit.*, as c. 1390. Miklos Boskovits, *Pittura Fiorentina alla vigilia del Rinascimento, 1370-1400*, 1975, p. 437 as 1390-1395.   11. The late Henry Tresham and William Young Ottley, *The British Gallery of Pictures . . .*, 1818, n.p., mention that "the late Mr Townley owned two or three other pieces from the same chapel." One of these is now at Rotterdam, which passed by descent to the 3rd Lord O'Hagan.   12. 1819 Catalogue (3).   13. 1893 Catalogue p. 5 (7).

2753   The Infant St. John presented to Zacharias

Fresco, 51.5 × 54 cm

Part of the composition of *The Naming of the Baptist*. The head and torso of Zacharias writing down the name of the Baptist is in the Camposanto, Pisa.[1]

See No. 2752.

Prov: Manetti Chapel, S. Maria del Carmine, Florence, sawn from the wall by Thomas Patch after 29 January 1771; probably bought by Roscoe at a Winstanley sale c. 1811, £10 0s 0d;[2] Roscoe sale, (6) bt. Mason £4 14s 6d; presented to the L.R.I., 1819;[3] deposited at the W.A.G., 1893;[4] presented to the W.A.G., 1948.

Ref: 1. Procacci, *op. cit.*, p. 218, 221, fig. 12.   2. Roscoe Papers 5315, Winstanley account datable post June 1811.   3. 1819 Catalogue (2).   4. 1893 Catalogue p. 4 (6).

STOKES, Marianne (nee Preindlsberger), 1855-1927

658   Polishing Pans

Canvas, 59 × 79.3 cm

Signed: *Marianne Stokes*

Prov: Presented by George Audley, 1928.

Exh: New English Art Club 1887 (23).[1] L.A.E., 1887 (378) as *Polished Pans*; L.A.E., 1928 (162) lent by George Audley.

Ref: **1.** Pall Mall Gazette Extra No. 34, *Pictures of 1887*, p. 88 as *Polished Pans* (repr.).

764   The Lesson

Canvas, 60 × 50.1 cm

The subject is a "Swiss child from the Haudères where they still wear picturesque costume."[1]

Prov: Purchased from the 1923 L.A.E. (£40).
Exh: R.A., 1923 (245); L.A.E., 1923, (826).
Ref: **1.** Letter from the artist, 29 November 1923.

2643   A Parting

Canvas, 88.3 × 133.3 cm

Signed: *Marianne Stokes*

Painted in Paris while the artist was studying under Colin and Courtois[1] (presumably Paul Alfred Colin and Gustave Claude Etienne Courtois).

Prov: Purchased from L.A.E., 1885 (£84).
Exh: Paris, *Salon*, 1884, No. 1973 as *Condamné à Mort*;[2] R.A., 1885 (17);[3] L.A.E., 1885 (268).
Ref: **1.** Wilfred Meynell *Mr and Mrs Adrian Stokes*, Art Journal, 1900, p. 197, but Meynell's wording is ambiguous.   **2.** Meynell, *op. cit.*, states that No. 2643 was exhibited at the Salon and this seems the most likely title.   **3.** Henry Blackburn, *Academy Notes*, 1885, p. 17 repr.

STRY, Jacob van, 1756-1815

738   Cattle in Landscape

Canvas, 53.3 × 65 cm

Signed: *Van Stry*

Prov: Bequeathed by Mrs Margaret Harvey, 1878.

SVEMPS, Leo, 1897-1975

349   Still Life

Canvas, 81.4 × 100.3 cm

Signed: *Leo Svemps 1937*

Prov: Presented by the Anglo Baltic Society, 1939.

TACCONI, Innocenzo, active early 17th century

2766 Assumption of the Virgin

Canvas, 232.5 × 161 cm

Signed: I.N.T.B.F./M.D.C.III.[1]

Commissioned by a member of the Bernardini family[2] presumably in 1603 as the altarpiece of the first chapel on the right on entering the Church of S. Alessandro Maggiore, Lucca.[3]

Prov: Removed from S. Alessandro Maggiore and sent to England by 1820.[4] W. H. Pease of Harpford House near Sidmouth; P. and D. Colnaghi; purchased from the Wavertree Bequest, 1955.

Ref: **1.** Not now visible but recorded in *Lucca pittrice nelle sue chiese* n.d. MSS Lucca Biblioteca Governativa 3299 (Misc.), int. 13.f.2 cited in Erich Schleier, *Innocenzo Tacconi 1603*, Burlington Magazine, Vol. 113, 1971, p. 665; presumably the signature stood for *Innocenzo Tacconi Bolognese fecit.* No. 2766 was traditionally attributed to Annibale Carracci.   **2.** There is a Bernardini coat of arms on the copy painted by Stefano Tofanelli (1752–1812) to replace No. 2766 when it was sent to England (Schleier, *op. cit.*, p.665, also citing a *Libro delle Visite Locali* etc., 1678. Vol. 50. f. 961 MSS Lucca Archivo della Curia Vescovile, which associates the altar with a Lorenzo Bernardini, and Tomaso Trenta, *Guida del Forestiere per la citta e il contado di Lucca*, Lucca. 1820. p. 68). Tofanelli's copy (reproduced in Schleier, *op. cit.*) is still in S. Alessandro Maggiore but now hangs in the left aisle.   **3.** *Lucca pittrice, op. cit..*   **4.** Trenta, *op. cit.* The Bernardini coat of arms, which does appear on Tofanelli's copy, and the signature may have been obliterated at this point to conceal the origin of No. 2766.

TENIERS, David, 1610-1690, style of

37 Boors Smoking

Panel, 25 × 19.4 cm

Inscribed: *D. TENIERS*

38 Boors in a Landscape

Panel, 18.4 × 26.6 cm

Inscribed: *DTF* (in monogram)

39 Boors outside a Tavern

Panel, 19.5 × 25.5 cm

Inscribed: *DTF* (in monogram)

Apparently late imitations with forged signatures.

Prov: Bequeathed by Mrs Margaret Harvey, 1878 except No. 37 which was presented by Miss I. S. Carstairs, 1924.

TERBORCH, Gerard, 1617-1681, after

832 Woman pouring Wine

Canvas, 35.7 × 28.2 cm

A copy[1] after the original in the Brooklyn Museum, New York (Inv. 34.494).

Prov: Bequeathed by Mrs Margaret Harvey, 1878.
Ref: 1. S. J. Gudlaugsson, *Katalog der Gemalde Gerard Ter Borchs*, 1960, No. 78e, p. 97.

TILTON, John Rollin, 1833-1888

2659 Kom Ombos, Egypt

Canvas, 77.5 × 124.5 cm

The view is taken from the south; Tilton did apparently visit Egypt but the details of No. 2659 agree with the plan and section of the temple in Richard Lepsius, *Denkmaler aus Aegypten und Aethiopen, etc.*, 1849-58, Vol. 2, pl. 102, based on Lepsius's visit of 1842-45.[1]

If No. 2659 was No. 1016 at the 1873 Royal Academy, the only picture Tilton exhibited there, Henry James referred to it thus: "Ghostly enough to-day the career of Story's neighbour Tilton, the American painter of Italian and Egyptian landscape, who had his season of delusive fame, his flush of Turneresque eminence in London, for a year or two, at the Academy, on the 'line', and who not unnaturally supposed that, in the well-worn phrase, his fortune was made, whereas it was but to remain, for the long after-period, quite sadly, publicly, permanently unfinished; yet with such compensations of setting, of background, of incidence, of imputed, of possible association and experience, a kind of Roman felicity of infelicity, in the whole dim little drama."[2] The picture at the 1873 Royal Academy was also reviewed in the *Saturday Review*:[3] "the picture having won by desert a place on the line its peculiar technique can be closely examined . . . indeed the picture has been so toned down that little light is left in it." This painting was moreover praised by the President of the Royal Academy, Francis Grant, at the annual Academy Dinner.[4]

Another(?) *Kom Ombos* by Tilton was owned by Marshall O. Roberts of New York.[5] The quality of No. 2659 suggests that it may be a copy.

Prov: Presented by Charles W. Jones on behalf of the executors of the late Miss Janet Fisher, 1905.
Exh: ?R.A. 1873 (1016) as *Kom Ombos, Upper Egypt, early morning, spring, after the subsiding of the waters of the Nile when they are of a greenish colour.*
Ref: 1. Dr. D. Downes, *letter*, 9 August 1973.   2. Henry James, *William Wetmore Story and his Friends*, 1903, p. 345.   3. 21 June 1873, p. 814.   4. Clara Clement and L. Hutton, *Artists of the 19th century*, 1879, II, p. 297.   5. The version owned by Roberts was exhibited at the 1874 *National Academy of Design*, New York (186).

TINTORETTO, Jacopo Robusti called, 1518-1594, after

2850   The Last Judgement

Canvas, 115.9 × 68.2 cm including strips 9.2 cm wide added on the left and 8.2 cm wide added on the right.

A copy with small variations after the original in the Madonna del Orto, Venice which is arched at the top. The figures in the strips added at the sides of No. 2850 and in the part of No. 2850 corresponding with the spandrels of the Madonna del Orto altarpiece do not appear in the original. No. 2850 was listed as a sketch, not a copy, until 1884.[1]

Prov: Count Truchsess (The Truchsessian Gallery) sold Skinner Dyke & Co. 24-26 April 1806 (211)[2] £3. Roscoe Sale 1816 lot 66 bt. Mason £15 4s 6d; presented to the L.R.I., 1819; presented to the W.A.G., 1955.

Exh: Manchester, *Art Treasures*, 1857 (914); Leeds, *National Exhibition*, 1868 (165).

Ref: 1. In the Roscoe Sale Catalogue (see Provenance) and elsewhere; W. M. Conway, *The Gallery of Art of the L.R.I.*, 1884, p. 23 was the first to recognise No. 2850 as a copy.   2. See also *Catalogue of The Truchsessian Picture Gallery*, 1803, p. 131 with dimensions (3 ft 7 in × 2 ft 1 in) and *Summary Catalogue of the Pictures etc. at the Truchsessian Gallery*, 1804, No. 873, p. 35 in both of which No. 2850 is attributed to Tintoretto.

TIZIANO Vecellio, *c.* 1488/90-1576, after

2851   Holy Family with infant St. John the Baptist in a landscape

Canvas, 92 × 127 cm

The Meeting of Christ and the infant St. John the Baptist took place on the Holy Family's return from their flight into Egypt.

2851 is probably a near contemporary copy of a lost Titian, of which the best surviving version is Louvre 1580, now generally attributed to Polidoro Lanzani.[1] At least 5 other versions are known.[2] The infant St. John carrying the lamb also appears in *The Holy Family* in the Andrew Mellon Collection, Washington;[3] in a fragment of a Sacra Conversazione;[4] without his lamb, but with a scroll and cross in the *Holy Family with Saint Catherine and Saint John the Baptist* in the Museo Civico, Vicenza.[5] In that picture the Joseph is almost identical with the Joseph in 2851. The Virgin and Child also occur in a fragment representing the *Holy Family with Saint Catherine* in Lucca Pinacoteca.[6]

There is insufficient evidence to make an attribution for 2851, although it is clearly not by the same hand as Louvre 1580.[7]

A *Holy Family with St. John* attributed to Titian was in the sale of Thomas Wilkinson junior in 1811.[8]

Prov: Possibly sold T. Winstanley's 21-22 January 1840;[9] in the L.R.I. by 1843;[10] deposited at the W.A.G., 1893;[11] presented to the W.A.G., 1948.

Ref: **1.** Harold E. Wethey, *Titian*, I, 1969, p. 172 and letter of Jacques Vilain, 4 October 1972.   **2.** Wethey, *op. cit.*, p. 172, but in *Polidoro Lanzani, Problems of Titianesque Attributions*, Pantheon, 1976, p. 195 appears implicitly to deny a Titian archetype.   **3.** National Gallery of Art, *Summary Catalogue of European Paintings and Sculpture*, 1965, p. 129, No. 36 as Titian.   **4.** Bernard Berenson, *Venetian School*, 1957, I. p. 194, II, pl. 931, as Francesco Vecellio.   **5.** Franco Barbieri, *Il Museo Civico di Vicenza, Dipinti e Sculture dal XVI al XVIII Secolo*, 1962, pp. 251-2 as Francesco Vecellio.   **6.** Lucca Pinacoteca Nazionale No. 246 as School of Titian.   **7.** Harold E. Wethey, *Polidoro Lanzani, Problems of Titianesque Attributions*, Pantheon, 1976, pp. 194-5 as Polidoro Lanzani (or copy after) circa 1550.   **8.** Thomas Wilkinson, Junr. sale, Winstanley and Son, 34 Russell Square, London, 29 June 1811 (45) *Holy Family with St. John*, Titian £11 0s 6d, but apparent measurements recorded in ink do not agree 5h4.3h.   **9.** Advertisement in the *Liverpool Mercury*, January 10, 1840, 4th Page. Winstanley also bought a Titian *Holy Family* for £13 13s 0d at Mr Proctor's sale, Christie's, 6 June 1842, unnumbered lot.   **10.** 1843 Catalogue, No. 81, p. 23.   **11.** 1893 Catalogue, No. 83, p. 30.

TOGNOLLI, Giovanni, 1786-1862

3040   The Finding of Aesculapius

Canvas, 198.5 × 296 cm

Attributed on entry into the collection to Ludovico Tagliani,[1] No. 3040 is listed in the Earle Sale Catalogue[2] (see Prov.) as by Tognolli who taught at the British Academy in Rome[3] and thus would have had contact with English patrons like Earle.[4] If by Tognolli, No. 3040 must date from after 1822 when he first started to paint in oil.

Prov: William Earle sold Winstanley Liverpool 17-18 April 1839 lot 48 Tognoli *The Discovery of Aesculapius*, 116 × 78 in, bt. Aikin, 60 gns. Presented by James Aikin, 1876.

Exh: Liverpool Mechanics Institution, *Second Exhibition of Objects Illustrative of the Fine Arts etc.*, 1842, No. 530.

Ref: **1.** 1885 Catalogue No. 108 p. 28.   **2.** Tognolli and Tagliani could easily be confused.   **3.** S. Weber, *Artisti trentini*, 1933, p. 280 and Francesco Ambrosi *Scrittori ed artisti trentini*, 1894, p. 288. There seems to be no record giving Tognolli's dates as a teacher at the British Academy. Kathleen M. Wells *The Return of the British Artists to Rome after 1815*, University of Leicester Ph.D. Thesis, 1974, is no help but the *Art Union*, 1845, p. 161, records that Tommaso Minardi was then appointed Professor of Drawing after considerable opposition to the appointment of any Italian.   **4.** Earle was an early patron of John Gibson and Sir Charles Lock Eastlake and lived in Rome in the 1820's and 1830's see Robert Syers, *History of Everton*, 1830, p. 255 and T. Algernon Earle, *Earle of Allerton Tower*, Transactions of the Historic Society of Lancashire and Cheshire, Vol. 42, 1890, pp. 48-51 and the Earle Sale Catalogue cited under provenance. A number of paintings by "G. Tegnoli" were in the sale of Sir P. Hesketh-Fleetwood Bt. M.P. at Rossall Hall, Lancs. on 6 June 1844.

ULLMAN, Eugene Paul, 1877-1953

2418   Femme au Chambre

Panel, 66.3 × 53.3 cm

Signed: *Eugene Paul Ullman*

Prov: Bequeathed by C. E. Ashworth, 1932.

VECCHIETTA, Pietro di Lorenzo, called, 1410-1480, studio of

2758 St. Bernardino Preaching

Canvas transferred from panel, 32 × 79.2 cm

St. Bernardino of Siena (1380-1444) was canonized in 1450. He especially cultivated the veneration of the Holy Name, holding up during his sermons a tablet inscribed with the initials I.H.S. as in this picture. The subject was first identified by Scharf.[1] The suggestion that 2758 represents the Appearance of San Bernardino[2] is unconvincing.[3] The lines incised by the artis to form the framework for the pavement and architecture are still clearly visible.

The coat of arms that hangs from the trumpet over the altar in the centre of the picture does not appear to correspond with those of any Sienese family although it is close to that of the Verdelli family which has four doves rather than two.[4] The leading figures of the groups on the right and left edges may well be portraits of the patron and his family.

Vecchietta's name was first proposed by Fairfax Murray.[5]

Two other predella panels of approximately the same height at Munich[6] and in the Vatican[7] are in a very similar style. Neither, however, has the step up to the pavement that appears in 2758. Compton plausibly suggests that they might have flanked 2758 and have formed part of the St. Bernardino altarpiece from the Cloister of San Francesco, Siena,[8] burnt in 1655.[9]

A fourth predella panel in the Uffizi,[10] not from the same altarpiece, appears to be closely related in style. The architectural conception in all four panels shows some similarity with the work of Francesco di Giorgio Martini, whose name was proposed by Crowe and Cavalcaselle,[11] and it is possible that he had some part in 2758 as an assistant in Vecchietta's studio. The figure types, however, are Vecchiettesque of the period of the Accademia *Sportelli*[12] and the predella to the Pienza *Madonna and Saints*.[13] Weaknesses in the drawing of the buildings in the Vatican panel[14] and other variations in style within the panels may suggest that more than one artist from the studio was involved in the execution.[15]

The carpet which hangs from San Bernardino's pulpit is of the so-called Holbein type produced in Western Anatolia.[16]

Prov: Probably Col. Crewe "Masaccio, A Congregation", Christie's 1 December 1810 (74) bt. in 5 gns, and 2 February 1811 (61) bt. Woodburn 4 gns; seen at Woodburn's by Ottley.[17] William Roscoe, his sale, 1816 (13) bt. Dr. Traill,[18] £31 10s 0d; presented to the L.R.I. by 1819;[19] deposited at the W.A.G., 1893;[20] presented to the W.A.G., 1948.

Exh: Manchester, *Art Treasures*, 1857 (72); Leeds, 1868 (23); R.A., 1881 (224).

Ref: **1.** MS notes on 1858 Proof Catalogue (20) (L.R.I. archives 63.14).   **2.** Robert L. Mode, *San Bernardino in Glory*, Art Bulletin, Vol. 55, 1973, p. 71.   **3.** H. W. van Os, *Vecchietta and the Franciscan Predella: A Renaissance Artist and his Workshop*, in Festoen (Festschrift Annie Zadoks), 1976, p. 464, n. 2.   **4.** Letter of Enzo Carli, 11 November 1976 who thinks it is invented.   **5.** L.R.I. Annual Report 1893, p. 48. Gertrude Coor, *Neroccio de'Landi*, 1961, p. 26 n.

49, 36 n. 90, however, still accepts the attribution proposed by Bernard Berenson, *The Central Italian Painters of the Renaissance*, 1897, p. 134 to Benvenuto di Giovanni.   **6.** Munich Alte Pinakothek 1020 *Miracle of St. Anthony of Padua* 32 × 65.5 cm. Ernst Buchner, *Alte Pinakothek Munchen*, 1957, p. 37 as Francesco di Giorgio Martini and Rolf Kultzen, *Alte Pinakothek Munchen, Italienische Malerei*. 1975, pp. 136-7 as Vecchietta. This relation was noted by Paul Schubring, *Cassoni*, 1915, p. 133. The panel has incised lines like 2758; letter of H. van Os (undated but September, 1976).   **7.** *Guida della Pinacoteca Vaticana*, 1933, (inside cover dated 1934) p. 67 No. 233 (142-A) *Miracle of a Saint* (probably St. Louis of Anjou) as Vecchietta.   **8.** 1963 Catalogue, pp. 195-6.   **9.** Giorgio Vigni, *Lorenzo di Pietro detto il Vecchietta*, 1937, p. 85.   **10.** Luciano Berti, *The Uffizi*, 1971, p. 31 (13) *Stories from the life of St. Benedict*, 28 × 193 cm as Neroccio di Bartolommeo Landi with Francesco di Giorgio Martini.   **11.** Crowe and Cavalcaselle, 1864-6, II, p. 371, III, p. 68.   **12.** Vigni, *op. cit.*,pl. III-V.   **13.** Vigni, *op. cit.*, pl. XX.   **14.** Van Os, *op. cit.*, p. 458-9.   **15.** Van Os, *op. cit.*, p. 459-460.   **16.** Compare the carpets reproduced by Wilhelm von Bode and Ernst Kühnel, *Antique rugs from the Near East*, 1970, p. 34 pl. 15 and Kurt Erdmann, *Oriental Carpets. An account of their history*, 1960, fig. 20 for carpets with similar designs in Italian fifteenth century pictures. Carpets of comparable size with only one row of repeated ornament hang from balconies in the background of a Cassone panel representing a tournament in Piazza S. Croce. Kurt Erdmann, *Orientalische Tierteppiche auf Bildern des XIV und XV Jahrhunderts*, Jahrbuch der preussischen Kunstsammlungen, L, 1929, pp. 285, 292, pl. 39c, 39d, 39e.   **17.** Letter of W. Y. Ottley to William Roscoe. 12 June 1812 (Roscoe Papers No. 2845 A).   **18.** A manuscript note at the front of E. K. Waterhouse's Copy of Roscoe's sale catalogue states that Traill bought on behalf of Thomas Coke of Norfolk, but the latter is also listed as a buyer in marked catalogues. Coke certainly expressed an interest in acquiring 2758 in a letter to Roscoe dated September 1 (?) 1816 (Roscoe Papers 912). He may have been persuaded to give it to the L.R.I.   **19.** 1819 Catalogue (7).   **20.** 1893 Catalogue p. 10 (20).

VEER, Abraham, Active 1674-1683

9127   A battle piece

Panel, 70.4 × 108.1 cm

Signed: *A VEER* (bottom left)

Recent cleaning revealed the signature. The artist is recorded as living in Heerestraat in Rotterdam in 1674 and may be identical with the Abraham Veer, the son of Abraham, the son of Thomas, who was baptized in the Lutheran church on 19 October 1635.

The composition in 9127 appears to have been a stock one with the artist.[1] Dr. van de Watering considers that 9127 "belongs to another, probably earlier period (shortly before 1680?)" than the other paintings known by him since the foliage is in a different style.[2]

Prov: Richard Rathbone; who presented it to the L.R.I. by 1859;[3] from whom transferred by the University of Liverpool to the W.A.G., 1976.

Ref: 1. Compare (a) a painting with Dr. Fr. Goldschmidt and Dr. V. Wallerstein, Berlin about 1933 panel signed 71 × 105 cm probably identical with a picture sold Frankfurt 7 October 1920 (417) (b) Baden-Baden sale, 17 June 1959 as Jan van

Huchtenburg and allegedly signed panel 73 × 83 cm probably cut at the right (c) Versailles sale 19 May 1974 (70) panel, signed and dated 16.3 (probably 1683), 68 × 93.5 cm. Another painting dated 1681 probably showing this composition was in a sale at Leyden 24 August 1802 (96) companion piece to (97). All the biographical and artistic information about Veer has been very kindly provided by Dr. van de Watering, *letter*, 7 January 1977.   **2.** Letter of Dr. van de Watering, 7 January 1977.   **3.** L.R.I. Catalogue, 1859 p. 66 (140) as Johan van Huchtenburg.

VENETIAN School, early 16th century

2820   Virgin and Child with Saints John the Baptist and Jerome

Panel, 32 × 46.3 cm

Condition: repaired in 1854 by Philip Westcott.[1]

The previous attribution of 2820 was to Basaiti, whose name was proposed by Berenson.[2] This type of composition stems ultimately from Giovanni Bellini.[3] The style, particularly the atmospheric sfumato of the modelling of the child reflect Bellini's early sixteenth century work. There are links with the works of Basaiti, such as with the Saint Jerome generally attributed to him in the Frari *Pala di San Ambrogio* begun by Alvise Vivarini and completed by Basaiti,[4] and with the bearded Saint in the foreground of the attributed altarpiece of San Pietro a Castello.[5] But the attribution is not totally convincing. Hesitancies leading to the redrawing of the Baptist's right arm and Christ's head suggest that 2820 may be the work of a young artist. The treatment of Saint John the Baptist is not unlike that of Christ in signed works of Rocco Marconi[6] whilst the Saint Jerome can be compared with the Saint Benedict in his *Madonna between Saints Francis and Benedict.*[7]

The attribution to Girolamo da Santacroce supported by many scholars since Waagen,[8] does not seem convincing. That artist's earliest known work, the Chicago *Madonna* dated 1516 already displays the landscape formula that was to be one of his trademarks.[9]

Prov: Entered the L.R.I. Collection between 1836 and 1843;[10] deposited at the W.A.G., 1893;[11] presented to the W.A.G., 1948.

Ref: **1.** Letter of Philip Westcott to John Finnie 30 January 1855 (L.R.I. Archives 17).   **2.** Bernard Berenson, *Italian Pictures of the Renaissance*, 1932, p. 53. 2820 is omitted from the latest list of Basaiti works, E. Bassi, s.v. BASAITI, Marco in *Dizionario Biografico degli Italiani*, VII, 1965, p. 54   **3.** Georg Gronau, *Giovanni Bellini*, 1930, pl. 86, 152.   **4.** Rodolfo Pallucchini, *I Vivarini*, n.d. p. 141, pl. 278.   **5.** Fritz Heinemann, *Giovanni Bellini e I Belliniani*, II, 1963, pl. 458.   **6.** *Christ and the Adulteress*, (Accademia, Venice) Bernard Berenson, *Italian Pictures of the Renaissance, Venetian School*, II, pl. 909 and *Christ between Saints Andrew and Peter* (San Giovanni e Paolo, Venice) Heinemann, *op. cit.*, I, p. 120 (S206), II, pl. 568.   **7.** Heinemann, *op. cit.*, I, p. 20 (59e), II, pl. 557.   **8.** G. F. Waagen, *Treasures of Art in Great Britain*, 1854, III, p. 237, No. 75; followed most recently by Heinemann, *op. cit.*, p. 163, S493.   **9.** Ryerson Collection 33.1008 *Paintings in the Art Institute of Chicago*, 1961, p. 40.   **10.** 1843 Catalogue, p. 12 (39).   **11.** 1893 Catalogue, p. 13 (32).

VENETIAN School, mid-16th century

2849   Madonna and Child enthroned with the infant Saint John and an angel

Copper, 28.5 × 16.3 cm

There is a pentimento in the archway, where there seems once to have been a column.

The angel is about to throw roses at the Madonna as commanded in the Song of Songs II 5, "fulcite me floribus . . . quia amore langueo," (sustain me with flowers . . . because I am sick with love). The text is very appropriate for a small devotional picture, since the desired feelings of the spectator on his knees before the picture would be the same as the Virgin's toward Christ.

2849 has been assigned to a follower of Giuseppe Salviati.[1] Links with this artist are not strong enough to maintain so definite an attribution. Compton correctly noted a relationship between 2849 and a group of paintings sometimes attributed to the young Tintoretto.[2] A painting possibly by the same artist as 2849 was on the Lucerne art market in 1960.[3]

Prov: Entered the collection of the L.R.I. between 1836 and 1843;[4] deposited at the W.A.G., 1893;[5] presented to the W.A.G., 1948.

Ref: 1. 1963 Catalogue, p. 176.   2. Rodolpho Pallucchini, *La Giovinezza del Tintoretto*, 1950, pp. 76-78, figs. 66-71.   3. *The Mystic Marriage of Saint Catherine*, attributed to Giovanni de' Galizzi. Sale of Galerie Fischer, Lucerne, 25 June 1960 (1758).   4. 1843 Catalogue p. 31 (113).   5. 1893 Catalogue p. 24 (65).

VENETIAN School, 17th century

2864   Adoration of the Shepherds

Copper, 46 × 22.8 cm

Attributed to Lodovico Carracci[1] on entry into the L.R.I.

Prov: Acquired by the L.R.I. between 1836 and 1843; deposited at the W.A.G., 1893; presented to the W.A.G., 1948.

Ref: 1. 1843 Catalogue No. 107

VENETIAN School, 18th century

6106   View on the Grand Canal

Canvas, 32.8 × 48.9 cm

The north west end of the Grand Canal including the churches of Santa Lucia and the Scalzi.

No. 6106 bears an old attribution to Jacopo Marieschi and is a reduced copy of a picture owned by the Leger Galleries, July 1962 then wrongly attributed to Francesco Tironi.[1]

Prov: A Gentleman removed from Venice sold Christie's 22 June 1875 lot 224, *A Pair of Views by Canaletto*, bt. Young £52 10s.[2] Presented by Miss Mary Cassie, 1961.

Ref: **1.** Compare the signed view now at the Staatliche Kunsthalle, Karlsruhe, No. 425.   **2.** Christie's Stencil 587A.

VERBOECKHOVEN, Eugene Joseph, 1798-1881

400   Sheep and Hens in Barn

Panel, 60 × 86 cm

Signed: *Eugene Verboeckhoven ft 1874*

There is a label on the back of the picture containing a declaration that No. 400 is an original painting, it is signed by the artist and dated 1874.

Prov: Bequeathed by George Audley, 1923.

1762   Sheep

Canvas, 56.7 × 48.7 cm

Signed: *Eugene Verboeckhoven ft. 1874*

There is a label on the back of the picture containing a declaration that No. 1762 is an original painting, it is signed by the artist and dated 1874.

Prov: Bequeathed by John Hughes, 1895.

VERONA, School of, 16th century

2786   Madonna and Child with the Infant St. John

Panel, 99 × 78.7 cm

Condition: Poor. Much rubbed.

This has been attributed to Liberale da Verona.[1] More recently Eberhardt has suggested Antonio da Pavia.[2] Neither of these names seems satisfactory. 2786 is closer to Antonio da Vendri in the typology of the children of his signed and dated *Madonna and Child and two angels* of 1518.[3] 2786 cannot be earlier than *c.* 1500 in view of the presence of strong Leonardesque characteristics.

The open book held by the Madonna is illustrated with a miniature of Pentecost. The text below, which is only partially legible, would seem to be that familiar from the Small Office of the Virgin, Ad Matutinum.

Domine, labia mea aperies
Et os meum annuntiebit laudem tuam
Deus, in adjutorum meum intende
Domine, ad adjuvandum me festina
Gloria Patri. Sicut erat. Alleluja.

It has not been possible to read the second text that follows.

Prov: Joseph Brooks Yates;[4] his sale, Winstanley's, 14 May 1857, (40), bt. William Rathbone, who presented it to the L.R.I., 1857-8;[5] deposited at the W.A.G., 1893;[6] presented to the W.A.G., 1948.

Ref: **1.** 1963 Catalogue, pp. 96-7.   **2.** Hans-Joachim Eberhardt orally.   **3.** Lionello Puppi, *Schedule per la storia della pittura veronese tra la fine del '400 e l'inizio de '500*, Arte Antica e Moderna, 1964, pl. 130c.   **4.** J. B. Yates made a number of purchases during his first visit to Italy in 1826. Roscoe Papers 343, 344.   **5.** L.R.I. Annual Report 1857/8.   **6.** 1893 Catalogue p. 14 (36).

VERONESE, Bonifazio, 1487-1553

2762   Virgin and Child with Saints Elizabeth, John the Baptist, Margaret, Anthony Abbot and Jerome

Canvas, 145.7 × 206 cm

The rabbits in the foreground, as defenceless animals, symbolize mankind, whose only hope for salvation is in Christ and his Passion.[1] The goldfinch and bullfinch perched on the base of the column, also, allude to Christ's sacrifice and Passion.[2]

The attribution goes back at least to 1840.[3] A typical work of the artist. Westphal[4] regards it as a workshop derivation from the *Sacra Conversazione* once in the Palazzo Giovanelli.[5] There is a general resemblance in the grouping of Saints Anthony and Jerome to those of Saints James and Jerome, and of Saints Peter and Mark in that picture. The Saint John the Baptist is very like the same saint (in reverse) in the Pitti *Madonna with Saint Elizabeth and a donor*.[6]

A weaker picture dependent on 2762 with the addition of St. Joseph, a female saint and a cherub in the sky, and with Saint Anthony Abbot transformed into Saint Andrew, once at Blenheim, is at Greenville, South Carolina.[7]

Prov: Bought in Venice:[8] John Ashton Yates (seal on the reverse); the Misses Yates;[3] Miss Yates of the Dingle; who bequeathed it to the L.R.I.;[8] entered the L.R.I., 18 April 1878;[9] deposited at the W.A.G., 1893;[10] presented to the W.A.G., 1948.

Exh: Liverpool, Mechanics Institution, 1840, Picture Gallery (131).[3] Liverpool, Society of Fine Arts, 1860 (186).

Ref: **1.** George Ferguson, *Signs and Symbols in Christian Art*, 1974, p. 20.   **2.** Herbert Friedmann, *The Symbolic Goldfinch*, 1946, p. 9.   **3.** Liverpool Mechanics Institution, *Catalogue of the Exhibition of objects Illustrative of the Fine Arts, Natural History, Philosophy, Machinery, Manufacturers, Antiquities, etc.*, 1840, p. 48 (131).   **4.** Dorothée Westphal, *Bonifazio Veronese*, 1931, p. 93 No. 40.   **5.** Westphal, pl. 40, now Columbia Museum of Art (62-929) S. H. Kress Foundation K 207.   **6.** Bernard Berenson, *Venetian School*, 1957, II, pl. 1137.   **7.** *Supplement to the Catalogue of the Art Collection, Bob Jones University*, 1963-8, No. 221, p. 76. 63⅛ × 89⅜ in.   **8.** L.R.I. Archives 17, letter of Eliz. Thompson, niece of Miss Yates of the Dingle, to the President of the L.R.I., 25 March 1878.   **9.** L.R.I. Archives 37, Presents Book, 18 April 1878.   **10.** 1893 Catalogue, p. 13 No. 31.

VERONESE, Paolo Caliari, called, 1528-1588, studio of

2854   The Finding of Moses

Canvas, 153 × 255 cm

Condition: cut[1] at bottom (*c.* 14 cm) and the top (*c.* 41 cm)[2]

The engraving by Delignon[2] and a drawing in the Villa Bogstad[3] in the same direction, both show minor, but differing variations from the picture, as well as revealing the loss of the upper parts of the trees and part of the foreground with the edge of the dress of the woman holding Moses.

Crosato has recently put forward the name of Benedetto Caliari.[4] The suggested comparison with the *Nativity of the Virgin* in the Scuola dei Mercanti is not convincing.

A drawing attributed to Veronese of the carriage in the middle distance dated 1582 is in the Baron von Hirsch Collection in Basle.[5] Cocke reasonably suggests that 2854 dates *c.* 1582.[6] Workshop participation in the execution seems clear.

The *Finding of Moses* was a favourite subject of Veronese's studio. Fastnedge list a number of versions.[7] Pace Crosato,[4] 2854 does not derive from that in Turin, although a carriage also occurs in the background of that picture.

Prov: Etienne Texier, Marquis d'Hautefeuille (died 1703);[8] the Duke of Orleans by 1727;[9] sold 1792 to Walkuers, a banker in Brussels;[10] Monsieur Laborde de Mereville who shipped it to London;[10] sold to Bryan (acting on behalf of the Duke of Bridgewater, the Earl of Carlisle and Lord Gower);[10] Bryan sale 26 December 1798 (149) bt. Maitland 40 gns;[11] John Maitland (deceased) sale of pictures removed from Woodford Hall, Essex, Christie's, 30 July 1831 (37) bt. Barnett 40 gns; presented to the L.R.I. by J. W. Gibsone, 1843;[12] deposited at the W.A.G., 1893;[13] presented to the W.A.G., 1948.

Exh: The Lyceum, The Strand, 26 December 1798-July 1799 (149).

Ref: **1.** Ralph Fastnedge, *Two Italian pictures recently restored at Liverpool*, Liverpool Bulletin, 3, Nos. 1 & 2, 1953, p. 27 and p. 27, n. 3; and W.A.G., *Cleaned Pictures*, 1955, p. 45.   **2.** J. Couché, *Galerie du Palais Royal*, Vol. II, 1808, XIe tableau, gives the measurements 6 pieds 5 pouces × 7 pieds 10 pouces. Using the conversion 1 pouce = 2.707 cm (see F. J. B. Watson, *The Wrightsman Collection*, II, 1966, p. 590) the measurements = 208.439 × 254.458 cm. The picture, when compared with the engraving has lost almost three times as much at the top as at the bottom.   **3.** Norsk Fokemuseum Bo 312 56 × 39 cm inscribed on the back P. Veronese (pencil) No. 19 (ink).   **4.** Lucian Larcher Crosato, *Note su Benedetto Caliari,* Arte Veneta, XXIII, 1970, p. 114, Teresio Pignatti, *Veronese,* 1976, Vol. 1, pl. 569, Vol. 2, pp. 147, 189, A151 as Benedetto and the bottega of Veronese.   **5.** Richard Cocke, *Observations of some drawings by Paolo Veronese,* Master Drawings, XI, No. 2, 1973, p. 141 and pl. 9.   **6.** Cocke, *op. cit.,* p. 142. Bernard Berenson, *Italian Pictures of the Renaissance, Venetian School,* I, 1957, p. 133 had already suggested that it was a late work in great part autograph.   **7.** *Cleaned Pictures,* p. 45.   **8.** Galleria Sabauda 575.   **9.** (L. F. Dubois de Saint Gelais), *Description des Tableaux du Palais Royal,* Paris, 1727, p. 385, as from the collection of M. de Hautefeuille. This could also refer to Gabriel Etienne Louis Texier, Marquis d'Hautefeuille (died 1743), but is more probably Etienne Texier, Marquis d'Hautefeuille, grand prior of Aquitaine and ambassador of Malta, since he is recorded as having a fine collection of paintings by Mariette (*Abecedario* II, *Archives de l'Art Francais,* IV, 1853-4, p. 345).   **10.** W. Buchanan, *Memoirs of Painting,* I, 1824, p. 18-19.   **11.** W. Buchanan, *op. cit.,* p. 135.   **12.** L.R.I. Annual Report 1843-4 and L.R.I. Presents Book, 6 November 1843 (L.R.I. Archives 37). 2854 may have been in William J. Keene sale, Christie's, 8 June 1839 (44) £6 15s 0d; but there was another *Finding of Moses* attributed to Veronese in London in the early nineteenth century, which appeared in an anonymous sale, Robins, 29 May 1811, £3 15s 0d; and the prices suggest that these two may be identical.   **13.** 1893 Catalogue p. 31 (86).

VERONESE, Paolo Caliari, called, after

2855   The Feast in the House of Levi

Canvas, 167 × 357 cm

Inscribed: *FECIT D. COVI MAGNV LEVI/LVCA CAP V/AD MDLXXIII/DIE XX APR*

A reduced copy of the picture dated 20 April 1573 painted for the Refectory of SS. Giovanni e Paolo, now in the Accademia, Venice (No. 203).[1]

A manuscript at Knowsley dated September 28, 1723 records "To Mr Casteel for Paul Veronese and Petro Cortone . . . 26:160 (Crossed out), 630 (written above)."[2]

The text is from St. Luke 5.29 in the Vulgate "Et fecit ei convivium magnum Levi in domo suo." The inscription abbreviates Convivium to Covi and D. presumably stands for Dominus.

Prov: Purchased for £60 for the Earl of Derby, Knowsley, before 1729;[3] sold Christie's 27 May 1909 (73) bt. Sir William P. Hartley 2 gns, who presented it to the W.A.G., 1914.

Ref: **1.** 550 × 127.8 cm; Giuseppe Fiocco, *Paolo Veronese, 1528-1588,* 1928, pp. 87-8, 185.   **2.** Knowsley MSS. Casteel is probably Peter Casteels III (1684-1749) who died in Richmond. The Earl of Derby owned pictures of *Peacocks Hens and Pigeons* and *Ducks and other Fowls* by Casteels. MS *Catalogue of Paintings at Knowsley Hall taken in 1801,* p. 7 (31), 14(145).   **3.** *Original Paintings and Prints collected by the Rt. Honourable James. Earl of Derby at Knowsley,* 1729

(MS Catalogue at Knowsley prepared for the printers I. Hunter and I. Fairhurst) Part 1 (90). G. Scharf, *Catalogue of Pictures at Knowsley Hall*, 1875, pp. 117-120 (203); MS *Catalogue of Pictures at Knowsley*, undated, after 1736, p. 6 records 2855. *A Catalogue of the paintings at Knowsley taken in 1782*, Prescot, 1790, p. 8 recorded in the "Dressing Room at top o' th' back stairs." MS *Catalogue of Paintings at Knowsley Hall taken in 1801*, (Victoria and Albert Museum Library), p. 17 (187) in the Dining Room as purchased for £60. *Catalogue of Painting at Knowsley Hall taken in 1801*, 1802, p. 17. MS *List of the Pictures in Knowsley Hall*, 1860 (Knowsley), (221) as on the North side of the Sitting Room; *A Catalogue of the Collection of Pictures at Knowsley Hall* compiled by Mary, Countess of Derby, 1887, p. 18 (200) with MS note as in the Tudor Sitting Room .

6943 The Crucifixion

Canvas, 121 × 101 cm

A copy after the picture from the Collection of Louis XIV, now in the Louvre.[1] A large section on the right containing the view of Jerusalem is omitted.

Prov: Presented to the L.R.I. by J. W. Gibsone, between 1857 and 1859;[2] presented by Liverpool University, 1969.
Exh: Leeds, *National Exhibition*, 1868 (175).
Ref: 1. Louis Hautecoeur, *Catalogues des Peintures*, *Musée National du Louvre*, II, 1926, p. 42, No. 1195, reproduced Giuseppe Fiocco, *Paolo Veronese*, 1928, pl. LXXXIII.   2. 1859 Catalogue p. 49 (92b). The type for the 1859 Catalogue was set up in 1858. Scharf does not mention 6943 in his notes on the proof placed in his hands for comments on April 12, 1858, or 1859 (L.R.I. Archives 63.14), but it does appear as a manuscript addition by Scharf to the proof (L.R.I. Archives 63).

VICENTINO, Andrea Michieli, called, 1539-1614

2847 The Court of Heaven

Canvas, 80 × 61.5 cm

At the top are Christ on the right with the globe, the Dove of the Holy Ghost and the Virgin on the left. Below are a number of saints, patriarchs, kings and prophets some of whom are identifiable. At the bottom on the left is St. Jerome, above him perhaps Moses with the tablets of the laws, above him two bishops perhaps St. Augustine and St. Ambrose. At the bottom on the right is St. Sebastian with an arrow, above him St. Catherine with a wheel, to the left of her perhaps St. Michael with the scales, above and to the right of her probably King David with a harp. At the bottom to the left of St. Sebastian is perhaps St. Lawrence with a gridiron; in the centre just below Christ and the Virgin is perhaps St. Andrew with his cross. At the bottom in the centre are two putti. The iconography is broadly similar to that of Jacopo Tintoretto's *Paradiso* in the Doge's Palace, Venice and No. 2847 has been incorrectly described as a sketch for this work.[1]

No. 2847 was first attributed to Vicentino by T. Mullaly[2] who associated with it another very similar but slightly larger sketch (116 × 86.4 cm) then owned by Hans Calmann, London. More doubtfully he described both these sketches as modelli for Vicentino's *Christ and the Virgin in Glory and Saints* now hanging to the left of the doorway on the end (north) wall of the left (north) transept of the Frari in Venice.[3]

Prov: ?John Pitt; William Morton Pitt sold Christie's 1 June 1811, lot 99 "*The Heavens by Tintoretto, a spirited picture freely coloured*" bt. Woodburn Senior £34 13s 0d. Probably the "Sketch by Tintoretto" bought by Roscoe from Thomas Winstanley in 1811;[4] Roscoe Sale 1816 lot 39, bt. Ballantyne[5] £11 11s 0d; presented to the L.R.I., 1819; deposited at the W.A.G., 1893; presented to the W.A.G., 1948.

Exh: Manchester, *Art Treasures*, 1857, No. 914. Leeds, *National Exhibition*, 1868, No. 165. W.A.G., *Cleaned Pictures*, 1955, No. 23.

Ref: 1. F. P. B. Osmaston, *The Paradise of Tintoretto*, 1910, frontispiece but even there he described the connection as doubtful and M. Pittaluga, *Il Tintoretto*, 1925, p. 231.   2. *Two Modelli by Andrea Vicentino*, Burlington Magazine, Vol. 106, 1964, pp. 507-509.   3. Giulio Lorenzetti, *Venice and its Lagoon*, 1961, p. 599.   4. Roscoe Papers, No. 5315.   5. Presumably the John Ballantyne of Edinburgh who sold Roscoe Sale 1816 Catalogues there (see the Catalogue title page).

VICTORS, Jan, 1620-1676

963   Landscape with a Cow in a Boat

Canvas, 83 × 115.3 cm

Signed: *Jan Victors ft.*

Of a type[1] perhaps datable early in Victors's career.[2]

Prov: Presented by Alfred Tomlinson on behalf of the family of John Tomlinson, 1949.

Ref.   1. Another well known example is the *Dutch Pastoral Scene*, (ex. Paul Drey Gallery, New York), ill. in W. Bernt, *Die Nederlandischen Maler des 17 Jahrhunderts*, 1948, III, p. 938 and exhibited Montreal Museum of Fine Arts, 1969, *Rembrandt and his Pupils*, No. 117.   2. H. Gerson verbally 11 August 1967; a date in the 1630's was seen on No. 963 in about 1954 but No. 963 shows little sign of the influence of Rembrandt whose pupil Victors was in the 1630's.

VINCENZO degli Azani da Pavia, called il Romano, active 1518, died 1557

2749   St. Catherine of Alexandria

Panel, 150 × 63.5 cm; painted area, 145 × 56.5 cm

The Saint stands on the Emperor Maximian or Maxentius, who according to legend martyred her.

Exh: Leeds, 1868 (87).

2748   St. Leonard

Panel, 150 × 62.7 cm; painted area, 145 × 56.5 cm

Exh: Leeds, 1868 (102).

2750   Madonna and Child in Glory

Panel, 150 × 86.5 cm; painted area, 144 × 81 cm

The attribution was first made by Bologna.[1] With 2748 and 2749, 2750 probably formed part of a polyptych executed for the Confraternity of San Leonardo in the old quarter at Mussomeli, a small Sicilian town between Palermo and Agrigento. On 10 January 1541 Vincenzo contracted with the Confraternity of San Leonardo to paint an altarpiece containing "imaginem intemerate Marie Virginis in medio cum imagine Iesu Christi in brachijs et ex uno latere Sancti Leonardi et ex alio latere imaginem Sancte Catherine . . ." There were to be figures of apostles below, which were to be painted and not in relief[2]—a specification that suggests that there might have been sculpture in other parts of the altarpiece. The whole complex was to follow the format of the high altarpiece of Sancta Maria La Nuova in Palermo. That church was rebuilt in the second half of the sixteenth century and there is no surviving record of the altarpiece's appearance.[3] Although the three panels are of the same height, the landscape is not continuous. 2750, therefore, may belong to a different tier from 2748 and 2749. Vincenzo was to set the altarpiece in place within 7 months. He was to be paid 55 *once* in instalments; 15 at the ordering of the altarpiece, 20 in August 1541 and the remaining 20 at Easter 1542.[2]

Comparison with Vincenzo's dated 1540 *Madonna of The Rosary* in San Domenico, Palermo confirms that 2750 and its companion panels date from the early 1540's.

Prov: San Leonardo, Mussomeli; in the nineteenth century on the wall of the "*Cappellone in cornu evangelii*"; transferred to San Leonardo's mother church, the Chiesa della Matrice, San Lodovico, prior to the closing of San Leonardo; sold in 1840 for about 40 onze with another painting probably by Vincenzo[5] with the aid of Salvatore Loforte, a painter, to a foreigner;[6] said to have been in a religious establishment in Palermo and to have been brought to this country by an agent of the late Pope;[7] William Brett;[8] from whom is was purchased for 100 guineas by the L.R.I. between February and April 1842;[9] deposited at the W.A.G., 1893;[10] presented to the W.A.G., 1948.

Ref: **1.** F. Bologna quoted by Dr. M. Picone, *letter*, 10 April 1959.   **2.** Giuseppe Cosentino, *Nuovi Documenti sul celebre pittore Vincenzo degli Azani detto il Romano*, Archivo Storico Siciliano Palermo, N.S., 37, 1912/13, pp. 501-2 published the contract in Arch. di Stato in Palermo. Atti di not. Antonio Occhipinti, Vol. 3707.   **3.** Gioacchino di Marzo, *Vincenzo da Pavia detto il Romano*, Palermo, 1916, p. 51.   **4.** A. Venturi, *Storia dell'arte Italiana*, IX part V, 1932, fig. 459.   **5.** Giuseppe Sorge, *Mussomeli dall'Origine all'abolizione della Feudalità*, II, Catania, 1916, p. 407-8. Dr. Ferretto of the Biblioteca Nazionale, Palermo kindly informed the compiler of this and the following reference, *letter*, 5 July 1975. The church of San Leonardo was rebuilt on its old site in the early seventeenth century. The new building was begun in March 1605. The Cappella Maggiore was finished in 1610 and the whole church completed by 1629. Sorge, *op. cit.*, pp. 406-7.   **6.** Giuseppe Sorge, *Mussomeli nel sec.XIX 1817-1900*, *Cronache*, Palermo, 1931, p. 56.   **7.** 1843 Catalogue p. 27 (97-99). The late Pope in 1843 would have been Pius VIII (1829-1830).   **8.** The Label on the reverse of 2748 consigns the picture by railway to him at No. 12 Bold Street. Nobody of this name is listed there in the Liverpool street directories of the nineteenth century. A. Littlejohn & Sons, Ironmongers were there between 1839 and 1914. This John Brett is probably the same man who exhibited two paintings of *The Temptation* and *The Expulsion* by Dubufe in Liverpool before 1845 to encourage subscribers to engravings of them. After 20,000 shares were taken, the pictures were to be raffled. But no engravings were made. (Joseph Mayer Papers, Liverpool Public Libraries, Newspaper Cuttings dated 1847.) A Mr Brett sold No. 960 Flinck to the L.R.I. A John? William Brett owned a copy of Rembrandt's *Night Watch* in the National Gallery (289). No picture dealer of this name is recorded in the London street directories, but a William Brett, cabinet maker listed at 22 Guildford Place, Spa Fields, London, from 1835 to 1848, whose probable relative another cabinet maker John is listed from 1838 to 1840 and 1844 to 1848.   **9.** L.R.I. Archives 41 Minute Book, undated between 24 February and 7 April.   **10.** 1893 Catalogue, pp. 25-26 (70-72).

VINCI, Leonardo da, 1452-1519, after

2785   Portrait of Mona Lisa

Panel, transferred from canvas, 82 × 56.5 cm

It has been suggested that the transfer from canvas to an old soft wood panel may have been made to heighten the impression of antiquity.[1]

An early copy of the portrait in the Louvre (No. 1601) which shows rather more of the columns behind the sitter and of the balusters of the chair arm than is now visible in the original.[2] The sitter is often thought to represent Lisa Gherardini (born 1479), who married Francesco del Giocondo in 1495. The Louvre painting probably dates *c.* 1503-6.[3]

Prov: W. R. Crompton-Stansfield of Esholt Hall, Yorkshire and afterwards of Frimley Park; by descent in 1875 to the widow of his nephew, Herbert Crompton Herries; at Frimley Park until 1900; R. S. Herries, Gloucester Street, London S.W. until 1907; Mrs Herbert Herries, 53 Warwick Square, London S.W.; on her death in March 1912 passed to W. H. Herries;[4] his sale, Christie's, 19 July 1912 (130) bt. Rathbone 105 gns; Harold S. Rathbone, who presented it to the W.A.G., "on behalf of an anonymous donor", 1915.

Exh: W.A.G., L.A.E., 1914 (1016A) as lent by Harold Rathbone.

Ref: **1.** Ralph Fastnedge, *W.A.G. Cleaned Pictures*, Liverpool, 1955, p. 34ff and 1963 *Catalogue*, p. 203-4.   **2.** The Louvre picture has been cut at the sides losing part of the columns. Letter of Charles Sterling, 10 December 1953. But it has not been cut at the bottom, letter of M. Foucart, 27 January 1977.   **3.** For other copies in Stuttgart and the Prado see Staatsgalerie, Stuttgart, 1971-1972, *Bild und Vorbild*, (1) and (4).   **4.** Letter of R. S. Herries to *The Times*, 9 August 1912.

VINNE, Jan Vincentsz van der, 1663-1721

9126   A riverside battle

Canvas, 91.5 × 114 cm

Signed: *J v Vinne 1686* $\frac{10}{20}$ or *11* (bottom right)

Probably painted just after the artist's arrival in England on 10 May 1686,[1] if one assumes the inscription is an abbreviation. Some of the figures appear to be Turkish suggesting that the action represented took place in the Austro-Turkish wars. Perhaps 9126 represents the Siege of Buda[2] recaptured from the Turks on 2 September 1686.[3]

Prov: Entered the collection of the L.R.I. between 1836 and 1843;[4] from whom transferred by the University of Liverpool to the W.A.G., 1976.

Ref: 1. A. van der Willigen, *Les Artistes de Harlem*, 1870, p. 312. Ulrich Thieme and Felix Becker, *Allgemeines Lexicon der Bildende Kunstler*, XXXIV, 1940 p. 392.   2. Dr Q. Hughes, *orally*, 1976, also Dr Miklos Horvath, *letter*, 14 February 1977 who however thinks that 9126 is not based on a contemporary engraving.   3. Nicholas Henderson, *Prince Eugen of Savoy*, 1964, p. 23.   4. L.R.I. Catalogue, 1843, p. 26 (94).

VISSCHER, Cornelis, about 1619-1662, after

3418   The Ratcatcher

Panel, 40.9 × 31.6 cm

A copy after Visscher's etching of 1655[1] but without the landscape.

An old label on No. 3418 reads; "Scuola Alemanda etc. No. 92/Theodoro Visscher in vece di Nettscher[2] rap (presentan) di un contadino con suo assistente che fanno veder topi e vendono polvere per (avvenel) arli."[3]

Prov: Bequeathed by Lord Wavertree, 1937.

Ref: 1. Eugene Dutuit, *Manuel de L'amateur d'estampes*, Vol. 6, 1885, p. 478, No. 43.   2. Presumably Casper Nettscher, 1639-1684.   3. I am indebted to Miss A. Zaina for help in deciphering this label.

VLAMINCK, Maurice de, 1876-1958

3025   Environs de Rouen

Canvas, 46 × 55 cm

Signed: *Vlaminck*

Painted in the spring of 1910;[1] at this time the artist was living at Vesinet, about 12 miles from Paris down the Seine, but he made frequent excursions further down the Seine, presumably as far as Rouen.[2]

Prov: Bought from the artist by D. H. Kahnweiler Spring 1910;[3] sold Hotel Drouot, Paris, 13-14 June, 17-18 November 1921, or 4 July 1922 (Ventes des tableaux etc. composant la collection de la galerie Kahnweiler, objet d'une mesure de sequestre de guerre).[4] Bruce Maxwell; Redfern Gallery; Anton Walbrook sold Sotheby's 6 May 1959 lot 80, bt. Kalman £2,200 from whom it was purchased 1959.

Exh: ?Grafton Galleries, 1910, *Manet and the Post-Impressionists*, No. 107, *Le Remorqueur*, (lent by M. Kahnweiler).[5]

Ref: 1. D. H. Kahnweiler, *letter*, 14 May 1959 who gives there the title of No. 3025. Kahnweiler had been buying all Vlaminck's paintings since 1907 (D. H. Kahnweiler, *My Galleries and Painters*, 1971, pp. 35-6 see also Andre Derain, *Lettres à Vlaminck*, 1955, pp. 191-2 and Florent Fels, *Vlaminck*, 1928, p. 91).   2. See Maurice Vlaminck, *Dangerous Corner*, 1961 (translated from *Le Tournant Dangereux*, 1929), pp. 70ff; the subdued mood of No. 3025 may reflect the artist's own feelings—he wrote: "when in 1910 under an angry sky the Seine overflowed its banks and flooded houses and trees the grandeur of the scene moved me deeply. All seemed to be overshadowed by desolate sadness etc." (*op. cit.*, p. 74).   3. Kahnweiler *op. cit.*   4. D. H. Kahnweiler, *letter*, 7 July 1959 stated that No. 3025 was included in one of these sales; it was probably lot 105, 17-18 November 1921, *Le Vapeur*, signé en bas a gauche, 46 × 55 cm bt. M. Grassat 500 francs; Grassat was buying at the sale for Kahnweiler (Malcolm Gee, *letter*, May 1977). No. 3025 has a Kahnweiler label with Inv. No. 534 on it.   5. A different picture according to D. H. Kahnweiler, *letter*, 14 May 1959.

VLIET, Hendrik Cornelisz van, 1611/12-1675

Loan 25   The New Church at Delft with the Tomb of William of Orange

Canvas, 127 × 85.5 cm

(?)Signed and dated 1667 at foot of centre pier (now illegible)

The Tomb of William I (of Orange or "the Silent") was begun in 1614 by Hendrik de Keyser and completed in 1622 by his son Pieter. Jantzen[1] lists four other versions of this composition by Van Vliet; No. 146 in the former Leuchtenberg Collection, signed and dated 1659,[2] No. 231 in the Schloss Georgium Dessau, signed and dated 1663; Nos. 683 (signed) and 464 (attributed now to Gerrit Houckgeest), both in the National Museum, Stockholm. The Stockholm versions and the Dessau version are taken from the same view point as the Liverpool picture but vary in other respects; the Leuchtenberg version is now untraced. A frontal view of the tomb by Van Vliet was in the Brod Gallery, London in 1967, and a view similar to No. 25 but from the other side of the Tomb is in the Nelson Gallery of Art, Kansas City (No. 70-17).[3]

Prov: R. V. Yates who presented it to the Liverpool Mechanics Institution, 1833[4]; lent by the Governors of the Liverpool Institute to the W.A.G.

Exh: Liverpool Mechanics Institution, *Exhibition of Objects Illustrative of the Fine Arts* etc., 1840, No. 640A.

Ref: 1. Hans Jantzen, *Das Niederlandishce Architecturbild*, 1910 p. 172, Nos. 532, 539, 554 and 583.   2. But apparently attributed in earlier catalogues of this collection to Emmanuel de Witte with figures by Weenix.   3. For other views in this church see Timothy Trent Blade, *Two Interior Views of the Old Church at Delft*, Museum Studies, Art Institute of Chicago, Vol. 6, 1971, pp. 34ff.   4. Minutes of the Committee of Directors of the Liverpool Mechanics Institution, 10 July 1833, Liverpool City Libraries, 373 1/1/1/.

VOLAIRE, Jean Antoine, 1750-1820

6130   The Eruption of Vesuvius

Canvas, 103 × 128 cm

Innumerable versions and variants exist.[1] The artist certainly saw the eruption of 14 May 1771[2] and his view of it from nature, differing considerably from No. 6130, was engraved by Guttenberg.[3]

Prov: Presented to the L.R.I. by Richard Rathbone in 1842-1843;[4] presented by the University of Liverpool in 1962.

Exh: Liverpool Mechanics Institution, *First Exhibition of Objects illustrative of the Fine Arts etc.*, 1840. No. 271 (as by Wright of Derby).

Ref: **1.** Henry Blundell of Ince Blundell owned one (*An Account of the Statues, Busts etc at Ince, Collected by H.B.*, 1803, p. 227 No. LIII): Henry Blundell Hollinshead another (exhibited at the Liverpool Royal Institution, *Old Masters*, 1823 (132)); Charles Townley of Townley Hall another (sold Christie's 27 February 1948 (65)); all vary slightly from each other—for lists of other versions see Napoli, Palazzo Reale, *Il Paesaggio Napoletano nella Pittura Straniera*, 1962, No. 98, pp. 84-5 with further references. **2.** Abbe Richard de Saint Non, *Voyage Pittoresque ou Description des Royaumes de Naples et de Sicile*, 1781, I, p. 210. **3.** Saint Non, *op. cit.*, opposite p. 210. **4.** No. 6130 is one of the pictures "added since this catalogue was printed" in the 1843 Catalogue (No. 126).

VOLLMAR, Ludwig von, 1842-1884

49 The Zither Player

Canvas, 81.1 × 95.3 cm

Signed: *L. Vollmar/Munchen*

Presumably the picture listed by Boetticher[1] as "Der kleine Virtuos, Ein zitherspielender Knabe, dem die Geschwister und eine Alte voll Staunen zuhoren"; according to Boetticher it was painted in 1877, completely reworked in 1879 and reproduced in *The Graphic*, 1879[2] and in the *Deutsche Illustriert Zeichnung* in November 1884.

H. Holland noted Defregger's influence on No. 49.[3]

Prov: Bequeathed by John Hughes, 1895.

Ref: **1.** F. von Boetticher, *Malerwerke des 19 Jahrhunderts*, 1891-1901, Vol. 2, p. 946. **2.** But not there located by the compiler. **3.** In *Allgemeine Deutsche Biographie*, 1896, under Vollmar, also with the date 1877.

VUILLARD, Edouard, 1868-1940

6217 Madame Hessel au Sofa

Board, 54.6 × 54.6 cm

Inscribed: *E. Vuillard.*[1]

The artist met Mme. Hessel in 1900 and the hairstyle of the sitter can perhaps be dated to 1899-1901[2] suggesting a date of 1900-1901 for this portrait. Antoine Salomon however prefers a date around 1908[3] and Andre Chastel dates another nearly identical version of No. 6217 to 1900-1905.[4]

For Mme. Hessel and her influence on the artist see particularly *Edouard Vuillard/K-X Roussel*, Orangerie des Tuileries, 1968, p. 101, No. 113.

Prov: In the artist's studio at his death; Mme. K.-X Roussel.[5] Hanover Gallery; bought in 1947[6] by G. G. O. Cross; bought from his heirs by the Gallery 1964.

Ref: 1. Frits Lugt, *Marques de Collections*, Supplement, 1956, 2497a, p. 363 (red not violet).   2. Anne Buck, *letter*, 4 November 1968.   3. Letter 31 May 1972.   4. Andre Chastel, *Vuillard*, 1946, p. 60 (rep.) pp. 69-71—this version inscribed *a mon amie Lucie Hessel Vuillard.*   5. Frits Lugt, *op. cit.*   6. Erica Brauser, *letter*, 29 October 1968.

WATERLOO, Anthonie, about 1610-1690, after

872   Landscape with Waterfall

Panel, 81 × 58 cm

A copy with variations, after the etching the *Water Mill*[1] by Waterloo.

Prov: Bequeathed by Mrs Margaret Harvey, 1878.

Ref: 1. Adam Bartsch, *Le Peintre Graveur*, 1854, Vol. II, p. 107, No. 103.

WESTCHILOFF, C.

1536   Les Faraglioni a Capri

Canvas, 60.3 × 73 cm

Signed: *C. Westchiloff*

The Faraglioni are off the south eastern corner of the island. The view is taken from the north west probably from the Strada di Tragara.

Prov: Presented by Lord Wavertree, 1927.

Exh: L.A.E., 1927 (859).

WESTERHOUT, Arnold van, 1651-1725 and LENARDI, Giovanni Battista, 1656-1704, after

2896   Theological Allegory with the Assumption of the Virgin

Canvas, 207 × 166 cm

Inscribed: lower l. corner: *Joannes Bart. Lenardus Romanus Invent. et delin* and in the r. much worn, apparently: *Arnoldus Van Westerhout Antwerp Ferd. Mag. Princ. Etruriae sculptor fecit Romae super perm*

Anno 1695 and in the c.: *Explicabuntur publice in Collegio Romano a Comite Emerico Csakii de Keresztszegh perpetuo Terre Scepusiensis Domino Abbate B. M. Virginis de Curru/Cathedralis ecclesie Agriensis (Erlau) Canonico Hungaro Collegii Germanici et Hungarici Alumno Anno 1695 Mensis . . .* The Central cartouche carries a dedication to Pope Innocent XII. Theological theses are inscribed on the columns. The trophies representing battles have further inscriptions on them.

A copy after an engraving of 1695 by Westerhout after Lenardi.[1] The engraving commemmorates a disputation of Count Emerich Csaky at the Collegium Romanum on 5 September 1695 after which he was made a Doctor of Theology.[2]

The theses he sustained are inscribed on the columns of the engraving. No. 2896 differs slightly from the engraving in that there is a new trophy on the right hand side inscribed: *Victoria Temesvarica Duce Principe Eugenio A° 1716*[3] and a new trophy on the left hand side inscribed *Victoria Belgradensis Duce Principe Eugenio A° 1717* .[4] No. 2896 was therefore presumably painted shortly after 1717 and the artist[5] was able to add some new victories to those already recorded on the trophies of the engraving. The figures in the medallions at the top have also been changed to King Stephen(?) and Queen Margaret(?) from the two generals of the engraving.

Prov: Presented by James Aspinall, 1859.

Ref: **1.** The engraving was published in a number of parts; there is an incomplete set at the Bibliotheque Nationale, Paris, Bb 22c Fol. Didier Bodart, *L'Oeuvre du graveur Arnold van Westerhout,* 1976 should be consulted.   **2.** Described at length in F. Buonani. *Numismata pontificum romanorum etc.,* 1699, I, pp. 364ff and in A. Steinhuber, *Geschiehte des Kollegium Germanikum Hungarikum in Rom,* II. 1906, p. 133.   **3.** The capture of the fort at Temesirar by Prince Eugene and his army.   **4.** The Capture of Belgrade by Prince Eugene and his Army in 1717.   **5.** The 1885 Catalogue give his name as Bernardo Luigi Lorente. apparently an unrecorded artist.

WESTPHALIA or the Lower Rhine about 1500, School of

1229   The Presentation in the Temple

Panel, 47.3 × 33.4 cm

Inscribed: *UNUS EST DEU* on the edge of the altar and *Di?i/?g/d?/ti??* in a niche above the altar.

One of a group of the *Seven Sorrows of the Virgin*[1] which together formed all or part of an altarpiece; the thin painted bands of blue and black along the top of No. 1229 and of blue and white along the right hand side of No. 1229 suggest that this panel was at the bottom left corner of this composite altarpiece or of a wing of it; the coloured bands would have provided the barriers between individual scenes. Moreover the panel is painted up to the edges only at the top and along the right hand side (painted area, 46.8 × 33 cm). Two other panels a *Flight into Egypt* (on loan from the Dutch government to the Gemeentemuseum Arnhem) and an *Entombment*[2] (Stedelijk Museum, Bruges) have similar painted bands, similar dimensions and a similar system of grooving on the back; they therefore probably belonged to the same altarpiece.[3] Presumably there were four other panels from this altarpiece still untraced—a *Christ among the Doctors*, *Christ carrying the Cross*, *Crucifixion* and *Descent from the Cross*.

Prov: Acquired by the L.R.I. between 1836 and 1843;[4] presented to the W.A.G., 1948.
Exh: Manchester, *Art Treasures*, 1857 (411).
Ref: **1.** For the iconography see W. H. Gerdts, *The Sword of Sorrow*, Art Quarterly, Autumn 1954, pp. 213ff and Louis Reau, *Iconographie de l'Art Chretien*, 1957, II, II, p. 108ff who states that the subject of the Seven Sorrows of the Virgin appeared first in Flanders at the end of the 15th Century.   **2.** H. Pauwels, *Catalogus*, 1960, No. 16.   **3.** Guido de Werd and Gerard Lemmens, *letters*, 15 January 1970 to 31 May 1972.   **4.** 1843 Catalogue No. 48 as by Wohlgemuth.

ZEZZOS, Alessandro, 1848-1913/14

2886   Outside St. Mark's

Canvas, 186 × 147 cm

Signed: *A Zezzos 1876*

Presumably the painting Boito described thus:[1] "Dello Zezzo, che fece recentemente un grande quadro con dentro due ragazzine le quali sedute sullo zoccolo della chiesa di San Marco, giocano con i colombi, cosa piuttosto insipida, ci rammentiamo il primo dipinto, lodato dai giornali veneziani" but in No. 2886 there are three girls not two.

Prov: Presented by Col Thomas Wilson, 1912.
Exh: (?)Paris, *Société des artistes francais*, 1876 (2087) as *Les Pigeons de Saint Marc*.
Ref: **1.** Camillo Boito, *Scultura e Pittura d'Oggi*, 1877, p. 128.

ZOBEL, Fernando, born 1924

6128   To the Hive

Canvas, 182 × 130 cm

Signed: *Zobel*

Inscribed: (on back of canvas) *417/COLMENAR/Zobel/Junio 1961/*

The artist has written:

"The title, *Colmenar*, is only remotely connected with beehives. Colmenar is the name of a small town in the province of Madrid. In 1961 I was doing a long series of abstractions and, rather than assign them numbers, I made up an alphabetical list of towns in the province of Madrid and assigned town-names to the paintings in the order in which they were completed. I find that I can identify individual paintings by name more easily than by number, no matter how arbitrary the name. I am sorry if this procedure has created problems in interpretation.

Most of the pictures in the series, including *Colmenar* have to do with what I can only describe as 'frozen motion', the contradiction involved resulting in a kind of tension that I found fascinating at the time. All the pictures in this series were executed in black and white. Eventually effects of light and shade appeared that I found intriguing, and these eventually led me back to my present concern with color.

At the time I was not particularly concerned with the conveying of particular emotions, though subjective reactions on the part of the audience are far from unwelcome. In other words, if the spectator senses the effect of an explosion, say, that is fine by me, though I rather think that the effect of this particular painting would tend to be less violent. More in the nature of, for instance, a flight of large birds. That, however, remains pretty subjective. The artist in this case had no desire to evoke any particular response beyond a sense of swift movement held under restraint."[1]

The statement in the 1963 Catalogue that No. 6128 evoked the atomic explosion at Hiroshima is incorrect.[2]

Prov: Purchased from O'Hana Gallery Ltd., London, 1962.
Exh: Arts Council, *Modern Spanish Painting*, 1962, No. 87.
Ref: 1. Letter, 11 May 1972. Colmenar is Spanish for apiary. See also Magaz Sangro, *Zobel*, 1959 and Antonio Lorenzo, *Zobel*, 1963. 2. Letter from the artist, 20 May 1972.

ZOFFANY, Johann, 1734/5-1810

1513 George, 3rd Earl Cowper

Canvas, 115.6 × 85 cm

An oval half length version[1] without the landscape background of the three quarter length portrait of about 1773 now owned by Viscount Gage.[2]

For the sitter see No. 1227 (by Mengs), *Horace Walpole's Correspondence* (ed. Lewis) 1937 onwards passim, Manners and Williamson,[3] Sutton[4] and Millar.[5]

Prov: By descent to Lord Lucas[6] (8th Baron) of Wrest Park Bedfordshire sold by Lady Lucas, Christie's 6 November 1917, lot 129 bt. Thrift £199 10s 0d; A. Tooth and Sons, H. A. Buttery; Leggatt Bros; Lord Brocket sold Sotheby's 16 July 1952 lot 102 bt. for W.A.G.
Ref: 1. Lady Victoria Manners and G. C. Williamson, *John Zoffany R.A.*, 1920, p. 236. 2. Manners and Williamson, *op. cit.*, Addenda et Corrigenda, also noting yet another version; Denys Sutton, *Paintings at Firle Place*, The Connoisseur, Vol. 137, 1956, Supplement, p. 81, pl. 2; Oliver Millar, *Zoffany and his Tribuna*, 1966, pl. 12, p. 10 who dates it to about 1773 and states that the landscape background is Cowper's Villa Palmieri, Florence. National Portrait Gallery, *Johan Zoffany*, 1976, No. 77, p. 60. 3. *Op. cit.* 4. *Op. cit.* 5. *Op. cit.* 6. See Burke's *Peerage* under Lucas.

2395   The Family of Sir William Young

Canvas, 114.3 × 167.8 cm

Sir William Young (1725-1788) was the son of William Young, a doctor in the West Indies who is said to have emigrated there from Scotland after the 1715 rebellion. His first wife died childless; his second wife was Elizabeth (1729-1801), only child of Brook Taylor of Bifrons, Kent, whom he married in 1747.[1] She is seated next to Sir William Young in No. 2395. The other figures in No. 2395 are, except for the negro servant, their children—from left to right: Brook, second son, at Eton 1762-6, John, fourth son, baptised at Antigua 10 September 1761, who married Jane Blizzard and died without issue at 14 Brock Street, Bath in 1834, Henry, third son, who died of wounds in the American War of Independence, Sarah Elizabeth, eldest daughter, who married Richard Ottley in 1770 and died in 1825, Elizabeth, who married a Mr Summers and died in 1823 at Margaret Street, Cavendish Square, London, Portia who died unmarried in 1832, in front of them, the youngest daughter Olivia who died unmarried in 1815, on the right, Mary who married a Mr Sewel and William (1749-1815) the eldest son and second baronet.[2] Sir William Young was successively Lieutenant Governor of Dominica (1768), and finally Governor of Dominica (1770-1774).[3] He purchased the Manor of Delaford, Iver, Bucks, in 1767 and was created a baronet in 1769.[4] Sir William Young is playing the cello, his wife Elizabeth and daughter, Olivia, are playing the theorbo.

The place represented in No. 2395, if indeed the setting is not imaginary, has not been certainly identified. Manners and Williamson assert that it "must be Delaford"[5] but Young's property there only contained an Elizabethan Manor House (demolished about 1800).[6] A. Atkinson suggested that it was "St. Dunstan's Park, Thatcham,"[7] by which he presumably meant Dunston House, Thatcham, built 1722-3, demolished 1798,[8] the residence of Richard Ottley husband of Sarah Elizabeth;[9] a record of the appearance of only one facade survives and this facade was not similar to the architecture in No. 2395.[10]

Two replicas of or studies for the extreme left hand and right hand groups[11] are owned by Sir William Young Bt. (the first contains Brook, John, Henry and the negro servant, the second William (junior) and Mary). Photographs are in the National Portrait Gallery.

No. 2395 has been dated to 1770,[12] the year of Sir William Young's appointment to the governorship of Dominica, the year after the grant of his baronetcy and the year of the marriage of his eldest daughter Sarah Elizabeth who has a very prominent place in No. 2395; if indeed the setting of No. 2395 is Dunston House (or St. Dunstan's Park), the residence of Sarah Elizabeth's new husband Richard Ottley, this would provide further evidence that No. 2395 was painted in 1770 on the occasion of this marriage. The Vandyke dress moreover of No. 2395 suggests a date in the 1770's when it was at its most popular.[13] However, William Young and his wife were friends of David Garrick from whom they tried to borrow scenery and costumes for a private production of *Julius Caesar* in 1758;[14] theatrical costume would therefore have been expected from them even at an earlier date and Mary Webster relying on the appearance of the eldest and youngest sons suggests a date about 1766 for No. 2395.[15] Despite his various official appointments Sir William Young was probably in England at least 1768-1772.[16]

Prov: Probably "my family picture at the old Road" bequeathed by the sitter Sir William Young to "Billie Young my grandson".[17] Julian Young sold Christie's 14 December 1928 (96) bt. Knoedler £7,350. Sir Philip Sassoon sold Christie's 2 July 1937 (34) bt. in; purchased from Sir Philip Sassoon, 1937.

Exh: 25 Park Lane, London, *English Conversation Pieces*, 1930 (7). Amsterdam, *Loan Exhibition of British Art*, 1936 (183).

Ref: **1.** *Complete Baronetage*, ed. G. E. C. Vol. 5, 1906, p. 153.   **2.** Charles Robson, *letter*, 14 August 1937. This list of children is largely confirmed by Sir William Young's Will and its Codicils of 1784-8 (Public Record Office 11/1168/20320, proved 29 July 1788) but at that time Elizabeth was married to a James Hartley and Brook was dead, John's marriage took place 1784-8 and there are references to various negro slaves. This will was partly reprinted in Vere L. Oliver, *History of the Island of Antigua*, 1899, Vol. 3, pp. 281ff where his children are also again listed in an extensive family tree, for Brook see R. A. Austen Leigh, *The Eton College Register*, 1753-1790, 1921, p. 582. For the second baronet see the *Dictionary of National Biography*; there is a portrait of him by Benjamin West at Eton see L. Cust, *Catalogue of Eton Portraits*, 1916, No. 16; he also appears in a *Conversation Piece* attributed to Richard Brompton painted at Rome 1773-4 and now at Audley End (R. J. B. Walker, *Catalogue of the Pictures in the State Rooms Audley End*, 1973, p. 26, No. 10).   **3.** T. Southey, *Chronological History of the West Indies*, 1827, Vol. 2, pp. 398 and 407 and Sir Alan Burns, *History of the British West Indies*, 1965, p. 505.   **4.** *Complete Baronetage*, op. cit.   **5.** Lady Victoria Manners, and Dr. G. C. Williamson, *John Zoffany*, 1920, p. 247.   **6.** W. H. Ward and K. S. Block, *A History of Iver*, 1933, pp. 198-9, p. 205.   **7.** A. Atkinson, *William Young Ottley Artist and Collector*, Notes and Queries, 2 April 1938, p. 236 and 12 November 1938, p. 346.   **8.** S. Barfield, *Thatcham, Berks and its Manors*, 1901, Vol. I, pp. 331-3. It was certainly not occupied by the Ottley family until after 1759.   **9.** Burke's *Landed Gentry*, 4th Edition 1863, p. 1135. The Ottleys were another West Indian family.   **10.** Barfield, *op. cit.*, Vol. I, pl. IV opposite p. 48.   **11.** Reproduced in Manners and Williamson, *op. cit.*, facing pages 244 and 246. According to G. C. Williamson, *English Conversation Pictures*, 1931, pp. 3, 19, the two godparents of the respective children in each group ordered them as later autograph replicas. S. Sitwell, *Conversation Pieces*, 1936, p. 38 also calls them replicas or adaptations. Mary Webster however in National Portrait Gallery, *Johan Zoffany*, 1976, Nos. 39-40, p. 42 describes them as "perhaps studies". The one with Brook, John and Henry is inscribed *Zoffany and Stubbs pinx 1770*.   **12.** Christie's Catalogue, 14 December 1928, p. 35 (see provenance).   **13.** J. L. Nevinson, *Vandyke Dress*, Connoisseur, Vol. 157, 1964, pp. 166ff. Zoffany's group portrait of the royal family in Vandyke dress also dates from 1770 (see Oliver Millar, *Pictures in the Royal Collection, Later Georgian Pictures*, 1969, pp. 149ff, No. 1201).   **14.** *Letters of David Garrick*, ed Little and Kahrl, 1963, Vol. I, Nos. 208-9.   **15.** Letter, 11 October 1976 and in *Johan Zoffany, op. cit.*, No. 41. I am indebted to Mary Webster for help in this entry.   **16.** Letters of David Garrick, *op. cit.*, Vol. 2, Nos. 586, 596, pp. 845-6.   **17.** Oliver, *op. cit.*, p. 281 in the second codicil of Sir William Young's Will.

ZUCCOLI, Luigi, 1815-1876

318   Card Players

Canvas, 36.4 × 43.5 cm

Signed and inscribed: *Luigi Zuccoli/Roma*

Genre scenes are generally dated to the latter part of Zuccoli's career and he seems to have been in Rome in the 1860's.

Prov: Bought from W. G. Herbert 1871 (bill 27 July MS W.A.G.) £63 by George Holt; bequeathed by Emma Holt, 1944.

CATALOGUE OF DRAWINGS AND WATERCOLOURS

ALBANI, Francesco, 1578-1660, after

**5082 Venus and Cupid surprised by a satyr
verso: Christ in glory**

Black chalk, 17.9 × 31 cm

The pose of the Venus and Cupid is very close to that of the same two figures in Albani's *Venus and Adonis* in the Villa Borghese (Inv. No. 44).

Prov: Presented by David Pennant to the L.R.I. before 1841; deposited at the W.A.G., 1893; presented to the W.A.G., 1948.

ALMA-TADEMA, Lawrence, 1852-1909

179 Sunday Morning

Watercolour, 34.3 × 22.5 cm

Signed: *L Alma Tadema 1870*

A version, with slight differences, of the right hand side of the oil painting of 1868 *The Visit: A Dutch Interior*, now in the Victoria and Albert Museum.[1] A further version also entitled *Sunday Morning* now in the Tate Gallery was painted in 1871;[2] it is very close to No. 179 but has an additional seated figure and a different view through the window.

Prov: ?Gambart.[3] Bt. by George Holt from Stephen T. Gooden about 1889 (£260); bequeathed by Emma Holt, 1944.
Exh: Glasgow Royal Institute of Fine Arts, 1888 (1226).
Ref: **1.** Inv. No. CA1.16; Victoria and Albert Museum, *Summary Catalogue of British Paintings*, 1973, p. 1. Was this the *Birth Chamber, Seventeenth Century* listed by R. Dircks, *List of Works by Alma-Tadema*, The Art Journal, Christmas Number, 1910, p. 27, No. LXVIII as 1869.   **2.** Inv. No. 3527, *The Collections of the Tate Gallery*, 1967, p. 1, Dircks, *op. cit.*, No. XCVI.   **3.** Most of Alma-Tadema's works at this period were painted for Gambart, see J. Maas, *Gambart*, 1975, pp. 215ff.

2430 Autumn

Watercolour, 24.8 × 61 cm

Signed: *L Alma Tadema op CXXVIII*

Inscribed: *IMPCAESDIV/PARTHICIFIL/DIVINERVAE/VS HADRIANVS*

The inscription of the marble seat refers to the Emperor Hadrian, adopted son of Parthicus (Emperor Trajan), adopted son of the Emperor Nerva.

No. 2430 was painted in 1874 and while at the Society of Painters in Watercolours Exhibition in that year was extensively reviewed by the Athenaeum critic: "In its class the chief work here is Mr Alma-Tadema's *Autumn* (249), the pathetic suggestion of which is deeply moving. There is fine and noble art in this picture, which represents the outskirts of a sparse beech wood, probably near Rome or some great Roman city, or it may be that the trees, whose ruddy leafage strews the ground, and whose huge serpent-like trunks rise before us, are but a screen in some public garden designed to veil the city, whose "Autumn" is suggested by the inscription recording Hadrian on the large crescent-shaped marble bench, which is conspicuous in the work, and sustains three figures of men, resting and meditating in an apparently mournful manner. The draughtmanship of this bench, its modelling, and its curiously characteristic colour, about the grey tones and lichens of which there is a certain pathetic sadness, is creditable even to an artist so distinguished as Mr Tadema is, and always has been. Its foreshortening is a marvel, so deftly have the beautiful curves of the sweeping back of the seat been given; and the perspective of the seat itself—planes varying as they recede from and again approach the plane of the picture—is a delight to the eye. Almost equally delightful are the colour and the solidity of the marble: the latter is due in no small degree to the modelling of the material and the exquisitely faithful treatment of the light."

The oil painting, No. 119 at the 1877 R.A., also entitled *Autumn* has an entirely different composition.[3]

Prov: Sold by the artist to Gambart the dealer.[4] Andrew Maxwell (by 1876).[5] Arthur Sanderson; The French Gallery (Wallis and Son) from whom purchased 1912.

Exh: Society of Painters in Watercolour 1874 (249); Royal Scottish Academy 1876 (795); Salon, Paris, 1878 (2348); Grosvenor Gallery *Exhibition of the Works of Sir Lawrence Alma Tadema* 1882 (262); Royal Academy *Exhibition of Works by the late Sir Lawrence Alma Tadema* 1913 (9).

Ref: **1**. R. Dircks, *List of Works by Alma-Tadema*, Art Journal, Christmas Number, 1910, p. 27. Anna Alma-Tadema, *letter*, 6 March 1913 MS Walker Art Gallery, states that it was finished on 6 April 1874. **2**. *The Athenaeum*, 25 April 1874, p. 565. Another shorter review appeared in the *Saturday Review* 25 April 1874, p. 53. **3**. Now in the Birmingham City Art Gallery 62'11 see their *Catalogue of Oil Paintings*, 1960, pp. 8-9. **4**. Anna Alma-Tadema, letter *op. cit.* **5**. Reviewed there by Robert Waller, *Mr Andrew Maxwell's Collection*, Magazine of Art, 1894, pp. 223-4, repr. p. 227.

ANROOY, Anton van, born 1870

91 Miss Rachel Keith

Watercolour, 48.5 × 34.4 cm

Signed: *A van Anrooy 08*

The sitter, daughter of George Keith, superintendent of customs in the Channel Islands,[1] married the artist on 24 April 1912.

Prov: Purchased from the 1909 L.A.E. (£25).
Exh: L.A.E. 1909 (645).
Ref: 1. Letter from the artist, 29 October 1909.

BANDINELLI, Baccio, 1493-1560, Studio of

2137 Six figures seated around a fire

Pen and brown ink, 20.2 × 36.4 cm

Inscribed: *di Raffaele d'Urbinis* (brown ink)

William Roscoe catalogued the drawing as Donatello, but it had been attributed to Bandinelli when in the Spencer collection. While close to Bandinelli's style the mechanical care with which the lines are drawn suggests that it is a copy of a drawing by Bandinelli, done by one of his pupils.

Prov: Earl Spencer (Lugt 1530); his sale, T. Philipe 10 June 1811 (14) bt. in at 5s; bt. from Philipe by William Roscoe 1 July 1811 for 9s,[1] Roscoe sale 1816 (23) bt. Esdaile 16s; William Esdaile (1758-1837) (Lugt 2617);[2] Alister Mathews from whom purchased, 1958.

Ref: 1. Roscoe Papers 2965.   2. Lot 18 in Esdaile's sale, Christie, 18 June 1840 was a pen drawing attributed to Donatello from the Spencer Collection described as four figures seated. It was bought with lot 17 for 3/-.

4158 Nude man kneeling

Pen and brown ink, 22.2 × 27.2 cm

Inscribed: *See page 255 Vol 4th* (pencil)[1]/*B. Bandinelli* (brown ink)

A careful copy of a drawing now in the Louvre (Inv. 105)[2] for the kneeling man in the top right corner of the relief of the *Baptism of Christ* on the tomb of Leo X in Santa Maria sopra Minerva, Rome.[3] Bandinelli received the commission in 1536, and completed that part of the monument by 1540. Pouncey suggested that 4158 might be by Vincenzo de Rossi (1525-1587),[4] one of Bandinelli's pupils. Certainly it is probably from Bandinelli's studio.

Prov: Roscoe sale, 1816 (82) bt. Ford 11/-; John Walter; his sale, Sotheby's, 12 November 1959, part of (56a) bt. C. G. Boerner; P. & D. Colnaghi & Co. Ltd., from whom purchased, 1960.

Ref: 1. A reference to William Roscoe, *Life of Leo X*, IV, Liverpool, 1805, p. 255 which mentions Bandinelli's work on the relief of the *Birth of the Virgin* at Loreto.   2. Maria Grazia Ciardi Duprè, *Per la cronologia dei disegni di Baccio Bandinelli fino al 1540*, Commentari, XVII, 1966, p. 163, fig. 27.   3. Duprè, *op. cit.*, p. 165, fig. 30.   4. P. M. R. Pouncey, orally, 8 July 1968.

BARTELS, Hans von, 1856-1913

2222 Returning from Work

Gouache, 97.8 × 78.2 cm

Signed: *Hans Bartels 1910*

The artist wanted No. 2222 returned to him to make the woman taller in 1910 but it is unclear if any alterations were in fact carried out.[1]

Prov: Purchased from the L.A.E., 1910 (£100).

Ref: 1. Letters between the Curator of the W.A.G. and the artist of 26 October 1910 and 6 January 1911 (MSS W.A.G.) The artist had seen the reproduction in *The Studio*, Vol. 51, 1910-11, pp. 230-1 where the acquisition of No. 2222 by the W.A.G. is reported.

BARTOLOMMEO, Fra, 1472-1517

8698 Madonna adoring the Christ Child (recto) Creation of Eve (verso)

Black chalk, pen and brown ink, brown wash, heightened with white (recto) Black chalk (verso); 25 × 21.3 cm

The attribution and related drawings are discussed at length in the article cited below.[1] The Madonna in 8698 originally was not in profile, but in three quarter view. The same figure occurs minus a head in Uffizi 290E verso and Staatliche Museen Preussischer Kulturbesitz, Berlin (West) KdZ 458 verso. All three drawings are closely connected to the early style of Fra Bartolommeo, when he was still influenced by Piero di Cosimo. The verso is close in style to drawings for Saint Peter in the Louvre *Marriage of Saint Catherine* signed and dated 1511 (Museum Boymans-van Beuningen M128 verso).

Prov: Sir Peter Lely (Lugt 2092); Earl Spencer (Lugt 1531); his sale, Thomas Philipe, 15 June 1811 (646) bt. R (probably Roscoe) £4 4s 0; Roscoe sale, 1816 (163) bt. Esdaile £5; William Esdaile (Lugt 1617); possibly his sale, Christie's, 18 June 1840 part of (76) with (77) bt. Sheath 2s 6d; Thomas Thane (Lugt 2461); Mr Husband, Bridgwater by 27 June 1952;[2] his sale[3] Christie's, 25 June 1974 (203) bt. H. M. Calmann, from whom purchased, 1974, with the aid of a grant from the National Art-Collections Fund.

Ref: 1. Martin Hopkinson, *A Fra Bartolommeo drawing once owned by William Roscoe*, Walker Art Gallery Bulletin and Annual Report, V, 1974-5, pp. 50-59.   2. Label on backing.   3. Letter of Mrs I. Husband, 17 November, 1974.

BARTOLOMMEO, Fra, follower of

5085 Head of a Man

Black chalk, 27.3 × 19.9 cm

The traditional attribution was to Fra Bartolommeo,[1] and 5085 is remarkably close in pose to the head of the second apostle from the left in his fresco of the *Last Judgement* painted for Santa Maria degli Angeli.[2] Venturi[3] and Shearman[4] accept the attribution, but Berenson thought it by Sogliani.[5]

The drawing appears to have been damaged by overcleaning and to have been redrawn. Venturi illustrates it prior to the damage.[6]

Prov: David Pennant, who presented it to the L.R.I. before 1841; deposited at the W.A.G., 1893; presented to the W.A.G., 1948.

Ref: **1.** 1859 Catalogue p. 74 (180). **2.** Reproduced in Christian von Holst, *Fra Bartolommeo und Albertinelli*, Mitteilungen des Kunsthistorischen Institutes in Florenz, 1974, p. 301, fig. 29. **3.** A. Venturi, *Storia dell'Arte Italiana*, IX, pt. 1, 1925, p. 294 note 2. **4.** John Shearman, letter 27 October 1961. **5.** Bernard Berenson, *The drawings of the Florentine Painters*, II, 1938, p. 349 (2726A) and *I disegni dei pittori Fiorentini*, II, 1961, p. 590 (2726A). **6.** Venturi, *op. cit.*, IX pt. 1, fig. 211.

BASSANO, Jacopo da Ponte, 1515/16-1592

1216   A hound

Black and brown chalks on blue paper, 20.8 × 28.9 cm

The attribution to Jacopo Bassano is traditional.[1] 1216 belongs to a small group of exceptionally fine studies of animals from life which Ballarin suggests were made by Jacopo from animals kept in his garden.[2] This is recorded by Ridolfi.[3]

Kultzen claims that 1216 is related to the Munich *Sacrifice of Noah*.[4] A closer connection exists with the Kromeriz *Entry of the Animals into the Ark*.[5] The legs of the hound in 1216 are incomplete, either because No. 1216 is a copy or perhaps because the artist intended to hide them in the painting as in the case with the Kromeriz picture. Similar dogs occur in a number of paintings by Jacopo Bassano and his studio of the 1580's, accompanied however by a loss of freshness and vitality.[6]

Prov: David Pennant; presented to the L.R.I. before 1841; deposited at the W.A.G., 1893; presented to the W.A.G., 1948.

Ref: **1.** 1859 Catalogue p. 74 (187) followed for instance by Edoardo Arslan, *I Bassano*, I, 1960, p. 169 with previous literature. **2.** Alessandro Ballarin, *L'Orto del Bassano*, Arte Veneta, 1964, p. 67. **3.** Carlo Ridolfi, *Le Maraviglie dell'Arte*, 1648, p. 389. **4.** Rolf Kultzen and Peter Eikemeier, *Alte Pinakothek Munchen Venezianische Gemalde des 15 und 16 Jahrhunderts*, 1971, I, p. 49, II, pl. 61. **5.** Arslan, *op. cit.*, II, pl. 199. **6.** Similar hounds occur in the Uffizi *Entry into the Ark* (Arslan, *op. cit.*, II, pl. 346) and in reverse in the Castello Sforzesco *Spring* (Arslan, *op. cit.*, II, pl. 345) and in a *Rustic Scene* with Leger, 1964.

BASSANO, Jacopo da Ponte, after

1215   A man stricken by the plague

Black chalk and grey wash on faded blue paper, 20.3 × 32.7 cm

A copy of the man in the bottom left corner of Jacopo Bassano's *St. Roche blessing the Plague Stricken*, now in the Brera, Milan, but formerly in San Rocco, Vicenza. The altarpiece is generally dated shortly after 1575.[1] The drawing which was formerly attributed to Jacopo Bassano,[2] was assigned to the workshop by the Tietzes.[3] But both E. Arslan[4] and Wethey[5] think that the drawing is not 16th century. The drapery in the man's lap is misunderstood, but the provenance of 1213 to 1216 is the same, which may suggest that they all came from the Bassano workshop.

Prov: David Pennant; who presented it to the L.R.I. before 1841; deposited at the W.A.G., 1893; presented to the W.A.G., 1948

Ref: **1.** Edoardo Arslan, *I Bassano*, I, p. 171, II, pl. 169.   **2.** 1859 Catalogue, p. 74 (186).   **3.** Hans Tietze and E. Tietze-Conrat, *The Drawings of the Venetian Painters in the 15th and 16th Centuries*, 1944, p. 51 (157).   **4.** Arslan, *op. cit.*, p. 349.   **5.** Harold E. Wethey, *orally*, 19 September 1975.

BASSANO, Studio of the, after Paolo VERONESE

1214   Doge Andrea Contarini with soldiers

Black chalk on faded blue paper, 42 × 28.7 cm

A copy of the middle group of *the Return of Doge Contarini to Venice after his victory at Chioggia* by Veronese and his studio in the Palazzo Ducale, Venice, painted probably in the late 1580's.[1]

The traditional attribution to Jacopo Bassano[2] was rejected by the Tietzes who assigned it to the Bassano workshop.[3] E. Arslan felt that it was close to Francesco Bassano.[4] The drawing has certain similarities, for instance, in the coarse broken line to Leandro, and it may be from his workshop.

Prov: David Pennant, who presented it to the L.R.I. before 1841; deposited at the W.A.G., 1893; presented to the W.A.G., 1948.

Ref: **1.** Giuseppe Fiocco, *Paolo Veronese*, 1928, pp. 109, 184, fig. 72.   **2.** 1859 Catalogue, p. 74 (185).   **3.** Hans Tietze and E. Tietze-Conrat, *The Drawings of the Venetian Painters in the 15th and 16th Centuries*, 1944, p. 51, (157 bis) pl. CXCVII.   **4.** Edoardo Arslan, *I Bassano*, I, 1960, p. 349.

BASSANO, Leandro da Ponte, 1557-1622, Studio of

1213   Kneeling man

Brown wash heightened with white on grey paper, 20.5 × 22.7 cm

The present attribution is due to the Tietzes,[1] who compare it with the drawing for the *Martyrdom of St. Lucy* in the Louvre (inv. 5284).[2] It was traditionally assigned to Jacopo Bassano.[3] E. Arslan suggests that it is a 17th century or 18th century derivation.[4]

Prov: David Pennant, who presented it to the L.R.I., before 1841; deposited at the W.A.G., 1893; presented to the W.A.G., 1948.

Ref: **1.** Hans Tietze and E. Tietze-Conrat, *The Drawings of the Venetian Painters in the 15th and 16th Centuries*, 1944, p. 57 (221).   **2.** Tietze and Tietze-Conrat, *op. cit.*, p. 58.   **3.** 1859 Catalogue p. 74 (184).   **4.** Edoardo Arslan, *I Bassano*, I, p. 349.

BOLOGNESE School, early 17th century

5094 Study of a male nude lying on his back

Red chalk on buff paper, 25 × 21.6 cm

Inscribed: *An Carraccio*

The 1967 Catalogue suggested an attribution to Antonio Carracci.

Prov: Unknown Collector with a flower as a mark. Presented by David Pennant to the
L.R.I. before 1841; deposited at the W.A.G., 1893; presented to the W.A.G.,
1948.

BOLOGNESE School, early 17th century

5127 St. Eligius and the devil disguised as a woman

Pen, ink, wash and black chalk, 36 × 20.1 cm

Inscribed: *T. Zuccaro*

St. Eligius was forced to shoe a horse which under the influence of the
devil, kicked anyone who approached it. He cut the leg off, shod it and
then restored the leg to the horse making the sign of the cross. He then
pulled the devil's nose with his pincers. The devil, as here, is often shown
in the form of a woman with horns.

The present attribution is due to Philip Pouncey.[1]

Prov: Presented by David Pennant to the L.R.I. before 1841; deposited at the W.A.G..
1893; presented to the W.A.G., 1948.
Ref: 1. *Letter* 26 July 1961.

BOUCHER, Francois, 1703-1770, after

2517 Three Putti in Clouds

Red chalk, 25.7 × 21.4 cm

After a drawing formerly in an American Private Collection.[1]

Prov: ?William Roscoe; bequeathed by Mrs A. M. Roscoe, 1950.
Ref: 1. P. and D. Colnaghi, *Old Master Drawings*, 1950 plate XIII. Anon sold Christie's, 5 April 1977 lot 135. The original drawing was engraved as plate 1 of *Cin-
quieme Livre de grouppes d'enfans Inventeés par F. Boucher et Gravé par Huquier
fils* n.d.

BRUEGHEL, Jan the elder, 1568-1625

6352   The Crossing of the Red Sea by the Israelites and the Destruction of Pharoah's Armies

Pen and wash in blue and brown inks, 28.8 × 41 cm

Inscribed: *Rijmdijk's Museum*

The subject is taken from Exodus XIV. No. 6352 has been cut on the right hand side so that the drowning of the Egyptians is now missing.[1] On the left Moses is examining the bones of Joseph which he took with them (Exodus XIII, 19); in the centre is the Egyptian treasure which the Israelites borrowed (Exodus XII, 35-36).

Attributed by Matthias Winner[2] to Jan Brueghel the elder largely by comparison with the *Continence of Scipio* at Munich,[3] No. 6352 is dated by him to about 1600 and described by him as Jan Brueghel's most fully worked out drawn figure composition. Many rather similar paintings of this subject are recorded by Frans Francken the younger to whom this drawing was attributed in the 1967 Catalogue.[4]

Prov: Jan van Rijmsdijk.[5] Robert Udnev not identified in his sale T. Philipe, 4 May 1803. Roscoe Sale 1816 lot 458 bt. Lord Stanley[6] 18s. Anon sold Sotheby's 1 July 1965 lot 116 bt. L'Art Ancien from whom purchased with the aid of a grant from the National Art-Collections Fund 1966.

Ref: **1.** Compare the size of No. 6352 given in the Roscoe Sale Catalogue (12½ × 20 in) see provenance.   **2.** *Neubestimmtes und Undbestimmtes in zeichnerischen Werk von Jan Brueghel d.A.*, Jahrbuch der Berliner Museen, Vol. 14, 1972, p. 146.   **3.** For which see Alte Pinakothek Munchen, *Deutsche und Niederlandische Malerei zwischen Renaissance under Barock*, 1963, p. 18, No. 827.   **4.** Lists of such works are in the 1967 Catalogue and in Staatliche Kunsthalle Karlsruhe, *Katalog Alte Meister*, 1966, p. 119.   **5.** Lugt 2167.   **6.** Later 13th Earl of Derby.

CAMPIGLIA, Giovanni Domenico, 1692-1768

5086   The Death of Laocoon and of his two sons

Black chalk, 51.6 × 39.4 cm

Inscribed: *Campiglia del*

After the well known Hellenistic group still in the Vatican.

Prov: (?)William Lock of Norbury Park; probably his sale Sotheby's 3 May 1821 part of lot 88 bt. Emery. David Pennant; presented to the L.R.I. by 1841; deposited at the W.A.G., 1893; presented to the W.A.G., 1948.

5087   The Borghese Warrior

Black chalk, 38.8 × 30 cm

Inscribed: *Ino Domenico Campiglia del Lucca 1692-176*

5088   The Borghese Warrior

Black chalk, 38.6 × 29.3 cm

Inscribed: *Campiglia del*

After the well known antique statue then in the Borghese Collection in Rome but now in the Louvre.

Prov: William Lock of Norbury Park sold Sotheby's 3 May 1821 lot 405[1] bt. David
            Pennant £0 19s 0d; presented to the L.R.I. before 1841; deposited at the
            W.A.G., 1893; presented to the W.A.G., 1948.
Ref: 1. Both are inscribed *Lock's Sale 405* on the verso.

5089   An antique bust

Black chalk on buff paper, 28.1 × 20.2 cm

Inscribed: *Campiglia del*

The bust has not been certainly identified; if rightly identified in the Lock Sale Catalogue No. 5089 was there described as representing the Emperor Elius Verus. Busts similar to No. 5089 are in Lowther Castle and Althorp House.[1]

Prov: ?William Lock of Norbury Park, probably at his sale Sotheby's 3 May 1821, lot
            405 bt. Pennant £0 19s 0d. David Pennant; presented to the L.R.I., before 1841;
            deposited at the W.A.G., 1893; presented to the W.A.G., 1948.
Ref: I.C.C. Vermeule, *letter*, December 1966.

5090   An antique bust

Black chalk, 28.3 × 20.3 cm

Inscribed: *Campiglia del* (on verso)

The bust has not been identified.[1]

Prov: William Lock of Norbury Park sold Sotheby's 3 May 1821 lot 405[2] bt. David
            Pennant £0 19s 0; presented to the L.R.I. before 1841; deposited at the W.A.G.,
            1893; presented to the W.A.G., 1948.
Ref: 1. *Emperor Hadrian* is inscribed on the verso but this is not correct.   2. *Lock's
            sale 405* is also inscribed on the verso.

5091   The Albani Antinous

Black chalk, 35 × 29.2 cm

After the relief found in Hadrian's Villa in 1735, later acquired by Cardinal Albani and still in the Villa Albani. No. 5091 shows the relief before restoration.[1]

The attribution dates back to the 1859 Catalogue.[2]

Prov: ?William Lock of Norbury Park, probably at his sale Sotheby's, 3 May 1821, lot 88 bt. Emery. David Pennant; presented to the L.R.I. before 1841; deposited at the W.A.G., 1893; presented to the W.A.G., 1948.

Ref: 1. It appears after restoration in J. J. Winckelmann, *Monumenti Antichi Inediti*, Vol. 2, 1767, p. 235, pl. 180 in an engraving by N. Mogalli after N. Mosman. 2. 1859 Catalogue No. 210 (or perhaps Nos. 208 or 209).

CIPRIANI, Giovanni Battista, 1727-1785

5092 (?)Antique Statue of Paris

Black and white chalk, 43.7 × 27.3 cm

Inscribed: *Cipriani del/Cipriani*

Undraped the statue would in reverse be nearly identical to an antique statuette of Paris in the Vatican.[1] The drapery, the torch or *fasces* and indeed perhaps the whole statue may be modern.[2] There is a plaster cast of it in the Palazzo degli Anziani, Lucca. In 1859 the artist was "supposed to be G. D. Campiglia".[3]

Prov: (?)William Lock,[4] probably at his sale Sotheby's 3 May 1821 lot 192 bt. David Pennant £1 9s 0d; presented to the L.R.I. before 1841; deposited at the W.A.G., 1893; presented to the W.A.G., 1948.

Ref: 1. W. Amelung, *Die Sculpturen des Vaticanischen Museums*, 1903, Vol. 1. p. 532, No. 343. 2. As suggested in the 1967 Catalogue. 3. 1859 Catalogue No. 211. 4. See No. 5122, footnote 2.

5095 Bacchus by Jacopo Sansovino

Black chalk on buff paper, 45.4 × 28 cm

Inscribed: *Cipriani del*

Very close to Marco Alvise Pitteri's engraving[1] after Jacopo Sansovino's statue then in the Uffizi now in the Museo Nazionale, Florence. The inscription however is presumably accurate.[2]

Prov: William Lock of Norbury Park sold Sotheby's 3 May 1821 part of lot 192[3] bt. David Pennant £1 9s 0d; presented to the L.R.I. before 1841; deposited at the W.A.G., 1893; presented to the W.A.G., 1948.

Ref: 1. A. F. Gori, *Museum Florentinum*, 1734 (Statuae Antiquae Deorum Vol. 3) No. 54; the engraving is inscribed *Campiglia del*. 2. The 1859 Catalogue No. 213 and the 1967 Catalogue follow the inscription. 3. *Lock's sale 192* is inscribed on the verso; the catalogue attributes No. 5095 to Cipriani. See No. 5122, footnote 2.

5096 Antique Statue of a seated Nymph

Black chalk, 40.6 × 25.8 cm

Inscribed: *Cipriani del*

Watermark: *crowned fleur de lys*

After the Hellenistic *Seated Nymph*, then (and now) in the Uffizi, Florence.[1]

Prov: William Lock of Norbury Park sold Sotheby's 3 May 1821 part of lot 192[2] bt. David Pennant £1 9s 0d; presented to the L.R.I. before 1841; deposited at the W.A.G., 1893; presented to the W.A.G., 1948.

Ref: 1. Guido A. Mansuelli, *Galleria degli Uffizi, Le Sculture*, Vol. 1, 1961, No. 52, pp. 80ff.   2. *Lock's Sale 1821, 192* is inscribed on the verso. See No. 5122, footnote 2.

5122   Antique Statue of a Muse

Red chalk and gouache on buff prepared paper, 29.9 × 18.9 cm

Inscribed: *Cipriani del* (on verso)

After the so-called *Urania* now in the Palazzo dei Conservatori, Rome.[1]

Prov: William Lock of Norbury Park sold Sotheby's 3 May 1821 part of lot 188[2] bt. David Pennant £0 10s 6d; presented to the L.R.I. before 1841; deposited at the W.A.G., 1893; presented to the W.A.G., 1948.

Ref: 1. *A Catalogue of the Ancient Sculptures preserved in the Municipal Collections of Rome*, Vol. 2, *Palazzo dei Conservatori* ed. H. Stuart Jones, 1926, p. 20, Scala 2, 1, Plates Volume, pl. 10.   2. *Lock's Sale 188* is inscribed on the verso. A note in the sale catalogue states that the drawings by Cipriani were given to Lock by the artist.

5123   Antique Statue of a Discobulus

Pencil, 30 × 18.8 cm

No. 5123 is very close to the engraving in Cavaceppi's *Raccolta*;[1] the discus is however held in a different way. The attribution to Cipriani[2] must be regarded as doubtful.

The original statue was bought by William Lock of Norbury Park from Bartolomeo Cavaceppi,[3] bought at his sale by Charles Duncombe of Duncombe Park, Helmsley,[4] where it still is.[5]

Prov: (?)William Lock; presumably at his sale, Sotheby's, 3 May 1821;[6] David Pennant; presented to the L.R.I. before 1841; deposited at the W.A.G., 1893; presented to the W.A.G., 1948.

Ref: 1. B. Cavaceppi, *Raccolta d'Antiche Statue*, 1768-1770, Vol. 3, pl. 42.   2. 1967 Catalogue. But in the 1859 Catalogue, No. 228, it is listed as by an unknown artist.   3. Cavaceppi *op. cit.*   4. Christie's, 16 April 1785, lot 54. See also A. Michaelis, *Ancient Marbles in Great Britain*, 1882, p. 295.   5. Duncombe Park Estate Office, *letter*, 6 January 1976.   6. Lot No. 87 at that sale was *Antique Statues of the Discobulus by Joh Casanova in black chalk, very fine, 3* bt. Emery £1 2s 0d. See No. 5122, footnote 2.

5124 Antique Statue of a Muse

Red chalk on grey prepared paper, 21.7 × 15.9 cm

Inscribed: *Cipriani del* (on verso)

The original statue has not been identified.[1]

Prov: William Lock of Norbury Park sold Sotheby's 3 May 1821 part of lot 188[2] bt.
          David Pennant £0 10s 6d; presented to the L.R.I. before 1841; deposited at the
          W.A.G., 1893; presented to the W.A.G., 1948.
Ref: 1. For very similar statues see Salomon Reinach, *Repertoire de la Statuaire Grec-
          que et Romaine*, Vol. 1, 1897, pp. 256-283.   2. *Lock's Sale 1821, 188* is
          inscribed on the verso. See No. 5122, footnote 2.

5125 (?)Antique statue of a Muse

Red chalk on grey prepared paper, 17.9 × 11.8 cm

Possibly after an antique statue of a Muse similar to the so called *Thalia*
in the British Museum[1] but also possibly after a 17th century statue[2]
—William Lock collected both antique and modern sculpture.

No. 5125 was probably catalogued as by an unknown artist in the 1859
Catalogue.[3]

Prov: William Lock of Norbury Park sold Sotheby's 3 May 1821 part of lot 188[4] bt.
          David Pennant £0 10s 6d; presented to the L.R.I. before 1841; deposited at the
          W.A.G., 1893; presented to the W.A.G., 1948.
Ref: 1. *A Description of the Collection of Ancient Marbles in the British Museum*,
          1818, Vol. 3, No. 5.   2. As suggested in the 1967 Catalogue.   3. Probably
          No. 227.   4. *Lock's Sale 1821 188* is inscribed on the verso. See No. 5122,
          footnote 2.

5126 Study of two nude soldiers in helmets holding rods and bound man.

Red chalk on pink/grey prepared paper, 18.6 × 20.6 cm

Inscribed: *Cipriani* (on verso)

Catalogued as by an unknown artist in the 1859 Catalogue.[1]

Prov: William Lock of Norbury Park sold Sotheby's 3 May 1821 lot 188[2] bt. David
          Pennant £0 10s 6d; presented to the L.R.I. before 1841; deposited at the
          W.A.G., 1893; presented to the W.A.G., 1948.
Ref: 1. No. 231.   2. *Lock's Sale 18 . . .188* is inscribed on the verso. See No. 5122,
          footnote 2.

CLAUDE Gellee, called Claude Lorrain, 1600-1682

6176 Study of trees with two figures

Pen, ink and brown wash on blue paper, 24 × 16.5 cm

Basically a drawing from nature but elaborated into a composition by the dark *motif* at the bottom right, the figures, the distant hills etc; dateable to about 1640.[1]

Prov: Jonathan Richardson Senior.[2] John Barnard.[3] Roscoe Sale. 1816 lot 576 bt. Bree[4] £1 14s 0d. Louisa Julia Manners. Emilius Ralph Norman. Miss Elizabeth Norman sold Sotheby's 21 May 1963 lot 69 bt. for the Gallery.

Ref: 1. M. Rothlisberger, *Claude Lorrain, the Drawings*, 1968, p. 184. No. 412 with further details.   **2.** Lugt 2183.   **3.** Lugt 1419.   **4.** A Liverpool art master see *Liverpool Mercury* 26 August 1814.

DEBILLEMONT-CHARDON, Mme Gabrielle, born 1860

2175 Deux Vieux Paysans

Watercolour on ivory, 10.2 × 14.2 cm

Signed: *G. Debillemont*

Portraits of M. and Mme Changenet of Chenove near Dijon, France, painted in August 1894.[1] The artist was born at Dijon.

Octave Uzanne commented on the realism of No. 2175, unusual in miniatures.[2]

Prov: Purchased from the 1907 L.A.E. (£35).

Exh: Paris *Société des artistes francais*, 1895, No. 2195 (7) as *Deux vieux Bourguignons* R.A. 1897 (1549) as *Two old Burgundians: man and wife*. L.A.E. 1907 (1796).

Ref: 1. An inscription on the back reads, *Portrait du pere et de la mere/ Changenet/Chenove Aout 1894/G. Debillemont.*   2. *Mme. Debillemont-Chardon's Miniatures*, The Studio, Vol. 48, 1909-10, p. 215.

DETAILLE, Jean Baptiste Edouard, 1848-1912

219 Grenadier du Regiment de Lorraine

Pen, ink, wash and gouache, 22.5 × 13 cm

Signed: *EDOUARD DETAILLE/1886*

Copied from a gouache by Johan Christian Becker painted by him between 1757 and 1763 from a soldier seen by him in Weimar during the Seven Years War.[1] Detaille has however added a grenade on to the grenadier's hat. The higher sword, the *fleuret* or *epée de duel* identifies the grenadier as a *maitre d'armes* or instructor in duelling with the sword.

Prov: Bought by George Holt from Cremetti, Hanover Gallery 1891 (bill 11 March, MS W.A.G.); bequeathed by Emma Holt 1944.

Ref: 1. A reproduction of Becker's gouache is in the Musee de l'Armée, Paris. I am indebted to Colonel M. MacCarthy for this and all the other military information (his letter 8 December 1975).

DIZIANI, Gasparo, 1689-1767

5097 **The Virgin and Child enthroned with Saints Peter, Jerome, (?)Ambrose and (?)Roch**

Pen, ink, grey wash and red chalk, arched top, 40 × 22.5 cm

Inscribed: *Diziani*

Prov: Presented by David Pennant to the L.R.I. before 1841; deposited at the W.A.G., 1893; presented to the W.A.G., 1948.

DURER, Albrecht, 1471-1528, after

5099 **Study for the statue of Albrecht, Count of Hapsburg**

Pen and ink, 25.1 × 16.9 cm

The statue was intended for the tomb of Emperor Maximilian in Innsbruck; Durer was working on this project 1514-1515.

Durer's drawing was obliterated by over-cleaning and No. 5099 in its present state is entirely re-drawn; it is illustrated in its original state by Winkler.[1]

Prov: Jonathan Richardson[2] sold Cock 6 November 1747 part of lot 1. David Pennant who presented it to the L.R.I. before 1841; deposited at the W.A.G., 1893; presented to the W.A.G., 1948.

Ref: **1.** *Die Zeichnungen Albrecht Durers*, 1938, Vol. 3, No. 677 with a full discussion of the original drawing. The most recent discussion of the original drawing is in Walter L. Strauss *The Complete Drawings of Albrecht Durer*, 1975, Vol. 3, p. 1574, No. 1515/50.   **2.** Lugt No. 2184. The drawing did not subsequently pass into the Denon Collection as Winkler (*op. cit.*) suggests as there is nothing on the verso. This provenance of course refers to the original drawing.

DURER, Albrecht, Imitator of

5098 **Pilate washing his hands**

Pen and ink, 14.7 × 12. 8 cm

A combination of the right hand group of figures from Durer's *Pilate Washing his Hands*[1] and of the left hand group of figures from his *Ecce Homo*,[2] both from the engraved *Little Passion*.

Prov: Presented by David Pennant to the L.R.I. before 1841; deposited at the W.A.G., 1893; presented to the W.A.G., 1948.

Ref: **1.** A. Bartsch, *Le Peintre Graveur*, Vol. 7, 1866, No. 11.   **2.** Bartsch *op. cit.*, No. 10.

DYCK, Sir Anthony van, 1599-1641, after

2436 Count Hendrik van der Bergh (about 1573-1638)

Black chalk, sepia wash, gouache on grey paper, 54.6 × 42 cm

Inscribed: *Van Dyck*

A copy after one of the versions of Van Dyck's portrait, probably that in the Prado of 1629-32 (Inv. No. 1486).

Prov: Marquess of Torre Soto, Seville. George A. Lockett sold Christie's 19 June 1942 bt. Nicholson Gallery from whom purchased 1944.

ERTZ, Edward Frederick, 1862-1954

440 The Water Carrier

Watercolour, 87.7 × 58.7 cm

Signed: *E. ERTZ*

Prov: Presented by Sir Oliver and Lady Lodge, Miss E. Holt, Mr Hemelryk and Hugh Rathbone 1914 through Mrs F. Hamel Calder.
Ref: 1. Letter from Mrs F. Hamel Calder 26 September 1914; she says No. 440 "was purchased for the permanent collection" by these subscribers implying perhaps that No. 440 dates from 1914.

FACIUS, Georg Siegmund or Johann Gottlieb, about 1750-after 1802

5093 Male Nude Study

Red chalk on buff paper, 38.6 × 25.2 cm

Inscribed: *Facius*

Prov: Presented by David Pennant[1] to the L.R.I. before 1841, deposited at the W.A.G., 1893; presented to the W.A.G., 1948.
Ref: 1. *North of Dean Street in 1821* is inscribed on the verso.

FENILE, G. di after SARGENT, John Singer, 1856-1925

9167   Lord Wavertree

Watercolour over pencil, 9.8 × 8 cm

Inscribed: *G di Fenile*

The sitter is William Hall Walker, Col. the Rt. Hon. Lord Wavertree (1856-1933), third son of Sir Andrew Barclay Walker, the donor of the W.A.G. He was Conservative M.P. for Widnes, 1905-1919 and created a Baron in 1919. He was a leading figure on the turf and active in the Volunteer Movement.[1] He was Deputy-Chairman of the Arts and Exhibition Sub-Committee of the Liverpool City Council for thirty-one years and was a major benefactor of the W.A.G.

9167 is a copy of the drawing signed and dated 1919, exhibited by Sargent in Liverpool in 1925 and last recorded in a private collection in New Zealand.[2] The copy was made in 1919.[3] Another copy with different drapery is in the W.A.G. (955),[5] and there are also portraits by R. E. Morrison (2569) H. C. Dickinson (2666) and Lynwood Palmer (2629) in the collection.

Prov: Lord Wavertree, who gave it as a Christmas present to his younger brother, Andrew Barclay Walker, fifth son of Sir Andrew Barclay Walker, Bart, 1919,[4] by descent to Sir Ian Walker-Okeover, who presented it, 1976.

Ref: **1.** For full details of his career see *Who's Who* and press cuttings, Liverpool Record Office, Liverpool Public Library.   **2.** L.A.E. 1925 (164) rep. p. 29 and also rep. *The Illustrated Sporting and Dramatic News* February 11 1933. There is a companion drawing of Lady Wavertree.   **3.** Inscription on backing in ink *Watercolour from J. Sargent/drawing dated 1919/by G. di Fenile 1919.*   **4.** Inscription on backing in pencil *To Barclay/from/Willie/Xmas 1919.*   **5.** See p. 196.

FERRANTI, Giulio Cesare de

5998   Two children, one wearing a tartan sash

Gouache, 26.6 × 21.6 cm (oval)

Signed: *C. Ferranti 64*

5999   Two Girls with blue ribbons

Gouache, 27 × 21.6 cm (oval)

Signed: *C. Ferranti 64*

Presumably the children in No. 5998 are Mary Eveline Melly (born 1854) and George Henry Melly (born 1860) while those in No. 5999 are Florence Elizabeth (born 1856) and Ellen Beatrice (born 1858), all the children of George and Sarah Melly.[1]

The artist was primarily a photographer[2] so possibly Nos. 5998-9 are copies (by another hand?) after photographs.

Prov: Presented by the descendants of George Melly 1944.[3]
Ref: **1.** See W. H. Rawdon Smith, *The George Mellys*, 1962 for further details of the sitters. There is no evidence that these children are the sitters beyond the date and provenance of Nos. 5998-9. The MSS Correspondence of George Melly (Liverpool City Libraries) has not been examined.   **2.** The Liverpool Directory of 1865 lists him as a photographer at 130 Bold Street, Liverpool. Two trade cards of 1870 and 1878 in the archives of Ferranti Ltd, Hollinwood, describe him as having a "photographic and art studio." See also G. Z. de Ferranti and R. Ince, *The Life and Letters of Sebastian Ziani de Ferranti*, 1934, pp. 16ff.   **3.** A typescript "*List of Furniture etc. in drawing room at 90 Chatham Street Liverpool selected for W.A.G.*" of 1944 (now in W.A.G.) lists Nos. 5998-9 simply as *Pair of oval watercolour drawings Family Groups in marquetrie frame—£3 3s 0d.* George Melly and Sarah Bright moved to 90 Chatham Street in the 1850's and it remained the family home until 1944.

FRENCH School, 17th century

5100   Triumph of Galatea

Brown ink and grey wash on grey prepared paper, 17.8 × 28.4 cm

Attributed since 1859 to Martin Freminet.[1]

Prov: Presented by David Pennant to the L.R.I. before 1841; deposited at the W.A.G., 1893; presented to the W.A.G., 1948.
Ref: **1.** 1859 Catalogue p. 75 (195).

FRENCH School, 18th century

5106   Study of a Male Nude

Red chalk on greyish paper, 27.8 × 25.7 cm

5107   Study of a Male Nude

Red chalk, 21.1 × 24.6 cm

Inscribed: *Poussin*

The pose of No. 5107 seems to be derived from the Farnese Hercules.

Prov: Presented to the L.R.I. by David Pennant before 1841; deposited at the W.A.G., 1893; presented to the W.A.G., 1948.

6617 Isaiah showing Hezekiah the shadow on the Dial

Black chalk, 18.2 × 26 cm

Inscribed: *Nicolo Poussino*

The subject is taken from II Kings XX, 8-11. The shadow on the sun dial goes back ten degrees as a sign that Hezekiah will recover from his illness.

Prov: N. Hone[1](?) sold Hutchins 9 February 1785 part of lot 28 (£1) C. Rogers[2] sold Thomas Philipe 18 April 1799 part of lot 501 (£0 12s 0d) acquired by William Roscoe from Thomas Philipe 28 January 1809 (£0 10s 6s);[3] Roscoe Sale 1816 lot 567 bt. Davies (£0 11s 0d). Mary Montgomery (in 1953). R. T. Clough sold Henry Spencer and Sons, Retford 28 March 1968 lot 874 bt. W.A.G.

Ref: 1. Roscoe Sale Catalogue (see provenance). 2. Roscoe Sale Catalogue (see provenance) and his mark (Lugt 624). 3. Roscoe Papers No. 5404.

GENNARI, Benedetto, 1633-1715

5101 Male Nude posed as Hercules holding a block of wood

Red chalk on buff paper, 43.3 × 29.3 cm

Inscribed: *di Gio Bene Gennari, nipote del Guercino*

Prov: Presented by David Pennant to the L.R.I. before 1841; deposited at the W.A.G., 1893; presented to the W.A.G., 1948.

GERMAN School, 19th century

7450 Landscape with castle and river

Pen, ink and grey wash, 15.5 × 23.3 cm

7450 was in a collection of drawings and engravings attributed to Nathaniel George Philips (1795-1831), some of which were bound in a scrapbook containing *Views in Lancs. and Cheshire from pictures by N. G. Philips* and other sketches and studies by Philips and other artists. The title page of the scrapbook was inscribed *Caroline Philips, Sep. 1841.* The items in the collection acquired by the Walker Art Gallery appear to be by various hands. Colin Bailey suggests that 7450 is German and possibly by a view painter working in Heidelberg.[1]

Prov: Caroline Philips (?); F. Weatherhead & Sons, Aylesbury, from whom purchased, 1970.

Ref: 1. Colin J. Bailey, *orally*, 11 February, 1977.

7451 Terracina

Pen and ink, 26 × 39.3 cm

Inscribed: *Terracina* (bottom right)

7451 like 7450 was in a collection of drawings and engravings attributed to Nathaniel George Philips (1795-1831). The present attribution was first suggested by Dr An Zwollo.[1] Colin Bailey suggests that it is by a follower of J. A. Koch.[2]

Prov: Caroline Philips (?); F. Weatherhead & Sons, Aylesbury, from whom purchased, 1970.
Ref: **1.** *Orally*, 7 February, 1976.   **2.** *Orally*, 11 February, 1977.

GIMIGNANI, Lodovico, 1643-1697

5105 Holy Family

Grey chalk, wash and gouache on buff paper, 37.9 × 21.5 cm

Inscribed: *GIMIGNANI*

A finished study for Gimignani's *Holy Family* in Santa Maria dell'Assunzione at Ariccia completed by 1665.[1] A modello for this painting was lot 6 Christie's at Villa Miani, 15 October 1970 and other drawings are in the Gabinetto Nazionale, Rome.

Prov: Presented to the L.R.I. by David Pennant by 1841; deposited at the W.A.G., 1893; presented to the W.A.G., 1948.
Ref: **1.** G. Incisa della Rocchetta, *Notizie sulla Fabbrica della Chiesa Collegiata di Ariccia*, Rivista dell'Istituto di Archeologia e Storia dell'Arte, 1924, p. 349 with many further details.

GIOVANNI Mauro della Rovere, called Il Fiammenghino, *c.* 1575-1640

9218 The Assumption of the Virgin

Pen and brown ink and wash, heightened with white over black chalk, 33.4 × 23.2 cm

The traditional attribution was to Pordenone.[1] Pouncey's suggestion that 9218 is by Giovanni Mauro della Rovere[2] is confirmed by comparison with the signed and dated 1596 *St. Anthony Abbot in Ecstasy*[3] and designs for angels in pendentives[4] both of which have angels of similar typology to the figures in 9218.

Prov: Jonathan Richardson Senior (Lugt 2184); Jonathan Richardson Junior (Lugt 2170); John Thane (Lugt 1544); William Young Ottley; his sale, Thomas Philipe, 15 June 1814 (1026) bt. by Roscoe through Philipe £2 12s 0d;[5] William Roscoe; Roscoe sale, 1816 (260) bt. Esdaile £1 17s 0d; William Esdaile (Lugt 2617) sold Christie's 20 June 1840 (443) bt. Sheath 316; C. R. Rudolf; from whose executors purchased by private treaty, 1977.

Ref: 1. Inscription by Richardson on the back associating it with a work in S. Rocco, Venice. 2. C. R. Rudolf, (sale), Sotheby's, 19 May 1977 (40). 9218 was withdrawn before the sale. 3. Bt. Colnaghi. 4. Now in the collection of Professor Moir. 5. Roscoe Papers 5404.

GOLTZIUS, Hendrick, 1558-1616

1629 Portrait of a Humanist

Pen and brown ink, 20.2 × 22.2 cm

Signed in monogram: *HG A° 1608*

One of a group of imaginary and real portraits of scholars and others made by Goltzius at this time.[1]

Prov: Presented to the L.R.I. by David Pennant before 1841; deposited at the W.A.G., 1893; presented to the W.A.G., 1948.
Ref: 1. E. K. J. Reznicek, *Hendrick Goltzius Zeichnungen*, 1961, Vol. 1, pp. 126, 386, No. 324, Vol. 2, pl. 423 who lists other similar drawings and engravings.

GRIMALDI, Giovanni Francesco, 1606-1680

6169 Landscape with Figures beside a River

Pen, ink and brown wash, 13.3. × 22.7 cm

Signed: *Gio: fran: co Grimaldi: fec:*

Inscribed: *No. 4*

Prov: Roscoe Sale 1816, part of lot 435 bt. Stanley[1] £0 13s 0d. Anon sold Sotheby's 21 February 1962 lot 182 bt. Hopton; Sir Harry Luke, K.C.M.G. sold Sotheby's 31 September 1962 lot 91 bt. Appleby from whom purchased 1963.
Ref: 1. Later 13th Earl of Derby.

GRIMM, Samuel Hieronymus, 1733-1794

8143 Fete for the Nymphs of the River Naethus

Pen, ink, watercolour and gouache, 24 × 32.5 cm

Signed: *S. H. Grimm fecit 1767*

8163   Marriage of Daphnis and Phyllis

Pen, ink, watercolour and gouache, 24.3 × 32.3 cm

Signed: *S. H. Grimm fecit 1767*

Two illustrations to Salomon Gessner's *Daphnis*, first published in 1754. At the beginning of Book I the shepherds and shepherdesses gather to propitiate the Nymphs of the River Naethus so that the river will not flood their fields; here Daphnis falls in love with Phyllis. At the end of Book II Daphnis marries Phyllis.

Grimm's early poetry shares with Gessner's writing a pastoral, idyllic and sentimental approach, together with an emphasis on "a return to nature". They may have known each other in Switzerland around 1750-1765 when Grimm was in Berne and Gessner in Zurich. Both contributed to A. Zingg's *Stammbuch*, Grimm's contributions being dated February 1766[1] and Gessner's 30 May 1766.[2] Grimm was in Paris 1765-1768; by then Gessner's works were well known there, *Daphnis* having been first published in a French translation by M. Huber in Paris in 1764.

Prov: Anon. sold Sotheby's, 26 October 1960, lot 52, bt. Fine Art Society; presented by C. F. J. Beausire, 1972.

Exh: W.A.G. *English Watercolours in the Collection of C. F. J. Beausire* 1970, Nos. 19-20.

Ref: 1. Rotha Mary Clay, *Samuel Hieronymus Grimm*, 1941, p. 28.   2. Letter from H. J. Walch, 8 December 1969.

GUERCINO, Il, Barbieri, Giovanni Francesco, 1591-1666

9213   A Monstrous Animal and a Peasant

Pen, ink and brown wash, 15 × 22.2 cm

A number of similar fantastic drawings by Guercino are recorded, they do not relate to paintings and were probably drawn for the amusement of the artist and his friends.[1] The style of this drawing suggests that it dates from around the 1620's.[2]

Prov: Earl Spencer[3] sold T. Philipe, 13 June 1811, lot 369 bt. in £0 5s 0d; bought by William Roscoe from Philipe July 1811 £0 15s 0d,[4] his sale Winstanley 25 September 1816. lot 400, bt. Heber[5] £0 13s 0d. William Dyce sold Christie's, 5 May 1865, lot 206, F. Bartolomeo etc. 9 items bt. Robinson £2 4s 0d; Sir John C. Robinson;[6] John Malcolm[7] by descent[8] to Geoffrey Gathorne-Hardy;[9] purchased from the executors of Robert Gathorne-Hardy 1977 with the aid of a contribution from the National Art-Collections Fund.

Exh: P. and D. Colnaghi, *Loan Exhibition of Drawings by Old Masters from the Collection of Mr. Geoffrey Gathorne-Hardy*, 1971, No. 33.

Ref: 1. Bologna, Palazzo dell'Archiginnasio, *Il Guercino, Disegni*, 1968, No. 243, p. 217. A very similar drawing is No. 2672 in the Print Room, Windsor Castle, but it lacks the figure of the peasant and its head is clearly that of a dog.   2. Denis Mahon, *verbally*, April 1977.   3. Lugt. 1530.   4. Roscoe Papers No. 5404 and 2964.   5. Identified as Richard Heber of Hodnet in the British

Museum Print Room Copy of the Roscoe Sale Catalogue but not at his sale, Stanley, London, 15 May 1834. **6.** Lugt 1433 and 2141b. **7.** J. C. Robinson, *Descriptive Catalogue of Drawings of John Malcolm of Poltalloch*, 1869, No. 288. **8.** *Descriptive Catalogue of Drawings in the possession of the Hon. A. E. Gathorne-Hardy*, 1902, No. 21. **9.** See exhibition catalogue cited under exhibitions.

HERMAN, Josef, born 1911

6548   Tractor and Farm Worker

Pen, ink, pencil and wash, 19.5 × 25 cm

Inscribed with colour indications

Drawn in Suffolk, 1964-5.[1]

Prov: Purchased from the Piccadilly Gallery, 1966.
Ref: 1. The artist, *letter*, 8 April 1976.

HUET, Paul, 1803-1869

8160   The Beach at Le Havre

Watercolour, 26.4 × 45 cm

Signed: *Paul Huet*

Very close indeed to the *Le Havre et les ramasseurs de galets* of 1829[1] and presumably dateable to that year.[2] In both watercolours pebbles are being gathered from the beach.

Prov: M. Perret Carnot, who married the artist's grand-daughter; Heim Gallery; C. F. J. Beausire who bequeathed it 1972.
Exh: Heim Gallery, *Paintings by Paul Huet and some contemporary French Sculpture* 1969 (30); W.A.G., *English Watercolours in the Collection of C. F. J. Beausire* 1970 (25).
Ref: 1. Pierre Miquel, *Paul Huet, De l'aube romantique a l'aube impressioniste*, 1962 repr. opp. p. 62 and there dated 1829. According to the *Heim Gallery Catalogue*, cited under exhibitions, further versions exist.   2. But the *Heim Gallery Catalogue* cited above says about 1828. 1828 was the year of the artist's visit to Normandy see Rene Paul Huet, *Paul Huet*, 1911, pp. 103ff.

ITALIAN School, 18th century

5130   A kneeling youth, throwing up his arms in surprise

Red over black chalk, 33.9 × 27.9 cm

Inscribed: *Carlin Dolci N°. 110*

5130 is not related to the drawing style of Dolci.[1] This highly finished drawing approaches that of academic artists of the 18th century,[2] although it may reflect a 17th century prototype. The action of the youth suggests that the subject is perhaps an Apostle in a Transfiguration, or Moses and the Burning Bush.

Prov: Presented by George Higgins, 1955.

Ref: **1.** Mina Gregori, *letter*, 10 October 1957 and P. M. R. Pouncey, *orally*, 8 July 1968. **2.** Mina Gregori, *letter*, 10 October 1957 and Charles McQuorquodale, *orally*, 1975.

KOCH, Joseph Anton, 1768-1839

8781 Landscape with William Tell

Pen, ink and watercolour, 73.7 × 111.5 cm

Signed: *Comp e del par Coch a Rome 1799*

The Austrian Governor Gessler on horseback points to the apple on the head of Walther, William Tell's son. William Tell lifts his crossbow to shoot at the apple. The second arrow with which he intended to shoot Gessler had he hit his son with his first arrow protrudes from the right shoulder of his jerkin. On the right a halberdier guards the imperial hat symbolizing the power of Austria over Switzerland, before which Tell had had refused to bow.[1]

No. 8781 was probably painted as a reaction to the French invasion of Switzerland of 1797-8 since the Legend of William Tell was closely associated with Swiss Nationalism, although Koch had earlier sympathized with the ideals of the French Revolution.[2] Koch returned to the theme in 1816 when the Baron vom Stein commissioned an oil painting of this subject as a companion to *The Tyrolean Landsturm* 1809, a subject from the Austrian War of Liberation; only drawings however survive of the William Tell subject from this commission.[3]

There are a large number of borrowings from Durer's engravings and woodcuts; most notably the buildings on the right are taken from Durer's woodcut *The Sojourn of the Holy Family in Egypt* and No. 8781 is an important work in the rediscovery of Durer in the late 18th and early 19th centuries.[4]

Prov: Sent to England before 1817;[5] probably acquired by the Earls of Sefton 1837-1851;[6] certainly in their collection by 1946;[7] accepted by H.M. Government in lieu of death duties 1973; presented to the W.A.G., 1975.

Ref: **1.** The complete story is retold in C. J. Bailey, *Joseph Anton Koch's Landscape with William Tell. An Early Watercolour Rediscovered*, Annual Report and Bulletin of the W.A.G., Vol. 5, 1974-5, p. 62 with many further references. **2.** Bailey, *op. cit.*, pp. 61ff. Many English Liberals turned against the French Revolution after the invasion of Switzerland. **3.** Bailey, *op. cit.*, pp. 64ff. **4.** Bailey, *op. cit.*, pp. 64ff. The Durer woodcut is No. 90 in A. Bartsch, *Le Peintre Graveur*, Vol. 7, 1866. **5.** Otto von Lutterotti, *Joseph Anton Koch*, 1940, p. 183, p. 303, No. Z972. **6.** The frame makers stamp is that of J. Haill of Tarleton Street, Liverpool; John Haill, Carver and Gilder, was at that address 1837-1851. **7.** Typescript inventory made by Lawrence Haward now in the National Portrait Gallery.

LEGROS, Alphonse, 1837-1911

2534 The Fisherman

Watercolour, 74.5 × 125 cm

Signed: *A. Legros 1868*

The right hand side of No. 2534 is very close to Legros's drypoint *Les Pecheurs d'Ecrevisses*.[1] Monique Geiger[2] does not however doubt the attribution.

Prov: Presented by Herbert Bickersteth 1949.
Ref: 1. A. Poulet-Malassis and A. W. Thibaudeau, *Catalogue raisonnée de l'oeuvre gravé et lithographié de M. Alphonse Legros* 1877, No. 74, p. 48. 2. *Letter*, 16 February 1970.

3198 Study from the antique

Pencil and black chalk, 40.3 × 30.8 cm

Signed: *A. Legros*

3199 Study from the antique

Pencil and black chalk, 41.7 × 30.7 cm

Signed: *A. Legros*

"Drawn from the antique before the Students of the Slade School, London University 1878."[1] Legros was professor at the Slade School 1876-1892. The cast from which Nos. 3198-9 were drawn does not survive there.[2] For Legros's teaching methods see particularly Holroyd's reminiscences.[3] See also pp. 103-4, 392-3.

Prov: Presented by the artist 1878.
Ref: 1. Labels on the backs of both No. 3198 and No. 3199. 2. Visit by the compiler 1971. 3. Charles Holroyd, *Some personal Reminiscences*, Burlington Magazine, Vol. 20, 1911-12, p. 274.

9195 Bords de rivière

Pen, ink, brown and grey wash, 24.6 × 39.5 cm

Signed: *A. Legros*

Prov: Presented by the family of W. A. McDonald, 1977.

LIPCZINSKY, Albrecht, 1875-1974

8802 Fanny

Red chalk, 23 × 28.9 cm

Signed: *All Lipczynski*

The drawing probably dates from 1918.[1] Fanny was the white greyhound belonging to the artist's wife, Doonie.[2]

Ref: **1.** Inscription on the back. **2.** C. H. Reilly, *Scaffolding in the Sky*, 1938, p. 110.

8803 A Caricature of George Harris

Black chalk, 36.5 × 25 cm

The sitter (1878-1929) was a Liverpool theatrical designer associated with the Sandon Studios Society, with whom Lipczinsky also exhibited.

8804 Madge Enett

Black chalk, 47.5 × 29.2 cm

Prov: H. Tyson Smith; Geoffrey Tyson Smith, from whose estate purchased, 1975.

MAURIER, George Louis Palmella Busson du, 1834-1896

4663 More Complimentary than it seems

Pen and ink, 12.9 × 19.2 cm

Signed: *DU MAURIER*

Inscribed on mount: *More complimentary than it seems./Papa (concluding the fascinating tale) "And he was turned into a beautiful Prince, and married Beauty!"*
Minnie (after a pause) "Papa, were you a Beast before you married Mamma?"

This cartoon was published in *Punch*, 19 February, 1876, p. 58.[1]

Prov: Purchased, 1911.
Ref: **1.** Identified by Leonee Ormond, *letter*, 27 June 1976.

4664 Things one would wish to have expressed differently

Pen and ink, 25.3 × 35.6 cm

Signed: *du Maurier*

Inscribed: *Things one would wish to have expressed differently./Guest: "Well, goodbye, old man!—and you've really got a very nice little place here!"*
Host: "Yes, but it's rather bare, just now. I hope the trees will have grown a good bit before you're back, old man!" (twice with variations)/*G. du Maurier/Hampstead/Oct 87*

Also inscribed with a letter perhaps to the Editor of *Punch* not related to No. 4664.

This cartoon was published in *Punch*, November 5, 1887, p. 210.

4665 The Latter-Day Taste

Pen and ink on card,[1] 31.5 × 21 cm

Signed: *du Maurier*

Inscribed: *¼ p G. du Maurier Oxford St. Nov 95*
on reverse: *Dec. 7.95*
The Latter-Day Taste
Author: "I've got here some short stories that I am anxious to publish"
Publisher: "Let me warn you. May I ask if they're written in an unintelligible Scotch dialect?"
Author: "Certainly not."
Publisher: "Then I'm afraid they're not the slightest use to us."

This cartoon was published in *Punch*, December 7, 1895, p. 274.

Ref: **1.** Stamped *Bristol Board.*

4666 Trop de Zele (An Aristocratic tip)

Pen and ink, 25.6 × 35.7 cm

Signed: *du Maurier*

Inscribed: *Trop de Zèle (An Aristocratic Tip)*
The New Companion (fresh from Girtham College)./"Yes, Lady Jane, I saw Her with Her Habitual Hypocrisy Holding out Her Hand to Him as He was Haranguing at His Hotel—"
Lady Jane: "Good gracious, child, don't stick in your H's so carefully as all that! People'll think your father and mother dropped 'em, and that you're tryin' to pick 'em up!"
(And People wouldn't be very far wrong).
G. du Maurier/Hampstead/May 92/¼ Punch reduce

This cartoon was published in *Punch*, June 11, 1892, p. 286.

4667 The Force of Habit

Pen and ink, 19.9 × 31.8 cm

Signed: *du Maurier*

Inscribed: *Hampstead—Dec. 94—Geo du Maurier/Punch ½p*
on reverse: *The Force of Habit*
The Vicar's daughter: "Oh, Papa dear, did you hear old Mr. Rogers snoring in his pew this afternoon?"
The Vicar: "No, my love, during the sermon, I suppose?"
The Vicar's daughter: "No! that's the funny part of it!"

This cartoon was published in *Punch*, December 22, 1894, p. 294.

4668 The New Craze

Pen and ink, 25.5 × 35.5 cm

Signed: *du Maurier*

Inscribed: *The New Craze*
Provincial Manager (to scion of aristocracy who has come to commence): So, my Lord, you're here at last! We've had three rehearsals without you—and it's produced to-morrow./I suppose you've been studying since you've been here?"/Lord Plantagenet (pleasantly): "Oh-ah-no, I've not begun yet. The fact is (still more pleasantly) I'd no idea that Plumborough was such a jolly place!"
Punch ½ page /With 2 CHM Initials & 6 CHM ½ pages also 1 P. social.

This cartoon was published in *Punch*, May 12, 1883, p. 222.

4669 Blasé

Pen and ink, 25.4 × 35.6 cm

Signed: du Maurier

Inscribed: *Six guineas (£6.6)* (on reverse)
Blasé
"Don't you think it would be nice if/we all went abroad this year, Willy?"
"Oh, bother abroad! I've been there!"
George du Maurier/Hampstead/May 93/¼ Punch/65

This cartoon was published in *Punch*, June 17, 1893, p. 286.

4670   Crede Experto

Pen and ink, 25.5 × 15.8 cm

Signed: *du Maurier*

Inscribed: *"Crede Experto!"/Q.C.: "Yes, I like the army as a profession. I mean to put my son into it."*
Little Snooks (who was Gazetted the week before last): "Ah you take the advice of a man who knows all about it—and don't!" G. du Maurier /Hampstead/Dec. 92

This cartoon was published in *Punch*, January 7, 1893, p. 10. There are pencil sketches, perhaps for No. 4670, on the back.

4671   As Worn

Pen and ink, 18.4 × 25.4 cm

Signed: *du Maurier*

Inscribed: *As Worn*
"Dear Uncle Ben,—you're always so kind! would you sit on my bonnet a little. I've taken out the pins."
G. du Maurier/Hampstead/June 90/½p. Punch

This cartoon was published in *Punch*, June 21, 1890, p. 294.

4672   Christmas Eve at the Moated Grange

Pen and ink on paper, 19.7 × 25.5 cm

Signed: *du Maurier*

Inscribed: *Christmas Eve at the Moated Grange./Emily (in the midst of Aunt Mariana's blood-curdling Ghost Story): "Hush! Listen! There's a door banging somewhere down-stairs! and yet the servants have gone to bed. George, do just run down and see what it can be!"*
(George wishes himself back at Charterhouse)
G. du Maurier/Hampstead/Dec 90/½p. Punch—great care

This cartoon was published in *Punch*, December 27, 1890, p. 306.

4673   The Laws of Heredity Illustrated

Pen and ink, 25.5 × 17.9 cm

Signed: *du Maurier*

Inscribed: *The Laws of Heredity Illustrated./Grigson (who has tripped up his friend Professor Grumpson's campstool just as the latter was sitting down on it).* "*Hi! Don't! It's no good cutting up rough, you known—I in-herited a tendency to practical joking, and can't help it—you said so your-self!!!*"

Grumpson: "*Quite so, my dear fellow; you're not to blame a bit! but I've inherited a tendency to kick practical jokers, and can't help it either.*"

(Kicks him). This inscription appears twice with variations and dele-tions./*G. du Maurier/Hampstead/Aug. 88/¼p. reduce*

This cartoon was published in *Punch*, September 1, 1888, p. 100.

4674   The Holiday Task

Pen and ink, 25.5 × 26.8 cm

Signed: *du Maurier*

Inscribed: *The Holiday Task/December 4-5* (?)/¼ *page*

This cartoon was published in *Punch*, 1 October 1881, p. 147.

4675   Party Politics

Pen and ink, 25.4 × 35.8 cm

Signed: *du Maurier*

Inscribed: *Party Politics*
"*I'm very glad Sir Percia Plantagenet was returned, Miss!*"
"*Why,—are you a Primrose dame?*"
"*No, Miss,—but my 'Usband is!*" (twice with variations)
G. du Maurier/Hampstead/Aug. 92

This cartoon was published in *Punch*, August 27, 1892, p. 90, but there the title was changed to *An Earnest Politician*.

4676   The Spread of Culture Downwards

Pen and ink on card,[1] 19.2 × 31.6 cm

Signed: *Du Maurier*

Inscribed: *Legend at Back/Half page Punch/G. du Maurier/56 Hamp-stead/Oct 93/SALVE*
on reverse: *The spread of culture downwards*
"*Ullo, Mary, what's this? Name of the 'Ouse?*"
"*No, Mr. Ignorance; it's a Latin word, and means 'Please to wipe your feet!'* "

This cartoon was published in *Punch*, November 11, 1893, p. 222.

Ref: **1.** Stamped *BRISTOL BOARD.*

4677 An Honest Penny

Pen and ink, 31.5 × 18.8 cm

Signed: *du Maurier*

Inscribed: ¼ *p G. du Maurier. March 96 Oxford St.*
on reverse: *Punch April 11th, 1896*
An Honest Penny
"What have you been doing all day?"
"Writing an article for the Gadfly."
"Who about?" "Robert Browning,"
"Suppose you've read a lot of him?"
"Not I! But I met him once at an Afternoon Tea."

This cartoon was published in *Punch*, April 11, 1896, p. 169.

4678 Distinguished Amateurs—The Pianist

Pen and ink, 25.1 × 35.4 cm

Signed: *DU MAURIER*

Inscribed: *Distinguished Amateurs—The Pianist/Grigsby: "I trust you will favour us this evening, Mr. Belmains!"/Mr. Belmains:"Well-er-no-hardly . . . They don't care for serious pianoforte-playing in this house, you know. I hope you will give us 'the's(?) got 'em on', Mr. Grigsby?"/Mr. Grigsby: "Well-I-er think not—scarcely! . . . you see, in this house they don't appreciate serious comic-singing!"* (inscribed twice with variations and deletions)
           social/reduce to ½ page

This cartoon was published in *Punch*, 24 December 1881, p. 291 and reprinted in *Society Pictures from Punch*, 1891, p. 141.

4679 Cookiana

Pen and ink, 30.5 × 23 cm

Signed: *DU MAURIER*

Inscribed: *upright ½ page for social/Nov 14/1874*
Inscribed on reverse: *Cookiana*
Cook (Engaging, and early engaging look): "And now, Ma'am, may I ask how many servants you keep besides myself, if I come?"
Lady: 'Only Two!"
Cook: "Ah! then I'm afraid I must decline! The fact is, I can't get on without my Rubber of an Evening!"

This cartoon was published in *Punch*, November 14, 1874, p. 209, with a slightly different caption.

4680   Lawn Tennis

Pen and ink, 30.5 × 23 cm

Signed: *du Maurier*

Inscribed: *Sept 12/1874*
Inscribed on reverse: *Lawn Tennis*
Miss Maud: "How do we stand?"
Captain Lovelace. "They are Six to our Love, and 'Love' always means nothing you know."
Miss Maud: "Always?"

This cartoon was published in *Punch*, September 12, 1874, p. 105.

4681   A True Friend

Pen and ink, 25.3 × 21.3 cm

Signed: *DU MAURIER*

Inscribed: *Part 1/Page 177/1874*
on reverse: *A True Friend*
Humble Host: "I suppose you find Swell Society very delightful, don't you, Topsawyer?"
Gorgeous Guest: "I believe yer, my Boy! Why, last night at Dinner, Now, There was I with a Baronet's Lady on one side, and a Dowager Viscountess on the other, and a Lord Alfred something sitting just opposite, and everything else to match! But Lor' Bless you, I'm quite content to come and dine with you, Dear old Boy, and drink your half-crown sherry!"
(Helps himself to another glass)

This cartoon was published in *Punch*, May 23, 1874, p. 221.

Prov: Presented by the Trustees of the late George du Maurier, in 1931, (Nos. 4664-4681).

MAYER-MARTON, George, 1897-1960

2144   Water over stones

Watercolour, 51.8 × 71 cm

Prov: Presented by John Moores, 1958.
Exh: W.A.G., 1958, *Liverpool Academy* (58).

6101 A Welsh Lake

Watercolour and ink, 56.8 × 77.5 cm

Painted in 1949.[1] The lake may be Llyn Llydaw, five miles south east of Llanberis.[2]

Prov: Presented by the artist's sister Mrs C. Friend, 1961.
Exh: W.A.G. and Derby, 1961, *Memorial Exhibition* (13).
Ref: 1. Mayer-Marton's MS workbook. Collection of Mrs H. J. Braithwaite.
2. Identified by Mrs W. Moran, 1961.

6102 Lake Balaton, Hungary[1]
Verso: A Mountain with trees and a cottage

Watercolour, 38 × 52.7 cm

Signed: mayer marton/38 (ink)

Prov: Presented by the artist's sister, Mrs C. Friend, 1961.
Exh: W.A.G. and Derby, 1961, *Memorial Exhibition* (3).
Ref: 1. Mayer-Marton's MS workbook. Collection of Mrs. H. J. Braithwaite.

9162 Anglers, Danube

Watercolour, 38.3 × 53.3 cm

Signed: mayer marton/33 (pencil)

Prov: Bequeathed by the artist to his sister, Mrs C. Friend, and presented by the latter to her daughter, Mrs H. J. Braithwaite, by whom presented, 1976.

MESDAG, Hendrik Willem, 1831-1915

920 On the Dutch Coast

Watercolour, 47 × 64 cm

Signed: *H. W. Mesdag*

Very similar in composition to and possibly a sketch for the oil painting *Marine (retour de la peche)*, No. 832 at the 1909 Société National des Beaux Arts (pl. 77 in the *Catalogue Illustré*).

Prov: Sent to the L.A.E., 1909 at the request of the Curator of the W.A.G.,[1] purchased there (£50) by the Gallery.
Exh: L.A.E., 1909 (359) *Retour de la Peche*.
Ref: 1. Letter to the artist from the Curator 11 June 1909. The Curator and the Chairman of the Committee governing the Gallery, John Lea, had earlier visited the artist at the Hague.

MEYER, Christoffel, 1776-1813

8170   Fair Scene in a Dutch Town

Pen, ink and grey wash, 36 × 44.5 cm

Signed: *C. Meyer*

Inscribed: (on inn sign): *WYN BIER/BRANDEWYN/EN GEDISTE/LEERD* (and on building on right) *SCHOUBURG*

Most of Meyer's known works show views in Rotterdam but No. 8170 does not appear to represent any part of that city nor has any inn with the name *The Lion in the Cradle* (corresponding with the inn sign in No. 8170) been identified there.[1]

Prov: Fine Art Society; C. F. J. Beausire who bequeathed it 1972.
Exh: W.A.G. *English Watercolours in the Collection of C. F. J. Beausire* 1970, No. 33.
Ref: 1. B. Woelderink, *letter*, 28 July 1969.

MOSER, George Michael, 1704-1783

5110   Seated Male Nude

Black chalk on buff prepared paper, 52.4 × 38.6 cm

5111   Male Nude posed as Ixion

Black chalk on grey prepared paper, 49.6 × 37 cm

5112   Seated Male Nude

Black chalk on grey prepared paper, 49.5 × 39.3 cm

5113   Male Nude with a Pole

Black chalk on grey prepared paper, 56.1 × 42.1 cm

5114   Male Nude posed as Apollo

Black chalk on pale brown prepared paper, 55.8 × 34.3 cm

5115   Study of a River God

Black chalk and gouache on grey prepared paper, 50.3 × 38.1 cm

Watermark: Fleur-de-Lys in circle crowned

5116   Seated Male Nude

Black chalk on buff prepared paper, 38.4 × 50.9 cm

5117   Seated Male Nude holding a tree branch

Black chalk and gouache on grey prepared paper, 41.9 × 46.5 cm

5118   Male Nude posed as a thinker

Black chalk on grey blue prepared paper, 51.8 × 38.6 cm

5119   Male Nude holding a pole

Black chalk and gouache on grey prepared paper, 48.6 × 36.8 cm

5120   Seated Male Nude

Black and white chalk on red/brown prepared paper, 46.3 × 33.1 cm

5121   Satyr resting

Black chalk and gouache on grey/blue prepared paper, 26.2 × 39.2 cm

Academic life studies by Cipriani with poses similar to those in Nos.
5111 and 5114 are in the British Museum. No. 5121 has a drawing probably of the Hellenistic *Satyr*[1] in the Uffizi Florence showing through. The
model in No. 5110 is also used in Nos. 5116-7 and in No. 5119. The
attribution is due to the 1843 Catalogue (p. 34) and to an inscription on
the back of No. 5115. Moser had a drawing school in Salisbury Court
which merged with the St. Martin's Lane Academy in about 1745;[2] subsequently as keeper of the Royal Academy he taught life drawing there.

Prov: William Lock of Norbury Park Surrey sold Sotheby's 3 May 1821 part of lot 214
or 215 both lots bt. David Pennant 11s and 7s.; presented to the L.R.I. before
1841; deposited at the W.A.G., 1893; presented to the W.A.G., 1948.

Ref: **1.** Guido A. Mansuelli, *Galleria degli Uffizi, Le Sculture*, Vol. I, 1958, No. 51 p.
80, pl. 51.   **2.** The most recent and most critical account, with many references, of Moser's early career is in R. Paulson, *Hogarth His Life, Art and Times*,
1971, Vol. 2, p. 437, note 26. For Moser's importance as a teacher see particularly *The Works of Sir J. Reynolds*, ed. Malone, 1798, Vol. I, pp. xlvi, xlvii.

MOYAERT, Claes Cornelisz, before 1600-about 1669

6939   The Return of Tobit

Pen, ink and wash and gouache on vellum, varnished, 11 × 20.3 cm

The preparatory drawing for Moyaert's etching *The Return of Tobit* from his set of four etchings on the story of Tobit.[1]

Prov: Roscoe Sale, 1816 part of lot 530 bt. Bree £0 16s 0d. Robert Hay sold Sotheby's 9 July 1968 lot 41 bt. Colnaghi for W.A.G.

Ref: 1. J. Philip van der Kellen, *Le Peintre Graveur hollandais et flamand*, 1866, No. 19. F. W. H. Hollstein, *Dutch and Flemish Etchings*, *Engravings and Woodcuts*, Vol. 14, 1956, p. 56, No. 19.

NEIZVESTNY, Ernst, born 1926

6255   Seated Male Nude

Pen and ink, 29 × 20.5 cm

Signed: *E. Neizvestny. 61*

Prov: Presented by Eric Estorick 1964.

NORTH ITALIAN School, late 16th century

4160   The Holy Family with St. Elizabeth and St. John the Baptist and angels.

Pen and ink and brown wash, 16.8 × 12.7 cm

Inscribed: *Schiavone*

Although acquired as a Palma Giovane the drawing appears to be much closer in style to a pair of drawings of the *Adoration of the Shepherds* and of the *Adoration of the Magi* in the Albertina, Vienna (inv. nos 1576 and 1577).[1] These drawings were originally published by Mrs Frohlich-Bum as the work of Schiavone,[2] but the Tietzes considered them to be later than Schiavone and not Venetian.[3] Another drawing possibly by the same hand is an *Adoration of the Shepherds* in Ottawa.[4]

Prov: Charles Rogers 1711-1784 (Lugt 624) possibly part of (749) his sale, Philipe, 23 April 1799; bt. by William Roscoe from T. Philipe 22 November 1808 for 7/6;[5] Roscoe sale, 1816 part of (285) bt. Ford 11/0; John Walter; his sale, Sotheby's 12 November 1959 part of (56a) bt. C. G. Boerner; P. & D. Colnaghi & Co. Ltd., from whom purchased, 1960.

Ref: 1. Alfred Stix and L. Frohlich-Bum, *Albertina*, *Die Zeichnungen der Venezianischen Schule*, 1926, p. 42 (63) and (64).   2. L. Frohlich-Bum, *Andrea Meldolla genannt Schiavone*, Jahrbuch der Kunsthistorischen Sammlungen des allerhochstes Kaiserhauses, XXXI, 1910, p. 173.   3. Hans Tietze and E. Tietze-Conrat, *The Drawings of the Venetian Painters in the 15th and 16th centuries*, 1944, p. 254 (A1458 and A1459).   4. A. E. Popham and K. M. Fenwick, *European Drawings in the Collection of the National Gallery of Canada*, 1965, p. 30 (37).   5. Roscoe Papers 5404.

NUCCI, Avanzino, 1552-1629

5083 Madonna and Child with Saints Anthony Abbot and Anthony of Padua

Black and red chalks squared for transfer, 26.6 × 18.6 cm

The attribution is traditional and is confirmed by comparison with the *Madonna and Child adored by three Saints* in San Francesco, Serra San Quirico, particularly in the similarity of the figures of Saint Anthony of Padua. The typology of both the Madonna and the Child in 5083 resembles that of the Madonna and Child in the *Madonna and Child enthroned with the infant St. John the Baptist and two saints* attributed to the Cavalier d'Arpino in the church of San Lucia, Serra San Quirico.[1]

Carandente's identification of the right hand saint as Saint Anthony of Padua,[2] is supported by his attributes, the blazing heart, the book and the lily.[3] Possibly the drawing is for an altarpiece for the Minor Observants.[4]

Prov: Jonathan Richardson 1665-1745 (Lugt 2183); David Pennant, who presented it to the L.R.I. before 1841; deposited at the W.A.G., 1893; presented to the W.A.G., 1948.

Ref: 1. Letter of Dr. H. Rottgen, 15 April 1968.   2. Letter of G. Carandente, 13 February 1968.   3. Louis Reau, *Iconographie de l'art chrétien*, III, I, 1958, p. 118.   4. Letter of G. Carandente, 13 February 1968.

PAGGI, Giovanni Battista, 1554-1627

5128 The Assumption of the Virgin with the Apostles standing round the Tomb
Verso: Study for the head and shoulders of the Apostle with a stick, on the left of recto

Recto: Pen and brown wash over black chalk
Verso: Black chalk, 40 × 28.4 cm

Pouncey first suggested that 5128 was probably by Paggi. It is a finished study for the altarpiece in the Church of the Carmine, Genoa.[2] The figures are less closely packed in the drawing, but otherwise differences are slight. Mary Newcome has pointed out[3] that Alizeri mentions the *Assumption* as being by Paggi; but that he notes that it is unlike the style of the *Adoration*, another picture by Paggi in the same church.[4] She has suggested that both the *Assumption* and the drawing for it are by Giulio Benso (c. 1601-1668), a pupil of Paggi and that they are datable around 1620.[5] The style of 5128 is certainly close to that of a drawing in the Albertina of the *Adoration of the Magi* bearing a traditional attribution to Benso.[6]

Prov: David Pennant, who presented it to the L.R.I. before 1841; deposited at the W.A.G., 1893; presented to the W.A.G., 1948.

Ref: 1. P. M. R. Pouncey, *letter*, 26 August 1961.   2. A. Venturi, *Storia dell'Arte Italiana*, IX, pt. VII, 1934, pp. 857, 859 fig. 475.   3. Mary Newcome, *letter*, 21 March 1973.   4. Federigo Alizeri, *Guida artistica per la citta di Genova*, I, 1846, pp. 570-1.   5. Mary Newcome, *letter*, 21 March 1973.   6. Alfred Stix and Anna Spitzmuller, *Albertina, Die Schulen von Ferrara, Bologna, Parma, Modena, Der Lombardei, Genuas, Neapels, und Siziliens*, 1941, p. 47 (507) pl. 109.

PARMIGIANINO, Girolamo Francesco Maria Mazzola, called, 1503-1540

1261 A maiden

Metalpoint, pen and brown ink and brown wash heightened with white, 14.7 × 8 cm

A study for the right canephoros on the south side of the vaulting of the transept of S. Maria della Steccata, Parma. The commission to paint the apse and barrel vaulting was given to Parmigianino in 1531. Most of the work was executed after 1535 and never finished by the artist. The closeness of the study to the figure as executed except in the vase would suggest that it is fairly late in the sequence of studies very close to the drawing in the Albertina.[1] Popham originally accepted the attribution,[2] but recently has voiced doubts as to whether 1261 is actually by Parmigianino himself,[3] and has suggested that some of the drawings related to Canephoroi were repetitions made for show, rather than studies for the figures.[4] This seems unlikely in the case of 1261.

There is a copy of it in Munich Staatliche Graphische Sammlung (nr 273).

Prov: Earl of Arundel; A. M. Zanetti; W. Y. Ottley, his sale, Philipe 6 June 1814 lot 814; Sir Thomas Lawrence (Lugt. 2445). Albert Tomlinson, by whom presented 1951.

Exh: Lawrence Gallery, fourth exhibition, 1836 (9).

Engr: Giannantonio Faldoni dedicated to N. Edelinck published by Antonio Zanetti, 1724;[5] John Baptist Jackson dedicated to Consul Smith[6] (both in reverse).

Ref: 1. A. E. Popham, *The Drawings of Parmigianino*, 1971, I, 190 (626) II, pl. 334.   2. A. E. Popham, *letter*, 3 December 1952.   3. A. E. Popham, *The Drawings of Parmigianino*, I, 1971, p. 85 (159).   4. Popham, *op. cit.*, p. 24.   5. Victor Weiner, *Eighteenth-Century Italian Prints*, The Metropolitan Museum of Art, Bulletin, January, 1971, pl. 7; Rudolf Weigel, *Die Werke der Maler in ihren Handzeichnungen*, 1865, p. 480 (5721).   6. Weiner, *op. cit.*, pl. 8.

PARMIGIANINO, Imitator of

4161 Three figures after an antique relief

Pen and brown ink, 14.8 × 11.9 cm

The present attribution is due to Philip Pouncey. William Roscoe catalogued the drawing as a Baccio Bandinelli.[1] 4161 is a copy after part of a famous antique relief, *Uncovering of Ariadne,* now in Blenheim Park, formerly owned by the Cavalier de Massimis and in the Palazzo della Valle, Rome.[2]

Prov: Roscoe sale, 1816, part of (82) bt. Ford 11s; John Walter; his sale, Sotheby's 12 September 1959, part of (56a) bt. C. G. Boerner; P. & D. Colnaghi & Co. Ltd. from whom purchased 1960.

Ref: 1. Note on old mount.   2. Fredrich Matz, *Die Dionysische Sarkophage*, Vol. 1, 1968, pp. 149-150 (45) plates 18-19, listing 9 different copies.

PASSAROTTI, Bartolommeo, 1529-1592

8467 Portrait of Giovanni II Bentivoglio

Pen and brown ink, 42.1 × 26.3 cm

Inscribed: *IOANNES BENTIVOLVS. Z vs HANIB. FIL.* (on scroll) *michelagnolo* (brown ink) with *Paserotto* written over it in pencil

Giovanni II Bentivoglio (1443-1508), the son of Annibale Bentivoglio, ruled Bologna from 1462 to 1506.

8467 is based on the lost portrait, the best record of which is a marble relief signed ANTONIVS BAL and dated 1497 in San Giacomo Maggiore, Bologna[1] and which was also the source for the image on the medal made by Francesco Francia in 1494.[2] The armour that Bentivoglio is wearing is the same as is recorded in the Sperandio medal dated by Hill before 1482,[3] and in the portrait in the Ambras Collection series of copies of portraits in the collection of Paolo Giovio.[4]

A similar portrait to 8467 in pen and brown ink by Passarotti of Ercole I Bentivoglio,[5] bound together in an album with eleven other drawings representing the most celebrated jurists of the Studio bolognese was in Christie's sale 6 December 1972 (42). The size of 8467 precludes any suggestion that it belonged to the same series.[6] But all the drawings may date from early in Passarotti's career and their technique suggests that they may have been intended to be engraved.

Prov: Roscoe sale 1816 part of (57) as Michelangelo bt. Davies[7] £1; William Sharp of Manchester, Sotheby, 1-14 March 1878 part of (279) bt. Riggall, £1 7s 0d; Sotheby's 18 December 1935 (57) bt. D. L. Oppé;[8] by descent to Miss A. Oppé; her sale, Christie's, 29 June 1971 (4) bt. for W.A.G.

Ref: 1. Georg Habich, *Die Medaillen der Italienischen Renaissance*, 1924, p. 100 pl. 38. 2. George Francis Hill, *A Corpus of Italian Medals of the Renaissance before Cellini*, 1930, I, p. 155 (606), II pl. 108. 3. Hill, *op. cit.*, I, p. 100 (391), II, pl. 71. 4. Friedrich Kenner, *Die Portratsammlung des Erzherzogs Ferdinand von Tirol*, Jahrbuch des Kunsthistorischen Sammlungen der allerhochsten Kaiserhauses, XVIII, 1899, pp. 199-200, now in Vienna Kunsthistorisches Museum Munzkabinett. See also Pompilio Totti, *Ritratti et Elogii di Capitani illustri*, Rome, 1635, p. 158. 5. *Burlington Magazine*, June 1970, Supplement, pl. XIV. 6. Their measurements average 27 × 19 cm. In 1970 they were with Stanza del Borgo and were exhibited in Milan and Florence, *Visi e figure in disegni italiani e stranieri dal Cinquecento all'Ottocento* 1970, (10-21) and Burlington Magazine, Supplement to December 1976, pl. XII. 7. Liverpool bookseller identified by British Museum Print Room Copy of Roscoe Sale Catalogue. This is John Davies, dealer in old books and prints listed in Liverpool Street Directories between 1805 and 1849. 8. Letter of Hugh Macandrew, 11 October 1974.

PERINO del Vaga, 1501-1577, after

5129 An old man

Pen and ink and brown wash on buff paper, 29.8 × 13.3 cm

After one of the figures executed by Perino to replace the wooden panelling in the Stanza della Segnatura destroyed during the sack of

Rome in 1527.[1] The old attribution was to Polidoro da Caravaggio,[2] to whom the figures were attributed in the 19th century.[3] Lot 70 in the sale of William Lock of Norbury Park was "friezes by P. da Cortona after Polidoro pen and indian ink heightened with white chalk".[4]

Prov: L.R.I., which deposited it in 1893 and presented it in 1948.

Ref: **1.** First recognized as such by John Shearman letter 28 August 1961. The relevant figure is reproduced by Fiorella Sricchia Santoro, *Daniele da Volterra*, Paragone, XVIII, 213, November 1967, fig. 11, pp. 14-15, who suggests that Perino was assisted by Daniele da Volterra. **2.** Old mount. **3.** Stendhal, *Promenades dans Rome*, 18 Sept. 1827, ed. Jean Jacques Pauvert, 1955, p. 65. **4.** Sotheby's 3 May 1821 (70) bt. Carey 8s.

PISA, Albert, 1864-1931

6980 Sunday Morning

Pen and ink, 25.7 × 17.5 cm

Signed: *A. Pisa*

A sketch after *Sunday Morning*, exhibited at the 1894 L.A.E. (No. 392). No. 6980 was made by the artist for reproduction in the Illustrated Catalogue of that exhibition (p. 82). The painting was also exhibited at the Royal Academy 1899 (No. 266).[1]

Prov: W. Woffenden, 61 Lord Street, Liverpool, one of the editors of the L.A.E. Illustrated Catalogues; by descent to Mrs T. K. Bradshaw from whom purchased 1969.

Ref: **1.** Described in Henry Blackburn, *Academy Notes*, 1899, p. 18.

PLESSIS, Hercules Enslin du, born 1894

1047 Fields at Tossa

Pencil and watercolour, 29 × 47.2 cm

Signed: *du Plessis*

Tossa is presumably Tossa del Mar, Spain.

Prov: Selected from the stock of Thos. Agnew and Son for the 1936 L.A.E.,[1] purchased from there by the Gallery, (£7 7s 0d).

Exh: L.A.E. 1936 (428).

Ref: **1.** Letter from Hugh Agnew to the Curator of the W.A.G., 14 September 1936.

POLIDORO da Caravaggio, 1499/1500-1543, after

4159   Figures from a frieze

Pen and ink and wash heightened with white on green paper, 22 × 16.9 cm

A good quality copy of a group to the left of centre of the lower frieze painted by Polidoro on the Palazzo Milesi.[1] The frieze was frequently copied, for instance, by Rubens whose copy of the man leading the horse is now in the British Museum.[2] 4159 is a fragment of a complete copy of the frieze which measured 9 × 20 in when it appeared in William Roscoe's sale.

Prov: Roscoe sale, 1816, part of (190*), bt. Ford £1 13s; John Walter, his sale, Sotheby's 21 September 1959 part of (56a), bt. C. G. Boerner; purchased from P. & D. Colnaghi & Co. Ltd., 1960.

Ref: **1.** Alessandro Marabottini, *Polidoro da Caravaggio*, II, 1969, pl. CXLVII for engraving of the facade by E. Maccari. The facade is described by Vasari, ed. Milanesi, 1880, V p. 149.   **2.** Philip Pouncey and J. A. Gere, *Italian Drawings in the Department of Prints and Drawings in the British Museum, Raphael and his Circle*, 1962, I, pp. 129-130, II, pl. 196.

PROCACCINI, Giulio Cesare, 1570-1625, after

5104   Madonna and Child with Saint Charles Borromeo and Saint Latinus

Red chalk heightened with white, on grey paper, 27.6 × 18.9 cm

A copy of the altarpiece in Sant' Afra, Brescia.[1] The drawing has probably been cut at the right as the picture shows all the right hand of St. Latinus holding the crozier.

At its entry into the collection the drawing was attributed to Maratti.[2]

Prov: David Pennant; presented to the L.R.I., before 1841; deposited at the W.A.G., 1893; presented to the W.A.G., 1948.

Ref: **1.** Milan, Palazzo Reale, 1973, *Il Seicento Lombardo Catalogo dei dipinti e delle sculture*, p. 44 (98) pl. 113.   **2.** 1859 Catalogue, p. 77 (202).

PROSDOCIMI, Alberto, born 1852

7788   Fountain in the Courtyard of the Doge's Palace, Venice

Watercolour, 67.1 × 167.7 cm

Signed: *A. Prosdocimi F.*

Prov: Unknown; found in Municipal Offices, Dale Street, Liverpool 1972.

RENI, Guido, 1575-1642, Follower of

5108   Virgin and Child

Red chalk on grey prepared paper, 18.7 × 41.5 cm

Inscribed: *Guido Reni*

Closely connected with Reni's early etchings of the Holy Family.[1]

Prov: Presented to the L.R.I. by David Pennant before 1841; deposited at the W.A.G., 1893; presented to the W.A.G., 1948.

Ref: 1. A. Bartsch, *Le Peintre Graveur*, 1808, Vol. 18, pp. 284-7, Nos. 9-11, particularly No. 10.

RUITH, Horace van, 1838/9-1923

6994   Be thou the rainbow to the Storms of Life

Black and white chalk on grey-blue paper, 25.4 × 16.7 cm

Inscribed: *HORACE V. Ruit* (black chalk)/*'Be thou the rainbow to the/Storms of Life.'/Byron./Horace van Ruith/5. Sᴛ James's Square London W* (blue ink)

6994 appears to have been drawn for a blockmaker for an illustrated catalogue of an exhibition,[1] but the artist does not seem to have exhibited any works of this title either at the Royal Academy or at the Liverpool Autumn Exhibitions. Possibly the artist originally intended to exhibit a painting with this composition, but never in fact did so.

He gave his address as 5 St James's Square between 1907 and 1916.

The quotation is taken from Byron's *The Bride of Abydos*, Canto II, Stanza 20 verse 399.

Prov: W. Woffenden;[2] by descent to Mrs T. K. Bradshaw, from whom purchased 1969.

Ref: 1. Pencil instructions for the size of the block are on the verso. The provenance also suggests that it was intended for an illustration.   2. W. Woffenden, blockmaker, was the editor of the L.A.E. Catalogue.

6997   Attentive Listeners

Pencil, 20 × 32.2 cm

Inscribed: *H.R.* (monogram in pencil) *"Attentive Listeners"/To Messrs D. MARPLES & Co/Publishers/from Mr. H. Van Ruith./London 18 Holland Park Rd.* (dark blue ink)

Presumably a drawing made for the blockmaker[1] after the oil exhibited at the Royal Academy in 1893 (9) and later at the L.A.E. in 1893 (41). It was not used in the L.A.E. Catalogue.

Prov: D. Marples & Co;[1] W. Woffenden;[2] by descent to Mrs. T. K. Bradshaw, from whom purchased, 1969.

Ref: **1.** D. Marples & Co. were the publishers of the L.A.E. Catalogue. **2.** See above.

SALVIATI, Francesco dei Rossi, 1510-1563

6171   Study for an allegorical female figure

Pen and brown ink heightened with white over black chalk under drawing on blue prepared paper, 27.6 × 18.9 cm

Inscribed: *F:S.*

The attribution is due to Popham.[1] The drawing probably dates from the mid to late 1540's. The style is close to a drawing of *Tarquin and Lucretia* in the Louvre (8796).[2]

Prov: William Roscoe;[3] T. Jones, his sale, Christie's 25 March 1963 (35) bt. by the W.A.G., through P. & D. Colnaghi & Co. Ltd.

Ref: **1.** Letter of J. Byam Shaw, 20 March 1963. It has however been doubted by David McTavish, *letter*, 8 February 1977. **2.** Catherine Monbeig-Goguel, *Inventaire Général des dessins italiens, I, Maîtres toscanes nés après 1500, morts avant 1600. Vasari et son temps*, 1972, p. 120 (143). **3.** Christie's, 25 March 1963 (35). Roscoe bought a female figure attributed to Salviati from T. Philipe 5 October 1808 for 9s. Roscoe Papers 5404. But the drawing cannot be traced in Roscoe's sale.

SARGENT, John Singer, 1856-1925

1271   Study of a Head

Charcoal, 30.2 × 20.4 cm

Signed: *J.S. 10*[1]

Prov: Presented by Mrs Francis Ormond and Miss Emily Sargent (both sisters of the artist) 1930.

Ref: **1.** Hitherto read as *J.S. 70* but No. 1271 is not in Sargent's early style.

SARTO, Andrea del, 1486-1531, after

5084   St. Peter

Red and black chalk on greyish paper, 21.9 × 14.8 cm

A good quality copy[1] of the head of St. Peter in Sarto's *Madonna with Saints*, formerly in the Kaiser Friedrich Museum, Berlin. The altarpiece, dated 1528, was painted for the Church of San Domenico, Sarzana.[2] The head is at a slightly different angle to that in the picture, which perhaps suggests that it is a copy of a study for the head of St. Peter, rather than of the picture.[3]

Popham attributed the drawing to Francesco Salviati,[4] but it does not seem to Michael Hirst[5] or the compiler to be by the same hand as other probable early Salviati drawings such as the red chalk study of a child after Sarto in the Ashmolean Museum, Oxford.[6] The traditional attribution was to Fra Bartolommeo.[7]

Prov: Jonathan Richardson 1665-1745 (Lugt 2184); David Pennant. Presented to the L.R.I., before 1841; deposited at the W.A.G., 1893; presented to the W.A.G., 1948.

Ref: 1. First identified as a copy after Sarto by Fairfax Murray L.R.I. Annual Report 1893, p. 51. (179).   2. John Shearman, *Andrea del Sarto*, 1965, I, pl. 159, II, p. 275 (88).   3. John Shearman, *letter*, 28 August 1961.   4. Note on mount.   5. Orally, November 1966.   6. Shearman, *op. cit.*, I, pl. 169b.   7. 1859 Catalogue (179).

SCHOONHOVEN Jan. J., born 1914

7778   T70-7

Ink and pencil, 40 × 25.5 cm

Signed: *Schoonhoven/1970*

Prov: Purchased from Lucy Milton Gallery 1971.
Exh: ?Lucy Milton Gallery, *Schoonhoven*, 1971.

SILVESTRO dei Gherarducci, Don, also known as Don Silvestro Camaldolese, 1352-1399

2764   The Birth of St. John the Baptist

Vellum, 28.8 × 30.1 cm (main subject 24 × 17.8 cm)

The Virgin holds the infant Baptist, as in the Andrea Pisano doors of the Florentine Baptistery. Her presence is unusual but does occur in Fra Domenico Cavalca's life of the Baptist written *c.* 1320-1342.[1]

At least 8 other miniatures attributed to Don Silvestro were in the collection of William Young Ottley with 2764.[2] The style of 2764 is very similar to those in Corale 2 (Gradual) in the Biblioteca Laurenziana,[3] which is dated 1370 and 1377. This manuscript came from the Camaldolite monastery of Santa Maria degli Angeli, where Don Silvestro was a monk. 2764 is said to have come "from the celebrated mass-book formerly in the monastery of Camaldoli."[5] Two leaves (fol. 97 and fol. 104) are missing from Corale 2 at the point at which the Feast of St. John the Baptist is celebrated.[6] Folio 97 probably originally contained 2764.[7] The song for the Feast of St. John the Baptist begins at folio 96 thus:

Ioannes. B. Hic ve / nit ut testimo / nium phibe / ret de lumine pa / rare domino plebe / perfectam. / In nativitate. S. / Johannis bap.te / promis maiore. iti, while folio 98 continues O altissime. prius q. / te formarem in utero / novite et anteq. ea / res de ventre sactificavi / te.

The dating of 2764 to 1390-1395 by Boskovits[8] seems too late in view of the stylistic resemblances to Corale 2.

Prov: William Young Ottley, who purchased it in Italy;[5] William Roscoe, sale (10) passed; in the L.R.I. by 1819;[9] deposited at the W.A.G., 1893;[10] presented to the W.A.G., 1948.

Exh: Manchester, *Art Treasures*, 1857 (44).

Ref: 1. Marilyn Aronberg Lavin, *Giovannino Battista*, Art Bulletin, XXXVII, 1955, p. 87. Mrs Jameson comments on the rarity of the Virgin's presence in *Legends of the Madonna*, 1904, p. 299.   2. Mirella Levi d'Ancona, *Don Silvestro dei Gherarducci e il maestro delle canzoni*, Rivista d'Arte, XXXII, 1957, p. 9. Two of these *The Death and Glorification of the Virgin* and *A royal saint with six smaller half-length figures of saints* were in the Rev. J. Fuller Russell sale, Christie's 18 April 1885, (124), bt. Colnaghi and (125), bt. Wood respectively. See also Francis Russell, *Don Silvestro dei Gherarducci and an illumination from the Collection of William Young Ottley*, Burlington Magazine, CXIX, 1977, pp. 192-5.   3. d'Ancona, *op. cit.*, pp. 9, 13.   4. Letter of Dott. Morandini, 29 January 1975; and Miklos Boskovits, *Su Don Silvestro, Don Simone e la Scuola degli Angeli*, Paragone, Vol. 265. 1972. p. 59 note 65.   5. Roscoe Sale Catalogue, p 123.   6. Letter of Dott. Morandini, 16 January 1975.   7. Letter of Mirella Levi d'Ancona, 14 October 1959, notes that folio 97 should have contained the Birth of the Baptist.   8. Miklos Boskovits, *Pittura Fiorentina alla vigilia del Rinascimento 1370-1400*, 1975, p. 423.   9. 1819 Catalogue (5).   10. 1893 Catalogue p. 7 (12).

STRADANUS, Jan van der Straet, called 1523-1605

6312   The Prophet Micah

Pen and ink over red and black chalks, squared for transfer, 18.6 × 12.5 cm (oval)

Inscribed: *joan. stradanus faciebat* (the latter two words crossed out)/*jan stradanus.*

6312 is one of a pair of drawings once owned by William Roscoe. Its companion, *Elisha*, is now in the Lugt Collection.[1] 6312 was engraved as plate 14 in *Icones Prophetarum Veteris Testamenti a Ioanne Stradano delineatae a Theodoro Gallaeo excusae*, published in Antwerp in 1613.[2] A copy of 6312 in the same direction as it, in the Ashmolean Museum, is signed *Gulielmus Bogdani fecit*. It appears unlikely that Bogdani's drawing was made for the engraver since the engraving follows 6312 more closely in that the back of the prophet overlaps the oval frame.

The engraving of Micah is accompanied by the inscription *Plango, et vt Israel maestus, mecu, rogo, plangat. MICHAEAS. Christi ortum, et magni iussa revelo Dei.* "I lament and ask that sad Israel should lament with me. MICAH. I reveal the rise of Christ and orders of mighty God."—a reference to the opening chapter from the Book of Micah and to his role as prophet of the coming Messiah.

Other drawings by Stradanus for this series are Jeremiah (National Gallery of Scotland D1526),[3] Amos (with Yvonne Tan Bunzl, 1970),[4] Sophonias (with William H. Schab, 1975)[5] and Gad (sold Sotheby's 4 December 1969 (31)).[6]

A number of other drawings of Old and New Testament figures in ovals are known which were presumably intended for engravings but perhaps were never engraved.[7]

Prov: ?W. Richardson;[8] Roscoe sale, 1816 (460) with the Lugt drawing bt. Lord Stanley 14s. Anon sold Sotheby's, 1 December 1964 (141) bt. Shaeffer; sold Sotheby's, 22 July 1965 (98) bt. P. & D. Colnaghi & Co. Ltd., from whom purchased, 1965.

Ref: 1. Identified by Dr. van Hasselt, *letter* of 23 July, 1976. Previously Sotheby 1 December 1964 (160) bt. Jeudwine.   2. Copies in the National Library of Congress, Washington and the National Gallery of Art, Washington containing 20 engravings including the title page. The Rijksprentenkabinett in the Rijksmuseum, Amsterdam own a set of 26 engravings including the title page (number 1 to 21 and 23 to 27) and one more number 22 is presumably missing. The link between the series of Stradanus drawings and this book was first noticed in William H. Schab Inc., *Catalogue Fifty-Six, Graphic Arts of Five Centuries*, 1975 pp. 22-3 (10). A further set of engravings in Antwerp Royale Musée des Beaux Arts Print Room bears a different title page also published in Antwerp. *Icones Prophetarum Veteris Testamenti à Stradano delineatae, à Ioanne Gallaeo excusae, à Corn Gallaeo sculptae*, with no publication date. J. J. P. Van Den Bemden, *De Familie Galle...*, Antwerp, 1863, p. 18 (4) mentions a set of engravings *Icones Prophetarum Majorum et Minorum veteris Testamenti* by Philippe Galle which may also be related. F. W. H. Hollstein, *Dutch and Flemish Etchings, Engravings and Woodcuts, ca. 1450-1700*, VII, 1952 p. 49 (4-30) as engraved by Cornelis Galle.   3. *Icones Prophetarum...* pl. 5.   4. *Icones Prophetarum...* pl. 11. *Old Master Drawings and Paintings presented by Yvonne Tan Bunzl exhibited at the premises of Faerber and Maison Ltd.*, 1970 (48) as Saint Joseph. This had previously appeared at Sotheby's, 1 July 1969 (303) as by Tiarini and as a Carmelite Saint. The halo in this drawing suggests that the person represented was not originally intended to be Amos.   5. *Icones Prophetarum ...* pl. 17. William H. Schab, Inc, *op. cit.*, Earlier at Sotheby, 22 November 1974 (22).   6. *Icones Prophetarum...* pl. 27. Identified by Carlos van Hasselt, *letter*, 23 July, 1976. With Stanza del Borgo, Milan, 1972 (letter from Keith Andrews, 13 May 1974). It had been earlier exhibited *Visi e figure in disegni italiani e stranieri dal Cinquecento all'Ottocento*, 1970 (9).   7. Unknown prophet, J. Q. van Regteren Altena collection, Amsterdam (letter Carlos van Hasselt, 23 July 1976); Unknown prophet, Sotheby, 4 December 1969 (32) later P. & D. Colnaghi, 1970, *Old Master and English Drawings* (7); Martha, National Gallery of Scotland D1691. P. & D. Colnaghi, *Old Master Drawings. A Loan Exhibition from the National Gallery of Scotland*, 1966 (32); Abraham and Isaac, and Saint John the Evangelist, Sotheby's Parke-Bernet, 22 October 1970, (33) and (34), both from the Victor Sordan Collection; the latter appeared in Faerber and Maison Ltd., *Old Master Drawings and Paintings presented by Yvonne Tan Bunzl*, 1971, (49). Simeon and the Christ Child, Witt Collection, 1287, Courtauld Institute of Art, *Hand-list of drawings in the Witt Collection*, 1956, p. 130; Anna, J. A. G. Weigel Sale, Gutekunst 15 May 1883 (1012), later Sotheby's, 8 June 1972 (179) and Cologne sale, 24 October 1973 (1973) pl. 42; A high priest, possibly Zachariah, though not the same as the engraving, probably J. A. G. Weigel sale, Gutekunst, 15 May 1883 (1012), sold Sotheby's, 10 December 1968 (49), with Yvonne Tan Bunzl, 1976; and Lazarus and Nicodemus, J. A. G. Weigel sale, Gutekunst, 15 May 1883 (1012). (The information about the drawings in the Weigel sale, Carlos Van Hasselt, *letter*, 23 July 1976).   8. William Roscoe purchased four drawings by "Stradan" from the print dealer W. Richardson 3 June 1808 for 5s (Roscoe Papers 5404).

TAMAGNI da San Gimignano, Vincenzo, 1492-after 1538

4162 A woman with a distaff

Pen and brown ink with black chalk on pink prepared paper, 15.6 × 12.4 cm

The attribution to Tamagni was first proposed by Francis Richardson.[1] A drawing in the British Museum in pen and brown ink assignable to him in a similar style is also on pink prepared paper (1951-2-10-1).[2]

The drawing since Resta's time had been attributed to Raphael.[3]

Prov: Padre Resta by 1707;[3] Jonathan Richardson 1665-1745 (Lugt 2184); Thomas Philipe?[4] Roscoe sale, 1816 (part of 175) bt. Ford £1 10s 0d; John Walter, his sale, Sotheby's, 12 November 1959, part of (56a) bt. C. G. Boerner; P. & D. Colnaghi & Co. Ltd., from whom purchased, 1960.

Ref: **1.** David E. Rust, *The drawings of Vincenzo Tamagni da San Gimignano*, National Gallery of Art Report and Studies in the History of Art, 1968, p. 88 B27 fig 20. **2.** Rust, *op. cit.*, p. 86 B21 fig 11. **3.** Padre Resta, *Parnaso de Pittori*, 1707, f. 61 as Una Donna ginocchione, che fila-: di RAFFAELE d'Urbino, qua scapata per inadvertenza tra i Michelangeleschi. **4.** Roscoe bought a volume with Padre Restas Drawings from old Pic from Philipe 13 June 1808 for £3 13s 6d (Roscoe Papers 5404).

TINTORETTO, Jacopo Robusti, 1518-1594, after

5109 The Entombment

Pen and brown wash with slight black chalk under drawing, 40.6 × 25.7 cm (shaped top)

Inscribed: $G^A VR^T?$

A copy of Tintoretto's *Entombment* painted for San Francesco della Vigna, Venice, now in the Duke of Sutherland's collection probably painted in the 1560's.[1] 5109 records the altarpiece before the lower half was removed leaving only the angel holding the crown of thorns which is now lost. This happened before 1648 when Ridolfi recorded the altarpiece as mutilated.[2] The altarpiece was engraved by Jacob Matham in 1594.[3] The inscription on the drawing may be an attribution to Tintoretto to whom it was assigned when it was first recorded.

Prov: David Pennant, who presented it to the L.R.I. before 1841; deposited at the W.A.G., 1893; presented to the W.A.G., 1948.

Ref: **1.** First identified as a copy after Tintoretto by Fairfax Murray, L.R.I. Annual Report, 1893, p. 51 (188), Hans Tietze, *Tintoretto*, 1958, p. 353 fig. 141. **2.** Carlo Ridolfi, *Delle Maraviglie dell'arte*, 1648, p. 32. **3.** Adam Bartsch, *Le Peintre Graveur*, III, 1854, p. 179 (191).

TIZIANO Vecellio, *c*. 1488/90-1576, after

6011   Venus and Adonis

Pen and black ink, 22.5 × 32.6 cm

A copy of the version of *Venus and Adonis* now in the Prado, which was completed in 1554.[1] It is perhaps by an early 17th century artist and the technique suggests that it may be after an engraving.[2]

Prov: Bt. from a dealer in Oxford by R. D. Radcliffe in 1863. In the collection before 1966.
Ref: **1.** Harold E. Wethey, *The Paintings of Titian*, III, 1975, pp. 188-190, pl. 84.   **2.** Harold E. Wethey, orally, 19 September 1975.

TOPOLSKI, Feliks, born 1907

4998   Hyde Park, London during the Coronation of Queen Elizabeth II, 1953

Ink, 17.1 × 23.8 cm

Signed: *F.T.*

For details of the artist's coverage of this event see *Topolski's Buckingham Palace Panoramas*, 1977, n.p.

Prov: Presented by Mrs G. Milman 1955.

VELDE, Esaias van de, about 1591-1630

Loan 228   Winter Landscape

Black chalk and grey wash, 18.6 × 30.4 cm

Signed: *E. V. VELDE 1628* (?)

Unidentified Watermark

There is a copy after No. 228 in the Museum Boymans van Beuningen, Rotterdam, Inv. No. F.G. 173.[1]

Prov: Bought by the Liverpool City Libraries about 1956; on loan to the W.A.G.
Ref: **1.** Dr. A. Zwollo, *letter*, 24 May 1976, George S. Keyes, *letter*, 24 August 1976.

VIOLET, Pierre Noel, 1749-1819

2213   Portrait of Jean Baptiste Vallerieau

Watercolour on ivory, 10.2 × 8 cm (oval)

Signed: *P. Violet*

The sitter was apparently in 1785 a servant of the Ployart de Thellusson family.[1] Subsequently he assumed the name of Picard (his family having originated in Picardy) and settled in Ashford, Kent as a tailor; he may have been connected with Sackville Tufton, 9th Earl of Thanet; he died at Ashford.[2]

Prov: By descent to the great grandson of the sitter, Arthur Vallerieau Wilkinson who presented it 1945.

Ref: **1.** MS Certificate of good conduct signed by Julie Ployart de Thellusson and dated 9 May 1785 (W.A.G.).   **2.** Information from the donor February 1945. A John Pickard died at Ashford on 22 April 1824, aged 72 (Ashford Parish Church Records, communicated by Caron A. K. W. Wright, *letter*, 13 January 1976); he was probably the sitter in No. 2213.

WATERLOO, Anthonie, 1609/10-1690

6172   A wood at the side of a river

Black chalk and gouache on blue paper, 26.4 × 41.4 cm

Prov: Roscoe[1] Sale 1816, part of lot 540, bt. Davies £0 14s 0d. T. Jones sold Christie's, 25 March 1963 (37), bt. W.A.G.

Ref: **1.** Roscoe bought a landscape attributed to Waterloo from T. Philipe in July 1809 for £2 2s 0d, (Roscoe Papers No. 5404).

WAUGH, Frederick Judd, 1861-1940

427   Snowdrifts

Pastel, 43.8 × 59.6 cm

Signed: *F. J. Waugh/1904*

Reproduced on page 62 of *Paintings of the Sea by Frederick Judd Waugh*, New York, 1936. *The Silent Fen* was an alternative title for No. 427.[1]

Prov: Purchased from the L.A.E., 1904 (£18).

Exh: L.A.E., 1904 (601).

Ref: **1.** George R. Havens, *Frederick J. Waugh*, 1969, pp. 79, 90, 275, No. 14 quoting from the artist's ledgers.

ZUCCHI, Jacopo, 1541-1589/1590

6558 Pope Leo X blessing King Francis I of France

Pen and ink and wash with white heightening over black chalk on olive green paper, 30.1 × 24.9 cm

Inscribed: *Luca delle Zucche* (in Greek and Italian)

A drawing for the painting in the ceiling of the *Sala di Leone X*.[1] The meeting of Pope Leo X and King Francis took place in Bologna in 1515.

There are a number of significant variations from the painting; Francis I wears a crown, his legs are uncovered below the knee, his helmet held by the putto behind him is not yet adorned with the lilies of the French royal arms and a figure at the top left hand corner is blowing a trumpet. 6558, however, is closer to the painting than the drawing in the Louvre for the whole ceiling (2175), where Pope Leo X is seated on a throne up a flight of steps, and King Francis bends to the ground to kiss his feet.[2]

No artist of the name of Luca delle Zucche is recorded. The inscription probably refers to Jacopo Zucchi, with whose early drawing style 6558 is compatible.[3] He was one of Vasari's assistants when he was working in the Sala di Leone X.[4] Although no other evidence of his active participation in the decoration of the room has yet come to light, the uncertainty in the handling would support the suggestion that 6558 was a young man's work.

Work on the paintings in the ceiling had begun by January 1560. Work on the next room started by 3 June 1561.[5]

Prov: Robert Udney (Lugt 2248); his sale, Philipe and Scott, 9 May 1803, part of (515) 2/0; William Roscoe;[6] Alister Mathews, from whom purchased, 1967.

Ref: **1.** Piero Bargellini, *Scoperta di Palazzo Vecchio*, 1968, pp. 115-116, pl. 154 and Giorgio Vasari, *I Ragionamenti*, ed. G. C. Sansoni, 1882, pp. 145-6.   **2.** Paola Barocchi, *Vasari Pittore*, 1964, pl. 64, and Catherine Monbeig-Goguel, *Inventaire Général des dessins italiens, I, Maîtres toscanes nés après 1500, morts avant 1600. Vasari et son temps*, 1972, pp. 162-4 (211).   **3.** For his drawing style see Edmund Pillsbury, *Drawings by Jacopo Zucchi*, Master Drawings, XII, 1974, pp. 3-33.   **4.** Edmund P. Pillsbury, *Jacopo Zucchi: His Life and Works*, Courtauld Institute of Art, Unpublished Doctoral Dissertation, 1973, p. 37.   **5.** Karl Frey and Herman-Walther Frey, *Der Literarische Nachlass Giorgio Vasaris*, II, 1930, p. 875.   **6.** Note on back.

CATALOGUE OF TAPESTRIES

BRUSSELLS, School of, about 1525

4115   Triumph of Fortitude

Silk and wool, 411 × 533 cm

Inscribed: *Obiicit adversis interrita corda periculis/Virtus eque iuvat morte recepta salus.* / *ALEXANDER* / *COCLES* / *HOLOFERNES JUDICH* / *CHLOELIA* / *MUTIUS SCEVOLA* / *CINOPE* / *DENTATUS* / *SCEVA* / *FORTITUDO* / *PENTHESIEEA* / *THAMARIS* / *DAVID* / *NEEMIAS* / *HIERUSALEM* / *PHNEES* / *JAHEL* / *SISARAM* /*JOSUE*[1]

The inscription at the top may be translated: Virtue opposes fearless hearts to threatening dangers. In the same way salvation pleases when death is accepted.

The figures from left to right are Alexander the Great conquering a City (*ALEXANDER*); Publius Horatius Cocles swimming in the River Tiber having jumped from the bridge he was defending (*COCLES*); Judith beheading Holofernes (*HOLOFERNES* and *JUDICH*); Cloelia escaping from Porsenna's camp (*CHLOELIA*); Mutius Scaevola burning his right hand in Porsenna's camp (*MUTIUS SCEVOLA*); Eleazer killing the elephant with a sword—I Macabees VI, 46; Cinope, one of the nine "preuses"[2] (*CINOPE*); two lions, usual symbols of Fortitude; Sicinius Dentatus, the Roman tribune and warrior (*DENTATUS*); Cassius Scaeva at the Battle of Dyrrhachium (*SCEVA*); an eagle; Fortitude (or Samson?) with her usual symbol, the column (*FORTITUDO*); Penthesilea, Queen of the Amazons, (*PENTHESIEEA*); Thomyris with the head of Cyrus (*THAMARIS*); David offered water from the well of Bethlehem—2 Samuel XXIII, 15 (*DAVID*); Hercules killing the Nemaean lion, Milo of Crotona with the tree root, or Samson killing the lion—Judges XIV, 6; Nehemiah rebuilding Jerusalem—Nehemiah II, 20ff (*NEEMIAS);* Phinehas killing the adulterous Israelites—Numbers XXV, 7 (*PHNEES*); Jael killing Sisera—Judges IV, 22 (*JAHEL* and *SISARAM*); Joshua and Caleb entering the promised land with the Israelites—Joshua I, Numbers XIV, 30 and XXXII, 12 (*JOSUE*); and (?) Gideon breaking the jars with the burning torches inside—Judges VII, 16ff.[3]

Other slightly later versions of No. 4115 are in the Fine Arts Museum of San Francisco (Inv. No. 1957. 126), in the Chateau de Langeais, Val de Loire but only the lower left corner, at Chenonceaux (Indre et Loire) and at the Museo de Santa Cruz, Toledo but all with a different border. *The Triumph of Fortitude* was one of a series of "Triumphs" of the seven virtues, Prudence, Justice, Fortitude, Temperance, Faith, Charity and

Hope;[4] the series was woven several times at first with borders as in No.
4115 but later with floral borders as in the other versions of No. 4115.

Prov: Manuel de Soler; bought in 1933 by Sir Ronald Storrs; presented by Martins
Bank Ltd. 1953.

Ref: **1.** Not now visible but taken from the San Francisco version (see Text).   **2.**
The nine "worthy women" for whom see Louis Reau, *Iconographie de l'Art Chretien*, Vol. 2, Part 1, 1956, pp. 327ff. Cinope was among them according to Mme
Francois Souchal, *letter*, 2 March 1976.   **3.** Another slightly later set of the
Triumph of the Virtues is discussed by M. Carlberg, *Le Triomphe des Vertus
chretiennes*, Revue belge d'archeologie et d'histoire de l'art, Vol. 29, 1960, pp.
3-36 with very similar iconography. I am deeply indebted to Mme Francois
Souchal for help with this entry.   **4.** *Temperance*, however, does not survive in
any known version; one version of each of the other virtues from this series is
reproduced in Anna G. Bennett, *Five Centuries of Tapestry from the Fine Arts
Museums of San Francisco*, 1976, pp. 93ff who also provides detailed sources for
the iconography in No. 4115.

K

CATALOGUE OF SCULPTURE

ALBACINI, Carlo, 18th century

6537 Bust of Minerva

Marble, height 101.5 cm with base

A copy after one of the versions of the so-called Athena of Velletri.[1]

A copy by Pierre Petitot after another of these versions, signed and dated 1789, is at the Musée des Beaux Arts d'Angers (Inv. 105 (1949)).

Prov: Bought from the artist by Henry Blundell 1777;[2] by descent to Colonel Joseph Weld who presented it, 1959.

Ref: **1.** Some twenty are listed by Seymour Howard, *The Lansdowne Bust of the Athena of Velletri*, Los Angeles County Museum of Art Bulletin, Vol. XVII, 1965, No. 1, p. 13. Henry Blundell in his *An Account of the Statues, Bust etc. at Ince. Collected by H.B.*, 1803, p. 46, No. 101 states that the original copied by Albacini was at Rome.   **2.** Blundell, *op. cit.*

6538 Bust of Lucius Verus

Marble, height 89 cm with base

A copy after the antique bust then in the Villa Borghese, Rome,[1] but now in the Louvre.[2]

Blundell observed of this copy: "The hair of the head and the beard are reckoned a fine specimen of modern art".[3]

Another copy of this bust was being made in Albacini's studio when Canova visited it in 1780; Canova was told that it would involve 19 months work.[4] Yet another copy (also by Albacini?) is now at Chatsworth in the Devonshire Collections.

Prov: Bought from the artist by Henry Blundell 1777;[5] by descent to Colonel Joseph Weld who presented it, 1959.

Ref: **1.** (Henry Blundell) *An Account of the Statues, Busts etc. at Ince. Collected by H.B.*, 1803, p. 45, No. 100.   **2.** Heron de Villefosse, *Catalogue sommaire des marbres antiques*, 1896, No. 1170.   **3.** Blundell, *op. cit.*   **4.** Hugh Honour, *Antonio Canova and the Anglo Romans*, The Connoisseur, Vol. 143, 1959, p. 244.   **5.** Blundell, *op. cit.*, No. 101.

6900 Bust of Bacchus

Marble, height 64.8 cm with base

A copy after a bust now in the Capitoline Museum described by Blundell as "Ariadne as many beautiful heads are, when the person represented is not known"[1] but now listed as Dionysus.[2]

Prov: Bought from the artist by Henry Blundell 1777;[3] by descent to Colonel Joseph Weld who presented it, 1959.

REf: 1. (Henry Blundell), *An Account of the Statues, Busts etc. at Ince. Collected by H.B.*, 1803, p. 46, No. 102.   2. *Catalogue of the Ancient Sculptures preserved in the Municipal Collections of Rome*, Vol. I, *The Sculptures of the Museo Capitolino*, ed. H. Stuart Jones, 1912, p. 344, No. 5 pl. 86. (Stanza del Gladiatore).   3. Blundell, *op. cit.*

9106   Bust of Alexander the Great

Marble, height 69 cm

After the so-called *Bust of Alexander* now in the Capitoline Museum.[1]

Blundell wrote of No. 9106:[2] "There is something very grand and noble in the character of this bust which denotes a great man. The open countenance and fine flowing head of hair give it a superior elegance to almost any other head."

Prov: Bought by Henry Blundell from the artist in 1777;[3] by descent to Colonel Joseph Weld who presented it 1959.

Ref: 1. *Catalogue of Ancient Sculptures preserved in the Municipal Collection of Rome*, ed. Stuart Jones, Vol. 1, *Museo Capitolino*, 1912, p. 341, No. 3, Plates Volume pl. 85.   2. (Henry Blundell), *An Account of the Statues, Busts etc. at Ince. Collected by H.B.*, 1803, No.103, p. 46.   3. Blundell, *op. cit.*, No. 102.

ALESSI, Andrea, about 1425-1503/5

7278   St. Jerome reading in a Cave

Stone relief,[1] 44.5 × 37.8 cm

Inscribed: *A L* (around a double headed eagle)

One of a considerable number of reliefs of St. Jerome[2] by Alessi[3] mainly still in Dalmatia.[4]

The arms and initials at the bottom are those of Alvise Lando the Venetian governor of Trogir in Dalmatia 1470-1472;[5] since Alessi hardly ever left Dalmatia No. 7278 can be dated to those years. The lion, St. Jerome's usual attribute, frightens off a dragon, presumably representing paganism, while above, the eagle, representing Christ, fights with the serpent, one of the symbols for Satan.[6]

Prov: Signora T. Ventura, Florence (by 1955); E. A. Martin, London; Cyril Humphris, from whom purchased 1970 with the aid of a contribution from the National Art-Collections Fund.

Ref: 1. Brac or Brazza stone according to Anthony Radcliffe, unpublished report, copy in W.A.G., p. 1.   2. St. Jerome was a native of Dalmatia and enjoys a strong local cult there.   3. No. 7278 was first attributed to Alessi by Cvito Fiskovic, *Radovi Nikole Firentinca u Zadru*, Peristil, Vol. 4, 1961, pp. 69ff.   4. The best lists are in Radcliffe, *op. cit.*, pp. 1ff, Inventaire des Collections publiques francaises, *Sculpture italienne, Musée Jacquemart-André*, 1975, p. 126 and in Cvito Fiskovic, *Alesijev reljef u Londonu*, Peristil, Vols. 10-11, 1967-8, pp. 47ff, which contains detailed evidence for the attribution of No. 7278 to Alessi.   **5.** Fiskovic, 1967-8, *op. cit.*, p. 49. The arms on No. 7278 are barely visible but the initials A L and the double headed eagle signifying that the bearer was an imperial count are conclusive. The arms of the Lando family are given in Count Pompeo Litta, *Celebri famiglie italiane*, 1819-98, Vol. 8. According to Radcliffe, *op. cit.*, p. 9 Lando did not leave Trogir until 1473; in 1471 he commissioned Alessi and Niccolo Fiorentino to carve reliefs in the City Loggia at Trogir (Fiskovic, 1967-8, *op. cit.*, p. 49).   **6.** Only the lion is traditional for St. Jerome; for the other animals see particularly Rudolf Wittkower, *Eagle and Serpent*, Journal of the Warburg Institute, Vol. II, No. 4, 1938-9 pp. 293ff. The Venetian iconography of St Jerome is most recently discussed in Millard Meiss, *The Painter's Choice*, 1976, pp. 194ff.

ANGELINI, Joseph, 1735-1811

6530   Head of Jupiter

Marble, height 89 cm with base

Signed: *Joseph Angelini 1780*

A copy made from an antique cornice[1] after the original in the Vatican Museum.[2] Possibly the *Head of Jupiter* seen by Canova in Angelini's studio in 1780; Canova preferred the carving of the beard in Angelini's copy to the original.[3]

Prov: Bought by Henry Blundell from Giovanni Volpato;[4] by descent to Colonel Joseph Weld who presented it, 1959.

Ref: **1.** (Henry Blundell), *An Account of the Statues, Busts etc. at Ince. Collected by H.B.*, 1803, p. 45, No. 99.   **2.** Blundell *op. cit.*, states that No. 6530 was copied "from that fine antique head of Jupiter in the Vatican Museum"; presumably he meant the head of the *Statue of the Seated Jupiter* (Walther Amelung, *Die Sculpturen des Vaticanischen Museums*, 1908, Vol. II, p. 519, No. 326, Plates Volume II, pl. 73) to which however No. 6530 is not identical.   **3.** Hugh Honour, *Antonio Canova and the Anglo Romans*, The Connoisseur, Vol. 143, 1959, p. 242.   **4.** Blundell, *op. cit.*

ARNOLFO di Cambio, died probably 1302, studio of

6639   Relief of a deacon holding a curtain

Marble, height 91 cm

Probably part of a tomb designed by Arnolfo di Cambio about 1290, but executed in his studio.[1] Martinelli however believes that No. 6639 and a *Head of a Deacon* in the Museo Capitolare di Perugia came from the tomb erected in the Cathedral of Perugia to Pope Urban IV who died there in 1264;[2] this tomb was attributed by Vasari to Giovanni Pisano[3] but by Martinelli to Arnolfo; by the 16th century it had already been dismantled.[4] If No. 6639 were as early as this it would be the first example of the use of attendant figures opening or closing curtains in front of the deceased in Italian tomb sculpture[5]—the best known example is the Tomb of Cardinal Guillaume de Braye by Arnolfo begun in 1282.

Prov: Found in Tuscany by Count Lanckoronski in the 1880's[6] sold Christie's, 18 June 1968, lot 160, bt. for the W.A.G.

Ref: **1.** Julian Gardner, *A Relief in the Walker Art Gallery and thirteenth century Italian Tomb Design*, Liverpool Bulletin, Vol. 13, 1968-70, pp. 5ff. Earlier attributions were to Fra Guglielmo (A. Venturi, *Storia dell'Arte italiana*, 1906, IV, pp. 65ff, fig. 43 and K. Frey in G. Vasari, *Le Vite*, 1911, p. 896); or to "zwischen Arnolfo und Fra Guglielmo" (H. Keller, *Der Bildhauer Arnolfo di Cambio und seine Werkstatt*, Jahrbuch der preussischen Kunstsammlungen, 1934, Vol. 55, pp. 205-228 and 1935, Vol. 56, pp. 22-43); P. Toesca first attributed No. 6639 to Arnolfo alone in *Il Trecento*, 1951, p. 214, note 22.   **2.** Valentino Martinelli, *Arnolfo a Perugia,* Atti del sesto Convegno di Studi Umbri, 1968, I, pp. 4ff.   **3.** G. Vasari, *Le Vite*, ed. Milanesi, I, 1878, p. 508.   **4.** Vasari, *op. cit.*   **5.** See Gardner, *op. cit.*, pp. 5-10 and John White, *Art and Architecture in Italy 1250-1400*, 1966, p. 56 who argues that at least in the de Braye tomb the deacon is closing the curtains not holding them back as maintained by Gardner, *op. cit.*, at p. 5. In No. 6639 the deacon certainly seems to be holding them back.   **6.** Baron Martin Koblitz, *letter*, 27 June 1968, quoting from a telephone conversation with Countess Lanckoronska.

ARONSON, Naoum, active *c*. 1900-1940

1525 Tete d'Enfant[1]

Marble bust, height 49.5 cm

Signed: *N. Aronson*

Reproduced as *La petite fille au bonnet* by C. de Danilowicz[2] who was presumably describing No. 1525 when he wrote: "Une de ses têtes d'enfant, espiègle, mutine, coiffée d'un petit bonnet, comme d'un casque, a dans les commissures des lèvres un sourire etrange, troublant. C'est une Joconde enfant que cette petite dont les yeux souriants et amusés cachent cependant je ne sais quelle profondeur d'idée, comme si, jouant à la poupée, l'enfant eût entrevu dans un éclair le Golgotha de toute vie humaine."[3]

Prov: Purchased from the artist at the 1908 L.A.E. (£40).

Exh: *Société Nationale des Beaux Arts*, Paris, 1908 (1834). L.A.E., 1908 (2071).

Ref: **1.** Entitled thus in the Société Nationale des Beaux Arts 1908 Catalogue and in the 1908 L.A.E. Catalogue.   **2.** C. de Danilowicz, *Naoum Aronson*, 1911 opposite p. 2.   **3.** Danilowicz, *op. cit.*, p. 28.

AUGSBURG, School of, 16th century

7397 Stag

Gilt bronze, height 37.2 cm excluding base

The head, body and legs of the Stag were cast as one piece; the antlers and ears were cast separately and attached.

No. 7397 has been associated[1] with a group of works assembled by Bange[2] around Hans Reisinger and the Augsburg School of the 16th century but it could be considerably later in date.

Prov: Heim Gallery, purchased, 1970.
Exh: Heim Gallery, *Mannerist Paintings and Sculpture*, 1970, No. 23.
Ref: **1.** Originally in the Heim Gallery Catalogue cited under Exhibitions.   **2.** E. F. Bange, *Die Deutschen Bronzestatuetten des 16 Jahrhunderts*, 1949, Nos. 157-166, pp. 142ff.

BARTELS, Wera von, born 1886

1526   Panther

Bronze, height 24.8 cm

Signed: *WERA V BARTELS*

Inscribed: *GUSS V A BRANDSTETTER/MUNCHEN*

Prov: The artist exhibited another cast of No. 1526 at the 1913 L.A.E. (No. 2005); this was purchased by Professor W. Baldwin Spencer; the Curator of the Walker Art Gallery however wrote to the artist on 2 February 1914 saying "that it is almost certain that my Committee will allow me to buy for the Gallery a replica of the Panther just purchased by Professor Spencer". This replica, presumably No. 1526, reached the Gallery on 17 February but by this time the Curator was absent ill. He returned to his duties late in May but does not seem to have submitted this replica to the Committee. War broke out with Germany in August; it therefore became impossible to return the replica or to submit it to the Committee.

BARTOLINI, Lorenzo, 1777-1850

8990   Portrait of J. A. D. Ingres

Marble, diameter 30.6 cm

Nearly identical to the bronze medallion of about 1806 now in the Ecole nationale des Beaux Arts, Paris.[1] The plaster (for this medallion and No. 8990?) was presented by the sculptor to Adolf von Sturler.[2] No. 8990 lacks the inscriptions of the names of sitter and sculptor visible in the plaster and bronze.

Prov: Heim Gallery, from whom purchased, 1975.
Ref: **1.** M. Tinti, *Lorenzo Bartolini*, 1936, Vol. II, p. 26, pl. III. G. Hubert, *Les sculpteurs italiens en France, 1790-1830*, 1964, p. 67, fig. 26. Arts Council of Great Britain, *The Age of Neo-Classicism*, 1972, p. 474, No. 962.   **2.** Hugo Wagner, *The Kunstmuseum in Bern*, Connoisseur, Vol. 192, p. 179, the plaster is now in the Kunstmuseum, Bern, Inv. No. P223.

BARYE, Antoine Louis, 1796-1875

1527   Panther and Hyena

Bronze, height 22.2 cm

Signed: *BARYE*

The original plaster and wax model was exhibited in 1889, as *Panthère saisissant un Zibeth*[1] and is now in the Louvre under that title.[2] It differs slightly from No. 1527 and other bronze versions.[3] Bronzes of this subject are first listed in Barye's 1855 Catalogues.[4]

Prov: Purchased by James Smith from Alexander Reid, 1899 as *Panther and Hyena*; bequeathed to the W.A.G., 1927.

Ref: 1. *Catalogue des oeuvres de Barye exposees a l'Ecole des Beaux Arts*, 1889 (644).   2. Inv. No. R.F.2274; *Collection Carle Dreyfus leguée aux Musees nationaux et au Musée des Arts decoratifs,* Exposition au Cabinet des Dessins du Musée du Louvre, 1953 (229).   3. For example the bronze version in the Louvre, Inv. No. O.A.5757.   4. These catalogues are reproduced in Roger Ballu, *L'Oeuvre de Barye*, 1890 and *Panthere surprenant un zibet* is there listed as Nos. 59, 71 and 69 (pp. 171, 175 and 179) at 40 francs, 45 francs and 50 francs respectively but the dimensions given are 11 cms high and 23 cms long—half the size of No. 1527.

1528   Centaur and Lapith

Bronze, height 31.4 cm

Signed: *BARYE*

Reduced replica about a quarter of the full size of the model for *Un Centaure et un Lapithe* or *Thésée combattant le Centaure Biénor* commissioned by the Minister of the Interior in 1849. The plaster model was exhibited at the 1850 Salon, No. 3171 and a bronze taken from it in 1877 is in the Louvre (Inv. No. OA 67 22). The original bronze is now at the Musee du Puy-en-Velay. Small bronzes presumably similar to No. 1528 are first listed in Barye's 1855 Catalogues.[1]

Prov: Purchased by James Smith from W. B. Paterson, 1898; bequeathed to the W.A.G., 1927.

Ref: 1. Roger Ballu, *L'Oeuvre de Barye*, 1890 where these catalogues are reproduced; Nos. 15, 20 and 18 (pp. 170, 174 and 178) are "Esquisses du meme sujet"(i.e. *Thésée combattant le Centaure Biénor*) 35 cm high; 35 cm long.

BERTOS, Francesco, active 1683-1733

6597   Homage to Sculpture (?)

Gilt Bronze, height 75 cm

A larger version differing slightly from No. 6597 and not gilded, was in the collection of Lionel Harris.[1] No. 6597 is the only known gilt bronze by Bertos. The subject of No. 6597 and the precise meaning, if there ever was one, are obscure.[2] At the bottom are sculptors at work; supported on a pedestal decorated with broken columns, laurel and a ram's head appears the Rape of Dejanira by the Centaur Nessus who holds a snake in the form of a circle, presumably a symbol of eternity.

Prov: Paul Wallraf, who bought it in 1953;[3] Cyril Humphris Ltd., from whom it was purchased 1967 with the aid of a contribution from the National Art-Collections Fund.

Exh: Arts Council, *Italian Bronze Statuettes*, 1961 (201) Rijksmuseum, Amsterdam, *Meesters van het brons der Italiaanse Renaissance*, 1962 (195).

Ref: 1. W. L. Hildburgh, *Some Bronze Groups by Francesco Bertos*, Apollo, Vol. 27, 1938, p. 84, fig IV as *Sculpture*; fig. V is another group by Bertos entitled *The Drama* which Hildburgh plausibly describes as a companion piece to *Sculpture* but no gilded version of *The Drama* is known. The composition of No. 6597 is very characteristic of Bertos, see Hildburgh, *op. cit.*, L. Planiscig, *Francesco Bertos*, Dedalo, Vol. 9, 1928-9, pp. 209-21 and *Dieci opere di Francesco Bertos conservate nel Palazzo Reale di Torino*, Dedalo, Vol. 9, 1928-9, pp. 561-75.   2. See H. R. Weihrauch, *Europaische Bronze-Statuetten*, 1967, p. 430.   3. *Letter*, 7 November 1967.

BOLOGNA, Giovanni, 1529-1608, after

6156   Rape of A Sabine Woman

Bronze, height 57.7 cm

After the marble group in the Loggia dei Lanzi, Florence,[1]

Prov: Purchased from Alfred Spero, 1962.

Ref: 1. For the relationship between the marble group and the numerous bronzes after it see particularly H. R. Weihrauch, *Europaische Bronze-Statuetten*, 1967, pp. 218ff.

BONHEUR, Rosa, 1822-1899

6165   Recumbent Ewe

Bronze, height 10 cm

Signed (on base): *Rosa B.*

Stamped: PEYROL

The original, also cast by Hippolyte Peyrol, was exhibited at the 1848 Paris Salon (No. 4261 as *Une brebis, bronze*).[1] Hippolyte Peyrol edited all Bonheur's bronzes.

Prov: Purchased from Mallett at Bourdon House, 1962.

Exh: Mallett at Bourdon House, *The Animaliers*, 1962 (112).

Ref: 1. Anna Klumpke, *Rosa Bonheur*, 1908, p. 429 described No. 4261 at the 1848 Paris Salon as *Brebis couchée*.

BOURDELLE, Antoine, 1861-1929

4148 Head of Beethoven

Plaster, height 59.7 cm including base

Signed: *BOURDELLE sculp.*

A version of one of five variants of the fifth study of Beethoven made in 1901 in Paris.[1] These studies culminated in the large bronze bust of 1902 in the Metropolitan Museum, New York.

Prov: Bequeathed by Miss Dorothy Rimmer, 1953.
Ref: 1. Rhodia Dufet—Bourdelle, *letter*, 22 February 1961. For other variants of the fifth study see Musée Bourdelle, Paris, *Sous le signe d'Apollon*, 1959, Nos. 9 and 10; No. 4148 is very close to No. 9. For the entire series of Beethoven studies see E. Bondeville, *Beethoven et Bourdelle*, L'art et les artistes, Vol. 32, 1936, pp. 263-68, G. Chastel, *Beethoven et Antoine Bourdelle*, 1939, F. Poncet, *Beethoven, gestaltet von Bourdelle, Plastiken, Malerei, Graphiken, Zeichnungen*, Exhibition Catalogue Mainz, 1950 and M. Dufet, *Le Drame de Beethoven vecu par Bourdelle*, 1966.

CANOVA, Antonio, 1757-1822, after

4101 Self-Portrait

Marble, height 58.5 cm

A variant of the 1812 self portrait of which there are plaster and marble versions at Possagno.[1] Many studio replicas and students' copies are recorded.[2]

Prov: Presented by John Neale Lomax, 1877.
Exh: L.A.E., 1877 (1298).
Ref: 1. Elena Bassi, *La Gipsoteca di Possagno*, 1957, No. 214, p. 202 and No. 309, p. 275. 2. G. Hubert, *La Sculpture dans l'Italie napoléonienne*, 1964, p. 140.

4223 Cupid and Psyche

Marble, height 132 cm

A reduced copy of the group of 1792 now at the Louvre.

Prov: Richard Naylor, Hooton Hall Sale, Christie's 2-12 August 1875, (475) bt. Torr £85 10s 0d; presented by John Torr M.P., 1875.

CAVACEPPI, Bartolomeo, 1716-1799

6535   Girl before a round Temple

Marble relief, 73 × 68 cm

J. J. Winckelmann described No. 6535 as "einem der schonsten erhobenen Arbeiten aus dem Altertume"[1] but Ashmole[2] holds it to be a work of the late 18th century. A drawing nearly indentical to No. 6535 was formerly owned by the Dukes of Dessau,[3] heirs of the Prince of Anhalt Dessau for whom Cavaceppi worked at Worlitz. Blundell was also a considerable patron of Cavaceppi but he did not know that No. 6535 was by Cavaceppi[4]—if indeed it is.

The female figure in No. 6535 is nearly identical to the central figure in the *Borghese Relief* or *Woman with a Candelabrum* now in the Louvre[5] and the temple in No. 6535 seems to be derived from another antique relief *The Temple of Vesta* now in the Uffizi, Florence, which itself was restored by Cavaceppi.[6] The repairs in No. 6535 suggest that it was a deliberate forgery.

An avowedly modern extension to the right of No. 6535 showing an open door (also by Cavaceppi?) was removed between 1783 and 1809.[7]

Prov: According to Blundell placed by Pope Sixtus V in the Villa Negroni.[8] Bought from there in 1786 by Jenkins;[9] Lord Cawdor sold Skinner and Dyke 5-6 June 1800 lot 77 £118 13s 0d;[10] Henry Blundell: by descent to Colonel Joseph Weld who presented it, 1959.

Ref: **1.** *Anmerkungen uber die Baukunst der Alten*, 1762, p. 38. Following Winckelmann Carlo Fea in his 1783 edition of Winckelmann's works, *Storia dell arti del disegno etc. tradotta dall'abbate Carlo Fea*, III, pl. 18, p. 495 is no less enthusiastic describing No. 6535 as a work "che forse non ha l'eguale in bassirilievi" and "di una perfetta conservazione suorche la mano colla quale tiene la ghirlanda con un pezzo della stessa ghirlanda sotto e sopra e buona parte dei piedi". The Cawdor Sale Catalogue (see provcnance supra) stated that "This Basso Relievo was purchased out of the Negroni Collection originally formed by Pope Sixtus Quintus and is justly esteemed the finest specimen of ancient sculpture that has reached our times". James Dallaway described it in his *Anecdotes of the Arts in England*, 1800, p. 388 noting that it fetched 113 guineas at Lord Cawdor's Sale. By 1806 a cast after it was in the Felix Meritis Gallery, Amsterdam (see the painting of the gallery by Adriaan de Lelie of 1809 exhibited in the Council of Europe, *The Age of Neoclassicism*, 1972, No. 183, p. 119). Henry Blundell in his *Account of the Statues, Busts etc. at Ince. Collected by H.B.*, 1803, p. 178, No. 521 mentioned that "the elegant figure of the nymph etc. have always rendered this bass-relief very valuable in the eyes of the connoisseurs".   **2.** Bernard Ashmole, *A Catalogue of the Ancient Marbles at Ince Blundell Hall*, 1929, No. 304, p. 110 but Adolf Michaelis, *Ancient Marbles in Great Britain*, 1882, pp. 399-400, No. 304 believed most of No. 6535 to be antique.   **3.** William H. Schab Gallery, New York, *Great Old Master Prints and Drawings, 1500-1800*, 1967, No. 166, p. 143. The drawing is inscribed *Poussin*: it includes the undoubtedly 18th century extension of No. 6535 to the right removed between 1783 and 1809.   **4.** Blundell, *op. cit.*   **5.** S. Reinach, *Repertoire de la statuaire grecque et romaine*, 1897-1910, I, p. 58. Heron de Villefosse, *Catalogue sommaire des marbres antiques*, 1896, No. 1641, It had been discovered by 1664 for it is engraved in Pietro Santo Bartoli *Admiranda Romanorum Antiquatum*, 1664-7, pl. 75.   **6.** Guido A. Mansuelli, *Galleria degli Uffizi, Le Sculture*, 1961, I, p. 168, No. 143, who states that it was in the Villa Medici by 1670.   **7.** This extension appears in the engraving by Gir. Carattoni, drawn by Vinc. Dolcibeni in Fea, 1783, *op. cit.*, but not in the engraving by W. Skelton drawn by H. Howard in Henry Blundell's *Engraving and Etchings of the Principal Statues etc. at Ince*, 1809, pl. 123. Fea but not Winckelmann, *op. cit.*, realized that it was a modern extension.   **8.** Blundell, 1803, *op. cit.* Was he just misinterpreting the statement in the Cawdor Sale Catalogue quoted in footnote 1.   **9.** Blundell, 1803, *op. cit.*   **10.** Dallaway, *op. cit.*

6580-1 Posidippus and Menander

Terracotta, each 51 cm high

Both modelled by Cavaceppi from the statues then in the Villa Negroni,[1] now in the Vatican.[2]

Prov: Henry Blundell,[1] by descent to Colonel Joseph Weld who presented them, 1959.
Ref: **1.** (Henry Blundell) *An Account of the Statues, Busts etc. at Ince. Collected by H.B.*, 1803, p. 33 Nos. 69-70. **2.** Walther Amelung, *Die Sculpturen des Vaticanischen Museums*, 1908, II, p. 469, No. 271 and p. 577, No. 390, Plates Volume II, pl. 54; according to Amelung Menander is wrongly identified. These two statues were of great importance to neo-classical sculptors, see for example Gerard Hubert, *La Sculpture dans l'Italie napoléonienne*, 1964, p. 452 on Thorwaldsen who owned casts of their heads.

6628 Bust of the Younger Faustina

Marble, height 57 cm with base

A copy after the so-called *Younger Faustina* now in the Capitoline Museum, Rome.[1]

The attribution to Cavaceppi is made by Howard[2] and presumably No. 6628 is the *Faustina* listed in Blundell's catalogue as bought from Cavaceppi.[3] However Ashmole[4] found another *Younger Faustina* in the garden at Ince not now traceable and not traceable in Blundell's catalogue; No. 6628 therefore need not be the *Faustina* bought from Cavaceppi by Blundell; it no longer bears the number of Blundell's catalogue.

The only other copy of this antique bust certainly by Cavaceppi was sold at Sotheby's, 15 December 1967 by the Duke of Northumberland and is now owned by A. M. Clark;[5] others attributed to Cavaceppi are listed by Howard.[6]

Cavaceppi had also restored the original antique Capitoline bust.[7]

Prov: (?)Bought from Bartolomeo Cavaceppi by Henry Blundell;[8] by descent to Colonel Jospeh Weld who presented it, 1959.
Ref: **1.** *The Sculptures of the Museo Capitolino*, ed. H. Stuart Jones, 1912, pp. 198ff pl. 52, No. 39. **2.** Seymour Howard, *Bartolomeo Cavaceppi and the Origins of Neo Classic Sculpture*, Art Quarterly, Vol. 33, No. 2, 1970, p. 132. **3.** (Henry Blundell) *An Account of the Statues, Busts etc. at Ince. Collected by H.B.*, 1803, p. 74, No. 201. Blundell apparently believed this bust to be antique. **4.** Bernard Ashmole, *Catalogue of the Ancient Marbles at Ince Blundell Hall*, 1929, p. 72, Nos. 189 and 189a. Both Ashmole and A. Michaelis, *Ancient Marbles in Great Britain*, 1882, p. 371, No. 189, believe No. 6628 to be modern. **5.** It is signed: BARTOLOMEUS CAVACEPPI FECIT ROMA. **6.** Howard, *op. cit.* **7.** Howard, *op. cit.*, p. 131. **8.** Blundell, *op. cit.*, but see above.

6629 Pseudo Artemis

Marble, height 61.5 cm

Blundell conceded that "the head is modern but in a fine style," and notes that he bought No. 6629 from Cavaceppi[1] to whom the head together with the neck, forearms, torch and drapery at the waist, all of which Ashmole believes to be modern,[2] can therefore presumably be attributed. According to Ashmole the antique parts of No. 6629 would have been part of a statue of Aphrodite or a nymph which Cavaceppi changed into a Diana.

Prov: Bought from Cavaceppi by Henry Blundell, by descent to Colonel Joseph Weld who presented it, 1959.

Ref: 1. (Henry Blundell) *An Account of the Statues, Busts etc. at Ince. Collected by H.B.*, 1803, p. 62, No. 160.   2. Bernard Ashmole, *A Catalogue of the Ancient Marbles at Ince Blundell Hall*, 1929, No. 81, p. 34, substantially following Adolf Michaelis, *Ancient Marbles in Great Britain*, 1882, p. 358, No. 81.

6895   The Emperor Trajan

Terracotta, height 69.8 cm

Henry Blundell wrote of No. 6895: "This statue of Trajan in terracotta was modelled and gilt to placed on that interesting painted pillar in the marble room. It was modelled from the original statue[1] which formerly stood on that venerable piece of antiquity Trajan's Column in Rome etc."[2] Blundell's "interesting painted pillar"was apparently made by Cavaceppi and then "painted by an eminent artist"[3] from the reliefs around Trajan's column so that ultimately Cavaceppi could carve a reduced replica of that column but the project was never completed.[4] It therefore seems probable but by no means certain that No. 6895 was made by or under the direction of Cavaceppi. Certainly it seems to have been made in Rome in about 1791.[5] The left hand of No. 6895 probably once held a globe.

Prov: Henry Blundell; by descent to Colonel Joseph Weld who presented it, 1959.

Ref: 1. Blundell does not seem to have known that the original statue was lost in the middle ages. Or did he think that the 18th (?)century reconstruction of a statue of Trajan now (and then) in the Uffizi (Guido A. Mansuelli, *Galleria degli Uffizi, Le Sculture*,Vol. 2, 1961, No. 83, p. 82), to which No. 6895 is very close, was the original or a copy of it. The only authentic records of Trajan are presumably Roman Coins—see for example Anne S. Robertson, *Roman Imperial Coins in the Hunter Coin Cabinet*, 1971, Vol. 2, p. 24, Nos. 151-4, pl. 5. In 1788 Charles Percier published a reconstruction see Rome, Academie de France, *Restaurations des monuments antiques de Rome par les architectes pensionnaires de l'Academie de France à Rome: Colonne Trajane par Percier*, 1877, pl. 1 but Percier's *Trajan* is not identical to No. 6895.   2. (Henry Blundell), *Account of the Statues, Busts etc. at Ince. Collected by H.B.*, 1803, No. 82, p. 38.   3. Was the "eminent artist" Percier (see footnote 1) or Piranesi whose *Trofeo o sia magnifica colonna coclide di marmo ove si veggone scolpite le due guerre daciche fatto da Trajano etc* appeared in 1775. A much earlier publication of Trajan's Column was Pietro Santo Bartoli's *Colonna Traiana eretta dal Senato etc. scolpita etc. da Pietro Santi Bartoli etc.*, n.d., pl. 1 which has a reconstruction of the figure of Trajan fairly similar to No. 6895.   4. Blundell, *op. cit.*, No. 470, p. 163. The painted pillar is now apparently lost. It was carved in wood, and then the reliefs painted on to the wood see S. H. Spiker, *Travels through England, Wales and Scotland in the year 1816*, 1820, p. 317. Another such replica, also with the gilt figure of the Emperor reconstructed on the top but in a much more baroque style than in No. 6895 was made from 1774-1780 by Luigi Valadier, Bartholomaus Hecher and Peter Ramoser in Rome and was acquired in 1783 by Prince Karl Theodor of Bavaria; it is now in the Schatzkammer of the Munich Residenz; for full details see Hans Thoma and H. Brunner, *Katalog der Schatzkammer der Residenz Munchen*, 1964, p. 355, No. 1221.   5. MS letter from J. Thorpe in Rome to Henry Blundell, 15 October 1791: "No boat is yet ???? to carry away the Bacchus and the gilded Trajan" (Tempest Archives).

COUSTOU, Guillaume, 1677-1746

7241   Bust of Nicolas Coustou, 1658-1733

Marble, height 57 cm

A version of the terracotta bust now in the Louvre[1] which perhaps dates from about 1720-1730.[2] F. Souchal believes No. 7241 to be "une version contemporaine de la terre cuite exécutée sinon par Guillaume Coustou lui même du moins par son atelier"[3] but the possibility remains that No. 7241 is a much later copy of the Louvre terracotta; one such marble copy is now in the Versailles Museum.[4] Sculptor and sitter were brothers.

Prov: Bought at a Paris sale in about 1959 by M. Ambroselli from a lady eighty years old living in Lyons;[5] Heim Gallery from whom it was purchased, 1969, with the aid of a contribution from the National Art-Collections Fund.

Exh: Heim Gallery, *French Portraits in Painting and Sculpture 1565-1800*, 1969, No. 23.

Ref: **1.** Inv. No. MR 3520; it was given to the Musée des Monuments Francais in 1802 by Charles Pierre Coustou, grand nephew of the sculptor and sitter (A. Lenoir, *Archives du Musee des Monuments Francais* in *Inventaire générale des richesses d'art de la France*, 1883, Vol. I, pp.139-140): see also Lady Dilke, *Les Coustou*, Gazette des Beaux Arts, 1901, Vol. 25, p. 204 where the Louvre terracotta is reproduced.   **2.** F. Souchal, *letter*, 9 Febraury 1970.   **3.** F. Souchal, *letter*, 25 June 1969; Francis Watson and Terence Hodgkinson agree, letter from the latter 1 August 1969.   **4.** Signed *J. Nogaret de Lyon 1803*. Michael Levey however in W. G. Kalnein and Michael Levey, *Art and Architecture of the Eighteenth Century in France*, 1972, p. 361 believes No. 7241 to be autograph.   **5.** Heim Gallery, *letter*, 25 September 1969 and F. Souchal, *letter*, 9 February 1970; the Coustou family came from Lyons.

CRUNELLE, Leonard, 1872-1944

4538   Wisconsin Academy Medallion

Bronze, 7.4 × 4.9 cm, arched top

Signed: *L.C.*

Struck in 1920 to commemorate the 50th anniversary of the foundation of the Wisconsin Academy of Sciences, Arts and Letters.[1]

Prov: Presented by the Wisconsin Academy of Sciences, Arts and Letters, 1921.

Ref: **1.** For full details of the Medallion including biographies of those represented on it see E. A. Birge, *The Medallion of the Academy*, Wisconsin Academy Review, Special Centennial Issue, 1970, Vol. 17, No. 1, pp. 13ff.

DALOU, Aime Jules, 1838-1902

367   The Hunter

Bronze, height 63.5 cm with base

Signed: *DALOU*

Inscribed: *CIRE PERDU/A A HEBRARD/(3)*

One of the 10 casts from the model for a projected life size group for the staircases of the Chateau de Vallières; the group was commissioned by the Duc de Gramont in 1898-1900 but never executed owing to the death of the artist.[1] A smaller, earlier?, model for this group also exists at the Petit Palais (No. 192) and this too was cast in bronze by Hebrard in an edition of 10.

Prov: Purchased from A. Spero, 1956.
Ref: 1. H. Caillaux, *Dalou*, 1935, p. 148 as *Le Chasseur*; the plaster model is at the Petit Palais, No. 217, other casts are in the Barber Institute, Birmingham were at Mallett, Bourdon House, 1964, *Sculpture by Jules Dalou*, No. 78 as *Meleager* and at Sotheby's, London 22 June 1966, lot 71, 2 July 1969, lot 138 and 30 November 1972, lot 32. See also M. Dreyfous, *Dalou, sa vie et son oeuvre*, 1903, p. 242 for the *écorché* related to this group.

DANNECKER, Johann Heinrich von, 1758-1841, after

4224   Ariadne on the Panther

Marble, height 78.8 cm

Reduced copy after the original[1] formerly in the von Bethmann Museum, the Ariadneum, in Frankfurt am Main which was destroyed during the second world war.

Prov: Presented by William Adamson, 1904.
Ref: 1. Photograph No. 3476/12, Historisches Museum, Frankfurt-am-Main. For the original see A. Spemann, *Dannecker,* 1909, pp 67-73, figs. 59-61.

EPSTEIN, Jacob, 1880-1959

387   Bust of Albert Einstein

Bronze, height 43.8 cm

Signed: *Epstein*

The sittings for this bust at a Cromer refugee camp in 1933 are described by the artist; the sitter had just fled from Germany and the bust was not completed when he had to leave for Princeton in the same year.[1]

Many casts exist.[2] The first to be exhibited appeared at Arthur Tooth and Sons, London in December 1933 (not numbered).

Prov: Purchased from Charles A. Jackson of Manchester, 1948.

Ref: 1. J. Epstein, *Autobiography*, ed. Buckle, 1963, pp. 77-8.   2. The most extensive list is in the Tate Gallery Catalogues, *The Modern British Paintings, Drawings and Sculpture*, 1964, p. 168.

758   Israfel

Bronze, height 53.3 cm

Modelled in 1930 from Sunita whose real name was Amina Peerbhoy[1] and first exhibited at the Leicester Galleries 1931.[2] Epstein wrote of it: "taken from an Indian model but it is purely Greek in feeling (or at any rate seems to me to be so)".[3] Israfel, Israfeel or Israfil was the Archangel of Music in the Koran and is the subject of a poem *Israfel* by Edgar Allan Poe of 1831.

Prov: Purchased from the artist, 1940.

Exh: R.A., *United Artists Exhibition*, 1940, No. 1276; Bluecoat Chambers, *Contemporary British Art*, 1940, No. 100.

Ref: 1. Richard Buckle, *Jacob Epstein, Sculptor*, 1963, p. 181 with much information about the model Amina Peerbhoy on p. 141ff and on other busts and heads of her pp. 146, 150, 154, 170, 182-3.   2. *Catalogue of an Exhibition of New Sculpture by Jacob Epstein*, Leicester Galleries, February 1931, No. 2.   3. Jacob Epstein to Arnold L. Haskell, *The Sculptor Speaks*, 1931, p. 94. The curator of the W.A.G. in 1940, Frank Lambert, put this note on the Gallery files referring to No. 758: "?Head of figure from a projected group of Satan between two fallen angels." He seems to have known the artist quite well and may have recorded a remark made by Epstein.

898   Man of Aran ("Tiger" King)

Bronze, height 44.5 cm

The sitter, Colman or "Tiger" King was the principal character in Robert Flaherty's film *Man of Aran* of 1933.[1] Flaherty and the artist shared an interest in primitive races[2] and Flaherty brought King to Epstein's studio to be modelled,[3] probably in 1933.[4]

Prov: Bought in 1935 by Mr S. Samuels from the Leicester Galleries;[5] presented by Mr and Mrs S. Samuels 1956 in commemoration of the tercentenary of the return of Jews to Britain.

Ref: 1. Arthur Calder Marshall, *The Innocent Eye*, 1963, pp. 141ff with references to earlier literature on Flaherty.   2. Marshall, *op. cit.*, p. 187. Richard Buckle, *Jacob Epstein*, 1963, p. 200.   3. Buckle, *op. cit.*   4. So Buckle implies. The bust was first exhibited at the Leicester Galleries, March 1935, No. 14.   5. Leicester Galleries, *letter*, 10 February, 1956. A copy of the invoice is in the Gallery files.

1312   Sonia

Bronze, height 52 cm

Made in 1931 as a result of a commission from the Leicester Galleries; the sitter was Mrs Sonia Heath.[1]

No. 1312 is perhaps a unique cast as the sculptor sold the copyright in it to the Walker Art Gallery with the bust.[2]

The sitter was Winifred Cicely Stratford, born 20 June 1904, in about 1925 she married a merchant navy captain, Leslie Heath; for a time in London she was a model and did some film work; the sculptor apparently saw here in the Regents Park tea garden and was so impressed by her features that he asked her to sit for him; Cecil Phillips of the Leicester Galleries was however also a friend of the Stratford family; subsequently the sitter married succesively Major Reginald Oldham and a Mr Templer; she died at Hove on 14 August 1974.[3]

Prov: Purchased from the 1933 L.A.E.
Exh: *Jacob Epstein Exhibition*, Leicester Galleries, May 1933, No. 17 as *Sonja (Mrs Heath) 1931*. L.A.E., 1933 (1571).
Ref: **1.** Richard Buckle, *Jacob Epstein*, 1963, p. 184. Lady Kathleen Epstein, *letter*, 21 June 1976.   **2.** The legal documents are in the Gallery files. Lady Kathleen Epstein, *letter*, op. cit., however states that there was another cast—the original commissioned cast.   **3.** Mrs M. M. Bell, *letter*, 7 December 1976.

ESTE, Antonio d' 1754-1837 and LISANDRONI, Ferdinando

8777   Head of Anchirrhoe

Marble, height 32.6 cm

A restoration of the late 18th century[1] to the antique statue of Anchirrhoe[2] (now Merseyside County Museums), which was removed in about 1960 leaving the statue headless.

Prov: Bought by Henry Blundell from the Duke of Modena out of the Villa d'Este;[3] by descent to Colonel Joseph Weld who presented it, 1959.
Ref: **1.** E. Q. Visconti, *Il Museo Pio Clementino descritto*, 1782-1807, Vol. III, p. 73 who writes of the statue: "This very singular statue formerly was in the Villa d'Este where it had been very ill repaired; at present it is restored with elegance by Signors Lisandroni and d'Este, eminent and accurate sculptors" (Henry Blundell's translation in his *Account of the Statues, Busts, Bass-relieves etc. at Ince. Collected by H.B.*, 1803, p. 290).   **2.** Bernard Ashmole, *A Catalogue of the Ancient Marbles at Ince Blundell Hall*, 1929, p. 21, No. 37 with further references. The statue in its restored state is reproduced in *Engravings and Etchings of the Principal Statues etc. at Ince*, Vol. I, 1809, pl. 16 and in Ashmole, *op. cit.*, pl.23.   **3.** Blundell, *op. cit.*, p. 16 No. 16 referring to the whole statue; No. 8777 was probably made after the statue's removal from the Villa d'Este and from the Duke of Modena's ownership.

FEDI, Pio, 1816-1892

4226   La Fiorentina

Marble, height 155 cm

Signed: *PIO FEDI FECE IN FIRENZE NEL 1874*

Inscribed: *LA FIORENTINA*

The original plaster model was presumably in the studio of Pio Fedi preserved as a museum by his heirs in Florence but dispersed in about 1966.[1]

Prov: Presented by Colonel Bourne, 1877.[2]

Ref: 1. Sandra Pinto, *letter*, 23 July 1976, it was lot 78 in the artist's sale, G. Sangiorgi, Florence, 28 April-1 May 1894 as *La Bella Fiorentina, modele en platre de la statue executée en marbre pour la Russie*, lots 172, 242 and 246 at the same sale were other versions and variants, lot 172 a plaster reduction and lots 242 and 246 unfinished reduced marbles. **2.** U. Thieme and F. Becker, *Allgemeines Lexikon*, 1915, Vol. II, p. 337 give the wrong date, 1872, relying on the 1885 *Catalogue*, No. 199.

FIX-MASSEAU, Pierre Felix, born 1869

4118 Convoitise

Bronze, height 30.5 cm

Inscribed: (?) *HONWILLER-Fondeur*

Prov: Purchased from the 1910 L.A.E. (£16).
Exh: Paris, *Société Nationale des Beaux Arts*, 1910, No. 1811; L.A.E., 1910, No. 2345.

FONTANA, Giovanni Giuseppe, 1821-1893

4167 Bust of Charles Dickens

Plaster, height 73.5 cm

Signed: *GIOVANNI FONTANA/Copyright reserved*

Inscribed: *(on pedestal) PICKWICK/C. DICKINS (sic)/ALL THE YEAR ROUND*

Nearly identical to the marble bust of 1872, see No. 7601 below.

Prov: Presented by the artist, 1876.

4168 Juliet at the Window

Marble relief, 82.5 × 72 cm

Inscribed: *"WHAT LIGHT THROUGH YONDER/WINDOW BREAKS"*

The inscription and subject are taken from Shakespeare's *Romeo and Juliet*, Act 2, Scene 2.

The Art Journal recorded that No. 4168 "holds the central position and deserves high commendation" at the 1874 R.A. exhibition.[1]

A *Romeo* by Fontana was exhibited at the L.A.E. 1878 (1039).[2]

Prov: Presented by George Holt, 1874.
Exh: R.A., 1874 (1581); L.A.E., 1874 (1093).
Ref: **1.** 1874, p. 335. **2.** Photograph (Joseph Mayer Papers, Liverpool City Libraries).

4227   Jepthah and his Daughter

Marble, height 157.5 cm

Signed: *GIOVANNI FONTANA SC*

Inscribed with title

The subject is taken from Judges II, 29ff. After his victory over the Ammonites Jepthah promised to sacrifice whoever came to meet him—this proved to be his daughter.

Prov: Presented by Mrs Fontana, the sculptor's widow, 1898.
Exh: R.A., 1860 (953) as *Jepthah and his Daughter: "Thou hast brought me very low"*; Liverpool Society of Fine Arts 1860 (891) priced at £250.

7263   The Fairy Queen

Marble relief, 106.6 × 66 cm (semicircular top)

Signed: *G. FONTANA SC.*

Inscribed with title

Presumably the subject is Titania from *A Midsummer Night's Dream.*

Prov: (?)George Holt; found at Sudley formerly his house, 1969.
Exh: L.A.E., 1876 (1139) as *The Fairie Queen.*

7597   Bust of Thomas Wright

Marble, height 66 cm

Inscribed: *T. WRIGHT F.S.A.*

Thomas Wright 1810-1877 was an antiquarian and historian—for further details see the *Dictionary of National Biography*. See 7600 for the plaster version of this bust.

A bust of Thomas Wright—presumably No. 7597 or a version of it—was taken in 1881 from Mrs Wright's house to the Society of Antiquaries's Rooms in Burlington House, London (Correspondence between H. S. Milman and C. Roach Smith of September 1881, Mayer Papers, Liverpool City Libraries).

7598   Bust of Joseph Clarke ·

Plaster, height 59 cm

Joseph Clarke (1802-1895) was an antiquarian and naturalist. He was closely associated with the Saffron Walden Museum of which he was a trustee. He assisted Charles Roach Smith (see No. 7612) with the drawings for his *Collectanea Antiqua* and Joseph Mayer (see No. 7599) with the arrangement of his antiquities. Many of his letters to Mayer are in the Liverpool City Libraries. There is a long obituary in the *Essex Review*, Vol. 4, 1895, pp. 205-10. See No. 7608 below for the marble version (with arms) of this bust.

Exh: (?)R.A., 1866 (883).

7599   Bust of Joseph Mayer

Marble, height 59 cm

Inscribed: *IOSEPH MAYER*

Joseph Mayer (1803-1886) was a celebrated Liverpool collector and antiquarian. See the *Dictionary of National Biography* for further details.

7600   Bust of Thomas Wright

Plaster, height 69 cm

Inscribed with name of sitter (?)

See No. 7597 above.

7601   Bust of Charles Dickens

Marble, height 74 cm

Signed: *G. FONTANA SC. 1872*

Inscribed: *PICKWICK/DICKENS/ALL THE YEAR ROUND*

See No. 4167 above. On September 14, 1871 the sculptor wrote to Joseph Mayer: "I have already fixed (?) the marble for the Bust (of Dickens)" (Mayer Papers, Liverpool City Libraries) and No. 7601 was first exhibited in January 1872 at a lecture entitled *Souvenirs of Charles Dickens* given by George Grossmith of London at the Free Library Hall, Bebington and then permanently placed in that Hall (unidentified press cuttings dated 23 January and 2 September 1872, Mayer Papers, Liverpool City Libraries).

Earlier versions presumably exist because Joseph Clarke wrote to Joseph Mayer on 5 September 1870 (Mayer Papers, Liverpool City Libraries) saying that he was "hoping to see a cast of the bust of Dickens".

Exh: ?L.A.E., 1875 (1106).

7603   Bust of Joseph Mayer

Marble, height 64 cm

Signed: *GIOVANNI FONTANA SC. 1868*

Identical to the bust and head of No. 7822 below. See also No. 7599 for the sitter.

Joseph Clarke in 2 letters to Mayer of 26 August 1867 and 24 November 1868 (Mayer Papers, Liverpool City Libraries) refers to two busts of Mayer then being made by Fontana at the same time as No. 7822.

Exh: ?R.A., 1868 (1013).

7604   Jane Mayer

Marble relief, 56 × 42 cm

Signed: *G. FONTANA SC. 1872*

Inscribed: *JANE MAYER*

Jane Mayer, 1806-1892, was Joseph Mayer's sister (see No. 7599) and kept house for him—see Margaretta Byers, *Notes on the Family of Mayer*, n.d. pp. 31-3.

No. 7604 was placed in the Free Library Hall, Bebington in 1872 (Unidentified press cutting dated 2 September 1872, Mayer Papers, Liverpool City Libraries).

7605   Bust of Homer

Marble, height 54 cm

After the well known antique bust the best known versions of which are in the Louvre and in the Museo Nazionale, Naples.

7608   Bust of Joseph Clarke

Marble, height 84 cm

Signed: *GIOVANNI FONTANA SC 1865/211 King's Road/Chelsea, London*

Inscribed: *ZOOLOGICAL   SOCIETY   OF   LON-DON/VOL.4/BRITISH BIRDS/CATALOGUE ???????/HISTORIC SOCIETY/ARCHAEOLOGIA VOL.38/* (on books)

See No. 7598 for the plaster version and the sitter. There is another marble version in the Saffron Walden Museum, Essex.

7609 Bust of Thomas Reay

Marble, height 62 cm

Signed: *GIOVANNI FONTANA SC/KINGS ROAD CHELSEA/LONDON*

Inscribed: *THOMAS REAY*

Thomas Reay was a cutler and surgical instrument manufacturer at 8 Church Street, Liverpool; by 1864 he is listed as a Gentleman at 312 Canning Street, Liverpool. He was a founder member of the Historic Society of Lancashire and Cheshire.

7610 Bust of "Peggy"

Marble, height 81 cm

Inscribed: *AN OFFERING TO THE MEMORY OF PEGGY WHOSE ELEGANT MANNERS CULTIVATED TASTE AND AFFECTIONATE FRIENDSHIP MADE HER A DELIGHTFUL COMPANION IN MY PILGRIMAGES TO SHRINES OF ART AND ANTIQUITIES IN MANY LANDS BY JOSEPH MAYER F.S.A.*

Presumably the sitter was Margaret Harrison. See also No. 7640. Joseph Clarke writing to Joseph Mayer on 12 June 1866 (Mayer Papers, Liverpool City Libraries) saw "Poor Peggy" at the Royal Academy Summer Exhibition "a pleasing resemblance to her but nothing more." Perhaps this was No. 7610.

Exh: ?R.A., 1866 (884) as *Marble bust of a lady; posthumous.*

7611 Bust of Josiah Wedgwood

Marble, height 63.5 cm

Signed: *G. FONTANA SC. 1864*

Perhaps after the relief of 1803 by Flaxman on the Wedgwood monument in Stoke-on-Trent Parish Church, (so *Portraits of Joseph Mayer and his Friends* referred to below states, mistaking the medallion at Stoke-on-Trent for a bust). Another version of No. 7611 at the Wedgwood Memorial Institute, Burslem was engraved in E. Meteyard, *Life of Josiah Wedgwood*, Vol. 2, 1866, p. 615, fig. 153.

A Bust of Wedgwood the potter in marble by Fontana was No. 162 in Mayer's *A Selection from a Series of Illustrations for a History of the Rise and Progress of the Arts of Sculpture, Painting, etc.* 1871, (p. 11).

No. 7611 was in the Free Library Hall, Bebington by 1871 (Unidentified press cutting dated 4 September 1871, Mayer Papers, Liverpool City Libraries).

Another *Bust of Wedgwood* perhaps identical to No. 7611 was being made by Fontana in 1858 (MS letter of 7 September 1858 from the artist to Joseph Mayer, Mayer Papers, Liverpool City Libraries).

7612   Charles Roach Smith

Marble relief, 52.5 × 43 cm (oval)

Signed: *G. FONTANA SC.*

Inscribed: *C. R. SMITH F.S.A.*

Charles Roach Smith (1807-1890) was a well known antiquarian and collector. For further details see *Dictionary of National Biography*.

Fontana intended to despatch a medallion to Smith on 3 February 1857 (letter of 3 February 1857 from Fontana to Smith, Joseph Mayer Papers, Liverpool City Libraries).

7613   Joseph Mayer

Marble relief, 52.5 × 44 cm (oval)

Signed: *G. FONTANA SC. 1856*

See No. 7599 for the sitter. Casts after this or another relief of Mayer by Fontana are referred to in letters of 3 & 5 February 1857 from Charles Roach Smith to Mayer (Mayer Papers, Liverpool City Libraries).

7614   Clarke Aspinall

Marble relief, 59 × 46 cm (oval)

Signed: *G. FONTANA SC.*

Inscribed: *CLARKE ASPINALL J.P.*

The sitter, 1827-1891 was a solicitor becoming coroner of Liverpool in 1867 a post he retained until his death. He was a town councillor 1859-1867. For further information see W. Lewin, *Clarke Aspinall*, 1893.

7615   Thomas Dodd

Marble relief, 58 × 47 cm (oval)

Signed: *G. FONTANA SC.*

Inscribed: *THOMAS DODD*

Thomas Dodd (1771-1850) was an auctioneer and print seller. For further details see *Dictionary of National Biography*.

7616 Samuel Mayer

Marble relief, 56.3 × 45 cm (oval)

Inscribed: *SAMUEL MAYER J.P.*

The father of Joseph Mayer for whom see No. 7599. He was born at Newcastle-under-Lyme in 1767, carried on a business there as a saddler and carrier but also developed a pottery, was Mayor in 1833 and died there in 1838.

7617 William Upcott

Marble relief, 53 × 40.5 cm (oval)

Signed: *G. FONTANA SC.*

Inscribed: *WILLIAM UPCOTT*

William Upcott (1779-1845) was an antiquarian and collector of manuscripts. For further details see *Dictionary of National Biography.*

7618 Margaret Maddock

Marble relief, 58 × 45 cm (arched top)

Signed: *G. FONTANA*

Margaret Maddock was born in 1854 and died on 27 January 1871 (see *Portraits of Joseph Mayer and his friends* referred to below).

7619 Thomas F. Redhead

Marble relief, 52.5 × 42.2 cm (oval)

Signed: *G. Fontana Sc. 1881*

Inscribed: *T. F. REDHEAD D.D. F.S.A.*

Thomas F. Redhead was Vicar of St. Peter's, Rock Ferry—near Joseph Mayer's home at Bebington. In 1863 he published *On the growth of fruits: in a letter to Joseph Mayer* to encourage fruit growing in England.

On 10 September 1880 and in a(?) subsequent undated letter the sitter wrote to Mayer about his arrangements for sitting for Fontana (Mayer Papers, Liverpool City Libraries). The medallion was nearly complete by 24 January 1881 (letter of 24 January 1881 from Fontana to Mayer, Joseph Mayer Papers, Liverpool City Libraries) and was despatched to Mayer by 3 February (letter of 3 February 1881 from Fontana to Mayer, Joseph Mayer Papers, Liverpool City Libraries) Mayer paid Fontana £15 for it (Receipt dated 14 June 1881, Joseph Mayer Papers, Liverpool City Libraries).

7639 Memorial to Thomas Dodd

Marble relief, 79.2 × 71.3 cm

Inscribed: *THOMAS DODD*

For the sitter see No. 7615 above.

7640 "Peggy"

Marble relief, 51 × 41.2 cm (oval)

Signed: *G. FONTANA SCulp 1856, 11 Lower Belgrave Place, Pimlico London*

Inscribed: *PEGGY*

For the sitter see No. 7610.

Nos. 7597-7601, 7603-7604, 7608-7610, 7612-7619, 7639-7640 were part of Joseph Mayer's "Gallery of Friends"[1]—busts and reliefs of his family and friends most of whom shared his antiquarian interests.

Prov: (Nos. 7597-7601, 7603-7605, 7608-7619, 7639-7640) Joseph Mayer; The Mayer Trust (at Mayer Hall, Bebington); presented to the W.A.G. by Bebington Corporation, 1969.

Ref: 1. *The List of the Articles bequeathed to the Bebington Museum and Free Library by the late Joseph Mayer*, MSS Liverpool City Libraries lists Nos. 7597, 7599, 7600, 7601, 7604, 7605, 7609, 7610, 7611, 7612, 7614, 7615, 7617. The Mayer Trust, *Handlist of Drawings, Prints, Sculpture etc. contained in the Upper Room of the Mayer Hall, Bebington etc. bequeathed by Joseph Mayer F.S.A.*, n.d. lists No. 7597 (?as No. 208), No. 7598 (as No. 195), No. 7599 (as No. 190), No. 7600 (?as No. 208), No. 7601 (as No. 214), No. 7603 (as No. 202), No. 7604 (as No. 201), No. 7605 (as No. 194), No. 7608 (as No. 195), No. 7609 (as No. 216), No. 7610 (?as No. 191), No. 7611 (as No. 199), No. 7612 (as No. 209), No. 7614 (as No. 212), No. 7615 (as No. 192), No. 7616 (as No. 196), No. 7617 (as No. 215), No. 7618 (?as Nos. 200 or 213), No. 7619 (as No. 193), No. 7639 (as No. 211), No. 7640 (?as No. 207). *Portraits of Joseph Mayer and his Friends*, MSS Liverpool City Libraries, Hf 920 MAY has photographs of No. 7597 (as plate 21), No. 7601 (as plate 14), No. 7603 (as pl. 7), No. 7604 (as pl. 26), No. 7608 (as pl. 24), No. 7609 (as pl. 22), No. 7610 (as pl. 30), No. 7611 (as pl. 12), No. 7612 (as pl. 18), No. 7613 (as pl. 6), No. 7614 (as pl. 13), No. 7615 (as pl. 19), No. 7616 (as pl. 11), No. 7617 (as pl. 20), No. 7618 (as pl. 28), No. 7640 (as pl. 29). Frederick Boyle, *Memoirs of Thomas Dodd, William Upcott and George Stubbs R.A.*, 1879 has photographs of No. 7615 (as frontispiece) and of No. 7617 (as frontispiece to section on Upcott).

7817 Statue of Samuel Robert Graves

Marble, height 224 cm

Inscribed: *S. R. GRAVES M.P./FOR LIVERPOOL FROM 1865 UNTIL HIS DEATH IN 1873/ERECTED BY PUBLIC SUBSCRIPTION*

Samuel Robert Graves (1818-1873) was born in Ireland, settled in

Liverpool and became a well known merchant and ship owner; he was Mayor 1860-1861 and Conservative M.P. for Liverpool 1865-1873.

A meeting was held at the Town Hall on 22 January 1873 to discuss steps to commemorate his public services at which the suggestion was made that a statue of him should be placed in St. George's Hall.[1] The Graves Memorial Fund was set up on the 25 January at a Public Meeting held at the Town Hall.[2] The fund was to be raised in subscriptions of not more than 5 guineas each.[3] The fund had reached £200 by 18 February when it was suggested that a statuette of Graves should be presented to his widow in addition to the proposed statue in St. George's Hall.[4] The fund ultimately reached £2,450 and "a number of the most celebrated artists were invited to send in models in competition for the execution of the statue and bust" (the statuette). Ten statues and six busts were submitted in model and the selection took place at the top of the first flight of steps at the entrance to the Town Hall on 18 June. Fontana was given the commission for the statue G. G. Adams for the bust. It was estimated that the statue would cost about £1,000 and the bust about £250. The residue of the fund was to be given to a public charity. Fontana's model (and the completed statue) represented Graves as addressing the House of Commons.[5] The "bronzed design to be executed in marble" for No. 7817 was exhibited at the L.A.E., 1873 (1045). The statue was complete by 11 December 1875,[6] and the ceremony of the unveiling was performed by the Home Secretary, the Right Hon. R. A. Cross on 29 December 1875.[7]

Prov: See above, transferred by the City Estates Committee to the W.A.G. 1972, but still in St. George's Hall.

Ref: **1.** Liverpool Mercury 23 January 1873 (Town Clerk's Newscuttings Book, June 1872-June 1873, pp. 207-8; Liverpool City Libraries). **2.** Liverpool Mercury, 28 January 1873 (Town Clerk's Newscuttings Book, June 1872-June 1873, p. 209; Liverpool City Libraries). **3.** Presscutting dated June 19, 1873 (Joseph Mayer Papers, Liverpool City Libraries). **4.** Liverpool Daily Post, 18 February, 1873 (Town Clerk's Newscuttings Book, June 1872-June 1873, p. 235; Liverpool City Libraries). **5.** Liverpool Mercury, 19 June 1873 (Town Clerk's Newscuttings Book, June 1873-October 1874, p. 7; Liverpool City Libraries). **6.** Liverpool Mercury, 11 December 1875 (Town Clerk's Newscuttings Book, October 1875-November 1876, p. 44; Liverpool City Libraries). **7.** Liverpool Daily Post, 30 December 1875 (Town Clerk's Newscuttings Book, October 1875-November 1876, pp. 56-59; Liverpool City Libraries).

7822 Statue of Joseph Mayer

Marble, height 225 cm

Signed: *SCULPTOR GIOVANNI FONTANA*

Inscribed: *JOSEPH MAYER F.S.A.*

Liverpool Town Council resolved on April 3, 1867 to commemorate Mayer's gift of part of his great collection of works of art and antiquities to the Town Council (now in the Merseyside County Museums) by a statue in St. George's Hall.[1] The Sculptor was selected by the sitter.[2] Fontana submitted a small model on May 23, 1867 and was asked then to produce a few sketches.[3] Terms of agreement were approved on September 26, 1867. Fontana was to receive £1,000.[4] His enthusiasm was such that he got up every morning at five o'clock to kneed the clay with which he was building up the statue and his wife was reported to be "in such extasies that she says she will never want again."[5] Fontana was paid £250 on report of the completion of a large model on December 12, 1876.[6] A photograph of this model is now in the Liverpool City Libraries, Binns Collection, Vol. 30, p. 97. Mayer himself received reports on Fontana's progress from his friend, Joseph Clarke.[7] The status was cut out in the rough and the lower half nearly finished by November 24, 1868.[8] The work was almost complete by March 22, 1869 when Fontana asked for permission to exhibit it at the Royal Academy, or if he was unable to finish it by April 7 for permission to exhibit the model.[9] In the event he did not exhibit either.[10] The statue was finished by May 2.[11] Fontana brought the statue to Liverpool by June 17.[12] and it was set in place by June 23.[13] Both the City Architect, E. R. Robson[14] and Josiah Boult[15] noted that the statue did not suit the niche selected, the latter justly remarking "from the set of the head it is impossible to obtain a proper view of the full face without going into the orchestra."[11] The statue was unveiled on September 28, together with Theed's statue of the Earl of Derby.[16]

Mayer holds in his hand the deed of gift by which the Town of Liverpool received part of his collection, [17] whilst behind him on his right is one of the pieces of Egyptian sculpture which he presented.[18] See also No. 7603.

Prov: See above; transferred by the City Estates Committee to the W.A.G., 1972, but still in St. George's Hall.

Ref: **1.** Liverpool Corporation Libraries, Museums and Education Committee Minute Book 3 April, 1867 (Liverpool City Libraries). The Committee had proposed the statue at their meeting of 28 March 1867 as was reported in the local newspapers on 29 March 1867 (Joseph Mayer Papers, Liverpool City Libraries).   **2.** Letter of 17 April 1867 from Fontana to C. Roach Smith (Joseph Mayer Papers, Liverpool City Libraries), presscutting dated 4 May 1869 (Joseph Mayer Papers, Liverpool City Libraries) and *Illustrated London News*, 14 August 1869, p. 169. Fontana had solicited the support of Charles Roach Smith as "under the circumstances Mr Mayer could not propose for me," letter of March 30, 1867 from Fontana to C. R. Smith (Joseph Mayer Papers, Liverpool City Libraries).   **3.** Liverpool Corporation Library, Museum and Education Committee Minute Book, 23 May 1867 (Liverpool City Libraries). See also *Art Journal*, May 1867, p. 126.   **4.** Liverpool Corporation Library, Museum and Education Committee Minute Book, 26 September 1867 (Liverpool City Libraries); Fontana had previously suggested a price of between £800 and £1,000. Letter from Fontana to J. A. Picton, 19 April 1867, Liverpool Corporation Libraries, Museum and Education Committee Minute Book 25 April 1867 (Liverpool City Libraries).   **5.** Letter from Joseph Clarke to Joseph Mayer, August 26, 1867 (Joseph Mayer Papers, Liverpool City Libraries).   **6.** Liverpool Coroporation, Library, Museum and Education Committee Minute Book, 12 December 1867 (Liverpool City Libraries).   **7.** In a letter of 8 July 1868 Clarke notes that Fontana was working on Mayer's nose (Joseph Mayer Papers, Liverpool City Libraries).   **8.** Letter of 24 November 1868 from Clarke to Mayer (Joseph Mayer Papers, Liverpool City Libraries).   **9.** Letter from Fontana to the Gentlemen of the Committee of the Mayer Statue, Liverpool Corporation Library, Museum and Education Committee Minute Book 25 March, 1869.   **10.** He decided not to exhibit the statue for fear of damage. Letter from Clarke to Mayer 2 May, 1869. (Joseph Mayer Papers, Liverpool City Libraries) Fontana was already doubtful about exhibiting the statue for this reason in January. Letter from Clarke to Mayer 24 January 1869 (Joseph Mayer Papers, Liverpool City Libraries).   **11.** Letter from Clarke to Mayer, May 2 1869 (Joseph Mayer Papers, Liverpool City Libraries). The Town Clerk was instructed to write to Fontana requesting that he should keep the statue in his studio for a short time. Liverpool Corporation Library, Museum and Education Committee Minute Book 10 May 1869 (Liverpool City Libraries).   **12.** Liverpool Corporation Library,

Museum and Education Committee Minute Book 17 June 1869 (Liverpool City Libraries).   **13.** Liverpool Corporation Library, Museum and Education Committee Minute Book 24 June 1869 (Liverpool City Libraries).   **14.** Letter from E. R. Robson to J. A. Picton of July 22, 1869 certifying that the statue and that of the Earl of Derby by Theed were "securely fixed". Liverpool Corporation Library, Museum and Education Committee Minute Book 22 July, 1869 (Liverpool City Libraries).   **15.** Letter from Josiah Boult to Mr Samuelson 23 June 1869. Liverpool Corporation Library, Museum and Education Committee Minute Book 24 June 1869 (Liverpool City Libraries).   **16.** Press Cuttings (Joseph Mayer Papers, Liverpool City Libraries). A review had already appeared in *Art Journal*, June 1869, pp. 194-5.   **17.** *Illustrated London News*, 14 August 1869, p. 169.   **18.** Noted by Clarke when only at the model stage referring to it as a "priest". Letter of 8 July 1868 to Mayer (Joseph Mayer Papers, Liverpool City Libraries). It was a votive statue made for Amen-Neb given by Mayer to the Liverpool City Museums (Inv. No. M13503) but destroyed in the Second World War; it is plate 27 in *Objects of Antiquity from Ancient Egypt*, prepared for Joseph Sams, 1839 (Dorothy Downes, *letter*, 2 February 1977).

FRACCAROLI, Innocenzo, 1805-1882

4169   Venus of Milo

Marble, height 107 cm

Reduced copy after the late Hellenistic statue now in the Louvre. It was discovered in 1820 and entered the Louvre in 1821. The copyist was not identified when No. 4169 was presented to the Gallery.[1]

Prov: Presented by James Harrison, 1877.
Ref: 1. Extracts of the Libraries, Museums and Arts Committee of the Liverpool Town Council 12 August 1876 which gave "an anonymous donor through Messrs. Agnew".

FRENCH School, 17th century

6012   Leda visited by Jupiter disguised as a Swan

Marble relief, 22.8 × 35.5 cm

The present attribution was suggested by Ulrich Middeldorf.[1]

Prov: Presented to the L.R.I. by David Pennant before 1841,[2] presented to the W.A.G., 1948.
Ref: 1. *Letter*, 14 May 1976.   **2.** 1843 Catalogue p. 34. For Pennant see Walker Art Gallery, *Old Master Drawings and Prints*, 1967, p. 4.

FRENCH School, about 1700

6134   Helmet

Bronze, height 56 cm

Either a ceremonial parade helmet or part of a dismantled monument. Quite similar to, but probably rather smaller than, the helmet formerly at the corner of the destroyed equestrian monument to Louis XIV by Jacques Desjardins at Lyon.[1]

Prov: Purchased from Mallett at Bourdon House, 1961.
Ref: 1. The engraving by B. and J. Audran is reproduced in Ragnar Josephson, *Martin Desjardins*, La Revue de l'Art, 1928, Vol. 53, p. 173, fig. 3; the similarity was first noticed by Lorenz Seelig and Dr Jennifer Montagu.

FRENCH School, 18th century

6245 Cupid holding a laurel wreath

Bronze, height 44 cm

Nearly identical to a bronze[1] now in the Louvre which has, apparently, as its pair a *Hercules strangling the Serpent.*[2] A pair of bronzes corresponding in size and subject with the Louvre pair were in the Crozat sale of 1772 without attribution.[3]

Prov: Baron Alphonse de Rothschild, Vienna;[4] S. & R. Rosenberg (by about 1948); R. Fribourg sold Sotheby's, 28 June 1963, lot 158 (as Francois Girardon) bt. Peel and Humphris Ltd., from whom purchased 1964.
Exh: Peel and Humphris, *Spring Exhibition, Sculpture and Works of Art,* 1964, (not numbered).
Ref: 1. Musée National du Louvre, *Catalogue des Bronzes et Cuivres,* 1904, No. 238, p. 202. 2. Catalogue des Bronzes, *op. cit.*, No. 237, p. 201. Dr J. Montagu, *letter,* 27 November 1964 doubts that they really are a pair. Both bronzes were sent to the Louvre by the Garde-Meuble National in 1900. 3. *Catalogue des estampes, vases ... Figures ... etc ... du cabinet de feu M. Crozat, baron de Thiers, par P. Remy,* Paris 26 February 1772, No. 899. But J. D. Draper, *letter,* 8 April 1971, believes that both the Louvre and the W.A.G. *Cupid holding a Laurel Wreath* are by Robert Le Lorrain. 4. Rosenberg and Stiebel, *letter,* 31 August, 1964.

FRENCH School, 19th century

4422 Head of a Man

Marble, height 29.3 cm

Apparently a work of the 14-15th centuries, but probably a 19th century forgery.[1]

Prov: Presented by Professor J. M. Whittaker, 1946.
Ref: 1. J. G. Beckwith, *letter,* 25 October 1961.

6122 Reclining Ox

Bronze, height 17.8 cm

Prov: Mr Goldschmidt;[1] Arcade Gallery from whom purchased, 1962.
Ref: 1. Arcade Gallery, *letter,* 12 April 1962.

6131 ?Cat

Wax painted to simulate bronze, height 10.1 cm

Prov: Purchased from Alfred Spero, 1962.

6166 Baigneuse

Bronze, height 42 cm

Related to the marble *Baigneuse* of about 1767 by Christophe-Gabriel Allegrain now at the Louvre.[1]

Prov: Purchased from Alfred Spero, 1962.
Ref: 1. P. Vitry, *Catalogue des sculptures du moyen age, de la renaissance et des temps modernes*, 1922, No. 884.

FUCHS, Emil, 1866-1929

4228 The Sisters

Marble, height 66 cm

Signed: *EMIL FUCHS 1913*

The small reduced model for a memorial to Lady Alice Montagu and her sister Lady Mary Montagu[1] intended for Kimbolton Church, Huntingdonshire; it was commissioned by Consuelo, Duchess of Manchester, their mother, but never erected.[2]

Prov: Presented by the artist, 1913.
Exh: R.A., 1913, No. 2003 as *The Sisters*; L.A.E., 1913 No. 369 as *The Sisters*.
Ref: 1. They were twins and died unmarried in 1900 and 1895 respectively: see Burke's *Peerage* under Manchester.   2. Emil Fuchs, *Memories of a Court Sculptor*, II, The World Today, 1925, pp. 222-3 and *With Pencil, Brush and Chisel*, 1925, pp. 38-43. The artist was a close friend of Lady Alice Montagu.

GAUDIER-BRZESKA, Henri, 1891-1915

4112 Bust of Alfred Wolmark

Plaster painted brown, height 67.3 cm

Signed in monogram and dated *13*

Listed by the artist on 9 July 1914 thus:
Année, 1913, *Nature*, Al Wolmark, buste,
Matière, Platre, *Dimension*, 1½ fois nature,
Vente, Donné, *Proprietaire*, Al Wolmark
Addresse, 47 Broadhurst Gdns., Hampstead,
Remarque, Cubique.[1]

The artist apparently met Wolmark in 1913;[2] Wolmark painted two portraits of Gaudier in the same year, one showing him at work on No. 4112.[3] No. 4112 and the contemporary *Bust of Horace Brodzky*[4] are Gaudier's first "cubist" sculptures and mark a decisive stylistic advance.[5] A pencil drawing entitled *Portrait of Wolmark* by Gaudier-Brzeska was exhibited at the Tib Lane Gallery, Manchester, 1965 *Jacob Epstein, Henry Gaudier-Brzeska*, No. 27. There are drawings by Gaudier of Wolmark in the Leicester Museum[3] and Art Gallery, in the collection of Eric Wolmark and in the Southampton Art Gallery, all possibly related to No. 4112; see No. 4113 below for casts of this bust.

Prov: Alfred Wolmark: Philip Granville from whom purchased, 1954.

Exh: Allied Artists Association, 1913, No. 1217, as *Alfred Wolmark*. Allied Artists Association, 1916, No. 39 as *Alfred A. Wolmark* (lent by the sitter).

Ref: 1. H. S. Ede, *A Life of Gaudier-Brzeska*, 1930, pp. 196-7. For Wolmark see the Fine Art Society Ltd., *Alfred Wolmark*, 1970 and *The Times*, January 7, 1961. 2. Musée des Beaux Arts d'Orleans, *Henri Gaudier*, 1956, p. 12. The Fine Society Ltd., *Alfred Wolmark*, 1970 n.p. 3. Ede, *op. cit.*, p. 165; Ede states that one was in 1930 in America. The other is in the Musée des Beaux Arts d'Orleans (*Henri Gaudier*, 1956, No. 98, p. 30). A photograph of 1914 showing Wolmark with No. 4112 is reproduced in The Fine Art Society Ltd., *Alfred Wolmark*, 1970, n.p. 4. Exhibited at the Musée des Beaux Arts d'Orleans, *Henri Gaudier*, 1956, No. 13 from the collection of H. Brodzky. 5. See particularly Scottish Gallery of Modern Art, Edinburgh, *Henri Gaudier-Brzeska*, 1972, Nos. 19 and 20, p. 19. Richard Cork however in his *Vorticism and Abstract Art in the first Machine Age*, Vol. 1, 1976, p. 169 sees the *Bust of Horace Brodzky* as "cubist" but No. 4112 as "Copying the Romantic abandon of Bourdelle;" to the compiler both works seem equally "cubist". According to the Edinburgh catalogue these two busts caused an "uproar in the press" when exhibited at the Allied Artists Exhibition, 1913. P. G. Konody in The Observer, 13 July 1913, described No. 4112 as "frenzied cubism"(quoted in Horace Brodzky, *Henri Gaudier-Brzeska*, 1933, p. 106); Cork, *op. cit.*, p. 171 refers to the same unfavourable critical reaction in 1913 to No. 4112 and to the artist's other works at the 1913 Allied Artists Association.

4113 Bust of Alfred Wolmark

Bronze, height 67.3 cm

Signed in monogram and dated *13*

A cast of No. 4112 above. Six in all were cast, including No. 4113, by the Art Bronze Foundry (London) Ltd., between 1954 and 1960 using the lost wax process; of these one is in the Southampton Art Gallery, one in the York City Art Gallery and another in the Musée d'Art Moderne, Paris.

Exh: Edinburgh, Scottish National Gallery of Modern Art, *Gaudier-Brzeska*, 1972, No. 20.

GERMAN School, 16th century

6215 A Bearded Man, robed and in armour

Oak, height 165 cm including base

Probably made in Xanten or at least in the area of the lower Rhine early in the 16th century[1] and perhaps originally polychromed in a realistic manner.[2]

The figure bears the insignia of the Golden Fleece around his neck but Baxandall believes that he was intended to be a martial saint.[3]

Prov: Scarisbrick Hall Sale, H. Spencer and Sons, 29 November 1963 lot 66, bt. W.A.G. (with another similar but female figure (No. 6219) which was certainly a 19th century pastiche).

Ref: 1. M. D. K. Baxandall, *verbally*, 25 June 1964 and in a *letter* from J. Pope Hennessy 6 May 1964. The style of armour however suggests a date later in that century (Michael Clayton, *letter*, 8 February 1965 and A. R. Dufty, *letter*, 27 June 1974). Dr A. Schadler, *verbally*, 30 April 1968 and Professor Gert von der Osten, *verbally*, 23 February 1975, also suggest an origin in the lower Rhine for No. 6215 but Dr F. Grossman, *letter*, 10 August 1965, and Professor Peter Metz, *letter*, 11 June 1965, note strong Antwerp or at least Netherlandish influence. Certainly some of the woodwork for Scarisbrick Hall came from Antwerp and other parts of Belgium in the 1830's and 1840's as part of Pugin's re-modelling, see Mark Girouard, *Scarisbrick Hall, Lancashire*, Country Life, 13 March 1958, p. 508.   2. Dr A. Schadler, *op. cit.*, doubts this. There are no certain traces of gesso on the figure now.   3. Baxandall, *op. cit.* On acquisition the figure was carrying a sword in his left hand but this may have been a 19th century reconstruction. The cockle shells suggest that the subject may have been St. James of Compostella. On the other hand von der Osten *op. cit.*, suggests he may have been "an ancestor" analogous to those on the tomb of the Emperor Maximilian I in the Hofkirche, Innsbruck.

GERMAN School, 16th century, style of

7279   Dog Scratching its Ear

Bronze, height 5.5 cm

The most recent discussion of this type, and the most complete list of versions and references, is that of William D. Wixom.[1] The idea seems to have originated around 1530 in Nuremberg with revivals in that city around 1600 and in the 19th century.[2]

Prov: Purchased from David Peel, 1970.

Ref: 1. *Renaissance Bronzes from Ohio Collections*, Cleveland Museum of Art, 1975, No. 180. See also particularly H. R. Weihrauch, *Europaische Bronzestatuetten*, 1967, p. 286 and E. F. Bange, *Die Deutschen Bronzestatuetten des 16 Jahrhunderts*, 1949, p. 125, No. 84.   2. Weihrauch, *op. cit.*, pl. 343 illustrates the earliest type; Wixom, *op. cit.*, illustrates the type of about 1600.

HOSMER, Harriet Goodhue, 1830-1908

9117   Puck

Marble, height 77 cm

Signed: *H. HOSMER FECIT. ROMA*

Inscribed: *PUCK*

The first version is generally dated to 1855-6[1] and was certainly finished by 26 September 1856.[2] *Puck* established the sculptor's reputation[3] and some 30 versions are believed to have been made[4] providing a profit of over 30,000 dollars for the artist.[5] The *Will-o'-the-wisp* of 1858 was the pendant.[6]

The Crown Princess of Germany later the Empress Frederick is stated to have exclaimed on seeing a version of Puck in the artist's studio: "Oh, Miss Hosmer, you have such a talent for toes!"[7] A more conventional reaction is quoted by Carr:[8]

"This little forest elf is the very personification of boyish self-will and mischief. With his right hand he grasps a beetle, and seems about to throw it; with his left he presses unconsciously a lizard. In all the lines of the face, in all the action of the body, gleams forth the mischievous self-will of a being scarcely aware of the pain he causes, whilst rollicking in the consciousness of his tiny might.

What a moment of fun and drollery was that in which he was conceived! What delicious pertness in that upturned toe! It is a laugh in marble."

Of considerable stylistic interest as a flagrant departure from neoclassical principles by the favourite pupil of John Gibson.[9] It is however by no means typical of her work which remained broadly neoclassical. Hosmer's source may have been Sir Joshua Reynolds's *Puck* of 1789 now owned by the Earl Fitzwilliam.

Prov: Probably the version bought by the Prince of Wales (later Edward VII)[10] in 1859.[11] Kendal Museum; purchased from the South Lakeland District Council, 1976.

Exh: International Exhibition, London 1862.[12]

Ref: **1.** *Art Journal*, 1875, p. 312 says in or about 1855; Susan van Rensselaer, *Harriet Hosmer*, Antiques, Vol. 34, 1963, pp. 425-6 says 1855, Vassar College Art Gallery, Poughkeepsie, *The White Marmorean Flock*, 1972, No. 5, n.p. says 1856.   **2.** Harriet Hosmer, *Letters and Diaries*, ed. Carr, 1913, p. 76.   **3.** Art Journal, *op. cit.*, H. W., *Lady—Artists in Rome*, Art Journal, 1866, p. 177; Hosmer, *op. cit.*, p. 278 Rensselaer, *op. cit.* Vassar College, *op. cit.*   **4.** Lorado Taft, *The History of American Sculpture*, 1903, p. 205. Among them for the Duke of Hamilton (Art Journal, 1875, *op. cit.*), F. Dixon Hartland (Art Journal, 1875, *op. cit.*), the Earl of Portarlington (Hosmer, *op. cit.*, p. 123). A version was exhibited at the Boston Athenaeum 1857 (Rensselaer, *op. cit.*)   **5.** Taft, *op. cit.*   **6.** Hosmer, *op. cit.*, p. 123 repr. p. 222.   **7.** Hosmer, *op. cit.*, p. 343.   **8.** Hosmer, *op. cit.*, p. 343.   **9.** Gibson continued to preach neoclassical purity to her, see for example his letter to her of September 1858 quoted in Hosmer, *op. cit.*, p. 133.   **10.** A tradition to this effect still exists at Kendal Museum where both No. 9117 and a version of Hosmer's *Sleeping Faun* (of which the Prince of Wales also had a version see below) were exhibited until 1976.   **11.** The purchase by the Prince of Wales of his version of *Puck* is recorded by Hosmer, *op. cit.*, p. 343 in which she states: "I have no souvenir of another royal visitor, the Prince of Wales, but he has two of me, my *Puck* and my *Sleeping Faun*. It was during one of his first visits to the continent that he bought the former. He was traveling with Empress Frederic (then Crown Princess) and her husband, and just married. The whole party came to my studio, and the Prince was quite taken with Puck, and nothing would do but he must buy it. Afterwards General Ellis (then Colonel) told me the Prince was not allowed to make any purchases on this trip except with his own pocket-money, so the Puck came out of his pin-money!" This probably refers to the Prince of Wales's visit to Rome in November 1862, but in fact his *Puck* was already in his rooms in Oxford in October 1860 (Hosmer, *op. cit.*, p. 163) so it was probably bought during the Prince's visit to Rome in early 1859; for this visit see S. Lee, *Edward VII*, 1925, Vol. 1, p. 60 who records that the Prince met Harriet Hosmer while touring

314

artists' studios under the guidance of Harriet Hosmer's master, John Gibson. The Prince wrote in his diary for 24 February 1859. "After this we saw the Studio of Miss Hosmer a young American Sculptress who was working at a large model in clay of a statue of Zenobia which promises to be a noble work. The conception is very good, the attitude dignified and the idea of motion is admirably given"—the Prince Consort had allowed the Prince of Wales to make purchases of "different minor works" and £300 had been allocated for this purpose (Sir Robin Mackworth-Young, *letter*, 11 August 1976 relying on the Royal Archives quoted by the gracious permission of Her Majesty the Queen). The Prince probably also met Harriet Hosmer on his later visit to Rome of November 1862 (for which see Lee, *op. cit.*, p. 151) and Harriet Hosmer later confused these two visits and possibly a later one in 1872 (for which see Lee, *op. cit.*, p. 326). **12.** Hosmer, *op. cit.*, pp. 184-5. *Art Journal Catalogue of the International Exhibition*, 1862-3, p. 319 repr. and *Official Catalogue of the Fine Art Department*, International Exhibition, 1862, p. 144, not numbered.

ITALIAN School, 16th century (?)

9105   Bust of a Satyr

Bronze with marble base, height 59 cm

There is some resemblance to certain busts of Socrates.[1]

Prov: Henry Blundell;[2] by descent to Colonel Joseph Weld who presented it 1959.
Ref: 1. See G. M. A. Richter, *The Portraits of the Greeks*, 1965, Vol. 1, p. 114, No. 23, figs. 524-6.   **2.** No. 566 is painted on to No. 9105. (Henry Blundell) *An Account of the Statues, Busts etc. at Ince. Collected by H.B.*, 1803, does not reach that figure implying that No. 9105 was acquired by him after 1803.

ITALIAN School, about 1600

6236   Perfume Burner or Ink Stand

Bronze, height 23.5 cm

Similar objects are often attributed to the studio of Niccolo Roccatagliata.[1]

Prov: Purchased from Julius Goldschmidt.
Ref: 1. John Pope-Hennessy, *Bronzes from the Samuel H. Kress Collection*, 1965, p. 132, No. 486 with many further references; L. Planiscig, *Venezianische Bildhauer der Renaissance*, 1921, fig. 665 (to which No. 6236 is very close); Arts Council of Great Britain, *Andrea Palladio*, 1975, p. 60, No. 108.

6243-4   Pair of Candlesticks

Bronze, height 23.5 cm

Possibly modern imitations.

Prov: Purchased from Julius Goldschmidt, 1964.

L

ITALIAN School, 17th century

6532-3 Two Busts of Unknown Men

Porphyry and coloured marble, height 64 cm and 62 cm

"Said to be portraits of the two celebrated Roman Consuls, Marcus and Sylla" according to Blundell.[1] Ashmole[2] believes the busts to be modern and suspects that the heads are too. A set of 17 similar busts are in the Galleria Borghese, Rome, attributed to an unknown 17th century sculptor.[3]

Prov: "Bought at Roehampton out of the collection of the late Lord Bessborough by Mr T— (presumably Thorpe) April 1801";[4] by descent to Colonel Joseph Weld who presented them to Liverpool Corporation, 1959.

Ref: 1. (Henry Blundell), *An Account of the Statues, Busts etc. at Ince. Collected by H.B.*, 1803, p. 185, No. 542. Presumably he meant Marius and Sulla.   2. Bernard Ashmole, *A Catalogue of the Ancient Marbles at Ince Blundell Hall*, 1929, p. 80, Nos. 216, 216a. A. Michaelis, *Ancient Marbles in Great Britain*, 1882, p. 373, Nos. 216 and 216a presumes the two busts are antique and describes them as emperors or generals.   3. Italo Faldi, *Galleria Borghese, Le Sculture dal Secolo XVI al XIX*, 1954, p. 16, No. 11; the Borghese busts were described as antique as early as 1700 (Faldi, *op. cit.*), but J. J. Winckelmann, *Geschichte der Kunst des Altertums,* 1764, (1830), II, pp. 827ff described them as 17th century.   4. Blundell, *op. cit.*

ITALIAN School, 18th century

6526 Lion attacking a Horse

Marble, height 41 cm

A free copy after the Hellenistic group now in the Palazzo dei Conservatori.[1] If No. 6526 is to be identified with No. 543 in Blundell's *Account*[2] he believed it to be "a good specimen of the later style of ancient sculpture" and "found in the neighbourhood of Smyrna". Michaelis[3] however identifies No. 543 in Blundell's *Account* with the second engraving in Blundell's *Engravings and Etchings*, pl. 103[4] which is certainly not No. 6526.

A group of about the same size as No. 6526 but closer to the original appears in a conversation piece by James Russel in the collection of Captain David Tyrwhitt Drake.[5] Another similar group was at Rousham Park, Oxfordshire by the 1730's.

Prov: ?Bought at Roehampton out of the collection of the late Lord Bessborough by Mr T— (presumably Thorpe) April 1801"[6] by descent to Colonel Joseph Weld who presented it, 1959.

Ref: 1. *A Catalogue of the Ancient Sculptures preserved in the Municipal Collections of Rome, The Sculptures of the Palazzo dei Conservatori*, ed. H. Stuart Jones, 1926, pp. 249-50, pl. 96. For this theme see Basil Taylor, *George Stubbs, The Lion and Horse Theme*, Burlington Magazine, 1965, p.. 81ff who notes that Blundell owned one of Stubbs's paintings of this subject (still in the family collection, last exhibited in Russell-Cotes Art Gallery and Museum, Bournemouth, *Paintings from Lulworth Castle Gallery*, n.d. No. 14). Both the Palazzo dei Conservatori group, then in the Capitol, and another marble antique *Lion attacking a Horse* then in the Pitti Palace were very popular with 18th century English visitors, see J. and J. Richardson, *An Account of Some of the Statues etc. in Italy etc.*, 1722, p. 59.   2. (Henry Blundell), *An Account of the Statues, Busts etc. at Ince. Collected by H.B.*, 1803, p. 185, No. 543.   3. A. Michaelis, *Ancient Marbles in Great Britain*, 1882, p. 391, No. 274. Bernard Ashmole, *A Catalogue of the Ancient Marbles at Ince Blundell Hall*, 1929 apparently does not identify Blundell's No. 543 at all.   4. (Henry Blundell), *Engravings and Etchings of the Principal Statues etc. at Ince*, 1809.   5. See Ralph Edwards, *A Conversation Piece by James Russel*, The Burlington Magazine, 1965, pp. 126-7.   6. Blundell, 1803, *op. cit.* (if No. 543). No. 6526 was not at Bessborough's Sale, Christie's, 5-7 February 1801.

6534   Head of a Youth

Bronze, height 36 cm

Identified by Ashmole[1] with No. 169 in Blundell's *Account*[2] in which case Blundell believed it to have been found at Orvieto and to have come from the Negroni Collection. Ashmole however believes it to be probably modern[3] and Seymour Howard[4] suggests the studio of Cavaceppi as its origin.

Prov: Henry Blundell; by descent to Colonel Joseph Weld who presented it, 1959.
Ref: 1. Bernard Ashmole, *A Catalogue of the Ancient Marbles at Ince Blundell Hall*, 1929, No. 171, p. 67.   2. (Henry Blundell), *An Account of the Statues, Busts etc. at Ince. Collected by H.B.*, 1803, p. 65, No. 169.   3. Ashmole, *op. cit.*, A. Michaelis, *Ancient Marbles in Great Britain*, 1882, p. 369, No. 171 presumes it is antique.   4. Verbally, 1966.

6536   Bust of a Man

Porphyry and white marble, height 84 cm with base

The sitter was identified by Blundell as Julius Caesar.[1] Ashmole described No. 6536 as a modern porphyry head of Roman.[2]

Prov: "Bought in London at a sale of the Duke of Buccleugh's effects many years ago",[3] Henry Blundell; by descent to Colonel Joseph Weld who presented it, 1959.
Ref: 1. (Henry Blundell) *An Account of the Statues, Busts etc. at Ince. Collected by H.B.*, 1803, p. 52, No. 122.   2. Bernard Ashmole, *Catalogue of the Ancient Marbles at Ince Blundell Hall*, 1929, No. 144, p. 59. A Michaelis, *Ancient Marbles in Great Britain*, 1882, p. 366, No 144 quotes Bernoulli's opinion that the head is probably modern and states that the bust is certainly modern.   3. Blundell, *op. cit.*, The Duke of Buccleuch acquired much of his antique sculpture from the Marquis of Monthermer but Michaelis was unable to trace a Buccleuch sale (Adolf Michaelis, *Ancient Marbles in Great Britain*, 1882, pp. 93 and 126) and James Dallaway, *Anecdotes of the Arts in England*, 1800, pp. 337-9 does not mention No. 6536 in his list of the Monthermer-Buccleuch Collection.

6896   Torso and Head of a Nymph

Marble, height 22.8 cm

The wooden base bears the number 568[1] presumably the original Ince number.

Prov: ?Henry Blundell; by descent to Colonel Joseph Weld who presented it, 1959.

Ref: 1. (Henry Blundell), *An Account of the Statues, Busts etc. at Ince. Collected by H.B.*, 1803, does not reach No. 568 indicating that No. 6896 was acquired after 1803: Bernard Ashmole, *A Catalogue of the Ancient Marbles at Ince Blundell Hall*, 1929, p. 33 confuses Ince Nos. 568 and Ince No. 72 and effectively does not mention No. 6896 which he presumably regarded as modern.

6901   Bust of a Man

Marble, height 53 cm

A copy after the bust and head only of the so-called *Genius of the Vatican* or the *Eros of Centocelle* in the Vatican Museum.[1] See also No. 9109.

Prov: ?Henry Blundell;[2] by descent to Colonel Joseph Weld who presented it, 1959.

Ref: 1. Walther Amelung, *Die Sculpturen des Vaticanischen Museums*, 1908, II, No. 250, pp. 408ff, Plates Volume II, pl. 45. The original was found by Gavin Hamilton at Centocelle and bought by Pope Clement XIV. Napoleon I brought it to Paris.   2. (Henry Blundell), *An Account of the Statues, Busts etc. at Ince. Collected by H.B.*, 1803, No. 183 as a copy after the "Genius of Rome" in the Vatican.

6902   Children Playing

Marble relief, 24.8 × 69.8 cm

A copy[1] after an antique relief formerly owned by Prince Mattei in Rome.[2]

Prov: Henry Blundell; by descent to Colonel Joseph Weld who presented it, 1959.

Ref: 1. (Henry Blundell), *An Account of the Statues, Busts etc. at Ince. Collected by H.B.*, 1803, p. 87, No. 248 and *Engravings and Etchings of the Principal Statues etc. at Ince*, 1809, Vol. II, pl. 91.   2. R. Venuti, *Vetera Monumenta etc. Matthaeiorum*, 1779, III, 36, 1.

6905   Medallion with head of woman in high relief

Marble, diameter 28 cm

Probably described by Blundell as "Juno: This head is on a patera, in alto-relievo. It is modern, but the sculpture is good."[1]

Prov: Henry Blundell; by descent to Colonel Joseph Weld who presented it, 1959.

Ref: 1. (Henry Blundell), *An Account of the Statues, Busts etc. at Ince. Collected by H.B.*, 1803, No. 224, p. 79.

7491   Bust of Seneca

Bronze, height 31.5 cm

A close modern variant[1] of the antique bronze so-called *Bust of Seneca*.[2]

Prov: ?Henry Blundell;[3] by descent to Colonel Joseph Weld who presented it, 1959.

Ref: 1. Bernard Ashmole, *A Catalogue of the Ancient Marbles at Ince Blundell Hall*, 1929, No. 217e, p. 81, but A. Michaelis, *Ancient Marbles in Great Britain*, 1882, p. 373, No. 217e says "Antique?".   2. The best known versions are in the Museo Nazionale, Naples (Museo Nazionale di Napoli, *Guida Illustrata*, per cura di A. Ruesch p. 217, No. 879), and in the Uffizi, Florence (Guido A. Mansuelli, *Galleria degli Uffizi, Le Sculture*, Vol. 2, 1961, Nos. 9-11, pp. 26ff) J. J. Bernoulli, *Griechische Ikonographie*, 1901, Vol. 2, p. 166 calls it the *Pseudo-Seneca* and describes No. 7491 as probably modern.   3. The Ince number of No. 7491, according to Ashmole, *op. cit.*, is 572. (Henry Blundell), *An Account of the Statues, Busts etc. at Ince. Collected by H.B.*, 1803, does not reach that number suggesting that Blundell acquired No. 7491 after 1803.

9107   Bust of Apollo

Marble, height 47 cm

Despite modern restorations, particularly the joining of head and bust, No. 9107 is probably a modern forgery or imitation not an antique bust.[1]

Prov: Henry Blundell;[2] by descent to Colonel Joseph Weld who presented it, 1959.
Ref: 1. B. Ashmole, *A Catalogue of the Ancient Marbles at Ince Blundell Hall*, 1929, No. 145b, pl. 24.   2. No. 598 is written on to No. 9105 Henry Blundell's *An Account of the Statues, Bust etc. at Ince. Collected by H.B.*, 1803, does not reach that figure implying that No. 9107 was acquired by him after 1803.

9108   Bust of Venus

Marble, height 61 cm

Very close but not identical to the head and bust of the *Statue of Aphrodite* now in the Capitoline Museum.[1] Possibly No. 9108 is the modern copy after the antique head of Venus formerly owned by A. R. Mengs to which Blundell refers in his *Account*.[2]

Prov: ?Henry Blundell; by descent to Colonel Joseph Weld who presented it, 1959.
Ref: 1. *Catalogue of Ancient Sculptures preserved in the Municipal Collections of Rome*, ed. Stuart Jones, Vol. I, *Museo Capitolino*, 1912, p. 182, No. 1, Plates Volume, pl. 45.   2. (Henry Blundell), *An Account of the Statues, Busts etc. at Ince. Collected by H.B.*, 1803, No. 185, p. 69.

9109   Bust of a Man

Marble, height 59 cm

A copy after the bust and head only of the so-called *Genius of the Vatican* or the *Eros of Centocelle* in the Vatican Museum.[1] See also No. 6901.

Prov: Henry Blundell;[2] by descent to Colonel Joseph Weld who presented it, 1959.
Ref: 1. Walther Amelung, *Die Sculpturen des Vaticanischen Museums*, 1908, II, No. 250, pp. 408ff, Plates Volume II, pl. 45. The original was found by Gavin Hamilton at Centocelle and bought by Pope Clement XIV. Napoleon I brought it to Paris.   2. (Henry Blundell), *An Account of the Statues, Busts etc. at Ince. Collected by H.B.*, 1803, No. 121 as a copy after the "Genius of Rome".

9110 Bust of Livia

Marble, height 57 cm

Blundell wrote of No. 9110:[1] "This head is finely wrought; and though modern deserves a place among reputable sculpture."

Prov: Prince Mattei, Villa Mattei;[1] Henry Blundell; by descent to Colonel Joseph Weld who presented it, 1959.

Ref: **1.** Henry Blundell, *An Account of the Statues, Busts etc. at Ince. Collected by H.B.*, 1803, No. 164, p. 64. No. 9110 is also engraved in Henry Blundell *Engravings and Etchings of the Principal Statues etc. at Ince*, 1809, No. 145, 3 and is noted as modern by B. Ashmole, *Catalogue of the Ancient Marbles at Ince Blundell Hall*, 1929, No. 143, p. 59.

9111 Bust of Apollo

Marble, height 67 cm

Despite numerous restorations Ashmole[1] concludes that No. 9111 is an 18th century forgery.

Prov: Henry Blundell;[2] by descent to Colonel Joseph Weld who presented it, 1959.

Ref: **1.** B. Ashmole, *Catalogue of the Ancient Marbles at Ince Blundell Hall*, 1929, No. 145a, p. 60.   **2.** No. 597 is painted on to No. 9111; Henry Blundell's *An Account of the Statues, Busts etc. at Ince. Collected by H.B.*, 1803 does not reach that figure implying that No. 9111 was acquired by him after 1803.

9112 Bust of Otho

Marble, height 77 cm

The head has been joined to the bust and there are other small restorations. Despite this No. 9112 is an 18th century imitation or forgery[1] probably by B. Cavaceppi[2] probably after the bust now in the Capitoline Museum.[3]

Prov: Prince Mattei, Villa Mattei, Rome;[4] Henry Blundell;[5] by descent to Colonel Joseph Weld who presented it, 1959.

Ref: **1.** B. Ashmole, *A Catalogue of the Ancient Marbles at Ince Blundell Hall*, 1929, No. 86, p. 41, pl. 35.   **2.** P. F. S. Poulsen, *Greek and Roman Portraits in English Country Houses*, 1923, pp. 18ff and Seymour Howard, *Bartolomeo Cavaceppi and the Origins of Neo-Classic Sculpture*, Art Quarterly, 1970, Vol. 33, p. 128.   **3.** *Catalogue of the Ancient Sculptures preserved in the Municipal Collections of Rome*, Vol. I, *The Sculptures of the Museo Capitolino*, ed. H. Stuart Jones, 1912, p. 192, No. 19, pl. 49.   **4.** R. Venuti, *Vetera Monumenta etc. Matthaeiorum*, 1779, Vol. 2, 14, 1.   **5.** (Henry Blundell), *An Account of the Statues, Busts etc. at Ince. Collected by H.B.*, 1803, p. 42, No. 92. Blundell believed the bust to be antique and remarked: "Visconti, Venuti and Amadizzi always maintained this to be a real head of Otho."

9113 Bust of Nero

Marble, height 34 cm

Listed by B. Ashmole[1] as "probably modern" despite restorations.

Prov: Henry Blundell;[2] by descent to Colonel Joseph Weld who presented it, 1959.

Ref: 1. *Catalogue of Ancient Marbles at Ince Blundell Hall*, 1929, No. 158, pl. 35. Seymour Howard, *letter*, 12 July 1976, suggests an attribution to Cavaceppi.   2. Ashmole, *op. cit.*, states that No. 9113 is No. 136 in (Henry Blundell), *An Account of the Statues, Bust etc. at Ince. Collected by H.B.* 1803 and Blundell certainly did identify his No. 136 as a bust of Nero but No. 9113 is inscribed *142* and Blundell's No. 142 was identified by him as a Hercules.

9114 Bust of Bacchus

Marble, height 37.5 cm

Nearly identical to an antique bust now in the Palazzo dei Conservatori[1] and, despite restorations, presumably a modern pastiche based on it.

Prov: (?)Henry Blundell; by descent to Colonel Joseph Weld who presented it, 1959.

Ref: 1. *Catalogue of Ancient Sculptures preserved in the Municipal Collections of Rome*, ed. Stuart Jones, Vol. 2, *Palazzo dei Conservatori*, 1926, p. 126, No. 94, Plates Volume, pl. 43.

9115 Bust of Vitellius

Marble, height 32 cm

A modern copy[1] after the bust at the Museo Archeologico, Venice,[2] despite the extensive restorations in No. 9115. Blundell wrote of No. 9115: "This is a real portrait of that Roman emperor, as is proved from medals."[3]

Prov: Henry Blundell;[4] by descent to Colonel Joseph Weld who presented it, 1959.

Ref: 1. According both to B. Ashmole, *A Catalogue of the Ancient Marbles at Ince Blundell Hall*, 1929, No. 116, p. 50 and to P. F. S. Poulsen, *Greek and Roman Portraits in English Country Houses*, 1923, p. 19. Seymour Howard, *letter*, 12 July 1976, suggests an attribution to Cavaceppi.   2. J. J. Bernoulli, *Romische Ikonographie*, 1882-1894, Vol. 2, 2, pl. 5.   3. (Henry Blundell), *An Account of the Statues, Busts etc. at Ince. Collected by H.B.*, 1803, No. 144, p. 58.   4. Blundell, *op. cit.*, No. 9115 is engraved in *Engravings and Etchings of the Principal Statues, Busts etc. at Ince*, 1809, pl. 64, 2.

ITALIAN School, 19th century

4149 Bust of Michelangelo

Marble, height 56 cm

Formerly attributed to Canova.[1] Apparently a neoclassical derivation from the bust by or after Daniele da Volterra now known in many versions, the best perhaps now in the Louvre.[2]

Prov: Presented by John Neale Lomax, 1877.

Exh: L.A.E., 1877 (1294).

Ref: 1. See Exhibition Catalogue cited above.   2. E. Steinmann, *Die Portratdarstellungen des Michelangelo*, 1913, p. 64, pl. 62; or No. 4149 might depend on other derivations from this bust for example Steinmann, *op. cit.*, p. 84, pl. 82 or p. 66 pl. 64.

4221   Venus

Marble, height 157.5 cm

A copy after the *Medici Venus* now in the Uffizi, Florence. Attributed by the donor to Lorenzo Bartolini[1] possibly by comparison with his copy of 1816 after the *Medici Venus* now at Chatsworth, Derbyshire.[2]

Prov: Presented by Thomas Carey, 1874.
Ref: **1.** *Letter*, 9 September 1874.   **2.** Mario Tinti, *Lorenzo Bartolini*, 1936, Vol. 2, p. 36, No. XXVI.

LAURENS, Henri, 1885-1954

7192   Femme à la Mandoline

Terracotta, height 36 cm

Inscribed: 6/6 (on base)

One of an edition of six executed in 1967 by Jean van Dongen for the Galerie Louise Leiris;[1] the "Epreuve O" from this edition is in the Musée National d'Art Moderne, Paris[2] and the original plaster of 1919 is still owned by the Galerie Louise Leiris;[3] this original plaster was itself derived from a wooden *Joueuse de Guitare* also of 1919.[4]

Prov: Galerie Louis Leiris; Gimpel Fils Ltd. from whom it was purchased, 1969.
Ref: **1.** Galerie Louise Leiris, *letters*, 10 February 1970 and 20 February 1970. **2.** *Henri Laurens, Exposition de la Donation aux Musées Nationaux,* Grand Palais, 1967, No. 112.   **3.** Galerie Louise Leiris, *letter*, 20 February 1970.   **4.** Marthe Laurens, *Henri Laurens, sculpteur*, (1955), pl. V, p. 75.

LEONI, Leone, 1509-1590, after

6235   Bust of Emperor Charles V

Bronze, height 21.5 cm

Probably derived from the bust of about 1549 now in the Kunsthistorisches Museum, Vienna, Inv. No. 5504.[1]

Prov: Bought from J. Goldschmidt, 1964.
Ref: **1.** See Kunsthistorisches Museum, Vienna, *Karl V* Exhibition Catalogue, 1958, No. 63, pl. 37.

LEPAUTRE, Pierre, 1660-1744, after(?)

6155   Atalanta

Bronze, height 46.3 cm (including base)

Closely related both to the Hellenistic marble now in the Louvre[1] and to the marble after it by Lepautre signed and dated 1704[2] on the strength of which No. 6155 and a number of other similar bronzes[3] are associated with Lepautre's studio.

Prov: Alfred Beit; Otto Beit[4] sold Sotheby's, 7 October 1948, lot 103, bt. V. Korda £28; bought by the W.A.G. from Mallett at Bourdon House Ltd., 1962.

Ref: 1. *Catalogue sommaire des marbres antiques*, 1922, No. 522.   2. *Catalogue des Sculptures des Jardins du Louvre, du Carrousel et des Tuileries*, Musees Nationaux, Palais du Louvre, 1931, No. 33, p. 39. This statue is now in the Louvre but originally stood near the Bassin des Carpes, Marly.   3. For example those at the Rijksmuseum, Amsterdam. Inv. No. 1383, the Allentown Art Museum, the Musée des Beaux Arts, Dijon and in the collection of Jacques Fischer, Paris.   4. *Catalogue of the Collection of Pictures and Bronzes in the possession of Mr Otto Beit*, 1913, No. 295 as Italian 17th century; the Beit Inventory No. 295 is painted on the base of No. 6155.

LEVIS, Giuseppe de, active 1577-1605

6925   Bust of a Man

Bronze and marble, height 68.6 cm

Signed: *IOSEH / DE˙ LEVIS / VER. F / MDC*

The only bust—and indeed the only large scale figurative bronze—known so far by this artist who often cast to the designs of others.[1] C. Avery believes however that No. 6295 was both designed and cast by de Levis.[2]

Prov: Purchased from the Heim Gallery, 1969, with the aid of a contribution from the National Art-Collections Fund.

Exh: Heim Gallery, *Baroque Paintings, Sketches and Sculptures for the Collector*, No. 63.

Ref: 1. Charles Avery, *Giuseppe de Levis of Verona etc.*, The Connoisseur, Vol. 181, 1972, pp. 179ff, Vol. 182, 1973, pp. 87ff, Vol. 185, 1974, pp. 123ff, and Vol. 194, 1977, pp. 115ff, for full details of his career and works.   2. Charles Avery, *Bust of a Man by Giuseppe de Levis*, Liverpool Bulletin, Vol. 13, 1968-70, p. 23.

LORENZI, Stoldo di Gino, 1533/4-1583

6528   Mars and Venus

Marble, 51.5 × 39 cm

Although it has been suggested that 6582 is an eighteenth century neoclassical relief,[1] eighteenth century artists are generally more archaeological in their treatment of antique armour than the artist of 6528.[2] Further the poses are more openly erotic than in eighteenth century reliefs of similar subjects and the treatment is more akin to the spirit of the sixteenth century. Middeldorf first suggested that 6528 could be by Battista Lorenzi or Stoldo Lorenzi.[3] Similarities are closest with the latter's Holkham *The provinces of Tuscany paying homage to Duke Cosimo I*[4] and with Pierino da Vinci's *Cosimo I founding the University of Pisa and dispelling the diseases of the marshes around Pisa*[5], which Pierino left unfinished according to Vasari and Borghini,[6] and which Utz thinks was completed by Stoldo.[7] 6528 lacks the refinement of the work of Pierino himself and the modelling is coarser and more fleshy than in his reliefs.

Mythological subjects of the type of 6528 were popular in mid six-teenth century Florence.[8]

Prov: Acquired by Henry Blundell between 1803 and 1809;[9] by descent to Colonel Joseph Weld who presented it, 1959.

Ref: **1.** Most recently by Sir John Pope-Hennessy 21 February 1976, *orally*; a view also held by Charles Avery.   **2.** A. Norman, *orally*, 13 February 1976.   **3.** Professor U. Middeldorf, *letter*, 6 April 1976.   **4.** Hildegard Utz, *Pierino da Vinci e Stoldo Lorenzi*, Paragone, 211/31, September, 1967, pp. 47-69, fig. 52, citing in pp. 54, 65n.35, Raffaello Borghini, *Il Riposo*, IV, Florence, 1584, p. 608. A comparison suggested by Middeldorf, *letter*, 6 April 1976.   **5.** Utz, *op. cit.*, fig. 51,   **6.** Vasari ed. Milanesi, VI, pp. 128-9 and Borghini, *op. cit.*, IV, p. 476 cited by Utz, *op. cit.*, pp. 51, 63 n.16.   **7.** Utz, *op. cit.*, p. 56, who also believes that the Holkham relief was created as a pendant. Pierino died in January 1553 and the iconography of the Holkham relief suggests a terminus post quem of April 1555. For other reliefs attributed to and by Pierino see Ursula Schlegel, *"Leda mit dem Schwan" und andere Flachreliefs des Pierino da Vinci*, Storia dell'arte, 6, 1970, pp. 151-154 who p. 152 n.6 does not accept Utz's hypothesis with respect to the Vatican relief, and Hildegard Utz, *Neue Dokumente und Amerkungen zu einigen Werken des Pierino da Vinci*, Storia dell'arte, 14, 1972, pp. 101-123.   **8.** Hildegard Utz, *Skulpturen und andere Arbeiten des Battista Lorenzi*, Metropolitan Museum Journal, 7, 1973, pp. 59-60. Compare also the marble relief of a pair of lovers with dolphin, possibly Alpheus and Arethusa, from a fountain in the Bargello (Inv. No. 282), Utz, 1972, *op. cit.*, pp. 102-103, fig. 1.   **9.** 6528 does not appear in Blundell's *Account of the Statues, Busts etc. at Ince. Collected by H.B.*, of 1803, but it is engraved without attribution in the *Engravings and Etchings of the Principal Statues etc. at Ince*, 1809, No. 127.

MADERNO, Stefano, about 1576-1636, after

4134   St. Cecilia

Marble, 49 × 24 cm

After the original in S. Cecilia in Trastevere, Rome.

Prov: Unknown; probably acquired by the Gallery in about 1870.[1]
Ref: **1.** In the Collection by 1882; 1882 Catalogue No. 221, p. 49.

MARIA, Giacomo de, 1762-1838

6652   Death of Virginia

Marble, height 214 cm

Signed: *G D M. B*[1]

Carved between 1806 and 1810 partly as instruction for the students at the Accademia di Belle Arti, Bologna, the marble having been purchased by some citizens of Bologna anxious to improve the facilities for studying sculpture at Bologna.[2] The subject of No. 6652 was apparently among those set for the Premio Curlandese at the old Accademia Clementina in 1790.[3]

The sculptor wrote that No. 6652 was "one of the works of greatest difficulty that a sculptor can undertake since the multiplicity of points of view, the interweaving of the lines and the problems of execution turn out more difficult than in any other operation in sculpture. The marble is of perfect beauty, there being no marks which distract the spectator from the forms and expression, quite apart from such merit as there may be in the work.

The mass of this group is such that only with difficulty could the companion be found. In fact one frequently sees antique statues but rarely groups and even more rarely of this size."[4]

The full size plaster for No. 6652 is still in the Accademia delle Belle Arti, Bologna (No. 3332) and impressions of the engravings after it drawn by G. dalla Valle and engraved by Francesco Rosaspina are in the W.A.G.[5]

Prov: Seen by a Mr Starkie in Bologna in 1819 and purchased by him for 740 Louis d'Or;[6] shipped from Trieste to Liverpool 1820;[6] purchased from G. P. Le G. Starkie of Huntroyde Hall, Burnley, 1968

Ref: 1. Presumably stands for Giacomo de Maria bolognese.   2. L. Sighinolfi, *Commemorazione del celebre scultore Giacomo de Maria*, Atti e Memorie della Reale Accademia Clementina, Vol. III, 1938-41, pp. 33 and 37; Sighinolfi only implies the dates 1806-1810 and he also states *op. cit.*, p. 38 that Suvorov nearly bought the group when he was in Bologna during his successful campaign in Italy of 1799 implying that drawings at least existed by then; the conception of No. 6652 was closely connected with Napoleon's encouragement to Italian artists and particularly teachers of art to exhibit in public (Sighinolfi, *op. cit.*, p. 33)—for these exhibitions see Gerard Hubert, *La Sculpture dans L'Italie napoléonienne*, 1964, pp. 247ff. Adamo Tadolini was helping the sculptor with the plaster model for No. 6652 in the plaster model for No. 6652 see his *Ricordi Autobiographici*, 1900, pp. 17-18.   3. Sighinolfi, *op. cit.*, p. 34. The prize had been instituted by Duke Peter of Courland in the late 1780's. Pietro Fancelli's painting *The Death of Virginia* (now Collezioni Comunale d'Arte di Bologna) was awarded a prize in the 1791 Concorso Curlandese see Guido Zucchini *Catalogo delle Collezioni Comunali d'Arte di Bologna*, 1938, p. 136. Was the subject politically inspired? Like Canova de Maria does not seem to have had any specific political affiliation. De Maria's low relief *Brutus Condemns his Sons* of about 1810 is in the Sala Vidoniana, Palazzo del Comune (Zucchini, *op. cit.*, p. 60).   4. Quoted in Sighinolfi, *op. cit.*, p. 38.   5. They are undated and G. dalla Valle has not been identified; the engravings were presented to the Gallery by G. P. le G. Starkie, 1968, see p. 431.   6. Sighinolfi, *op. cit.*, p. 38. This Mr Starkie was presumably Le Gendre Starkie of Huntroyde Hall, 1790-1822. For the whole family see Burke's *Landed Gentry*. Letters from the Starkie Family in Italy 1818-1819 are now in the Kent Country Record Office, Maidstone (U908 C80/6-9, C84/1-7, U980 C79/2-6); No. 6652 does not seem to be mentioned but Le Gendre Pierce Starkie (born 1796), Le Gendre's younger brother, wrote to his sister Charlotte on 6 June 1818 and 30 May 1819 revealing that he was in Bologna 25-27 May 1818 and in early May 1819 (U908 C80/7 and 9) (Felix Hull, *letter*, 29 March 1977). The group presumably went straight from Liverpool to Huntroyde Hall; Sighinolfi states incorrectly that it "dominated a Liverpool square," it is listed in the Huntroyde Hall inventory of 1877 prepared by Agnew's of Manchester.

MENE, Pierre Jules, 1810-1879

6168   (?)Two Pointers

Bronze, height 25 cm

Signed: *P. J. Mene*

Apparently a cast of No. 57, *Groupe Chiens au Repos (Race Saint-*

ongeoise), in the catalogues issued by the artist from rue de l'Entrepot from 1857 onwards.[1]

The title is traditional; the dogs are probably from a breed of early French Pointers, the modern equivalent of which would be the Braque d'Auvergne.[2]

Prov: Purchased from Mallett at Bourdon House, 1962.
Exh: ?Paris Salon, 1857, as No. 5009, *Chiens Anglais.*
Ref: 1. According to Jane Horswell, *Bronze sculpture of Les Animaliers*, 1971, p. 141. The *Race Saintongeoise* was a type of bloodhound now extinct. 2. The Kennel Club, *letter*, 15 May 1974.

MOZIER, Joseph, 1812-1870

7607 Bust of a Woman

Marble, height 58 cm

Signed: *J. Mozier Sc Florence 1850*

Probably a version of the *Star Gem'd Aurora*—another version or possibly No. 7607 was exhibited at the National Academy of Design, New York in 1850.[1]

Prov: ?Joseph Mayer; presented by Bebington Corporation, 1971.
Ref: 1. No. 7 lent by Ogden Haggerty (R. P. Wunder, *letter*, 18 August 1976).

NEUJD, Axel Herman, 1872-1931

4123 The Picture Book

Bronze, height 21.6 cm

Signed: *H. NEUJD / 05*

Prov: Purchased from the artist 1912 (£15).
Exh: Stockholm, April 1906, *Gunnar Hallstrom, Oskar Hullgren, John. E. Osterlund, Herman Neujd,* No. 11 as *Bilderboken;* Norkoping 1906, *Konst Utstallningen i Konst och Industri Utstallningen*, No. 331; Stockholm, May 1908, *Bror Hillgren, Herman Neujd, Werner Sundblad, Gusten Widerback, Mathilde Wigert-Osterlund, John Osterlund*, No. 38. L.A.E., 1911 (2420).

NIMPTSCH, Uli, 1897-1977

2630 Olympia

Bronze, height 58.5 cm

Signed: *UN* (under left foot)

The first cast, now in the Tate Gallery, was made in 1956,[1] the artist having worked on the figure from 1953 until 1956.[2] The wax is still in the artist's possession.[3]

Prov: Purchased 1957 from the artist with contributions from the P. H. Holt Trust and Lord Cohen of Birkenhead.

Ref: 1. It was exhibited at the Royal Academy 1957 (1468) as *Reclining Figure*. The new title for No. 2630 has no significance (Uli Nimptsch, *letter*, 12 May 1974). 2. Tate Gallery Catalogues, *The Modern British Paintings, Drawings and Sculpture*, 1964, p. 492. 3. It is reproduced on the cover of W.A.G., Liverpool, *Sculpture by Uli Nimptsch*, 1957. The artist apparently agreed with the Tate Gallery in 1957 that only six or perhaps four casts from this wax were to be made (Uli Nimptsch, *letter, op. cit.* and MSS insurance list for W.A.G., *Sculpture by Uli Nimptsch*, 1957).

NORTH ITALIAN School, 16th century

6362 The Virgin teaching the Infant Christ to read

Marble, height 41 cm

Attributed by John Pope-Hennessy to Antonio Perolo.[1] For the subject see Louis Reau, *Iconographie de l'Art Chrétien*, 1957, II, II, pp. 284-5.

Prov: Sir Thomas Barlow; Alfred Spero from whom purchased, 1966.

Ref: 1. Letter 25 May 1966 on the basis of the signed relief, the *Virgin and Child*, dated 1521 in the Castello Sforzesco, Milan (S. Vigezzi, *La Scultura in Milano*, 1934, Vol. I, pp. 184-5, No. 589, Vol. II pl. XXX).

6561 Virgin and Child

Terracotta, painted brown, height 112 cm

An attribution to Alfonso Lombardi was made by Roberto Longhi[1] in about 1964 but Antonio Begarelli[2] seems a no less probable candidate for No. 6561.

Prov: A "vecchia casa bolognese";[3] Swiss Private Collection;[4] Heim Gallery from whom purchased,1967.

Ref: 1. Heim Gallery, *letter*, 21 March 1967. 2. See Gino Magnani, *Antonio Begarelli*, 1930, particularly p. 30 for the group in S. Domenico, Modena, *Christ in the house of Martha and Mary with Lazarus* etc. attributed by Vasari to Begarelli (*Opere*, ed. Milanesi, Vol. 6, 1881, p. 483). 3. Heim Gallery, *letter, op. cit.* 4. Heim Gallery, *letter, op. cit.*

PARTRIDGE, William Ordway, 1861-1930

8230 Bust of George Washington

Bronze, height 48 cm

Signed: *ORDWAY PARTRIDGE SC*

Inscribed: *THE HENRY BONNARD BRONZE CO/MT. VERNON. N.Y./U.S.A./U.S.A.*

Based on the bust of 1785 by Jean Antoine Houdon.[1]

Prov: Liverpool Town Hall; transferred to the Gallery, 1972.
Ref: 1. Louis Reau, *Houdon*, 1964, I, pp, 405-6, II, No. 204, p. 46.

PESCI, Ottilio, born 1877

6167 Portrait of a man

Bronze, height 51.7 cm

Signed: *Ottilio Pesci / Paris 1912 + 1*

Inscribed: *C. VALSUANI . Cire Perdue*

Prov: Purchased from Alfred Spero, 1962.

PINEAU, Ludovic

4202 Tristesse

Bronze, height 71.1 cm

Signed: *L^{vic} PINEAU*

Prov: Presented by Mrs J. R. Logan, 1933.

PIRANESI, Giovanni Battista, 1720-1778, reworked by

6527 Antique Vase

Marble, 64 cm (height) × 47 cm (diameter)

"Found in a cave near Monticelli in the Sabine Country and was so much decayed and corroded that it was necessary to re-work several parts and new polish the figures; this gave it the appearance of being modern which lessens much the value of it. It was bought from Volpato; the pedestal and repairs by Piranesi."[1] The pedestal is still at Ince Blundell, on the lawn.

Prov: Bought by Henry Blundell from Giovanni Volpato; by descent to Colonel Joseph Weld who presented it, 1959.
Ref: 1. (Henry Blundell), *An Account of the Statues, Busts etc. at Ince. Collected by H.B.*, 1803, pp. 91-2, No. 270. Bernard Ashmole *A Catalogue of the Ancient Marbles at Ince Blundell Hall*, 1929, p. 121, No. 404 says "entirely reworked." No. 6527 does not appear in Piranesi's *Vasi, Candelabri, etc.*

RAUCH, Christian Daniel, 1777-1857, after

4206 Bust of Alexander von Humboldt

Marble, height 53.3 cm

Inscribed with the sitter's name

After the bust of 1823;[1] the original plaster cast was at the Rauch Museum, Schloss Charlottenburg, Berlin (No. 191) and is now with the Skulpturenabteilung of the Staatliche Museen, Berlin. On entry into the collection No. 4206 was listed as by R. Willig; perhaps this was an error for Richard Willis[2] or for Hermann Wittig[3] or August Wittig[4] any of whom may have executed No. 4206 after Rauch.

Prov: Bequeathed by A. H. Lemonius, 1898.
Ref: **1.** F. and K. Eggers, *Christian Daniel Rauch*, 1873-1891, Vol. 2, pp. 231ff, 236, 294, Vol. 4, pp. 43, 285, Vol. 5 pp. 48, 87, pl. 41. **2.** A. Graves, *The Royal Academy of Arts A Complete Dictionary of Contributors*, 1906, Vol. 8, p. 300. **3.** As assumed in Ulrich Thieme and Felix Becker, *Allgemeines Lexikon*, 1947, Vol. 36, p. 138. **4.** August Wittig did work with Rauch see Eggers, *op. cit.*, Vol. 3, p. 310, Vol. 4, pp. 46, 179, 338.

6961 Bust of Heinrich Wilhelm Mattaus Olbers (1758-1840)

Plaster, height 66.8 cm

The original of 1830-1 is in the University Library, Bremen.[1]

Prov: Presented by ?Focke to the L.R.I., 11 February 1839;[2] presented to the W.A.G., 1969.
Ref: **1.** Dr. Wolfgang Kruger, *letter*, 21 November 1975. See also F. and K. Eggers, *Christian Daniel Rauch*, 1873-91, Vol. 3, p. 56 and Vol. 5, pp. 58 and 176. **2.** *Presents Book*, L.R.I. Archives 37.

RENOIR, Pierre Auguste, 1841-1919

3175 The Little Blacksmith

Bronze, height 33 cm

Inscribed: *CIRE / VALSUANI / PERDUE*

One of an edition of ten cast by Valsuani for Renou and Poyet apparently in 1953-4 after a plaster then owned by the Renoir family.[1]

A number of plasters and one terracotta of this subject—apparently varying slightly among themselves—were made in 1916 by Richard Guino working under Renoir's direction.[2] Presumably No. 3175 was cast from one of these plasters.

No. 3175 can also be entitled *Fire* or *The Young Shepherd*.[3]

Prov: Purchased from Alex Reid and Lefevre[4] by Morton Oliphant, 1955; presented by
        him, 1955.
Ref: 1. Alex Reid and Lefevre, *letter*, 24 January 1955 and Renou and Poyet, *letter*, 15
        February 1954. The Renoir Collectors Mark, Lugt 2137b appears inside No.
        3175   2. Julius Meier—Graefe, *Renoir*, 1929, pp. 396–7; Paul Haesaerts,
        Renoir Sculptor, 1947, pp. 30-31, 42. One of these plasters, not the one used for
        No. 3175 but presumably the *Recherches de Sculpture* reproduced in Ambroise
        Vollard, *Tableaux, Pastels et Dessins de Pierre Auguste Renoir*, 1918, Vol. I, Nos.
        446-7, p. 112, was cast by Vollard in 1916—a cast is reproduced in Meier—
        Graefe, *op. cit., pp.* 406-17 and in W. George, *L'Oeuvre Sculpté de Renoir*,
        L'Amour de l'Art, 1924, p. 339 while further details are given in V. E. Johnson,
        Ambroise Vollard editeur, 1944, pp. 133-4; another of these plasters is repro-
        duced in Haesaerts, *op. cit.*, pl. XXVIII, XXIX, and XLIII. In the 1960's Guino
        claimed a considerable part in the conception of these works; his claim was not
        generally accepted see *L'affaire Guino*, Gazette des Beaux Arts (Chronique des
        Arts), April 1974, Vol. 83, p. 5.   3. Haesaerts, *op. cit.*, p. 42. Its pair was called
        Water or *The Stooping Washerwoman* or *The Small Bather*, see Haesaerts, *op.
        cit.*, p. 42, Nos. 20-21.   4. Alex Reid and Lefevre bought the entire edition
        from Renou and Poyet, letter from the former, *op. cit.*

RICHE, Louis, born 1877

3174   Cat

Marble painted black, apparently formerly painted grey,[1] height 27 cm

Signed: *L. RICHE*

Prov: Purchased from the 1907 L.A.E. £20.
Exh: Paris, *Société des artistes francais*, 1907, No. 3305 as *Etude de chat*; L.A.E., 1907,
        No. 1924 as *Etude de chat*.
Ref: 1. Described as marble in the L.A.E. Catalogue cited above and as grey marble in
        the 1927 Catalogue p. 154.

RINALDI, Rinaldo, 1793-1873

4107   The Parable of the Wise and Foolish Virgins

Marble, height 172 cm

Signed: *R. Rinaldi f/Roma 1855*

Unfavourably reviewed by the Art Journal critic, who had presumably
seen an earlier version, thus: " . . . struck me as a decided failure in point
of conception. It is no study of the Bible parable; there is neither haste nor
dignity nor indignation in the action of the wise virgin, rising up in haste to
meet the Bridegroom and sternly disregarding the earnest prayers of her
imploring companion—but they are represented as two affectionate and
sympathising sisters, the virgin bearing the lighted taper stooping over
her fellow as though in the act of rekindling her extinguished lamp. The
execution of this group which I am surprised to find has made some noise
at Rome is also very feeble".[1]

Prov: Bought by R. C. Naylor from the sculptor in Rome 1855;² sold Christie's, 2-12 August 1875 lot 727 bought Agnew. Bequeathed by Daniel Busby 1887.

Ref: 1. *A Walk through the Studios of Rome*, Art Journal, 1854, p. 288.   **2.** Note in Christie's 1875 Catalogue.

7143   Bust of Elizabeth Mary, 2nd Marchioness of Westminster

Marble, height 66 cm with base,

Inscribed: *LADY ELIZ. H. BELGRAVE*

Signed: *RINALDI/ROME/1836*

The sitter is Lady Elizabeth Mary Leveson-Gower (1797-1891) who married in 1819 Richard Grosvenor, Viscount Belgrave, who became 2nd Marquis of Westminster in 1845 on the death of his father.[1] The "H" of the inscription is probably an error.

The sitter and her husband and children were in Rome from 25 March until 30 May 1836, she sat to Rinaldi in May.[2]

Prov: Passed presumably from Eaton Hall, Cheshire to an engineering works in Macclesfield; thence to an antique dealer; purchased from the brother of this dealer through the personal column of the Sunday Times in about 1951 by R. Melinin-Warner;³ sold Sotheby's, 24 July 1969, lot 124, bt. W.A.G.

Ref: 1. See *Dictionary of National Biography* under Grosvenor for her husband and *Burke's Peerage* under Westminster; for her literary works see *British Museum Catalogue of Printed Books* under Grosvenor, Elizabeth Mary. The sitter of No. 7143 could reasonably be the same person as in Sir Thomas Lawrence's *Portrait of Lady Elizabeth Leveson-Gower* of 1818 (now owned by the Duke of Sutherland).   **2.** Gervas Huxley, *Lady Elizabeth and the Grosvenors*, 1965, p. 157 relying on the sitter's diary now owned by Count Guy de Pelet.   **3.** R. Melinin-Warner, *letter*, 30 September 1969.

ROBBIA, Andrea della, 1435-1525, studio of

9025   A cherub's head, part of a semicircular architrave

Relief in polychrome enamelled terracotta, 28.7 × 58.3 cm

Fragments from another architrave of this type are in the Victoria and Albert Museum.[1] Terracottas like 9025 inspired the production at the Della Robbia Pottery Company, Birkenhead founded by Harold S. Rathbone, son of P. H. Rathbone, in 1893.[2]

Prov: P. H. Rathbone; by descent to Miss E. M. Moore; presented by the executors of her estate, 1975.

Ref: 1. John Pope-Hennessy and Ronald Lightbown, *Catalogue of Italian Sculpture in the Victoria and Albert Museum*, 1964, I, pp. 229-230, III, pl. 231-234.   **2.** For details of the Company's work see Bruce Tattersall, *The Birkenhead Della Robbia Pottery*, '*Il Progresso sia il Nostro Scopo*', Apollo, 97, 1973, pp. 164-168.

RODIN, René Francois Auguste, 1840-1917

3176 (?) Unlasting Love

Bronze, height 39 cm

Signed: *A. Rodin*

Identical to a plaster of 1885 in the Musee Rodin[1] and very close to a marble in the National Gallery of Art, Washington.[2]

Prov: Bought by James Smith from Alex Reid 1899; bequeathed by James Smith 1927.
Ref: 1. Reproduced in R. Descharnes and J. -F. Chabrun, *Auguste Rodin*, 1967, p. 125 as *Love that passes*; listed by I. Jianou and C. Goldscheider, *Rodin* 1967, p. 99 as *Unlasting Love*, not listed in Georges Grappe, *Catalogue du Musée Rodin*, 1929, but a variant of No. 91 *Jeune Mere* in this catalogue; No. 3176 was described by James Smith as *La Nymphe et l'enfant* (MSS list, W.A.G.).   2. Inventory No. A-83, as *Woman and Child*.

3177   Sister and Brother

Bronze, height 39 cm

Signed: *A. Rodin*

Identical to a bronze in the Musée Rodin of 1890 or 1891.[1] A marble version, presumed also to be from Rodin's plaster, exists.[2]

Prov: Bought by James Smith from Glaenzer and Co. 1901; bequeathed by him, 1927.
Ref: 1. George Grappe, *Catalogue du Musée Rodin*, 1929 No. 192 pp. 80-81 giving 1890 as the date. I. Jianou and C. Goldscheider, *Rodin*, 1967, p. 104 favour 1891 and give a list of other versions. The cast in the Fitzwilliam Museum, Cambridge, is stated to be "the first cast, 1890" (their *Annual Report for the year ending 31 December 1959*, 1960, p. 4).   2. Arts Council of Great Britain, *Rodin*, 1970, No. 69 p. 73.

4179   The Danaid

Bronze, height 30.5 cm

Signed: *A. Rodin* and *A. Rodin* on stamp inside bronze

A marble version of 1885 is in the Musée Rodin.[1] The Danaids were the 50 daughters of King Danaus of Argos, all but one of whom murdered their husbands, the 50 sons of Aegyptus, on their wedding night. They were punished by having to spend eternity filling a sieve with water.[2]

Prov: Bought by James Smith from the artist 1902; bequeathed by him 1923.
Exh: Arts Council, *Rodin*, 1966-7, No. 13; Arts Council, Hayward Gallery, *Rodin*, 1970 (21).
Ref: 1. Georges Grappe, *Catalogue du Musée Rodin*, 1929, p. 52, No. 96. I Jianou and C. Goldscheider, *Rodin*, 1967, p. 90 with a long list of other versions.   2. It is generally stated that No. 4179 was originally conceived as part of the *Gates of Hell*, but not in J. Cladel, *Rodin, The Man and his Art*, 1917, p. 299 who dates *The Danaid* to 1890.

4180   Eve

Bronze, height 76 cm

Signed: *A. Rodin.*

A reduced version of the *Eve au Rocher* of 1881[1] originally conceived for the Gates of Hell.[2]

Prov: Bought by James Smith from the artist 1902; bequeathed by him, 1923.

Exh: Venice, 1901, *Quarta Esposizione Internazionale d'Arte*. 1902, Sala E., *Mostra delle Sculture Auguste Rodin*, pp. 46-7, No. 15.[3] L.A.E., 1906, No. 1456

Ref: 1. Georges Grappe, *Catalogue du Musée Rodin*, 1929, p. 41, Nos. 56 and 58 for their life size versions; another list of versions is in I. Jianou and C. Goldscheider, *Rodin*, 1967, p. 89 to which may be added the marble reduced versions—the same size as No. 4180—one now in Gemaldegalerie Neue Meister, Staatliche Kunstsammlungen Dresden, their *Katalog*, 1975, p. 124, No. 1890 and the other commissioned by M. Ricorne and sold Christie's, 29 June 1976 lot 241.   **2.** For the Gates of Hell see particularly Albert E. Elsen, *Rodin's Gates of Hell*, 1960, pp. 66 and 89.   **3.** Old label.

4181   Minerva

Marble with a bronze helmet, height 48 cm

Signed: *A. Rodin*

Very close to a plaster of 1896 in the Musée Rodin;[1] the figure is stated to have been inspired by Mrs Russell (Nee Mariana Mattioco della Torre).[2]

Prov: Bought by James Smith from the artist 1907 for 6000 francs,[3] bequeathed by him 1923.

Exh: Arts Council, Hayward Gallery, *Pioneers of Modern Sculpture*, 1973, No. 39.

Ref: 1. Georges Grappe, *Catalogue du Musée Rodin*, 1929, No. 229 p. 92 as *Pellas au casque*. I. Jianou and C. Goldscheider, *Rodin*, 1967, p. 101 where the version in the Musee Rodin is described as a bronze. There is a marble *Minerve sans casque* close to No. 4181 but without the bronze helmet in the National Gallery of Victoria Melbourne (Felton Bequest, 1905).   **2.** Grappe, *op. cit.*, Jianou and Goldscheider, *op. cit.*, a wax bust of Mrs Russell of about 1888-1889 is in the Musée Rodin, Grappe, *op. cit.*, No. 174. p. 75 as 1889, Jianou and Goldscheider. *op. cit.*, as about 1888 with a list of other versions.   **3.** James Smith had asked the price of No. 4181 in a letter to the artist of 15 November 1905; the bust did not reach him until November 1907 having been delayed by the casting of the helmet (Monique Laurent, *letter*, 23 July 1974, relying on letters from James Smith to the artist now in the Musée Rodin). Letters of 1907 (MSS W.A.G.) from the artist to James Smith confirm the price and the date of delivery.

4182   La Mort d'Athenes

Marble group, height 42 cm

Signed: *A. RODIN*

Not very close in composition to the plaster of about 1902 with the same title in the Musée Rodin.[1] The only other marble version is in the Thyssen-Bornemisza Collection, Castagnola,[2] to which No. 4182 is nearly identical. Grappe briefly discusses the subject matter of the Musée Rodin plaster describing it[3] as the "composition ou l'artiste a noblement symbolisé tout son regret de l'art antique dont les ruines n'apparaissent plus que ca et la sous les sables" but it lacks the crowning figure of the dying nude girl, present in No. 4182 and presumably symbolizing Athens.

Prov: Bought from the artist by James Smith 1903[4] for 12,000 francs[5] bequeathed by
          him , 1923.
Ref: 1. Georges Grappe, *Catalogue du Musée Rodin,* 1929, No. 296. p. 112. Dated
          there 1904 but the plaster presumably preceded the marble; I. Jianou and C.
          Goldscheider, *Rodin,* 1967, p. 109 suggest 1902 which is more likely.   2.
          Sammlung Schloss Rohoncz, Villa Favorita, Castagnola, *Katalog,* 1958, p. 134,
          K56c (4), bought directly from the artist by August Thyssen.   3. *Op. cit.* For
          Rodin's attitude to Greek art see particularly J. Cladel, *Rodin, The Man and his
          Art,* 1917, pp. 218ff.   4. In a letter of 27 September 1903 now in the Musée
          Rodin James Smith and his wife informed the artist that they would definitely buy
          the marble version (No. 4182) not a bronze version (Monique Laurent, *letter,* 23
          July 1974).   5. Letter of 3 October 1903 from the artist to James Smith pre-
          sumably relating to No. 4182 (MSS W.A.G.).

ROSSETTI, Antonio, born 1819

4237   Secret Love

Marble, height 101.5 cm

Signed: *A Rossetti Fece / Roma 1876*

Inscribed: *AMOR SECRETO*

The revival of the veiled figure in Italian 19th century sculpture was largely due to Raffaelle Monti.[1]

For the Renaissance origins of the subject of No. 4237 see particularly Erwin Panofsky, *Studies in Iconology,* 1939, pp. 95ff.

Prov: Bequeathed by Sir William B. Forwood, 1928.
Ref: 1. Anthony Radcliffe, *Monti's Allegory of the Risorgimento,* Victoria and Albert
          Museum Bulletin, 1965, Vol. I, No. 3, pp. 25ff.

4238   Time is Precious

Marble, height 117 cm (without base)

Signed: *A. Rossetti/Roma 1873*

The donor referred to this marble as *Self Help.*[1] An unsigned, undated version is in the Lichfield District Gallery.

Prov: Presented by G. C. Schwabe, 1877.
Exh: L.A.E., 1877 (1316).
Ref: 1. *Letter,* 3 February 1877 read before the Libraries, Museums and Arts Commit-
          tee of Liverpool Town Council, 8 February 1877.

SCHADOW, Rudolf, 1786-1822

8227   The Spinner

Marble, height 122 cm

A version of the statue best known by the version formerly in the Royal Palace, Berlin[1] but now destroyed.[2]

Prov: Unknown;[3] in Liverpool Town Hall by 1966; transferred by the City Estates Committee to the W.A.G. 1972 but still in the Town Hall.

Ref: 1. The engraving by D. Marchetti after J. Podio in Wolfgang von Goethe, *Erlauterungen der Abbildungen von den Bildhauer—Arbeiten des Johann Gottfried Schadow und seines Sohnes Ridolfo Schadow*, 1849, Blatt XXX is inscribed *Rudolph Schadow in marmore fecit Romae 1816*; Goethe writes (p. 7): "eins oder zwei nach England gingen"—one is still at Chatsworth, was the other No. 8227?   2. Dr. Peter Bloch, *letter,* 22 May 1974. A surviving version is in the Galleria d'Arte Moderna, Milan.   3. A version was in the collection of Henry Bright at Ashfield, Liverpool in 1882: see *The Private Collections of England,* The Athenaeum, No. 2864, 1882 p. 376.

SOUTH GERMAN School, 18th century

6103-4   Two Saints

Limewood,[1] each height 132 cm

Dr. Albrecht Miller[2] suggests a connection with the workshop of Anton Sturm around 1720-30. Presumably originally polychrome and part of an altar group; there are many old fractures in both statues.

Prov: Anon sold Christie's, 24 November 1960 (as South German) lot 5, bt. in; Arcade Gallery from whom they were purchased, 1961.

Exh: Manchester City Art Gallery, *German Art 1400-1800*, 1961 (214).

Ref: 1. Tilia vulgaris according to Joyce Plesters, *letter*, 29 May 1961.   2. *Letter*, 15 June 1970.

SUSINI, Antonio, about 1550-1624, after (?)

6314   The Farnese Bull

Bronze, height 46 cm

Stamped three times with "crowned C"

Fairly close to Susini's signed bronze of 1613 in the Galleria Borghese[1] after the antique marble now in the Museo Nazionale, Naples.[2] The "crowned C" stamps, if genuine, indicate that No. 6314 was made or sold in Paris between 1745 and 1749.[3]

Prov: Purchased from Cyril Humphris Ltd., 1965.

Ref: 1. Italo Faldi, *Galleria Borghese, Le Sculture dal Secolo XVI al XIX*, 1954, No. 59, p. 61.   2. A. Ruesch, *Guida del Museo Nazionale di Napoli*, n.d., pp. 80ff, fig. 29, No. 260.   3. See Pierre Kjellberg, *Nouvelles precisions a propos du C Couronné*, Connaissance des Arts, No. 169, March 1966, pp. 13-15.

TACCA, Ferdinando, 1619-1686

7398   Mercury and Juno

Bronze, height 43 cm

One of a group of small two figure bronzes by Tacca.[1] Another cast of this bronze was in the French Royal Collections[2] and a third is in the Germanisches Nationalmuseum, Nurnberg, (Inv. Pl. O. 2826). The subject is unclear; the seated female figure may not in fact be Juno.[3]

Prov: ?The Dukes of Ferrara.[4] The Heim Gallery, London, presented by the National
        Art-Collections Fund 1970 "to mark the long and successful term of Hugh Scrutton as Director of the Gallery, 1952-70."

Ref: **1.** *Angelica and Medoro* is at the Royal Palace, Madrid, *Roger and Angelica* and
        Apollo and Daphne are at the Louvre, *Venus and Adonis* is at the Museum of Fine
        Arts, Budapest and *Hercules and Omphale* is in a private collection in U.S.A.
        (Anthony Radcliffe, *letter*, 3 August 1970). A more complete list appears in
        Anthony Radcliffe, *Ferdinando Tacca, the missing link in Florentine Baroque
        Bronzes*, Kunst des Barock in der Toskana, 1976, pp. 14ff. There is no documentary evidence for attributing any of these bronzes to Tacca.   **2.** J. Guiffrey,
        Testament et inventaire apres deces de Andre le Nostre, Bulletin de la Société de
        l'Histoire de l'Art francais, 1911, p. 224; André Le Notre gave the bronze to the
        king in 1693. It was last recorded in the Parisian art market in 1970.   **3.** The
        cast in the French Royal Collections was described in 1693 as *Juno and Mercury*
        (Guiffrey, *op. cit.*) but the cast in the collection of the Duke of Ferrara was simply
        described in 1684 as *Un Mercurio con vaso in mano avanti a una figura di donna
        coronata posta a sedere* (*Documenti inediti per servire alla storia dei musei d'Italia*,
        III, Rome, 1880, p. 26).   **4.** No. 7398 may well have been the cast owned by
        the Duke of Ferrara and kept by him in 1684 in his casino outside the Porta Castello, Ferrara (*Documenti inediti, op. cit.*).

TAKIS, born 1925

6894   Signals, Series III

Chromium plated brass tube, cast iron, plastic and three light bulbs, maximum height 230 cm adjustable.

Inspired by electric railway signals the first *Signals* by Takis were made in 1954 or 1955.

Prov: Purchased from Unlimited, Widcombe Manor, Bath 1968.

TENERANI, Pietro, 1789-1869

8556   Bust of a Woman

Marble, height 67.5 cm

Signed: *PRO. TENERANI FVA. 1853*

Prov: Bought from the Heim Gallery, 1973.

THORWALDSEN, Bertel, 1770-1844, after

7503-4   Day and Night

Marble reliefs, diameter 78.2 cm

The original models of 1815 are in the Thorwaldsen Museum, Copenhagen, Nos. 369-70.

Prov: Bought by a Mr Ram(?) in Rome 1827;[1] Henry Robertson Sandbach of Hafodunos Hall, purchased from Kent House School, Hafodunos Hall, 1971.

Ref: 1. List of Statues at Hafodunos Hall, 15 February 1933, MSS National Museum of Wales, Cardiff. Neither Sandbach nor Mr Ram are mentioned in Thorwaldsen's account books; if Nos. 7503-4 were the reliefs being made in Thorwaldsen's studio in 1825-6 the executant was Luigi Bienaimé (Bjarne Jornaes, *letter*, 4 November 1970).

UECKER, Gunther, born 1930

6653   Ball of Nails

Nails, canvas and wood on metal base, diameter of ball 58 cm

The artist has written:[1]

"In 1959 I made the first ball of nails.

For me it was a consequence: to show a spatial extension in an extensive dimension, to part from the plane picture and the limited situation of a plane wall. My preceeding "structure plates" already showed a tendency to this development: the edges were completely nailed which made it impossible to frame the pictures. The illusional plane had the tendency to become an object, a real thing for itself, without any prospectional illusion. This nailing of the edging zones of a picture I did for the first time in 1958.

In 1959 I produced the first ball of nails—"Gliding Glide"—which now is in the Busch Reisinger Museum, Cambridge, Mass. From this time I worked with and studied objects of spatial dimension: cubes, free standing squares and rectangles, discs. In 1960 I showed the first moving discs with a lateral flashing of light: articulated light in a motoric movement. I think this should be seen in connection with the ball of nails."

No. 6653 dates from 1966.[2]

Prov: Purchased by the Contemporary Art Society 1966;[2] presented by the Contemporary Art Society, 1968.

Exh: Contemporary Art Society, *Recent Acquisitions*, 1968, No. 132.

Ref: 1. *Letter*, 12 December, 1968.   2. Contemporary Art Society, *Annual Report 1966-7* n.p.

VENETIAN School, late 16th century (?)

6132   Doorknocker

Bronze, height 21.2 cm

Variants were at the Casa Diedo a S. Giovanni in Oleo, Venice[1] and at the Casa Fonda, later Spalletti Trivelli, Reggio Emilia[2] and two more are still in the Collezione Auriti[3] and at Berlin.[4]

Prov: Bought from Alfred Spero, 1962.
Ref: **1.** *Raccolta dei Bataori a Venezia*, 1758 (ed. G. B. Brusa, 1879 as *Raccolta di Battitori a Venezia*), fig. 16.   **2.** Andrea Balletti *Gli ultimi battenti in bronzo a Reggio dell'Emilia*, Rassegna d'Arte, Vol. 3, 1903, p. 121.   **3.** Museo di Palazzo Venezia *La Collezione Auriti*, 1964, pp. 21-2, pl. 23.   **4.** Berlin Staatlichen Museen, *Die Italienischen Bildwerke der Renaissance und des Barock, Bronzestatuetten Busten und Gebrauchsgegenstande*, 1930, No. 299, pl. 86, p. 62 where Bode dates it to the end of the 16th century.

VOGEL, Karel, 1897-1961

8469   Bust of Frank Lambert

Bronzed plaster, height 33 cm

The sitter (1884-1973) was Director of Leeds City Art Gallery 1927-31 and Director of the W.A.G., Liverpool 1931-1952.[1]

The artist was presumably the K. Vogel who exhibited a head at the 1940 Royal Academy (No. 1567) from 38 Redcliffe Road, London S.W.10 and two heads at the 1953 Royal Academy (Nos. 1254 and 1274) from 6 Hartington Road, London W.4. He also made a bust of Oskar Kokoschka.[2]

Prov: Presented by the executors of the sitter, 1973.
Ref: **1.** Obituary in *The Times*, 16 January 1973 and 18 January 1973.   **2.** Exhibited at the Victoria and Albert Museum, *Homage to Kokoschka*, 1976, No. 84, p. 47.

WEIGELE, Henri, 1858-1927

4217   Athenienne

Marble and bronze,[1] height 89 cm (including base)

Signed: *H. Weigele*

Prov: Purchased from the artist 1906, L.A.E. (£120).
Exh: L.A.E., 1906 (1461).
Ref: **1.** Possibly not bronze but brass or copper; it was formerly gilded—listed in the L.A.E. Catalogue as *Marbre et Bronze Doré*.

WOLFF, Emil, 1802-1879

4184   The Goat Herd

Marble, height 127 cm

Signed: *E. WOLFF / F. C. ROM. 1839*

The conception at least dates from 1830.[1]

Prov: Richard Vaughan Yates.[2] Presented by Colonel W. M. Belcher, 1916.
Exh: ?Royal Berlin Academy of Art 1838, No. 1015 as *Eine Hirtin* (another version).
        ?Royal Academy, 1839, No. 1306 as *A Girl with a Goat and Tambourine*. Liver-
        pool, Mechanics Institution, *Ist. Exhibition of Objects Illustrative of the Fine Arts*,
        1840 (332).[3]
Ref: **1.** Engraved in Giornale di belle Arti (ossia Pubblicazione mensuale delle mig-
        liori degli Artisti moderni), anno 1, 1830, pl. 27, p. 57 as *Une Bergere* drawn by
        Baumgarten, engraved by F. Cartoni and invented by Emilio Wolff.   **2.** A
        Statuette, *A German Maiden with a Lamb* by Wolff was also apparently made for
        Yates and exhibited at the Crystal Palace in 1854 (see Mrs Jameson, *A Hand-
        book to the Courts of Modern Sculpture*, 1854, p. 83, No. 268).   **3.** No. 4184 is
        reviewed in the *Liverpool Journal*, 18 June 1840, p. 10.

CATALOGUE OF SILVER

AALBORG, School of, *c.* 1725

3369 A Peg Tankard and Cover

Height, 17 cm

Inscribed with the mark of Thore Sorensen of Aalborg,[1] the date 1725[2] and the initials *BJS/KED*

The cover is inset with a coin of King Frederick III of Norway dated 1649.

Prov: Presented by Lord Wavertree, 1933.
Ref: **1.** Christian Boje, *Danske Guld og Solv Smedemaerker for 1870*, 1946, p. 181, (1280), 1954 (1478). This reference was kindly pointed out by Fritze Lindahl of the Nationalmuseet, Copenhagen in a letter of 20 April 1976. **2.** Arthur Grimwade, *The Wavertree Bequest of Racing Trophies at the W.A.G., Liverpool, Part II*, The Connoisseur, February, 1975, p. 125.

AMSTERDAM, School of, 1849

3379 A Circular Bowl with corded rim

Width, 20.4 cm diameter

Inscribed with the marks *JGM* over a crater (J. G. Meyer of Amsterdam), *P* and the mark for the first class silver in the Netherlands.[1]

The piece dates from 1849.[2]

Prov: Presented by Lord Wavertree, 1933.
Ref: **1.** Marc Rosenberg, *Der Goldschmiede Merkzeichen*, IV, 1928, p. 394 (7544). **2.** The maker and date were first noted by Arthur Grimwade in 1967 and confirmed by Dr. J. Verbeek, *letter*, 31 May 1976.

AUGSBURG, School of, late 17th century

3374 A Beaker, parcelgilt

Height, 13.1 cm

Inscribed with the marks of Augsburg (half-effaced)[1] and Cornelius Poppe.[2]

Prov: Presented by Lord Wavertree, 1933.

Ref: 1. Marc Rosenberg, *Der Goldschmiede Merkzeichen*, I, 1922, pp. 30-31. 2. Rosenberg, *op. cit.*, p. 161 (731) and Arthur Grimwade, *The Wavertree Bequest of Racing Trophies at the W.A.G., Liverpool, Part II*, The Connoisseur, February, 1975, pp. 126-7.

COPENHAGEN, School of, 1728

3382 A Peg Tankard and Cover

Height, 25.3 cm

Inscribed on the cover with the marks of Copenhagen dated 1728,[1] of Copenhagen for 21 January—18 February,[2] of Warden Conrad Rudolf,[3] and the mark of David Buur,[4] the body inscribed with the date 1755 (twice), the initials *JJF, JJL* and *RR*, the mark of Copenhagen with the initials *PM* beneath it, and the mark *1728*, and the inscription *Vagt 112 Lot*.

The cover is inset with a medal relating to betrothal or marriage. The cover dates from January 1728, the body from the 19th century.

Prov: Presented by Lord Wavertree, 1933.

Ref: 1. Chr. A. Boje, *Danske Guld og Solv Smedemaerker for 1870*, 1954, p. 27 (51). 2. Chr. A. Boje, *Danske Guld og Solv Smedemaerker for 1870*, 1954, p. 30 and Rosenberg, *op. cit.*, p. 157 (5618). 3. Rosenberg, *op. cit.*, p. 156 (5607) and Boje, *op. cit.*, p. 29 4. Chr. A. Boje, *Danske Guld og Solv Smedemaerker for 1870*, 1954, p. 60 (344).

COPENHAGEN, School of, 1742

3366 A Tankard and Cover

Height, 15 cm

Inscribed with the Copenhagen mark of 1742,[1] the mark for the period 23 September to 22 October,[2] the mark of Warden Pet Nikolai von Haven,[3] and on the cover with the initials *JKS* and the date *1742*.

The cover is inset with a coin of Frederick IV of Denmark and Norway dated 1704.

Prov: Presented by Lord Wavertree, 1933.

Ref: 1. Arthur Grimwade, *The Wavertree Bequest of Racing Trophies at the W.A.G., Liverpool, Part II*, The Connoisseur, February, 1975, pp. 125-6. cf Chr. A. Boje, *Danske Guld og Solv Smedemaerker for 1870*, 1954, p. 27. 2. Boje *op. cit.*, p. 30 3. Marc Rosenberg, *Der Goldschmiede Merkzeichen*, IV, 1928, p. 155 (5608), and Boje, *op. cit.*, p. 29 mark listed as in use 1732-1749.

DUTCH School, *c.* 1650

3375/3376   A pair of communion Beakers

Height, 18.2 cm each

Both inscribed with maker's mark, a crowned heart,[1] with the inscription *Ter Lief de van den Ghecruysten De Kercke van Bommenede vereert Door: P:B:Anno 1651* around an engraving of a church, and with the inscription *L V C: 22:V:19:DOET: DAT:TOT:MYNDER:- GEDACHTENIS:*

It has been suggested that the mark is that of a maker at the Hague where a similar mark is recorded for 1653,[2] or that the beakers were made in Dordrecht.[3]

The inscription around the view of the village church reads "For the love of the Crucified One. Offered to the Church of Bommenede by P. B. Anno 1651". Bommenede, a fishing village on the north-east coast of the island of Schouwen in the province of Zeeland was inundated on 26 January 1682 and the church was destroyed a few days later. The church in the engravings does not correspond with the recorded appearance of Bommenede church, which was cruciform with two towers.[4] A possible explanation is that the engraver had not visited Bommenede.

The P.B. of the inscription is Pieter Bolle who presented the beakers to the church.[5]

The second inscription refers to Luke 22 v. 19 "Do this in remembrance of me".

Prov: Presented to the Church of Bommenede by Peter Bolle 1651; rescued from the church after the flood of 26 January 1682; sold in Middelburg in 1795;[6] Mrs K. Hocke Hogenboom by 1870;[5] Lord Wavertree, by whom presented, 1933.

Exh: Middelburg, *Oud-en merkwaardigheden in de provincie Zeeland*, 1870, (284).[5]

Ref: **1.** Arthur Grimwade, *The Wavertree Bequest of Racing Trophies at the W.A.G., Liverpool, Part II*, The Connoisseur, February 1975, pp. 126-7.   **2.** Grimwade *op. cit.*, and Elias Voet Jr. *Merken van Haagsche Goud-en Zilversmeder*, 1941, p. 159 (18) pointed out to the compiler by Dr. B. Jansen, *letter*, 23 June 1976.   **3.** J. de Bree, *Avondmaalsbekers uit de Kerk van Bommenede, verloren gewaand, maar teruggevonden*, Antiek, December 1975, pp. 509-511 quoting Dr. ter Molen, who confirmed his opinion by letter, 19 August 1976.   **4.** Grimwade, *op. cit.*, quoting information from K. Citroen.   **5.** de Bree, *op. cit.*, p. 509 and letters, 14 March 1975 and 2nd May 1975.   **6.** Letter of Betsy Fokker, 3 April 1976.

DUTCH School, mid 17th century

3383   A Circular Dish

Width, 22.4 cm diameter

Inscribed with a 19th century Dutch control mark and inset with coins dated 1565, 1566, 1568 and 1569 of Sigismund, Duke of Lithuania and 1777 of Stanislaus, King of Poland.

DUTCH School, late 17th century

3380   A oval Bowl and Cover

Height, 13.3 cm

Inscribed on the cover with the initials *GFW* and *AGF* and the date *1857*.

The two coats of arms engraved on the bowl, one of which bears the initials *JLS*, have not been identified.

DUTCH School, *c.* 1850

3385   A Sugar Bowl and Cover

Height, 13 cm

Unmarked.

GERMAN School, *c.* 1700

3386   A Beaker

Height, 7.7 cm

Bearing the inscription *P.P.S. M.N.D.* around the rim and inset with coins of King Christian V of Denmark and Norway dated 1693, 1694 and 1696, and with a coin of the Emperor Leopold dated 1700 bearing the arms of the city of Cologne.

GRONINGEN, School of, 1695/6

3378   An oval Ecuelle and Cover

Width, 22.5 cm

Inscribed with the mark of Groningen[1] for 1695/6[2] and the maker's mark of Jan Entinck[3] (*IE*) and engraved with an unidentified coat of arms.

The snake on the top is probably a 19th century addition.

Prov: Presented by Lord Wavertree, 1933 (3383, 3380, 3385,3386, 3378).
Ref: **1.** First identified by Richard Norton, *letter*, 23 August, 1960 see also Arthur Grimwade, *The Wavertree Bequest of Racing Trophies at the W.A.G., Liverpool, Part II*, The Connoisseur, February, 1975 p. 127.   **2.** Identified by J. M. Leopold, letter of 1 June 1976. Jan Entinck was admitted in 1695, and his last known work is marked 1716/17.

343

INDIAN School, 19th century

3388 A Bowl chased and engraved with foliage and geometrical ornament

Width, 24.5 cm

Inscribed with indecipherable mark and with mark *6EC*

According to John Lowry[1] 3388 may be a piece of Chinese export silver, or Indian or South-east Asian.

Prov: Presented by Lord Wavertree, 1933.
Ref: **1.** *Letter*, 23 April 1976.

LOWER SAXON School, late 17th century

3387 An oval Bowl on three ball feet

Width, 22 cm diameter

Inscribed with the initials *CFL*, the date *1767*, a standard mark *XII* and with the maker's mark, *P. 2*

Grimwade attributed 3387 to the German or Baltic School of the 17th century.[1] Dr. Jedding's suggestion that it is North German of the second half of the 17th century,[2] is confirmed by the mark XII, which was used in Jever[3] and Oldenburg.[4]

Prov: Presented by Lord Wavertree, 1933.
Ref: **1.** Valuation list, 1967(MSS W.A.G.).   **2.** Letter of 9 August, 1976.   **3.** Wolfgang Scheffler, *Goldschmiede Niedersachsens*, II, 1965, pp. 864-865, 1257 (1646)—a reference pointed out to the compiler by Dr. Hermann Jedding, 1 November 1976.   **4.** Letter of Dr. Hermann Jedding, 1 November 1976.

MOSCOW, School of, 1752

3368 A Tankard and Cover parcelgilt

Height, 15.3 cm

Inscribed with the Moscow marks of 1752,[1] and with the marks *M* (MG),[2] of Timofey Siluyanof[3] and the mark *A.M.* (probably Chester for 1895-6)[4] (on the base of the tankard, on the rim of the cover and on the inside of the cover) and *M* (MG)[2] (on the body).

The tankard was almost certainly restored in Chester in 1895-6. It has been suggested that the star on the cover may be part of the restoration.[5]

Prov: Presented by Lord Wavertree, 1933.

Ref: **1.** Arthur Grimwade, *The Wavertree Bequest of Racing Trophies at the Walker Art Gallery, Liverpool, Part II*, The Connoisseur, February, 1975, p. 126, cf. Marc Rosenberg, *Der Goldschmiede Merkzeichen*, IV, 1928, p. 467 (8149).   **2.** The mark of an unknown master assayer active 1752-1767, see M. M. Postnikova-Loseva *Russian jewellery, its centres and masters*, 1974, p. 251 (594). This reference was pointed out by Dr. I. V. Porto, *letter*, 9 June 1976.   **3.** Postnikova-Loseva, *op. cit.*, p. 265 (1011). This reference was also pointed out by Dr. I. V. Porto, *letter*, 9 June 1976.   **4.** Sir Charles James Jackson, *English Goldsmiths and their marks*, 1905, p. 377, a reference pointed out by Dr. M. Postnikova-Loseva, *letter*, 12 August 1976.   **5.** M. Postnikova-Loseva, *letter*, 12 August 1976.

NURENBERG, School of, *c.* 1645

3365   A Tankard and Cover, silvergilt

Height, 14.2 cm

Inscribed with the mark of Andreas Michel of Nurenberg on the cover[1] and the mark *BM* under the base.

Prov: Presented by Lord Wavertree, 1933.

Ref: **1.** Marc Rosenberg, *Der Goldschmiede Merkzeichen*, III, 1925, p. 198 (4165) and Arthur Grimwade, *The Wavertree Bequest of Racing Trophies at the W.A.G., Part II*, The Connoisseur, February, 1975, p. 124.

OPORTO, School of, *c.* 1750

3377   A Sugar-bowl and Cover, silvergilt

Height, 16.1 cm

Inscribed with the marks of Oporto[1] and the maker *GS*.[2]

Prov: Presented by Lord Wavertree, 1933.

Ref: **1.** Arthur Grimwade, *The Wavertree Bequest of Racing Trophies at the W.A.G., Liverpool, Part II*, The Connoisseur, February 1975, p. 127.   **2.** Manuel Goncalves Vidal, *Marcas de Contrastes e ourives portugueses desde o seculo XV a 1950*, 1958, No. 1000.

RIGA, School of, late 17th century

3371   A Tankard and Cover, parcelgilt

Height, 25 cm

Inscribed with the mark of Riga (nearly obliterated), with indistinct maker's mark perhaps of Caroli Israel (*JC*)[1] with the date *1696* and the arms and name of Matthias Lithander[2] and *lot 131½*. The cover inscribed *Oberster Matse Firanuiwiftz Niclurioff.*

The body and cover are inset with medals relating to marriage one of which bears the monogram *IB*.

Caroli Israel was enrolled as a master in 1691 and died in 1709.[1]

Matthias Lithander obtained nobility in 1690 and became a member of the City Council of Tartu (Estonia).[1]

The medallist I.B. may be Johann Buchheim (1624-1683) or Johann Bensheimer (active 1670-1680).[1]

Prov: Presented by Lord Wavertree, 1933.
Ref: 1. Letter of Ida Cekule, undated, but June 1976, reporting information from A. Jursone. 2. Arthur Grimwade, *The Wavertree Bequest of Racing Trophies at the W.A.G., Liverpool, Part II*, The Connoisseur, February, 1975, p. 124.

SWEDISH School, 17th century

3372 A Tankard and Cover, parcelgilt

Height, 23 cm

Inscribed on the cover with the date *1656* and with two coats of arms with the names of Hennig Ecklef and Salome Ecklefen in a wreath.[1]

Prov: Presented by Lord Wavertree, 1933.
Ref: 1. Arthur Grimwade, *The Wavertree Bequest of Racing Trophies at the W.A.G., Liverpool, Part II*, The Connoisseur, February 1975, p. 125.

TALLINN, School of, *c.* 1700

3373 A Peg Tankard

Height, 18.1 cm

Inscribed with the marks of Tallinn (Reval)[1] and indistinctly of Franz Johann Dreyer,[2] and on the cover with the monogram *IJT* or *A, VK*.

Prov: Presented by Lord Wavertree, 1933.
Ref: 1. Marc Rosenberg, *Der Goldschmiede Merkzeichen*, IV, 1928, p. 185 (5756). 2. Rosenberg, *op. cit.*, p. 187 (5773), and Arthur Grimwade, *The Wavertree Bequest of Racing Trophies at the W.A.G., Liverpool, Part II*, The Connoisseur, February, 1975, p. 125.

VASA, School of, *c.* 1700

3367   A Tankard and Cover

Height, 17.1 cm

Inscribed with the mark of the maker Daniel Meijer of Vasa,[1] and of Olaf Lofvander Junior (1774-1823)[2] and of Lulea (Sweden).[3] The cover is engraved with the names of Jacob Estlander and Britha Farbus and is inset with a coin of Charles XII of Sweden dated 1697.

The mark of Olaf Lofvander Junior probably indicates repair or resale by him.[4]

Prov: Presented by Lord Wavertree, 1933.

Ref: 1. Letter of Dag Wigman 21 May 1976. Meijer was master at Vasa from 1687 to 1695.   2. Marc Rosenberg, *Der Goldschmiede Merkzeichen*, IV, 1928, p. 485 (8416).   3. Rosenberg, *op. cit.*, p. 888 (5394).   4. Arthur Grimwade, *The Wavertree Bequest of Racing Trophies at the W.A.G., Liverpool, Part II*, The Connoisseur, February, 1975, pp. 124-5, 127.

VIBORG, School of, early 18th century

3370   A Peg Tankard and Cover

Height, 18.6 cm

Inscribed with the marks of Johan Aage Kop[1] and of Viborg[2] (Jutland) and with the date *1706* and with the initials *B.O.S.S./D.I.D.G./* and *M.R.L.-B.P.D.*

The cover is inset with a coin of the Duke of Saxony dated 1623.

Prov: Presented by Lord Wavertree, 1933.

Ref: 1. Chr. A. Boje, *Danske Guld og Solv Smedemaerker for 1870*, 1954, p. 290 (3500).   2. Boje, *op. cit.*, p. 289 (3488) and Arthur Grimwade, *The Wavertree Bequest of Racing Trophies at the W.A.G., Liverpool, Part II*, The Connoisseur, February, 1975, p. 125.

M

CATALOGUE OF CERAMICS

The attributions are mainly due to Edward Owens, May 1930 and have been confirmed by J. G. Ayers, *letter*, 3 June 1976.

K'ANG HSI 1661-1722

3706   Oviform vase and cover with Vandyke pattern

17.7 cm (height)

3707, 3708   A pair of bottles with feather and bottle pattern

18.4 cm (height)

3709   Aster bottle

20.2 cm (height)

3710   Vase with floral pattern in panels

21.6 cm (height)

3711   Oviform vase with floral pattern and wooden cover

14.6 cm (height)

3713   Vase with floral pattern in twisted panels and wooden cover

11.5 cm (height)

3714   Vase and cover with label pattern

20.2 cm (height)

3716   Cylindrical jar with feather and bottle pattern

20.2 cm (height)

3717   Cylindrical jar with bottle and stool pattern

19.7 cm (height)

3718   Barrel shaped vase with medallion front and wooden cover

12 cm (height)

3719 Incense burner with wooden lid

12.7 cm (height)

Late in the period

3720 Hawthorne ginger jar with wooden cover

12.7 cm (height)

3721, 3722, 3723 Three tall cups and saucers

Cups, 8.2 cm (height); Saucers, 12.7 cm (diameter)

3724 Hawthorne ginger jar with wooden cover

15.2 cm (height)

3725 Hawthorne ginger jar with wooden cover

14 cm (height)

3726 Hawthorne ginger jar with wooden cover

15.2 cm (height)

3727 Hawthorne ginger jar with wooden cover

15.2 cm (height)

The Hawthorne ginger jars 3720 and 3724-3727 bear similar petalled patterns.

3728 Tall bowl with deer and tree pattern

15.9 cm (height)

3729 Bowl with panels of decoration

12.7 cm (diameter)

3730 Squat bowl

5.1 cm (height)

3731 Sprinkler bottle

12.1 cm (height)

3733 Pear shaped bottle with dragon pattern

14 cm (height)

3734 Mustard pot and lid with floral pattern

7.6 cm (height)

3735 Oviform vase and cover with circular medallions

19.1 cm (height)

3736 Oviform vase with dragon and Hoho bird and wooden cover

14.7 cm (height)

3737 Small Lyzen vase

10.2 cm (height)

3738 Oviform vase with dragon pattern and wooden cover

14 cm (height)

Prov: Bequeathed by James Smith of Blundellsands, 1927.

3739 Lyzen vase with single figures in panels with silver neck

12.1 cm (height)

Prov: Said to have been in the collection of Marie Antoinette;[1] bequeathed by James
Smith of Blundellsands, 1927.
Ref: 1. MS list of 1927 of works of art *To go to the Liverpool Corporation (now held in
trust by E. Smith, The Knowle, Blundellsands).*

3741 Oviform Lyzen vase and cover with figure pattern

16.5 cm (height)

3742 Oviform vase with Hoho bird pattern and wooden cover

10.8 cm (height)

3744, 3745 A pair of tall Lyzen jars and covers

14 cm (height)

3746, 3747 A pair of Lyzen bottles

17.2 cm (height)

3748 Tall Lyzen with silver cover

14.6 cm (height)

3749 Oviform Lyzen vase with silver cover

16.5 cm (height)

3750 Pale Hawthorne ginger jar with carved wooden cover

35.6 cm (height)

3751 Hawthorne ginger jar with medallion

22.8 cm (height)

3753 Ginger jar and cover

19.3 cm (height)

Prov: Bequeathed by James Smith of Blundellsands, 1927.

3763 Vase with long neck with floral pattern

48.3 cm (height)

3764 Lyzen vase with travellers at an inn

45.8 cm (height)

3765 Oviform jar and cover with a landscape with deer and a heron

44.5 cm (height)

Prov: Presented by Mrs Sutton Timmis, 1945.

K'ANG HSI, 1661-1722 or YUNG CHENG, 1723-1735

3712 Gourd shaped bottle

22.8 cm (height)

3740 Oviform vase with pale blue dragon pattern

15.2 cm (height)

Both these attributions are due to J. G. Ayers.[1]

Prov: Bequeathed by James Smith of Blundellsands, 1927.
Ref: 1. Letter, 8 June 1976.

YUNG CHENG, 1723-1735

3732 Bottle with small figures and a bridge

17.8 cm (height)

3743 Sweetmeat box with figures

9.5 cm (diameter)

Prov: Bequeathed by James Smith of Blundellsands, 1927.

CATALOGUE OF PRINTS AND PHOTOGRAPHS

ABBATE, Niccolo dell', 1509-1571

9124   Two Roman Women

Etching, 19.1 × 11.6 cm

The figures are probably derived from classical relief sculpture.

The traditional attribution to Primaticcio[1] was first denied by Dimier,[2] and the affinities with the drawings of Niccolo dell'Abbate pointed out by Béguin[3] strongly suggest his authorship of 9124.[4]

Prov: William Roscoe, his sale, Winstanley, 14 September 1816 as Battista del Moro with the latter's "large landscape with cattle and figures"[5], (676)[6] bt. Ford[7] 15s; Charles Robert Blundell; by descent to Col. Sir Joseph Weld; his sale, Christie's, 30 June 1976 (172) as School of Fontainebleau, bt. in; from whom purchased with the aid of donation from the Trustees of the Eleanor Rathbone Trust, 1976.

Ref: **1.** Adam Bartsch, *Le Peintre Graveur*, XVI, 1818, pp. 305-6 (1).   **2.** L. Dimier, *Le Primatice, peintre, sculpteur, et architecte des rois de France*, 1900, pp. 115, 507 (138) as anonymous after Primaticcio. Jean Adhemar, *Bibliothèque Nationale Département des estampes Inventaire des fonds français, graveurs du seizième siècle*, II, 1938, p. 61, also implicitly denies the attribution.   **3.** Sylvie Béguin, Henri Zerner, *Ecole de Fontainebleau, Gravures*, Revue de l'Art, 1969, p. 105, fig. 8.   **4.** The attribution has been accepted by Hamish Miles, *The "Treasure-House of Marvels" at Paris*, Burlington Magazine, 1973, p. 35; although H(enri). Z(erner)., *L'Ecole de Fontainebleau*, Paris, Grand Palais, 1972 p. 327 (426) still included it under the heading Primatice? He dates it after 1553.   **5.** Colonel Sir Joseph Weld sale, Christie's, 30 June 1976 (171) bt. Colnaghi.   **6.** Both 9124 and Weld's Battista dal Moro bear the inscription 676 in pencil on their old mounts.   **7.** Identified by a MS note in the British Museum Copy of Roscoe's sale catalogue as Will. Ford, bookseller. He was born in Manchester in 1771 and died in Liverpool in 1832. He suffered financial difficulties soon after Roscoe's sale, and in consequence was forced to sell his stock of books, prints and manuscripts in two sales held by Winstanley in Manchester ((James) C(rossley) in *The Admission Register of the Manchester School*, II, 1868, pp. 79-81). 9124 does not appear in the print sales of 8 December 1816 and the following days and of 21 March 1817.

ABBEY, Edwin, 1852-1911, after

7490   Oh Mistress Mine

Photogravure, 52.8 × 33.2 cm

Inscribed: *Reproduced by permission from the Original Painting in the Possession of the Liverpool Corporation. Copyright 1905: London and*

Washington by the Fine Art Publishing Co., Ltd., Charing Cross House, London, Printed in England. Oh, Mistress Mine, Edwin Abbey, R.A. *BURLINGTON PROOF*

Prov: Acquired 1905.

ALBERS, Joseph, born 1888

7184   White Line Squares IX

Screenprint, 39.7 × 39.7 cm

Signed: *A'66* (in pencil lower right) *WLS 62-125* (pencil lower left)

Prov: Purchased from Waddington Galleries, 1969.
Exh: W.A.G., *Lithograph and Screenprints from the Waddington Galleries*, 1969 (27).

7185   White Line Squares XV

Screenprint, 39.7 × 39.7 cm

Signed: *A'66* (in pencil lower right) *W.L.S. XV 62-125* (in pencil lower left)

White Line Squares were published by Gemini G.E.L., Los Angeles.[1] According to Hopkins the genesis of the series was in 1964.[2] Work actually began in January 1966 and after 9 months Albers had produced sixteen prints.[3] Albers painted a series of small color studies in oil in connection with the project.[4] Albers points out that when a white line "is placed within a so-called" "Middle colour," (as in this series), "even when the color is evenly applied it will make the colour look like two different shades or tints of that color."[5] A second series of 8 colour lithographs of this title was published in 1967.[6]

Prov: Purchased from Waddington Galleries, 1969.
Exh: W.A.G., *Lithograph and Screenprints from the Waddington Galleries*, 1969 (30).
Ref: **1.** *Art in America*, January-February, 1967, p. 121 and Donald H. Karshan, *American Printmaking 1670-1968*, Art in America, July-August, 1968, p. 50.   **2.** H. T. H., *The New Lithographs* in *Josef Albers White Line Squares*, Los Angeles County Museum of Art, 1966.   **3.** Kenneth E. Tyler, foreword to *Josef Albers White Line Squares*, Los Angeles County Museum of Art, 1966.   **4.** H. T. H., *op. cit.*   **5.** Josef Albers, *White Line Squares* in *Josef Albers White Line Squares*, Los Angeles County Museum of Art, 1966.   **6.** *Art in America*, May-June, 1967, p. 85.

ANTONINI, Annapia, born 1942

7798   Large Green Landscape (Grand Paysage Vert)

Aquatint, 29.5 × 39 cm

Signed and inscribed: *27/30 "Grand paysage vert A. Antonini* (pencil)

7802   Jar (Cruche)

Aquatint, 11.3 × 14.7 cm

Signed and inscribed: *6/15 "Cruche,, A. Antonini* (pencil)

Prov: Purchased from Anthony Dawson, 1969.

APPEL, Karel, born 1921

6223   The Racecourse

Colour lithograph, 55.2 × 75.6 cm

Inscribed: *Appel 60/ 90* (pencil)
$\overline{125}$

Prov: Redfern Gallery; the Medici Gallery, Liverpool from whom purchased 1964.
Exh: ?Redfern Gallery, *Deux Mille gravures en couleur*, 1961/2 (11).

BARTOLOZZI, Francesco, 1725-1815 after LAWRENCE, Thomas, 1769-1830

3181   Elizabeth Farren, later Countess of Derby (1759-1829)

Stipple engraving, 55.5 × 35.4 cm

Inscribed: lower margin: *T. Lawrence Pinxt. Publish'd Jany 1792 by Bull & Jeffryes Ludgate Hill London. F. Bartolozzi Sculpt. R.A. Engraver to his Majesty.*

Fourth state.[1] After the portrait by Lawrence exhibited at the Royal Academy in 1790 (171), now in the Metropolitan Museum of Art, New York.[2] The engraving was begun by Knight and finished by Bartolozzi.[3]

Prov: Leggatt Bros.; Major R. Sutton Timmis, by whom presented, 1933.
Ref: 1. A. De Vesme, *Francesco Bartolozzi*, 1928, pp. 280-1 (1075).   2. K. Garlick, *Sir Thomas Lawrence*, 1954, p. 37, pl. 3.   3. J. T. Herbert Baily, *Francesco Bartolozzi*, 1907, p. 6.

BARTOLOZZI, after MARTIN, William, active 1765-1831

7008   Lady Macduff and family surprised and murdered by order of Macbeth

Stipple engraving, 49 × 60 cm

Inscribed: (lower margin) *Wm. Martin Historic Painter to His Majesty Pinxt F. Bartolozzi R.A. Sculpt/LADY MACDUFF AND FAMILY SURPRISED AND MURDERED BY ORDER OF MACBETH. Vide Shakespeare's Tragedy of Macbeth, Act. IV. Sc2/Enter murderers. Lady Macduff.—"What are these faces?" Murderer "Where is your husband?" Lady Macduff "I hope in no place so unsanctified where such as thou may'st find him."/to the CORPORATION and INHABITANTS of the Borough of Liverpool this plate of LADY MACDUFF./is most respectfully dedicated; by their much obliged and obedient servant, William Martin./Engraved from the Original Picture 12 feet by 9 (presented by the artist &) placed in the Exchange of Liverpool—Published for the Proprietor August 11th 1804 by Wm. Martin, Windsor Castle and H. Macklin, 39 Fleet Street, London/DEUS NOBIS. HAEC OTIA. FECIT* (on scroll beneath coat of arms of Liverpool)

Undescribed 5th state. The first state dates from 1792.[1] After the painting exhibited at the Royal Academy in 1791 (84).

Until the building of the New Exchange, which was begun in 1803, the Town Hall was known as the Exchange. *Gore's Liverpool General Advertiser* made the following announcement on November 24, 1791.[2].

"We have authority to inform the public, that Mr William Martin, Historical Painter (pupil to the late Mr Cipriani) has presented to the town of Liverpool ten pictures, two of which are now in the Exchange, and the whole are intended to be placed in the dining room, when the alterations are completed. Prints are engraving from four of the pictures) the subjects of which are, *Lady Macduff surprised in her Castle at Fife*, and *Cleopatra arming Antony*, will be ready for delivery early in the spring, and the other two in December following, the subjects of these latter are, *Queen Katharine's Vision*, and *Ferdinand's first interview with Miranda*. The six other are smaller ones, to be painted in Chairo Scuro (sic), intended to fill compartments, the subjects being, *History*, *Painting*, *Sculpture*, *Architecture*, *Astronomy*, and *Geometry*.

The pictures now in the Exchange are taken down for the present, but will be put up in the Assembly Room the middle of next week."

No engravings after *Queen Katharine's Vision* and *Ferdinand's first interview with Miranda* are recorded by de Vesme. It is therefore possible that these paintings were never executed. Both scenes are Shakespearian (*Henry VIII* Act 4 Scene 2, and *The Tempest* Act 1 Scene 2).

The other pictures were presumably destroyed in the fire[3] which wrecked the interior of the Town Hall on 18 January 1795. Only the furniture in the basement storey was saved.[4]

Martin had earlier painted a pair of pictures of *Edward and Eleanora* and of the *Death of Lady Jane Gray*, which he presented in 1787 to the Corporation of Norwich, his home town.[5]

Prov: Presumably presented to Liverpool Corporation, 1804; transferred from the Town Hall, 1962.

Ref: **1.** de Vesme, *op. cit.*, p. 463 (1834).   **2.** *Gore's Liverpool General Advertiser*, November 24, 1791, p. 3.   **3.** Matthew Gregson sale, Winstanley, 26 October 1830 (794).   **4.** Liverpool Town Hall and Exchange Minute Book 1795-1797. No. 9 Report of John Foster Junr Surveyor dated 2nd February 1795 (Liverpool Public Library).   **5.** de Vesme, *op. cit.*, p. 135 (518), 140 (530), and *A Catalogue of the Portraits and Paintings in St. Andrew's Hall*, 1905, p. 14 (9) and (10).

7007   Lady Macduff and her family surprised and murdered by order of Macbeth

Coloured stipple engraving, 43.2 × 58.2 cm

Inscribed: *Wm, Martin Historic Painter to his Majesty. Pinxt. F. Bartolozzi R.A. Sculp.*

Undescribed state.[1]

Prov: Presumably presented to Liverpool Corporation; transferred from the Town Hall. 1967.
Ref: **1.** de Vesme, *op. cit.*, p. 463 (1834).

7009   Cleopatra and her attendants assisting to arm Antony

Stipple engraving coloured; 45.2 × 60.8 cm

Inscribed: *Wm. Martin Historic Painter to his Majesty, Pinxt. F. Bartolozzi R.A. Sculpt.* (lower margin)

Undescribed. Without either the publication date of the first described state (November 15, 1792) or the dedication of the second state.[1]

Prov: Presumably presented to Liverpool Corporation; transfered from the Town Hall, 1967.
Ref: **1.** de Vesme, *op. cit.*, pp. 464-5 (1838).

7010   Cleopatra and her attendants assisting to arm Antony

Stipple engraving, 49.1 × 60.9 cm

Inscribed: (lower margin) *Wm. Martin Historic Painter to His Majesty, Pinxt. F. Bartolozzi. R.A. Sculpt./CLEOPATRA AND HER ATTENDANTS ASSISTING TO ARM ANTONY. vide Shakespeare's tragedy of Antony & Cleopatra, Act IV. sc4./Cleopatra. "sooth, la, I'll help: thus it must be." Antony. "Well, well; we shall thrive now–"/to the CORPORATION and INHABITANTS of the Borough of Liverpool this plate of ANTONY and CLEOPATRA is most respectfully dedicated, by their much obliged and obedient humble servant, William Martin./ Engraved from the Original Picture 12 feet by 9 (presented by the artist &) placed in the Exchange of Liverpool. Published for the Proprietor August 11th. 1804, by Wm. Martin, Windsor Castle; and H. Macklin, 39 Fleet Street, London./ DEUS. NOBIS HAEC OTIA. FECIT* (on scroll beneath coat of arms of Liverpool)

Second state.[1]

The picture was destroyed by the fire which wrecked the interior of the Town Hall on 18 January 1795.[2]

Prov: Presumably presented to Liverpool Corporation, 1804; transfered from the Town Hall, 1967.
Ref: 1. de Vesme, *op. cit.*, p; 464-5 (1838).   2. Matthew Gregson sale, Winstanley, 26 October 1830 (794).

BARTSCH, Adam von, 1757-1821 after WEENIX, Jean Baptiste, 1621-1663

7180   A seated man caressing a dog

Etching, 19.5 × 14.5 cm

Signed: *A. Bartsch sc.* (on plate)

Le Blanc 353.[1] After an unsigned etching attributed to Weenix.[2]

Prov: Presented by Charles Ross, 1969.
Ref: 1. Ch. Le Blanc, *Manuel de l'amateur d'estampes*, I, 1854, p. 181.   2. Adam Bartsch, *Le Peintre Graveur*, I, 1845 p. 394 (2).

BARTSCH, after VAN DE VELDE, Adriaen, 1636-1672

7181   Man with crutch and woman with laundry basket

Etching, 12.8 × 12.4 cm

Signed: *A. Bartsch sc.* (on plate)

Le Blanc 352. Third State.[1]

Prov: Presented by Charles Ross, 1969.
Ref: 1. Ch. Le Blanc, *Manuel de l'amateur d'estampes*, I, 1854, p. 181.

BARTSCH after POTTER, Paulus, 1625-1654

7182   Recumbent Cow

Etching, 10.6 × 14.5 cm

Signed: *A Bartsch sc.* (on plate)

Le Blanc 147. Second State.[1]

Prov: Presented by Charles Ross, 1969.

Ref: 1. Ch. Le Blanc, *Manuel de l'amateur d'estampes*, I, 1854, p. 178.

BARTSCH after FICKE, Nicholaes active 1642, dead by 1702

7183 Tethered Horse

Etching, 12.2 × 18.3 cm

Signed: *A. Bartsch sc* (on plate)

Inscribed: *N. Fick 1643* (in reverse on plate)

A copy of Ficke's dated etching of 1643.[1]

Prov: Presented by Charles Ross, 1969.

Ref: 1. F. W. W. Hollstein, *Dutch and Flemish Etchings, Engravings and Woodcuts ca. 1450-1700*, VI, (1952) p. 244.

BECCAFUMI, Domenico, 1486-1551, after

9123 The four doctors of the church

Chiaroscuro Woodcut (two blocks; black and olive green), 22.4 × 17.7 cm

Inscribed: *Dal mecherino*

Watermark: Indistinct

An earlier state exists without the inscription.[1] Whilst the design is clearly Beccafumi's, the authorship of the print is much disputed,[2] the attribution to Beccafumi himself being upheld by Servolini[3] and Sanminiatelli.[4] A related drawing is in the National Gallery of Art, Washington (B-25, 802) bearing an attribution on it to Sebastiano Mazzoni Fiorentino (died 1683).[5]

Prov: Thomas Philipe; from whom bought by William Roscoe, 16 October 1811 5s;[6] his sale, Winstanley, 19 September 1816, with "A Philosopher raising his mantle over his shoulder with his right hand, a pair of compasses in his left, on the ground a globe"[7] as Beccafumi (1281)[8] bt. Robinson £2; Thomas H. Robinson; his sale, Winstanley, 26 March 1819 (906) again with the "Philosopher" 29s bt. in; his sale, Winstanley, Manchester 19 May 1820 again with the "Philosopher" (218); Charles Robert Blundell; by descent to Colonel Sir Joseph Weld; his sale, Christie's, 30 June 1976 (147) bt, in; from whom purchased with the aid of a donation from the Eleanor Rathbone Charitable Trust, 1976.

Ref: 1. Donato Sanminiatelli, *Domenico Beccafumi*, 1967, pl. V cat. Incisioni, n. 3. 2. Adam Bartsch, *Le Peintre Graveur*, XII, 1866, p. 84 (35); J. Judey, *Domenico Beccafumi*, 1932, p. 132; Antony De Witt, *Galleria degli Uffizi, La Collezione delle stampe*, 1938, p. 43 (76); Maria Fossi, *Mostra di Chiaroscuri*

Italiani nei secoli XVI, XVII, XVIII, Florence, Gabinetto Disegni e Stampe degli Uffizi, 1956 (54) and Carlos von Hasselt, *Clairs-obscurs Gravures sur bois imprimées en couleurs de 1500 à 1800 provenant de collections Hollandaises*, Paris, Institut Néerlandais, 1965, p. 27 (45) and *Acquisitions récentes de toutes époques*, Fondation Custodia, *Collection Frits Lugt*, Paris, Insitut Néerlandais, 1974, p. 44 (122), all consider it to be after Beccafumi. **3.** Luigi Servolini, *La xilografia a chiaroscuro italiana nei secoli, XVI, XVII & XVIII*, 1928, p. 77. **4.** Donato Sanminiatelli, *Le esposizione di chiaroscuri agli Uffizi*, Paragone, 73, 1956, p. 58 as between 1524/5 and 1529/32, s.v. BECCAFUMI, Domenico in *Dizionario Biografico degli Italiani*, VII, 1965, p. 421 as between 1524 and 1528 and *Domenico Beccafumi*, 1967, p. 132 (3) as *c.* 1527-30. **5.** *Recent acquisitions and promised gifts*, National Gallery of Art, Washington, 1974, p. 199 rep. as Beccafumi *Study of River Gods*. **6.** Roscoe Papers 5404. **7.** Col. Sir Joseph Weld sale, Christie's, 30 June 1976 (159) bt. Colnaghi. **8.** 1281 inscribed in pencil on old mount.

BEJOT, Eugène, 1867-1931

4618   Port St. Bernard, Paris

Etching, 21.1 × 22.7 cm

Signed: *Eug Bejot Paris 1913* (on plate) *Eug Bejot* (pencil)

Fourth state. From an edition of 60.[1] A view from a window on the Quai Henri IV looking across to Montagne Sainte-Genevieve and the Pantheon.[1]

Prov: Presented by James Connell & Sons, London, 1917.
Ref: 1. Jean Laran, *L'Oeuvre Gravé d'Eugène Béjot*, 1937, pp. 181-2 (309).

BEUTLICH, Tadek, born 1922

6201   Two Fighting Insects

Coloured woodcut, 52.1 × 78.7 cm

Signed: *7/24/"Two Fighting Insects"*, *Tadek Beutlich* (pencil below plate).

Prov: Grabowski Gallery?; the Print Centre, from whom purchased, 1964.
Exh: ?Grabowski Gallery, *Tadek Beutlich*, 1963 (5).

6355   Heatwave in Antarctica

Blockprint, 85.1 × 59.7 cm

Signed: *19/75 "Heatwave in Antarctic" Tadek Beutlich* (pencil)

Prov: Purchased from Prestons Art Gallery, Bolton, 1966.

BLANCHARD, Thomas Marie Auguste, 1819-1898 after HUNT, William Holman, 1827-1910 and MORELLI

4001 The Finding of the Saviour in the Temple

Line engraving, 53.3 × 74.9 cm

Inscribed: *London, Published Aug. 1st. 1867, by E. Gambart and Co, No. 1 Kings Street, St. James* (upper margin) *W. Holman Hunt Aug. Blanchard* (pencil below plate) Printsellers' Association stamp *FHD*

Around the mount there is a white slip with gold lettering bearing the inscription: *The finding of the Saviour in the Temple./And he went with them, and came to Nazareth, and was subject unto them; but his mother kept all these sayings in her heart./And when they found him not, they turned back again to Jerusalem seeking him. And after three days they found him in the Temple./And when they saw him. They were amazed; and his mother said unto him. Son, why hast thou thus dealt with us behold, thy father and I have sought thee sorrowing./And he said unto them, how is it that ye sought me? wist yet not that I must be about my Father's business?*

After Hunt's picture in the City Art Gallery, Birmingham, which was first exhibited at the German Gallery from 1860 to 1862.[1] Morelli had already begun a black chalk drawing after the picture for Gambart by November 1860. Gambart proposed to print from 1,000 to 2,000 artist's proofs at 15 guineas, 1,000 before letters proof at 12 guineas, 1,000 proofs at 8 guineas and 10,000 prints at 5 guineas and expected that the orders could amount to 50,000 guineas in four years.[2] The picture was temporarily withdrawn from the exhibition in August 1861 so that Morelli could complete the drawing after which Blanchard produced his engraving.[3] Morelli's drawing was completed by the end of January 1863.[4] The engraving was originally published 2 June 1863.[5] This version of it was with the printers when Hunt visited Gambart in Paris on the way back from Italy in 1867, and "there was still a touch or two to be given to the plate."[6] On 2 November 1867 the Athenaeum announced that the plate which had occupied Blanchard for no less than 7 years would shortly be published,[7] and on 19 November Hunt informed Gambart that he would call on him to sign the proofs.[8]

Prov: Presented by Mrs Margaret Harvey, 1878.
Ref: 1. *William Holman Hunt*, W.A.G., 1969, pp. 39-41 with full bibliography. 2. Jeremy Maas, *Gambart Prince of the Victorian Art World*, 1975, pp. 131-2 quoting a memorandum addressed by Gambart to the printseller George Pennell dated 12 November 1860. (Gillott Papers). 3. *The Athenaeum*, August 24, 1861, p. 256. 4. *The Athenaeum*, January 31, 1863, p. 157. 5. *An alphabetical list of engravings declared at the Printsellers Association*, 1892, p. 123. 6. Letter of W. Holman Hunt to J. W. Burney, dated Sept. 30, 1867. 7. *The Athenaeum*, November 2, 1867, p. 579 cited by Maas, *op. cit.*, p. 205. 8. *Letter*, John Rylands Library, University of Manchester MS 1268 cited by Maas, *op. cit.*, p. 205.

BLANCHARD, Thomas Marie Auguste, 1819-1898 after ALMA-TADEMA, Lawrence, 1836-1912

4002 Spring

Steel engraving, 47 × 26.6 cm

Inscribed: *London. Published october 1st. 1879 by Pilgeram & Lefevre, 1a King Street, St. James's* (upper margin)/*L Alma Tadema Spring Aug Blanchard* (pencil lower margin) PRINTSELLERS ASSOCIATION Stamp *GC*

After the picture exhibited at the Royal Academy 1877 (117).

4003   Summer

Steel engraving, 47.9 × 26.8 cm

Inscribed: *London. Published october 1st. 1879 by Pilgeram & Lefevre, 1a. King Street, St. James's* (upper margin)/*L Alma Tadema Summer Aug Blanchard* (pencil lower margin) PRINTSELLERS ASSOCIATION Stamp *JY*

After the picture exhibited at the Royal Academy 1877 (118).

4004   Autumn: Vintage Festival

Steel engraving, 47.8 × 26.6 cm

Inscribed: *London. Published october 1st. 1879 by Pilgeram & Lefevre, 1a. King Street, St. James's* (upper margin) /*HERCVLAII/NONI* (on amphora) *L Alma Tadema Aug Blanchard* (pencil lower margin) PRINTSELLERS ASSOCIATION Stamp *NU*

After the picture exhibited at the Royal Academy 1877 (119), now at the City Art Gallery, Birmingham (62' 11)

4005   Winter

Steel engraving, 47.8 × 26.2 cm

Inscribed: *London. Published october 1st. 1879 by Pilgeram & Lefevre, 1a. King Street, St. James's* (upper margin) *L Alma Tadema Aug Blanchard* (pencil lower margin) PRINTSELLERS ASSOCIATION Stamp *RO*

After the picture exhibited at the Royal Academy 1877 (120). The set was reviewed enthusiastically and at length in *The Academy*, 1 May, 1880 p. 331.

Prov: Purchased 1880.[1]
Ref: 1. Libraries, Museums and Arts Committee Extracts Volume, 18 March 1880. Purchased for £21 unframed.

BLUVBERG, Zeilik Grigor'evich, born 1912

6286   Monument to an unknown sailor, Odessa

Colour woodcut, 28.7 × 42 cm

Prov: Presented by the City of Odessa through a delegation, 1965.

BOITARD, Louis Philippe, active 1738-1770 after WANDELAAR, Jan, 1690-1759

7466 Illustration of the muscles of a man walking to the left

Engraving, 55.8 × 40.4 cm

Inscribed: *TAB.IX.* (upper margin) *L. P. Boitard Sculp. Impensis J. & P. Knapton, Londini, 1748* (lower margin)

7470 Illustration of the muscles of a man

Engraving, 55.7 × 40.2 cm

Inscribed: *TAB. II.* (upper margin) *L. P. Boitard Sculp. Impensis J. & P. Knapton, Londini, 1747* (lower margin)

Published by John and Paul Knapton in an English translation of Bernard Siegfried Albinus' *Tabulae Sceleti et Musculorum Corporis Humani* published in 1749.[1] The pose in 7466 is the same as in Ravenet's pl. III in the same set (7467) illustrating a skeleton whilst the pose in 7470 is the same as in Grignion's plates in the same set illustrating muscles (7471 and 7472). The engravings are based on those by Jan Wandelaar in the original 1747 Leiden edition of Albinus.

Prov: Presented by Liverpool College of Art, 1970.
Ref: 1. For further details of this and earlier editions see Judy Egerton in, *George Stubbs anatomist and animal painter*, The Tate Gallery, 1976, pp. 56-57 (6).

BONASONE, Giulio di Antonio, active 1531-1574, after CARRUCCI, Jacopo, called Il Pontormo, 1494-1557

9184 The Birth of Saint John the Baptist

Engraving, 28.4 × 43 cm

Inscribed: *IACOBVS FLORENTINVS IN VENTOR/NATIVITAS BEATI JOANNIS BAPTISTAE/.IVLIO. B.F.* (on pedestal) *Petri de Nobilibus/ANT. LAFRERI./SEQUANI. FORMIS.* (on plate)

The only known engraving by Bonasone after Pontormo. Third state.[1] In the niches in the background are two prophets, Abraham and Isaac, Moses and the Fall of Adam, presumably because the birth of the Baptist provides the bridge between the Old and the New Testament in that the Baptist proclaimed the coming of the Messiah, Christ who was to fulfil the prophecies of the Old Testament.

Prov: William Roscoe; his sale, Winstanley, 11 September 1816 (310) with the *Virgin with the dead Christ*[2] bt. Robinson £1 18s 0d; Thomas H. Robinson sale, Winstanley, 17 March 1819 (191) 9s 6d, bt in; his sale, Winstanley, Manchester, 18 May 1820 (59) with an earlier state 22/6; Charles Robert Blundell; by descent to Colonel Sir Joseph Weld; his sale, Christie's, 7 October 1976 (11) with 9173-9183 bt. in; purchased from Colonel Sir Joseph Weld with 9173-9183, 1976.

Ref: **1.** Adam Bartsch, *Le Peintre Graveur*, XV, 1867, pp. 131-132 (76) does not mention this state. See also Maria Catelli Isola, *Giulio Bonasone e un disegno di Michelangelo in una stampa sconosciuta*, Studi di storia dell'arte bibliogia, ed erudizione in onore di Alfredo Petrucci, 1969, p. 24 n. 9. **2.** Bought by Roscoe for 7s 6d from Philipe 12 August 1808 (Roscoe Papers 5404); Thomas H. Robinson Sale, Winstanley, Manchester, 18 May 1820 part of (57); Colonel Sir Joseph Weld sale, 30 June 1976 (166) bt. Colnaghi.

BONNARD, Pierre, 1867-1947

6633   Children's Garden. Roundabout in the Champs Elysées (Jardins des enfants. Rond-Point des Champs Elysees)

Etching, 33.5 × 25.8 cm

Signed: *P. BONNARD* (on plate)

From the Series *Paris—1937.*

Prov: Purchased from the Folio Fine Art Ltd., 1968.

BOURDON, Sebastien, 1616-1671

9170   The Holy Family with the infant Saint John the Baptist and a bird (La Vierge à l'oiseau)

Etching, 12.8 × 17.3 cm

Signed: *Seb. Bourdon inuent. et fecit* (on plate)

Second state with the address effaced.[1] The bird is probably a goldfinch symbolizing the Passion.

Prov: William Roscoe;[2] his sale, Winstanley, 19 September 1819 (1191)[3] with 9171-9172 and three others[4] bt. Slater 17s; Charles Robert Blundell; by descent to Colonel Sir Joseph Weld; his sale Christie's, 7 October 1976 (12) with 9169 Rosa, 9171-9172; purchased from Colonel Sir Joseph Weld, 1976.

Ref: **1.** A.-P.-F. Robert-Dumesnil, *Le Peintre-Graveur français*, I, 1835, pp. 143-4 (21). **2.** Roscoe bought two etchings by Bourdon on 3 June 1808 from W. Richardson for 12s 6d (Roscoe Papers 5404). **3.** Lot number inscribed in pencil on the back of the mount. **4.** Colonel Sir Joseph Weld sale, Christie's, 30 June 1976 (208) bt. Somerville and Simpson and (209-210) bt. Tunick.

9171   The Holy Family with the Infant Saint John the Baptist (La Vierge à l'ecuelle)

Etching, 16.6 × 16.7 cm (circular)

First state.[1]

Prov: William Roscoe;[2] his sale, Winstanley, 19 September 1816 (1191) with 9170 and
9172[3] and three others[4] bt. Slater 17s; Charles Robert Blundell; by descent to
Colonel Sir Joseph Weld; his sale, Christie's, 7 October 1976 (12) with 9169-
9170 and 9172; purchased from Colonel Sir Joseph Weld, 1976.

Ref: **1.** A.-P.-F. Robert-Dumesnil, *Le Peintre-Graveur français*, I, 1835, p. 139
(12).   **2.** Roscoe bought two etchings by Bourdon on 3 June 1808 from W.
Richardson for 12s 6d, (Roscoe Papers 5404).   **3.** Mounted with 9172 probably by Roscoe.   **4.** Colonel Sir Joseph Weld Sale, Christie's, 30 June 1976
(208-210).

9172   The Flight into Egypt

Etching, 27.9 × 24 cm

Signed: *S. Bourdon, in. et sculp. ex cum priuil.* (on plate)

First state.[1]

Prov: J. B. of 2 Russell Court.[2] William Roscoe, his sale Winstanley, 19 September
1816 (1191) with 9170-9171[3] and three others,[4] bt. Slater 17s; Charles Robert
Blundell; by descent to Colonel Sir Joseph Weld; his sale, Christie's, 7 October
1976 (12) with 9169-9171 bt. in; purchased from Colonel Sir Joseph Weld, 1976.

Ref: **1.** A.-P.-F. Robert-Dumesnil, *Le Peintre-Graveur franéais*, I, 1835, p. 142
(18).   **2.** Inscription in pen on verso, (he is presumably John Barnard—see
Miss Olive Lloyd-Baker sale, Sotheby, 29 June 1965).   **3.** Mounted with
9171.   **4.** Colonel Sir Joseph Weld Sale, Christie's, 30 June 1976 (208-210).

BRAQUE, Georges, 1882-1963

2730   The bird and his nest

Lithograph, 34 × 51.1 cm

Inscribed: *G. Braque* (on block) *G. Braque 54/400* (below block)

2730 is based on the sketch of 1955,[1] for the large painting of 1956 in
the Musée Nationale d'Art Moderne, Paris.[2]

Prov: Purchased from the Redfern Gallery, through the New Shakespeare Theatre Art
Gallery, 1958.

Exh: New Shakespeare Theatre Art Gallery, Liverpool, December, 1958 (4).

Ref: **1.** M. Knoedler & Co., Inc., New York, *Georges Braque 1882-1963, An American Tribute, The Late Years (1940-1963) and The Sculpture*, 1964, (34) in the
collection of John Richardson, New York.   **2.** Musee du Louvre, *Presentation
de la Donation Braque*, 1965 (11).

BRUNET-DEBAINES, Alfred Louis, born 1845

4621   Interior of the Temple Church

Engraving, 25.4 × 18.4 cm

Signed: *A. Brunet Debaines/1878* (on plate)

4622 Fountain Court, The Temple

Engraving, 25.5 × 19.7 cm

Signed: *A. Brunet-Debaines del et ft* (?) (on plate)

4623 Temple Bar

Engraving, 20.9 × 24.7 cm

Signed: *A. Brunet-Debaines Temple Bar 1477*

4624 Lincoln's Inn Fields

Engraving, 16 × 19.8 cm

Signed: *A. Brunet-Debaines*

4625 St. Pauls from Bankside

Engraving, 17.3 × 22.7 cm

Signed: *A. Brunet-Debaines*

4626 The Thames below London Bridge

Mezzotint, 21.2 × 16.5 cm

Signed: *A. Brunet-Debaines* (on plate)

Prov: Purchased 1881.

BRUNET-DEBAINES, Alfred Louis after COROT, Jean-Baptiste-Camille, 1796-1875

4627 Landscape

Etching, 9.1 × 11.9 cm

Inscribed: *COROT* (on plate)

Signed: *A. Brunet Debaines Sₜ.* (lower margin)

Prov: Presented by James Smith of Blundellsands, 1923.

BURGKMAIR, Hans the elder, 1473-1531

6328 A Bactrian Camel with a rider holding a Cartouche

Woodcut, 38.6 × 37.9 cm

Watermark: Double headed eagle bearing a crown; and IF

Inscribed: *23* (on block)

No. 23 from the *Triumphal Procession of the Emperor Maximilian*
which was intended to supplement Durer's *Triumphal Arch* of 1515. The
programme for the *Triumphal Procession*, a series of 135 woodcuts, was
conceived by the Emperor himself and worked out by his secretary Max
Treitzsaurwein in 1512. Burgkmair himself designed only 67 of the
woodcuts; his collaborators included Durer and Altdorfer. The original
programme was never completed, nor were any of the woodcuts, most of
which were designed between 1516 and 1518, published until 1526, after
the Emperor's death.[2] 6328 belongs to the third edition published by
Bartsch in Vienna in 1796.

Prov: Bequeathed by M. D. and B. P. Legge, 1962.
Ref: **1.** F. W. H. Hollstein, *German Engravings, Etchings and Woodcuts ca. 1400-
1700*, V. 1962, p. 120 (574).   **2.** Erwin Panofsky, *The Life and Art of Albrecht
Durer*, 1955, p. 179; and Heinrich Geissler, *Hans Burgkmair Das Graphische
Werk*, Stadtische Kunstsammlungen, Augsburg, 1973 (203).

CARRACCI, Annibale, 1560-1609

9190   Christ mocked

Etching, 17.5 × 13.2 cm

Signed: *Anib. Carracius in. et. fecit. 1606* (on plate)

Second state.[1] A preparatory drawing is at Chatsworth (inv. 430.)[2].

Prov: William Roscoe, his sale, Winstanley 14 September 1816 (727)[3] with 9191[4] bt.
Slater 9s 6d; Charles Robert Blundell; by descent to Colonel Sir Joseph Weld; his
sale, Christie's, 7 October 1976 (16) with 9191 bt. in; purchased from Colonel Sir
Joseph Weld by the Liverpool Daily Post and Echo Ltd, by whom presented,
1976.
Ref: **1.** Adam Bartsch, *Le Peintre Graveur*, XVIII, 1818, p. 182 (3) and Maurizio Calvesi and Vittorio Casale, *Le Incisioni dei Carracci*, Rome, 1965, p. 70
(219).   **2.** Ralph Holland, *The Carracci Drawings and Paintings*, The Hatton
Gallery, Newcastle upon Tyne, 1961 (158) and J. Byam Shaw, *Old Master Drawings from Chatsworth*, Washington and New York, 1969/70 p. 21 (24).   **3.** Lot
number inscribed in pencil on back of mount.   **4.** Mounted with 9190, probably by William Roscoe.

9191   The Adoration of the Shepherds

Etching, 10.4 × 13.1 cm

Signed: *Annibal Caracius fecit et inue* (on plate)

Second state.[1] The design is related to a composition by Correggio
known from a drawing in the Fitzwilliam Museum, Cambridge.[2] A preparatory drawing by Annibale is at Windsor.[3] Posner argues that since a

discarded study for 9191 was made on the back of a proof impression of the 1606 print of *Christ Mocked*, 9191 dates about 1606.[4] The connection, however, is unproven. Mahon[5] and Calvesi and Casale[6] date it about 1604, whilst Wittkower[7] accepts Bodmer's[8] dating at the end of the artist's career.

Prov: C. M. Cracherode (Lugt 606);[9] William Roscoe; his sale, Winstanley, 14 September 1816 (727) with 9190[10] bt. Slater 9s 6d; Charles Robert Blundell; by descent to Colonel Sir Joseph Weld; his sale, Christie's, 7 October 1976 (16) with 9190 bt. in; purchased from Colonel Sir Joseph Weld by the Liverpool Daily Post and Echo, by whom presented, 1976.

Ref: **1.** Adam Bartsch, *Le Peintre Graveur*, XVIII, 1818, p. 181 (2).   **2.** Corrado Ricci, *Correggio*, 1930, p. 171 and Donald Posner, *Annibale Carracci, A Study in the Reform of Italian Painting around 1590*, I, 1971, p. 167 n. 80.   **3.** R. Wittkower, *The drawings of the Carracci in the collection of Her Majesty the Queen at Windsor Castle*, 1952, p. 147 (356) fig. 50.   **4.** Posner, *op. cit.*, II pp. 47-8, 73 (175).   **5.** Denis Mahon in *Mostra dei Carracci, Disegni*, Bologna, 1956, pp. 174-175 (263) as perhaps around 1604-5.   **6.** Maurizio Calvesi and Vittorio Casale, *Le Incisioni dei Carracci*, Rome, 1965, p. 69 (215).   **7.** Wittkower, *op. cit.*, p. 147.   **8.** Heinrich Bodmer, *Bemerkungen zu Annibale Carraccis graphischen Werk*, Die Graphischen Kunste, III, 1938, p. 117.   **9.** Inscription in verso in pencil *c.m.c.—1961/no. 49.*   **10.** 9190 and 9191 were mounted together, probably by Roscoe.

CARRACCI, Annibale, after

9121   Christ and the Samaritan Woman at the Well

Engraving, 29.1 × 41.7 cm

Inscribed: *Anibal Car. invent et sculp./1610/Petrus Stephanonius formis Cum Privilegio*

Watermark: Fleur de lys

Second state.[1] The first state is dated 1595 and is unsigned and bears no inscription. After the painting in the Brera.[2] The attribution of the print has been much disputed. Traditionally given to Reni,[3] Malvasia suggested Francesco Brizio as the author,[4] whilst Bodmer,[5] Anthony de Witt[6] and Calvesi and Casale[7] include it among Annibale's own etchings, the latter, however, expressing some doubt as to the validity of the attribution. Posner, however, assumes that the attribution to Annibale on this state is an error by the publisher,[8] and thinks that it is possibly by Reni.[9]

Prov: William Roscoe; his sale, Winstanley, 14 September 1816 (732) as by Fr. Brizio with 9191 and one other item;[10] bt. Slater [11] 15s; Charles Robert Blundell; by descent to Colonel Sir Joseph Weld; his sale, Christie's, June 30, 1976 (178) bt. National Art-Collections Fund by whom presented 1976.

Ref: **1.** Adam Bartsch, *Le Peintre Graveur*, XVIII, 1818, pp. 304-5.   **2.** Donald Posner, *Annibale Carracci—A Study in the Reform of Italian Paintings around 1590*, 1971, I, p. 33 (77).   **3.** Carlo Cesare Malvasia, *Felsina Pittrice*, 1678, pp. 102-3 followed by Bartsch *op. cit.*   **4.** Malvasia, *op. cit.*   **5.** Heinrich Bodmer, *Bemerkungen zu Annibale Carraccis graphischen Werk*, Die Graphischen Kunste, III, 1938, pp. 111, 114, fig. 8.   **6.** Anthony de Witt, *Galleria degli Uffizi. La Collezione delle stampe*, 1938, p. 162.   **7.** Maurizio Calvesi and Vittorio Casale, *Le Incisioni dei Carracci*, Rome, 1965, pp. 65-66 (208).   **8.**

Posner, *op. cit.*, 1971, I, p. 26.   **9.** Posner, *op. cit.*, I, p. 33.   **10.** 9191 is Annibale Carracci's *Adoration of the Magi* (Bartsch false, I; Calvesi and Casale 210) which was in Colonel Sir Joseph Weld sale, Christie's, 7 October 1976 (17).   **11.** Slater, a Catholic clergyman acted for Blundell at both Roscoe's prints and drawings sales. MS notes in British Museum copy of Roscoe sale catalogue. He is almost certainly the Benedictine, Dom Edward B. Slater (1774-1832) born in Liverpool, who served at Croston in Lancashire between 1804 and 1814, who later was created Bishop of Ruspa *in partibus infidelium* and Vicar Apostolic of the Mauritius. This information was kindly provided by Father Francis Edwards S. J., *letter*, 4 October, 1976.

CARRACCI, Lodovico, 1555-1619

9188   The Madonna and Child with the infant Saint John the Baptist

Drypoint, 21.1 × 13.5 cm

Signed: *Ludouico Caratio fece/1604* (on plate)

Generally accepted as by Lodovico,[1] although Bodmer considers that it is by a pupil after Lodovico's design.[2] A preparatory drawing is at Chatsworth,[3] and the final study indented for the engraving and blackened on the verso for transfer was in the Ellesmere Collection.[4]

Prov: William Roscoe; his sale, Winstanley, 14 September 1816 (712) with 9189 bt. Slater[5] 8s; Charles Robert Blundell; by descent to Colonel Sir Joseph Weld; his sale, Christie's, 7 October 1976 (18) with 9189 bt. in; purchased from Colonel Sir Joseph Weld by the Liverpool Daily Post and Echo, by whom presented, 1976.

Ref: 1. Adam Bartsch, *Le Peintre Graveur*, XVIII, 1818, p. 25 (3) and Maurizio Calvesi and Vittorio Casale, *Le Incisioni dei Carracci*, Rome, 1965p. 57 (190).   **2.** Heinrich Bodmer, *Lodovico Carracci*, 1939, p. 156 (2) pl. 99.   **3.** Bodmer, *op. cit.*, p. 148 (9).   **4.** Sotheby's, 11 July 1972 (7). On loan to the Fitzwilliam Museum, Cambridge.   **5.** For Slater see 9121 CARRACCI, Annibale after.

CARRACCI, Lodovico, after

9189   The Madonna and Child with the infant Saint John the Baptist

Etching, 18.9 × 12.8 cm

A copy after 9188 not mentioned by Bartsch under Lodovico.

Prov: William Roscoe, his sale, Winstanley, 14 September 1816 (712) with 9188 bt. Slater 8s; Charles Robert Blundell; by descent to Colonel Sir Joseph Weld; his sale, Christie's, 7 October 1976 (18) with 9188 bt. in; purchased from Colonel Sir Joseph Weld, 1976.

CHAGALL, Marc, born 1887

636 Moonlight (Clair du Lune)

Colour lithograph, 68.3 × 49.5 cm

Inscribed: 1949 MArc ChAgAll (plate) MARC CHAGALL (black ink)

Prov: Purchased from the Redfern Gallery, 1957 at *Modern Colour Lithographs* Exhibition.

Exh: ?Redfern Gallery, *An Exhibition of Colour lithographs, etchings, aquatints, lithographed affiches, pochoirs*, 1956/7, (41); W.A.G., *Modern Colour Lithographs*, 1957 (22).

CHAHINE, Edgar, born 1874

433 Quartier du Combat

Etching and aquatint, 20 × 25.5 cm

Signed: *Edgar Chahine* (pencil)

Prov: Purchased from the artist at the L.A.E., 1909.
Exh: L.A.E., 1909 (1422).

4635 Ghemma in a black turban (Ghemma en turban noir)

Drypoint, 49.9 × 29.9 cm

Signed and inscribed: *Edgar Chahine 1/50* (pencil) *ED SAGOT/EDITEUR/PARIS* (stamp) *Ghemma en Turban noir* (pencil)

Chahine also produced a drypoint of Ghemma standing.[1]

Prov: Purchased from the artist at the L.A.E., 1910.
Exh: L.A.E., 1910 (1334).
Ref: 1. Librairie Auguste Blaizot; Paris, *Chahine Exposition de son Oeuvre illustré*, 1974 (52) as 1907.

4636 Lara

Drypoint, 34.9 × 45.8 cm

Signed: *Edgar Chahine 3/50 (pencil)*

Prov: Purchased from the artist at the L.A.E., 1912.
Exh: L.A.E., 1912, (1751).

CHRISTO, Javacheff, born 1935

8481 Wrapped monument to Leonardo

Photo-lithograph, 68.1 × 55.3 cm

Signed and inscribed: *WRAPPED MONUMENT TO LEONARDO (PROJECT FOR PIAZZA DELLA SCALA, MILANO) PHOTO SHUNK KENDER* (on block *322*/(pencil) *999* (on block) *Christo* (pencil below block)

Prov: Purchased from Prue O'Day, Don Anderson, "Modern Prints", 1973.

8482 Wrapped Monument to Leonardo

Photo-lithograph, 68.4 × 55.5 cm

Signed and inscribed: *WRAPPED MONUMENT TO LEONARDO (PROJECT FOR PIAZZA DELLA SCALA, MILANO)* (on plate) *332*/(pencil) *999* (on block) *Christo* (pencil below block).

The project dates from 1970.

Prov: Purchased from Prue O'Day, Don Anderson, "Modern Prints", 1973.

CLOUWET, Albertus, 1636-1679

8569 Portrait of Baccio Bandinelli

Engraving; 17.0 × 11.9 cm

Inscribed: *BARTHELEMY SURNOME BACCIO/BANDINELLI Sculpteur et Peintre/Né à Florence en 1487. Mort dans la même Ville/en 1559/A Paris chez Odieuvre C.P.R.*

This engraving was mounted behind 4161, a drawing by an imitator of Parmigianino, which was attributed to Bandinelli when in Roscoe's collection.

The engraving was published in Dreux du Radier's *L'Europe Illustré*, volume VI in both the 1765 and 1777 editions. The engraving is by the same hand as the portraits of Michelangelo and Peter Brueghel the Elder in the same volume. The technique is very close to the portrait of Guercino, which is signed Ab. Clouwet.

Bandinelli is wearing a shell with a cross, the badge of the knighthood of St. James conferred on him by the Emperor Charles V.

Prov: William Roscoe; John Walter, his sale, Sotheby's, 12 November 1959, part of (56a) bt. C. G. Boerner; P. & D. Colnaghi & Co. Ltd., from whom purchased, 1960.

370

COLIN, Paul Emile, born 1877

4660   Unloading (on décharge)

Woodcut, 7.5 × 12.1 cm

Signed and inscribed: *P E Colin/"La Terre et l'Homme"/d'Anatole France/faisant suite a/"Les Travaux et les Jours" d'Hesiode/On décharge* (pencil)

Exh: L.A.E., 1911 (1603).

4659   Haymaking in the Vosges (Les Foins dans les Vosges)

Woodcut, 6.8 × 12.1 cm

Signed and inscribed: *P E Colin/"La Terre et l'Homme"/d'Anatole France/faisant suite a "Les Travaux et Les Jours" d'Hesiode/Les Foins dans les Vosges* (pencil)

Exh: L.A.E., 1911 (1605).

4658   Driving Sheep (Le Troupeau)

Woodcut, 8.3 × 12.1 cm

Signed and inscribed: *P. E. Colin/"La Terre et l'Homme"/d'Anatole France/Le Troupeau* (pencil)

Exh: L.A.E., 1911 (1613).

4657   Harvest time at Domrémy, Meuse (La Moisson à Domrémy, Meuse)

Woodcut, 6.2 × 12.1 cm

Signed and inscribed: *P. E. Colin/La Terre et l'Homme/d'Anatole France/faisant suite a/Les Travaux et les Jours d'Hesiode/La Moisson à Domrémy* (pencil)

Exh: L.A.E., 1911 (1606).

4 of 20 illustrations by Colin to Anatole France's *La Terre et l'Homme*, exhibited in Liverpool. Colin produced 114 woodcuts in all for *Les Travaux et les jours d'Hesiode, traduction de Paul Mazon, suivis de la Terre et l'homme, par Anatole France*, which was published in Paris in 1912.

Prov: Purchased from the artist at the L.A.E., 1911.

COROT, Jean-Baptiste-Camille, 1796-1875

332 Souvenir of Tuscany (Souvenir de Toscane)

Etching, 13.4 × 18.2 cm

Signed: *C.C.* (on plate)

Third state.[1] Delteil dates it around 1845. Corot's journey to Italy in 1843 probably inspired this etching. It was not completed until about 1865.

Prov: Bequeathed by James Smith of Blundellsands, 1923.
Ref: **1.** Loys Delteil, *Le Peintre-Graveur Illustré*, V, *Corot*, 1910 (1).

COTTINGHAM, Robert, born 1935

8557 "Orph"

Photo-lithograph, 59.7 × 90.5 cm

Signed: *223/300 Cottingham* (pencil)

From *10 documenta super realists* portfolio, published by Shorewood Atelier, NYC, edition of 300 in 1972.[1] Cottingham was an art director in advertising before becoming a full time painter and expressed his fascination with advertising signs particularly of the nineteen thirties and forties in an interview with Linda Chase and Ted McBurnett.[2]

Prov: Purchased from Prue O'Day, Don Anderson "Modern Prints", 1973.
Ref: **1.** Art in America, November-December 1972, p. 161 (repr.) also reproduced in Kunstverein Braunschweig and elsewhere, 1973-4, *Amerikanischer Fotorealismus Grafik* (10).   **2.** *The Photo-Realists: 12 Interviews*, Art in America, November-December, 1972, p.77.

DAUPHIN, Eugene Baptiste Emile, active 1880-1907

1318   The Quai at Toulon (Le Quai de Toulon)

Colour etching and aquatint, 46.7 × 58.3 cm

Signed: *E. Dauphin No. 39* (pencil)

Prov: Purchased from the artist at the L.A.E., 1906.
Exh: *L.A.E.*, 1906 (1060).

DINE, Jim, born 1935

7809 Rainbow

Colour lithograph on Hodgkinson's hand made paper, 37 × 45 cm

Signed: *Jim Dine 120/150 1972* (pencil)

From the edition donated by the artist in aid of the National Council for Civil Liberties and Release. Issued by Petersburg Press Ltd., 59a Portobello Road, London W.11. The Rainbow has been a recurring theme in this artist's work.[1]

Prov: Purchased from Prue O'Day, Don Anderson, Modern Prints, 1972.
Ref: 1. For instance, Museum Boymans-van Beuningen, Rotterdam, 1971, *Jim Dine* (5), (56), and Whitechapel Art Gallery, 1970/1 *3——→00: new multiple art*, (172).

DOS SANTOS, Bartolomeu, born 1931

6927 Bishops' Meeting[1]

Aquatint, 25 × 29.9 cm

Signed and inscribed: *38/50 Bishop's Meeting Bartolomeu '62* (in pencil below plate)

Prov: London Graphic Art Associates from whom purchased, 1969.
Ref: 1. Wayne Dynes, *Bartolomeu Dos Santos, Graphic Works*, n.d. (*c.* 1967), pl. 2.

6145 The Thames

Colour aquatint, 33 × 86.3 cm

Signed and inscribed: *24/30 The Thames Bartolomeu—62* (pencil)

Dos Santos has also produced an etching and aquatint in colours of this subject in an edition of 70.[1]

Prov: Purchased from St. George's Gallery, 1962.
Ref: 1. Wayne Dynes, *Bartolomeu Dos Santos, Graphic Works*, London, n.d. (*c.* 1967), pl. 13 as 1963/66.

DUFY, Raoul, 1877-1953

637 Harvest time (Le Moisson)

Lithograph, 61.5 × 50 cm

Inscribed: *115/200* (pencil) *Raoul Dufy* (ink)

Prov: Purchased from the Redfern Gallery, 1957.
Exh: ?Redfern Gallery, *An exhibition of colour lithographs, etchings, aquatints, lithographed affiches, pochoirs*, 1956/7 (84). W.A.G., *Modern Colour Lithographs*, 1957 (35).

638 Flags, Nice (Drapeaux, Nice)

Lithograph, 51.5 × 43.4 cm

Inscribed: *Raoul Dufy* (on block) *Raoul Dufy* (ink) *71/200* (pencil)

Prov: Purchased from the Redfern Gallery, 1957.
Exh: ?Redfern Gallery, *An exhibition of colour lithographs, etchings, aquatints, lithographed affiches, pochoirs*, 1956/7 (88). W.A.G., *Modern Colour Lithographs*, 1957 (37).

6224 The Parade (La Parade)

Colour lithograph, 35.5 × 45 cm

Inscribed: *Raoul Dufy* (on block)

Prov: Redfern Gallery; the Medici Gallery, Liverpool from whom purchased 1964.
Exh: The Medici Gallery, Liverpool, 1964, *Modern Lithographs* (15).

DUFY, Raoul, after

2731 Orchestral troup (Troup d'orchestre)

Lithograph, 51.7 × 43.5 cm

Inscribed: *Raoul Dufy* (on block) *Raoul Dufy 127/200* (pencil)

After the central area of the 1948 oil *Le Grand Concert* in the Musee de Nice.[1]

Prov: Purchased from the Redfern Gallery though the New Shakespeare Theatre Art Gallery, 1958.
Exh: ?Redfern Gallery, *An exhibition of colour lithographs, etchings, aquatints, lithographed affiches, pochoirs*, 1956/7 (76). New Shakespeare Theatre Art Gallery, Liverpool 1958 (19).
Ref: 1. Lille, Palais des Beaux-Arts, 1964, *Raoul Dufy*, pl. 20.

DURER, Albrecht, 1471-1528

4527 The Promenade

Engraving, 19.3 × 12.1 cm

Signed: *AD* in monogram

First state.[1] Panofsky dates it about 1498,[2] Ravenel about 1497[3] and Levin about 1496-7.[4] The composition is foreshadowed in a drawing of a strolling couple at Hamburg of about 1492-3[5] and in a drawing at Oxford.[6]

The meaning of this engraving is discussed by R. Wustmann.[7]

Prov: John Tetlow (Lugt 2868); James Smith of Blundellsands, who bequeathed it in 1923.

Ref: **1.** F. W. H. Hollstein, *German Engravings, Etchings and Woodcuts 1400-1700*, VII, 1962, p. 78 (83). **2.** Erwin Panofsky *Albrecht Durer*, 1945, I, p. 69, II p. 28 (201). **3.** Guillard F. Ravenel, in *Durer in America, His Graphic Works*, National Gallery of Art, Washington, 1971, pp. 120-1 (13). **4.** William R. Levin, *Images of Love and Death in Late Mediaeval and Renaissance Art*, The University of Michigan Museum, 1975-1976, p. 75 (35). **5.** Friedrich Winkler, *Die Zeichnungen Albrecht Durers*, I, 1936, pp. 40-41 (56). **6.** Winkler, *op. cit.*, I, pp. 110-11 (163). **7.** *Von einigen Tieren und Pflanzen bei Durer*, Zeitschrift fur bildende Kunst, 1911, p. 112. See also *Europe in Torment: 1450-1550*, Rhode Island School of Design, Providence, 1974, pp. 104-5 (39).

4528 St. John the Baptist and St. Onuphrius

Woodcut, 21.4 × 14.3 cm

Panofsky dates the original woodcut about 1504.[1] No. 4528 is a later impression.[2]

Prov: Thomas Bewick (stamp unrecorded by Lugt on verso); Miss Isabella Bewick; her sale, Newcastle, Davison, 6 February 1884 (343); Edwin Sanderson;[3] James Smith of Blundellsands, who bequeathed it, 1923.

Ref: **1.** Panofsky, *op. cit.*, II, p. 40 (332). **2.** Hollstein, *op. cit.*, p. 186 (230). **3.** Stamp on backboard.

4529 Frederick the Wise, Elector of Saxony (1463-1525)

Engraving, 19.3 × 12.7 cm

Inscribed: *AD* in mongram. *CHRISTO. SACRVM./.ILLE. DEI VERBO. MAGNA PIETATE. FACIEBAT./.PERPETVA. DIGNVS. POSTERITATE. COLI./.D. FRIDR. DVCI. SAXON. S.R. IMP./.ARCHIM. ELECTORI./ALBERTVS. DURER. NVR. FACIEBAT. B.M.F.V.V./M..D. XXIIII.*

First state.[1] A preliminary drawing for this engraving is in the Ecole des Beaux Arts, Paris.[2] Frederick the Wise, Elector of Saxony (1463-1525) was the Founder of the University of Wittenburg, supporter of Luther and the most important patron of Cranach. He was in Nurenburg between November 1522 and February 1523.[3]

Prov: Bequeathed by James Smith of Blundellsands, 1923.
Ref: **1.** Hollstein, *op. cit.*, VII, p. 93 (102). **2.** Friedrich Winkler, *Die Zeichnungen Albrecht Durers*, IV, 1939, p. 76 (897). **3.** *1471 Albrecht Durer 1971*, Germanischen Nationalmuseums, Nurnberg, 1971, p. 296 (547).

4531 Samson fighting with a lion

Woodcut, 38.4 × 28 cm

Signed: *AD* in monogram

Hollstein (107).[1] Panofsky dates it 1497-8.[2] The pose of Samson is based on an engraving of *c.* 1475 by Israel van Meckenen. The figure, however, is transformed through knowledge of the Italian Renaissance.[3]

Prov: W. L. Kerry, who presented it to the L.R.I., before 1859;[4] deposited at the W.A.G., 1893; presented, 1948.

Ref: **1.** Hollstein, *op. cit.,* VII, p. 98.   **2.** Panofsky, *op. cit.,* II, p. 31 (222).   **3.** Ravenel, *op. cit.,* p. 163 (86).   **4.** 1859 Catalogue p. 74 (183).

DURER, Albrecht, Imitator of

4530   The Entombment

Engraving, 23.6 × 17.7 cm

Inscribed: *AD* in monogram (on tablet hanging from tree) *1507* (on tomb) *SICVT IN ADA OM/NES MORIVNTVR/ITA ET IN CHRIS-TO/OMNES VIVIFICAB/VNTVR* (on tablet held by cherub).

A forgery,[1] as was already realized in 1830.[2]

Prov: Robert Balmanno (Lugt 214); his sale Sotheby's, May 4, 1830 part of (786) bt. Palier 9s 6d; James Smith of Blundellsands, who bequeathed it, 1923.

Ref: **1.** J. Heller, *Albrecht Durers Leben und Werke,* II, Band, II Abteilung, Bamberg, 1827, p. 839 (2254).   **2.** The Robert Balmanno sale catalogue describes it "the Entombment after him Durer, (in Kilian's style)," a reference to the Augsburg family of engravers of the 17th and 18th centuries.

ERNST, Max, born 1891

2734   The wood and the blue moon (Bois et la lune bleu)

Lithograph, 54 × 43.8 cm

Inscribed: *max ernst* (bottom right and left)

Probably a reproduction of a tapestry pulled from a lithograph, *Forest,* in the collection of Katy Sursok, Geneva.[1]

Prov: Purchased from the Redfern Gallery through the New Shakespeare Theatre Art Gallery, 1958.

Exh: New Shakespeare Theatre Art Gallery, Liverpool, 1958 (27).

Ref: **1.** Giuseppe Gatt, *Max Ernst,* 1970, p. 37. It is much smaller in size than the original print 123 × 98 cm

6225   The evening and the blue moon (Le soir et la lune bleu)

Colour lithograph, 30.5 × 41.3 cm

Inscribed: *Max Ernst* (pencil)

Prov: Redfern Gallery; the Medici Gallery, Liverpool from whom purchased 1964.

Exh: ?Redfern Gallery, *Deux Mille Gravures en Couleur,* 1961/2 (470); The Medici Gallery, Liverpool, 1964, *Modern Lithographs* (21).

FANTUZZI, Antonio, active 1537-1550 after ROSSO Fiorentino, 1495-1540

9119   Contest between Minerva and Neptune

Etching, 26.1 × 40.9 cm

The subject is the competition between the two gods for the land of Cecrops in Attica. Victory went to Minerva, who is being crowned with a wreath. For her gift of the olive tree (in front of her) was preferred to Neptune's of the horse, which he holds in a grouping reminiscent of the *Horsetamers* on the Capitol in Rome. The contest is watched by Jupiter with his thunderbolts, Saturn or Time with his Scythe and other deities in the clouds, whilst Mercury, the messenger of the Gods stands behind Minerva. The figure on the ground with the tower on her head is Athens. The exact literary source for this composition is unknown since the horse is not mentioned in the principal sources for the myth.[1] Far more figures appear than in other 16th century representations of the story.[2]

The end wall of the *Galerie Francois Ier* in the Palace of Fontainebleau contains a painting by Jean Alaux (1788-1864) after the composition by Rosso reflected in 9119, but there is no evidence that the subject was ever included in the original decoration of the Gallery. It is possible that the Rosso composition was only planned and never executed.[3] A partial copy of Fantuzzi's print is in the Louvre (Inv. 8738).[4] An engraving sometimes attributed to Rene Boyvin also reflects the Rosso design, but is much squatter in format, includes more at the sides and less at the top than the Fantuzzi.[5]

The subject of the composition, the contest resulting in the creation of the horse a symbol of war and passion and of the olive tree, a symbol of peace and prosperity,[6] could refer to a decision of Francis I to turn from a warlike to a peaceful policy.

Zerner dates 9119 to 1542.[7]

Prov: Thomas Thane (Lugt 2433); William Roscoe, his sale, Winstanley, 14 September 1816 (672) with *Cadmus, with the monogram AFI*[9] as Primaticcio bt. Slater £1 18s 0d;[10] Charles Robert Blundell;[11] by descent to Colonel Sir Joseph Weld; his sale, Christie's, June 30, 1976 (173) bt. by the National Art-Collections Fund, by whom presented, 1976.

Ref: 1. A. Pigler, *Barockthemen*, II, 1974, p. 184 for instance cites Ovid, *Metamorphoses*, VI, 70-82. The earliest reference to the horse that the compiler can trace is Maurus Servius Honoratus Grammaticus on Virgil, *Georgics*, I, 12ff where the other elements in the story are not mentioned. An edition was published in Paris in 1532, but presumably there is a late 15th or early 16th century source which includes all the elements of the story.   2. Pigler, *op. cit.*, p. 184 lists other examples.   3. Kurt Kusenberg, *Le Rosso*, 1931, pp. 196-7, n. 159.   4. Dora and Erwin Panofsky, *The Iconography of the Galerie Francois Ier at Fontainebleau*, Gazette des Beaux Arts, 1958, pp. 176-177 n. 112 and Sylvie Beguin, *Henri Zerner, Ecole de Fontainebleau, Gravures*, Revue de l'Art, 1969, p. 105. H. Z(erner), *Les estampes et le style de l'ornement*, in *La Galerie Francois Ier au Chateau de Fontainebleau*, Revue de l'Art, Numero special, 1972, p. 115 argues that the composition would not have fitted the space if the disposition of the west wall of the Gallery was the same as that of the east wall.   4. Beguin, *op. cit.*, p. 105.   5. The attribution proposed by A. P. F. Robert-Dumesnil, *Le Peintre-Graveur*, VIII, 1850, p. 45 (67), is accepted by F. Herbet, *Catalogue de l'Oeuvre de Fantuzzi*, Les Graveurs de l'Ecole de Fontainebleau, II, Annales de la Societe historique et archeologique du Gâtinais, 1896 (1897), Fontainebleau, p. 25 (26), and A. Linzeler, *Bibliotheque Nationale Departement des estampes, Inventaire des fonds francais Graveurs du seizieme siecle*, I, 1938, p. 177; but is doubted by Jacques Levron, *Rene Boyvin graveur angevin du XVIe siecle*, 1941, p. 75 and H(enri). Z(erner). in *L'Ecole de Fontainebleau*, Grand Palais, Paris, 1972-1973, p. 265 (312). **6.** Dora and Erwin Panofsky, *op. cit.*, p. 176, n. 112. **7.** Henri Zerner, *L'eau forte a Fontainebleau, le role de Fantuzzi*, Art de France, 1964, p. 75, and H(enri). Z(erner). *op. cit.*, p. 265 (312). See also Henri Zerner, *The School of Fontainebleau Etchings and Engravings*, 1969, A.F.32. **8.** This number appears on the back of the old mount in pencil. **9.** Colonel Sir Joseph Weld, sale, Christie's, June 30, 1976 (174) bt. Colnaghi also with the number 672 on the back of the old mount in pencil. **10.** Slater acted for Blundell at the Roscoe prints' and drawings' sales. For further details see CARRACCI, Annibale, after 9121. **11.** Mounted originally in an album bearing the typed title *No. 3 Italian Etchings*, (Colonel Sir Joseph Weld Sale, Christie's, May 25, 1977, lot 237).

FRANCO, Giovanni Battista called Il Semolei, 1498-1561

9185   Melchisedech offering bread and wine to Abraham

Etching and burin, 26.7 × 41 cm

Signed: *Batista franco fecit* (on plate)

Watermark: Two crescents

Second state.[1] The print illustrates *Genesis XIV* 18-20.[2]

Prov: William Roscoe, his sale, Winstanley, 14 September 1816 (694) as *Presents brought to Solomon* bt. Slater 10s 6d; Charles Robert Blundell; by descent to Colonel Sir Joseph Weld; his sale, Christie's, 7 October, 1976 (52) bt in; purchased by the Liverpool Daily Post and Echo Ltd., by whom presented, 1976.

Ref: **1.** Adam Bartsch, *Le Peintre Graveur*, XVI, 1818, p. 120 (5). **2.** For other examples of this subject see A. Pigler, *Barockthemen*, I, 1974, pp. 34-37. **3.** Lot number inscribed in pencil on back of mount.

GIORDANO, Luca, 1632-1705

9174   The Assumption and Coronation of Saint Anne

Etching, 32 × 25.2 cm

Signed: *Lucas Jordanus In et sculp.* (on plate)

Second state.[1] Milkovich dates the etching after Giordano's return from Spain.[2]

Prov: ?Cecchi, from whom bought by William Roscoe, December 1812 for 3s 6d;[3] ?William Roscoe his sale, Winstanley, 16 September 1816 (878) bt. Robinson 14s 0d; Thomas Robinson sale, Winstanley, 22 March 1819 (591) 10s, Charles Robert Blundell; by descent to Colonel Sir Joseph Weld his sale, Christie's, 7 October 1976 (11) with 9173, 9175-9184 bt. in; purchased from Colonel Sir Joseph Weld, 1976.

Ref: **1.** Adam Bartsch, *Le Peintre Graveur*, XXI, 1821, p. 177 (6) and Oreste Ferrari and Giuseppe Scavizzi, *Luca Giordano*, I, 1966, pl. XLV.   **2.** Michael Milkovich in *Luca Giordano in America*, Brooks Memorial Art Gallery, Memphis, Tennessee, 1964, p. 37 (41).   **3.** Roscoe Papers 5404.

GODEFROY, Jean, 1771-1839 after GERARD, Baron Francois, 1770-1837

4008 Napoleon at the Battle of Austerlitz

Engraving, 54 × 101.2 cm

Inscribed: *F. Gerard Pinxt. 1810 J. Godefroy Sculpt. 1813/a Paris chez J. Godefroy rue Bellefond No. 37/F. B. Montmartre* (below plate)

After the picture at Versailles.

Prov: Presented by R. Wingfield, 1877.[1]

Ref: **1.** The gift to the Gallery of 4008 by Mr Wingfield of 4 Baltic Buildings, Red Cross Street was accepted on 24 January 1877 (Libraries, Museums and Arts Committee Extracts Volume, Liverpool Public Library).

GOINGS, Ralph, born 1928

8559 Van outside Garage

Photo-lithograph, 46.3 × 65.8 cm

Signed: *Ralph Goings* (pencil bottom right); *H.C.VI* (pencil bottom left)

Issued in an edition of 200.[1]

In an interview with Brian Doherty, Goings has expressed his interest in the randomness in any given segment of the environment. "I believe in a kind of random order in the way reality has put itself together—a functional arrangement rather than a visual arrangement."[2]

Prov: Purchased from the D.M. Gallery, 1973.

Ref: **1.** Kunstverein Braunschweig and elsewhere, 1973-4, *Amerikanischer Fotorealismus Grafik*, (20) repr.   **2.** *The Photo-Realists: 12 Interviews*, Art in America, November-December, 1972, p. 88.

GRIGNION, Charles I, 1717-1810 after WANDELAAR, Jan, 1690-1759

7469   Illustration of the muscles of a man with his back turned

Engraving, 57.2 × 41 cm

Inscribed: *TAB.VIII.* (upper margin) *C. Grignion Sculp Impensis J. & P. Knapton Londini, 1748* (lower margin)

7471   Illustration of the muscles of a man

Engraving, 56.4 × 40.5 cm

Inscribed: *TAB.III* (upper margin) *C. Grignion Sculp. Impensis J. & P. Knapton Londini. 1747* (lower margin)

7472   Ilustration of the muscles of a man

Engraving, 54.1 × 38 cm

Inscribed: *TAB.IV.* (upper margin) *C. Grignion Sculp. Impensis J. & P. Knapton, Londini, 1747* (lower margin)

Published in 1749 in Bernard Siegfried Albinus' *Tabulae Sceleti et Musculorum Corporis Humani.*[1] The pose in 7469 is the reverse of the pose in 7471 and 7472 and of Boitard's plate in the same series (7470), and the same as in Scotin's plate II in the same series (7468). The engravings are based on those by Jan Wandelaar in the original 1747 Leiden edition of Albinus.

Prov: Presented by Liverpool College of Art, 1970.
Ref: 1. For further details of this and earlier editons see Judy Egerton in, *George Stubbs anatomist and animal painter*, Tate Gallery, 1976, pp. 56-57 (6).

GRIMALDI, Giovanni Francesco, 1606-1680

9186   The rest on the flight from Egypt

Etching, 31.5 × 21.8 cm

Signed: *Gio franco. Grimaldi bolognese inuen. et. fec.* (on plate)

Bartsch 15.[1]

Two angels offer a bowl of roses to the Child, probably symbolizing the Passion.

Prov: William Roscoe; his sale, probably (797)[2] with 9187 and two others bt. Slater 8s; Charles Robert Blundell; by descent to Colonel Sir Joseph Weld; his sale, Christie's, 7 October 1976 (61) with 9185 bt. in; purchased with 9187 by the Liverpool Daily Post and Echo Ltd., by whom presented, 1976.

Ref: **1.** Bartsch, *op. cit.*, XIX, pp. 92-93 (15).   **2.** Lot number 796 inscribed on the back of the mount in the Roscoe sale was *Four large landscapes with figures* by Grimaldi bt. Traill £1, but since 9187 was in lot 797 bt. Slater, who is known to have acted for Blundell, the inscription is probably an error.

9187 The two goats

Etching, 31.5 × 21.8 cm

Signed: *Gio franco. grimaldi fec.* (on plate)

Bartsch 14.[1]

Prov: William Roscoe, his sale, Winstanley, 16 September 1816 (797)[2] with three others, possibly including 9186 bt. Slater 8s; Charles Robert Blundell; by descent to Colonel Sir Joseph Weld; his sale, Christie's, 7 October 1976 (61) with 9186 bt. in; purchased with 9186 by the Liverpool Daily Post and Echo Ltd. by whom presented, 1976.

Ref: **1.** Adam Bartsch, *Le Peintre Graveur*, XIX, 1819, p. 92 (14).   **2.** Lot number inscribed in pencil on the back of the mount.

HAMILTON, John McLure, 1851-1936

4881 Professor Tyndall

Lithograph, 26.9 × 38.5 cm

Hamilton exhibited 4881 at the Liverpool Autumn Exhibition of 1911 as a number of the Senefelder Club. 4881 is related to an oil in the National Portrait Gallery of Professor Tyndall reading seated in an armchair with a pile of books at his elbow.[1] Either the National Portrait Gallery oil or an oil which was in the collection of Mrs Tyndall,[2] was probably exhibited at the Liverpool Autumn Exhibition of 1894 (251).[3] Hamilton stayed at "The Hut", Hindhead close to the Tyndall's home, when he was painting him. Professor Tyndall was an invalid at the time.[4]

The sitter, John Tyndall (1820-1893), F.R.S. was Professor of Natural Philosophy at the Royal Institution from 1853. As well as publishing a number of important papers on a wide variety of topics in the natural sciences, he did much to popularize science.

Prov: Purchased from the artist at the L.A.E., 1911.
Exh: L.A.E., 1911, (1303).
Ref: **1.** J. McLure Hamilton, *Men I have painted*, 1921, reproduced between pages 90 and 91.   **2.** Hamilton, *op. cit.*, p. 99.   **3.** The same or another portrait of Professor Tyndall had been exhibited at the Society of Portrait-Painters in 1893 (68). *The Saturday Review*, May 20, 1893, p. 539   **4.** Hamilton, *op. cit.*, pp. 94-5.

6971   Young Britons Coursing

Half tone proof corrected in pencil on card, 13.2 × 16.5 cm

Inscribed: *Hamilton* (in pencil)

A sketch intended for a proposed illustration in the L.A.E. Catalogue of 1890 after the picture exhibited at the R.A. (391) and at the L.A.E., (949) of that year. It appears never to have been used.

Prov: W. Woffenden;[2] by descent to Mrs T. K. Bradshaw, from whom purchased, 1969.
Ref: 1. An inscription on the back in black ink gives the title and the artist's address as Alpha House, Regent's Park, London.   2. W. Woffenden was manager of Goodall and Suddick Limited of Venice Chambers, 61 Lord Street, Liverpool, and the editor and blockmaker of the L.A.E. Illustrated Catalogue.

HARBUTT, Charles, born 1935

9204   Liverpool 1971

Photograph, 35.4 × 28.0 cm

Signed: *Charles Harbutt* (lower right in black ink)

The artist took the photograph during a visit to Liverpool in 1971 when he came to see a Merseybeat Revival Concert. His paternal grandfather was a Liverpool dock-worker.[1]

The photograph shows Lime Street Station from the fire escape of the Adelphi Hotel, where he stayed for the one night of his visit.[2] The buildings in the foreground have since been demolished and replaced by a coach park.

This particular photograph is said to have sparked the idea for the Arts Council *Other Eyes* exhibition. It was published in Charles Harbutt, *Travelog*, M.I.T. Press, 1974.[3]

Prov: Purchased from the artist, 1977.
Exh: Arts Council, *Other Eyes*, 1976 (64) illustrated.
Ref: 1. Letter of the artist, 9 December, 1976.   2. The artist, *orally*, 19 April 1977.   3. The book won the prize for the best photographic book of the year 1974 at the Arles Festival, France

HAYDEN, Henri, born 1883

6546   Landscape

Lithograph, 38 × 51 cm

Signed: *41/220 Hayden/61* (pencil below block)

Prov: Purchased from the Piccadilly Gallery, 1966.

HELLEU, Paul-Cesar, 1859-1927

5081 Head of a lady

Drypoint, 54.3 × 33.3 cm

Signed: *Helleu/6* (pencil)

Prov: Bequeathed by Alderman John Lea, J.P., 1927.

HERMAN, Josef, born 1911

6359 Two Miners

Lithograph, 49.8 × 71.2 cm

Signed: *48/50 Josef Herman* (pencil)

6359 was commissioned by the St. George's Gallery. The artist made it in the studios of the Curwen Press[1] in 1960/1. It is on Barchem Green Crisbrook waterleaf in one colour, black, only.[2] A lithograph of this subject in three colours was published by the Curwen Press in 1962.[3]

Prov: Purchased from Prestons Art Gallery, Bolton. 1966.
Ref: **1.** Letter from the artist 8 April 1976. **2.** Letter of Stephen Reiss, 25 May 1976. **3.** *Curwen Prints* Catalogue, March 1976, Joseph Herman 5 (2) reproduced.

HEYDEMANN, Willie, active 1886-1917 after PIFFARD, Harold H., active 1895-1899

4009 His Last Review

Etching, 48 × 59.3 cm

Signed and inscribed: *London. Published May 2nd. 1898 by the Fine Art Society Lim, 148, New Bond Street, W* (upper margin). *Entered according to act of Congress in the year 1898 by The Fine Art Society Lim, in the Office of the Librarian of Congress at Washington* (lower margin) *H. Piffard* (ink on lower margin) *W. Heydemann* (pencil on lower margin)

After the picture exhibited at the Royal Academy in 1897 (527) Napoleon is shown at St. Helena in 1820 with the children of General Bertrand. His head also appears on the lower margin.

Prov: Purchased from the artist at the L.A.E., 1898 by an anonymous buyer, who withdrew when he learnt that the price was £5 not 5s as he had understood. The purchase was taken on by the Gallery instead.
Exh: L.A.E., 1898 (1346).
Ref: **1.** Old Register II, p. 122.

HEYMAN, Charles, 1881-1915

4888 Demolitions, Rue Chanoinesse, Paris

Etching, 23.2 × 25.5 cm

Signed: *Ch. Heyman* (on plate); *Ch. Heyman 12/30 Demolitions rue Chanoinesse* (pencil below plate)

Prov: Purchased from the artist at the L.A.E., 1912.
Exh: *L.A.E.*, 1912 (1723).

HOLLAR, Wenzel, 1607-1677 after VAN AVONT, Peeter, 1600-1632

3193 View of the Abbey of Groenendael

Etching, 15.2 × 20.9 cm

Inscribed: *W Hollar fec: 1647* (inside print) *R:do admodum D.n̄o D: Petro Parys, Canonicorum Regularium Ordinis S. Augustini Congregationis Windesemensis per Ger-/maniam inferiorem Commisario, nec-non Ecclesiae Bte. Mariae in Viride Valle Priori dig:mo hoc Monasterij sui simulacrum, D. C. Q. Petrus van Avont* (lower margin)

First state.[1] There is also a large bird's eye view of Groenendael Abbey.[2] Both are after Hollar's friend Van Avont.[3]

Prov: Bequeathed by Charles Marten Powell through the National Art-Collections
          Fund, 1929.
Ref: **1.** Gustav Parthey, *Wenzel Hollar*, 1853, p. 174 (849).   **2.** Parthey, *op. cit.*, p.
          175 (850).   **3.** F. W. H. Hollstein, *Dutch and Flemish Etchings, Engravings
          and Woodcuts*, IX, 1953, p. 70.

3192 View of the Abbey of Rothendael

Etching, 15.0 × 21.1 cm

Inscribed: *W Hollar fecit 1648* (inside print) *Rdo. Admodum Dno. D: Adriano Van der Reest Ecclesiae S. Pauli Ordinis Canonicorum Regu S: Augusti Congreg:is Winde-/semensis Priori dignissimo, hanc Monasterij sui Rubrae Vallis Imaginem, Observantiae ergo D:C. Q. Petrus van Avont.* (lower margin)

First state.[1] Like 3193 after van Avont.[2]

Prov: Bequeathed by Charles Marten Powell through the National Art-Collections
          Fund, 1929.
Ref: **1.** Parthey, *op. cit.*, p. 185 (886).   **2.** Hollstein, *op. cit.*, IX, p. 70.

384

HOLLAR, after WILDENS, Jan, 1586-1653

3191   Landscape with Horseman

Etching, 14.4 × 21.5 cm

Inscribed: *Ioannes Wildens inventor. W. Hollar fecit 1650 I. Meyssens excudit.*

After Wildens and printed by Meyssens (1612-1670).[1]

Prov: Bequeathed by Charles Marten Powell through the National Art-Collections Fund, 1929.
Ref: 1. Parthey, *op. cit.*, p. 262 (1226) and Hollstein, *op. cit.*, IX, p. 71.

HUMBERT, Suzanne, 1913-1952

6227   The park and the Eiffel Tower (Le Parc et la Tour Eiffel)

Colour lithograph, 45.7 × 33.7 cm

Signed: *26/65 Suz. Humbert* (pencil)

6227   was published *c.* 1950.[1]

Prov: Redfern Gallery; the Medici Gallery, Liverpool from whom purchased 1964.
Exh: Medici Gallery, Liverpool, 1964, *Modern Lithographs* (27).
Ref: 1. Letter from Hubert Prouté, 23 September 1976.

6338   The racecourse (Le champ de Courses)

Colour lithograph, 29.8 × 40 cm

Signed: *Suz. Humbert 62/65*

6338 was published *c.* 1950.[1]

Prov: Purchased from Prestons Art Gallery, Bolton, 1966.
Ref: 1. Letter from Hubert Prouté, 23 September 1976.

ITALIAN School, mid 16th century

9178   The Triumph of Venus

Etching, 11.9 × 17.4 cm

Inscribed: *Petri de Nobilibus Formis* (on plate)

Watermark: B over a circle

Attributed by Bartsch to Bonasone,[1] but considered to be by an anonymous follower of Marcantonio Raimondi by Passavant.[2]

Prov: Charles Robert Blundell; by descent to Colonel Sir Joseph Weld; his sale, Christie's, 7 October, 1976 (11) with 9173-9177, 9179-9184 bt. in; purchased from Colonel Sir Joseph Weld with 9173-9177, 9179-9184, 1976.

Ref: 1. Adam Bartsch, *Le Peintre Graveur*, XV, 1867, p. 38 (7)   2. J. D. Passavant, *Le Peintre-Graveur*, VI, 1864, p. 84 (74). For other examples of the subject see A. Pigler, *Barockthemen*, II, p. 265.

ITALIAN School, mid 16th century after SALVIATI, Francesco, 1510-1563

9173   The birth of Adonis and the Metamorphosis of Myrrha

Engraving, 28.9 × 43 cm

Trimmed so that it lacks the margin, the date 1544 and the inscription described by Bartsch.[1] The literary source is Ovid *Metamorphoses* X 503-514.[2] Adonis was the offspring of the unwittingly committed incestuous union of Cinyras, King of Cyrpus and his daughter Myrrha. Cinyras on discovering his true relationship with Myrrha attempted to kill her (this scene is in the right background). Myrrha fled to Arabia, where she was changed into a tree called *myrrh*, in which form she was when she gave birth.

Voss thinks that 9173 was one of a series of five prints after drawings by Salviati dating around 1540 and not much later entrusted to different engravers between 1542 amd 1544.[3] The other etchings represent *Adam and Eve*, *Adam and Eve Lamenting the Death of Abel*, *The Flaying of Marsyas* and the *Continence of Scipio* (9176), the first three of which Voss associates with Girolamo Fagiuoli,[4] to whom according to Vasari Salviati gave some drawings for engraving before leaving Bologna.[5]

Prov: Edward Peart (Lugt 892); Charles Robert Blundell; by descent to Colonel Sir Joseph Weld; his sale, Christie's, 7 October 1976 (11) with 9174-9184 bt. in; purchased from Colonel Sir Joseph Weld with 9174-9184, 1976.

Ref: 1. Adam Bartsch, *Le Peintre Graveur*, XV, 1867, p. 42.   2. A. Pigler, *Barockthemen*, II, 1974, p. 10.   3. Hermann Voss, *Kompositionen des Francesco Salviati in der italienischen Graphik des XVI Jahrhunderts*, II, Die graphischen Kunste, Mitteilungen der Gesellschaft für vervielfaltigende Kunst, XXXV, 1912, pp. 61-63, pl. 5.   4. Voss, *op. cit.*, pp. 61-63, pl. 1-4.   5. Vasari ed. G. Milanesi, VII, p. 18.

9176   The Continence of Scipio

Engraving, 30 × 43 cm

Inscribed: *1542* (on a stone) *AVRVM . QVOD . PRO . REDIMENDA CAPTIVA . VIRGINE . PARENTES ./ATTVLERANT LVCEIO . SPONSO . TRADIT . SCIPIO . ROMAE . EXCD/AN T SAL.* (on plate)

Considered by Bartsch to be by an anonymous Florentine master approaching the style of Agostino Veneziano.[1] Voss recognised that it was based on a design by Francesco Salviati.[2]

Prov: Charles Robert Blundell; by descent to Colonel Sir Joseph Weld; his sale, Christie's, 7 October 1976 (11) with 9173-9175 and 9177-9184 bt. in; purchased from Colonel Sir Joseph Weld with 9173-9175 and 9177-9184, 1976.

Ref: **1.** Adam Bartsch, *Le Peintre Graveur*, XV, 1867, p. 30 (3). **2.** Hermann Voss, *Kompositionen des Francesco Salviati in der italienischen Graphik des XVI Jahrhunderts*, II, Die Graphischen Kunste, Mitteilungen der Gesellschaft für vervielfaltigende Kunst, XXXV, 1912, pp. 61-63, pl. 4, *Die Malerei der Spatrenaissance in Rom und Florenz*, I, 1920, p. 250. See A. Pigler, *Barockthemen*, II, 1974, pp. 424-429 for other examples of the subject and its literary sources.

JAQUES, Bertha Evelyn, born 1863

9147 The Tangle, Chioggia

Etching, 22.7 × 15.2 cm

Signed: *Bertha E. Jaques* (pencil)

Inscribed: *To Geoffrey H. Wedgwood—1929/The Tangle—Chioggia—Italy*

Reproduced in *Modern Etchings, Mezzotints and Dry-points* edited by Charles Holme, 1913, p. 125 and discussed on p. 110 by E. A. Taylor.

Prov: Presented by Geoffrey Heath Wedgwood, 1976.

Exh: Paris, *Société des artistes français*, 1912 (4879) *The Tanghe (Chioggia)* (sic) one of *Trois Gravures*, the others being *Pallazzo Minelli (Venise)* and *A Sunney-Corner (Villefranche)*.

JAWLENSKY, Alexis von, 1864-1942

6226 Head, green and black harmony (Tête harmonie verte et noire)

Colour lithograph, 58.4 × 51.5 cm

Inscribed: *24/125* (pencil) *a jawlensky* (on block)

Prov: Redfern Gallery; the Medici Gallery from whom purchased 1964.

Exh: ?Redfern Gallery, *Deux Mille Gravures en Couleur*, 1961/2 (591).[1] Medici Gallery, Liverpool, 1964, *Modern Lithographs* (15).

Ref: **1.** Another lithograph of this title was exhibited at the Redfern Gallery, *Gravures en Couleur*, 1958/9 (359).

KANDINSKY, Wassily, 1866-1944, after

639   Landscape (Paysage)

Colour lithograph, 35 × 54.7 cm

Inscribed: *KANDINSKY 1911* (on block) *KANDINSKY* (ink)

Published by Galerie Maeght. After *Impression IV*, an oil in a private collection.[1]

Prov: Purchased from the Redfern Gallery, 1957.
Exh: W.A.G., 1957, *Modern Colour Lithographs* (51).
Ref: 1. Paris, UNESCO, *Catalogue of colour reproductions of paintings—1880-1957*, Paris, 1957 (383). The picture is called *Komposition 4*, 1911 by the present owners. Dusseldorf, Kunstsammlung Nordrhein-Westfalen, *Malerei des zwanzigsten Jahrhunderts*, 1968 (35).

6231   Lyric (Lyrique)

Colour lithograph, 37.5 × 28.6 cm

Inscribed: *LK/24/KANDINSKY* (on block)

After the oil in the collection of the Galerie Maeght, Paris.[1]

Prov: Redfern Gallery; the Medici Gallery from whom purchased, 1964.
Exh: ?Redfern Gallery, *Deux Mille Gravures en Couleur*, 1961/2 (610).[2] Medici Gallery, 1964, *Modern Lithographs* (ex catalogue).
Ref: 1. Maria Volpi Orlandini, *Kandinsky dall'art nouveau alla psicologia della forma*, 1968, rep as *Accompagnamento nero*.   2. A lithograph of this title was also exhibited at the Redfern Gallery, *Gravures*, 1958/9 (379).

KITAJ, Ronald B., born 1933

6299   Photography and Philosophy

Screenprint, 49.5 × 77.5 cm

Signed: *R. B. Kitaj 6/40* (black ink)

Issued in 1964.[1]

Prov: Purchased from Marlborough Fine Art Ltd., 1965.[2]
Ref: 1. Arts Council, 1970, *Kelpra Prints*, List of Screenprints made at Kelpra Studio 1961-1970; but according to Museum Boymans-van Beuningen, Rotterdam, 1970, *R. B. Kitaj, Catalogus van het volledige grafische kunst* (3) issued in 1963.   2. Reproduced Marlborough New London Gallery, *Marlborough Prints* (List of Prints), July 1965, and *Opening of the Print Department*, 1964 (15).

6908 Truman in the White House

Screenprint, 53.5 × 79 cm

Signed and inscribed: *TRUMAN IN THE WHITE HOUSE (A ROMANCE BY R. B. KITAJ)/ (note: The irregular shapes above, except for the red ones, are transformations of Mondrian Brushstrokes)* (on block) *KITAJ 59/70* (pencil)

Issued in 1966.[1]

Prov: Purchased from Marlborough Fine Art Ltd., 1969.
Ref: **1.** Museum Boymans-van Beuningen, Rotterdam, *op. cit.*, (14) and Arts Council, 1970, *Kelpra Prints*, List of Screenprints made at Kelpra Studio 1961-1970.

8483 Charles Olson

Colour screenprint and collage, 76 × 57.5 cm

Signed and inscribed: *PHOTOGRAPHIC MEMORY used in Chinese-translation machine/contains several hundred thousand dictionary-like entries, any/one of which can be found in a twenty-thousandth of a second./Over 50 million "bits" of information are embodied in a dot code,/which forms the narrow gray bands at the edge of the disk. The/disk, only half of which is shown, is printed two-thirds actual size.* (on block) *Kitaj A/P* (pencil)

One of ten screenprints making up *First Series Some Poets* from an edition of 70 issued in 1969.[1] Ohff says that the series "Zeigt erstaunlich akademisch gezeichnete Kopfe . . .und umrankt sie mit einer Art von Seelenlandschaft."

Prov: Purchased from Prue O'Day, Don Anderson "Modern Prints", 1973.
Ref: **1.** Museum Boymans-van Beuningen, Rotterdam, *op. cit.*, (26f). **2.** Heinz Ohff, *R. B. Kitaj—Das Gesamte Graphische Werk*, Das Kunstwerk, June-July, 1972, p. 85.

KLEIN, Johann Anton, 1792-1875

7460 New Year's Card

Etching, 9.8 × 11.1 cm

Signed: *Zum/neuen Jahr/1818./JAK.* (in monogram)[1] *fec. 1817* (on plate)

A little girl is cutting up a calendar inscribed *Kalend/fur 1817* (on plate). One of a series of New Year's Cards produced by Klein from 1808 to 1830 (for 1831).[2] Second state.[3]

Prov: ?N. G. Philips; purchased from F. Weatherhead & Sons, 1970.
Ref: **1.** Georg Kaspar Nagler, *Die Monogrammisten*, I, 1919, p. 353. **2.** C. Jahn, *Das Werk von Johann Klein*, pp. 4 (11), 66 (169), 70 (181), 91 (227), 113 (273), 118-119 (286), 120 (289), 122-3 (295). **3.** Jahn, *op. cit.*, p. 80 (202).

LANSKOY, Andre, 1902-1976

2736 Landscape (Paysage)

Lithograph, 58.4 × 48.2 cm

Inscribed: *28/200 LANSKOY* (pencil)

Prov: Purchased from the Redfern Gallery through the New Shakespeare Theatre Gallery, 1958.
Exh: New Shakespeare Theatre Art Gallery, 1958 (31).

LATENAY, Gaston de, born 1859/60

392 The Rain (La Pluie)

Etching, 17.8 × 18.8 cm

Signed: *G. DE LATENAY* (on plate) *38/50 G. DE LATENAY* (pencil)

Another impression was reproduced in *Modern Etchings Mezzotints and Dry-Points* edited by Charles Holme, 1913, p. 173.[1]

Prov: Purchased from the artist, 1911.
Exh: L.A.E., 1910 (1433).
Ref: 1. See also E. A. Taylor, *France*, in *Modern Etchings Mezzotints and Dry-Points* edited by Charles Holme 1913, p. 159.

LE CORBUSIER, Charles Edouard, called Jeanneret, 1887-1965

2747 The Modular (Le Modulor)

Lithograph, 69.8 × 52.1 cm

Inscribed: *L-c/50/ami du Modulor, cherche par/toi-même invente découvre . . ./Apporte tes inventions, elles seront/utiles/merci, ami/Paris* <u>20</u>.56 *Le Corbusier*
 2

Prov: Purchased from Mazo, Paris, 1958.

LEFEVRE, Achille 1798-1864 after MURILLO, Bartholome Estevan, 1618-1682

4018 The Immaculate Conception

Engraving, 80.1 × 56.5 cm

Inscribed: *Murillo Pinxt./Ach. Lefevre Sculpt.* (on plate)

After the picture in the Louvre known as the Soult *Immaculate Conception*[1] which was once in the collection of Louis Phillipe.

Prov: Presented by Mrs Margaret Harvey, 1878.
Ref: **1.** August L. Mayer, *Murillo*, 1913, pl. 166.

LEGER, Fernand, 1881-1955, after

640 Construction

Colour lithograph, 56.5 × 39.2 cm

Inscribed: *F. LEGER* (ink) *176/200* (pencil)

After *Composition aux deux oiseaux sur fond jaune* painted a few weeks before the artist's death.[1]

Prov: Purchased from the Redfern Gallery, 1957.
Exh: ?Redfern Gallery, *An Exhibition of Colour Lithographs, etchings, aquatints, lithographed affiches, pochoirs*, 1956/7, (176). W.A.G., 1957, *Modern Colour Lithographs* (6).
Ref: **1.** Paris, Musee des Arts Decoratifs, 1956, *Fernand Leger 1881-1955* (162).

6339 Woman and Child (Femme et l'Enfant)

Colour lithograph, 34.9 × 24.8 cm

Inscribed: *F. LEGER/21* (on block)

Published by the Galerie Maeght. After an oil in a private collection.[1]

Ref: **1.** Paris, UNESCO, *Catalogue of Colour Reproductions of Paintings—1860 to 1957*, Paris, 1957 (446).

6340 Musicians in the Countryside (Musiciens à la Campagne)

Colour lithograph, 34.3 × 44.4 cm

Inscribed: *F. LEGER/45* (on block)

After an oil in the collection Aimé Maeght.[1]

Prov: Purchased from Prestons Art Gallery, Bolton, 1966.
Ref: **1.** Paris, Musée des Arts Decoratifs, 1956, *Fernand Leger 1881-1955* (115) reproduced.

LEGROS, Alphonse, 1837-1911

1476   The finding of the lost sheep (Le mouton retrouvé)

Etching, 42.7 × 31.5 cm

Signed: *A. Legros* (on plate)

Inscribed: *Tirê a 50 épreuves/Planche détruite/No. 33* (red stamp below plate)

Second state.[1]

Ref: 1. A. P. Malassis and A. W. Thibaudeau, *Catalogue Raisonné de l'Oeuvre Gravé et Lithographe de M. Alphonse Legros, 1855-1877*, 1877 p. 55 (86).

3200   The woodcutters (Les bucherons)

Etching, 41.6 × 66.5 cm

Signed: *A. Legros* (on plate)

Inscribed: *TIRE A 100 EPREUVES/No. 74* (red stamp below plate)

Second state.[1] Legros produced another version of the same subject.[2]

Prov: Presented by the artist, 1876.[3]
Ref: 1. Malassis and Thibaudeau, *op. cit.*, p. 60 (95).   2. Malassis and Thibaudeau, *op. cit.*, p. 56 (80).   3. P. H. Rathbone reported the receipt of four etchings by Legros (that is 1476, 3200, 3202 and 3203) to the Arts and Exhibition Sub Committee on 7 January 1876 and the Committee returned thanks to Mr Legros for his donation (Libraries, Museums and Arts Committee Extracts Volume, Liverpool Public Library).

3201   Head of an old man

Drypoint, 38.4 × 25.1 cm.

Signed: *A. Legros* (ink below plate)

Drawn and etched from the life before the Students of the Slade School, London University, 1877.[1] See also pp. 103-4, 256, 393.

Prov: Presented by the artist, 1878.
Ref: 1. Label on the back of the mount.

3202   Head of a young man

Drypoint, 37.8 × 27.2 cm

Signed: *A. Legros* (ink below plate) *Tiré à 50 épreuves/Planche detruite/No 33* (red stamp below plate)

3203 Cardinal Manning

Etching, 52.8 × 35 cm

Signed: *A Legros* (ink below plate)

Third state.[1] Cardinal Manning, Roman Catholic Archbishop of Westminster (1808-1892) was a leading ecclesiastical statesman.

Prov: Presented by the artist, 1876.[2]
Ref: 1. Malassis and Thibaudeau, *op. cit.*, p. 24 (43). 2. P. H. Rathbone reported the receipt of four Legros etchings to the Arts and Exhibition Sub Committee on 7 January 1876 (Libraries, Museums and Arts Committee Extracts Volume, Liverpool Public Library).

3204 Head of a young man

Drypoint, 27.2 × 22.1 cm

Signed: *A. Legros* (ink below plate)

Drawn and etched from life before the students of the Slade School, London University, 1877.[1]

Ref: 1. Label on the back of the mount. For Legros' choosing of models for his prints see Thomas Okey, *Alphonse Legros: Some Personal Reminiscences,* 2, Burlington Magazine, 1911-1912, p. 276.

3205 Head of an old man

Drypoint, 33.5 × 25.3 cm

Signed: *A. Legros* (pen below plate)

Drawn and etched from life before the students of the Slade School, London University, 1877.[1] See also pp. 103-4, 256, 392.

Prov: Presented by the artist, 1878.
Ref: 1. Label on back of mount.

8607 Tree trunk

Drypoint, 30.3× 25.2 cm

Second state.

8608 The Refectory

Etching, 21.1 × 30.9 cm

Third state.[1] Wright dates it about 1862.[2]

Ref: **1.** A. P. Malassis and A. W. Thibaudeau, *Catalogue Raisonné de l'Oeuvre Gravé et Lithographé de M. Alphonse Legros, 1855-1877*, 1877, pp. 34-5 (55).   **2.** Harold J. L. Wright, *The Etchings, Drypoints and Lithographs of Alphonse Legros 1837-1911, being a lecture delivered to the Print Collectors Club on Friday November 20, 1911*, 1934, p. 5 pl. IV.

8609   The Death of Saint Francis

Etching, 19.5 × 29.7 cm

Sixth state. Legros painted an oil of this subject.[1]

Ref: **1.** National Gallery, 1912, *Alphonse Legros* (35) lent by G. Knowles.
Prov: Purchased from P. and D. Colnaghi Ltd, 1971.

8610   Study of a man's head

Etching, 31.3 × 24.8 cm

Signed: *A. Legros* (on plate)

Third state.[1] The subject is Alessandro di Marco, a Piedmontese, who also served as a model for Poynter and other artists. Legros signed an oil portrait of him and dated it in 1868. That portrait was also in the Bliss Collection.[2]

Prov: Howard Mansfield; Frank E. Bliss;[3] P. & D. Colnaghi Ltd from whom purchased, 1971.
Exh: ?National Gallery, *Loan Collection of works by Alphonse Legros*, 1912 (120) lent by Frank E. Bliss.
Ref: **1.** National Gallery, *Catalogue of Loan Collection of works by Alphonse Legros, June to September, 1912*, p. 16 (120), *and A Catalogue of the Etchings, Drypoints and Lithographs by Professor Alphonse Legros (1837-1911) In the Collection of Frank E. Bliss*. 1923, pl. VII.   **2.** 32.7 × 42.5 cm *Paintings . . . from the Collection of Frank E. Bliss, Esq. op. cit.*, p. 69 (302).   **3.** Collector's stamp.

8611   Siesta in the Countryside

Drypoint, 28.6 × 21.3 cm

Signed: *AL* (stamp on plate) *A. Legros* (in pencil)

Probably the drypoint listed as La Sieste by Béraldi.[1]

Ref: **1.** H. Béraldi, *Les Graveurs du XIXe Siècle*, IX, 1889, p. 104 (217).
Prov: Purchased from P. and D. Colnaghi Ltd, 1971.

8612   Death and the Woodcutter (No. 2)

Etching, 40.5 × 28.4 cm

Signed: *A. Legros* (on plate)

Third state. Thibaudeau lists only three proofs and three counter-proofs, one of which at least was in the Gueraut Collection.[1] Béraldi lists three other prints of this subject.[2] *Death and the Woodcutter No. 2* is the reverse of *Death and the Woodcutter No.1.*[3] The National Gallery of Canada owns an oil signed by Legros based on *Death and the Woodcutter No. 2,*[4] and Legros exhibited a piece of sculpture of this subject at the Grosvenor Gallery in 1882.[5]

Prov: R. Gueraut; Wm. Tipping;[6] P. & D. Colnaghi Ltd; from whom purchased, 1971.

Ref: 1. Malassis and Thibaudeau, *op. cit.*, p. 92 (142).   2. Béraldi, *op. cit.*, pp. 101 (141), 103 (181), 104 (213).   3. M. C. Salaman, *op. cit.*, pl. 4.   4. Gabriel P. Weisberg, *Alphonse Legros and the theme of Death and the Woodcutter*, The Bulletin of the Cleveland Museum of Art, April 1974, pp. 131-2.   5. *The Magazine of Art*, 1882 p. 437 (rep).   6. Inscription on the verso in pencil.

8613   F. Régamey

Drypoint, 22.8 × 16.5 cm

Signed: *A. Legros* (on plate)

Fifth state. Régamey (1849-1925) was a French draughtsman, engraver and lithographer, who worked for a number of periodicals. He produced an etched portrait of Legros at the age of forty, which was used as the frontispiece of the first book on Legros prints.[1] Legros etched another portrait of Régamey of which only one state is recorded.[2]

Prov: F. G. Stephens; F. E. Bliss; P. & D. Colnaghi Ltd., from whom purchased, 1971.

Exh: ?P. & D. Colnaghi & Co., Grosvenor Galleries, 1922, *Paintings, Drawings, Etchings and Lithographs from the Collection of Frank E. Bliss, Esq.*, (93).

Ref: 1. Malassis and Thibaudeau, *op. cit.*, frontispiece.   2. P. & D. Colnaghi & Co., Grosvenor Galleries, 1922, *op. cit.*, p. 74 (316).

8614   Sir Edward Poynter

Etching, 25.6 × 16.9 cm

Signed: *A. Legros* (on plate)

Watermark: VAN/GELDER/PORTFOLIO

Fifth state, published in *The Portfolio* No. 85, January, 1877.[1] Legros succeeded his friend Poynter (1836-1919) as Slade Professor at University College, London in 1876.

Ref: 1. Malassis and Thibaudeau, *op. cit.*, pp. 23-24 (42).

8615   M. Champfleury

Lithograph, 24.3 × 19.4 cm

Signed: *A. Legros* (on plate)

Dated: *1875* (on plate)

Jules Husson, called Fleury or Champfleury (1821-1889), a leading French novelist of the realist school, was one of those who encouraged Legros to take up printmaking and was an early purchaser of his prints.[1] Legros illustrated Champfleury's version of the popular legend of the "Bonhomme Misère' with 6 etchings,[2] published in 1877.[3]

Ref: 1. Wright, *op. cit.*, p. 15.   2. Wright, *op. cit.*, p. 16.   3. M. C. Salaman, *Alphonse Legros*, 1926, p. 5.
Prov: Purchased from P. & D. Colnaghi, Ltd., 1971.

9011   Jules Dalou[1]

Etching, 25.2 × 16.5 cm

Signed: *A. Legros* (on plate)

Watermark: VAN GELDER ZONEN

Jules Dalou (1838-1902) made a bronze portrait of Legros.[2]

Prov: Sir Frank Short;[3] purchased from N. W. Lott and H. J. Gerrish, Ltd., 1975.
Ref: 1. Malassis and Thibaudeau, *op. cit.*, p. 22 (40).   2. *Paintings . . . from the Collection of Frank E. Bliss, Esq.*, *op. cit.*, (315).   3. Pencil inscription beneath image.

9012   The walk of the convalescent (La Promenade du convalescent)

Drypoint, 27.8 × 19.7 cm

Inscribed: *Impr par A. Delâlre, Paris* (on plate)

Watermark: HP in an elaborate shield topped by a crown bearing a crescent moon, two five leafed clover like flowers and two tusks, with a budding flower as a finial beneath.

Second state. One of only six impressions.[1]

Prov: Purchased from N. W. Lott and H. J. Gerrish Ltd., 1975.
Ref: 1. Malassis and Thibaudeau, *op. cit.*, p. 45 (68).

9083   The Ambulance (L'Ambulance)

Drypoint, 36.8 × 26.9 cm

The only state.[1] Bliss owned another impression which had been retouched by the artist and signed and dated 1861.[2]

Prov: The artist?;[3] Frank E. Bliss (Lugt 265); Mr McDonald; by descent to his son, B. McDonald, from whom purchased, 1976.
Ref: 1. A. P.-Malassis and A.-W. Thibaudeau, *Catalogue Raisonné de l'oeuvre gravé et lithographé de M. Alphonse Legros*, 1877, p. 82 (124).   2. *Paintings from the collection of Frank E. Bliss, Esq.*, *op. cit.*, (144).   3. The drypoint listed in *A Catalogue of the Etchings, Drypoints and Lithographs by Professor Alphonse Legros (1837-1911) in the Collection of Frank E. Bliss*, 1923, p. 30 (124) was acquired from the artist. This might however be the later impression.

LEHEUTRE, Gustave, born 1861

4901 The lock on the New Canal at Troyes (L'ecluse du Nouveau Canal, à Troyes)

Etching, 21.8 × 33.8 cm

Signed: *G. Leheutre 1907* (on plate) *G. Leheutre 4 Sep/No. 42* (pencil) *Ed Sagot/editeur/paris* (stamp) *L'Ecluse du Nouveau Canal à Troyes Planche detruite* (pencil)

5th state.[1]

Prov: Purchased from the artist at the L.A.E. 1909.
Exh: *L.A.E.*, 1909 (1413).
Ref: **1.** Loys Delteil, *Le Peintre-Graveur Illustré*, *XII*, *Gustave Leheutre*, 1921 (81).

LE MOAL, Jean, born 1909

6232 Autumn (L'Automne)

Colour Lithograph, 58.6 × 45.9 cm

Signed: *80/140 Jean Le Moal* (pencil)

Prov: Redfern Gallery; the Medici Gallery, Liverpool, from whom purchased, 1964.
Exh: ?Redfern Gallery, *Deux Mille Gravures en Couleur*, 1961/2, (733). Medici Gallery, Liverpool, 1964, *Modern Lithographs* (35).

LEPERE, Auguste Louis A., 1849-1918

344 The arrival at the mill (L'arrivée au moulin)

Etching, 16.2 × 20.3 cm

Signed: *A. Lepere 17/35* (pencil)

Watermark: The letter A and a snail

Prov: Purchased from the artist at the L.A.E., 1909.
Exh: *L.A.E.*, 1909 (1423).

345 The thatched cottage at Rousseau (La Chaumière a Rousseau)

Etching, 15.6 × 22.7 cm

Signed: *A. L.* (on plate) *A Lepere 15/35* (pencil)

Prov: Purchased from the artist at the L.A.E., 1912.
Exh: *L.A.E.*, 1912 (1718).

4902   The watering place at Port Marie (L'abbreuvoir au Port Marie)

Etching, 19.9 × 26.7 cm

Signed and inscribed: *A Lepère* (pencil on plate) *Ed. Sagot/editeur/paris* (stamp)

First state.[1]

Prov: Purchased from the artist at the L.A.E., 1910.
Exh: L.A.E., 1910 (1392)
Ref: 1. Inscription on verso.

LIAO, Shiou Ping, born 1936

6642   Paris B 1966

Colour etching, 48 × 34.2 cm

Signed: *16/20 PARIS B 1966 Shiou-Ping Liao*, and with monogram (pencil below plate)

6643   Bonheur 1967

Colour etching, 49 × 29 cm

Signed: *14/20 Bonheur Shiou-Ping Liao* and with monogram twice (pencil below plate)

6644   Winter 1968 (L'Hiver 1968)

Colour etching, 39.5 × 43.2 cm

Signed: *4/30 L'hiver 1968 Shiou-Ping Liao* and with monogram twice (pencil below plate)

Prov: Purchased from Anthony Dawson, 1968.

LLOYD, Charles, born 1932/3

6923   Rusting Landscape

Zinc plate etching in colour and aquatint printed in intaglio; 49.2 × 34.6 cm

Signed and inscribed: *2/25 Rusting Landscape C. Lloyd '68* (pencil below plate)

Described by the artist as "a mood landscape in olives and orange of our urban environment—the scrap we throw away can be the starting point for the creative eye to find and then reusing this transform it into a new graphic image." Two plates were used, one plate being printed first (green), then the second plate (orange) over the first printing.[1]

Prov: Purchased from Gorner and Millard Prints, 1969.
Ref: 1. Undated notes by the artist in the Gallery files.

LUND, Niels Moller, 1863-1916

543   Corfe Castle[1]

Etching, 15.8 × 18.9 cm

Signed: *N.M.L.* (on plate) *Niels M. Lund* (pencil)

Prov: Purchased from the artist 1914.
Exh: L.A.E., 1914 (1388)
Ref: 1. *The Studio*, LXIV, 1915, p. 181, 182 rep.

544   Pevensey

Etching, 26 × 36.2 cm

Signed: *NML./PEVENSEY* (on plate) *Niels M. Lund* (pencil)

Prov: Presented by the artist, 1914.
Exh: L.A.E., 1914 (1379).

MANDEL, Johann August Edward, 1810-1882, after RAPHAEL, 1483-1520

4022   The Sistine Madonna

Steel engraving, 85 × 59.7 cm

Signed: *E. Mandel* (below plate in ink)

After Raphael's painting now at Dresden.

Prov: Purchased, 1884.

MANNOZZI, Giovanni, called Giovanni da San Giovanni, 1592-1636, after

9175 An allegorical subject

Etching, 19.5 × 20.1 cm

Inscribed: /Joan:a S. Joan:inv: (on plate)

Probably by a late 18th century engraver, close to Francesco Zuccarelli, after a drawing then attributed to Giovanni da San Giovanni,[1] now in the British Museum, Inv. No. 1946-7-13-90. This drawing was probably engraved while in C. Rogers's Collection.[2]

Fame crowns a ruler seated on a lion with a laurel wreath, probably one of the Medici family, since he holds in his left hand a laurel branch. Prudence holds a mirror up to his face, whilst behind Prudence stands Fortitude. In front of these two is Charity represented by a mother with a group of children, one of whom raises a flaming heart towards the ruler. In the foreground with his back to the spectator lies Time with a dog. There are three other allegorical female figures two of them carrying swords, one of these latter who appears to be receiving from the ruler or giving to him a laurel branch.

Prov: Charles Robert Blundell;[3] by descent to Colonel Sir Joseph Weld; his sale, Christie's, 7 October 1976 (11) with 9173-9174, 9176-9184 bt. in; purchased from Colonel Sir Joseph Weld with 9173-9174, 9176-9184.

Ref: **1.** A. E. Popham, *Catalogue of Drawings in the Collection formed by Sir Thomas Phillips Bart, F.R.S.* . . . Vol. 1, 1935, p. 163.   **2.** It bears part of his collector's mark (Lugt 624) reversed.   **3.** William Roscoe sale, Winstanley, 9 September 1816 (80) is described as *Different Masters of the Florentine School Eight Imitations of Drawings various.* It was bought by Slater, who acted for C. R. Blundell at the sale, for 9s 6d.

MARINI, Marino, born 1901

7190 Trio 1954

Etching, 35.2 × 29.2 cm

Signed: *35/50* marino (pencil below plate)

From Marini Album No. I, made up of 12 original etchings published by XXème siècle, Paris and Leon Amiel, New York, printed on 15 May 1968 by Lacourière on Rives vellum.[1]

Prov: Purchased from London Graphic Arts, 1969.
Ref: **1.** Patrick Waldberg and G. di San Lazzaro, *Marino Marini, L'Oeuvre Complet*, Paris, 1970, pp. 481-482 (50d).

MASTER E.M. after HUET, Jean Baptiste Marie, 1745-1811

6879 (a) The Stag

Lithograph, 33 × 47.5 cm

Inscribed: *Drawn on Stone by E.M. Printed by George Smith, Liverpool. Dessiné d'apres nature par Huet ainé/THE STAG.—LE CERF.*

One of four lithographs in Volume I of 7 volumes. It is the reverse to Nicolas Huet's colour lithograph after Jean-Baptiste Huet's design (No. 27) in the set of animals published in Paris by Basset, Md d'Estampes et Fabricant des Papiers peints, rue St. Jacques No. 670.

6880 (d) The Hunted Roebuck

Lithograph, 33 × 47.5 cm

Inscribed: *Drawn on Stone by E.M. Printed by George Smith, Liverpool. Dessiné d'après nature par Huet ainé/THE HUNTED ROEBUCK.—LE CHEVREUIL POURSUIVI.*

One of four lithographs in Volume III of 7 volumes. The lithograph is the reverse of Nicolas Huet's colour lithograph (No. 29) after Jean-Baptiste's design, published in Paris.

For the other lithographs in the set see below.

MASTER E.M. after HUET, Nicolas, called HUET le fils, 1772-1852

6879 (b) The Dromedary

Lithograph, 33 × 47.5 cm

Inscribed: *Drawn on Stone by E.M. Printed by George Smith, Liverpool. Dessiné d'après nature par Huet fils/THE DROMEDARY.—LE DROMEDAIRE.*

(c) The Jaguar

Lithograph, 33 × 47.5 cm

Inscribed: *Drawn on Stone by E.M. Printed by George Smith, Liverpool. Dessiné d'après nature par Huet fils/THE JAGUAR.—LE JAGUAR.*

(d)   The Polar Bear

Lithograph, 33 × 47.5 cm

Inscribed: *Drawn on Stone by E.M. Printed by George Smith, Liverpool. Dessiné d'après nature par Huet fils/THE POLAR BEAR.—OURS BLANC DU NORD.*

Three of four lithographs in Volume I of 7 volumes. They are the reverse of the colour lithographs Nos. 21, 26 and 9 respectively in the set published in Paris. The Jaguar No. 26 in that set is inscribed as engraved by Nicolas Huet after a design by Jean Baptiste Huet, his father. The other two were engraved by Lambert Frères after designs by Nicolas Huet. The Dromedary and the Polar Bear are also the reverse of the colour lithographs (plates 33 and 9) in the *Collection de Mammiferes du Museum d'Histoire Naturelle.*[1] Nicolas Huet exhibited a drawing of the Polar Bear at the Salon of 1808 (307).[2]

6880   (a) The Zebra

Lithograph, 33 × 47.5 cm

Inscribed: *Drawn on Stone by E.M. Printed by George Smith, Liverpool/THE ZEBRA.—LE ZEBRE.*

(b)   The Bengal Tiger

Lithograph, 33 × 47.5 cm

Inscribed: *Drawn on Stone by E.M. Printed by George Smith, Liverpool. Dessiné d'après nature par Huet fils/THE BENGAL TIGER. —TIGRE DU BENGALE.*

(c)   The Barbary Ram

Lithograph, 33 × 47.5 cm

Inscribed: *Drawn on Stone by E.M. Printed by George Smith, Liverpool. Dessiné après nature par Huet fils/THE BARBARY RAM.—LE BELIER DU BARBARE.*

Three of four lithographs in Volume III of 7 volumes. *The Bengal Tiger* and *The Barbary Ram* are the reverse of the coloured lithographs (Nos. 11 and 16) by Lambert Frères after the designs of Nicolas Huet, published in Paris. *The Zebra* however differs in pose from the colour lithograph of that animal (No. 14) in the Paris set, also by Lambert Frères after Nicolas Huet, but is the reverse of the colour lithograph (plate 52) in the *Collection de Mammiferes du Museum d'Histoire Naturelle.*[1] Nicolas Huet exhibited a drawing of *The Barbary Ram* at the Salon of 1806 (271).[2]

The covers of Volumes, I, III and IV call Nicolas Huet, Painter to the Menagerie of the Late Majesty the Empress Queen, and to the Museum of Natural History at Paris. Huet became painter to the menagerie of the Empress Josephine and painter to the Musée d'Histoire Naturelle in October 1804. The Empress Josephine died in 1814.

George Smith the printer is recorded in the Liverpool Street directories from 1824. In 1834 his firm became Smith Brothers, in 1839 George Smith & Co. and finally in 1848 George Smith, Watts & Co.

The E.M., who produced the lithographs might be Edward Matthews, a lithographic printer first recorded in the Liverpool street directories in 1839, who set up his own firm of copperplate, lithographic and letterpress printers in 1841. He is last recorded in 1860. It is possible that he began his career with George Smith.

For other lithographs in the series see under Jean Baptiste Huet and Jacques Christophe Werner (see above and below).

MASTER E.M. after WERNER, Jacques Christophe 1798-1856

6881 Animals drawn on stone IV

(a) The Horned Monkey

Lithograph, 33 × 47.5 cm

Inscribed: *Drawn on Stone by E.M. Printed by George Smith, Liverpool. Dessiné d'après nature par Werner/VARIETY OF THE HORNED MONKEY.—VARIÉTÉ DU SAJOU CORNOU.*

(b) The Civet

Lithograph, 33 × 47.5 cm

Inscribed: *Drawn on Stone by E.M. Printed by George Smith, Liverpool. Dessiné d'après nature par Werner/THE CIVET.—LE CIVETTE.*

(c) The Gnu

Lithograph, 33 × 47.5 cm

Inscribed: *Drawn on Stone by E.M. Printed by George Smith, Liverpool. Dessiné d'après nature par Werner/THE GNU.—GNOU FEMELLE.*

(d) The Mococo

Lithograph, 33 × 47.5 cm

Inscribed: *Drawn on Stone by E.M. Printed by George Smith, Liverpool. Dessiné d'après nature par Werner/THE MOCOCO.—LE MOCOCO.*

Volume IV of 7 volumes.

The Civet and the Gnu are the reverse of the colour lithographs by Nicolas Huet after Jean Baptiste Huet (plates 13 and 41) in the *Collection de Mammiferes du Museum d'Histoire Naturelle.*[1] The *Gnu* represented may be the one presented by M. Janson, Governor of the Cape to the Empress Josephine and by her to the Museum. It was obtained as a result of an expedition of 1800-1804.[3] The Cape Civet (viverra mellivora) may be the one brought to the Museum by M. Delahande.[4]

6882 Animals drawn on stone V

(a) The Rhinoceros

Lithograph, 33 × 47.5 cm

Inscribed: *Drawn on Stone by E.M. Printed by George Smith, Liverpool. Dessiné d'après nature par Werner/THE RHINOCEROS.—RHINOCEROS UNICORNE.*

(b) The Elephant

Lithograph, 33 × 47.5 cm

Inscribed: *Drawn on Stone by E.M. Printed by George Smith, Liverpool/THE ELEPHANT.—L'ELEPHANT*

(c) The Zebu

Lithograph, 33 × 47.5 cm

Inscribed: *Drawn on Stone by E.M. Printed by George Smith, Liverpool. Dessiné d'après nature par Werner/THE ZEBU.—ZEBU FEMELLE*

(d) The Chamois

Lithograph, 33 × 47.5 cm

Inscribed: *Drawn on Stone by E.M. Printed by George Smith, Liverpool. Dessiné d'après nature par Werner/THE CHAMOIS.—CHAMOIS FEMELLE*

Volume V out of 7 volumes. The Elephant is identical with the colour lithograph (plate 30) by Nicolas Huet after Jean Baptiste Huet in the *Collection de Mammiferes du Museum d'Histoire Naturelle* whereas the Zebu is the reverse of the colour lithograph (plate 50) in the same volume.[1] Nicolas Huet exhibited a drawing of the *Rhinoceros* at the Salon of 1817 (439), after an animal shown in Paris in 1815.[2] The Rhinoceros may have lived at Versailles.[5]

6883 Animals drawn on stone VI

(a) The Senegal Jackal

Lithograph, 33 × 47.5 cm

Inscribed: *Drawn on Stone by E.M. Printed by George Smith, Liverpool. Dessiné d'après nature par Werner/THE SENEGAL JACK-ALL.—CHACAL DU SENÉGAL*

(b) Lion Cubs

Lithograph, 33 × 47.5 cm

Inscribed: *Drawn on Stone by E.M. Printed by George Smith, Liverpool. Dessiné d'après nature par Werner/LION CUBS.—LIONCEAUX ÂGES D'UN JOUR.*

(c) The Axis or Ganges Stag

Lithograph, 33 × 47.5 cm

Inscribed: *Drawn on Stone by E.M. Printed by George Smith, Liverpool. Dessiné d'après nature par Werner/THE AXIS OR GANGES STAG.—AXIS*

(d) The Genet

Lithograph, 33 × 47.5 cm

Inscribed: *Drawn on Stone by E.M. Printed by George Smith, Liverpool. Dessiné d'après nature par Werner/THE GENET.—GENETTE*

Volume VI of 7 volumes.

The Genet is identical with the colour lithograph by Nicolas Huet after Jean Baptiste Huet (plate 13) in the *Collection de Mammiferes du Museum d'Histoire Naturelle.*[1] The Senegal jackal may be that sent to the Menagerie by M. Leschenault and described as follows "This last is a new species, remarkable for its slender make and tapering head." It was mated with an Indian jackal and produced young.[6] The Lion cubs may have been born in captivity in the menagerie.[7]

6884　Animals drawn on Stone VIII

(a)　The Serval

Lithograph, 33 × 47.5 cm

Inscribed: *Drawn on Stone by E.M. Printed by George Smith, Liverpool. Dessiné d'après nature par Werner/THE SERVAL.—LE SERVAL*

(b)　The Mouflon of Corsica

Lithograph, 33 × 47.5 cm

Inscribed: *Drawn on Stone by E.M. Printed by George Smith, Liverpool. Dessiné d'après nature par Werner/THE MOUFLON OF CORSICA.—MOUFLON DE CORSE.*

There is also an engraving by Demarteau after a drawing by J. B. Huet of the *Mouflon*.[8]

(c)　The Kevel

Lithograph, 33 × 47.5 cm

Inscribed: *Drawn on Stone by E.M. Printed by George Smith, Liverpool. Dessiné d'après nature par Werner/THE KEVEL.—KEVEL.*

(d)　The Coati

Lithograph, 33 × 47.5 cm

Inscribed: *Drawn on Stone by E.M. Printed by George Smith, Liverpool. Dessiné d'après nature par Werner/THE COATI.—LE COATI*

Last of 7 volumes entitled *Animals, drawn on Stone after plates from original drawings* by M. Huet and M. Werner respectively. Werner produced drawings for the last 4 volumes, despite the front cover of book IV which attributes them to Huet.

Jacques Christophe Werner was the natural history painter at the Jardin des Plantes, Paris. He published 5 lithographic plates of the Orang-Outang and the Chimpanzee, Paris, 1836.

For discussion of the other two books in the collection, see under Huet 6879, 6880.

Prov:　Transferred from Liverpool City Museum, 1968.

Ref:　**1.** *Collection de Mammiferes de Muséum d'Histoire Naturelle classée suivant la Methode de M. Cuvier, Secrétaire perpétuel de l'Institut, et Professeur d'anatomie comparée du Museum d'Histoire Naturelle . . .,* 1808.　**2.** C. Gabillot, *Les Huet,* 1892, p. 156.　**3.** M. Deleuze, *History and Description of the Royal Museum of Natural History,* I, 1823, pp. 92-3.　**4.** Deleuze, *op. cit.,* II, p. 316.　**5.** Deleuze, *op. cit.,* II, p. 325.　**6.** Deleuze, *op. cit.,* II, p. 565.　**7.** Deleuze, *op. cit.,* II, p. 319.　**8.** Rudolf Weigel, *Die Werke der Maler in ihren Handzeichnungen,* 1865, p. 323 (3901).

MATISSE, Henri, 1869-1954

641 Design in five colours (Dessein en cinq couleurs)

Lithograph, 54.1 × 49.7 cm

Inscribed: *matisse 52* (on block) *Henri matisse* (ink) *184/200* (pencil)

Exh: ?Redfern Gallery, *An Exhibition of Colour lithographs, etchings, aquatints, lithographed affiches, pochoirs*, 1956/7 (190).[1] W.A.G., *Modern Colour Lithographs*, 1957 (71).

Ref: 1. Lithographs of this title were also exhibited at the Redfern Gallery, *Summer Exhibition*, 1954 (515) and *Summer Exhibition*, 1956 (528).

MATISSE, Henri, after

642 Still life by the window (Nature morte à la fenêtre)

Lithograph, 75.5 × 56.3 cm

Inscribed: *Matisse 47* (on block) *Henri-Matisse* (ink) *69/200* (pencil)

After the *Still life with Pomegranate (Nature morte à la grenade)* in the Musée Matisse Nice-Cimiez.[1]

Exh: ?Redfern Gallery, *An Exhibition of Colour lithographs, etchings, aquatints, lithographed affiches, pochoirs*, 1956/7 (194); W.A.G., *Modern Colour Lithographs*, 1957 (73).

Prov: Purchased from Redfern Gallery, 1957.

Ref: 1. Arts Council of Great Britain, Hayward Gallery, 1968, *Matisse 1869-1954* (118).

MAYER-MARTON, George, 1893-1960

9163 Quartet

Etching and drypoint, 34.8 × 39.8 cm

Signed: *mayer marton/Probedrück* (in pencil below plate)

Executed in 1927.[1]

Ref: 1. Information from Mrs H. J. Braithwaite, 1976.

9164 Skating rink

Etching and drypoint, 24.8 × 32 cm

Signed: *G mayer marton/Probedrück* (pencil below plate)

Executed in Vienna in 1924.[1] The original plate was lost in transit from Austria at the time of the artist's emigration to England.[2]

Ref: **1.** Mayer-Marton's MS workbook Collection of Mrs H. J. Braithwaite.
          2. Information from Mrs H. J. Braithwaite, 1976.

9165   Harbour: sun sails

Etching and drypoint, 31.1 × 29 cm

Signed: *Mayer marton* (pencil below plate)

Executed in 1927.[1] The original plate was lost in transit from Austria at the time of the artist's emigration to England.[2]

Ref: **1.** Mayer-Marton's MS workbook. Collection of Mrs H. J. Braithwaite.
          2. Information from Mrs H. J. Braithwaite, 1976.

9166   Old Town with boats

Etching and drypoint, 40.3 × 29.4 cm

Signed: *mayer marton* (pencil below plate)

Executed in 1928.[1]

Prov: Bequeathed by the artist to his sister, Mrs C. Friend, and presented by the latter to her daughter, Mrs H. J. Braithwaite, by whom presented, 1976.
Ref: **1.** Mayer-Marton's MS workbook. Collection of Mrs H. J. Braithwaite.

MECKENEM, Israhel van, active 1466, died 1503 after SCHONGAUER, Martin, active 1469, died 1491

9122   The Third Foolish Virgin

Engraving, 11.2 × 6.7 cm

Signed: *I.M.* (beneath the Virgin's feet slightly to the right)

After Schongauer's print (Lehrs 83).[1]

Prov: Charles Robert Blundell; by descent to Colonel Sir Joseph Weld, his sale, Christie's, 30 June 1976 (64) bt. National Art-Collections Fund, by whom presented, 1976.
Ref: **1.** Max Lehrs, *Geschichte und kritischer Katalog des Deutschen, Niederlandischen und Franzosischen Kupferstichs im XV Jahrhundert*, IX, 1934, p. 334 (426) cites 20 examples.

MERYON, Charles, 1821-1868

546 Le Pont Neuf

Etching, 18.2 × 18 cm

Signed: lower margin: *C Meryon del. sculp. 1853*

Inscribed: *Imp A. Delâtre Rue de la Bucherie no6.*

7th state.[1] The 6th state of this etching contains in the lower margin the following poem, traces of which are still visible in this state.

Ci-gît du vieux Pont-Neuf	O savants médecins
L'exacte ressemblance	Habiles chirurgiens
Tout radoubé de neuf	De nous pourquoi ne faire
Par récente ordonnance	Comme du pont de pierre

Two drawings for the etching are known in the Bibliothèque Nationale, Paris (A.C. 8523)[2] and in Toledo Museum of Art (23.3106).[3]

Prov: P. D. (Lugt 2074);[4] Dowdeswell; bt. 1891 by James Smith of Blundellsands,[5] who bequeathed it in 1927.

Ref: 1. Loys Delteil, (edited by Harold J. L. Wright), *The Etchings of Charles Meryon*, 1924 (33); reproduced Martin Hardie, *Charles Meryon and his eaux-fortes sur Paris being a lecture delivered to the print collectors quarterly club on Thursday 11th March 1931*, 1931, pl. XVI.   **2.** James D. Burke, *Charles Meryon Prints & Drawings*, Toledo Museum of Art, Yale University Art Gallery and St. Louis Art Museum, 1974-1975, p. 60.   **3.** Burke, *op. cit.*, pp. 60-61 (48) rep. who also mentions a finished drawing in the MacGeorge collection in reverse, reproduced in William Aspenwall Bradley, *Some Meryon drawings in the MacGeorge Collection*, Print Collectors Quarterly, 1917, p. 241. See also Paul L. Grigaut, *Some unpublished or little-known Meryon drawings in the Toledo Museum of Art*, p. 233.   **4.** Unidentified by Lugt, possibly Dowdeswell.   **5.** MS notes in W.A.G.'s possession.

4950 Part of the City of Paris towards the end of the 17th century, on the left bank of the Seine between the Notre Dame bridge and the bridge by the Exchange (Partie de la Cité de Paris vers la fin du XVIIe siècle, sur la rive gauche de la Seine entre le Pont Notre Dame et le pont au Change).

Etching, 16.7 × 31.5 cm

Inscribed: on the hoarding above the buildings at the extreme right of the print: *AU REPU/LE SOBRE RESTA/POISSON FR.* In lower margin: *Delâtre Imp. r. des Feuillantines. 2 Paris/PARTIE DE LA CITÉ DE PARIS VERS LA FIN DU XVIIe SIECLE, SUR LA RIVE GAUCHE DE LA SEINE, ENTRE LE PONT Ne, DAME ET LE PONT AU CHANGE/N.B. Suivant toute probabilité la façade Méridionale des presentes maisons, habitées par tanneurs, formait un côté de la rue de la Pelleterie. Chose assez singulière, par les causes sur les quelles peut s'exercer la sagacité des curieux, des parties importantes du sujet, a savoir les Tours Notre Dame, le coin de la pompe Ne. De. les cheminées/des pignons du* pont, *manquent dans l'original, du moins le seul emplacement en est indiqué, tandis que des details, (que la gravure a dailleurs soigneusement reproduits), y sont faits avec minutie. En fin pour prendre la vie a ces lieux le graveur a cru pouvoir ajouter différents groupes de figures (Le dessin fait partie de la collection de Mr. Bonnardot.) Chez ROCHOUX. Quai de l'Horloge. 19.*

8th State.[1]

Prov: Dowdeswell, bt. 1891 by James Smith of Blundellsands,[2] who bequeathed it to the Gallery, 1927.

Ref: **1.** Loys Delteil (edited Harold J. L. Wright), *Catalogue Raisonne of the etchings of Charles Meryon,* 1924 (51).   **2.** MS notes in W.A.G.'s possession.

MIRO, Joan, born 1893

643   The animals (Les animaux)

Colour Lithograph, 35.5 × 26.3 cm

Inscribed: *miró* (on block)

One of a series commercially printed by Mourlot.

Prov: Purchased from the Redfern Gallery, 1957.

Exh: ?Redfern Gallery, *An Exhibition of Colour lithographs, etchings, aquatints, lithographed affiches, pochoirs,* 1956/7, (201); W.A.G., *Modern Colour Lithographs,* (75).

6228   Woman and birds (Femme et oiseaux)

Colour lithograph, 35 × 41.9 cm

Inscribed: *miró* (on block)

Prov: Redfern Gallery; the Medici Gallery from whom purchased, 1964.

Exh: ?Redfern Gallery, *Gravures,* 1958/9 (892); Medici Gallery, Liverpool, 1964 *Modern Lithographs* (37).

MUSIC, Antonio, born 1915

3172   The brown threads (Les Filets bruns)

Coloured aquatint, 42 × 53.4 cm

Signed: *11/90 Music* (pencil)

Prov: Ernest Musgrave; Redfern Gallery from whom purchased, 28 November 1956 by Frank Lambert, who presented it, 1959.

Exh: ?Redfern Gallery, *An Exhibition of Colour lithographs, etchings, aquatints, lithographed affiches, pochoirs,* 1956/7 (225).

NEL, Peter, born 1935

6922 Glennel landscape

Etching, 49 × 49 cm

Signed and inscribed: *27/50 Glennel landscape Peter Nel* (pencil)

"Glennel" is the name of the farm owned by the artist's father in Botswana. The etching is a "memory" of a painting of 1954/5. The artist states, "I tried to get the feeling of Africa in wintertime—crisp, dry and lonely."[1]

Prov: Purchased from Gorner and Millard Prints, 1969.
Ref: 1. Undated notes by the artist in the Gallery files.

OLITSKI, Jules, born 1922

7792 Pink Blue

Screenprint, 88.5 × 65.5 cm

Signed: $\frac{29}{150}$ /*Jules Olitski 70* (pencil)

Prov: Purchased from Leslie Waddington Prints Ltd., 1972.
Exh: Leslie Waddington (Prints), 1972.

PALMA, Jacopo called Il Giovane, 1544-1628

9179 Allegorical figure of Rome holding a statuette of Victory

Etching, 16.9 × 25.5 cm

Signed: *franco forma Con Priuilegio Palma* (on plate)

Bartsch 24.[1]

Prov: William Roscoe, his sale, Winstanley, 14 September 1816 (700)[2] with 9181-9183, bt. Money 9s; Charles Robert Blundell; by descent to Colonel Sir Joseph Weld; his sale, Christie's 7 October 1976 (11) with 9173-9178, 9180-9184 bt. in; purchased from Colonel Joseph Weld, 1976 with 9173-9178, 9180-9184.
Ref: 1. Adam Bartsch, *Le Peintre Graveur*, 1818 pp. 293-294 (24).   2. Lot number inscribed in pencil on the back of the mount.

9180   Holy Family with Saints Francis and Jerome

Etching, 11 × 16.7 cm

Signed: *Palma/fece* (on plate)

Bartsch 21.[1]

Prov: William Roscoe, his sale Winstanley's 14 September 1816 (698) with one other, bt. Robinson 10s 6d; Thomas H. Robinson sale, Winstanley, Manchester, March 22, 1819 (519) as *The Virgin and Child, adored by St. Jerome and two saints* (sic) with 9181 7s bt. in; Thomas H. Robinson his sale, Winstanley, Manchester, May 18, 1820 (142) again with 9181 7s; Charles Robert Blundell; by descent to Colonel Sir Joseph Weld; his sale, Christie's 7 October 1976 (11) with 9173-9179, 9181-9184 bt. in; purchased from Colonel Sir Joseph Weld, 1976 with 9173-9179, 9181-9184.

Ref: 1. Adam Bartsch, *Le Peintre Graveur*, XVI, p. 292 (21).

9181   Christ and the woman taken in adultery

Etching, 11 × 16.7 cm

Signed: *Palma fece.* (on plate)

Bartsch 20.[1]

Prov: William Roscoe; his sale Winstanley, 14 September 1816 (700)[2] with 9179 and 9182-9183 bt. Money 9s; Thomas H. Robinson sale, Winstanley, Manchester, March 22, 1819 (519) with 9180 7s bt. in; his sale, Winstanley, Manchester, May 18, 1820 (142) again with 9180 7s. Charles Robert Blundell; by descent to Colonel Sir Joseph Weld; his sale, Christie's 7 October 1976 (11) with 9173-9180, 9182-9184 bt. in. purchased from Colonel Sir Joseph Weld with 9173-9180 and 9182-9184, 1976.

Ref: 1. Adam Bartsch, *Le Peintre Graveur*, XVI, 1818, p. 292 (20).   2. Lot number inscribed on the back of the mount.

9182   Studies of ten heads, two backs, one torso, one leg, one arm, one knee and two feet

Etching, 14.4 × 20.3 cm

Signed: *Palma fece.* (on plate)

Bartsch 15.[1] 9179-9182 are four of the twenty-six etchings by Palma which were published in to volumes as *Regole per imparar a disegnar i corpi humani divise in doi libri delineati dal Famoso Pittor Giacomo Palma* printed by Giacomo Franco in 1611 and published in Venice by Marco Sadeler in 1636.[2] The other prints in the books were produced by Jacopo Franco and Luca Ciamberlano after Palma's designs.

Prov: Nathaniel Smith (cf Lugt 2298);[3] William Roscoe; his sale, Winstanley, 14 September 1816 (700)[4] with 9179, 9181, 9183 bt. Money 9s; Charles Robert Blundell; by descent to Colonel Sir Joseph Weld; his sale, Christie's, 7 October 1976 (11) with 9173-9181, 9183-9184 bt in; purchased from Colonel Sir Joseph Weld with 9173-9181, 9183-9184, 1976.

Ref:	1. Adam Bartsch, *Le Peintre Graveur*, XVI, 1818, p. 290 (15).	2. Carlo Pasero, *Giacomo Franco editore incisore e calcografo nei secoli XVI e XVII*, La Bibliofilia, XXXVII, 1935, pp. 333, 352.	3. Inscription in brown ink on the back of the mount no. 4 Oct 1499.	4. Lot number inscribed in pencil on the back of the mount.

PALMA, Jacopo, called Il Giovane, after

9183   The Adoration of the Shepherds

Etching, 28.5 × 21.3 cm

Inscribed: *Iacobus Palma Inuentor* (on plate below margin)

Watermark: a heart and undeciphered lettering

Prov:	William Roscoe; his sale, Winstanley, 14 September 1816 (700) with 9179, 9181-9182 bt. Money 9s; Charles Robert Blundell; by descent to Colonel Sir Joseph Weld; his sale, Christie's, 7 October 1976 (11) with 9173-9182 and 9184 bt. in; purchased from Colonel Sir Joseph Weld with 9173-9182 and 9184, 1976.

PENNELL, Joseph, 1860-1926

671   Coal—the Abomination of Works

Etching, 19.8 × 25.1 cm

Signed: *Jo Pennell imp* (pencil below plate)

From an edition of 50.[1]

Exh:	L.A.E., 1909 (1283).
Prov:	Purchased from the artist at the L.A.E., 1909.
Ref:	1. Louis A. Wuerth, *Catalogue of the Etchings of Joseph Pennell*, Boston, 1928, p. 183 (531).

672   The Grip (Serang)

Etching, 23.7 × 31.8 cm

Signed and inscribed: *MARIA* (on barge on plate) *Jo Pennell imp* (pencil below plate)

From an edition of 40.[1]

Exh:	L.A.E., 1910 (1281).
Prov:	Purchased from the artist at the L.A.E., 1910.
Ref:	1. Wuerth, *op. cit.*, p. 209 (609).

1300 On the way to Bessemer

Etching, 28.1 × 17.7 cm

Inscribed: *Approach to . . . mite / J Pennell July 1908* (on plate in reverse)

Signed: *Jo Pennell del fec imp* (on paper)

From an edition of 90.[1] Pennell described his excitement at finding his subjects. In this case he jumped off a trolley car to draw the subject after leaving the works. "It's all adventure—the adventure of Hunting for the Wonder of Work."[2]

Exh: L.A.E., 1909 (1280).
Ref: 1. Wuerth, *op. cit.*, p. 179 (520); Elisabeth Luther Cary, *Joseph Pennell: A Note*, Print Collector's Quarterly, XIV, 1927 p. 48 (repr.). 2. *Joseph Pennell's Pictures of the Wonder of Work*, 1916 (XIII).

1566 Standard Oil Works, Staten Island

Etching, 14 × 30.7 cm

Signed: *Jo Pennell imp* (pencil below plate)

From an edition of 50.[1] An earlier state without the horizontal lines in the river was illustrated in *The Studio*.[2]

Exh: L.A.E., 1909 (1277).
Ref: 1. Wuerth, *op. cit.*, p. 184 (536). 2. Hans W. Singer, *Some new American Etchings by Mr Joseph Pennell*, The Studio, 47, 1909, p. 27.

1567 The Cliffs of West Street, New York

Sandpaper mezzotint, 25.5 × 32.5 cm

Signed: *Jo Pennell imp Jo Pennell imp* (pencil below plate)

From an edition of 50 issued in 1908.[1]

Exh: L.A.E., 1909 (1278).
Ref: 1. Wuerth, *op. cit.*, p. 172 (500).

1568 Edgar Thomson Steelworks, Bessemer

Etching, 27.6 × 19.9 cm

Inscribed: *Jo Pennell July 1908/Bessemer* (in reverse on plate)

Signed: *Jo Pennell imp* (in pencil below plate over an earlier inscription *Jo Pennell imp*)

Watermark: ANDRIEUX

From an edition of 90.[1] This etching was published in *The Studio*, 1909.[2] Of this view Pennell wrote, "the only artists who see things in the world are engineers and a few architects, for the mill has taken the place of the Cathedral—and the great craftsmen who once worked for Popes now work for captains of industry—for art follows money."[3]

Exh: *L.A.E.*, 1909 (1279).
Ref: **1.** Wuerth, *op. cit.*, p. 178 (517).   **2.** Singer, *op. cit.* p. 25.   **3.** *Joseph Pennell's pictures of the Wonder of Work*, 1916 (XII).

1569   Among the Skyscrapers, New York

Etching and drypoint, 28 × 21.4 cm

Signed: *J. Pennell imp Jo Pennell imp* (pencil below plate)

From an edition of 75.[1]

Exh: *L.A.E.*, 1909 (1281).
Ref: **1.** Wuerth, *op. cit.*, p. 170 (494).

1570   New York from Brooklyn Bridge

Etching, 27.8 × 21.4 cm

Signed: *Jo Pennell imp* (pencil below plate)

From an edition of 150.[1] This etching was published in *The Studio*, 1909,[2] and was also used as the frontispiece in *Masterpieces of American painting*, New York, 1910.[1]

Exh: *L.A.E.*, 1909 (1282).
Ref: **1.** Wuerth, *op. cit.*, p. 169 (490).   **2.** Singer, *op. cit.*, p. 24.

1571   From Courtland Street Ferry, New York

Sandpaper mezzotint, 32.9 × 15.2 cm

Signed: *Jo Pennell del sc imp* (pencil below plate)

From an edition of 50 issued in 1908.[1] Drawn at night from a ferry boat.[2] Reviewed enthusiastically in *The Studio*, 48, 1909-10, p. 148.

Exh: *L.A.E.*, 1909 (1285).
Ref: **1.** Wuerth, *op. cit.*, p. 173 (502).   **2.** *Catalogue of an Exhibition of lithographs and etchings by Joseph Pennell of the Wonder of Work with an introduction and notes by the artist*, Bradford, 1913, p. 9 (29).

1572 Palisades and Palaces, New York

Etching, 27.8 × 21.5 cm

Signed: *Jo Pennell imp* (pencil below plate)

From an edition of 50 published in 1908.[1] This etching was published in *The Studio*, 1909.[2]

Exh: L.A.E., 1909, (1279).
Ref: **1.** Wuerth, *op. cit.*, p. 171 (496).   **2.** Singer, *op. cit.*, p. 23.

1573 West Street Building from Singer Building, New York

Etching, 27.5 × 21.2 cm

Inscribed: *Jo Pennell/1908* (on plate)

Signed: *Jo Pennell imp Jo Pennell imp* (pencil below plate)

Watermark: MXCCXXXV (repeated in reverse) D a shield with a rampant lion facing right HH (all repeated in reverse)

From an edition of 90.[1]

Exh: L.A.E., 1909 (1288).
Ref: **1.** Wuerth, *op. cit.*, p. 169 (491).

1574 The Mahoney Valley (The Mining Village)[1]

Etching, 17.9 × 22.9 cm

Inscribed: *Jo Pennell/July 1909* (in reverse on plate)

Signed: *Jo Pennell imp* (pencil below plate)

From an edition of 50.[1]

Exh: L.A.E., 1909 (1289).
Ref: **1.** Wuerth, *op. cit.*, p. 180 (524).

1575 Pittsburg No. 3

Etching, 21.6 × 29.5 cm

Signed: *J. Pennell imp* (pencil below plate)

From an edition of 60.[1] Pennell described Pittsburg as "the work-city of the world", and the view from the opposite side of the river as "the glorification of work."[2]

Exh: L.A.E., 1909 (1290).
Ref: **1.** Wuerth, *op. cit.*, p. 179 (519).   **2.** *Joseph Pennell's Pictures of the Wonder of Work*, 1916 (XI) (a later state).

1576 Main Street, Mahoney City

Etching, 28.1 × 21.7 cm

Signed: *Jo Pennell imp* (pencil below plate)

From an edition of 50.[1] A Pennsylvania mining town.[2]

Prov: Purchased from the artist at the L.A.E., 1909.
Exh: L.A.E., 1909 (1291).
Ref: 1. Wuerth, *op. cit.*, p. 180 (523).   2. *Catalogue of an Exhibition of Lithographs and Etchings by Joseph Pennell . . .*, Bradford, 1913, p. 10 (36).

1577 The Dump (Serang)

Etching, 23.7 × 31.4 cm

Signed: *Jo Pennell imp* (on paper)

From an edition of 50.[1]

Prov: Purchased from the artist at the L.A.E., 1910
Exh: L.A.E., 1910 (1818).
Ref: 1. Wuerth, *op. cit.*, p. 209 (611).

1610 Coal Wharves, Staten Island No. I

Etching, 14.2 × 31 cm

Signed: *Jo Pennell imp* (pencil below plate)

From an edition of 60.[1]

Exh: L.A.E., 1909 (1284).
Ref: 1. Wuerth, *op. cit.*, p. 185 (537).

1780 The Coalbreaker (The things that tower: Collieries)

Etching, 20.3 × 28.1 cm

Signed: *Jo Pennell imp* (pencil below plate)

From an edition of 50.[1] Pennell's own comments were "these huge buildings where the coal is screened and sifted look in the landscape like huge castles, and they are the castles of work."[2]

Exh: L.A.E., 1909 (1292).
Ref: 1. Wuerth, *op. cit.*, p. 181 (527).   2. *Catalogue of an Exhibition of lithographs and etchings by Joseph Pennell . . .*, Bradford, 1913, p. 9 (35).

1781 The Bridges, New York

Etching, 27.8 × 21.2 cm

Signed: *Jo Pennell imp* (pencil below plate)

From an edition of 50 issued in 1908.[1]

Prov: Purchased from the artist at the L.A.E., 1909.
Exh: *L.A.E.*, 1909 (1286).
Ref: 1. Wuerth, *op. cit.*, p. 170 (492).

PICASSO, Pablo, 1881-1974

2735 Music (Musique)

Lithograph, 39 × 48.2 cm

Inscribed: *Picasso/12 Mai 47 II* (on block) *17/200* (pencil)

Prov: Purchased from the Redfern Gallery through the New Shakespeare Theatre Art Gallery, 1958.
Exh: New Shakespeare Theatre Gallery, Liverpool, 1958 (35).

6229 The arrival of the knight (L'arrivée du chevalier)

Colour lithograph, 47 × 74.3 cm

Inscribed: *21.2.51* (on block) *217/350 Picasso* (pencil)

Picasso produced a number of works on the theme of the knight in 1951.[1]

Prov: Redfern Gallery; the Medici Gallery, Liverpool from whom purchased, 1964.
Exh; Medici Gallery, Liverpool, 1964 (39).
Ref: 1. For instance an oil *The Knight* (*Sport of Pages*) is dated 24/2/51 and a colour lithograph, *The Knight and his Page* was issued in that year. Arts Council, *Picasso*, 1960 (187) pl. 46f.

PIRANESI, Giovanni Battista, 1720-1778

6654 Temple of Fortunus

Etching, 40 × 59.7 cm

Inscribed: *Veduta del Tempio di Cibele della Bocca della Verita* (and with key) */Presso l'autore a Strada Felice vicino alla Trinita de'Monti A paoli due e mezzo./Piranesi Archit dis. ed incise*

The round temple by the Tiber, which was used for the church of S. Maria del Sole.[1] One of the *Vedute di Roma*.

Prov: Purchased from P. & D. Colnaghi & Co. Ltd., 1968.
Ref: 1. Arthur M. Hind, *Giovanni Battista Piranesi*, 1922, p. 52 (47).

PIRANESI, Giovanni Battista and others

7102 A book of views of Italy

(a) ITALIAN School, late 18th century

Eruption of Vesuvius, 1779

Engraving, 29 × 52.5 cm

Inscribed: *5* (upper margin) *Prospetto del Vesuvio veduto dal Molo di Napoli A. Montagna di Somma. B. Vesuvio. C. Rottura par dove nel 1767. dilavò l'eruzione D. riempiendo l'artio del Cavallo; e percorse fin a San Giorgio. Dalla medesima apertura. C. C. nel 1779, nella notte di Agosto, erutto incredible quantita di fuoco, ceneri,/pomici, e lapilli. Principiò il fenomeno ad ora una, e quasi minuti 15 della notte, con tanta energia, attività, e forza, che in pochi minuti si vede il fuoco di altezza circa a due Miglia dalla bocca, e le ceneri permiste di pomici superavano l'eruzione piu del doppio. Il fuoco eruttato cadeva dall'altezza in arco parabolico;/e diviso in pietre infocate di tanti ordini diversi, coprirono gran parte delle Montagne Vesuvio B. e di Somma A; danneggiando Ottaiano, e le Case, e Casini à suoi contorni; le Ceneri, le Pomici, e i Lapilli portate dall'attività dello Scirocco, che lentamente spirava in quell'ora, giunsero a Nola, e in altre terre attorno; e finalmente/le ceneri più leggiere in poche ore giunsero in Bovino, e in fino al di là di Foggia. Continuò l'eruzione simile nel giorno 9. dalla ore 15. infino alle ore 17. e finalmente nel giorno 11 dalle ore 18. infino alle ore 20. nel modo qui espresso.*

(b) PIRANESI, and NOLLI Giovanni Battista, 1692-1756

Titlepage of La Topografia di Roma

Etching, 46.8 × 68.3 cm

Inscribed: *34* (upper margin) *All E̅mo e R̅mo Sigr. Sigr. P̅ne Colmo̅/Il Sigr. Cardinale Alessandro Albani/Emo, e Rmo Principe/Ardisco offerire all'Emza Via ristretta in questa picciola Pianta la nuova/Topografia di Roma . . . Roma il di primo del 1748/Umo Divotis. e Oblmo Servitore/ Gio.Battista Nolli* (on cartouche) *LA TOPOGRAPHIA/DI ROMA/ DI GIO. BA̅TTA NOLLI/DALLA MAGGIORE/IN QVESTA MINOR/TAVOLA/DAL MEDESIMO RIDOTTA* (on remains of triumphal arch) *Piranesi/e Nolli/incisero* (on end of socle) Also an index and numerous identifying numbers and inscriptions.

The only plate in the *Nuova Pianta di Roma* (published 1748), which bears Piranesi's name. The views of St. Peters and other Roman buildings and monuments at the bottom are probably Piranesi's. The rest of the volume is probably engraved by Carlo Nolli, who signed two of the index plates.[1]

Ref: **1.** Arthur M. Hind, *Giovanni Battista Piranesi*, 1922, p. 78.

(c) View of the Piazza and Basilica of S. Giovanni in Laterano

Etching, 48.5 × 70.2 cm

Inscribed: *Veduta della Piazza, e Basilica di S. Giovanni in Laterano* (on scroll) *Cavalier Piranesi F.* (lower margin)

First state.[1]

Ref: **1.** Hind, *op. cit.*, p. 69 (117).

(d) View of the Pantheon

Etching, 47.4 × 69.5 cm

Inscribed: *Veduta del Pantheon d'Agrippa/oggi Chiesa di S. Maria ad Martyres/Piranesi F.* (on scroll with key)

Second state.[1]

Ref: **1.** Hind, *op. cit.*, p. 56 (60).

(e) View of the inside of the Pantheon

Etching, 47.8 × 56.2 cm

Inscribed: *Caval. Piranesi F./Veduta interna del Panteon. etc.*, (lower margin)

Second state.[1]

Ref: **1.** Hind, *op. cit.*, p. 62 (86).

(f) Trajan's Column

Etching, 54.4 × 40.6 cm

Inscribed: *Piranesi fecit/Colonna Trajana/Presso l'autore a Strada Felice nel Palazzo Tomati vicino alla Trinità de'monti* (lower margin with key)

Fifth state.[1]

Ref: **1.** Hind, *op. cit.*, p. 53 (51).

(g) View of the Campo Vaccino

Etching, 41 × 54.6 cm

Inscribed: *Veduta di Campo Vaccino/Presso l'autore a Strada Felice nel palazzo Tomati vicino alla Trinità de' monti/ Piranesi del. Sculp* (lower margin) and with key

Between the third and fourth states.[1]

A view of the Forum Romanum from the Campidoglio with the Colosseum in the distance.

Ref: 1. Hind, *op. cit.*, pp. 49-50 (40).

(h) View of the Roman Campidoglio with the staircase leading to the Church of Aracoeli

Etching, 40 × 54.1 cm

Inscribed: *Veduta del Romano Campidogli con Scalinata che va alla Chiesa d'Araceli/Architettura di Michelangelo Bonaroti/Presso l'autore a Strada Felice nel Palazzo Tomati vicino alla Trinità de monti/Piranesi del. scol.* (lower margin) and with key

First state.[1]

Ref: 1. Hind, *op. cit.*, p. 68 (111).

(i) View of the Flavian amphitheatre, called the Colosseum

Etching, 43.8 × 69.2 cm

Inscribed: *Veduta dell'Anfiteatro Flavio, detto il Colosseo/Presso l'autore a Strada Felice vicino alla Trinità de monti/Piranesi F.* (lower margin) and with key

Second state.[1]

Ref: 1. Hind, *op. cit.*, p. 55 (57).

(j) View of the Flavian amphitheatre called the Colosseum

Etching, 49.7 × 70.5 cm

Inscribed: *VEDUTA DELL'ANFITEATRO FLA-/VIO DETTO IL COLOSSEO* (scroll bottom left) *Cav. Piranesi F.* (scroll bottom right) and with key.

First state.[1] A bird's eye view.

Ref: 1. Hind, *op. cit.*, p. 71 (126).

(k)   Tomb of Caecilia Metella

Etching, 45.8 × 63.8 cm

Inscribed: *Sepolcro di Cecilia Metella/or detto Capo di bove fuori della porta/di S. Sebastiano su l'antica via Appia* (on scroll bottom left) *Piranesi F.* (bottom right).

Second state.[1]

Ref: **1.** Hind, *op. cit.*, p. 57-58 (67).

(1)   View of the waterfall at Tivoli

Etching, 47.5 × 70.5 cm

Inscribed: *VEDVTA. DELLA. CASCATA/DI. TIVOLI/Eques Piranesius del sculp/1766* (on masonry bottom right).

Second state.[1]

Ref: **1.** Hind, *op. cit.*, p. 59 (75).

(m)   View of the Basilica of St. Peter with its Portico and adjacent Piazza

Etching, 47.7 × 71.1 cm

Inscribed: *Veduta dell'insigne Basilica Vaticana coll'ampio Portico, e Piazza adjacente/Cavaliere Piranesi delin. ed inc.* (lower margin) and with key.

First state.[1]

Ref: **1.** Hind, *op. cit.*, p. 70 (120).

(n)   Internal view of the Basilica of St. Peter

Etching, 40.6 × 59.5 cm

Inscribed: *Piranesi fecit/Veduta della Basilica di S. Pietro in Vaticano./Presso l'autore a Strada Felice nel Palazzo Tomati vicino alla Trinità de'monti* (lower margin)

Fourth state.[1] View of the nave looking towards the choir.

Ref: **1.** Hind, *op. cit.*, p. 39 (4).

(o)   Internal view of the Basilica of St. Peter, close to the Choir

Etching, 48.7 × 67.3 cm

Inscribed: *Veduta interna della Basilica di/S. Pietro in Vaticano vicino alla Tribuna/Caval. Piranesi F.* (on tablet)

First state.[1] Beneath the dome.

Ref: **1.** Hind, *op. cit.*, p. 66 (102).

(p)   View of the Piazza di Monte Cavallo

Etching, 47.6 × 70.9 cm

Inscribed: *Veduta della Piazza di Monte Cavallo* (on scroll with key) *Cavalier Piranesi del. e inc.* (lower margin)

First state.[1] Looking across at the Palazzo Quirinale from behind the statues of the horse-tamers.

Ref: **1.** Hind, *op. cit.*, p. 66 (103).

(q)   View of the Piazza Navona

Etching, 46.9 × 70.1 cm

Inscribed: *Veduta di Piazza Navona/sopra le rovine del Circo/ Agonale/Cav. Piranesi F.* (on scroll)

First state.[1] With S. Agnese on the left.

Ref: **1.** Hind, *op. cit.*, p. 67 (108).

(r)   View in perspective of the Fontana di Trevi

Etching, 47.5 × 70.8 cm

Inscribed: *Veduta in prospettiva della gran Fontana dell'Acqua Vergine detta di Trevi Architettura di Nicola Salvi./Cavalier Piranesi F.* (lower margin)

First state.[1]

Ref: **1.** Hind, *op. cit.*, p. 66 (104).

(s)   View of the Palazzo Farnese

Etching, 41.8 × 66 cm

Inscribed: *Veduta del Palazzo/Farnese* (on scroll) *Cavalier Piranesi F.* (lower margin)

First state.[1]

Ref: **1.** Hind, *op. cit.*, p. 67 (107).

(t) View of the Villa of His Excellency Signor Cardinal Alessandro Albani outside the Porta Salaria

Etching, 44.3 × 69.5 cm

Inscribed: *Veduta della Villa dell'Emo Sigr. Card./Alesandro Albani fuori di Porta Salaria* (on masonry) *Cavalier Piranesi inc.* (lower margin)

First state.[1]

Ref: **1.** Hind, *op. cit.*, p. 63 (89).

(u) View of the Ponte and Castello Sant'Angelo

Etching, 37.7 × 58.6 cm

Inscribed: *Piranesi Architetto fec./Veduta del Ponte e Castello Sant'Angelo/Presso l'autore a Strada Felice nel palazzo Tomati vicino alla Trinità de'monti* (lower margin)

Fourth State.[1]

Ref: **1.** Hind, *op. cit.*, p. 46 (29).

(v) View of the Villa d'Este, Tivoli

Etching, 46.8 × 70.1 cm

Inscribed: *VEDVTA. DELLA/VILLA. ESTENSE/IN TIVOLI* (on masonry) *G. Piranesi inc.* (bottom right)

First state.[1]

Ref: **1.** Hind, *op. cit.*, p. 66 (105).

(w) View of the Piazza del Popolo

Etching, 40.5 × 54.9 cm

Inscribed: *Veduta della Piazza del Popolo/Presso l'autore a Strada Felice vicino alla Trinità de'monti* (lower margin) and with key

Fourth state.[1]

Ref: **1.** Hind, *op. cit.*, pp. 41-42 (14).

(x) View of the Temple of the Sibyl at Tivoli

Etching, 61.9 × 43.7 cm

Inscribed: *Altra Veduta del/tempio della Sibilla/in Tivoli/Piranesi F.* (on scroll with key)

Second state.[1]

Ref: 1. Hind, *op. cit.*, p. 57 (61).

The last twenty-two etchings are part of the series *Vedute di Roma*, which were published individually from 1748 to Piranesi's death.

Prov: Transferred by the City Estates, 1968.

POLIAKOFF, Serge, born 1906

2733   Abstraction

Lithograph, 57.5 × 43.7 cm

Inscribed: *Serge Poliakoff* (on block) *12/200* (in pencil)

Prov: Purchased from the Redfern Gallery, through the New Shakespeare Theatre Art Gallery, 1958.
Exh: ?Redfern Gallery, *An Exhibition of Colour lithographs, etchings, aquatints, lithographed affiches, pochoirs*, 1956/7 (271); New Shakespeare Theatre Art Gallery, Liverpool, 1958 (43).

POPOVA, Lijudmilla Gennadievna, born 1930

6290   Odessa, Potemkin stairway

Colour woodcut, 29.7 × 45.7 cm

Inscribed: *64* and with monogram

6291   Odessa Monument to A. S. Pushkin

Colour woodcut, 25 × 31.5 cm

Inscribed: *64* and with monogram

Prov: Presented by a delegation from Odessa, 1965.

RAIMONDI, Marcantonio, *c.* 1480-1527/34, after

4164   Venus and Cupid

Engraving, 17.2 × 13.1 cm

Watermark: A crown surmounting a shield flanked (?) by one or two rampant animals.

First of many copies of Marcantonio's engraving after Raphael.[1]

Prov: Cavalier Seratti; his sale £7 15s 0d;[2] William Roscoe; his sale, Winstanley, 11
         November 1816 part of (282) bt. Benson[3] £1 11s 0d; John Walter; his sale, 12
         November 1959 part of (56a) bt. C. G. Boerner; P. & D. Colnaghi; from whom
         purchased 1960.

Ref: 1. Adam Bartsch, *Le Peintre Graveur*, XIV, 1867, p. 225 (297) and Henri
         Delaborde, *Marc-Antoine Raimondi*, 1888, pp. 161-2. See also Sterling and
         Francine Clark Art Institute, Williamstown, 1975, *Durer with other eyes* (49)
         for a pasticle based on Marcantonio's engraving and on Durer's engravings of *St.
         Eustace* and *Hercules*.   2. Note on mount.   3. Identified as Robert Benson,
         Merchant, Liverpool in the British Museum copy of the Roscoe Sale Catalogue.

RAJON, Paul Adolphe, 1843-1888 after HOLL, Frank, 1845-1888

4973   George Rae

Etching, 32.8 × 25.6 cm

Signed and inscribed: *Frank Holl 1889* (sic) (on plate) *GEORGE
RAE./From the Portrait by Frank Holl, R.A.,/Painted for the North and
South Wales Bank. 1884.* (lower margin)/*Rajon* (pencil below plate)

After the picture exhibited at the Royal Academy 1884 (415) which is
now owned by the Midland Bank, 62 Castle Street, Liverpool. George
Rae (1817-1902) was a well known Liverpool banker and collector.

Prov: Presented by T. Rowland Hughes J.P., 1909.

RAUSCHENBERG, Robert, born 1925

9054   Horsefeathers Thirteen III, 1973

Lithograph, screenprint, pochoir (stencil) and collage embossed, 45.2
× 38.6 cm

Signed: *RAuschenberg 72 18/* (pencil below plate)
         80

One of a series of eight prints produced by Rauschenberg in 1972-3
and published by Gemini G.E.L., Los Angeles in 1973. Joseph Young
states that in *Horsefeathers Thirteen* Rauschenberg for the first time
incorporated numerous print media into one print.[1]

Prov: The Waddington Galleries,[2] Jonathan Rashleigh Phipps, from whom purchased,
         1975.
Ref: 1. Joseph Young, *Robert Rauschenberg*, Art News, March 1974, pp. 48-49. The
         publication of the series was reviewed in *The Print Collectors Newsletter*, IV,
         1973/4 pp. 37-38.   2. Label on backing.

RAVENET, Simon Francois, 1706-1774 after WAN-DELAAR, Jan, 1690-1759

7467 Skeleton of a man walking left

Engraving, 55 × 39.8 cm

Inscribed: *TAB.III.* (upper margin) *S. F. Ravenet Sculp. Impensis J. & P. Knapton, Londini, 1747* (lower margin)

Plate III of Bernard Siegfried Albinus' *Tabulae Sceleti et Musculorum Corporis Humani* published in 1749.[1] The pose is the same as in plate IX, Boitard's engraving (7466). The engraving is based on that by Jan Wandelaar in the original 1747 Leiden edition of Albinus.

7473 Nude Woman seen from behind

Engraving, 55.8 × 38.2 cm

Inscribed: *TAB.III.* (upper margin) *Impensis J. & P. Knapton, Londini, 1748. S. F. Ravenet Sculp.* (lower margin)

The parts of the body are also labelled with letters.

7474 Nude Woman

Engraving, 56 × 38.8 cm

Inscribed: *TAB.II.* (upper margin) *Impensis J. & P. Knapton Londini 1750. S. F. Ravenet Sculp.* (lower margin)

7473 and 7474 were published by John and Paul Knapton in 1750 in the Appendix to Albinus, *Three whole length anatomical figures representing the fore view of a man and two different views of a woman*, from Bidloo's Anatomy. Plate I is an engraving by Scotin (7475).

Prov: Presented by Liverpool College of Art, 1970.
Ref: 1. For further details of this and earlier editions see Judy Egerton in *George Stubbs anatomist and animal painter*, Tate Gallery, 1976, pp. 56-57 (6).

RENI, Guido, 1575-1642

9120 The Holy Family

Etching, 23 × 14.7 cm

Signed: *Guido Reni fecit* (on plate)

Watermark: O

Second state. Bartsch notes the influence of Parmigianino.[1]

Prov: ?W. Richardson;[2] William Roscoe, his sale, Winstanley, 14 September 1816 (740) with an impression of the first state[3] bt. Currie[4] 10s; Charles Robert Blundell; by descent to Colonel Sir Joseph Weld; his sale, Christie's, 30 June 1976 (185) bt. by the National Art-Collections Fund and presented by them to the Gallery.

Ref: 1. Adam Bartsch, *Le Peintre-Graveur*, XVIII, 1818, pp. 284-5 (9); and Max von Boehn, *Guido Reni*, 1910, p. 110 pl. 100.   2. Roscoe purchased a print of a Holy Family by Guido from Richardson for 2s 6d on 26 June 1808 (Roscoe Papers 5404). This could be either 9120 or its companion as lot 740 in Roscoe's sale.   3. Col. Sir Joseph Weld sale, Christie's, 30 June 1976 (184). Both this and 9120 bear the lot number in the Roscoe sale 740 on the back of the backing paper in pencil.   4. Identified in the British Museum Copy of the Roscoe sale Catalogue as a Liverpool Corn merchant. He is William Wallace Currie of Currie and Brice, Merchants.

RENI, Guido, 1575-1642 after CARRACCI, Lodovico, 1555-1619

9192   The Adoration of the Magi

Etching and burin, 22.2 × 18.1 cm

First state. After Ludovico Carracci's fresco in the Gessi Chapel of San Bartolomeo sul Reno, also called Santa Maria della Pioggia.[1] The etching after this picture by Justus Sadeler wrongly attributes the painting to Annibale.[2] Bartsch attributes the etching to one of the pupils of the Carracci, Sisto Badalocchio or Francesco Brizio.[3] Calvesi and Casale argue for its attribution to Reni on the grounds of links with the style of Reni's etching of *St. Roche giving alms*.[4]

Prov: William Roscoe, his sale, Winstanley, 14 September, 1816 (732) with a copy in reverse by Ludovico Matthiolis and 9121 bt. Slater,[5] 15s; Charles Robert Blundell; by descent to Colonel Sir Joseph Weld; his sale, Christie's, 7 October 1976 (17) bt. in; purchased from Colonel Sir Joseph Weld, by the Liverpool Daily Post and Echo, by whom presented, 1976.

Ref: 1. Carlo Cesare Malvasia, *Felsina Pittrice*, I, 1678, p. 88. For further details on the picture see Heinrich Bodmer, *Lodovico Carracci*, 1939, p. 131 (51) pl. 24 who dates it *c.* 1591-1592.   2. Malvasia, *op. cit.*, p. 88.   3. Adam Bartsch, *Le Peintre Graveur*, XVIII, 1818, pp. 199-200 (Annibale false 1) Roscoe also considered the attribution to Annibale doubtful, sale catalogue (732).   4. Maurizio Calvesi and Vittorio Casale, *Le Incisioni dei Carracci*, Rome, 1965, pp. 66-7 (210).   5. For Slater see 9121 after CARRACCI, Annibale.

RIBOT, Augustin Théodule, 1823-1891

9082   Frontispiece to a series of ten etchings

Etching, 31.8 × 23.4 cm

Signed: *.t.Ribot* (top right on plate) *7/10 Eaux-Fortes/Par t. Ribot* (on plate)

This etching does not appear to be listed by de Fourcaud[1] or Béraldi.[2]

Prov: Mr McDonald; by descent to his son, Brian McDonald, from whom purchased, 1976.

Ref: 1. L. de Fourcaud, *Théodule Ribot Sa vie et ses oeuvres*, 1885.   2. H. Béraldi, *Les Graveurs du XIXe Siècle*, XI, 1891.

RODE, Christian Bernhard, 1725-1797

9168 **Frederick William the Great Elector riding a sleigh about to cross the Frisches Haff with his infantry**

Etching, 38 × 61.2 cm

Inscribed: *Friedr. Wilh. d. Grosse führt sein Fussvolk auf Schlitten über d. frische Haff. nach d. Brand. Gesch. d. Kön. v. Pr./seiner Kom. Hoheit den ältesten Sohne des Prinzen von Preussen gewidmet von B. Rode.*

The inscription may be translated "Frederick William the Great Elector leads his infantry on sledges over the Frische Haff according to the Brandenburger *History of the Kings of Prussia/* dedicated to His Royal Highness, the eldest son of the Prince of Prussia by B. Rode."

The dedication is presumably to Frederick William III, King of Prussia (1770-1840), son of Frederick the Great's nephew, Frederick William II, who succeeded Frederick the Great in 1786.

One of a series of etchings representing incidents from the spectacular campaign of Frederick William, Elector of Brandenburg (1620-1688) against the Swedes in the winter of 1678/9.[1] The crossing took place from 16 to 18 January 1679. The Swedish army was driven in headlong flight along the Baltic Coast to Tallinn (Riga) losing all but 1500 men without a battle. The Frisches Haff is the long shallow lagoon between Gdansk (Danzig) and Kalinigrad (Konigsberg). Rode's other etchings showing the crossing of Frisches Haff and the liberation of Rathenau;[2] and two compositions showing *The Crossing of the Kurische Haff* further along the coast.[3] These latter three are dated 1786.[4]

Prov: William Roscoe; his sale, Winstanley, 17 September 1816 (916)[5] as *Russian travellers on sledges* with Rode's *Nero burning the Christians to illumine the Circus*[6] bt. Henshaw 15s; Charles Robert Blundell; by descent to Colonel Sir Joseph Weld; his sale, Christie's, 7 October 1976 (87) bt. in; purchased from Colonel Sir Joseph Weld, 1976.

Ref: 1. G. K. Nagler, *Neues allgemeines Kunstler-Lexikon*, XV, 1910, p. 30 (151). The literary source for Rode was probably either Samuel von Pufendorf, *De Rebus Gestis Friderici Wilhelmi Magni*, II, 1685, pp. 1283-1286 or in his *Friedrich Wilhelm des Grossen Khurfurstens zu Brandenburg Lebens und Taten*, 1710, pp. 816ff which included an engraving of the crossing of the Kurische Haff opposite p. 818.   2. Nagler, *op. cit.*, p. 30 (150).   3. Ch. Le Blanc, *Manuel de l'amateur d'estampes*, III, 1854, pp. 346-7, (175-176).   4. Nagler, *op. cit.*, p. 30 (150) and Le Blanc, *op. cit.*, p. 347 (175-176).   5. Lot number inscribed in pencil on old mount.   6. Colonel Sir Joseph Weld Sale, Christie's, 7 October 1976 (88).

ROSA, Salvator, 1615-1673

9169   Alexander the Great in the Studio of Apelles

Etching with drypoint, 45.3 × 27.3 cm

Inscribed: *Alexandro M.multa imperitè in officina disserenti/silentium comiter suadebat Apelles rideri eum dicens/a pueris, qui colores tererent Salvator Rosa Inv. scul.* (on plate)

Watermark: unidentified

Second state.[1] The inscription, which is based on the famous account of the Elder Pliny, *Natural History* XXXV 85-6 of the encounter between the most famous ruler and patron and the most famous painter of Antiquity[2] may be translated, "Alexander the Great used to talk about many things in the studio without any knowledge of them, and Apelles would advise him politely to be silent, saying that the boys grinding the colours were laughing at him."

The etching is a pair to *The Genius of Salvator Rosa*, an impression of which was in the same lot at William Roscoe's sale. The plate for the etching is in the Calcografia Nazionale, Rome (747e).[3] A preparatory black chalk drawing is in the Galleria Nazionale delle Stampe, Rome (F.N. 124.795),[4] whilst Carlo Antonini produced an engraving after 9169[5] and there is a drawing in the Uffizi (N.S. 6610) derived from 9169.[6]

Tomory considers it to be the earliest of Rosa's large figure subjects and dates it 1651-1656.[7] But a date of *c.* 1662 is more generally accepted on the grounds of style and of the link with *The Genius of Salvator Rosa*.[8]

Prov: William Roscoe;[9] his sale, Winstanley, 16 September 1816 (872)[10] the *Genius of Salvator Rosa* bt. Slater[11] 14s; Charles Robert Blundell; by descent to Colonel Sir Joseph Weld; his sale, Christie's, 7 October 1976 (12) with 9170-9172 Bourdon bt. in; purchased with 9170-9172 from Colonel Sir Joseph Weld, 1976.

Ref: **1.** Adam Bartsch, *Le Peintre Graveur*, XX, 1821, pp. 269-270 (4) and Mario Rotili, *Salvator Rosa Incisore*, 1974, p. 220 (102).   **2.** For Rosa's choice of this particular moment in the story see Richard Wallace in *Salvator Rosa*, Hayward Gallery, London, 1973, pp. 51, 61 (101). For other references to the story see Peter A. Tomory, in *Salvator Rosa. His etchings and engravings after his works*, John and Mable Ringling Museum of Art, Sarasota, 1971 (11) and A. Pigler, *Barockthemen*, II, 1974, p. 369. For Rosa's preaching in his prints see Alfredo Petrucci, *Poesia e superbia di Salvatoriello acquafortista*, Nuova Antologia, 443, May-August, 1948, pp. 267-275.   **3.** Rotili, *op. cit.*, p. 220.   **4.** Arturo Pettorelli, *Salvator Rosa, pittore, incisore, musicista, poeta*, 1924, p. 26 pl. 38 and Rotili, *op. cit.*, p. 220 pl. 102a.   **5.** Anna Barricelli in *Incisioni di Salvator Rosa*, Turin Galleria Sabauda, 1969, pl. 26.   **6.** Barricelli, *op. cit.*, and Rotili, *op. cit.*, p. 220.   **7.** Tomory, *op. cit.*, *Introduction* and (11).   **8.** Barricelli, *op. cit.*, Wallace, *op. cit.*, p. 61 (100); Rotili, *op. cit.*, pp. 89-90 as 1662, and p. 220 as in the central months of 1662; Christopher White in *Recent acquisitions and promised gifts*, National Gallery of Art, Washington, 1974, p. 151 (101).   **9.** Roscoe was offered a work by Rosa (whether it was a drawing or print is uncertain) by I. Edwards for 10s 6d, in a letter of 12 March 1789. He had wanted a *Banditti* which Edwards, however, had already sold. Roscoe Papers 1369.   **10.** Lot number in pencil half erased on the back of the mount.   **11.** For Slater, see CARRACCI, Annibale, after 9121.

ROSASPINA, Francesco 1762-1841 after MARIA, Giacomo de, 1762-1838

6892   The Death of Virginia (front view)

Engraving, 45.9 × 30 cm

Inscribed: *Giacomo de Maria inv: e sculpi—in Bologna/G. dalla Valle delineò/F. Rosaspina Inc./LA MORTE DI VIRGINIA/Gruppo in marmo alto metri 2 centim 3 0 palmi Romani 10 oncie 9.* (on plate)

6893   The Death of Virginia (back view)

Engraving, 45.7 × 29.9 cm

Inscribed: *Giacomo de Maria inv: e sculpi— in Bologna/G. dalla Valle delineò/F. Rosaspina Inc./LA MORTE DI VIRGINIA/Gruppo in marmo alto metri 2 centim 3/0 palmi Romani 10 oncie 9* (on plate)

After the marble by Giacomo de Maria (6652 p. 324)

Prov: Presented by G. P. Le G. Starkie, 1968.

ROSSIGLIANI, Giuseppe Nicola called Niccolo Vicentino, active first half of the 16th century after PARMIGIANINO, Francesco, 1503-1540

9177   The Adoration of the Magi

Chiaroscuro woodcut (three blocks; brown), 16.3 × 23.9 cm

First state, before the monogram of Andreani and the date MDCV.[1] The inscription has been obliterated by damage.

Oberhuber considers that the style belongs to the artist's Bolognese period or early in his second Parma period.[2]

A drawing by Parmigianino in the Louvre in the same direction as 9177 was used by Vicentino.[3]

There is also an etched copy by Schiavone.[4]

Prov: William Roscoe;[5] his sale Winstanley, Liverpool, 19 September 1816 (1285) with the second state of the same woodcut, and Vicentino's *Virgin and Child with Saints Margaret, Anthony the hermit and Philip, the Magdalen and an Angel*[6] bt. Slater 18s; Charles Robert Blundell; by descent to Colonel Sir Joseph Weld; his sale, Christie's, 7 October 1976 (11) with 9173-9176 and 9178-9184 bt. in; purchased from Colonel Sir Joseph Weld with 9173-9176 and 9178-9184, 1976.

Ref: 1. Adam Bartsch, *Le Peintre Graveur*, XII, 1866, p. 29 (2); William Roscoe sale (1285) included examples of both the first and second state. The second state owned by Roscoe appeared in the Colonel Sir Joseph Weld sale, Christie's, 30 June 1976 (134) bt. Beartz. Since 9177 has the Roscoe lot number 1285 inscribed in pencil on the back of the mount, it is very probable that it is the first state. **2.** Konrad Oberhuber in *Parmigianino und sein Kreis*, Vienna, Graphische Sammlung Albertina, 1963, p. 43 (98). **3.** M. Pittaluga, *Disegni del Parmigianino e corrispondenti chiaroscuri cinquecenteschi*, Dedalo, IX, 1928, p. 39; Oberhuber, *op. cit.*, p. 43 and A. E. Popham, *Catalogue of the Drawings of Parmigianino*, I, 1971, pp. 13, 134 (358), II pl. 124. **4.** Oberhuber, *op. cit.*, p. 43 points out that Bartsch, *op. cit.*, XVI, pp. 43-44 (8) is after 9177. **5.** Roscoe purchased an *Adoration des Roi after Parmo* from Thomas Philipe for 5s on 16 October 1811 (Roscoe Papers 5404). **6.** Colonel Sir Joseph Weld sale, Christie's, 30 June 1976 (134) bt. Beartz. **7.** Colonel Sir Joseph Weld sale, Christie's, 30 June 1976 (142) bt. Tunick. Lot number inscribed in pencil on the back of the mount. Roscoe understandably, but mistakenly identified it as *The Adoration of the Magi*.

ROULLET, Jean Louis, 1645-1699 after CARRACCI, Annibale, 1560-1609

4047　The Three Maries at the Tomb

Engraving, 51.8 × 61.4 cm

Inscribed: *Annibal Carraccius pinxit/Ioan Lud. Roullet./del et sculp./cum. privil. Regis* (on plate)

After the painting in the National Gallery (2923).[1] Engraved when in the Orleans collection.[2]

Prov:　　Presented by E. Swift, 1896.
Ref:　　**1.** Donald Posner, *Annibale Carracci*, 1971, pl. 177a. **2.** The picture had previously been in the collection of the Marquis de Seignelay. Michael Levey, *National Gallery, The 17th and 18th century Italian Schools*, 1971, p. 72.

RUSCHA, Edward, born 1937

8288　Royal Road Test

Book of photographs, 24 × 19.5 cm

The book contains 62 pages and 36 photographs. It was made in collaboration with Mason Williams and Patrick Blackwell and published by Heavy Industry Publications in 1967.

8289　Crackers

Book of photographs, 22.2 × 15 cm

The book contains 240 pages and 115 photographs. It was published by Heavy Industry Publications in 1969. Ruscha has also produced a lithograph of this title in an edition of 30.[1]

Ref:　　**1.** Amsterdam, Stedelijk Museum Prentenkabinett, 1976, *Edward Ruscha* (7) repr.

8290   Every Building on The Sunset Strip

Book of photographs, 18 × 14.3 cm

It contains an accordion-fold opening to 832.9 cm It was published in Los Angeles in 1966 by Heavy Industry Publications.

8291   Thirtyfour Parking Lots in Los Angeles

Book of photographs, 25.4 × 20.3 cm

The book contains 48 pages and 31 photographs and a fold out. It was published by Heavy Industry Publications in 1967.

8292   Real Estate Opportunities

Book of photographs, 17.9 × 14 cm

The book contains 48 pages and 25 photographs. It was published by Heavy Industry Publications in 1970. Ruscha has also produced a lithograph of this title in an edition of 30.[1]

Ref: 1. Amsterdam, Stedelijk Museum Prentenkabinett, 1976, *Edward Ruscha* (8) repr.

8293   A Few Palm Trees

Book of photographs, 17.7 × 14 cm

The book contains 64 pages and 14 photographs. It was published by Heavy Industry Publications in 1971. William C. Seitz has placed Ruscha's albums in relation to the Artificialism of Los Angeles County.[1]

Prov: Purchased from Nigel Greenwood Ltd., 1972.
Ref: 1. William C. Seitz, *The Real and the Artificial Painting of the New Environment*, Art in America, November-December, 1972, p. 70.

RYABCHENKO, Sergei Vasil'evich, born 1923

6287   Station Square, Odessa

Colour woodcut, 37.2 × 51.1 cm

6288   Potemkin stairway, Odessa

Colour woodcut, 24 × 62.7 cm

Inscribed: *61*, and with monogram

6289   Shevchenko Park. The Old Citadel, Odessa

Colour woodcut, 34.5 × 52.3 cm

Inscribed: *54r*, and with monogram

Prov: Presented by a delegation from Odessa, 1965.

SCOTIN, Louis Gérard, 1690-after 1755 or SCOTIN, Gérard Jean Baptiste, born 1698 after WANDELAAR, Jan, 1690-1759

7468   Skeleton of a man with his back turned

Engraving, 55.8 × 41.3 cm

Inscribed: *TAB. II* (upper margin) *G. Scotin Sculp. Impensis J. & P. Knapton Londini, 1747* (lower margin)

Published in 1749 in Bernard Siegfried Albinus' *Tabulae Sceleti et Musculorum Corporis Humani.*[1] The pose is the same as in Grignion's plate illustrating muscles in the same set, plate VIII (7469). The engraving is based on that by Jan Wandelaar in the original 1747 Leiden edition of Albinus.

7475   Male nude

Engraving, 55.8 × 39.9 cm

Inscribed: *TAB. I.* (upper margin) *Impensis J. & P. Knapton Londini, 1750. G. Scotin Sculp* (lower margin) Various parts of the body and bones are labelled with letters.

Published in 1750 in an Appendix to Albinus, *Three whole length anatomical figures representing the fore view of a man and two different views of a woman.* From Bidloo's Academy. The other two plates are by Ravenet (7473 and 7474).

Prov: Presented by Liverpool College of Art, 1970.
Ref: 1. For this and earlier editions see Judy Egerton, in *George Stubbs anatomist and animal painter*, Tate Gallery, 1976, pp. 56 -57 (6).

SKIOLD, Birgit, born 1928

6637   Sea Limits

Lithograph, 50.8 × 76.2 cm

Signed and inscribed: *Consider the sea's listless chime:/Time's self it is, made audible,-/The murmur of the earth's own shell./Secret continuance sublime/Is the sea's end: our sight may pass/No furlong further. Since time was,/This sound hath told the lapse of time./No quiet, which is death's-it hath/The mournfulness of ancient life,/Enduring always at dull strife./As the world's heart of rest and wrath,/Its painful pulse is in the sands./Last utterly, the whole sky stands,/Grey and not known, along its path//Listen alone beside the sea,/Listen alone among the woods;/Those voices of twin solitudes/Shall have one sound alike to thee:/Hark where the murmurs of thronged men/Surge and sink back and surge again,-/Still the one voice of wave and tree/Gather a shell from the strown beach/And listen at its lips: they sigh/The same desire and mystery-/The echo of the whole sea's speech./And all mankind is thus at heart/Not anything but what thou art:/And Earth, Sea, Man are all in each.* (on block) *Sea Limits/D. G. Rossetti/Birgit Skiold 68 49/100* (pencil below block)

The Sea Limits is Song XI of D. G. Rossetti's *Poems* published in 1870.

The artist states that the ideas for both 7795 and 6637 "came from the Archipelago, near Stockholm where I spent my childhood and I often go back, so most of my prints and drawings are to do with the sea."[1]

Prov: Purchased from Circle Press Publications, 1968.
Ref: 1. Birgit Skiold, *letter*, 28 April, 1976.

7795   Ocean waters

Coloured etching, 48.8 × 77 cm

Signed: *A/P Birgit Skiold—68* (pencil below plate)

Prov: Purchased from Anthony Dawson, 1969.

SOULAGES, Pierre, born 1919

2732   Composition

Lithograph, 62.8 × 48.6 cm

Inscribed: *89/200* (pencil) *Soulages* (ink)

Prov: Purchased from the Redfern Gallery, through the New Shakespeare Theatre Art Gallery, 1958.
Exh: ?Redfern Gallery, *An Exhibition of Colour lithographs, etchings, aquatints, lithographed affiches, pochoirs*, 1956/7 (288); New Shakespeare Theatre Art Gallery, Liverpool, 1958 (46).

STAEL, Nicholas de, 1914-1955, after

644   Cafe Music (Musique de Café)

Colour lithograph, 58.2 × 45 cm

Inscribed: *Stail* (on block) *Stael* (ink) *184/200*

After the 1952 oil *Les musiciens* in a private collection.[1]

Prov: Purchased from the Redfern Gallery, 1957.

Exh: ?Redfern Gallery, *An Exhibition of colour lithographs, etchings, aquatints, lithographed affiches, pochoirs,* 1956/7 (97); W.A.G., 1957, *Modern Colour Lithographs* (108).

Ref: **1.** Another reproduction of slightly different dimensions was published by Braun & Cie, Paris. Unesco, *Catalogue of Colour Reproductions of Paintings, 1860 to 1959,* Paris, 1959 (1094).

2728   Composition

Lithograph, 57.2 × 44.2 cm

Prov: Purchased from the Redfern Gallery through the New Shakespeare Theatre Art Gallery, 1958.

Exh: New Shakespeare Theatre Art Gallery, Liverpool, 1958 (24).

2729   Landscape (Paysage)

Lithograph, 34.7 × 43.5 cm

Prov: Purchased from the Redfern Gallery through the New Shakespeare Theatre Art Gallery, 1958.

Exh: New Shakespeare Theatre Art Gallery, Liverpool, 1958 (23).

STELLA, Frank, born 1936

8192   Club Onyx—Seven Steps

Lithograph, 38.2 × 55.7 cm

Signed: *G. II.* (stamps) $\frac{/25}{100}$ *F. Stella 67* (pencil)

One of 9 lithographs making up the Black Series 1. The publication has been discussed by Judith Goldman with particular reference to the "pin-striped" lines' relation to the framing edge.[1] A painting entitled *Seven Steps* of 1959 was at Sotheby Parke-Bernet, 18 November, 1970.[2]

Prov: Purchased from Bernard Jacobson, 1972.

Ref: **1.** Judith Goldman, *Frank Stella: Black Series and Star of Persian Prints,* Artist's Proof, VIII, 1968, pp. 67-8.   **2.** *Studio International,* November, 1970, p. X repr. For this painting's present location and for other related paintings and prints see Brenda Richardson, *Frank Stella, The Black Paintings,* Baltimore Museum of Art, 1976-7, passim.

8193   Newstead Abbey

Lithograph, 40.6 × 55.8 cm

Signed: $\frac{63}{75}$ *F. Stella '70* (pencil) *G. II.* (stamps on paper)

One of 9 lithographs making up the Aluminium Series. Stella has also produced two paintings called *Newstead Abbey* dating from 1960.[1]

Prov: Purchased from Bernard Jacobson, 1972.

Ref: **1.** (a) Frederick Castle, *What's That, the '68 Stella, Wow!*, Art News, January, 1969, p. 46 and Jean-Claude Lebenstejn, *57 Steps to Hyena Stomp*, Art News, September, 1972, pp. 62-3 in William Rubin Collection; (b) Bernhard Kerber, *Streifenbilder zur Unterscheidung ähnlicher Phänomene*, Wallraf-Richartz Jahrbuch, XXXII, 1970, pp. 247-8, fig. 173.

THAULOW, Frits, 1847-1906

1322   The marble steps, Venice (L'escalier de marbre, Venise)

Aquatint, 47.6 × 59.2 cm

Signed: *Frits Thaulow* (pencil)

The steps outside a church on the Grand Canal

Prov: Purchased at the L.A.E., 1906.
Exh: *L.A.E.*, 1906 (1036).

VASARELY, Victor, born 1908

6918   Exhibition poster—L'Art Vivant, 1965-1968, Fondation Maeght, Saint Paul

Screenprint, 71.3 × 40.2 cm

Inscribed: *L'ART VIVANT 1965-1968/13 AVRIL-30 JUIN, 1968/FONDATION MAEGHT/SAINT PAUL(AM)/Vasarely c. by Fondation Maeght/Ateliers Réunis Bagnolet*

6926   CTA Positif-Permutation III

Screenprint, 59.8 × 59.8 cm

Signed and inscribed: *114/150 Vasarely* (pencil below block) *EDITEUR DENISE RENE* and editor's monogram is a circle (stamp)

7197   Constellations-Plate V

Screenprint, 69.8 × 34.7 cm

Signed and inscribed: *36/150 V. Vasarely* (pencil) *EDITEUR DENISE RENE* and editor's monogram is a circle (stamp)

Fifth out of a series of eight seriographs.

Prov: Purchased from the London Graphic Art Associates, 1969.

VEBER, Jean, 1864-1928

553 The Lesson (La Leçon)

Colour lithograph, 33.8 × 47.5 cm

Signed: *Jean Veber/11* (pencil)
20

Two illustrations in the left margin show the cook coming to her mistress's bedside for orders (a first idea[1] for *The unhappy housekeeper* (*La ménagère dolente*[2]) and a child who did not know his lesson beginning to cry, whilst his mother in bed raises her arms to the sky in anger.

Prov: Purchased from the artist at the L.A.E., 1908.
Exh: L.A.E., 1908 (1346).
Ref: **1.** Pierre Veber and Louis Lacroix, *L'Oeuvre Lithographié de Jean Veber*, 1931 p. 49 (65) pl. 29. **2.** Veber and Lacroix, *op. cit.*, p. 66 (50) pl. 30.

1097 The cork players (Les joueurs de Bouchon)

Colour lithograph, 30.3 × 43.0 cm

Signed: *Jean Veber 51/100* (pencil)

Reproduction of a group in a decorative panel of the refreshment room of the Hotel du Ville, Paris.[1] E. Rimbault Dibdin, curator of the W.A.G., visited Veber before the exhibition and Veber sent eight lithographs to it which had interested him.[2]

Prov: Purchased from the artist at the L.A.E., 1909.
Exh: L.A.E., 1909 (1420).
Ref: **1.** Veber and Lacroix, *op. cit.*, pp. 26, 54 (96) pl. 47. **2.** Letter of Jean Veber to E. Rimbault Dibdin, 6 August 1909.

1170 The little suburban tavern (La petite guinguette)

Colour lithograph, 21.2 × 29 cm

Signed and inscribed: above and beside the doorway to the tavern *AUBERE/la CHOAILLE/ GALETTE/ BRIOCHE/DINER/ BIERE/CIDRE* (on block) *Jean Veber 50/150* (pencil)

Perhaps related to the panel he painted for the Hotel du Ville, Paris.[1]

Exh: L.A.E., 1909 (1501).
Ref: **1.** Veber and Lacroix, *op. cit.*, p. 7.

5037 The giant (Le géant)[1]

Colour lithograph, 27.3 × 34.8 cm

Signed: *Jean Veber/55/100* (pencil)

Veber produced another lithograph of this subject dated 1896, illustrating *Les Fleurs du Mal.*[2]

Prov: Purchased from the artist at the L.A.E., 1909.
Exh: L.A.E., 1909 (1411).
Ref: **1.** Veber and Lacroix, *op. cit.*, p. 47 (48).   **2.** Veber and Lacroix, *op. cit.*, p. 42 (9).

VENEZIANO, Agostino dei Musi, called, *c.* 1490—still active 1536

4163 Hercules strangling the serpents

Engraving, 21.9 × 17.7 cm

Signed: *A.V.* (on tablet) *1533*

Second state, with the alteration of the date, from 1532 to 1533. After Giulio Romano according to Bartsch,[1] but also related to a fresco by Giulio Campi at Rocca dei Principi di Soragna.[2]

Prov: Granwill Brux or Bruse (?);[3] William Roscoe, his sale part of (288) bt. Esdaile £1 9s 0d; his sale Christie 15 March 1838 (part of 439) bt. Smith 17/- (with lot 438). John Walter; his sale, Sotheby's 12 November 1959 part of (56a) bt. C. G. Boerner; P. & D. Colnaghi & Co. Ltd., from whom purchased, 1960.
Ref: **1.** Adam Bartsch, *Le Peintre Graveur*, XIV, 1867, p. 237 (315).   **2.** Aurelia Perotti, *I Pittori Campi da Cremona*, n.d., p. 26, fig. 17.   **3.** Old inscription on verso.

VLAMINCK, Maurice, de 1876-1958

645 The Shops (Les boutiques)

Aquatint, 26.7 × 33.6 cm

Inscribed: *8/20* (pencil) *Vlaminck* (on block)

Prov: Purchased from Redfern Gallery, 1957.
Exh: ?Redfern Gallery, *An Exhibition of Colour Lithographs, Etchings, Aquatints, Lithographed affiches, Pochoirs*, 1956/7 (331)[1] W.A.G., 1957, *Modern Colour Lithographs*, (125).
Ref: **1.** Prints of this title were also exhibited at the Redfern Gallery, *French and English Original Artists' Prints in Colour*, 1953/4, (218); *Summer Exhibition*, 1954, (551), and *Summer Exhibition*, 1956, (514).

WALTNER, Charles Albert, 1846-1925 after GALLAND, Pierre-Victor, 1822-1892

7375 Commemorative Diploma of the 1889 Paris Universal Exhibition

Engraving, 23 × 29 cm

Inscribed: *P. V. Galland mv./C.A.Waltner Sc.*

Prov: Presented to Liverpool Corporation by the French Government in 1889. Transferred to the W.A.G., before 1970.

WARHOL, Andy, born 1930

8474 Marilyn

Silkscreen print, 91.6 × 91.6 cm

Published by Sunday B. Morning. No. 94 in an edition of 250.[1]

Prov: Purchased from Bernard Jacobson, 1973.
Ref: **1.** Stamp on reverse.

WHISTLER, James McNeill, 1834-1903

676 The Pool

Etching, 13.8 × 21.5 cm

Signed: *Whistler 1859* (on plate)

Inscribed: *COOPER/Sᴛ GEORGE'S WF/NEW CRANE/TO LET* (on hoardings) *JANE No6* (on keel of boat)

Fourth state.[1] One of the sixteen etchings of scenes on the Thames.

Prov: Bequeathed by James Smith of Blundellsands, 1923.
Ref: **1.** E. G. Kennedy, *The etched works of Whistler*, 1910, I, (43 ɪᴠ).

677 Eagle Wharf

Etching and drypoint, 13.7 × 21.4 cm

Signed: *Whistler 1859* (on quay on plate)

Inscribed: *YZAK WHITELEY & Co/W. BROWN/SAIL MAKER/SHIP OWNER/EAGLE/WHARF* (on hoardings on plate)

Sole state.[1] No. 11 in series of sixteen etchings of scenes on the Thames.

Prov: Bequeathed by James Smith of Blundellsands, 1923.
Ref: **1.** Kennedy, *op. cit.*, I, (41).

1306 The Forge

Drypoint, 19.5 × 31.6 cm

Signed: *Whistler/1864* (on plate)

Third state.[1]

Prov: Bequeathed by James Smith of Blundellsands, 1923.
Ref: 1. Kennedy, *op. cit.*, I (68III).

1307 Thames Warehouses

Etching and drypoint, 7.5 × 20.2 cm

Signed: *Whistler 1859* (on plate)

Inscribed: *FREDκ VINK & Co/ROPE & SAIL MAKERS/SMITH & SON/HERMATAGE COAL WHARF/NORE'S WHARF* (on hoardings on plate)

Watermark: Heraldic with bricked arch.[1]

First state.[2] No. 13 in set of 16 scenes on the Thames.

Prov: Bequeathed by James Smith of Blundellsands, 1923.
Ref: 1. Identified by Margaret MacDonald.   2. Kennedy, *op. cit.*, I (38I).

1578 Landscape with the Horse

Etching, 12.8 × 20.2 cm

Signed: *Whistler 1859* (on plate)

Second state.[1]

Prov: Presented by Dr. H. Nazeby Harrington, 1910.
Ref: 1. Kennedy, *op. cit.*, (36II).

1579 The Music Room

Etching, 14.3 × 21.5 cm

Second state.[1] Seymour Haden (1818-1910), etcher and brother-in-law of Whistler is sitting reading a paper at a table with his wife Deborah, Whistler's half-sister and his assistant, the surgeon James Traer. Whistler lived with the Hadens for a short period on coming to England in May 1859.

Prov: Presented by Dr. H. Nazeby Harrington, 1910.
Ref: 1. Kennedy, *op. cit.*, I, (33II).

1580 Vauxhall Bridge

Etching and drypoint, 6.9 × 11.4 cm

Signed: *Whistler/1861* (on plate)

Second state.[1]

Prov: Presented by Dr. Nazeby Harrington, 1910.
Ref: 1. Kennedy, *op. cit.*, I, (70II).

1581 Fulham

Etching and drypoint, 13.4 × 20.7 cm

Inscribed: with butterfly (on plate) Printsellers Association stamp *GJ* (beneath plate)

Second state.[1] A view of Chelsea old church and old Battersea bridge.

Prov: Bequeathed by James Smith of Blundellsands, 1923.
Ref: 1. Kennedy, *op. cit.*, III (182II)

1582 Hurlingham

Etching and drypoint, 13.7 × 20.1 cm

Inscribed: with butterfly (on plate)

Third state.[1]

Prov: Bequeathed by James Smith of Blundellsands, 1923.
Ref: 1. Kennedy, *op. cit.*, III, (181III).

1583 Old Hungerford Bridge

Etching and drypoint, 13.7 × 21.3 cm

Signed: *Whistler* (on plate)

Third state.[1] One of set of sixteen etchings of scenes of the Thames.

Prov: Bequeathed by James Smith of Blundellsands, 1923.
Ref: 1. Kennedy, *op. cit.*, I, (76III).

1584 Becquet

Etching and drypoint, 25.6 × 19.2 cm

` Third state.[1] One of the set of sixteen etchings. The muskets in the lower right corner form part of an etching of West Point made by an old classmate of Whistler, which Whistler did not completely obliterate. The sitter (1829-1907) was a sculptor and amateur musician.

Prov: Bequeathed by James Smith of Blundellsands, 1923.
Ref: 1. Kennedy, *op. cit.*, I, (52III).

1585   The little pool

Etching and drypoint, 10.2 × 12.6 cm

Signed: *Whistler 1861* (on plate)

Eighth state.[1] One of sixteen etchings of scenes of the Thames. The man sketching is Percy Thomas, and the boy his brother, Ralph, who issued the first catalogue of Whistler etchings in London in 1874. The man standing is their father, Sergeant Thomas, printseller and publisher, who sold Whistler's Thames set.[2]

Prov: Bequeathed by James Smith of Blundellsands, 1923.
Ref: 1. Kennedy, *op. cit.*, I, (74VIII).   2. Margaret F. MacDonald, *Whistler. The Graphic Work:Amsterdam*, *London*, *Liverpool*, *Venice*, Thos. Agnew & Sons Ltd., W.A.G., and Glasgow Art Gallery and Museum, 1976, p. 15 (6).

1586   Millbank

Etching and drypoint, 10 × 12.6 cm

Inscribed: *1861* (on plate)

Watermark: Heraldic with bricked arch.[1]

Fifth state.[2] One of the sixteen etchings and scenes of the Thames.

Prov: Bequeathed by James Smith of Blundellsands, 1923.
Ref: 1. Identified by Margaret MacDonald.   2. Kennedy, *op. cit.*, I, (71V).

1587   Early Morning (Battersea)

Etching and drypoint, 11.3 × 15.1 cm

Signed: *Whistler* (on plate)

Watermark: Heraldic with a bricked arch.[1]

Sole state.[2] One of sixteen etchings of scenes of the Thames.

Prov: Bequeathed by James Smith of Blundellsands, 1923.
Ref: 1. Identified by Margaret MacDonald.   2. Kennedy, *op. cit.*, I, (75).

P

1588 Chelsea Bridge and Church

Etching and drypoint, 10×16.8 cm

Watermark: *E. ERVEN D. BLAU*

Third state.[1] One of the sixteen etchings of scenes of the Thames.

Prov: Bequeathed by James Smith of Blundellsands, 1923.
Ref: 1. Kennedy, *op. cit.*, II, (95III).

1589 Sketching No. I

Etching and drypoint, 12×16.5 cm

Signed: *Whistler* (on plate)

State Ia,[1] which is probably the same state as State II, the only difference arising in the printing.

Prov: Presented by Mrs J. G. Legge, 1947.
Ref: 1. Kennedy, *op. cit.*, II, (86Ia).

1590 The Punt

Etching and drypoint, 11.9×16.3 cm

Signed: *Whistler/861* (on plate)

Second state.[1]

Prov: Presented by Mrs J. G. Legge, 1947.
Ref: 1. Kennedy, *op. cit.*, II, (85II).

1782 The Lime-Burners

Etching and drypoint, 25.2×17.6 cm

Signed: *Whistler/1859* (on plate)

Watermark: Heraldic with bricked arch[1]

Second state.[2] One of the sixteen etchings of scenes of the Thames.

Prov: Bequeathed by James Smith of Blundellsands, 1923.
Ref: 1. Identified by Margaret MacDonald. 2. Kennedy, *op. cit.*, I, (46II).

1783 Rotherhithe

Etching and drypoint, 27.6×19.9 cm

Signed: *Whistler 1860* (on plate)

Watermark: Heraldic with a bricked arch.[1]

Third state.[2] One of the sixteen etchings of scenes of the Thames. Published as Wapping, but exhibited as Rotherhithe at the R.A. 1862 (93). Whistler drew the etching in a warehouse that was being repaired. A brick fell near Whistler and he stopped working abruptly, scratching the plate with a vertical line up the middle.[3]

Prov: Bequeathed by James Smith of Blundellsands, 1923.
Ref: **1.** Identified by Magaret MacDonald.   **2.** Kennedy, *op. cit.*, I, (66III).   **3.** Theodore Duret, *Whistler*, 1917, p. 19.

2494   Black Lion Wharf

Etching, 15.2 × 22.8 cm

Signed: *Whistler 1859* (on plate)

Inscribed: *HORE'S WHARF/HOARE'S WHARF./OLD SHIPPING CLIPPERS/TO LET EVERY DAY/GLASGOW/ GRANGE-MOUTH/INVERNES /PETERHA/St ANDREWS/BLAC LION W RF* (on hoarding on plate)

Third state.[1] One of the sixteen etchings of scenes of the Thames.

Prov: Bequeathed by James Smith of Blundellsands, 1923.
Ref: **1.** Kennedy, *op. cit.*, I, (42III).

2495   Thames Police

Etching, 15.3 × 22.8 cm

Signed: *Whistler 1859* (on plate)

Inscribed: *W PING WHART/YOR IRE BOTTLE COMPAN/THAMES POLICE* (on hoardings on plate)

Second state.[1] One of the sixteen etchings of scenes of the Thames.

Prov: Bequeathed by James Smith of Blundellsands, 1923.
Ref: **1.** Kennedy, *op. cit.*, I, (44II).

2496   Old Westminster Bridge

Etching, 7.5 × 20.2 cm

Watermark: Heraldic with bricked arch.[1]

Second state.[2] One of sixteen etchings of scenes of the Thames.

Prov: Presented by James Smith of Blundellsands, 1923.
Ref: **1.** Identified by Margaret MacDonald.   **2.** Kennedy, *op. cit.*, I, (39II).

2497 Limehouse

Etching and drypoint, 12.6 × 20.2 cm

Signed: *Whistler 1859* (on plate)

Inscribed: *CURTIS/GN/R MA* (on hoarding on plate)

Watermark: *DE ERVEN D BLAUV*

Third state.[1] One of the sixteen etchings of scenes of the Thames.

Prov: Presented by James Smith of Blundellsands, 1923.
Ref: 1. Kennedy, *op. cit.*, I, (40III).

7435 Liverdun

Etching, 10.7 × 15.3 cm

Signed: *J. Whistler Imp. Delatre, Rue St. Jacques. 171* (on plate)

Second state.[1] One of "Twelve Etchings from Nature." Whistler visited Liverdun on the Moselle and Marne-Rhine Canals near Nancy in 1858.

Prov: Bought at Paddy's Market, Liverpool and presented by Ian Campbell, 1970.
Ref: 1. Kennedy, *op. cit.*, I, (16II).

7436 Street at Saverne

Etching, 20.6 × 15.7 cm

Signed: *Whistler/Imp. Delatre. Rue St. Jacques* (on plate)

Fourth state.[1] One of "Twelve Etchings from Nature". Saverne is a small town north west of Strasbourg on the Marne-Rhine Canal.

Prov: Bought from Paddy's Market, Liverpool and presented by Ian Campbell, 1970.
Ref: 1. Kennedy, *op. cit.*, I, (19IV).

7437 The old woman at Loques (La vieille au Loques)

Etching, 20.9 × 14.6 cm

Signed: *Whistler/Imp. Delatre. Rue St. Jacques 171*

Second state.[1] One of "Twelve Etchings from Nature." The sitter has been identified as Madame Gerard,[2] who appears in two other early etchings.[3]

Prov: Purchased at Paddy's Market, Liverpool and presented by Ian Campbell, 1970.
Ref: 1. Kennedy, *op. cit.*, I, (21II). **2.** Inscription on verso in pencil. **3.** Kennedy, *op. cit.*, I, (11) and (12).

7786 Elinor Leyland

Drypoint, 21.3 × 13.8 cm

Inscribed: with butterfly (on plate)

Third state.[1] The sitter was the youngest daughter of F. R. Leyland, born 16 October 1861. 7786 dates from *c.* 1873.

Prov: Purchased from P. & D. Colnaghi & Co. Ltd., 1972.
Exh: P. & D. Colnaghi & Co. Ltd., *An Exhibition of Etchings, Drypoints and Lithographs by James McNeill Whistler*, 1971 (60).
Ref: 1. Kennedy, *op. cit.*, II, (109III)

7787 The little velvet dress

Drypoint, 16.3 × 11.9 cm

Signed: with butterfly (on plate) *Whistler 1st* (pencil below plate).

An unrecorded first state,[1] before the vertical lines at the lower right between the horizontals.[2] The sitter is Mrs Florence Leyland (1834-1910), wife of F. R. Leyland, the Liverpool shipowner and patron of Whistler. 7787 is the second of Whistler's drypoint portraits of Mrs Leyland done in 1873.

Prov: Purchased from P. & D. Colnaghi & Co. Ltd., 1972.
Exh: P. & D. Colnaghi & Co. Ltd., *An Exhibition of Etchings, Drypoints and Lithographs by James McNeill Whistler*, 1971 (56).
Ref::   1. Colnaghi, *Whistler*, 1971 (56).   2. Kennedy, *op. cit.*, II, (106).

9017 Florence Leyland

Drypoint, 21.2 × 13.4 cm

Inscribed: with butterfly in oval (on plate) *I am flo"* (on plate)

Watermark: Arms of Amsterdam

A very light sixth impression.[1] Born 2 September 1859, the second oldest daughter of F. R. Leyland.

Prov: Purchased from P. & D. Colnaghi & Co. Ltd., 1975.
Ref: 1. Kennedy, *op. cit.*, II, (110 VI).

9066 Speke Hall No.1

Pencil and pen over etching and drypoint, 22.4 × 14.9 cm

Signed: *Whistler 1870./Speke Hall.*

Watermark: *PD*

An unrecorded state between the 6th and 7th states[1] with additions in pencil and pen, the most important of which are the diagonal lines up the left hand side of the path, several horizontal lines on the right hand side of the path, brush strokes at the top of the woman's hat and particularly pencil work at the back of her dress and in the interior of her dress.

The woman's jacket is already fur trimmed as in the succeeding 7th state but the artist has not yet added the extra struts on the left hand gable of the house.

The figure in the foreground is probably Mrs Leyland, or her sister, Elizabeth Dawson, who was for a time engaged to the artist.

9066 is a view of the south front. But in place of the window of the Blue Drawing Room, Whistler has etched the main entrance porch and the bridge over the moat on the north front. MacDonald dates this impression about 1875.[2]

Prov: Mortimer Menpes (1860-1938),[3] Sotheby, Belgravia 7 October 1975 (130) purchased through Agnews, 1975.

Ref: **1.** Kennedy, *op. cit.*, p. 35 (96).   **2.** Margaret F. MacDonald, *Whistler The Graphic Work: Amsterdam, Liverpool, London, Venice*, Thos. Agnew & Sons Ltd., W.A.G., and Glasgow Art Gallery and Museum, 1976, p. 32 (61).   **3.** M. Menpes, *Whistler as I knew him*, 1904, rep. opp. p. 38.

9193   Fanny Leyland

Drypoint, 19.6 × 13.2 cm

Inscribed: on plate with butterfly, and in pencil on tab with butterfly and *"imp"*.

Sixth and final state.[1] The sitter was the eldest daughter of F. R. Leyland, born 29 October 1857. MacDonald thinks that she was about fifteen when she posed for this drypoint.[2] A pencil drawing is related.[3]

Prov: Thos. Agnew & Sons Ltd., from whom purchased, 1976.

Exh: Thos. Agnew & Sons, W.A.G., and Art Gallery and Museum, Glasgow, 1976, *Whistler, The Graphic Work: Amsterdam, Liverpool, London,.Venice* (67).

Ref: **1.** Kennedy, *op. cit.*, II, (108VI).   **2.** Margaret F. MacDonald, *Whistler The Graphic Work: Amsterdam, Liverpool, London, Venice*, Thos. Agnew & Sons Ltd., W.A.G., Art Gallery and Museum Glasgow, 1976, p. 34 (67).   **3.** E. R. & J. Pennell, *The Life of J. McN. Whistler*, 1919, reproduced opp. p. 181.

WINNER, Gerd, born 1936

8484   Holborn Underground

Screenprint, 63.3 × 63.5 cm

Signed: *Winner* (pencil bottom right) *AP* (pencil bottom left)

One of an edition of 75 published 1972. Printed by Kelpra Studios.[1]

Winner's prints of London Underground Stations were reviewed by Bud Shark in *Studio International*, May 1973.[2]

Prov: Purchased from Prue O'Day, Don Anderson "Modern Prints", 1973.
Ref: **1.** Rubber stamp on back.   **2.** Bud Shark, *Graphics*, Studio International 185, May 1973, p. 242.

8661   New York Canyon

Screenprint, 61.5 × 99 cm

Signed: *Winner 1973/49*
                  75

Printed by Chris Prater, Kelpra Studios and published by Kelpra Editions, 1973.[1]

Prov: Purchased from Prue O'Day, Don Anderson "Modern Prints", 1974.
Ref: **1.** Kunsthalle Bremen, 1975, *Gerd Winner Bilder und Graphik 1970-75* (61).

WUJCIK, Theo, born 1936

8660   Portrait of June Wayne

Hand coloured lithograph, 55 × 53.3 cm

Signed: *Theo Wujcik 1973/AP 13* and with a snail monogram

8660 was published by Brooke Alexandra. The artist drew June Wayne's image on the stone using a "black prism-color pencil rather than traditional lithographic grease pencils." He also used prism-color pencils for the hand colouring. "An impression of the lithographic key image was impressed onto a clean sheet of acetate. This was then cut through to form the stencil . . . The key image was printed over the colored sheet, using sinclair and valentine, stone Neutral Black, lithographic ink."[1]

Prov: Purchased from Prue O'Day, Don Anderson "Modern Prints", 1974.
Ref: **1.** Letter from the artist, 20 January, 1977

ZAO, Wou-ki, born 1921

6357   LXII

Colour lithograph, 47 × 62.8 cm

Inscribed: *'63/112* and with monogram (pencil)
             175

Prov: Purchased from Prestons Art Gallery, Bolton, 1966.

ZORN, Anders Leonard, 1860-1920

5079 Wet

Etching, 15.7 × 11.8 cm

Signed: *19Z11 ° ZORN 1911* (on plate) *Zorn* (in pencil below plate)

Third state.[1] One of 5 works exhibited in Liverpool by Zorn that year. 5079 is also known as *The Bather. Seated.*[2] Zorn also painted an oil of the same subject, but different in composition.[3]

Prov: Purchased from the artist at the L.A.E., 1912.
Exh: W.A.G., *L.A.E.*, 1912 (1383).
Ref: **1.** Karl Asplund, *Zorn's engraved work*, II, 1920, p. 374; Ernest M. Lang, *The Etchings of Anders Zorn*, 1923, p. XIV pl. 83.   **2.** J. Nilsen Laurvik, *Anders Zorn—Painter—Etcher*, Print Collectors Quarterly, I, 1911, p. 637.   **3.** Asplund, *op. cit.*, p. 374.

CONCORDANCE

Explanation

The first column gives the Gallery Inventory Number.

The second column indicates the medium of the work of art (P for painting, D for drawing or watercolour, E for print, S for sculpture, C for ceramics, T for tapestry, M for silver) thus enabling the reader to find the appropriate section of this catalogue for each work of art.

The third column has the attribution of each work in this catalogue.

The fourth column gives the attribution in the two post war Gallery catalogues of paintings (1963) and old master drawings and prints (1967)—see page 4 for full descriptions of these two catalogues—a dagger indicates that the work of art is to be found under the same name in those catalogues as in this present catalogue.

The fifth column indicates the attribution in the 1927 or 1928 catalogues—again see page 4 for full descriptions of these catalogues and again a dagger shows that the work of art is to be found under the same name in those catalogues as in this present catalogue—all works against which a number appears in the next (sixth) column will appear in the 1928 catalogue, the rest in the 1927 catalogue.

The sixth, seventh, eighth, ninth, tenth, eleventh and twelfth columns show the number under which each work appears in the catalogues of 1893/1915, 1885, 1859, 1851, 1843, 1836 and 1819—again see page 4 for full descriptions of these catalogues.

The last column gives the lot number of the work of art in William Roscoe's 1816 Sale Catalogue, see page 3 for full description of this catalogue.

A blank indicates that the work of art did not appear at all in the catalogue or catalogues concerned.

IN-VENTORY	MEDIUM	1977 ATTR.	1963/67 ATTR.	1927/28 ATTR.	1893/1915	1885	1859	1851	1843	1836	1819	1816
37	P	Teniers	†	†								
38	P	Teniers	†	†		51						
39	P	Teniers	†	†		52						

In-ventory	Medium	1977 Attr.	1963/67 Attr.	1927/28 Attr.	1893/1915	1885	1859	1851	1843	1836	1819	1816
49	P	Vollmar	†									
91	D	Anrooy		†								
109	P	Abbey		†								
110	P	Anderson		†		109						
119	P	Neapolitan School	†	Giordano		100						
120	P	Neapolitan School	†	Giordano		98						
127	P	Reni	†	Lanfranco		99						
134	P	Roos	†									
136	P	Italian School	Venetian School	Unknown		185						
141	P	Reni		Zampieri		176						
142	P	Claude	†									
144	P	Giordano	†	†	105		117	107	73			
145	P	Giordano	†	†	100		112	102	125			
150	P	Gimignani	†				122	112	90			
151	P	Garzi	Rosa									
175	P	Picknell		†			119	109	92			
177	P	Ruysdael	†									
178	P	Alma-Tadema										
179	D	Alma-Tadema										
180	P	Monmoyer	†									
181	P	Bonheur	†									
182	P	Bonheur	†									
183	P	Bonheur	†									
184	P	Bonheur	†									
185	P	Bonheur	†									

Inventory	Medium	1977 Attr.	1963/67 Attr.	1927/28 Attr.	1893/1915	1885	1859	1851	1843	1836	1819	1816
190	P	Boughton										
191	P	Browne										
202	P	Corot	†									
219	D	Detaille										
220	P	Martino	†									
226	P	Frere	†									
230	P	Gerome	†									
248	P	Koller	†									
255	P	Legras	†									
270	P	Merle	†									
298	P	Scheffer	†									
313	P	Beers	†									
318	P	Zuccoli	†									
332	E	Corot		†								
344-345	E	Lepere		†								
349	P	Svemps	†									
367	S	Dalou										
387	S	Epstein										
392	E	Latenay		†								
400	P	Verboeckhoven	†									
412	P	Parton				56						
427	D	Waugh		†								
433	E	Chahine		†								
440	D	Ertz		†								
508	P	Farasyn										

In-ventory	Medium	1977 Attr.	1963/67 Attr.	1927/28 Attr.	1893/1915	1885	1859	1851	1843	1836	1819	1816
543-544	E	Lund										
546	E	Meryon	†									
553	E	Veber		†								
566	P	Cossaar	†	†								
567	P	Cossaar	†	†								
613	P	Goyen	†									
619	P	Balestra	†									
636	E	Chagall										
637	E	Dufy										
638	E	Dufy										
639	E	Kandinsky										
640	E	Leger										
641	E	Matisse										
642	E	Matisse										
643	E	Miro										
644	E	Stael										
645	E	Vlaminck										
658	P	Stokes										
662	P	D'Orsay										
671	E	Pennell		†								
672	E	Pennell		†								
676	E	Whistler		†								
677	E	Whistler		†								
699	P	Cuneo		†								
723	P	Leys	†	†								

In-ventory	Medium	1977 Attr.	1963/67 Attr.	1927/28 Attr.	1893/1915	1885	1859	1851	1843	1836	1819	1816
729	P	Mazzotta	†	†	294							
738	P	Stry	†	†								
749	P	Fournier	†	†								
754	P	Muller	†									
755	P	Normann		†								
756	P	Prat	†	†								
758	S	Epstein										
764	P	Stokes		†								
769	P	Boughton		†								
817	P	Dutch School	†	Unknown								
818	P	Netherlandish School	Brunswick Monogrammist	Flemish School	53		55	56	52	44	36	100
819	P	Miereveldt	†									
820	P	Dutch School	†	Steen								
821	P	Master L.D.	†	Unknown Flemish School								
822	P	Batist	†	†								
823	P	Batist	†	†								
824	P	Post	Dutch School	Poost	114							
825	P	Netherlandishh School	†	Floris								
826	P	Eversdijk	†	Unknown	148							
827	P	Moro	Netherlandish School									
829	P	Netherlandish School	van Orley									
831	P	Dutch School	Ockers									
832	P	Terborch	†	†	10							
833	P	Netherlandish School	School Haarlem			48	48	57	42		Ms	

In-ventory	Medium	1977 Attr.	1963/67 Attr.	1927/28 Attr.	1893/1915	1885	1859	1851	1843	1836	1819	1816
834	P	Netherlandish School	†	Flemish School	61		66	60				
835	P	Momper	†	†	116a		1388	129	118			
867	P	Moucheron	†	†	112		132	123	95			
868	P	Kabel	Huysmans	Huysmans	117		139					
869	P	Asselijn	†	School Berchem	115		135	126	123			
870	P	Hondecoeter	†	†	114							
871	P	Slabbaert	†	Dou		9						
872	P	Waterloo	†	†		141						
873	P	Netherlandish School	Master of Groote Adoration	†	50		52	53	60	34	34	96
874	P	Molenaer	†	†	†		7					
898	S	Epstein		†								
915	P	Jones										
920	D	Mesdag		†								
941	P	Frieseke										
955	P	Sargent										
956	P	Dutch School	fol. Both									
957	P	Rembrandt	Bol	Bol	110		130	122	116			
958	P	Bor	†									
959	P	Fabritius	†									
960	P	Flinck	†	S. Koninck	111		131	121	100			
961	P	Heeremans	†	†	113		133	124	96			
962	P	Dutch School	C. Johnson II									
963	P	Victors	†									
1011	P	Rembrandt	†									

In-ventory	Medium	1977 Attr.	1963/67 Attr.	1927/28 Attr.	1893/1915	1885	1859	1851	1843	1836	1819	1816
1012	P	Netherlandish School	att. Master of Female Half-Lengths	Flemish School	57		60	39	54	39	31	82
1013	P	Netherlandish School	att. Master of Female Half-Lengths	Flemish School	56		59	38	53	38	30	82
1014	P	Master of the Virgo Inter Virgines	†	†	37		38	37	47	32	28	78
1015	P	Schongauer	Isenbrandt	Flemish School	60		65	45	50	37	32	83
1016	P	Netherlandish School	foll. C Engelbrechtsz	Krug	52		54	55	66	41	13	19
1017	P	Isenbrandt	†				64	59	56	33	15	29
1018	P	Mostaert	†	†	51		53	54	63	40	34	149
1019	P	Rembrandt	Horst									
1020	P	Master of Frankfurt	†	Unknown								
1021	P	Netherlandish School	att. J. Joest	Flemish School	55		57	58	51	7	17	20
1022	P	Ruysdael	†									
1023	P	Roman School	†									
1024	P	Dutch School	Verburgh									
1028	P	Bouchet	†	†								
1030	P	Geets	†	†								
1031	P	Master P. L.	†									
1047	D	Plessis										
1097	E	Veber		†								
1110	P	Kaufmann										
1126	P	Monticelli	†									
1127	P	Monticelli	†									
1128	P	Monticelli	†	†								

IN-VENTORY	MEDIUM	1977 ATTR.	1963/67 ATTR.	1927/28 ATTR.	1893/1915	1885	1859	1851	1843	1836	1819	1816
1129	P	Monticelli	†	†								
1130	P	Monticelli	†	†								
1170	E	Veber		†								
1177	P	Brueghel	†	†	62		67					
1178	P	Campin	†	†	38		39	42	55	43	29	81
1179	P	Hemessen	†	Unknown		360						
1180	P	Spanish School	Master of Mansi Magdalen				40	44	59	36	33	85
1181	P	Rubens	†	†								
1182	P	Dyck	†	Rubens		285						
1183	P	Arthois	†									
1184	P	Lucas	†	Flemish School	39							
1185	P	Lucas	†	Flemish School	40							
1186	P	Netherlandish School	†	Stoss			41	43	49	45	27	
1187	P	N. Italian School	Netherlandish School	Heemskerk	68							
1188	P	Netherlandish School	†									148
1189	P	Netherlandish School	School Brussels	Flemish School	59		63	41	65			
1190	P	Douven	†									
1191	P	Dyck	†									
1192	P	Netherlandish School	P. Coecke	School van Orley	58		62					
1193	P	Netherlandish School	Coffermans				61	40	58	35	21	
1195	P	Schuppen	†	†	95		106	130	115			
1213	D	Bassano	†	†	136		184					
1214	D	Bassano	†	†	137		185					
1215	D	Bassano	†	†	138		186					
1216	D	Bassano	†	†	139		187					

IN-VENTORY	MEDIUM	1977 ATTR.	1963/67 ATTR.	1927/28 ATTR.	1893/ 1915	1885	1859	1851	1843	1836	1819	1816
1217	P	Bassano	†	†	88		96	86	75			
1218	P	Bassano	†	†	89		97	87	84			
1219	P	Bassano	†									
1220	P	Roos	†				121	111	103			
1221	P	Baldung Grien	†	†	47		49	23	27			
1222	P	Krell	Cranach		49		51	51	68			97
1223	P	Cranach	†	†	48		50	52				
1224	P	Durer	†	†	46		47	47	67			
1225	P	Master of the Aachen Altarpiece	†	School Westphalia	41		42	49	62			
1226	P	Master of the Aachen Altarpiece	†	School Westphalia	41		43	50	64			
1227	P	Mengs	†									
1228	P	Roos	†	†	116		137					
1229	P	Westphalia	Austrian School	Flemish School	43		44	46	48			
1230	P	Levenstede	School Lower Saxony	German School	44		45	35				
1231	P	Levenstede	School Lower Saxony	German School	45		46	36				
1261	D	Parmigianino	†									
1271	D	Sargent										
1300	E	Pennell		†								
1306	E	Whistler		†								
1307	E	Whistler		†								
1308	P	French School	†	Clouet	54		56	57	1	1	18	75
1309	P	French School	Fragonard	Flemish School	109		129	120	102	3	MS	
1310	P	Dughet	†			289						

Inventory	Medium	1977 Attr.	1963/67 Attr.	1927/28 Attr.	1893/1915	1885	1859	1851	1843	1836	1819	1816
1311	P	Poussin	Dughet	†								
1312	S	Epstein										
1313	P	Poussin	†	†	108		126	117	86			
1314	P̄	Giulio	†	†	75		80	71	122			
1315	P	French School	†	†	63		68	34	61	46	37	
1318	E	Dauphin		†								
1322	E	Thaulow		†								
1327	P	Garrido	†	†								
1337	P	Langenmantel	†									
1351	P	Murillo	†									
1352	P	Murillo	†									
1476	E	Legros		†		164						
1486	P	Goyen	†									
1513	P	Zoffany										
1525	S	Aronson		†								
1526	S	Bartels		†								
1527	S	Barye										
1528	S	Barye										
1532	P	Mayan	†	†								
1536	P	Westchiloff	†									
1566-77	E	Pennell		†								
1578-88	E	Whistler		†								
1589-90	E	Whistler										
1600	P	Perugino	†									
1610	E	Pennell		†								

INVENTORY	MEDIUM	1977 ATTR.	1963/67 ATTR.	1927/28 ATTR.	1893/1915	1885	1859	1851	1843	1836	1819	1816
1629	D	Goltzius	†	†	143		191					
1762	P	Verboeckhoven	†	†								
1777	P	Bridgman		†		25						
1779	P	Bukovac	†	†								
1780-81	E	Pennell										
1782-83	E	Whistler										
1788	P	Coleman										
2127	P	Segantini	†	†								
2136	P	Marchand	†									
2137	D	Bandinelli	†									23
2144	D	Mayer-Marton										
2165	P	Gambardella		†		276						
2175	D	Debillemont-Chardon		†								
2213	D	Violet										
2222	D	Bartels										
2282	P	Dore	†	†		5						
2283	P	Fisher										
2359	P	Dahl										
2373	P	Le Sidaner	†	†								
2395	P	Zoffany										
2418	P	Ullman										
2430	D	Alma-Tadema		†								
2436	D	Dyck	†									
2494-97	E	Whistler										
2517	D	Boucher	†									

In-ventory	Medium	1977 Attr.	1963/57 Attr.	1927/28 Attr.	1893/1915	1885	1859	1851	1843	1836	1819	1816
2534	D	Legros										
2537	P	Kneller										
2571	P	Newton		†								
2590	P	Drury		Dury								
2593	P	Legros				179						
2630	S	Nimptsch										
2634	P	Sargent										
2641	P	Scherrewitz	†	†								
2643	P	Stokes		†								
2648	P	Schloesser	†	†		6						
2659	P	Tilton		†								
2689	P	Richir	†	†								
2728	E	Stael										
2729	E	Stael										
2730	E	Braque										
2731	E	Dufy										
2732	E	Soulages										
2733	E	Poliakoff										
2734	E	Ernst										
2735	E	Picasso										
2736	E	Lanskoy										
2739	P	Bertieri	†	†								
2740	P	Boughton		†								
2747	E	Le Corbusier										
2748	P	Vincenzo	†	Puligo	72		77	70	99			

In-ventory	Medium	1977 Attr.	1963/67 Attr.	1927/28 Attr.	1893/1915	1885	1859	1851	1843	1836	1819	1816
2749	P	Vincenzo	†	Puligo	71		76	69	98			
2750	P	Vincenzo	†	Puligo	70		75	68	97			
2751	P	Central Italian School	fol. Antoniazzo	School Parma	34*		35	32	43			
2752	P	Spinello	†	Florentine School	7		6	8	17	16	3	7
2753	P	Spinello	†	A. Lorenzetti	6		5	7	16	17	2	6
2754	P	Assereto	†	†	106a		123	114	88			
2755	P	Bartolommeo	†	†	17		17	14	28	24	8	14
2756	P	Bartolommeo	†	†	18		18	15	29	24	9	15
2757	P	Bellini	†	Rondinelli	33		33	30	40			
2758	P	Vecchietta	†	†	20		20	17	25	22	7	13
2759	P	Bicci	†	Florentine School	9		8	1	10			
2760	P	Bicci	†	Florentine School	10		9	2	11			
2761	P	Florentine School	Bicci di Lorenzo	†	11a		11	6	15	15		
2762	P	Veronese	Bonifazio	Bonifazio	31							
2763	P	Courtois	S. Rosa	Rosa		107						
2764	D	Silvestro	†	†	12		12	10	35	29	5	10
2765	P	North Italian School	School Verona	†	76		81	72	31			
2766	P	Tacconi	An. Carracci									
2767	P	Carracci	†	†	94		104	93	110			
2768	P	Casanova	†	†		287						
2769	P	Catena	†	†	81		87	77	6	4	23	63
2770	P	Catena	†	Venetian School	30		31	28	38	27	16	21
2771	P	Cavallino	†	Romanelli		288						
2772	P	Credi	†		24		25	22	2	9		

463

IN-VENTORY	MEDIUM	1977 ATTR.	1963/67 ATTR.	1927/28 ATTR.	1893/1915	1885	1859	1851	1843	1836	1819	1816
2773	P	Ercole	†	†	28		29	26	32	25	12	18
2774	P	Ferri	†									
2775	P	Lippi	†	School Botticelli	35*							
2776	P	Montagna	Fogolino	†	35		36	33	44			
2777	P	Garofalo	†	N. Italian School	77		82	101	79			
2778	P	Ferrarese School	att. Garofalo	†	26		27	24	34			
2779	P	Guercino	att. Gennari the Younger	Gennari the Elder	98a		110	97	114			
2780	P	Lucchese School	fol. Filippino Lippi	School Ghirlandaio								
2781	P	Gianfrancesco	†	Giovanni Francesco			24	21	33	21		
2782	P	Biondo	†	Sienese School	5		4	5	13	14	1	2
2783	P	Granacci	†	Unknown	13							
2784	P	Bissolo	†	Boccacino	79		85	75	4	2	20	64
2785	P	Vinci	†	†								
2786	P	Verona School	Liberale att.	N. Italian School	36		37					
2787	P	Martini	†	†	8		7	9	26	26	4	8
2788	P	Mazone	†	School Gentile da Fabriano	13							
2789	P	Michelangelo	†	†			69	61	3	10	19	32
2790	P	Neri	†	Liberatore								
2791	P	Niccolo	†	Unknown								
2792	P	Scarsellino	†	Tintoretto	85		91	83	76			
2793	P	Palmezzano	†	Palmezzano	29		30	27	37			
2794	P	Panini	†	†		106						
2795	P	Bertoia	†	N. Italian School	90		99	89	45	31		38
2796	P	Pesellino	†	Florentine School	14		14	11	18			

In- ventory	Medium	1977 Attr.	1963/67 Attr.	1927/28 Attr.	1893/ 1915	1885	1859	1851	1843	1836	1819	1816
2797	P	Pesellino	Pseudo Piero Francesco Fiorentino	Pier Francesco	19		19	16	23	18	11	16
2798	P	Pittoni	†									
2799	P	Preti	†	†	104		116	106	91	no. No.		
2800	P	Procaccini	†	†	99	111						
2801	P	Reni	†	Bolognese School	98	108	108	100				
2802	P	Italian School	Rocca	Solimena	106	118	118	108	78			
2803	P	Rosselli	†	†	15	15	15	12	19			
2804	P	Rosso	†	Dosso Dossi	82	88	79	9		12	22	72
2805	P	Santacroce	†	†	80	86	76	8		8	MS	
2806	P	Santacroce	†	School of Ferrara	34	34	31		41			
2807	P	Raphael	Sassoferrato	Sassoferrato	95	106	99		127			
2808	P	Master of Apollo and Daphne	Florentine School	Sellaio								
2809	P	Florentine School	Dido Master	Sellaio	21	21	18		22			
2810	P	Signorelli	†	†	25	26	78		36	20		
2820	P	Venetian School	att. Basaiti	School Bellini	32	32	29	29				
2828	P	Meifren	†	†								
2840	P	Florentine School	Bolognese XVIIc	att. L. Carracci	93	103	92		87			
2841	P	Raphael	Manzuoli aft Raphael	†								
2842	P	Raphael	†	†								
2843	P	Raphael	†	†	74		79					
2844	P	Raphael	†	†	73		78					
2845	P	Raphael	†	†								

In-ventory	Medium	1977 Attr.	1963/67 Attr.	1927/28 Attr.	1893/1915	1885	1859	1851	1843	1836	1819	1816
2846	P	Solimena	†									
2847	P	Vicentino	D. Tintoretto	J. Tintoretto	84		90	82	7	6	24	39
2848	P	Palma	†	Bolognese School	92		102	63	108			
2849	P	Venetian School	G. Salviati	School Tintoretto	65		71	64	113			
2850	P	Tintoretto	†	†			92a	84	5	11	25	66
2851	P	Tiziano	F. Vecellio	Manner of Titian	83		89	81	81			
2852	P	Florentine School	Vasari	Vasari	66		72	65	124			
2853	P	Fontana	Michelangelo	Venusti	64		70	62	111			
2854	P	Veronese	†	†	86		93	85	69			
2855	P	Veronese	†	†								
2856	P	Perugino	†	Fiorenzo di Lorenzo	22		22	20	24	23	6	11
2857	P	Florentine School	†	†	11		10	5	14			
2858	P	Roman School	†	Reni								
2859	P	Florentine School	†	†	67		73	66	80			
2860	P	Bolognese School	†	†	94a							
2861	P	Bolognese School	†	†	94a							
2862	P	Bolognese School	†	†	94a							
2863	P	Bolognese School	Tiarini	Reni	97		107	98	112			
2864	P	Venetian School	†	Bolognese School	91		101	91	107			
2865	P	Neapolitan School	Maratti	School Naples	107		125	116	101			
2866	P	Central Italian School	Umbrian School	N. Italian School	16		16	13	20			
2867	P	Raphael	Umbrian School	School Verona	27		28	25	30			
2868	P	Florentine School	†	†	69		74	67	104			
2869	P	Brescian School	†	della Vecchia	87		95	113	42	28	26	44

IN-VENTORY	MEDIUM	1977 ATTR.	1963/67 ATTR.	1927/28 ATTR.	1893/1915	1885	1859	1851	1843	1836	1819	1816
2870	P	Byzantine Greco-Venetian School	†									
2871	P	North Italian School	Roman School	att. Pulzone			94	80	10	5	14	
2872	P	Pasinelli	Bolognese School	Unknown	78	110	84	78	83			
2873	P	Flemish School	N. Italian School	Unknown		97						
2874	P	Derain	†	†								
2876	P	Gleyre	†	†								
2877	P	Gussow	†	†		11						
2878	P	Lamoriniere	†	†								
2885	P	Scheffer	†	†		19						
2886	P	Zezzos	†	Unknown								
2887	P	Preti	†	†	103		115	105	89	no No.		
2888	P	Preti	†		101		113	103	70	no No.		
2889	P	Preti	†	†	102		114	104	72	no No.		
2890	P	Pesellino	Pseudo Pier Francesco	Pier Francesco	23		23	29	33	19	10	17
2891	P	Rosa	†									
2892	P	Rosa	Montanini									
2893	P	Carracci	Reni									
2894	P	Reni	†	Unknown	96							
2895	P	Reni	†									
2896	P	Westerhout	†	Lenardi		95						
2897	P	Diest	†									
2898	P	Le Brun	Hoet			150						

INVENTORY	MEDIUM	1977 ATTR.	1963/67 ATTR.	1927/28 ATTR.	1893/1915	1885	1859	1851	1843	1836	1819	1816
2899	P	Loutherbourg	†									
2900	P	Bolognese School	†	Unknown		286						
2901	P	Gronland		†		327						
2903	P	Dolci	Manzuoli aft Dolci	Manzuoli								
2945	P	Lely										
2953	P	Hamdi	†	†								
2990	P	Delaroche	†	†								
2991	P	Italian School	Romano-Dutch School									
2992	P	Meulener	Netherlandish School									
2997	P	Miereveldt										
3017	P	Sargent		Skipworth								
3023	P	Kneller										
3024	P	Hayden	†									
3025	P	Vlaminck	†									
3032	P	Cavailles	†									
3033	P	Bompiani	†	†								
3034	P	Daguerre	†	†		104						
3035	P	Delobbe		†								
3036	P	Lamoriniere	†	†								
3038	P	Pulinckx	†	†		275						
3039	P	Schex	†	†		38						
3040	P	Tognolli	Tagliani	Tagliani		108						
3041	P	Lindholm	†	†		131						
3042	P	Master of Forli	†	Byzantine School	3							

In-ventory	Medium	1977 Attr.	1963/67 Attr.	1927/28 Attr.	1893/1915	1885	1859	1851	1843	1836	1819	1816
3043	P	Byzantine Greco-Venetian School	†	Byzantine School	1		1					
3044	P	Byzantine Greco-Venetian School	†	Byzantine School	4		3	3	12	13		
3045	P	Byzantine Greek School	†	Sienese School	2		2					
3046	P	Moscow School	†									
3047	P	Ottoman School	Turkish School									
3048	P	Novgorod School	†									
3049	P	N. Russian School	School Pskov									
3050	P	Moscow School	†									
3051	P	Byzantine Greco-Venetian School	†									
3052	P	Byzantine Greco-Venetian School	†									
3053	P	Byzantine, Greek School	†									
3054	P	Byzantine Greek School	†									
3055	P	Byzantine Greek School	†									
3073	P	Boughton		†								
3086	P	Blanchard										
3090	P	Legros		†		124						
3144	P	Pissarro										
3157	P	Mayer-Marton										
3172	E	Music										
3174	S	Riche		†								
3175	S	Renoir										

In-ventory	Medium	1977 Attr.	1963/67 Attr.	1927/28 Attr.	1893/1915	1885	1859	1851	1843	1836	1819	1816
3176	S	Rodin										
3177	S	Rodin										
3181	E	Bartolozzi	†									
3191-93	E	Hollar	†									
3198	D	Legros		†		161						
3199	D	Legros		†		162						
3200	E	Legros		†		156						
3201	E	Legros		†		159						
3202	E	Legros		†		157						
3203	E	Legros		†		160						
3204	E	Legros		†		164						
3205	E	Legros										
3276-3314	P	North Italian School	†									
3365	M	Nurenberg School										
3366	M	Copenhagen School										
3367	M	Vasa School										
3368	M	Moscow School										
3369	M	Aalborg School										
3370	M	Viborg School										
3371	M	Riga School										
3372	M	Swedish School										
3373	M	Tallinn School										
3374	M	Augsburg School										
3375	M	Dutch School										

Inventory	Medium	1977 Attr.	1963/67 Attr.	1927/28 Attr.	1893/1915	1885	1859	1851	1843	1836	1819	1816
3376	M	Dutch School										
3377	M	Oporto School										
3378	M	Groningen School										
3370	M	Amsterdam School										
3380	M	Dutch School										
3382	M	Copenhagen School										
3383	M	Dutch School										
3385	M	Dutch School										
3386	M	German School										
3387	M	Lower Saxon School										
3388	M	Indian School										
3418	P	Visscher	Fisher									
3419	P	Italian School	Giaquinto	Giordano		20						
3420	P	Neapolitan School	Giordano	Giordano								
3706-11	C	K'ang Hsi										
3712	C	K'ang Hsi or Yung Cheng										
3713-14	C	K'ang Hsi										
3716-31	C	K'ang Hsi										
3732	C	Yung Cheng										
3733-39	C	K'ang Hsi										
3740	C	K'ang Hsi or Yung Cheng										
3741-42	C	K'ang Hsi										
3743	C	Yung Cheng										
3744-51	C	K'ang Hsi										

471

In-ventory	Medium	1977 Attr.	1963/67 Attr.	1927/28 Attr.	1893/1915	1885	1859	1851	1843	1836	1819	1816
3753	C	K'ang Hsi										
3763-65	C	K'ang Hsi										
4001	E	Blanchard		†		89						
4002-5	E	Blanchard		†		154						
4008	E	Godefroy		†		155						
4009	E	Heydemann		†								
4018	E	Lefevre		†		166						
4022	E	Mandel		†								
4047	E	Roullet		†								
4097	P	Rubens	†									
4101	S	Canova		†		203						
4107	S	Rinaldi		†								
4112	S	Gaudier-Brzeska										
4113	S	Gaudier-Brzeska										
4115	T	Brussells School										
4118	S	Fix-Masseau		†								
4123	S	Neujd		†								
4134	S	Maderno		Unknown		221						
4148	S	Bourdelle										
4149	S	Italian School		Canova		210						
4158	D	Bandinelli	†									82
4159	D	Polidoro	†									190
4160	D	North Italian School	Schiavone									285
4161	D	Parmigianino	†									82
4162	D	Tamagni	†									175

In-ventory	Medium	1977 Attr.	1963/67 Attr.	1927/28 Attr.	1893/1915	1885	1859	1851	1843	1836	1819	1816
4163	E	Veneziano	†									288
4164	E	Raimondi	†									282
4167	S	Fontana				236						
4168	S	Fontana		†		246						
4169	S	Fraccaroli		†		211						
4179	S	Rodin		†								
4180	S	Rodin		†								
4181	S	Rodin		†								
4182	S	Rodin		†								
4184	S	Wolff		†								
4202	S	Pineau										
4206	S	Rauch		Willig								
4217	S	Weigele		†								
4221	S	Italian School		Bartolini		226						
4223	S	Canova		†		262						
4224	S	Dannecker		†								
4226	S	Fedi		†		199						
4227	S	Fontana		†								
4228	S	Fuchs		†								
4237	S	Rossetti										
4238	S	Rossetti		†		213						
4422	S	French School										
4527-29	E	Durer	†	†								
4530	E	Durer	†	†								
4531	E	Durer	†	†		135	183					

473

IN-VENTORY	MEDIUM	1977 ATTR.	1963/67 ATTR.	1927/28 ATTR.	1893/1915	1885	1859	1851	1843	1836	1819	1816
4538	S	Crunelle		†								
4618	E	Bejot		†								
4621-27	E	Brunet-Debaines		†								
4635-6	E	Chahine		†								
4657-4660	E	Colin		†								
4663-4681	D	Du Maurier		†								
4881	E	Hamilton										
4888	E	Heyman		†								
4901	E	Leheutre		†								
4902	E	Lepere		†								
4950	E	Meryon	†									
4973	E	Rajon		†								
4998	D	Topolski		†								
5037	E	Veber		†								
5079	E	Zorn		†								
5081	E	Helleu		†								
5082	D	Albani	†	†	149	197						
5083	D	Nucci	†	Avanzino	150	198						
5084	D	Sarto	†	Fra Bartolommeo	131	179						
5085	D	Bartolommeo	Sogliani	†	132	180						
5086	D	Campiglia	†	†	157	205						
5087	D	Campiglia	†	†	158	206						
5088	D	Campiglia	†	†	159	207						
5089	D	Campiglia	†	†	161(?)	208(?)						

Inventory	Medium	1977 Attr.	1963/67 Attr.	1927/28 Attr.	1893/1915	1885	1859	1851	1843	1836	1819	1816
5090	D	Campiglia	†	†	162(?)		209(?)					
5091	D	Campiglia	†	†	160(?)		210					
5092	D	Cipriani	†	Campiglia	163		211					
5093	D	Facius	†	Campiglia	164		212					
5094	D	Bolognese School	Carracci	Carracci	146		194					
5095	D	Cipriani	†	†	165		213					
5096	D	Cipriani	†	†	166		214					
5097	D	Diziani	†	†	156		204					
5098	D	Durer	†	†	133		181					
5099	D	Durer	†	†	134		182					
5100	D	French School	Freminet	Freminet	147		195					
5101	D	Gennari	†	Guercino	153		201					
5104	D	Procaccini	†	Maratti	155		203					
5105	D	Gimignani	†	Maratti	154		202					
5106	D	French School	†	Poussin	151		199					
5107	D	French School	†	Poussin	152		200					
5108	D	Reni	†	†	148		196					
5109	D	Tintoretto	Master GNR	†	140		188					
5110-21	D	Moser	†	Unknown	167-183		215-226		p. 34			
5122	D	Cipriani	†	Unknown	167-183		229-230					
5123	D	Cipriani	†	Unknown	167-183		228					
5124	D	Cipriani	†	Unknown	167-183		229-230					
5125	D	Cipriani	†	Unknown	167-183		227					

Q

INVENTORY	MEDIUM	1977 ATTR.	1963/67 ATTR.	1927/28 ATTR.	1893/1915	1885	1859	1851	1843	1836	1819	1816
5126	D	Cipriani	†	Unknown	167-183	231						
5127	D	Bolognese School	†	Zuccaro	141	189						
5128	D	Paggi	†	Zuccaro	142	190						
5129	D	Perino	Polidoro									
5130	D	Italian School	Dolci									
5599	P	Liebermann										
5608	P	Italian School										
5998	D	Ferranti										
5999	D	Ferranti										
6003	P	Formilli		†								
6011	D	Titian	†									
6012	S	French School							p. 30 p. 34			
6101	D	Mayer-Marton										
6102	D	Mayer-Marton										
6103	S	S. German School										
6104	S	S. German School										
6106	P	Venetian School	†									
6111	P	Courbet	†									
6112	P	Seurat	†									
6115	P	Kitaj										
6119	P	Biondo	†									9
6120	P	Biondo	†									9
6122	S	French School										
6126	P	Spanish School	Gutierrez			124	115	82				

In-ventory	Medium	1977 Attr.	1963/67 Attr.	1927/28 Attr.	1893/1915	1885	1859	1851	1843	1836	1819	1816
6128	P	Zobel	†									
6130	P	Volaire	†				146	133	126			
6131	S	French School										
6132	S	Venetian School										
6133	P	Monet	†									
6134	S	French School										
6145	E	Dos Santos										
6155	S	Lepautre										
6156	S	Bologna										
6165	S	Bonheur										
6166	S	French School										
6167	S	Pesci										
6168	S	Mene										
6169	D	Grimaldi	†									435
6171	D	Salviati	†									
6172	D	Waterloo	†									540
6173	P	Cerezo										
6174	P	Jenkins										
6176	D	Claude	†									576
6177	P	Balducci										
6201	E	Beutlich										
6215	S	German School										
6216	P	Matisse										
6217	P	Vuillard										
6223	E	Appel										

In- ventory	Medium	1977 Attr.	1963/67 Attr.	1927/28 Attr.	1893/ 1915	1885	1859	1851	1843	1836	1819	1816
6224	E	Dufy										
6225	E	Ernst										
6226	E	Jawlensky										
6227	E	Humbert										
6228	E	Miro										
6229	E	Picasso										
6231	E	Kandinsky										
6232	E	Le Moal										
6234	P	Denis										
6235	S	Leoni										
6236	S	Italian School										
6242	P	Cezanne										
6243	S	Italian School										
6244	S	Italian School										
6245	S	French School										
6254	P	Nikich-Krilichevski										
6255	D	Neizvestny										
6261	P	Pignone										
6272	P	Kneller										
6273	P	Guardi										
6274	P	Guardi										
6286	E	Bluvberg										
6287-9	E	Ryabchenko										
6290	E	Popova										
6291	E	Popova										

IN-VENTORY	MEDIUM	1977 ATTR.	1963/67 ATTR.	1927/28 ATTR.	1893/1915	1885	1859	1851	1843	1836	1819	1816
6299	E	Kitaj										
6312	D	Stradanus	†									460
6314	S	Susini										
6328	E	Burgkmair	†									
6338	E	Humbert										
6339	E	Leger										
6340	E	Leger										458
6352	D	Brueghel	Francken									
6355	E	Beutlich										
6357	E	Zao										
6359	E	Herman										
6362	S	North Italian School										
6366	P	Solimena										
6369	P	Montagna										
6370	P	Montagna										
6526	S	Italian School										
6527	S	Piranesi										
6528	S	Lorenzi										
6530	S	Angelini										
6532	S	Italian School										
6533	S	Italian School										
6534	S	Italian School										
6535	S	Cavaceppi										
6536	S	Italian School										
6537	S	Albacini										

Inventory	Medium	1977 Attr.	1963/67 Attr.	1927/28 Attr.	1893/1915	1885	1859	1851	1843	1836	1819	1816
6538	S	Albacini										
6546	E	Hayden										
6548	D	Herman										
6558	D	Zucchi										
6561	S	North Italian School										
6580	S	Cavaceppi										
6581	S	Cavaceppi										
6584	P	Scheffer										
6588	P	Le Sidaner										
6597	S	Bertos										
6610	P	Beerstraten										
6611	P	Backhuyzen										
6617	D	French School											567
6628	S	Cavaceppi										
6629	S	Cavaceppi										
6633	E	Bonnard										
6637	E	Skiold										
6639	S	Arnolfo										
6642-44	E	Liao										
6645	P	Degas										
6652	S	Maria										
6653	S	Uecker										
6654	E	Piranesi										
6879-84	E	Master E. M.										

In-ventory	Medium	1977 Attr.	1963/67 Attr.	1927/28 Attr.	1893/1915	1885	1859	1851	1843	1836	1819	1816
6892	E	Rosaspina										
6893	E	Rosaspina										
6894	S	Takis										
6895	S	Cavaceppi										
6896	S	Italian School										
6900	S	Albacini										
6901	S	Italian School										
6902	S	Italian School										
6905	S	Italian School										
6908	E	Kitaj										
6918	E	Vasarely										
6922	E	Nel										
6923	E	Lloyd										
6925	S	Levis										
6926	E	Vasarely										
6927	E	Dos Santos										
6939	D	Moyaert										530
6942	P	Floris						58				
6943	P	Veronese							92b			
6944	P	Flemish School						128	119	74			
6945	P	Barocci										
6961	S	Rauch										
6971	E	Hamilton										
6980	D	Pisa										
6994	D	Ruith										

481

IN-VENTORY	MEDIUM	1977 ATTR.	1963/67 ATTR.	1927/28 ATTR.	1893/1915	1885	1859	1851	1843	1836	1819	1816
6997	D	Ruith										
7007-7010	E	Bartolozzi										
7041	P	Brown										
7102	E	Piranesi										
7140	P	Gambardella										
7143	S	Rinaldi										
7180-3	E	Bartsch										
7184-5	E	Albers										
7188	P	Araeen										
7190	E	Marini										
7192	S	Laurens										
7197	E	Vasarely										
7241	S	Coustou										
7263	S	Fontana										
7274	P	Harpignies										
7278	S	Alessi										
7279	S	German School										
7375	E	Waltner										
7397	S	Augsburg School										
7398	S	Tacca										
7435-7	E	Whistler										
7450-1	D	German School										
7460	E	Klein										
7466	E	Boitard										

In-ventory	Medium	1977 Attr.	1963/67 Attr.	1927/28 Attr.	1893/1915	1885	1859	1851	1843	1836	1819	1816
7467	E	Ravenet										
7468	E	Scotin										
7469	E	Grignion										
7470	E	Boitard										
7471-2	E	Grignion										
7473-4	E	Ravenet										
7475	E	Scotin										
7490	E	Abbey										
7491	S	Italian School										
7503	S	Thorwaldsen										
7504	S	Thorwaldsen										
7597-7601	S	Fontana										
7603-7605	S	Fontana										
7607	S	Mozier										
7608-7619	S	Fontana										
7639-7640	S	Fontana										
7778	D	Schoonhoven										
7786-7787	E	Whistler										
7788	D	Prosdocimi										
7792	E	Olitski										
7795	E	Skiold										
7798	E	Antonini										

483

Inventory	Medium	1977 Attr.	1963/67 Attr.	1927/28 Attr.	1893/1915	1885	1859	1851	1843	1836	1819	1816
7802	E	Antonini										
7809	E	Dine										
7817	S	Fontana										
7822	S	Fontana										
8143	D	Grimm										
8160	D	Huet										
8163	D	Grimm										
8170	D	Meyer										
8192-3	E	Stella										
8227	S	Schadow										
8230	S	Partridge										
8288-8293	E	Ruscha										
8467	D	Passarotti										
8469	S	Vogel										
8474	E	Warhol										
8481-2	E	Christo										
8483	E	Kitaj										
8484	E	Winner										
8556	S	Tenerani										
8557	E	Cottingham										
8559	E	Goings										
8564	P	Kneller										
8569	E	Clouwet										
8607-8615	E	Legros										

Inventory	Medium	1977 Attr.	1963/67 Attr.	1927/28 Attr.	1893/1915	1885	1859	1851	1843	1836	1819	1816
8626	P	Gerard										
8660	E	Wujcik										
8661	E	Winner										
8698	D	Bartolommeo										163
8777	S	Este										
8781	D	Koch										
8802-8804	D	Lipczinsky										
8990	S	Bartolini										
9011-9012	E	Legros										
9017	E	Whistler										
9025	S	Robbia										
9054	E	Rauschenberg										
9066	E	Whistler										
9082	E	Ribot										
9083	E	Legros										
9098	P	Alma-Tadema										
9015	S	Italian 16th C.										
9106	S	Albacini										
9107	S	Italian 18th C.										
9108	S	Italian 18th C.										
9109	S	Italian 18th C.										
9110	S	Italian 18th C.										
9111	S	Italian 18th C.										

Inventory	Medium	1977 Attr.	1963/67 Attr.	1927/28 Attr.	1893/1915	1885	1859	1851	1843	1836	1819	1816
9112	S	Italian 18th C.										
9113	S	Italian 18th C.										
9114	S	Italian 18th C.										
9115	S	Italian 18th C.										
9117	S	Hosmer										
9119	E	Fantuzzi										672
9120	E	Reni										740
9121	E	Carracci										732
9122	E	Meckenem										
9123	E	Beccafumi										1281
9124	E	Abbate										676
9125	P	Bourdon					127	118	93			
9126	P	Vinne					134	125	94			
9127	P	Veer					140					
9128	P	Italian School										
9147	E	Jaques										
9162	D	Mayer-Marton										
9163	E	Mayer-Marton										
9164	E	Mayer-Marton										
9165	E	Mayer-Marton										
9166	E	Mayer-Marton										
9167	D	Fenile										
9168	E	Rode										916
9169	E	Rosa										872
9170	E	Bourdon										1191

IN-VENTORY	MEDIUM	1977 ATTR.	1963/67 ATTR.	1927/28 ATTR.	1893/1915	1885	1859	1851	1843	1836	1819	1816
9171	E	Bourdon										1191
9172	E	Bourdon										1191
9173	E	Italian School										
9174	E	Giordano										878
9175	E	Mannozzi										
9176	E	Italian School										
9177	E	Rossigliani										1285
9178	E	Italian School										
9179	E	Palma										700
9180	E	Palma										698
9181	E	Palma										700
9182	E	Palma										700
9183	E	Palma										700
9184	E	Bonasone										310
9185	E	Franco										694
9186	E	Grimaldi										797
9187	E	Grimaldi										797
9188	E	Carracci										712
9189	E	Carracci										712
9190	E	Carracci										727
9191	E	Carracci										727
9192	E	Reni										732
9193	E	Whistler										
9195	D	Legros										
9204	E	Harbutt										

In-ventory	Medium	1977 Attr.	1963/67 Attr.	1927/28 Attr.	1893/1915	1885	1859	1851	1843	1836	1819	1816
9213	D	Guercino										400
9218	D	Giovanni										260

GENERAL INDEX

This index includes all artists' names and all owners or locations (past and present) of works of art mentioned anywhere in the catalogue, it also includes all subjects of works of art now in the Gallery (except subjects which are too vague like *Landscape* or too frequent like *Virgin and Child*) and all significant exhibitions at which works of art now in the Gallery have been exhibited before their acquisition by the Gallery.

489

Bartolommeo di Giovanni, 13, 14, 15, 87, 118
Bartolommeo, Fra, 236, 275
Bartolotto, Antonio, 195
Bartolozzi, Francesco, 354–357
Bartsch, Adam, 357–358, 366
Baruchson, Arnold, 50, 101, 108
Barye, Antoine Louis, 288, 289
Basaiti, Marco, 214
Basel Historiches Museum, 156
Basel, Kunstmuseum, 44, 194
Bass, Major Edward, 184
Bassano, Francesco, the elder, see Ponte
Bassano, Francesco, the younger, 15, 16, 17, 238
Bassano, Jacopo, 15, 16, 17, 237, 238
Bassano, Leandro, 238
Batist, Karel, 17
Battista del Moro, 352
Battle, 47, 124, 213, 223
Battle, Sea, 54
Baudelaire, 439
Baumgarten, 339
Bawdsey Manor, Suffolk, 98
Be Thou the Rainbow to the Storms of Life, 273
Beach, 254
Bear, Polar, 402
Beatrizet, Nicolas, 124, 125, 126
Beatty, Mrs Chester, 46, 202
Beatty, Sir Alfred Chester, 46, 202
Beaumont Collection, 204
Beausire, C. F. J., 110, 253, 254, 265
Bebington Corporation, 300–306, 326
Bebington, Free Library Hall, 300–306
Bebington, Mayer Hall see Mayer Trust
Beccadelli, Lorenzo, 152
Beccafumi, Domenico, 11, 358
Becker, Johan Christian, 245
Beckett, I., 98
Becquet, 442, 443
Beers, Jan van, 17
Beethoven, 291
Begarelli, Antonio, 327
Bejot, Eugene, 359
Beit, Alfred, 323
Beit, Otto, 323
Belcher, Colonel W. M., 339
Belgian Village, 101
Belgrade, Capture of, 228
Belgrave, Lady Elizabeth, 331
Bell, J. R., 119
Bellin, Francois, 103
Bellini, Gentile, 18
Bellini, Giovanni, 18, 35, 41, 62, 195, 214
Bellini, Jacopo, 172
Bembo, Pietro, 163
Benedetto da Maiano, 160
Benedict, Saint, 194
Benjamin, B., 102
Bennecourt, 129
Bennett, William, 188
Benserade, Isaac de, 102
Bensheimer, Johann, 346
Benso, Giulio, 268
Benson, Robert, 426
Benson, Ambrosius, 142
Bentivoglio, Giovanni II, 270

Benvenuto di Giovanni, 213
Beolco, Angelo called Ruzzante, 153
Berchem, Nicolas, 11, 174
Berendt, 13
Bergamo, Accademia Carrara, 142
Bergh, Count Hendrik van der, 247
Berlin, Internationale Kunstaustellung 1891, 201
Berlin, Kaiser Friedrich Museum, 16, 87, 111, 275
Berlin, Royal Academy of Art, 89, 90, 199
Berlin, Royal Palace, 335
Berlin, Schloss Charlottenburg Rauch Museum, 329
Berlin, Staatliche Museen Preussischer Kulturbesitz, 38, 40, 41, 114, 164, 175, 236, 329, 338
Berlin, Staatliche Schlosser und Garten, 48
Bern Kunstmuseum, 288
Bernardini, Lorenzo and Family, 208
Bernardino of Siena, Preaching of Saint, 212
Bernheim, Georges, 130
Bernini, Pietro, 170
Berre, Etang de, Provence, 121
Bertelli, Ferando, 125
Bertieri, Genevieve, 19
Bertieri, Pilade, 18
Bertoia, Jacopo, 19
Bertos, Francesco, 289
Bertrand, Children of General, 383
Berwick, William Noel Hill 3rd Lord, 83, 94, 139, 140
Besancon, Musee des Beaux Arts et d'Archeologie, 48
Bessarion, Cardinal, 153
Bessborough, Lord, 316
Bessemer, 414
Bessemer, Edgar Thomson Steelworks, 414
Bethlehem, 282
Betrayal of Christ, 15
Betrothal, 186
Beutlich, Tadek, 359
Bewick, Isabella, 375
Bewick, Thomas, 375
Bicci di Lorenzo, 20, 69
Bickersteth, Herbert, 256
Bickley, J. Latty, 100
Bienaimee, Luigi, 337
Bienor, 289
Bievre, Vallee de la, 121
Biondo, Giovanni del, 21
Birmingham, Barber Institute, 296
Birmingham, City Art Gallery, 27, 234, 360, 361
Birmingham Repertory Theatre, 96
Bissolo, Francesco, 22
Blacksmith, 329
Blaise, Martyrdom of Saint, 193
Blakey, T. or J., 191
Blanchard, Pascal, 23
Blanchard, Thomas Marie Auguste, 8, 360, 361
Blat, Ognissanti, 194
Blenheim Palace, 217
Blenheim Park, 269
Bliss, F. E., 394, 395, 396
Bloemen, J. F. van, 179

491

R

503

Mene, Pierre Jules, 325
Mengs, Anton Raphael, 123, 230, 319
Menpes, Mortimer, 448
Mensing Collection, 169, 170
Mentmore, 158
Mercury, 336
Mereville, Laborde de, 218
Merit, 88
Meritis Gallery, Amsterdam, 292
Merle, Hugues, 124
Meryon, Charles, 409–410
Mesdag, Hendrik Willem, 264
Mesens, E. L. T., 46
Methuen, Lord, 159
Meulener, Pieter, 124
Meuse, River, 101
Meyer, Christoffel, 265
Meyer, J. G., 340
Meyssens, I, 385
Micah, 276
Michael, Saint, 22, 167, 220
Michel, Andreas, 345
Michelangelo Buonarotti, 73, 124, 270, 321, 370
Michiel, Giovanni, 169
Middelburg, 342
Miereveldt, Michiel, 127, 128
Miguel, Don of Spain, 60
Milan, Biblioteca Ambrosiana, 151, 153, 154, 155, 156, 157, 161, 162, 163, 164, 166
Milan, Brera, 132, 180, 237, 367
Milan, Castello Sforzesco, 237, 327
Milan, Galleria d'Arte Moderna, 335
Milan, Galleria Grubicy, 201
Milan, Museo Poldi Pezzoli, 180
Milan, Piazza della Scala, 370
Mill, 66, 397
Miller, John, 15, 188
Millet, Francois, 57
Milman, Mrs G., 279
Milo of Crotona, 282
Milton Gallery, Lucy, 275
Minardi, Tommaso, 211
Miners, 27, 383
Minerva, 284, 333, 377
Mirandola, Siege of, 158
Miro, Joan, 410
Mirola, Girolamo, 19
Mitchell, N., 8
Mniszech, Countess Andre, 85
Mocking of Christ, 92
Mococo, 404
Modena, Duke of, 298
Modena, S. Domenico, 327
Moir, Professor, 252
Mola, Pier Francesco, 24, 178
Molenaer, Klaes, 128
Molesworth, H. O., 13
Molinaer, John, 128
Molinary Collection, 152, 157
Momper, Jan de, 129
Mona Lisa, 223
Monaco, Lorenzo, 172
Monet, Claude, 129
Money, Mr, 411–413
Monkey, 119

Monkey, Horned, 403
Monnoyer, Jean-Baptiste, 130
Monroe, Marilyn, 440
Monsu X, 129
Montagna, Bartolomeo, 131, 132
Montagu, Lady Alice and Lady Mary, 311
Montague, George of Sawsey Forest, 184
Montanini, Pietro, 189
Montecavallo, S. Andrea del Noviziato, 65
Montgomery, Mary, 250
Monthermer, Marquess of, 317
Monticelli, 328
Monticelli, A. J. T., 133, 134
Moon, 376
Moonlight, 106, 369
Moore, Miss E. M., 331
Moores, John, 97, 263
Morales, 204
Morelli, 360
Moretti, 204
Morghen, Luigi, 163
Morley, 26
Morny, Duc de, 25, 138
Moro, Antonio, 77, 134
Moro, Battista del, 352
Morone, Domenico, 181
Morrison, Alfred, Mrs, 101
Morrison, R. E., 248
Moscow School, 135, 344
Moser, George Michael, 265, 266
Moses, 220, 240, 255, 362
Moses, Finding of, 218
Moshtawa Sherif, 90
Mosque, Door of, 134
Mostaert, Jan, 136
Moucheron, Frederick de, 137
Mouflon of Corsica, 406
Mount Trust, 14
Mourlot, F. 410
Moyaert, Claes Cornelisz, 266, 267
Mozier, Joseph, 326
Muller, C. L. L., 137
Muller, Theobald, 151
Mundler, Otto, 138
Munich, Bayerisches Staatsgemal-desammlungen, 59, 63, 92, 117, 123, 174, 192, 212, 237, 240
Munich, Staatliche Graphische Stammlung, 269
Munich Residenz, 294
Murder, The, 44
Mure, John, 188
Murillo, Bartholome Esteban, 66, 137, 138, 139, 391
Murray, David, 201
Murrieta, Messrs, 25
Muscles, 362, 380
Muse, 243, 244
Muselli Collection, 18
Musgrave, Ernest, 410
Music, 418, 435
Music, Antonio, 410
Music Room, The, 441
Musicians, 391
Mussomeli, Confraternity of S. Leonardo, 222
Mussomeli, S. Lodovico, 222
Myrrha, Metamorphosis of, 386

Onuphrius, Saint, 375
Oporto School, 345
Oppe, Miss A., 270
Oppe, D. L., 270
Orange Tree, 51
Oranges, Ladies playing with, 133
Orange, Prince of, 58
Orange, William of, 51
Orleans, Duke of, 102, 183, 432
Orleans, Musee des Beaux Arts, 312
Ormond, Mrs Francis, 274
Orsay, see D'Orsay, Count Alfred
Orsini, 96
Orvieto, 317
Oslo, 167
Oslo, Villa Bogstad, 218
Otho, 320
Ottawa, National Gallery of Canada, 71, 153, 267, 395
Ottley, William Young, 100, 125, 126, 206, 212, 252, 269, 275–276
Ottoboni, Cardinal, 204
Ottoman School, 168
Outhwaite, 53
Outposts, The, 101
Overschie, 85
Overstone, Lord, 138, 139
Ovid Metamorphoses, 57, 72, 102, 386
Oxen, 45, 310
Oxford, 279, 314
Oxford, Ashmolean Museum, 124, 176, 275, 276, 375
Oxford, New College, 131

Paddy's Market, Liverpool, 446
Padua, Museo Civico, 65, 194
Paggi, Giovanni Battista, 268
Palermo, 222
Palermo, S. Domenico, 222
Palermo, S. Maria La Nuova, 222
Palier, 376
Palma, Jacopo Il Giovane, 169, 267, 411
Palma, Jacopo Il Vecchio, 22
Palmer, Lynwood, 248
Palmezzano, Marco, 169
Panetti, Domenico, 65
Panigarola, Francesco, 161
Pangiavahli, 200
Panini, G. P., 170
Panshanger, 123, 131, 144
Panther, 288, 296
Pantocrator, The, 168
Parable of the Wise and Foolish Virgins, 330, 408
Paraskeva, Saint, 168
Pareja, Juan de, 205
Parenzo, Cathedral, 40
Parenzo, San Niccolo, 40
Paris, 242
Paris, City of, 50, 295, 398
Paris, Judgement of, 146
Paris, Bibliotheque Nationale, 228, 409
Paris, Champs Elysees, Rond-Point, 363
Paris, Ecole des Beaux Arts, 288, 375
Paris, Eiffel Tower, 385
Paris, Hotel du Ville, 438
Paris, Institut Neerlandais, see Lugt, Frits
Paris, Internationale Exhibition 1878, 199

Paris, Jardin des Plantes, 406
Paris, Left Bank, 409
Paris, Musee de L'Armee, 245
Paris, Musee d'Histoire Naturelle, 402–405
Paris, Musée Jacquemart André, 285
Paris, Musee du Jeu de Paume, 44
Paris, Musee National d'Art Moderne, 312, 322, 364
Paris, Musee National du Louvre, 14, 60, 79, 81, 84, 85, 102, 114, 156, 172, 183, 198, 210, 220, 223, 235, 236, 238, 241, 274, 284, 289, 291, 292, 295, 309, 310, 321, 322, 323, 336, 391, 431
Paris, Musee du Luxembourg, 85, 198
Paris, Musee Rodin, 332–334
Paris, Palais des Beaux Arts, 53
Paris, Palais Royal, 184, 219
Paris, Petit Palais, 296
Paris, Pantheon, 359
Paris, Pont Neuf, 409
Paris, Port St. Bernard, 359
Paris, Rue Chanoinesse, 384
Paris, Salon, 25, 31–32, 50, 103, 109–110, 137, 207, 234, 289, 326, 402, 405
Paris, Sambon Gallery, 15
Paris, Societe des Artistes Francais, 23, 27, 53, 75, 90–91, 121, 179, 229, 245, 330, 387
Paris, Societe Nationale des Beaux Arts, 19, 78, 80, 106, 188, 264, 287, 299
Paris, Universal Exhibition 1889, 439, 440
Park, Mrs Fanny, 101
Parma, Galleria Nazionale, 20
Parma, Palazzo Vecchio, 19
Parma, Palazzo del Giardino, 19
Parma, Palazzo del Comune, 19
Parma, Palazzo Lalatta, 19
Parma, Palazzo Visconti, 19
Parma, S. Maria della Steccata, 269
Parmigianino, Francesco, 146, 269, 370, 428, 431
Parrot, 76
Parting, A., 207
Parton, Ernest, 171
Partridge, William Ordway, 327
Pasajes, Guipuzcoa, 122
Pasinelli, Lorenzo, 73, 171
Passaro, Venice, 131
Passarotti, Bartolommeo, 165, 270
Passeri, Giuseppe, 94
Passion, Instruments of, 116, 204
Patch, Thomas, 205, 206
Patenir, Joachim, 199
Paterson, Mrs Barbara Jean, 78
Paterson, W. B., 134, 289
Paul, Saint, 20, 33, 71, 121, 140
Pavia, Certosa, 149
Pavia, Museo Malaspina, 205
Peach, 88
Pear, 88
Pearce, 87
Peart, Edward, 386
Pease, W. H., 208
Peel, David, 313
Peel and Humphris Ltd., 310
Peerbhoy, Anita, 297
Peggy, 303, 306

515

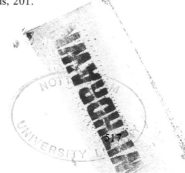